Covell ♦ Lupton
Principles of Remedies

Fifth edition

Previous Editions

First edition — W Covell and K Lupton, 1995
Second edition — W Covell and K Lupton, 2003
Third edition — W Covell and K Lupton, 2005
Fourth edition — W Covell and K Lupton, 2008

Covell ◆ Lupton
Principles of Remedies

Fifth edition

Wayne Covell
BA, LLB (Syd)
Solicitor and Trade Marks Attorney

Keith Lupton
BA, LLB (Syd), LLM, PhD (Lond)
Solicitor

Jay Forder
BL (Hons) (Zim), LLM (Lond), MSc (Bond)
Associate Professor, Bond University

LexisNexis Butterworths
Australia
2012

LexisNexis

AUSTRALIA	LexisNexis Butterworths
	475–495 Victoria Avenue, Chatswood NSW 2067
	On the internet at: www.lexisnexis.com.au
ARGENTINA	LexisNexis Argentina, BUENOS AIRES
AUSTRIA	LexisNexis Verlag ARD Orac GmbH & Co KG, VIENNA
BRAZIL	LexisNexis Latin America, SAO PAULO
CANADA	LexisNexis Canada, Markham, ONTARIO
CHILE	LexisNexis Chile, SANTIAGO
CHINA	LexisNexis China, BEIJING, SHANGHAI
CZECH REPUBLIC	Nakladatelství Orac sro, PRAGUE
FRANCE	LexisNexis SA, PARIS
GERMANY	LexisNexis Germany, FRANKFURT
HONG KONG	LexisNexis Hong Kong, HONG KONG
HUNGARY	HVG-Orac, BUDAPEST
INDIA	LexisNexis, NEW DELHI
ITALY	Dott A Giuffrè Editore SpA, MILAN
JAPAN	LexisNexis Japan KK, TOKYO
KOREA	LexisNexis, SEOUL
MALAYSIA	LexisNexis Malaysia Sdn Bhd, PETALING JAYA, SELANGOR
NEW ZEALAND	LexisNexis, WELLINGTON
POLAND	Wydawnictwo Prawnicze LexisNexis, WARSAW
SINGAPORE	LexisNexis, SINGAPORE
SOUTH AFRICA	LexisNexis Butterworths, DURBAN
SWITZERLAND	Staempfli Verlag AG, BERNE
TAIWAN	LexisNexis, TAIWAN
UNITED KINGDOM	LexisNexis UK, LONDON, EDINBURGH
USA	LexisNexis Group, New York, NEW YORK
	LexisNexis, Miamisburg, OHIO

National Library of Australia Cataloguing-in-Publication entry

Author:	Covell, Wayne.
Title:	Covell and Lupton Principles of remedies.
Edition:	5th edition.
ISBN:	9780409330953 (pbk).
	9780409330960
Notes:	Includes index.
Subjects:	Remedies (Law) — Australia. Damages — Australia.
	Restitution — Australia. Equity — Australia.
Other Authors/Contributors:	Lupton, Keith; Forder, Jay.
Dewey Number:	347.94077.

Typeset in Garamond and Futura.

Printed in China.

Visit LexisNexis Butterworths at www.lexisnexis.com.au

Contents

Contents

Preface

It has been four years since our last edition and 17 since our first. There have been many changes. Despite a generation of history and case law under the Trade Practices Act 1974 (Cth), on 1 January 2011 the Act was renamed the Competition and Consumer Act 2010 (Cth). To be sure it was not just a name change as there have been many substantive changes too. Chapter 16 has been amended accordingly and recent developments in case law have been incorporated throughout. As noted in the preface to our fourth edition, Mareva injunctions have become freezing orders (Chapter 10) and Anton Piller injunctions are now often referred to as search orders (Chapter 9). There is also the recent development of super-injunctions and anonymised injunctions (see Chapter 8). These new names could not have been predicted in our first edition. But our continuing challenge remains the same: to distil the law of remedies into the essential principles. As stated boldly in the second edition, we have rigorously eschewed prolixity in favour of brevity. It is encouraging to see that many of the stated principles in the first edition can still be traced in this fifth edition. Apart from name changes, what has also changed is that the law of remedies is now a vital and pragmatic subject for navigating the whole legal landscape.

Wayne and Keith are very pleased to welcome Associate Professor Jay Forder as a co-author. This is an exciting development for this book and we thank Jay for enthusiastically sharing his erudite learning with our readers. In preparing this manuscript Wayne has updated Chapters 1, 7, 8, 9 and 10, Keith has updated Chapters 1, 4, 5, 6, 11, 12, 13, 14 and 15 and Jay has updated Chapters 2, 3 and 16.

We owe thanks for the support of others in completing this book. Wayne thanks Robin Covell, James Covell, Daphne Covell and Martin Covell for their love, praise and encouragement. Robin has proof read all of Wayne's chapters since the first edition and any obstinate errors that remain are all his own. Jay thanks colleagues and family for their support and assistance; and for their tolerance of the idiosyncrasies brought out by the writing process. We are all grateful to our commissioning editor Serena Cubie at LexisNexis Butterworths for her persistence in publishing this book and to Susan Seccombe who carefully crafted our manuscript into this fifth edition.

The law is stated according to the materials that were available to us up to March 2012.

Wayne Covell
Keith Lupton
Jay Forder

Table of Cases

References are to paragraphs

Table of Cases

Table of Cases

Table of Cases

Table of Statutes

References are to paragraphs

Part 1

INTRODUCTION

CHAPTER

Introduction

SCOPE OF THE LAW OF REMEDIES

1.1 The law of remedies is as old as law itself. Every case or action in law has raised the question of the availability of a remedy. But the study of the law of remedies as a subject in its own right is a recent phenomenon. Traditionally, remedies have been treated almost as *addenda* to the 'substantive' subjects of contract, tort and equity. In English and Australian law, the first scholarly work devoted to remedies was F H Lawson's *Remedies of English Law*, first published in 1972.[1] Since then, many new works have appeared on the subject, but the contents of these works are often quite different. Beyond a few generally agreed core subjects, such as damages, injunctions and specific performance, there is no general consensus about what properly constitutes the law of remedies.[2] Given the absence of any judicial definition, there are at least four distinctions that help define the law of remedies.

---

1. Penguin Books, Harmondsworth, 1972.
2. S M Waddams, 'Remedies as a Legal Subject' (1983) 3 *Oxford Journal of Legal Studies* 113; R Zakrzewski, *Remedies Reclassified*, Oxford University Press, Oxford, 2005, pp 7–22.

Primary and secondary rights

1.2   First, a common starting point is the distinction between rights and remedies. According to the *Oxford English Dictionary*, the word 'remedy' derives from the Latin word *remedium*, meaning 'medicine, means of relief'.

The medical analogy is apt because remedies in law are often thought of, in a practical sense, as the medicine or means of relief for the violation of a legal right. In this context, the violation of a legal right is called a 'cause of action'; for example, a breach of contract, the commission of a tort, or a breach of an equitable or statutory duty. In *Letang v Cooper*, Diplock LJ (as he then was) said:

> A cause of action is simply a factual situation the existence of which entitles one person to obtain from the court a remedy against another person.[3]

1.3   The jurisprudential problem with the dichotomy between rights and remedies is that remedies are simply another species of rights. This was recognised by the philosopher John Austin[4] in the nineteenth century, when he drew a distinction between primary and secondary rights:

> Those which I call primary do not arise from injuries, or from violations of other rights and duties. Those which I call secondary … arise from violations of other rights and duties, or from injuries, delicts [torts], or offences.[5]

In terms of Austin's scheme, primary rights correspond with causes of action, and secondary rights correspond with remedies. Austin acknowledged that the distinction is illogical, because 'a primary right or duty is not of itself a right or duty, without the secondary right or duty by which it is sustained; and *e converso*'.[6] In this sense, there is truth in the old maxim *ubi jus ibi remedium* ('where there is a right there is a remedy').[7] So, why draw the distinction between rights and remedies? Austin's answer:

> The reason for describing the primary right and duty apart; for describing the injury apart; and for describing the remedy or punishment apart, is the clearness and compactness which results from the separation. The cause of the greater compactness is that the same remedial process is often applicable, not merely to this particular right, but to a great variety of classes of rights; and, therefore, if it be separated from the rights to which it is applicable, it may be disposed of at once; otherwise it must be frequently repeated.[8]

1.4   The 'clearness and compactness which results from the separation' of primary rights and remedies has attracted many lawyers — even those who

---

3.   [1965] 1 QB 232 at 242–3.

4.   Born 1790; died 1859.

5.   J Austin, *Lectures on Jurisprudence*, R Campbell (ed), 5th ed, John Murray, London, 1885, vol II, Lecture XLV, p 763.

6.   Austin, 1885, p 768. See also *Chase Manhattan Bank NA v Israel British Bank (London) Ltd* [1981] Ch 105 at 124 per Goulding J.

7.   Lord Denning was certainly at odds with most jurists when, in *Hill v C A Parsons & Co Ltd* [1972] 2 Ch 305 at 316, his Lordship declared that the maxim 'enables us to step over the trip-wires of previous cases and to bring the law into accord with the needs of today'.

8.   Austin, 1885, pp 767–8.

write books on contract and tort law, for they too invariably devote separate chapters to remedies. Books on remedies take that process a step further. Of course, it is not unknown for lawyers to find clarity in illogical distinctions. There is no difficulty here, though, as long as it is remembered that the purpose of drawing the distinction is not because it should be rigidly adhered to, but because it helps to describe the law. And as Waddams notes:

> The subject is worthy of study because it enables illuminating parallels to be drawn that cross the boundaries between contract and tort, and between law and equity.[9]

1.5   Austin's distinction between primary and secondary rights is reflected in the judgment of Lord Diplock in *Photo Production Ltd v Securicor Transport Ltd*,[10] where his Lordship said:

> Every failure to perform a primary obligation is a breach of contract. The secondary obligation on the part of the contract breaker to which it gives rise by implication of the common law is to pay monetary compensation to the other party for the loss sustained by him in consequence of the breach.[11]

His Lordship left aside 'those comparatively rare cases in which the court is able to enforce a primary obligation by decreeing specific performance of it'.[12]

1.6   For the most part, the distinction between primary and secondary rights works well in defining the boundaries of the law of remedies. However, even Austin acknowledged that in some cases 'so complete is the complication of the one branch of the law with the other, that some primary duties cannot be described with any approach to completeness in their own part of the law; they can only be apprehended by looking at the description of the corresponding injury'.[13] The clearest illustration of this integration of rights and remedies is torts where damage is an essential component of the cause of action, such as malicious falsehood, passing off and, most notably, the tort of negligence. In *Fairchild v Glenhaven Funeral Services Ltd* Lord Hoffmann, in considering the principles that govern a breach of duty and causation in negligence, said:

> ... it has long been recognised that the imposition of a duty of care in respect of particular conduct depends upon whether it is just and reasonable to impose it. Over vast areas of conduct one can generalise about the circumstances in which it will be considered just and reasonable to impose a duty of care: that is a consequence of *Donoghue (or M'Alister) v Stevenson*.[14] But there are still situations in which Lord Atkin's generalisation cannot fairly be applied and in which it is necessary to return to the underlying principle and inquire whether

---

9.   S M Waddams, 'Remedies as a Legal Subject' (1983) 3 *Oxford Journal of Legal Studies* 113 at 121.

10.   [1980] AC 827.

11.   [1980] AC 827 at 849. See B Dickson, 'The Contribution of Lord Diplock to the General Law of Contract' (1989) 9 *Oxford Journal of Legal Studies* 441 at 449. See also (1990) 10 *Oxford Journal of Legal Studies* 288.

12.   [1980] AC 827 at 848.

13.   Austin, 1885, p 768.

14.   [1932] AC 562; [1932] All ER Rep 1.

it would be just and reasonable to impose liability and what its nature and extent should be …

The same is true of causation. The concepts of fairness, justice and reason underlie the rules which state the causal requirements of liability for a particular form of conduct (or non-causal limits on that liability) just as much as they underlie the rules which determine that conduct to be tortious. And the two are inextricably linked together: the purpose of the causal requirement rules is to produce a just result by delimiting the scope of liability in a way which relates to the reasons why liability for the conduct in question exists in the first place.[15]

Remedies and procedure

1.7   Aside from the distinction between rights and remedies, the second basic distinction that assists in defining the law of remedies is the distinction between remedies and court procedure. According to the view adopted by the High Court in *Adam P Brown Male Fashions Pty Ltd v Philip Morris Inc*,[16] the distinction turns upon the difference between 'ends' and 'means'. Remedies are the 'ends' which the administration of justice seeks to achieve, and procedure is the 'means' for achieving those ends. Unfortunately, the distinction is difficult to apply in practice, and the truth is that a significant part of the law of remedies is procedural in nature.[17] That is particularly true of the law concerning interlocutory injunctions. Indeed, court practice and procedure has been fertile ground for the development of new remedies including super-injunctions, anonymised injunctions, freezing and search orders: see Chapters 8–10. The importance of interlocutory relief and procedural remedies is not to be underestimated. It may, as a practical matter, finally dispose of the proceedings: see 8.53.

Civil and criminal law

1.8   The third distinction that assists in defining the law of remedies is the difference between civil and criminal law. Except in so far as many crimes are also torts, we have confined our discussion to the civil law. Even so, punishment is not quite confined to the criminal law. The civil remedy of damages in tort manifests a punitive element in the form of exemplary damages: see 2.88–2.92.

Self-help and judicial remedies

1.9   The final distinction that we make, albeit with less justification than the above, is the distinction between self-help remedies and judicial remedies administered by the courts. Considerations of space have required us to exclude discussion of self-help remedies such as abatement of nuisance, eviction of trespassers, and, most importantly, termination of contracts for

---

15.   [2003] 1 AC 32 at [55]–[56].

16.   (1981) 148 CLR 170 at 176–7.

17.   See the discussion in *Goulandris Bros Ltd v Goldman (B) & Sons Ltd* [1958] 1 QB 74 at 99–100 per Pearson J.

breach. In these circumstances, the law concerning rescission of contracts poses a difficulty because the subject straddles the divide between self-help and judicial remedies. Rescission is, in theory, the act of the rescinding party. The role of the court is 'to adjudicate upon the validity of a purported disaffirmance … and, if it is valid, to give effect to it and make appropriate consequential orders'.[18] We have chosen to treat the law of rescission as a whole: see **Chapter 5**.

SCHEME OF THIS BOOK

1.10   This book discusses the major remedies in the four areas that comprise the law of obligations in common law jurisdictions; namely, tort, contract, equity and statute. Apart from adding the law of restitution, this is the traditional historical division and we have adhered to it, not because it is a logical division, but for the purposes of clarity and practicality. While we recognise the view that in some areas of remedial law the traditional historical divisions are of 'diminishing significance',[19] we have nonetheless distinguished in **Chapters 2** and **3** between damages in tort and damages in contract. This view is supported by the comments of Gleeson CJ, McHugh, Gummow and Hayne JJ in *Astley v Austrust Ltd*:

> … the conceptual and practical differences between the two causes of action remain of 'considerable importance'. The two causes of action have different elements, different limitation periods, different tests for remoteness of damage and … different apportionment rules.
>
> The theoretical foundations for actions in tort and contract are quite separate.[20]

The same reasoning applies to equitable compensation and to damages under the Competition and Consumer Act 2010 (Cth). Accordingly, these too are also dealt with separately in **Chapters 11** and **16**. Considerations of space make it impossible for us to discuss in any detail the multitude of statutory remedies enacted by the federal and state parliaments each year, so in **Part 5** of the book we have focused on the remedies available under the Contracts Review Act 1980 (NSW) and the Competition and Consumer Act 2010 (Cth).

---

18.   *Matt v Kruger* (1955) 94 CLR 216 at 224 per Dixon CJ, Webb, Kitto and Taylor JJ. See also *Cockburn v GIO Finance Ltd (No 2)* (2001) 51 NSWLR 624 at 638 per Ipp AJA (NSW CA).

19.   To adapt the words of Deane J in *Commonwealth v Amann Aviation Pty Ltd* (1991) 171 CLR 64 at 116 when discussing the historical division between contract and tort damages. See **2.3**.

20.   (1999) 197 CLR 1 at 23 (footnote omitted).

Part 2

COMMON LAW

CHAPTER

Damages in Tort

INTRODUCTION

2.1   Damages are an award of money by the court designed to compensate the plaintiff for injuries caused by the defendant's wrong. Damages in tort are intended to place the plaintiff, so far as money can, in the position he or she would have occupied had the tort not been committed. As explained by Lord Blackburn in *Livingstone v Rawyards Coal Co*:

> … where any injury is to be compensated by damages, in settling the sum of money to be given for reparation of damages you should nearly as possible get at that sum of money which will put the party who has been injured, or who has suffered, in the same position as he would have been in if he had not sustained the wrong for which he is now getting his compensation or reparation.[1]

The main common law exception to this 'cornerstone of tort law'[2] arises in those rare cases where exemplary damages are awarded. Here the principle is not one of compensation but, rather, punishment and deterrence: see **2.88–2.92**. The main statutory exceptions are the limits placed on the amounts that can be awarded as compensatory damages under the civil liability,[3] motor accident[4] and workers' compensation[5] legislation. But even under these reforms 'regard must still be had to the existing common law'.[6]

At the 'frontiers of tortious liability'[7] there is continuing uncertainty as to what is 'actionable damage' or an 'actionable injury'. Some injuries, even

---

1.   (1880) 5 App Cas 25 at 39; see also *Haines v Bendall* (1991) 172 CLR 60 at 63 per Mason CJ, Dawson, Toohey and Gaudron JJ.

2.   *Harriton v Stephens* (2004) 59 NSWLR 694; [2004] NSWCA 93 at [215] per Ipp JA.

3.   Civil Law (Wrongs) Act 2002 (ACT); Personal Injuries (Liabilities and Damages) Act 2003 (NT); Civil Liability Act 2002 (NSW); Civil Liability Act 2003 (Qld); Civil Liability Act 1936 (SA); Civil Liability Act 2002 (Tas); Wrongs Act 1958 (Vic); Civil Liability Act 2002 (WA).

4.   Motor Accidents (Compensation) Act 1979 (NT); Motor Accidents Compensation Act 1999 (NSW); Motor Accidents Act 1988 (NSW); Motor Accidents (Liabilities and Compensation) Act 1973 (Tas); Transport Accident Act 1986 (Vic).

5.   Safety, Rehabilitation and Compensation Act 1988 (Cth); Seafarers Rehabilitation and Compensation Act 1992 (Cth); Workers Compensation Act 1951 (ACT); Work Health Act 1986 (NT); Workers Compensation Act 1987 (NSW); Workers' Compensation and Rehabilitation Act 2003 (Qld); Workers Rehabilitation and Compensation Act 1986 (SA); Workers Rehabilitation and Compensation Act 1988 (Tas); Accident Compensation Act 1985 (Vic); Workers Compensation and Injury Management Act 1981 (WA).

6.   Dominic Villa, *Annotated Civil Liability Act 2002 (NSW)*, Law Book Co, 2004, p 128; compare Injury Prevention, Rehabilitation and Compensation Act 2001 (NZ) s 317 which abolishes the common law right to sue for personal injury.

7.   *Magill v Magill* (2006) 226 CLR 551 at [52] per Gummow, Kirby and Crennan JJ.

if reasonably foreseeable, might not give rise to a claim for damages. Three examples considered later in this chapter are the loss of a chance of a better outcome in medical negligence cases (see **2.28–2.30**), the negligent infliction of pure psychiatric harm (see **2.45–2.48**) and pure economic loss: see **2.49–2.52**. Also, the question as to whether 'wrongful birth' and 'wrongful life' claims amount to actionable damage was considered by the High Court in *Cattanach v Melchior*[8] and *Harriton v Stephens*.[9] The wrongful birth issue in *Cattanach* was whether the cost of raising a healthy but unplanned child conceived as a consequence of a doctor's negligence is actionable damage. A bare majority held that it was[10] and then several jurisdictions immediately passed laws to neutralise its effect.[11] It remains an actionable injury but the amount that can be awarded as compensation has been curtailed.[12] Writing extra-curially McHugh J concluded:

> … the epilogue to the High Court's decision in *Cattanach v Melchior* may be seen as revealing the impotence of the judiciary in resolving the significant controversies of the day. Such a view, however, entails an insufficiently sophisticated conception of the judicial contribution to pluralist democracy. In fact, the illustration is entirely consistent with the proposition that '[a]cts of judicial law-making have been known to set in motion a continuing process of reform'.[13]

2.2 By contrast, the High Court decision in favour of the defendant doctor in *Harriton v Stephens* has not 'set in motion a continuing process of reform'. The 6:1 majority refused to recognise 'wrongful life' as an actionable injury where a severely disabled plaintiff would not have been born but for a doctor's negligence. The doctor failed to diagnose rubella in the mother during pregnancy and she therefore lost an opportunity to terminate the pregnancy. The daughter, Alexia Harriton, was born with severe lifelong disabilities including blindness, deafness, mental retardation and spasticity. She claimed special damages for her past and future medical costs and general damages for pain and suffering. But the trial judge, Studdert J, found against her and so did the New South Wales Court of Appeal[14] and the High Court. In the High Court Crennan J in the majority held:

> A comparison between a life with disabilities and non-existence, for the purposes of proving actual damage and having a trier of fact apprehend the

---

8.   (2003) 215 CLR 1; [2003] HCA 38.

9.   (2006) 226 CLR 52; [2006] HCA 15 and see *Waller v James*; *Waller v Hoolahan* (2006) 226 CLR 136.

10.   McHugh, Gummow, Kirby and Callinan JJ (Gleeson CJ, Hayne and Heydon JJ dissenting); compare *McFarlane v Tayside Health Board* [2000] 2 AC 59; *Rees v Darlington Memorial Hospital NHS Trust* [2004] 1 AC 309.

11.   Civil Liability Act 2003 (Qld) Pt 5; Civil Liability Act 2002 (NSW) Pt 11; Civil Liability Act 1936 (SA) s 67.

12.   See *Harriton v Stephens* (2004) 59 NSWLR 694; [2004] NSWCA 93 at [165] per Mason P (in dissent).

13.   'The strengths of the weakest arm' (2004) 25 *Aust Bar Rev* 181 at 188 citing M H McHugh, 'The Law making Function of the Judicial Process' (1988) 62 *ALJ* 15 (Part I), 116 (Part II) at 124; see also Justice Kirby, 'Judicial Activism? A Riposte to the Counter Reformation' (2004) 24 *Aust Bar Rev* 21.

14.   (2004) 59 NSWLR 694; [2004] NSWCA 93.

nature of the damage caused, is impossible. Judges in a number of cases have recognised the impossibility of the comparison and in doing so references have been made to philosophers and theologians as persons better schooled than courts in apprehending the ideas of non-being, nothingness and the afterlife.

There is no present field of human learning or discourse, including philosophy and theology, which would allow a person experiential access to non-existence, whether it is called pre-existence or afterlife. There is no practical possibility of a court (or jury) ever apprehending or evaluating, or receiving proof of, the actual loss or damage as claimed by the appellant. It cannot be determined in what sense Alexia Harriton's life with disabilities represents a loss, deprivation or detriment compared with non-existence.[15]

The sole dissenting decision in favour of allowing the plaintiff's appeal was Kirby J's. His Honour came to the following conclusion:

Denying the existence of wrongful life actions erects an immunity around health care providers whose negligence results in a child who would not otherwise have existed, being born into a life of suffering. Here, that suffering is profound, substantial and apparently lifelong. The immunity would be accorded regardless of the gravity of the acts and omissions of negligence that could be proved. The law should not approve a course which would afford such an immunity and which would offer no legal deterrent to professional carelessness or even professional irresponsibility.

In virtually all matters where wrongful life remedies would be available by the application of common law principles, legislatures in Australia would ultimately have the last word. But just as parliaments have their functions in our governance and law-making, so have the courts. The courts develop the common law in a principled way. They give reasons for what they do. They constantly strive for the attainment of consistency with established legal principles as well as justice in the individual case.

In the present appeal, that approach favours the provision of damages to the appellant whose life of profound suffering and costly care is a direct result of the agreed negligence of the respondent. That is why this case is not really to be labelled as one about wrongful life. The appellant's life exists. It will continue to exist. No one suggests otherwise. The question is who should pay for the suffering, loss and damage that flow from the respondent's carelessness. That is why the proper label for the appellant's action, if one is needed, is 'wrongful suffering'. The ordinary principles of negligence law sustain a decision in the appellant's favour. None of the propounded reasons of legal principle or legal policy suggests a different outcome.[16]

2.3   This chapter discusses the principles of compensatory damages in tort, although there is an emphasis on negligence. Damages in contract, equity and under the Competition and Consumer Act 2010 (Cth) are dealt with in Chapters 3, 11 and 16 respectively. Recovery of money acquired by the defendant's tort and restitutionary damages based on the defendant's tort are dealt with in Chapter 4: see 4.33–4.35 and 4.36–4.39 respectively.

---

15.   (2006) 226 CLR 52; [2006] HCA 15 at [252]–[253].

16.   (2006) 226 CLR 52; [2006] HCA 15 at [153]–[155].

The layout of this chapter and the following chapter, 'Damages in Contract', is basically the same because many of the principles guiding the award of damages in contract and tort are similar; indeed, the main elements are identical. But the choice to use two separate chapters is based on practicality. For the most part practising lawyers still separate the remedy of damages into compartments based on the underlying causes of action. This approach finds support in many cases. In *Commonwealth v Amann Aviation Pty Ltd*, Deane J introduced the topic of damages in contract by observing:

> While the general principle is the same in both contract and tort, the rules governing its application in the two areas may differ in some circumstances. Those differences are largely the result of historical considerations in that they reflect distinctions between causes of action rather than reasoned development or exegesis of the law. They are of diminishing significance for most purposes (note, for example, the gradual assimilation of the tests of 'within the contemplation of the parties' (in contract) and 'reasonably foreseeable' (in tort): see, for example, *Parsons Ltd v Uttley Ingham & Co*[17] but cf., e.g., *C Czarnikow Ltd v Koufos*).[18] Nonetheless, the stage has not been reached where they can be ignored and it is arguable that the fact that actual damage is not an essential element of a cause of action in contract is important in relation to some aspects of the present case.[19]

But in *Astley v Austrust*,[20] a professional negligence case concerning a solicitor's concurrent liability in tort and contract, it was the differences between the actions that dominated the High Court's reasoning, rather than the similarities. The court has also warned on several occasions that it is not 'always sound' to 'assimilate' various causes of action, particularly those in contract and tort.[21]

ELEMENTS

2.4   If the plaintiff is to receive *compensatory* damages in tort, the court must find that:

a)   the plaintiff has a tortious *cause of action* against the defendant;

b)   the defendant's tort has *in fact caused* the plaintiff's loss;

c)   the plaintiff's loss *is not too remote*; and

d)   the plaintiff has not breached his or her 'duty' to *mitigate* unnecessary loss.

Arguably these 'elements' are better described as 'guidelines', but the choice to describe them as 'elements' is based on the notion that a failure to satisfy any one of them will be fatal to the plaintiff's case.

---

17.   [1978] QB 791.

18.   [1969] 1 AC 350.

19.   (1991) 174 CLR 64 at 116. The facts are discussed at 3.43.

20.   See (1999) 197 CLR 1 at [47] per Gleeson CJ, McHugh, Gummow and Hayne JJ and the extract at 1.10.

21.   *Commonwealth v Cornwell* (2007) 229 CLR 519 at [4] per Gleeson CJ, Gummow, Kirby, Hayne, Heydon and Crennan JJ.

2.5   Both at common law[22] and under the civil liability statutes[23] the plaintiff bears the burden of proving the first three elements with 'reasonable certainty' as opposed to 'absolute certainty'.[24] Certainty is not a separate element, but refers to the standard or standards of proof applicable to each element.[25] Generally, the plaintiff's cause of action must be proved on the balance of probabilities.[26] This does not mean this standard is to be applied rigidly to each element in damages. Where the loss cannot be easily measured or calculated,[27] such as where damages are presumed or assessed 'at large'[28] in defamation and passing off, a different approach is used in assessing the amount of the loss. There also appears to be a different approach in unusual cases involving several tortfeasors (see **2.31–2.36**).

2.6   In the last element, mitigation, the defendant bears the burden of proving[29] that the plaintiff has breached his or her 'duty' to mitigate loss flowing from the defendant's wrong. Put another way, the plaintiff is presumed to have taken reasonable steps towards mitigating unnecessary loss unless the defendant proves to the contrary. The word 'duty' in this context should be treated with caution, since, unlike other duties, if breached, it does not result in a cause of action, nor is the plaintiff regarded as being contributorily negligent. Breach of the duty merely reduces the amount of damages payable: see **2.53–2.56**.

The defendant will also bear the burden of proof where it is alleged that the plaintiff is guilty of contributory negligence: see **2.15–2.20**.

CAUSE OF ACTION

2.7   There is a long and diverse list of torts supporting a right to compensatory damages, including: assault, abuse of process, battery, conspiracy, conversion, deceit, defamation, detinue, duress, false imprisonment, inducing a breach of contract, injurious (or malicious) falsehood, interference with contract,

---

22. *Todorovic v Waller* (1981) 150 CLR 402 at 412 per Gibbs CJ.

23. The plaintiff bears the onus of proving on the balance of probabilities 'any fact relevant to the issue of causation': see Civil Law (Wrongs) Act 2002 (ACT) s 46; Civil Liability Act 2002 (NSW) s 5E; Civil Liability Act 2003 (Qld) s 12; Civil Liability Act 1936 (SA) s 35; Civil Liability Act 2002 (Tas) s 12; Wrongs Act 1958 (Vic) s 52; Civil Liability Act 2002 (WA) s 5D.

24. For a discussion on 'certainty' see Luntz, *Assessment of Damages for Personal Injury and Death*, 4th ed, LexisNexis Butterworths, Sydney, 2002, pp 94–123.

25. As reflected in the reasons of the majority in *Sellars v Adelaide Petroleum NL* (1994) 179 CLR 332 at 355–6 per Mason CJ, Dawson, Toohey and Gaudron JJ.

26. *Sellars v Adelaide Petroleum NL* (1994) 179 CLR at 351 and 355 per Mason CJ, Dawson, Toohey and Gaudron JJ. See also Civil Law (Wrongs) Act 2002 (ACT) s 46; Civil Liability Act 2002 (NSW) s 5E; Civil Liability Act 2003 (Qld) s 12; Civil Liability Act 1936 (SA) s 35; Civil Liability Act 2002 (Tas) s 12; Wrongs Act 1958 (Vic) s 52; Civil Liability Act 2002 (WA) s 5D.

27. See Luntz, *Assessment of Damages for Personal Injury and Death*, 4th ed, LexisNexis Butterworths, Sydney, 2002, pp 94–123.

28. The meaning of this phrase is considered at **2.76–2.77**.

29. See *Watts v Rake* (1960) 108 CLR 158 at 159 per Dixon CJ and 163 per Menzies J; *Purkess v Crittenden* (1965) 114 CLR 164; *Munce v Vinidex* [1974] 2 NSWLR 235 (CA); *Geest plc v Lansiquot* [2003] 1 All ER 383; [2002] UKPC 48; compare *Selvanayagam v University of the West Indies* [1983] 1 WLR 585 (PC).

malicious prosecution, misfeasance in public office, negligence, negligent misstatement, nuisance, passing off, trespass to land, trespass to goods and, perhaps, invasion of privacy (as to which, see 8.16).

The character and make-up of the cause of action have a dramatic effect on how the court examines the plaintiff's claim for damages. For example, in defamation, passing off, false imprisonment, interference with contract and malicious prosecution, damages are assessed 'at large'. There is a presumption that the natural and probable consequence of the tort is injury or damage. Issues involving causation and remoteness of damage, while not irrelevant, are much less pronounced. Actual damage may be shown but it is ordinarily immaterial in proving the commission of the tort even if damage is an element in the cause of action (as is the case with passing off). By contrast, in negligence the plaintiff lacks the benefit of any such presumption or notion that damages are 'at large'. Proof of actual injury or damage is an essential element in the cause of action itself, and thus the action will not accrue unless damage occurs.[30] Here, damage is said to be the 'gist of the action'[31] because without it, there is no action.

Apart from actions where damage is the 'gist of the action', establishing a tortious cause of action without proof of actual damage merely entitles the plaintiff to nominal damages.[32] Such an award, while insignificant, usually allows the plaintiff to be awarded the costs of the action. However, the plaintiff will be deprived of this too if the damages are categorised as contemptuous rather than nominal. Contemptuous damages (the 'smallest coin in the realm') indicate that the action should never have been brought. For example, in *Connolly v Sunday Times Publishing Co Ltd*[33] the jury awarded one shilling as damages and the High Court upheld the trial judge's decision to deny the plaintiff's costs of an 11-day trial and commissions to London and Victoria.

To obtain more than nominal or contemptuous damages the plaintiff must establish the balance of the elements discussed below.

CAUSATION

Introduction

2.8 The plaintiff's damage or loss must have *in fact* been caused by the defendant's tortious wrong. But this is not a straightforward issue — questions concerning causation create just as much havoc in law as they do in philosophy. The legal test needs to go beyond the logic of cause and effect. As observed by Mason CJ in *March v E & M H Stramare Pty Ltd*:

30. *Commonwealth v Cornwell* [2007] HCA 16; (2007) 234 ALR 148.

31. *Harriton v Stephens* (2006) 226 CLR 52; [2006] HCA 15 at [251] per Crennan J; (2004) 59 NSWLR 694; [2004] NSWCA 93 at [239], [253] per Ipp JA.

32. See, for example, *Wheeler v Riverside Coal Transport Co Pty Ltd* [1964] Qd R 113; *General Tire & Rubber Co v Firestone Tyre & Rubber Co Ltd* [1975] 1 WLR 819; *Spalding v Gamage* (1915) 32 RPC 273 (passing off).

33. *Connolly v Sunday Times Publishing Co Ltd* (1908) 7 CLR 263.

It has often been said that the legal concept of causation differs from philosophical and scientific notions of causation. That is, because 'questions of cause and consequence are not the same for law as for philosophy and science', as Windeyer J pointed out in *National Insurance Co of New Zealand Ltd v Espagne*.[34] In philosophy and science, the concept of causation has been developed in the context of explaining phenomena by reference to the relationship between conditions and occurrences. In law, on the other hand, problems of causation arise in the context of ascertaining or apportioning legal responsibility for a given occurrence. The law does not accept John Stuart Mill's definition of cause as the sum of the conditions which are jointly sufficient to produce it. Thus, at law, the person may be responsible for damage when his or her wrongful conduct is one of a number of conditions sufficient to produce that damage.[35]

Part of the coping mechanism in common law has been to split causation into two issues: namely, causation in fact and causation in law.[36] Causation in fact is usually decided by the application of the 'but for' test.[37] The court asks: but for the defendant's wrong, would the plaintiff have suffered the loss or damage complained of? If the loss or damage would have occurred despite the wrong, the claim must fail for lack of a causal connection. However, as discussed at **2.10–2.11**, this test, combined with the requirement of proof on a balance of probabilities, yields odd results where the court identifies several causes or multiple sufficient causes of the plaintiff's loss. In any event, if the court finds as a matter of fact that the defendant did cause the plaintiff's loss, it then decides whether there is causation in *law*. Some feel that policy and value judgments are to be taken into account at both stages of the enquiry;[38] but this view is also criticised because it allows uncertain policy factors to cloud what ought to be a factual issue.[39] The Civil Liability Acts (which, in this respect, alter the common law approach in negligence cases — see **2.12–2.13**) recognise this criticism by separating factual causation from the question whether the defendant *ought* to be liable — the latter question taking account of all relevant policy factors (whether previously taken into account in determining causation or remoteness). But, at least in cases which do not involve the Civil Liability Acts, the High Court[40] still favours the approach in

---

34. (1961) 105 CLR 569 at 591.

35. Citing in support *McLean v Bell* (1932) 147 LT 262 at 264 per Lord Wright; *Sherman v Nymboida Collieries Pty Ltd* (1963) 109 CLR 580 at 590–1 per Windeyer J.

36. *March v E & M H Stramare Pty Ltd* (1991) 171 CLR 506 at 515 per Mason CJ.

37. *March v E & M H Stramare Pty Ltd* (1991) 171 CLR 506; *Tabet v Gett* (2010) 240 CLR 537; [2010] HCA 12. The 'but for' test is also known by its Latin formulation: *causa sine qua non* (literally 'a cause without which [there would be] nothing'). See also the slightly different formulation of the factual causation test in the Civil Liability Acts, discussed at **2.12–2.13**.

38. See the views expressed in *March v E & M H Stramare Pty Ltd* (1991) 171 CLR 506 by Mason CJ at [19] and Deane J at [6]–[7].

39. See the views expressed by McHugh J in *March v E & M H Stramare Pty Ltd* (1991) 171 CLR 506 at [12]–[21]; and Ipp JA in *Ruddock & Ors v Taylor* [2003] NSWCA 262 at [85]–[88].

40. *Travel Compensation Fund v Robert Tambree t/as R Tambree and Associates* [2005] HCA 69 per Kirby J at [55] and Callinan J at [79]–[81]; *Tabet v Gett* [2010] HCA 12 per Kiefel J at [112]; *Amaca v Ellis* [2010] HCA 5; *Amaca Pty Ltd v Booth; Amaba Pty Ltd v Booth* [2011] HCA 53.

March v E & M H Stramare Pty Ltd,[41] which allows policy factors to intrude in the causation issue, with common sense as the yardstick.[42] Whichever approach is taken, the result is a policy cap on recoverable damages because the court might refuse to award, as a matter of *law*, damages for the loss even though in *fact* the loss was caused by the defendant.

2.9 Some of the difficulties with causation are a result of uncertainty about how the standard of proof is to be satisfied. Proof of an historical fact, such as causation, is ordinarily governed by the general civil standard.[43] In *Malec v J C Hutton Pty Ltd (No 2)*, Deane, Gaudron and McHugh JJ observed:

> A common law court determines on the balance of probabilities whether an event has occurred. If the probability of the event having occurred is greater than it not having occurred, the occurrence of the event is treated as certain; if the probability of the event having occurred is less than it not having occurred, it is treated as not having occurred.[44]

However, strict application of the requirement for proof on a balance of probabilities can produce unsatisfactory results when a number of events combine to cause the loss — as illustrated by the facts of *March v E & M H Stramare Pty Ltd*, discussed at **2.10**. The endorsement of the 'common sense' approach by the High Court in that case not only allows factual causation to be tempered by policy factors, but also enables courts to avoid some of these unsatisfactory results. The ways in which courts apportion liability (discussed in relation to contributory negligence, joint, concurrent and successive tortfeasors in **2.15–2.27**) illustrate this common sense approach. There remain, however, two situations in which requiring proof of causation on a balance of probabilities still causes difficulties: the loss of a chance and alternative causes where there is an 'evidential gap'. These are discussed at **2.28–2.36**.

Multiple causes and common sense

2.10 In *Amaca Pty Ltd v Booth; Amaba Pty Ltd v Booth*,[45] Gummow, Hayne and Crennan JJ noted that, for historical reasons, courts had used the 'but for' test to 'embrace a view of causation which assigned occurrences to a single cause'.[46] They mentioned two reasons: the preponderance of jury trials in which causation was seen as a question of fact to be decided by the jury; and the common law view that contributory negligence was an 'absolute defence'

---

41. (1991) 171 CLR 506.

42. See **2.10–2.11**.

43. *Sellars v Adelaide Petroleum NL* (1994) 179 CLR 332 at 355 per Mason CJ, Dawson, Toohey and Gaudron JJ; *Medlin v State Government Insurance Commission* (1995) 182 CLR 1 at 6 per Deane, Dawson, Toohey and Gaudron JJ (HCA); *Mallet v McMonagle* [1970] AC 166 at 176 per Lord Diplock; Civil Law (Wrongs) Act 2002 (ACT) s 46; Civil Liability Act 2002 (NSW) s 5E; Civil Liability Act 2003 (Qld) s 12; Civil Liability Act 1936 (SA) s 35; Civil Liability Act 2002 (Tas) s 12; Wrongs Act 1958 (Vic) s 52; Civil Liability Act 2002 (WA) s 5D.

44. (1990) 169 CLR 638 at 642–3.

45. [2011] HCA 53 at [65], [66].

46. A phrase used by Mason CJ in *March v E & M H Stramare Pty Ltd* (1991) 171 CLR 506 at 511.

which prevented courts from apportioning liability between a negligent plaintiff and defendant. However, as they pointed out,[47] these reasons have lost force with the decline in civil trials by jury and the introduction of apportionment legislation (as to which, see **2.15**).

The High Court acknowledged in the watershed case of *March v E & M H Stramare Pty Ltd* that the 'but for' test was 'inadequate or troublesome'.[48] The facts in *March v E & M H Stramare Pty Ltd* involved contributory negligence, but the difficulty applies equally to any set of multiple causes. The plaintiff was injured when, at about 1 am, the car he was driving hit the defendant's truck which was parked in the middle of the street. The evidence showed that the truck had its parking and hazard lights on, but that the plaintiff was drunk at the time of the collision. The trial judge found the way in which the defendant's truck was parked was negligent and in breach of the duty of care owed to other road users, including careless and drunk road users. However, the plaintiff was also negligent and the trial judge apportioned liability at 70 per cent attributable to the plaintiff and 30 per cent to the truck driver. The Full South Australian Supreme Court overturned this finding. Given that the truck driver's negligence was only 30 per cent to blame, it could not be said on the balance of probabilities (that is, with a more than 50 per cent probability) that the truck driver's negligence caused the loss. It held that the sole effective cause of the collision was the plaintiff's own negligence. On this reasoning it can be observed that if there had been four different causes, each equally to blame for the accident (25 per cent), none of them could be proven on a balance of probabilities to be an effective cause.

The plaintiff appealed to the High Court and won. The court found that the defendant's negligence in parking the truck was also a cause of the accident and it restored the judgment of the trial judge. Mason CJ referred to the 'well known difficulty … where there are two or more acts or events which would each be sufficient [in law] to bring about the plaintiff's injury'.[49] The application of the 'but for' test 'gives the result, contrary to common sense, that neither is a cause' because neither is more than 50 per cent to blame.[50] The Chief Justice then observed:

> In truth, the application of the test proves to be either inadequate or troublesome in various situations in which there are multiple acts or events leading to the plaintiff's injury … The cases demonstrate the lesson of experience, namely, that the test applied as an exclusive criterion of causation, yields unacceptable results and that the results which it yields must be tempered by the making of value judgments and the infusion of policy considerations.[51]

---

47.   [2011] HCA 53 at [67].

48.   *March v E & M H Stramare Pty Ltd* (1991) 171 CLR 506 at 516 per Mason CJ and 523 per Deane J.

49.   (1991) 171 CLR 506 at 516.

50.   J A Jolowicz and W V H Rogers, *Winfield and Jolowicz on Tort*, 13th ed, Sweet & Maxwell, London, 1989, p 134, cited with approval by Mason CJ (1991) 171 CLR 506 at 516. See also Deane J at 522–3; McHugh J at 534.

51.   (1991) 171 CLR 506 at 516, applied in *Chappel v Hart* (1998) 195 CLR 232.

This observation reinforces an earlier conclusion of the High Court in *Fitzgerald v Penn*.[52] Dixon CJ, Fullagar and Kitto JJ observed with characteristic brevity that causation 'is not susceptible of reduction to a satisfactory formula';[53] that the ultimate question was 'whether a particular act or omission … can fairly and properly be considered a cause of the accident',[54] and it was 'all ultimately a matter of common sense'.[55] In *March*, Mason CJ also favoured a test which incorporates or relies on 'common sense'[56] and Deane J was of a similar view.[57] By contrast, McHugh J preferred to limit causation to a factual enquiry. He doubted whether there was 'any consistent common sense notion of what constitutes a 'cause' '[58] and objected that:

> … if the 'but for' test is applied in a 'practical common sense way', it enables the tribunal of fact, consciously or unconsciously, to give effect to value judgments concerning responsibility for the damage.[59]

The court recognised, however, that, in the words of Mason CJ:

> the law's recognition that concurrent or successive tortious acts may each amount to a cause of the injuries sustained by a plaintiff is reflected in the proposition that it is for the plaintiff to establish that his or her injuries are "caused or materially contributed to" by the defendant's wrongful conduct …[60]

Where there are multiple causes, requiring the plaintiff to prove on a balance of probability that the defendant's negligent conduct *materially contributed* as a cause of the harm makes the requirement far more intuitive. Care should be taken, however, not to confuse material contribution as a cause of the harm with material contribution to the risk of harm — see **2.34–2.36**.

2.11   Where does this leave the 'but for' test? It has not been replaced; and, at least in cases that do not fall under the Civil Liability Acts, the views of Mason CJ and Deane J have prevailed over those of McHugh J. While courts no longer look for the single cause of a loss, they still use the 'but for' test as a useful starting point. Indeed, the High Court has confirmed in cases after *March* that the 'but for' test is to be applied (to adopt the words of Glass JA (in dissent) in *Alexander v Cambridge Credit Corporation Ltd*) in a 'practical common sense way'.[61] Thus in *Bennett v Minister of Community Welfare*, Mason CJ, Deane and Toohey JJ in a joint judgment held:

52.   (1954) 91 CLR 268; cited by Mason CJ in *March* (1991) 171 CLR 506 at 515.

53.   (1954) 91 CLR 268 at 278.

54.   *Fitzgerald v Penn* (1954) 91 CLR 268 at 276.

55.   (1954) 91 CLR 268 at 278.

56.   (1991) 171 CLR 506 at 518–19.

57.   (1991) 171 CLR 506 at 524. See also *Medlin v State Government Insurance Commission* (1995) 182 CLR 1 at 6 per Deane, Dawson, Toohey and Gaudron JJ.

58.   (1991) 171 CLR 506 at 532.

59.   (1991) 171 CLR 506 at 532.

60.   (1991) 171 CLR 506 per Mason CJ at [16].

61.   (1987) 9 NSWLR 310 at 315.

In the realm of negligence, causation is essentially a question of fact, to be resolved as a matter of common sense. In resolving that question, the 'but for' test, applied as a negative criterion of causation, has an important role to play but it is not a comprehensive and exclusive test of causation; value judgments and policy considerations necessarily intrude.[62]

Gaudron J in a similar vein held that 'it is now settled that, in the context of tortious liability, questions of causation are questions of fact to be answered as a matter of common sense and experience'.[63] More recent High Court cases all affirm this approach.[64]

Use of the common sense approach does not, however, relieve the court from explaining its reasons for imposing or withholding liability. In *Fairchild v Glenhaven Funeral Services Ltd* Lord Hoffman in the House of Lords said:

> … the causal requirements for liability are normally framed in accordance with common sense. But there is sometimes a tendency to appeal to common sense in order to avoid having to explain one's reasons. It suggests that causal requirements are a matter of incommunicable judicial instinct. I do not think that this is right. It should be possible to give reasons why one form of causal relationship will do in one situation but not in another.[65]

Causation under the Civil Liability Acts

2.12　　As a result of the recommendations of the Ipp Report,[66] the Civil Liability Acts[67] adopted the approach to causation preferred by McHugh J in *March v E & M H Stramare Pty Ltd*.[68] The New South Wales Act provides:

5D General principles

(1) A determination that negligence caused particular harm comprises the following elements:

(a) that the negligence was a necessary condition of the occurrence of the harm ("factual causation"), and

(b) that it is appropriate for the scope of the negligent person's liability to extend to the harm so caused ("scope of liability").

This approach requires the factual issue of causation to be treated as a separate question from whether there *ought* to be liability. Further discussion of the scope of liability — and the policy factors and value judgments which are to be taken into account — is included in the discussion of remoteness

---

62. (1992) 176 CLR 408 at 413; but note that the approach in negligence claims is now modified by the Civil Liability Acts.

63. (1992) 176 CLR 408 at 418–19. See also *Chappel v Hart* (1998) 195 CLR 232 at 238 per Gaudron J.

64. *Tabet v Gett* [2010] HCA 12; *Amaca Pty Ltd v Ellis* [2010] HCA 5; *Amaca Pty Ltd v Booth; Amaba Pty Ltd v Booth* [2011] HCA 53.

65. [2003] 1 AC 32 at [53].

66. Commonwealth of Australia, *Review of the Law of Negligence: Final Report*, (2002) at [7.26]–[7.51].

67. Civil Law (Wrongs) Act 2002 (ACT) s 45; Civil Liability Act 2002 (NSW) s 5D; Civil Liability Act 2003 (Qld) s 11; Civil Liability Act 1936 (SA) s 34; Civil Liability Act 2002 (Tas) s 13; Wrongs Act 1958 (Vic) s 51; Civil Liability Act 2002 (WA) s 5C. The Personal Injuries (Liabilities and Damages) Act 2003 (NT) does not have similar provisions dealing with causation.

68. (1991) 171 CLR 506 at [11]–[21].

at **2.41**. As for factual causation, in *Adeels Palace Pty Ltd v Moubarak*, the High Court acknowledged that the Act 'expresses the relevant questions in a way that may differ from what was said by Mason CJ, in *March v Stramare (E & M H) Ltd*',[69] but refused to speculate on whether and to what extent the different approaches might lead to different conclusions. The court made it clear that 'where the Civil Liability Act or equivalent statutes are engaged, it is the applicable statutory provision that must be applied'.[70] Despite this, in applying s 5D(1)(a), the court saw no difference between the 'but for' test and the 'necessary condition' test. It said 'the first of the two elements identified in s 5D(1) (factual causation) is determined by the "but for" test';[71] and later, 'In the present case, … the "but for" test of factual causation was not established. … [The breach of duty] was not a necessary condition of the occurrence of the harm …'.[72] In cases applying the necessary condition test, there has been no discernable difference in the outcome.[73]

2.13 So when are the Civil Liability Acts 'engaged'? Again, the wording is slightly different as between the various Acts, but their common ambit in this respect appears to be claims based in negligence, whether the claim is phrased in tort, contract, under statute or otherwise,[74] although most of the Acts contain exclusions relating to other more specific regimes, such as those applying to dust and smoking diseases, motor accidents compensation schemes and workers compensation.

Intervening events

2.14 Whichever approach to causation is to be used, the defendant may escape liability if the chain of causation is broken by a later event which is seen as the real cause of the loss.[75] Such an event is described as a new intervening act (*novus actus interveniens*). Even though the original wrongful act may have been a necessary condition for the harm to occur, the subsequent event is seen as overtaking the causal connection. The subsequent event must arise independently of the original wrong; and must disturb the sequence of events that would have been anticipated. Events which are reasonably foreseeable will not break the chain.[76]

---

69. [2009] HCA 48 at [43] per French CJ, Gummow, Hayne, Heydon and Crennan JJ.

70. [2009] HCA 48 at [44]. See also *Zanner v Zanner* [2010] NSWCA 343 per Tobias JA at [64].

71. [2009] HCA 48 at [45].

72. [2009] HCA 48 at [53]; and see *Strong v Woolworths Ltd* [2012] HCA 5 at [18].

73. See, for example, *Al Mousawy v Howitt Stevens Constructions Pty Limited* [2010] NSWSC 122; *Joranorski v Billbergia Pty Ltd* [2010] NSWSC 211; *Zanner v Zanner* [2010] NSWCA 343; and *Strong v Woolworths Ltd* [2012] HCA 5.

74. The approach and wording in the Acts is not entirely consistent, but see Civil Law (Wrongs) Act 2002 (ACT) s 41; Civil Liability Act 2002 (NSW) s 5A; Civil Liability Act 2003 (Qld) s 4; Civil Liability Act 1936 (SA) s 4 and 34(1); Civil Liability Act 2002 (Tas) s 10; Wrongs Act 1958 (Vic) s 44 and 45; Civil Liability Act 2002 (WA) s 5A. The Personal Injuries (Liabilities and Damages) Act 2003 (NT) does not have similar provisions.

75. *March v E & M H Stramare Pty Ltd* (1991) 171 CLR 506 at 512; *Bennet v Minister of Community Welfare* (1992) 176 CLR 408 at 413.

76. *Haber v Walker* [1963] VR 339; *Medlin v State Government Insurance Commission* (1995) 182 CLR 1.

A *novus actus interveniens* is to be distinguished from a subsequent tortious act that aggravates or contributes to the original damage, in which case the principles relating to successive tortfeasors discussed at **2.25–2.27** will apply.

Contributory negligence

2.15 The approach to causation and contributory negligence in *March v E & M H Stramare Pty Ltd*[77] was only made possible by legislation permitting responsibility to be shared. Such sharing was not possible at common law. If the defendant established that the plaintiff's own negligence contributed to the damage this was a complete bar to recovery. The common law 'defence' was harsh because proof of even a small amount of contributory negligence was sufficient to deny the plaintiff's claim in its entirety.[78] The courts responded by developing rules such as the 'last opportunity' rule, which allowed recovery if the defendant had the 'last opportunity' to avoid the harm.[79] There was also the 'agony of the moment' rule; that is, the plaintiff's negligence was ignored or an allowance was made for it if it occurred in the 'agony of the moment' caused by the defendant's negligence.[80] The need for such convoluted rules was overcome by the apportionment legislation enacted in all Australian jurisdictions and New Zealand.[81] With the exception of Western Australia, they were all originally modelled on s 1(1) of the English Law Reform (Contributory Negligence) Act 1945, which provides:

> Where any person suffers damage as the result partly of his own fault and partly of the fault of any other person or persons, a claim in respect of that damage shall not be defeated by reason of the fault of the person suffering the damage, but the damages recoverable in respect thereof shall be reduced to such extent as the court thinks just and equitable having regard to the claimant's share in the responsibility for the damage …

2.16 In New South Wales the key apportionment provision affecting contributory negligence claims is found in s 9(1) of the Law Reform (Miscellaneous Provisions) Act 1965. It provides:

> If a person (the *claimant*) suffers damage as the result partly of the claimant's failure to take reasonable care (*contributory negligence*) and partly of the wrong of any other person:
>
> (a) a claim in respect of the damage is not defeated by reason of the contributory negligence of the claimant, and
>
> (b) the damages recoverable in respect of the wrong are to be reduced to such extent as the court thinks just and equitable having regard to the claimant's share in the responsibility for the damage.[82]

---

77. (1991) 171 CLR 506.

78. See *Joslyn v Berryman* (2003) 214 CLR 552; [2003] HCA 34 at [17] per McHugh J.

79. See *Alford v Magee* (1952) 85 CLR 437; *Joslyn v Berryman* (2003) 214 CLR 552; [2003] HCA 34 at [18] per McHugh J.

80. See *Municipal Tramways Trust v Ashby* [1951] SASR 61.

81. Contributory Negligence Act 1947 (NZ).

82. See also Law Reform (Miscellaneous Provisions) Act 1955 (ACT) s 15(1); Law Reform (Miscellaneous Provisions) Act (NT) s 16; Law Reform Act 1995 (Qld) s 10(1); Law Reform (Contributory

Section 8 defines 'damage' as including 'loss of life and personal injury'. While s 13 goes on to provide that claims by relatives under the Compensation to Relatives Act 1897 (the New South Wales re-enactment of Lord Campbell's Act)[83] will not be defeated or reduced by the contributory negligence of the deceased, this is subject to s 5T(2) of the Civil Liability Act 2002 (NSW), which allows for such a reduction in most claims.[84] There are equivalent statutory provisions in other jurisdictions.[85] It is also important to note that there are statutory presumptions deeming contributory negligence, for example, where the injured person or deceased was intoxicated by alcohol or drugs[86] or was not wearing a seat belt or a safety helmet in a motor vehicle accident.[87]

2.17 *March v E & M H Stramare Pty Ltd*,[88] discussed above, provides one illustration of how apportionment legislation is applied; another instructive case focusing on deemed or presumed contributory negligence is *Joslyn v Berryman*.[89] On Friday 25 October 1996 Sally Joslyn and Allan Berryman commenced a 'drinking binge of heroic proportions'[90] in the lead-up to Mr Rowan Crisp's Saturday night 21st birthday party in Dareton, a town in south-western New South Wales. On the Saturday morning Mr Berryman said he felt 'fairly crook' but he still managed to work during the day and rest for a time before heading off to the party at about 9 pm.[91] Travelling in another car, Ms Joslyn had already arrived at the party at about 7 pm with a bottle of Grants Scotch Whisky 'which she seemed to demolish that night, perhaps without anyone else's assistance'.[92] Similarly, with only 'one interruption, at about 11.30 pm, Mr Berryman spent his time at the party … drinking alcohol'.[93] Meagher JA described the party as follows:

> The party went on for many hours. The consumption of alcohol seems to have been the principal event in the party. In traditional Australian manner, the men and women did their drinking in two separate groups, apart from each other, although Mr Berryman did, gallantly, spend some moments with,

Negligence and Apportionment of Liability) Act 2001 (SA) s 7; Wrongs Act 1954 (Tas) s 4; Wrongs Act 1958 (Vic) s 26(1); Law Reform (Contributory Negligence and Tortfeasors' Contribution) Act 1947 (WA) s 4; Contributory Negligence Act 1947 (NZ).

83. See also Civil Law (Wrongs) Act 2002 (ACT); Compensation (Fatal Injuries) Act 1974 (NT); Supreme Court Act 1995 (Qld) ss 13–23; Civil Liability Act 1936 (SA) Pt 5; Fatal Accidents Act 1934 (Tas); Wrongs Act 1958 (Vic) Pt III; Fatal Accidents Act 1959 (WA).

84. See also Civil Liability Act 2002 (NSW) ss 3B and 5A.

85. Civil Liability Act 1936 (SA) s 45.

86. See Civil Law (Wrongs) Act 2002 (ACT) s 95; Personal Injuries (Liabilities and Damages) Act 2003 (NT) s 14; Civil Liability Act 2002 (NSW) ss 48–50; Civil Liability Act 2003 (Qld) ss 46–49; Civil Liability Act 1936 (SA) ss 46–48; Civil Liability Act 2002 (Tas) s 5; compare Wrongs Act 1958 (Vic) s 14G; Civil Liability Act 2002 (WA) s 5L.

87. See, for example, Motor Accidents Compensation Act 1999 (NSW) s 138(2); Civil Liability Act 1936 (SA) s 49 (automatic 25 per cent reduction).

88. (1991) 171 CLR 506.

89. (2003) 214 CLR 552; [2003] HCA 34.

90. [2001] NSWCA 95 at [2] per Meagher JA.

91. (2003) 214 CLR 552; [2003] HCA 34 at [52] per Gummow and Callinan JJ.

92. [2001] NSWCA 95 at [16] per Meagher JA.

93. (2003) 214 CLR 552; [2003] HCA 34 at [52] per Gummow and Callinan JJ.

and talking to, Miss Joslyn. From the moment Mr Berryman and his friends arrived, they all intended to spend the night at the Crisps. They all caroused long after midnight.[94]

Some time around 4 am Mr Berryman went to sleep on the front seat of his 1987 Toyota Hilux Utility. The keys had been removed from the ignition by another guest and given to Ms Joslyn who had asked for them. About half an hour later Ms Joslyn was seen to be 'quite drunk and staggering about' (like most of the other guests at that time) and eventually she placed her swag on the ground beside Mr Berryman's vehicle. Later that Sunday morning, at about 7 am, they drove 15 minutes to Mildura for breakfast at a McDonald's café. Mr Berryman bought the food, drove to a park on the river bank, ate, and then started the drive back to Dareton. The weather was fine and the road was dry. But on this journey Ms Joslyn noticed that Mr Berryman was dozing off at the wheel. She insisted on driving. He let her do so, despite knowing that she had lost her driving licence after being convicted of driving under the influence and that she was an inexperienced driver who had not driven for some time. He also knew that his vehicle had a propensity to roll. Ms Joslyn did not know what the speed limit was and 'it would not have made much difference if she did, as the speedometer was not working'.[95] After driving about one kilometre, Ms Joslyn failed to negotiate a sharp turn. The vehicle rolled and crashed. Mr Berryman was seriously injured. At the time of the accident, at about 8.45 am, Ms Joslyn's blood sample indicated that she had a blood alcohol level of 0.138 g/100 ml and Mr Berryman's indicated 0.19 g/100 ml.

Mr Berryman sued both Ms Joslyn for negligent driving and the Wentworth Shire Council, claiming that it failed to provide proper warning signs. The New South Wales District Court trial judge, Boyd-Boland ADCJ, found both defendants negligent and held Ms Joslyn 90 per cent responsible and the council 10 per cent. But his Honour reduced Mr Berryman's damages by 25 per cent due to his contributory negligence in allowing Ms Joslyn to drive when he knew that she was unfit to do so. Mr Berryman appealed to the New South Wales Court of Appeal on the ground that a finding of contributory negligence should not have been made, and he was successful. Meagher JA (Priestley JA and Ipp AJA concurring) found he was not guilty of *any* contributory negligence, noting that at the time he let Ms Joslyn drive she showed no signs of intoxication. But, on further appeal, the High Court held that Mr Berryman was guilty of contributory negligence under s 74(2) of the Motor Accidents Act 1988 (NSW), which requires a finding of contributory negligence where the plaintiff is a voluntary passenger in a vehicle and is 'aware, or ought to have been aware' that the driver 'was impaired as a consequence of the consumption of alcohol'. Gummow and Callinan JJ said that the 'Court of Appeal erred in failing to have regard to, and to apply

---

94.   [2001] NSWCA 95 at [17] per Meagher JA.
95.   [2001] NSWCA 95 at [20] per Meagher JA.

s 74 of the Act'.[96] The case was remitted back to the Court of Appeal where Mr Berryman was found to be 60 per cent responsible and his damages were reduced accordingly.

2.18 Section 9(1)(b) of the Law Reform (Miscellaneous Provisions) Act 1965 (NSW) provides that damages are to be 'reduced to such extent as the court thinks just and equitable having regard to the claimant's share in the responsibility for the damage'.[97] The High Court in *Pennington v Norris* held that the criterion of responsibility is the degree of 'culpability' of the parties; that is, the respective degrees of departure from the standard of care of the reasonable person.[98] The court compares the culpability of each party, their whole conduct and the relative importance of their contribution in causing the damage.[99] But '[a]lmost any exercise which involves assessing the degree of contributory negligence must inevitably be somewhat rough and ready'.[100]

In *Pennington* the plaintiff pedestrian was injured when he was hit by the defendant's car on a wet and misty night. The plaintiff had been drinking at three different hotels in the previous two hours, but the evidence was that he had not been affected by alcohol. The defendant's car hit him at 30 mph on a road near the three hotels and his body came to rest almost 30 feet from the point of impact. The trial judge apportioned culpability at 50 per cent each, but the High Court said it should only be 20 per cent for the plaintiff and 80 per cent for the defendant. The court held that the defendant's negligence was:

> … more culpable, more gross, than that of the plaintiff. The plaintiff's conduct was *ex hypothesi* careless and unreasonable but, after all, it was the sort of thing that is very commonly done: he simply did not look when a reasonably careful man would have looked. We think too that in this case the very fact that his conduct did not endanger the defendant or anybody else is a material consideration.

2.19 In *Corr v IBC Vehicles Limited*[101] a 30-year-old maintenance engineer, Mr Corr, was employed in 1996 by IBC Vehicles, which manufactured light commercial Vauxhall branded vehicles. He was trying to fix a fault with an automated arm when, without warning, it picked up a metal panel on its sucker and swung it forcibly in the direction of Mr Corr. He was violently struck on the head and his right ear was severed. Lord Bingham in the House of Lords observed that '[h]e would have been decapitated had he not

---

96. (2003) 214 CLR 552; [2003] HCA 34 at [77]. See also Civil Liability Act 2002 (NSW) s 49; Civil Liability Act 1936 (SA) ss 46–48; Civil Liability Act 2003 (Qld) s 49.

97. Compare Motor Accidents Act 1988 (NSW) s 74(3) and the Motor Accidents Compensation Act 1999 (NSW) s 138(3), which require apportionment to be made by reference to nothing other than what 'the court thinks just and equitable': see *Berryman v Joslyn* [2004] NSWCA 121.

98. (1956) 96 CLR 10 at 16; *Imbree v Sierra* [2004] HCA 64 at [51] per Gleeson CJ, Gummow, Kirby and Hayne JJ.

99. *Wynbergen v Hoyts Corporation Pty Ltd* (1997) 149 ALR 25 at 29 per Hayne J, citing in support *Podrebersek v Australian Iron & Steel Pty Ltd* (1985) 59 ALR 529.

100. *Corr v IBC Vehicles Limited* [2008] UKHL 13 at [70] per Lord Neuberger.

101. [2008] UKHL 13.

instinctively moved his head'.[102] Apart from his serious disfiguring injuries, Mr Corr also suffered flashbacks, nightmares, severe headaches, post-traumatic stress disorder, clinical depression and was treated with electro-convulsive therapy. He sued his employer in 1999 claiming damages for his physical and psychological injuries. In 2002 he began to contemplate suicide and in May of that year, nearly six years after the accident, he jumped from the top of a multi-storey car park. The proceedings were then amended to substitute his widow and personal representative as claimant. It was common ground that the employer's negligence caused the original accident in 1996, the depression that followed and that Mr Corr had taken his own life as a consequence. However, the employer denied that it was responsible for the widow's financial loss caused by Mr Corr's suicide. On appeal it argued that the damages should be reduced due to Mr Corr's fault or contributory negligence in taking his own life. Lord Bingham, in the majority, rejected the employer's argument and held:

> I do not think that any blame should be attributed to the deceased for the consequences of a situation which was of the employer's making, not his. Consistently with my rejection of arguments based on *novus actus* and unreasonable conduct, I would similarly absolve the deceased from any causal responsibility for his own tragic death. I would accordingly assess his contributory negligence at 0%. That, in my opinion, reflects the responsibility of the deceased for his own loss …[103]

2.20   In *Wynbergen v Hoyts Corporation Pty Ltd*[104] the High Court found that the court cannot apportion 100 per cent of the damage to one party to the exclusion of the other as this would not be 'just and equitable'.[105] Still, in most jurisdictions *Wynbergen* has been reversed by legislation adopting the Ipp Report recommendation that contributory negligence should be able to 'defeat' a plaintiff's claim for damages.[106] For example, s 5S of the Civil Liability Act 2002 (NSW) provides:

> In determining the extent of a reduction in damages by reason of contributory negligence, a court may determine a reduction of 100% if the court thinks it is just and equitable to do so, with the result that the claim for damages is defeated.[107]

Joint and concurrent tortfeasors

2.21   Where the plaintiff's loss is caused by more than one defendant a three-fold classification is traditionally used: *joint* tortfeasors, *several concurrent* tortfeasors and *successive* tortfeasors. Joint tortfeasors are responsible for the

---

102. [2008] UKHL 13 at [2].

103. [2008] UKHL 13 at [22], Lords Walker, Mance and Neuberger concurring.

104. (1997) 149 ALR 25.

105. Compare *Chapman v Hearse* (1961) 106 CLR 112 at 123.

106. *Review of the Law of Negligence: Final Report 2002* (Cth), Recommendation No 30.

107. See also Civil Liability Act 2003 (Qld) s 24; Wrongs Act 1954 (Tas) s 4; Wrongs Act 1958 (Vic) s 63.

same tort and either act in concert[108] or are vicariously liable, such as employer and employee, master and servant, principal and agent. Several concurrent tortfeasors act independently and not in concert, but inflict the same damage, for example, two cars negligently collide with the plaintiff's car. Successive tortfeasors also act independently, but the distinguishing feature is that the damage is different. This is discussed at **2.25–2.27**. The focus here is on joint and several concurrent tortfeasors. The term 'concurrent tortfeasors' is the generic term used to describe both joint tortfeasors and several concurrent tortfeasors.[109]

At common law each concurrent tortfeasor is liable to the plaintiff for the *whole* loss. This is known as 'solidary liability'. The rule in *Merryweather v Nixan*[110] also provided that there was no right of contribution between the tortfeasors, but this was abolished by legislation in all jurisdictions similar to s 5(1)(c) of the Law Reform (Miscellaneous Provisions) Act 1946 (NSW).[111] It, and s 5(2), provide defendants with 'a right and a remedy'[112] to recover from other tortfeasors part of, or even the whole of, the sum paid to the plaintiff. Under s 5(2) the amount of the defendant's contribution is that which is 'found by the court to be just and equitable having regard to the extent of that person's responsibility for the damage'. In exercising this discretion the court may exempt a person from contribution, order partial contribution or even order a complete indemnity.

2.22 Section 5(1)(a) of the Law Reform (Miscellaneous Provisions) Act 1946 (NSW) also abolished the common law rule that judgment against one joint tortfeasor barred all further actions against other joint tortfeasors. Still, where a plaintiff does bring successive actions there is a sanction in s 5(1)(b) which prevents the plaintiff from recovering any more in a subsequent action than what was obtained in the first action. Further, the plaintiff is not entitled to costs unless the court is of the opinion that there were reasonable grounds for bringing the subsequent action.

Unfortunately, as observed by the High Court in *Amaca Pty Ltd v New South Wales*, the contribution provisions:

> ... have become notorious for the conceptual and practical difficulties they engender. Some of those difficulties stem from the fact that it is possible to bring proceedings for contribution that are heard and determined separately

---

108. See, for example, *Thompson v Australian Capital Television Pty Ltd* (1996) 186 CLR 574 where two independent television stations, Channels 7 and 9, were held to be joint tortfeasors for broadcasting the same defamatory comments.

109. *Baxter v Obacelo Pty Ltd* (2001) 205 CLR 635; [2001] HCA 66 at [24] per Gleeson CJ and Callinan J.

110. (1799) 8 Term Rep 186; 101 ER 1337.

111. Law Reform (Miscellaneous Provisions) Act 1955 (ACT) Pt IV; Law Reform (Miscellaneous Provisions) Act 1956 (NT) Pt IV; Law Reform Act 1995 (Qld) Pt 3 Div 2; Law Reform (Contributory Negligence and Apportionment of Liability) Act 2001 (SA) ss 5 and 6; Wrongs Act 1954 (Tas) s 3; Wrongs Act 1958 (Vic) Pt IV; Law Reform (Contributory Negligence and Tortfeasors' Contribution) Act 1947 (WA) s 7.

112. *James Hardie & Coy Pty Ltd v Seltsam Pty Ltd* (1998) 196 CLR 53; [1998] HCA 78 at [2] and [24] per Gaudron and Gummow JJ.

from proceedings establishing the liability in respect of which contribution is sought.[113]

2.23   Another difficulty, which arose in *Baxter v Obacelo Pty Ltd*,[114] is where the plaintiff settles with one tortfeasor but not with the other concurrent tortfeasor.[115] Baxter was employed as a solicitor in Whitehead's firm, which was retained by Obacelo in a conveyancing transaction. Baxter had conduct of the matter. Obacelo alleged it was handled negligently and claimed damages in excess of $430,000. In one action, Obacelo sued both Whitehead and Baxter, but framed its claim in both contract and tort based on the mistaken belief that Whitehead and Baxter were partners. Obacelo then learned that Baxter was an employee and could not be liable in contract. At the same time, in 1988, Obacelo and Whitehead agreed to settle the claim against Whitehead for $250,000 inclusive of costs. A deed of release was executed and consent judgment was entered in the New South Wales Supreme Court. The litigation, according to Kirby J, 'then fell into a slumber from which it was only awakened in 1998, apparently as a result of Mr Baxter's initiative in applying to have the claim against him summarily dismissed'.[116] This 'produced a belated flurry of pleadings'[117] with Obacelo continuing to pursue Baxter by amending its claim to one based on the negligence of Baxter as an employee. Baxter's defence was that Whitehead was vicariously liable for all Baxter's acts as an employee, the settlement was for the same damage which had been fully recovered from Whitehead and s 5(1)(b) prevented the plaintiff from recovering any more from Baxter.

Baxter's appeal to the High Court was unanimously dismissed. It held that neither s 5(1)(b) nor the common law rules of accord and satisfaction[118] precludes a plaintiff who partially settles against one joint tortfeasor from continuing against another joint tortfeasor to recover the balance. Gleeson CJ and Callinan J held:

> In the present case, the deed of release, the terms of settlement, and the conduct of the parties to the settlement, clearly showed that it was contemplated that the respondents would pursue their claim against the appellant, and that they were not accepting the sum of $250,000 in full satisfaction of the loss or damage they said they incurred. There is no reason why they should be prevented from continuing with their claim against the appellant.[119]

---

113. *Amaca Pty Ltd v New South Wales* (2003) 199 ALR 596; [2003] HCA 44 at [17] per McHugh, Gummow, Kirby, Hayne and Callinan JJ.

114. (2001) 205 CLR 635; [2001] HCA 66.

115. See also *Thompson v Australian Capital Television Pty Ltd* (1996) 186 CLR 574.

116. (2001) 205 CLR 635; [2001] HCA 66 at [85].

117. (2001) 205 CLR 635; [2001] HCA 66 at [85].

118. See (2001) 205 CLR 635; [2001] HCA 66 at [59]–[73] per Gummow and Hayne JJ; see also Andrew Broadfoot, 'Multiple defendant litigation and the rule against double recovery' (2002) 10 *TLJ* 255.

119. (2001) 205 CLR 635; [2001] HCA 66 at [55]; see also [75] per Gummow and Hayne JJ.

Their Honours did indicate, however, that a plaintiff would fail in a later action:

> If it would be unconscientious of the plaintiff to pursue a claim against another tortfeasor, or if the amount received pursuant to the settlement is, or ought to be regarded as, recoupment of the whole of the plaintiff's loss or damage, then action against another tortfeasor, whether in separate proceedings, or, where the other tortfeasor was a party to the original proceedings, by way of continuation of those proceedings, must fail. If, either expressly or by implication, a settlement agreement manifested a common intention of the parties to the agreement that the settlement sum was to be paid and received in full satisfaction of the rights of the plaintiff, against the defendant or anyone else, in relation to the loss or damage incurred, then, for both of those reasons, a further claim would fail. The most obvious way to negative such an intention would be by an express reservation of rights. While the effect of the settlement agreement, in the ordinary case, will be the most significant factor bearing upon either or both of the two possible grounds mentioned, it is not possible to eliminate any other circumstances which, in a given case, could indicate unconscientiousness, or loss of the subject matter of a claim. Bearing in mind the obligation to give credit for the amount already recovered, a defendant who could show that the actual loss or damage incurred by the plaintiff did not exceed the amount already recovered would succeed in any event. Leaving aside questions of onus of proof, to say that there is no such excess is simply to say that the loss has been fully recouped.[120]

Kirby J observed in a separate judgment that '[p]erhaps it would have been wiser for Mr Baxter to have let the sleeping dogs of litigation lie'.[121]

2.24   Under the civil liability reforms, there is a further change regarding apportionment. While the wording[122] and exact scope vary,[123] the general thrust of the Acts is that with claims arising from negligence (whether in tort, contract or otherwise) or under the statutory misleading or deceptive conduct provisions, where the damage is for pure economic loss or property damage (that is, excluding personal injury claims)[124] concurrent tortfeasors can only be proportionally, rather than wholly, liable for the plaintiff's loss. For example, s 35(1) of the Civil Liability Act 2002 (NSW) provides:

> (a)   the liability of a defendant who is a concurrent wrongdoer in relation to that claim is limited to an amount reflecting that proportion of the damage or loss claimed that the court considers just having regard to the extent of the defendant's responsibility for the damage or loss, and

---

120. (2001) 205 CLR 635; [2001] HCA 66 at [54]; see also [75] per Gummow and Hayne JJ.

121. (2001) 205 CLR 635; [2001] HCA 66 at [85].

122. For example, the NSW Act uses the words 'failure to take reasonable care' — see Civil Liability Act 2002 (NSW) s 34(1)(a); the Qld Act refers to 'a breach of duty of care' (and duty of care is defined as a duty to take reasonable care or to exercise reasonable skill) — see Civil Liability Act 2003 (Qld) s 28(1)(a) and Sch 2.

123. For example, the Qld Act excludes claims by consumers — see Civil Liability Act 2003 (Qld) s 28(3)(b); the NSW Act does not.

124. See, for example, Civil Liability Act 2002 (NSW) s 34(1)(a).

(b) the court may give judgment against the defendant for not more than that amount.[125]

In apportioning responsibility between defendants, the court should 'exclude that proportion of the damage or loss in relation to which the plaintiff is contributorily negligent under any relevant law' and the court may also 'have regard to the comparative responsibility of any concurrent wrongdoer who is not a party to the proceedings'.[126]

Successive tortfeasors and vicissitudes of life

2.25   Difficult issues arise in causation where there are successive tortfeasors. Not only is there the difficulty of applying the 'but for' test, there is also the problem of applying the principle that in assessing damages the contingencies or vicissitudes of life are to be taken into account. This means damages are reduced in order to take into account events which would have reduced the plaintiff's entitlement to income or profit. For example, typically in a personal injury action a plaintiff's damages award for lost income and profit is reduced by reference to factors such as unemployment, sickness, accidents and death: see **2.71**. Should this principle also take into account the effect of another tortious wrong (particularly where that wrong has already occurred) because the distinction between tortious and non-tortious vicissitudes is illogical?[127] The issues involved are highlighted by the House of Lords' decisions in *Baker v Willoughby*[128] and *Jobling v Associated Dairies*,[129] and the High Court judgment in *Faulkner v Keffalinos*.[130] These cases do not, however, provide a definitive answer to the question posed, and perhaps such an answer cannot be found, because 'the law must abstract some consequences as relevant, not perhaps on the ground of pure logic but simply for practical reasons'.[131]

In *Baker v Willoughby*[132] the defendant injured the plaintiff's leg in 1964 in a car accident. In 1967 the same leg was injured when a second tortfeasor and criminal, an armed robber, shot the plaintiff's leg during a robbery. The leg had to be amputated. At the trial, in 1968, the defendant denied liability after the second injury by arguing that the vicissitudes of life had to be taken into account. This was accepted by the English Court of Appeal which held that the damage caused by the defendant had been obliterated or overwhelmed by the amputation of the leg. But, on appeal, the House of Lords reversed this decision. In their Lordships' speech, the defendant continued to be responsible for the injury that he had caused and the armed robber was responsible for the

---

125. See also Wrongs Act 1958 (Vic) Pt IVAA; Civil Liability Act 2002 (WA) Pt 1F.
126. Civil Liability Act 2002 (NSW) s 35(3).
127. See *Nilon v Bezzina* [1988] 2 Qd R 420 at 427 per McPherson J.
128. [1970] AC 467.
129. [1982] AC 794.
130. (1970) 45 ALJR 80.
131. *Liesbosch, Dredger v SS Edison (Owners)* [1933] AC 449 at 460 per Lord Wright.
132. [1970] AC 467.

extra damage. The defendant had inflicted an injury which remained, in effect, a concurrent cause; therefore, it did not diminish the liability in damages.

2.26 Both Windeyer J of the High Court of Australia in *Faulkner v Keffalinos*,[133] and the House of Lords in *Jobling v Associated Dairies*,[134] refused to follow *Baker v Willoughby*.[135] In *Faulkner* the plaintiff was injured by the defendant's negligence in a car accident. The plaintiff suffered a partial loss of earning capacity as a result. Before the trial, the plaintiff was injured again in another car accident and suffered a total loss of earning capacity. The High Court reduced the defendant's liability for damages because the vicissitudes of life had to be taken into account. However, only Windeyer J explicitly referred to and refused to follow *Baker*.[136]

The approach of Windeyer J in *Faulkner* is supported by the House of Lords in *Jobling v Associated Dairies*.[137] In *Jobling* the plaintiff was partially disabled by a back injury which occurred at his place of employment. He sued his employer but, before the trial and not due to the prior injury, he developed a totally disabling illness — cervical myelopathy. The House of Lords held that the onset of this illness was 'one of the vicissitudes of life relevant to the assessment of damages'.[138] Thus, the first tortfeasor's liability was reduced to the extent that the later injury was a cause of the plaintiff's loss.

Successive tortfeasors and contributory negligence

2.27 This issue was considered by the House of Lords in *Fitzgerald v Lane*.[139] The plaintiff was hit by the first defendant's car when crossing a busy road at traffic lights which were green in the traffic's favour. A further serious injury resulted when the plaintiff was hit again, by the second defendant's car. It was impossible to determine precise responsibility for the injuries. The trial judge held that the plaintiff and both defendants were negligent and the responsibility for the serious injury was to be borne equally by all three. Both defendants appealed to the English Court of Appeal and argued the issues of causation, quantum and apportionment. They were only successful on apportionment. The court reduced their joint liability to 50 per cent, which was to be borne equally between them. A further argument by the second defendant — that the plaintiff had failed to prove affirmatively on the balance of probabilities

---

133. (1970) 45 ALJR 80.

134. [1982] AC 794.

135. [1970] AC 467.

136. In *Godden v Metropolitan Meat Industry Board* [1972] 2 NSWLR 183 at 191 (CA), after discussing *Faulkner* Kerr CJ and Jacobs JA reasoned that the majority in the High Court were in concurrence with the House of Lords in *Baker v Willoughby* and not Windeyer J; while in *DNM Mining Pty Ltd v Barwick* [2004] NSWCA 137 at [45] Giles JA preferred the approach of Windeyer J. *K Mart Australia Ltd v McCann* [2004] NSWCA 283 follows the approach taken in *Jobling v Associated Dairies Ltd* (1982) AC 794 and *DNM Mining Pty Ltd v Barwick* [2004] NSWCA 137 and this view seems to have been accepted in other courts — see, for example, *Acir v Frosster Pty Ltd* [2009] VSC 454 at [266]–[267].

137. [1982] AC 794; see also *DNM Mining Pty Ltd v Barwick* [2004] NSWCA 137.

138. [1982] AC 794 at 809 per Lord Edmund-Davies.

139. [1989] AC 328.

that the second defendant had caused the serious injury — was rejected. The House of Lords confirmed the decision of the Court of Appeal. In their opinion, the trial judge had erred because the plaintiff was substantially the author of his own misfortune.

The loss of a chance

2.28   An enduring problem when requiring proof of the cause of a loss on a balance of probabilities arises where the plaintiff has lost a chance or opportunity, but the evidence shows that the likelihood of the chance or opportunity bearing fruit is less than 50 per cent. The difficulty is well illustrated by the reasoning of the House of Lords in *Hotson v East Berkshire Area Health Authority*.[140] A 13-year-old boy fractured his hip and was taken to a hospital which failed to correctly diagnose the boy's injury or correct it for five days. The evidence showed that because of the injury there was a 75 per cent chance that the boy would develop a permanent serious deformity of the hip. The late diagnosis meant that the deformity became almost certain and in fact the boy developed the deformity. The boy sued claiming the loss of a 25 per cent chance of avoiding the deformity which the hospital's negligence made inevitable. The House of Lords denied the claim, since on the balance of probabilities the deformity would have occurred even if the hospital had not been negligent.[141] Thus, on the probabilities (as a finding of fact), the 'sole' cause of this damage (in law) was the fall, not the hospital's negligence. In *Gregg v Scott*,[142] a bare majority of the House of Lords subsequently affirmed the reasoning in *Hotson*.

2.29   For a time it looked as though Australian courts might take a different approach as a result of the NSW Court of Appeal's decision in *Rufo v Hosking*.[143] Ms Rufo suffered spinal microfractures due to osteoporosis. When treating Ms Rufo, the doctor had breached his duty of care, for example, by not prescribing the most suitable drugs. Despite these breaches, Ms Rufo's action failed at trial because of the lack of a causal connection between the breach and the loss. The court found there was a less than 50 per cent chance that the microfractures would have been avoided if the doctor had acted with reasonable care, and thus, on the balance of probabilities, it was more probable than not that the microfractures would have occurred anyway. This was reversed by the New South Wales Court of Appeal, which held that, even though there was a less than 50 per cent chance that the loss would have been avoided, Ms Rufo was entitled to damages for the loss of that chance. Santow JA drew on Lord Diplock's explanation of the court's role:

---

140. [1987] AC 750.
141. Compare *Sellars v Adelaide Petroleum NL* (1994) 179 CLR 332, where it was held in contract that a loss of a chance is recoverable in damages even if on the balance of probabilities the outcome created by the chance was unlikely. See also **3.46**.
142. [2005] UKHL 2.
143. [2004] NSWCA 391.

The role of the court in making an assessment of damages which depends upon its view as to what will be and what would have been is to be contrasted with its ordinary function in civil actions of determining what was. In determining what did happen in the past a court decides on the balance of probabilities. Anything that is more probable than not it treats as certain. But in assessing damages which depend upon its view as to what will happen in the future or would have happened in the future if something had not happened in the past, the court must make an estimate as to what are the chances that a particular thing will or would have happened and reflect those chances, whether they are more or less than even, in the amount of damages which it awards.[144]

Santow J pointed out that the result of the *Hotson* approach was that a plaintiff could be fully compensated where the loss of a chance exceeded 50 per cent, say 51 per cent, and yet receive nothing if the loss were, say, 49 per cent.[145] He went on to say:

> There is much to be said for consistency, whereby a chance above or below 50% obtains no more and no less in compensation than the corresponding percentage, instead of an all or nothing approach. That should not open floodgates to loss of chance claims either in the medical field or more generally. First, the loss of chance must itself be established on the balance of probabilities, as also that the chance if offered would have been taken. Second, it is the very nature of the doctor's duty of reasonable care and skill that directs it to achieving the best chance of a favourable medical outcome, subject to informed patient choice and what is practically available.[146]

The approach he adopted had already found favour in the High Court in contract and under the Trade Practices Act 1974 (Cth).[147] Where the lost chance amounts to more than mere speculation and can be proven to have existed on a balance of probability, the issue is then treated as a question of quantum rather than causation — the question becomes what is the value of the lost chance? And this is where the likelihood of the chance coming to fruition is taken into account.[148]

2.30 The High Court was called upon to choose between these two approaches in *Tabet v Gett*.[149] The plaintiff, a six-year-old patient at a children's hospital, was operated on after being diagnosed as having a brain tumour, but nevertheless suffered irreversible brain damage. The operation took place urgently after the plaintiff suffered a seizure on 14 January and a CT scan revealed the brain tumour. The trial court found that the defendant, a paediatrician at the hospital, was negligent for not having ordered a CT scan

---

144. [2004] NSWCA 391 at [20], citing Lord Diplock in *Mallett v McMonagle* [1970] AC 166 (HL) at 176.

145. [2004] NSWCA 391 at [45]. See also the High Court noting the all or nothing approach in *Malec v J C Hutton Pty Ltd* (1990) 169 CLR 638 at 643 per Deane, Gaudron and McHugh JJ.

146. [2004] NSWCA 391 at [52]; see also *State of New South Wales v Burton* [2006] NSWCA 12 at [66] per Basten JA.

147. See *Sellars v Adelaide Petroleum NL* (1994) 179 CLR 332.

148. See **3.46** and *Sellars v Adelaide Petroleum NL* (1994) 179 CLR 332 at 355 per Mason CJ, Dawson, Toohey and Gaudron JJ.

149. [2010] HCA 12.

the day before when the plaintiff suffered an episode during which it was noticed that her right pupil was not reacting. The plaintiff alleged that the doctor's negligence had materially contributed to the cause of her injuries, or alternatively, had at least caused the loss of a chance of a better outcome. At trial, she failed on the first argument, the court finding that on the balance of probabilities, detection and treatment of the tumour a day earlier would not have avoided the loss — the seizure and deterioration in her condition would have occurred anyway. But, following the approach taken in *Rufo*, the plaintiff succeeded on her alternative argument. She was held to have proven on a balance of probabilities that she had lost a chance of a better outcome and was awarded $610,000. On appeal, both the New South Wales Court of Appeal and the High Court refused to follow the *Rufo* approach. The Court of Appeal took the unusual step of refusing to follow its earlier decision, describing *Rufo* as 'plainly wrong'.[150] In the High Court, Heydon J held that, on the evidence, the alleged lost chance was entirely speculative and had not been proven at all, so he did not consider the lost chance argument. The other six judges agreed with the Court of Appeal. Hayne and Bell JJ, for example, said:

> … the language of loss of chance should not be permitted to obscure the need to identify whether a plaintiff has proved that the defendant's negligence was more probably than not a cause of damage (in the sense of detrimental difference). The language of possibilities (language that underlies the notion of loss of chance) should not be permitted to obscure the need to consider whether the possible adverse outcome has in fact come home, or will more probably than not do so.[151]

Gummow J's reasons included the conclusion that:

> … in personal injury cases the law of negligence as understood in the common law of Australia does not entertain an action for recovery when the damage … is characterised as the loss of a chance of a better outcome of the character found … in this case.[152]

The court was comfortable drawing a distinction between this case and the principles in *Commonwealth v Amann Aviation*[153] and *Sellars v Adelaide Petroleum*.[154] Kiefel J, for example, suggested there was a difference between a contemplated commercial benefit, which has value in itself, and the chance of a better medical outcome which derives its value from the extent of the final physical damage.[155] However, it is not clear where this dividing line will ultimately fall — there was little clarity in *Tabet v Gett* as to whether the High Court's reasoning should be restricted to medical negligence cases, or to all personal injuries, or to a broader category of negligence claims. If the approach applies to all negligence cases, it is equally unclear what will happen where there are alternative causes of action in tort and contract, perhaps even attracting the provisions of the Civil Liability Acts.

---

150. *Gett v Tabet* [2009] NSWCA 76 at [389].
151. *Tabet v Gett* [2010] HCA 12 at [69].
152. *Tabet v Gett* [2010] HCA 12 at [46].
153. [1991] HCA 54.
154. [1994] HCA 4.
155. *Tabet v Gett* [2010] HCA 12 at [124].

Alternative causes and the 'evidential gap'

2.31 A second enduring problem when requiring proof of the cause of a loss on a balance of probabilities arises where there are a number of alternative possible causes, only one of which could be the actual cause. With advances in science and technology, our understanding of cause and effect continually improves; and the problem is often resolved when expert evidence discloses which cause is more likely to be the actual cause. However, there are unusual cases where the evidence cannot disclose which of the alternatives should be seen as the cause in law. A solution gradually developed in the United Kingdom[156] and was finally accepted by the House of Lords in *Fairchild v Glenhaven Funeral Services Ltd*.[157] The case involved three appeals, heard concurrently, concerning employees who contracted mesothelioma by exposure to substantial quantities of asbestos dust. The evidence showed it was probably due to a cell mutation caused by a *single* asbestos fibre but, because each employee had been exposed to asbestos fibre by more than one employer, the Court of Appeal refused to award damages because the plaintiffs could not prove on the balance of probabilities which exposure had caused the disease. This result was overturned by the House of Lords. In their opinion, the asbestos exposure was a breach of the employers' duty of care owed to the employees and, despite current medical evidence not being able to attribute the onset of the condition to a particular employer, the plaintiffs were nonetheless entitled to recover the full amount from any one of the employers. Lord Bingham said:

> The crucial issue on appeal is whether, in the special circumstances of such a case, principle, authority or policy requires or justifies a modified approach to proof of causation.[158]

Their Lordships held that it did. On the balance of probabilities, the breach of the duty by each employer had 'materially increased the risk'[159] of contracting the disease and this was to be equated with proof that each employer had materially contributed in causing the disease. Lord Nicholls explained in his speech why the employees were not to be left without a remedy:

> The present appeals are another example of such circumstances, where good policy reasons exist for departing from the usual threshold 'but for' test of causal connection. Inhalation of asbestos dust carries a risk of mesothelioma. That is one of the very risks from which an employer's duty of care is intended to protect employees. Tragically, each claimant acquired this fatal disease from wrongful exposure to asbestos dust in the course of his employment. A former employee's inability to identify which particular period of wrongful exposure brought about the onset of his disease ought not, in all justice, to preclude recovery of compensation.

---

156. *McGhee v National Coal Board* [1973] 1 WLR 1; *Wilsher v Essex Area Health Authority* [1988] AC 1074.

157. [2003] 1 AC 32.

158. [2003] 1 AC 32 at [2].

159. [2003] 1 AC 32 at [65] per Lord Hoffmann, at [108]–[116] per Lord Hutton.

So long as it was not insignificant, each employer's wrongful exposure of its employee to asbestos dust and, hence, to the risk of contracting mesothelioma, should be regarded by the law as a sufficient degree of causal connection. This is sufficient to justify requiring the employer to assume responsibility for causing or materially contributing to the onset of the mesothelioma when, in the present state of medical knowledge, no more exact causal connection is ever capable of being established. Given the present state of medical science, this outcome may cast responsibility on a defendant whose exposure of a claimant to the risk of contracting the disease had in fact no causative effect. But the unattractiveness of casting the net of responsibility as widely as this is far outweighed by the unattractiveness of the alternative outcome.[160]

2.32   The Law Lords were aware of the dangers and expressed concern that their decision should be narrowly interpreted. Lord Nicholls, for example, went on to say:

I need hardly add that considerable restraint is called for in any relaxation of the threshold 'but for' test of causal connection. The principle applied on these appeals is emphatically not intended to lead to such a relaxation whenever a plaintiff has difficulty, perhaps understandable difficulty, in discharging the burden of proof resting on him. Unless closely confined in its application this principle could become a source of injustice to defendants. There must be good reason for departing from the normal threshold 'but for' test. The reason must be sufficiently weighty to justify depriving the defendant of the protection this test normally and rightly affords him, and it must be plain and obvious that this is so. Policy questions will loom large when a court has to decide whether the difficulties of proof confronting the plaintiff justify taking this exceptional course. It is impossible to be more specific.[161]

2.33   In the United Kingdom, the approach in *Fairchild* was affirmed in *Barker v Corus UK Ltd*.[162] Whereas in *Fairchild* all the potentially causal events were a result of the negligence of the defendants, the House of Lords in *Barker* extended the approach to situations where not all the exposures were negligently caused by the defendants; and it apportioned the loss between them. The latter aspect was overturned by subsequent legislation. It provides that, in cases of mesothelioma where the *Fairchild* approach applies, the defendant(s) will be liable for the *whole* loss suffered by the plaintiff, whether or not there might have been other tortious or non-tortious exposures to asbestos; and the loss is to be borne jointly and severally with other 'responsible persons'.[163] In what can be seen as a further extension, the United Kingdom Supreme Court has since applied the *Fairchild* approach where the defendant was the sole known source of occupational exposure to asbestos dust (the only other source being general environmental exposure) and the extent of the exposure was small.[164]

---

160. [2003] 1 AC 32 at [41]–[42].

161. [2003] 1 AC 32 at [43].

162. [2006] UKHL 20.

163. Compensation Act 2006 (UK), s 3.

164. *Sienkiewicz v Greif (UK) Ltd* [2011] UKSC 10.

The court also suggested there was no reason in principle why the *Fairchild* exception should be limited to mesothelioma.

2.34   The solution developed by the House of Lords in *Fairchild* relies on a 'material increase in the risk of harm'. The crux of the problem is that no evidence can show whether the increased risk actually caused the harm. It is thus an exception to the normal requirement that causation should be proven on a balance of probabilities. The *Fairchild* approach should be distinguished from other situations in which a material increase in the risk of harm might be helpful in proving causation. In the absence of expert evidence that directly tips the scales of the 'but for' test, it has always been possible to establish a causal connection by 'a robust and pragmatic approach to inferential fact finding'.[165] Dixon J in *Betts v Whittingslowe*,[166] when dealing with a statutory duty, explained inferential reasoning in relation to causation thus:

> ... the breach of duty coupled with an accident of the kind that might thereby be caused is enough to justify an inference, in the absence of any sufficient reason to the contrary, that in fact the accident did occur owing to the act or omission amounting to the breach of statutory duty. In the circumstances of this case that proposition is enough. For, in my opinion, the facts warrant no other inference ...

Unlike the *Fairchild* approach, the inference still has to be drawn to prove the cause on a balance of probability; a material increase in the risk of harm is not by itself sufficient proof of a causal link.[167]

2.35   In Australia, the High Court has yet to accept the *Fairchild* approach and, at least in New South Wales, the Supreme Court is inclined to await a High Court decision.[168] The Civil Liability Acts, however, make provision for a *Fairchild* exception. Thus, for example, the New South Wales Act says:

> (2) In determining in an exceptional case, in accordance with established principles, whether negligence that cannot be established as a necessary condition of the occurrence of harm should be accepted as establishing factual causation, the court is to consider (amongst other relevant things) whether or not and why responsibility for the harm should be imposed on the negligent party.[169]

This section can be contrasted with the general approach in the Civil Liability Acts separating factual causation from normative factors — it allows normative factors to be used to override the lack of causation. Apart from the limit that it only applies to 'exceptional case[s], in accordance with established principles', it appears to give courts a wide discretion. In effect, it enables

165.   *Evans v Queanbeyan City Council* [2011] NSWCA 230 per Allsop P at [48].

166.   (1945) 71 CLR 637 at 649. See also *Bradshaw v McEwans Pty Ltd* (1951) 217 ALR 1 at 5–6.

167.   *Amaca Pty Ltd v Ellis* [2010] HCA 5.

168.   *Evans v Queanbeyan City Council* [2011] NSWCA 230 per Allsop P at [52].

169.   Civil Liability Act 2002 (NSW) s 5D(2). While the wording is slightly different in some of the other acts, the effect appears to be the same.

a court to take the same approach as the House of Lords did in *Fairchild v Glenhaven Funeral Services Ltd*.[170]

It is unclear how courts will interpret the CLA's limiting terms — 'exceptional case[s]' and 'established principles'. In a number of cases, the High Court has clarified situations in which this section and the *Fairchild* approach do not apply. It does not apply, for example, where the evidence is capable of proving the normal causation requirement of a 'material contribution to the cause of the loss' on the balance of probabilities. Thus, in a case involving a traffic accident at a known 'black spot', the court was prepared to accept that the negligent design of the intersection had materially increased the risk of an accident; but refused to accept that this meant it materially contributed as a cause of the accident. The court was satisfied there was sufficient evidence to show that, on the balance of probabilities, the intersection's poor design was not a material factor — the cause of the accident was the inattention of both drivers (plaintiff and defendant).[171] Neither does the *Fairchild* approach apply where a court is required to postulate on what would have happened if, in the past, a party had taken a different course of action. In *Adeels Palace Pty Ltd v Moubarak; Adeels Palace Pty Ltd v Bou Najem*,[172] after a fight broke out in a busy restaurant during New Years Eve celebrations, a patron returned with a gun and shot the two plaintiffs. They sued the restaurant, alleging it had breached its duty of care towards them by not employing sufficient bouncers or security guards; and this materially contributed as a cause of their injuries. The court held that, even if a duty of care had been breached in this way, there was no proven causal link. A conclusion that more security guards *might* have prevented the loss was merely speculative and did not prove causation on a balance of probabilities. When invited to override the need to prove factual causation under the civil liability statute by holding this was an exceptional case, in accordance with established principles,[173] the court refused, suggesting it would be contrary to established principle, rather than in accordance with established principle, to hold the restaurant liable.[174]

The High Court has also avoided applying the *Fairchild* approach in cases involving diseases more analogous to the facts in *Fairchild*. In *Amaca v Ellis*,[175] the executor of Paul Cotton's estate sued two defendants who had negligently exposed Mr Cotton to asbestos fibres in his working life. Mr Cotton died of lung cancer, but he had also smoked 15–20 cigarettes per day for more than 26 years. The plaintiff abandoned any reliance on the *Fairchild* approach and tried to prove that the exposure to asbestos fibre was a necessary condition or a material contribution to the cause of the disease. The evidence, based on epidemiological (statistical) studies of large populations, could not apportion

---

170. [2003] 1 AC 32.
171. *Roads and Traffic Authority v Royal* [2008] HCA 19.
172. [2009] HCA 48.
173. Civil Liability Act 2002 (NSW) s 5D(2).
174. [2009] HCA 48 at [57].
175. [2010] HCA 5.

a probability greater than 23 per cent that the lung cancer was attributable to asbestos exposure. The High Court held that it had not been established that it was more probable than not that the asbestos exposure was a cause or necessary condition of the lung cancer. In *Amaca Pty Ltd v Booth; Amaba Pty Ltd v Booth*[176] the plaintiff had contracted mesothelioma, as in *Fairchild*. As a motor mechanic, he had worked on brake linings containing asbestos fibre for over 30 years. The two defendants were the manufacturers of most of the brake linings on which he had worked. Several other brief isolated exposures to asbestos fibre were overshadowed by the prolonged exposures during his working life. Unlike *Fairchild*, the medical evidence did recognise the possibility that cumulative exposure might increase the risk of catching the disease. The High Court upheld the trial judge's conclusion that there was sufficient evidence to establish that each of the defendants' negligence not only increased the risk of his contracting the disease, but causally contributed to it on a balance of probability.

2.36 In all the above cases, the High Court was content to draw inferences and conclusions about causation from the evidence, using the more traditional 'material contribution to the *cause* of the loss' approach rather than a 'material increase in the *risk* of harm'. One is lead to the conclusion that, if the Fairchild approach does find favour in Australia, it will be a very limited exception.

REMOTENESS

Reasonable foreseeability and direct causation

2.37 In contract and tort, even if the damage was in fact caused by the defendant, the damage must not be too remote. As discussed in **Chapter 3**, the test of remoteness in contract is the contemplation test, but in tort a different test developed. Prior to the landmark decision of the Privy Council in *Overseas Tankship (UK) Ltd v Morts Dock & Engineering Co Ltd (Wagon Mound (No 1))*,[177] a tortfeasor was liable for all damage *flowing directly* from the wrongful act,[178] otherwise known as the 'direct causation test' or the '*Polemis* test'. Under this test, issues of remoteness were rarely divorced from issues of causation in fact. But in negligence cases the test was rejected by the Privy Council in *Wagon Mound (No 1)* in favour of the reasonable foreseeability test. While the reasonable foreseeability test has since been applied to a number of other torts — see **2.43** — in negligence claims, the Australian landscape has changed slightly as a result of the Civil Liability Acts. These changes are described more fully after dealing with the reasonable foreseeability test.

2.38 *Wagon Mound (No 1)* concerned a charterer of a ship who negligently spilled oil into Morts Bay, Balmain while the ship was being loaded. The oil floated on the surface of Sydney Harbour and was eventually carried to the

176. [2011] HCA 53.

177. [1961] AC 388.

178. *Re Polemis and Furness, Withy & Co* [1921] 3 KB 560 (CA).

water beneath the plaintiff's wharf, where welding operations were being carried out. The oil was ignited by spatters of molten metal falling from the welding operations onto some cotton waste floating on the harbour. A fire resulted, and the plaintiff's wharf and equipment were destroyed, together with some nearby ships. The dockyard proprietors sued the charterer, but ultimately failed on appeal to the Privy Council. Had the *Polemis* direct causation test found favour with their Lordships, the plaintiff would have succeeded, but instead they replaced this test with one of reasonable foreseeability. The charterer was not liable for the damages to the dockyard because the damage resulting from the oil spill was not reasonably foreseeable. Their Lordships noted that the trial judge had found that the charterer neither knew, nor could have reasonably known, that the oil was capable of being set on fire when spread on water.

2.39   Determining the necessary degree of foreseeability is, however, a matter greatly affected by the evidence. *Overseas Tankship (UK) Ltd v The Miller Steamship Co (Wagon Mound (No 2))*[179] involved the same incident as *Wagon Mound (No 1)*, but the action was brought in both nuisance and negligence by the owner of a ship that was damaged at the wharf. Predictably, the trial judge held that the loss was not foreseeable and thus no damages were available in negligence. Nonetheless, his Honour held that the foreseeability test did not apply in nuisance. This meant the shipowner could recover all damage under the direct causation test of remoteness. On appeal, the Privy Council held that the foreseeability test applied to both nuisance and negligence actions, but the plaintiff still recovered the loss. Lord Reid said:

> In *The Wagon Mound (No 1)* the Board were not concerned with degrees of foreseeability because the finding was that the fire was not foreseeable at all … But here the findings show that some risk of fire would have been present to the mind of a reasonable man in the shoes of the ship's chief engineer. So the first question must be what is the precise meaning to be attached in this context to the words 'foreseeable' and 'reasonably foreseeable' …
>
> In the present case there was no justification whatever for discharging the oil into Sydney Harbour. Not only was it an offence to do so, but it involved considerable loss financially …
>
> In their Lordships' view a properly qualified and alert chief engineer would have realised there was a real risk here … If a real risk is one which would occur to the mind of a reasonable man in the position of the defendant's servant and which he would not brush aside as far-fetched, and if the criterion is to be what that reasonable man would have done in the circumstances, then surely he would not neglect such a risk if action to eliminate it presented no difficulty, involved no disadvantage, and required no expense …
>
> The most that can be said to justify inaction is that he would have known that this could only happen in very exceptional circumstances. But that does not mean that a reasonable man would dismiss such a risk from his mind and do nothing when it was so easy to prevent it. If it is clear that the reasonable man

---

179. [1967] 1 AC 617.

would have realised or foreseen and prevented the risk, then it must follow that the appellant is liable in damages.[180]

2.40   While the success of the plaintiff in the second action is perhaps best explained by the further evidence adduced indicating the real risk of fire, which would occur in the mind of a reasonable person, the *Wagon Mound* cases nevertheless demonstrate that the courts oscillate on the same facts as to whether damage is too remote or not. This oscillation reveals that in practice there is little difference between the direct *Polemis* test and the foreseeability test. The point is further illustrated by *Hughes v Lord Advocate*[181] and *Nader v Urban Transit Authority of NSW*.[182] In *Hughes v Lord Advocate* the House of Lords found that it was necessary only to foresee the general kind of damage and not the extent of damage that might result.[183] The defendant negligently left a kerosene lamp near a manhole. A boy tripped over the lamp, the kerosene escaped and caused an explosion. It was found to be reasonably foreseeable that a boy might be burnt by the escaped kerosene that caught on fire, but the explosion resulting in his extensive injuries was less predictable. However, the House of Lords rejected a distinction between foreseeable injury by burning and non-foreseeable injury by explosion, and held that the boy could recover full compensation for his damage.

In *Nader v Urban Transit Authority of NSW*[184] the plaintiff, a 10-year-old boy, fell from a bus and suffered minor cuts and bruising to his head. Two weeks after the accident he complained of headaches and a lack of concentration and became progressively withdrawn. There was no neurological damage, but the evidence showed that he had developed a serious psychiatric condition, known as 'Ganser Syndrome', which would inhibit the development of his emotional or economic independence. The syndrome was found to have been 'triggered' by the over-protective behaviour of his parents following the accident. The defendant argued that the development of the syndrome was too remote because it was not foreseeable, but the majority in the New South Wales Court of Appeal, Samuels and McHugh JJA, found that the damage was foreseeable and therefore recoverable.[185] Mahoney J, in dissent, preferred to emphasise the lack of factual causation between the fall and the syndrome.

The prevailing views in the House of Lords in *Hughes* and the New South Wales Court of Appeal in *Nader* allow for a very expansive interpretation of what is reasonably foreseeable. In *Tame v New South Wales; Annetts v Australian Stations Pty Ltd* (*Tame and Annetts*) McHugh J observed:

> Many of the problems that now beset negligence law and extend the liability of defendants to unreal levels stem from weakening the test of reasonable foreseeability ... Given the undemanding nature of the current foreseeability

180.   [1967] 1 AC 617 at 641–4.
181.   [1963] AC 837 (HL).
182.   (1985) 2 NSWLR 501 (CA).
183.   This principle was accepted by the High Court in *Mount Isa Mines Ltd v Pusey* [1970] HCA 60.
184.   (1985) 2 NSWLR 501 (CA).
185.   Compare ss 31 and 33 of the Civil Liability Act 2002 (NSW).

standard, an affirmative answer to the question whether damage was reasonably foreseeable is usually a near certainty.[186]

As discussed below, the 'undemanding nature of the current foreseeability standard' has ensured that it is not, if it ever was, the exclusive test of remoteness in tort.

The scope of liability under the Civil Liability Acts

2.41   Under the civil liability statutes, a defendant cannot be held to be negligent for non-foreseeable and insignificant risks—reasonable foreseeability is a requirement. In addition, under the broad causation requirement, the policy factors previously taken into account under the common law's reasonable foreseeability test will be equally relevant in determining whether it is appropriate for liability to extend to the harm caused. The two relevant provisions in New South Wales, for example, state:[187]

5B General principles

(1) A person is not negligent in failing to take precautions against a risk of harm unless:

     (a) the risk was foreseeable (that is, it is a risk of which the person knew or ought to have known), and

     (b) the risk was not insignificant, and …

…

5D General principles

(1) A determination that negligence caused particular harm comprises the following elements:

     (a) …

     (b) that it is appropriate for the scope of the negligent person's liability to extend to the harm so caused ("scope of liability").

…

(4) For the purpose of determining the scope of liability, the court is to consider (amongst other relevant things) whether or not and why responsibility for the harm should be imposed on the negligent party.

2.42   As pointed out in **2.12**, this is an attempt to keep factual causation separate from the policy factors and value judgments that are to be taken into account in determining the scope of liability. What is to be taken into account in deciding whether it is 'appropriate' for liability to extend to the harm caused is open-ended; a court is merely required under s 5D(4) to 'consider (amongst other relevant things) whether or not and why responsibility … should be imposed on the [defendant]'. Given the common law's rich history in developing the direct causation (*Polemis*) and reasonable foreseeability (*Wagon Mound*) tests of remoteness, each taking relevant policy factors into account, it

---

186. (2002) 211 CLR 317; [2002] HCA 35 at [98]–[99].

187. Civil Liability Act 2002 (NSW) ss 5B(1) and 5D(1)(b) and 5D(4); Civil Liability Act 2003 (Qld) s 9(1)(a) and (b). See also Civil Law (Wrongs) Act 2002 (ACT) ss 43 and 45; Civil Liability Act 2003 (Qld) ss 9 and 11; Civil Liability Act 1936 (SA) ss 32 and 34; Civil Liability Act 2002 (Tas) ss 11 and 13; Wrongs Act 1958 (Vic) ss 48 and 51; Civil Liability Act 2002 (WA) ss 5B and 5C.

is likely that courts will continue to take the same factors into account under the civil liability statutes. But the open-ended nature of the requirement would also allow courts to take other additional factors into account. It remains to be seen whether and in what ways the scope of liability test might differ from the common law.

Applicability of the remoteness tests

2.43   While the reasonable foreseeability test of remoteness developed in the law of negligence,[188] the approach in negligence claims has changed slightly as a result of the Civil Liability Acts. However, as discussed at **2.42** above, the reasonable foreseeability test is still relevant. The test also continues to apply to nuisance[189] and trespass.[190] But there is doubt about its application to conversion,[191] while the direct causation *Polemis* test still applies to the intentional torts of deceit[192] and malicious falsehood.[193] In torts where damages are 'at large', such as defamation and passing off, the issue of reasonable foreseeability is rarely a decisive issue as remoteness issues are much less pronounced. Judicial statements about remoteness and passing off need to be treated with caution because they are often made in cases concerning injunctions rather than damages. In *Erven Warnink BV v J Townsend & Sons (Hull) Ltd*[194] Lord Diplock favoured a 'reasonable foreseeability' test, while Lord Fraser favoured a more direct test requiring that the plaintiff was 'really likely to suffer' substantial damage. Lord Oliver in *Reckitt & Colman Products Ltd v Borden Inc*[195] adopted an approach similar to that of Lord Fraser when he said that damage in a *quia timet* (because he fears) action must be shown to be 'likely' to be suffered.[196]

The reasonable foreseeability test owes its development to the law of negligence, but even here it is subject to at least three qualifications. First, there is the so-called 'egg-shell skull' rule, according to which the defendant takes his or her victim as they are found. This is not affected by the reasonable foreseeability test of remoteness.[197] While one view is that this rule is an

---

188.   *Overseas Tankship (UK) Ltd v Morts Dock & Engineering Co Ltd (Wagon Mound (No 1))* [1961] AC 388.

189.   See *Cambridge Water Co v Eastern Counties Leather plc* [1994] 2 AC 264 at 300–1.

190.   See *Hogan v AG Wright Pty Ltd* [1963] Tas SR 44; *Svingos v Deacon* [1971] 2 SASR 126; compare *TCN Channel Nine Pty Ltd v Anning* (2002) 54 NSWLR 333 (CA).

191.   See *National Australia Bank Ltd v Nemur Varity Pty Ltd* (2002) 4 VR 252 (CA).

192.   *Palmer Bruyn & Parker Pty Ltd v Parsons* (2001) 208 CLR 388; *Smith New Court Securities Ltd v Scrimgeour Vickers (Asset Management) Ltd* [1997] AC 254; *National Australia Bank Ltd v Nemur Varity Pty Ltd* (2002) 4 VR 252 at 276 per Batt JA (CA); *Toteff v Antonas* (1952) 87 CLR 647; *Doyle v Olby* [1969] 2 QB 158 at 167 per Lord Denning (CA).

193.   *Palmer Bruyn & Parker Pty Ltd v Parsons* (2001) 208 CLR 388.

194.   [1979] AC 731; [1980] RPC 31.

195.   [1990] RPC 341; (1990) 17 IPR 1 (HL).

196.   See also *Spalding v Gamage* (1918) 35 RPC 101 at 117 (CA).

197.   *Smith v Leech Brain & Co* [1962] 2 QB 405; *Mount Isa Mines Ltd v Pusey* (1971) 125 CLR 383 at 406; *Commonwealth v McLean* (1996) 41 NSWLR 389 (CA).

application of the direct causation test by way of an exception to the reasonable foreseeability test,[198] another is that of Glass JA in *Havenaar v Havenaar*:

> It would doubtless be preferable to accord due respect to the proposition that foreseeability is the only criterion of remoteness by treating the eggshell skull principle as an accepted illustration of it. So regarded it does no more than recognize that the possession by the plaintiff of special proclivities capable of enlarging the lesser harm which would be suffered by others is always foreseeable as a possibility notwithstanding that the particular proclivity and the way in which it has worked itself out in producing special harm may not be foreseeable even as possibilities.[199]

2.44   The second and third qualifications are two types of negligently inflicted damage where the reasonable foresight test of remoteness is necessary, but not sufficient: *pure* psychiatric injury (see **2.45–2.48**) and *pure* economic loss (see **2.49–2.52**). As observed by Gleeson CJ in *Gifford v Strang Patrick Stevedoring Pty Ltd*:

> … just as it would place an unreasonable burden upon human activity to require people to anticipate and guard against all kinds of foreseeable financial harm to others that might be a consequence of their acts or omissions, so also it would be unreasonable to require people to anticipate and guard against all kinds of foreseeable psychiatric injury to others that might be a consequence of their acts or omissions.[200]

Pure psychiatric injury and pure economic loss are so-called because the plaintiff has not suffered any other form of injury to the person or property due to the defendant's negligence. Gleeson CJ in *Gifford*, said the 'distinction is not based on science or logic; it is pragmatic, and none the worse for that'.[201] In any event, for both types of damage the courts insist on the plaintiff satisfying further control mechanisms beyond reasonable foresight. The High Court has preferred to emphasise control mechanisms found in the cause of action rather than the remedy. For example, in *Tame and Annetts*[202] Gleeson CJ adopted the observation of Brennan J in *Jaensch v Coffey*:

> In my opinion, the exigencies of proof of the elements of the cause of action impose the appropriate limits upon the scope of the remedy. Those limits are likely to be at once more flexible and more stringent than limits imposed by legal rules which might be devised to give effect to a judicial policy of restraining the remedy within what are thought to be acceptable bounds.[203]

198. *March v E & M H Stramare Pty Ltd* (1991) 171 CLR 506 at 534 per McHugh J; *Tame and Annetts* (2002) 211 CLR 317; [2002] HCA 35 at [117] per McHugh J, at [199] and [203] per Gummow, Kirby JJ, at [279] per Hayne J.
199. [1982] 1 NSWLR 626 at 631 (CA).
200. (2003) 214 CLR 269; [2003] HCA 33 at [9].
201. (2003) 214 CLR 269; [2003] HCA 33 at [6].
202. (2002) 211 CLR 317; [2002] HCA 35 at [19].
203. (1984) 155 CLR 549 at 571; 54 ALR 417 at 434.

Pure psychiatric harm

2.45   If a plaintiff suffers pain and suffering due to a negligently inflicted physical injury, the courts routinely award damages for such harm: see **2.73**. Indeed, '[p]ersonal injury must be understood as embracing both physical and psychological injury'.[204] But, if a plaintiff suffers *pure* psychiatric injury unaccompanied by physical injury, commonly referred to as 'nervous shock',[205] the 'common law has long shown a marked reluctance to allow damages'.[206] In *Coultas v Victorian Railways Commissioners*[207] a pregnant Mrs Coultas was a passenger in a horse-drawn buggy at a level crossing when the gatekeeper negligently allowed it to cross in front of an oncoming train. The resulting near miss caused Mrs Coultas to faint and suffer a miscarriage. The jury in the Victorian Supreme Court awarded damages for shock and this was upheld by the Full Court. But, on appeal, the Privy Council found the damage to be too remote when unaccompanied by physical injury. Yet, ultimately, it is the jury's view in *Coultas* that has triumphed. The Privy Council's decision was eventually overcome by statute in all Australian jurisdictions. In New South Wales s 3 of the Law Reform (Miscellaneous Provisions) Act 1946 achieved this, but this was repealed and replaced by s 29 of the Civil Liability Act 2002 (NSW):

> In any action for personal injury, the plaintiff is not prevented from recovering damages merely because the personal injury arose wholly or in part from mental or nervous shock.[208]

An independent statutory cause of action and remedy for nervous shock suffered by close family members of the victim was also created.[209] This did not abolish but, rather, supplemented the common law[210] and indeed the latter continued to develop to the point where it 'outflanked' the statutory action.[211]

2.46   While reasonable foresight remains a necessary precondition both at common law[212] and under the statute,[213] it is not sufficient. First, the plaintiff's harm must be a 'recognisable' psychiatric illness or disorder. As Windeyer J

---

204.   *Corr v IBC Vehicles Limited* [2008] UKHL 13 at [7] per Lord Bingham.

205.   A term that 'operates as a common lawyer's shorthand for the categories of psychiatric harm which are compensable under the tort of negligence': *Tame and Annetts* (2002) 211 CLR 317; [2002] HCA 35 at [20] per Gummow and Kirby JJ.

206.   *Tame and Annetts* (2002) 211 CLR 317; [2002] HCA 35 at [98] per Hayne J.

207.   (1888) 13 App Cas 222.

208.   See also Law Reform (Miscellaneous Provisions) Act 1955 (ACT) s 23; Law Reform (Miscellaneous Provisions) Act 1956 (NT) s 24; the Civil Liability Act 1936 (SA) ss 33, 53 and 69; Wrongs Act 1958 (Vic) s 23.

209.   See Law Reform (Miscellaneous Provisions) Act 1946 (NSW) s 4 (now repealed).

210.   *Gifford v Strang Patrick Stevedoring Pty Ltd* (2003) 214 CLR 269; [2003] HCA 33.

211.   Dr Des Butler, '*Gifford v Strang* and the new landscape for recovery for psychiatric injury in Australia' (2004) 12 TLJ 1.

212.   *Tame and Annetts* (2002) 211 CLR 317; [2002] HCA 35 at [45] per Gaudron J; *Gifford v Strang Patrick Stevedoring Pty Ltd* (2003) 214 CLR 269; [2003] HCA 33 at [98] per Hayne J.

213.   Civil Law (Wrongs) Act 2002 (ACT) s 34; Civil Liability Act 2002 (NSW) s 32(1); Wrongs Act 1958 (Vic) s 72(1); Civil Liability Act 1936 (SA) s 33; Civil Liability Act 2002 (Tas) s 34; Civil Liability Act 2002 (WA) s 5S. Queensland and Northern Territory do not have equivalent provisions in their civil liability statutes.

observed in *Mount Isa Mines Ltd v Pusey*, '[s]orrow does not sound in damages'.[214] This principle has long been part of the common law and it now has statutory force.[215] In *Tame and Annetts* Gummow and Kirby JJ held:

> In Australia, as in England, Canada and New Zealand, a plaintiff who is unable affirmatively to establish the existence of a recognisable psychiatric illness is not entitled to recover. Grief and sorrow are among the 'ordinary and inevitable incidents of life'; the very universality of those emotions denies to them the character of compensable loss under the tort of negligence. Fright, distress or embarrassment, without more, will not ground an action in negligence. Emotional harm of that nature may be evanescent or trivial.[216]

Second, a majority of the High Court[217] in *Tame and Annetts* held that a relevant consideration at common law, but not an independent test or precondition for liability, is that a person of 'normal fortitude' might have suffered the psychiatric harm suffered by the plaintiff. By contrast, the minority[218] viewed this as a precondition to liability, a view which now has statutory force.[219] However, if the defendant is aware, or ought to have been aware, that the plaintiff has a particular susceptibility to psychiatric harm, then the 'normal fortitude' test will neither bar recovery at common law[220] nor under statute.[221]

Two further control mechanisms considered in *Tame and Annetts* were that the plaintiff's psychiatric damage should be caused by a 'sudden shock' and, in a similar vein, that the plaintiff should have 'directly perceived' the accident or its immediate aftermath. Both tests, however, were squarely rejected. While neither is a necessary precondition to recovery at common law, the High Court described them as relevant considerations.[222]

In deciding whether a duty of care is owed, the statutory provisions include these and other relevant factors.[223] Thus s 32(2) of the NSW Act says the 'circumstances of the case' to be taken into account include:

---

214. (1970) 125 CLR 383 at 394.
215. Civil Liability Act 2002 (NSW) ss 31 and 33; Workers Compensation Act 1987 (NSW) s 151P(b); Civil Liability Act 1936 (SA) s 53; Wrongs Act 1958 (Vic) ss 72 and 75; Civil Liability Act 2002 (WA) s 5S.
216. (2002) 211 CLR 317; [2002] HCA 35 at [193] (footnotes omitted); Gaudron J concurring at [44]; compare Gleeson CJ at [7].
217. (2002) 211 CLR 317; [2002] HCA 35 at [16] per Gleeson CJ, at [61]–[62] per Gaudron J, at [197], [199]–[203] per Gummow and Kirby JJ; see also *Gifford v Strang Patrick Stevedoring Pty Ltd* (2003) 214 CLR 269; [2003] HCA 33 at [98] per Hayne J, at [119] per Callinan J.
218. McHugh J at [109]–[119], Hayne J at [273]–[274] and Callinan J at [366].
219. Civil Law (Wrongs) Act 2002 (ACT) s 34; Civil Liability Act 2002 (NSW) s 32(1); Civil Liability Act 1936 (SA) s 33; Civil Liability Act 2002 (Tas) s 34; Wrongs Act 1958 (Vic) ss 72(1) and 74; Civil Liability Act 2002 (WA) s 5S; and see *Wicks v State Rail Authority (NSW)* [2010] HCA 22. Queensland and Northern Territory do not have equivalent provisions in their civil liability statutes.
220. *Tame and Annetts* (2002) 211 CLR 317; [2002] HCA 35 at [62] per Gaudron J, at [273]–[274] per Hayne J.
221. Civil Law (Wrongs) Act 2002 (ACT) s 34(4); Civil Liability Act 2002 (NSW) s 32(4); Civil Liability Act 1936 (SA) s 33(3); Civil Liability Act 2002 (Tas) s 34(4); Wrongs Act 1958 (Vic) ss 72(3) and 74; Civil Liability Act 2002 (WA) s 5S(4).
222. (2002) 211 CLR 317; [2002] HCA 35 at [18] per Gleeson CJ, at [66] per Gaudron J, at [188]–[191] and [204]–[225] per Gummow and Kirby JJ.
223. Civil Law (Wrongs) Act 2002 (ACT) s 34(2); Civil Liability Act 2002 (NSW) s 32(2); Wrongs Act 1958 (Vic) ss 72(3) and 74; Civil Liability Act 2002 (WA) s 5S(4). There are different approaches in Civil

(a) whether or not the mental harm was suffered as the result of a sudden shock,

(b) whether the plaintiff witnessed, at the scene, a person being killed, injured or put in peril,

(c) the nature of the relationship between the plaintiff and any person killed, injured or put in peril,

(d) whether or not there was a pre-existing relationship between the plaintiff and the defendant.[224]

In the narrower case of pure mental harm as a result of injuries or risk suffered by someone other than the plaintiff, some of the civil liability statutes specify as a requirement (rather than just a relevant consideration) that the plaintiff witnesses the 'person being killed, injured or put in peril' or has a close relationship with the victim before damages can be awarded.[225]

The meaning of s 32(2)(b) in the New South Wales Act was clarified by the High Court in *Wicks v State Rail Authority (NSW)*.[226] Two police officers attended a serious train accident. A number of people had been killed or injured and the officers were involved in the rescue operation. The New South Wales Court of Appeal held they could not recover damages for mental harm because they had not witnessed the victims being 'killed, injured or put in peril'. On appeal, the High Court reversed the decision, holding that the phrase should not be narrowly interpreted in this way. Witnessing victims being 'killed, injured or put in peril' did not refer only to the moment of the accident, since people were still being put in peril, for example, while rescue operations were being carried out.

The High Court in *Wicks* also explained the importance of understanding these statutory provisions against the background of the common law.[227] Considered below are the facts of three High Court cases explaining the common law approach more fully, namely, *Gifford v Strang Patrick Stevedoring Pty Ltd*[228] and two cases heard concurrently, *Tame* and *Annetts*.[229] *Tame* was like *Coultas* in that the plaintiff was the primary victim, whereas in *Gifford* and *Annetts* the plaintiffs were secondary victims alleged to have suffered psychiatric injury due to the death of a third person. The nature of the relationship between the plaintiff and the deceased, as well as the relationship

Liability Act 2002 (Tas) s 34(2) and Civil Liability Act 1936 (SA) s 33(2) arw s 53. Compare also *Tame and Annetts* (2002) 211 CLR 317; [2002] HCA 35 at [210] per Gummow, Kirby JJ who reason that in cases of protracted suffering as opposed to sudden shock, the issue is not one involving the duty of care, but rather, causation and remoteness.

224. Civil Liability Act 2002 (NSW) s 32(2). The Civil Liability Act 2002 (Tas) s 34(2) only includes the requirements in (a) and (d).

225. There are differences in the wording and the effect of some of these provisions, but see Civil Liability Act 2002 (NSW) s 30(1) and (2); Civil Liability Act 1936 (SA) s 53(1); Civil Liability Act 2002 (Tas) s 32(1) and (2); Wrongs Act 1958 (Vic) s 73(1) and (2).

226. [2010] HCA 22.

227. [2010] HCA 22 at [24].

228. (2003) 214 CLR 269; [2003] HCA 33.

229. (2002) 211 CLR 317; [2002] HCA 35.

between the plaintiff and the defendant, were important considerations in both *Gifford* and *Annetts*. These are also important statutory considerations under the civil liability reforms.[230]

2.47   In *Annetts*, James Annetts, a boy of 16, was offered a job as a jackaroo at Flora Valley, a remote cattle station in the Kimberley district of Western Australia. In what became a critical piece of evidence, before James left his parents' home in Binya, New South Wales, his mother telephoned the wife of the station manager, Mrs Loder, seeking assurances as to her son's well-being. Mrs Loder told Mrs Annetts that her son would be working under constant supervision, would share a room with one to four other men, all of his meals would be supplied for him and he would be well looked after. The day after James arrived at Flora Valley, Mrs Annetts again telephoned Mrs Loder to check that her son had arrived safely. On 13 October 1986, just seven weeks after James started, Mr Loder stationed James to work alone as a caretaker at Nicholson Station, a desolate property 100 km east of Flora Valley and about 270 km north of Balgo. On 3 December 1986 Mr Loder, the station manager, learned that James had disappeared and suspected the worst: grave personal injury or death. It took three days before a police officer in Griffith, New South Wales, telephoned Mr Annetts with news that hit like a 'thunderclap':[231] his son was missing and he believed that he had run away. Mr Annetts collapsed and Mrs Annetts took over the conversation. A search commenced for James and another missing teenager who had also been employed by the Loders. Mr and Mrs Annetts made many telephone calls to people living near Halls Creek seeking information on James' whereabouts. In January 1987 they went to Halls Creek and were shown some of their son's belongings that had been found, including a hat covered in blood. Mr and Mrs Annetts made several more trips to the area but they could not find their son. On 26 April 1987 Mr Annetts learned by telephone that the vehicle that James had been driving had been found bogged in the Gibson Desert some 133 km south of Balgo. Later that day Mr Annetts learned that two sets of human remains had been found near the abandoned vehicle. A couple of days later Mr Annetts returned to Halls Creek police station where he was shown a photograph of the skeletal remains of a person whom he identified as James.

The Coroner found that James had died on or about 4 December 1986 as a result of dehydration, exhaustion and hypothermia. The Annetts sued the station owner for the negligent infliction of psychiatric damage. Their difficulty was that they had neither suffered a sudden shock nor had they directly perceived the accident or its immediate aftermath. The High Court held that neither one of these facts were preconditions to recovery and the Annetts could maintain their action. Gleeson CJ observed:

---

230. Civil Law (Wrongs) Act 2002 (ACT) s 34(2)(c) and (d); Civil Liability Act 2002 (NSW) ss 32(2)(c) and (d); Wrongs Act 1958 (Vic) ss 72(2)(c) and (d); Civil Liability Act 2002 (WA) s 5S(2)(c) and (d). There are different approaches in Civil Liability Act 2002 (Tas) s 34(2) and Civil Liability Act 1936 (SA) s 33(2) arw s 53. See also *Burke v New South Wales* [2004] NSWSC 725; and *Wicks v State Rail Authority (NSW)* [2010] HCA 22.

231. (2002) 211 CLR 317; [2002] HCA 35 at [364] per Callinan J.

The process by which the applicants became aware of their son's disappearance, and then his death, was agonizingly protracted, rather than sudden. And the death by exhaustion and starvation of someone lost in the desert is not an 'event' or 'phenomenon' likely to have many witnesses. But a rigid distinction between psychiatric injury suffered by parents in those circumstances, and similar injury suffered by parents who see their son being run down by a motor car, is indefensible.

Here there was a relationship between the applicants and the respondent sufficient, in combination with reasonable foreseeability of harm, to give rise to a duty of care, though the applicants did not directly witness their son's death, and suffer a sudden shock in consequence. The applicants, on the assumed facts, who themselves had responsibilities for the care of their son, only agreed to permit him to go to work for the respondent after having made inquiries of the respondent as to the arrangements that would be made for his safety and, in particular, after being assured that he would be under constant supervision. Contrary to those assurances, he was sent to work, alone, in a remote location. In those circumstances there was a relationship between the applicants and the respondent of such a nature that it was reasonable to require the respondent to have in contemplation the kind of injury to the applicants that they suffered.[232]

The defendant's assurance that James would be constantly supervised also played a central role in the reasoning of Gaudron, McHugh, Gummow and Kirby, Hayne and Callinan JJ.[233] Both Gleeson CJ and Gaudron J relied on the notion that the defendants should have 'reasonably contemplated' the Annetts' psychiatric harm.[234] This bears a striking similarity to the remoteness test in contract cases: see **3.14–3.24**.

2.48   The relationship between the parties that was critical in *Annetts* was that between the employer, a young employee and his parents. The critical relationship in *Gifford v Strang Patrick Stevedoring Pty Ltd*[235] was between the employer, employee and his teenage children. A wharf labourer at Darling Harbour, Sydney, was crushed to death when a large forklift carelessly reversed over him. His estranged wife learned of the accident shortly after and his three children aged 19, 17 and 14 learned of their father's death later that day at their home in Woolloomooloo. Although the children did not live with their father, he saw them daily and maintained a close, loving relationship. The children were advised not to view their father's body due to the shocking crush injuries. The New South Wales Court of Appeal disallowed the wife's claim because while she had suffered emotional distress and grief this was not a recognised psychiatric illness. The children's claim was also disallowed because there had not been any direct perception of the accident or its aftermath. But this was reversed on appeal to the High Court which found, following *Annetts*, that direct perception was not a necessary prerequisite for recovery. While it was

232.   (2002) 211 CLR 317; [2002] HCA 35 at [36], [37].

233.   (2002) 211 CLR 317; [2002] HCA 35 at [54], [144], [237]–[239], [302] and [361] respectively.

234.   See also Gleeson CJ's comments in *Gifford* (2003) 214 CLR 269; [2003] HCA 33 at [8].

235.   (2003) 214 CLR 269; [2003] HCA 33.

relevant, the overriding consideration was that 'as a class, children form an obvious category of people who might be expected to be at risk of the kind of injury in question'.[236]

While both *Annetts* and *Gifford* involved secondary victims, *Tame*, heard and decided concurrently with *Annetts*, involved a primary victim. Mrs Tame suffered injuries after a drunk driver collided with her vehicle. The investigating police officer mistakenly attributed the drunk driver's alcohol reading to Mrs Tame. Although the error was corrected and not relied on in any way, Mrs Tame developed an obsession about the mistake which caused a psychotic depression. It was also found that she had a predisposition to such an illness due to her mistreatment as a child, the recent loss of a parent and marital problems. Her claim for damages for negligently inflicted psychiatric injury caused by the police officer and the state of New South Wales was rejected. The investigating police officer did not owe a duty of care in these circumstances and, even if he did, her injury was not reasonably foreseeable.[237]

Pure economic loss

Introduction

2.49   In many torts, the plaintiff suffers severe economic loss such as loss of profits, loss of income, loss of enjoyment of a service, costs of alternative transportation, loss of interest, financial loss and so on. An old common law rule applying to negligence, however, prohibited recovery of economic loss unless it was based on injury to the plaintiff's person or property. Or, put another way, pure economic loss was not recoverable. This rule of remoteness, however, was not of general application;[238] in particular, the following economic torts were exempt: passing off, injurious falsehood, inducing a breach of contract, interfering with contractual relations and wrongful dismissal. But, even in some of these torts, particularly passing off, the courts would search to find an injury to the plaintiff's property.

The Willemstad

2.50   In any event, while there is still a 'tendency to assume that physical injury to person or property is the paradigm case for the application of the law of negligence',[239] there has been a gradual acceptance of pure economic loss claims. Initially, this was achieved by the development of negligent misstatement and the notion of proximate cause. In 1964 the House of Lords

---

236.   *Gifford* (2003) 214 CLR 269; [2003] HCA 33 at [12] per Gleeson CJ; and see [86]–[89] per Gummow and Kirby JJ; and at [101] per Hayne J.

237.   *Tame and Annetts* (2002) 211 CLR 317; [2002] HCA 35 at [23]–[29] per Gleeson CJ; at [63] per Gaudron J; at [120]–[121] per McHugh J; at [231]–[234] per Gummow and Kirby JJ and at [298]–[300] per Hayne J; see also *Koehler v Cerebos (Australia) Ltd* (2005) 222 CLR 44; compare *Nationwide News Pty Ltd v Naidu* [2007] NSWCA 377 where intentional psychiatric injury to a primary victim was found to be foreseeable.

238.   *Perre v Apand Pty Ltd* (1999) 198 CLR 180 at [179] per Gummow J.

239.   *Tame and Annetts* (2002) 211 CLR 317; [2002] HCA 35 at [5] per Gleeson CJ.

in *Hedley Byrne & Co Ltd v Heller & Partners Ltd*[240] allowed for recovery of
pure economic loss not dependent upon physical or property injury where
there had been a negligent misstatement.[241] The High Court of Australia also
allowed for recovery of pure economic loss in *Caltex Oil (Australia) Pty Ltd
v The Dredge Willemstad*.[242] In *The Willemstad*, the master of a dredge severed an
oil pipeline on the bottom of Botany Bay. Caltex used the pipeline to receive
its refined oil at its terminal. The pipeline was owned by another company,
Australian Oil Refinery Pty Ltd (AOR), and the oil was transported at its risk.
AOR was compensated for the loss and the issue was whether Caltex could
be compensated for its loss. The severing of the pipeline not only resulted in
loss of oil but also caused economic damage to Caltex because it had to find
alternative means of transporting the refined oil.

At the trial both the master of the dredge and the company that supplied
the maps of Botany Bay to the master were found to be negligent. The loss
suffered by Caltex, however, was found to be purely economic and thus, on
this issue, judgment was entered for the defendants. Caltex appealed to the
High Court and won. Gibbs CJ said there was still an exclusionary rule that
economic loss was not recoverable where not consequential upon injury to
the plaintiff's person or property, even though such loss was foreseeable.[243]
But the Chief Justice was prepared to allow an exception if the defendant had
knowledge or ought to have known that a specific plaintiff would be likely to
suffer damage because of the defendant's negligence.[244] In deciding this issue
the court needed to examine all the facts to see if there was proximity. This
did not have to be physical proximity, so if the plaintiff and a third party were
engaged in a common adventure, as in *The Willemstad*, this would suffice.[245]

Stephen J also opted for a test based on proximity when considering whether
pure economic loss is recoverable. He criticised the general exclusionary rule
for economic loss, but said there was a need for 'some control mechanism'
based upon notions of proximity or sufficient proximity between the tortious
act and harm. On the facts Stephen J noted that the defendant's knowledge
of the economic loss, the nature of the loss (namely, loss of the pipeline) and
the nature of the damage to the plaintiff (namely, the expense of obtaining
alternative means of transporting the oil) were all 'salient features'[246] showing
a close degree of proximity and reasonable foreseeability.[247] His Honour also

---

240. [1964] AC 465.

241. See also *L Shaddock & Associates Pty Ltd v Parramatta City Council* (1981) 150 CLR 225; *San Sebastian Pty Ltd v Minister Administering the Environmental Planning and Assessment Act 1979* (1986) 162 CLR 340.

242. (1976) 136 CLR 529; compare *Candlewood Navigation Corp Ltd v Mitsui OSK Lines Ltd* (1985) 3 NSWLR 159 (PC).

243. (1976) 136 CLR 529 at 555.

244. A concept later developed into the 'vulnerability' principle in *Perre v Apand Pty Ltd* (1999) 198 CLR 180 at [11]–[15] per Gleeson CJ, and [50], [109] and [118] per McHugh J.

245. (1976) 136 CLR at 555.

246. (1976) 136 CLR 529 at 576–7.

247. This approach was followed in *Perre v Apand Pty Ltd* (1999) 198 CLR 180 at [201] per Gummow J.

held there was no issue of 'indeterminate liability',[248] a concept that stems from Chief Judge Cardozo's well-known judgment in the American case, *Ultramares Corp v Touche*,[249] where the plaintiff suffered pure economic loss after relying on negligently prepared accounts to invest in a company. In rejecting the claim the Chief Judge said:

> If liability for negligence exists, a thoughtless slip or blunder, the failure to detect a theft or forgery beneath the cover of deceptive entries, may expose accountants to a liability in an indeterminate amount for an indeterminate time to an indeterminate class.[250]

Willemstad to Woolcock

2.51   For many years after *The Willemstad* the High Court confirmed the need to satisfy both reasonable foreseeability and proximity in cases of negligently inflicted pure economic loss.[251] But neither test was confined to issues of remoteness. So, for example, in *Gala v Preston*[252] the High Court held that proximity was also relevant in deciding whether a duty of care was owed in the first place.

Despite its longstanding acceptance, the proximity doctrine was discarded by the High Court in both *Perre v Apand*[253] and *Woolcock Street Investments Pty Ltd v CDG Pty Ltd*.[254] In *Woolcock*, discussed below, the court held that 'proximity is no longer seen as the "conceptual determinant" in this area'.[255] Earlier, in *Esanda Finance Corporation Ltd v Peat Marwick Hungerfords*, Brennan J recognised 'something more' than reasonable foreseeability was needed,[256] and this was not proximity but, rather, the incremental development of 'novel categories of negligence'.[257] And in *Hill v Van Erp* McHugh J (in dissent) said that the proximity principle had 'not increased the predictability of judicial decisions'.[258]

In *Hill* a solicitor's negligence deprived a beneficiary of a half-share in the testatrix's house. Although the beneficiary was not the solicitor's client, the

---

248. (1976) 136 CLR 529 at 568.
249. 255 NY Rep 170 (1931).
250. 255 NY Rep 170 (1931) at 179–80.
251. See *Burnie Port Authority v General Jones Pty Ltd* (1994) 179 CLR 520; *Bryan v Maloney* (1995) 182 CLR 609; *Hill v Van Erp* (1997) 188 CLR 159 at 175 per Dawson J; *Esanda Finance Corporation Ltd v Peat Marwick Hungerfords* (1997) 188 CLR 241 at 254 per Dawson J and 260 per Toohey and Gaudron JJ.
252. (1991) 172 CLR 243.
253. *Perre v Apand Pty Ltd* (1999) 198 CLR 180 (property owner liable for a neighbour's pure economic loss due to the sowing of banned potato seeds).
254. (2004) 216 CLR 515; [2004] HCA 16.
255. (2004) 216 CLR 515; [2004] HCA 16 at [16] per Gleeson CJ, Gummow, Hayne and Heydon JJ; see also McHugh J at [80].
256. (1997) 188 CLR 241 at 249.
257. See also *Sutherland Shire Council v Heyman* (1985) 157 CLR 424 at 481; *Perre* (1999) 198 CLR 180 at [94]–[99] per McHugh J. A similar approach is taken in New Zealand—see *Rolls Royce NZ Ltd v Carter Holt Harvey Ltd* [2004] NZCA 97.
258. *Hill v Van Erp* (1997) 188 CLR 159 at 210; and see *Perre* (1999) 198 CLR 180 at [70]–[74] per McHugh J.

majority[259] held that the solicitor was liable. Dawson and Toohey JJ relied on proximity, while Gaudron J found this was not relevant where the beneficiary had lost a 'precise legal right ... closely analogous to property damage'.[260] Brennan CJ preferred his incremental approach, but as noted by Dawson J:

> ... the difference between the approach based on proximity and that suggested by Brennan J is, in my view, far less than the protracted debate on the subject would suggest, and is, perhaps more a difference of labelling than one of substance. Reasonable foreseeability of harm does not, of itself, always give rise to a duty to take care. Something more is required according to the category of the case in question, and that something more is called proximity.[261]

2.52   Despite Dawson J's observation, since *Woolcock* it appears that this 'something more' is now called the 'vulnerability' principle. But, as with proximity, it appears that Chief Judge Cardozo's influential 'indeterminacy' principle (see **2.50**) will continue to play a central role in pure economic loss claims; that is, the court should be careful to avoid the imposition of 'liability in an indeterminate amount for an indeterminate time to an indeterminate class'. The High Court has stressed this in every case from *The Willemstad* to *Woolcock*, and it is often relied on at the 'coal face'.[262]

In *Woolcock* all of the High Court judges referred to the indeterminacy principle as the reason why the vulnerability doctrine or other control mechanisms were needed.[263] In that case, consulting engineers CDG designed and supervised the building of a warehouse and offices in Townsville in 1987. CDG obtained a quote for a geotechnical investigation into the sub-soil conditions, but the owner refused to pay and chose its own structural footing sizes provided by the builder. The warehouse was sold to Woolcock in 1992. The contract neither contained a warranty that the building was free from defects nor a clause assigning to Woolcock any rights that the owner might have had against others including CDG. No expert was engaged by Woolcock to inspect the warehouse and it made no inquiries as to whether the building had structural defects. In 1994 the warehouse was subject to substantial structural distress and needed costly rectification work. Woolcock sued CDG in the Queensland Supreme Court relying on *Bryan v Maloney*,[264] where the High Court held that a builder of a house owes subsequent purchasers a duty of care to avoid the pure economic loss caused by latent defects due to negligent construction. On appeal the High Court, by a 6:1 majority, distinguished *Bryan v Maloney* and found that CDG did not owe Woolcock such a duty of care. In

---

259.   Brennan CJ, Dawson, Toohey, Gaudron and Gummow JJ.

260.   (1997) 188 CLR 159 at 198.

261.   (1997) 188 CLR 159; 142 ALR 687 at 700; and see *Pyrenees Shire Council v Day* (1998) 192 CLR 330 at [73] [76] per Toohey J (in dissent).

262.   See, for example, in *Johnson Tiles Pty Ltd v Esso Australia Pty Ltd* [2003] VSC 27 where Gillard J denied a pure economic loss claim based on a negligent interruption to gas supplied to 1.4 million customers.

263.   (2004) 216 CLR 515; [2004] HCA 16 at [21] per Gleeson CJ, Gummow, Hayne and Heydon JJ; at [46] [47] per McHugh J; at [154] [162], [166] per Kirby J; at [205], [225] [227] per Callinan J.

264.   (1995) 182 CLR 609.

a joint judgment, Gleeson CJ, Gummow, Hayne and Heydon JJ observed that '[c]laims for damages for pure economic loss present peculiar difficulty'[265] and then held:

> Since *Caltex Oil*, and most notably in *Perre v Apand Pty Ltd*, the vulnerability of the plaintiff has emerged as an important requirement in cases where a duty of care to avoid economic loss has been held to have been owed. 'Vulnerability', in this context, is not to be understood as meaning only that the plaintiff was likely to suffer damage if reasonable care was not taken. Rather, 'vulnerability' is to be understood as a reference to the plaintiff's inability to protect itself from the consequences of a defendant's want of reasonable care, either entirely or at least in a way which would cast the consequences of loss on the defendant. So, in *Perre*, the plaintiffs could do nothing to protect themselves from the economic consequences to them of the defendant's negligence in sowing a crop which caused the quarantining of the plaintiffs' land. In *Hill v Van Erp*, the intended beneficiary depended entirely upon the solicitor performing the client's retainer properly and the beneficiary could do nothing to ensure that this was done. But in *Esanda Finance Corp Ltd v Peat Marwick Hungerfords*, the financier could itself have made inquiries about the financial position of the company to which it was to lend money, rather than depend upon the auditor's certification of the accounts of the company.
>
> In other cases of pure economic loss (*Bryan v Maloney* is an example) reference has been made to notions of assumption of responsibility and known reliance. The negligent misstatement cases like *Mutual Life & Citizens' Assurance Co Ltd v Evatt* and *Shaddock & Associates Pty Ltd v Parramatta City Council (No 1)* can be seen as cases in which a central plank in the plaintiff's allegation that the defendant owed it a duty of care is the contention that the defendant knew that the plaintiff would rely on the accuracy of the information the defendant provided. And it may be, as Professor Stapleton has suggested,[266] that these cases, too, can be explained by reference to notions of vulnerability.[267]

Woolcock was not vulnerable because, first, it could have protected itself from the negligent infliction of pure economic loss by insisting on either a warranty in the sale contract that the building was free from defects or a provision assigning the vendor's rights against CDG.[268] Second, Woolcock could have made inquiries about, or obtained an expert opinion on, latent defects.[269] *Bryan v Maloney* was to be distinguished, not because it involved a residential dwelling as opposed to commercial premises, but because there the owner relied on the builder who assumed responsibility for its design.[270] By contrast, in *Woolcock*, the 'original owner asserted control over the

---

265. (2004) 216 CLR 515; [2004] HCA 16 at [21].

266. Citing 'Comparative Economic Loss: Lessons from Case-Law-Focused "Middle Theory"' (2002) 50 *UCLA Law Review* 531 at 558–9. See also Professor Stapleton, 'The golden thread at the heart of tort law: Protection of the vulnerable' (2003) 24 *Australian Bar Review* 135.

267. (2004) 216 CLR 515; [2004] HCA 16 at [23]–[24].

268. (2004) 216 CLR 515; [2004] HCA 16 at [31] per Gleeson CJ, Gummow, Hayne and Heydon JJ; and see [94]–[96] and [111]–[113] per McHugh J; [213] per Callinan J.

269. (2004) 216 CLR 515; [2004] HCA 16 at [32] per Gleeson CJ, Gummow, Hayne and Heydon JJ; and see [213] per Callinan J.

270. (2004) 216 CLR 515; [2004] HCA 16 at [26] per Gleeson CJ, Gummow, Hayne and Heydon JJ.

investigations which the engineer undertook for the purposes of performing its work'[271] in designing the warehouse.

Despite the rise to prominence of the vulnerability doctrine, the NSW Court of Appeal has concluded that it is only one of a number of factors to be taken into account. In *Caltex Refineries (Qld) Pty Ltd v Stavar*, Allsop P listed a non-exhaustive list of 17 'salient features' which ought to be considered when deciding whether there was a duty of care in novel circumstances.[272] Shortly thereafter, in *Makawe Pty Ltd v Randwick City Council*, Hodgson JA (with whom Campbell JA agreed) held it was wrong to treat the foreseeability of reliance by the plaintiff, control by the defendant and the vulnerability of the plaintiff as each being necessary requirements.[273] In *Makawe*, the owner of a unit in a building suffered economic loss as a result of flooding caused by fluctuations in the water table. The court was concerned with whether the Council, which approved the development and building applications, owed a duty of care to a subsequent purchaser of the property. The Court of Appeal held it was the cumulative effect of these salient features which had to be taken into account. After balancing these factors, the court agreed with the primary judge's conclusion that the Council did not owe the plaintiff a duty of care in this situation.

For claims that come under the Civil Liability Acts, the range of factors to be taken into account appears to be more open-ended — see the discussion at 2.42. However, the common law approach is still relevant and, now that the proximity doctrine has been discarded in favour of the vulnerability doctrine, it will be fascinating to see whether this is more than a mere label change and whether it can do what proximity could not, namely, increase 'the predictability of judicial decisions'.[274]

MITIGATION

2.53 There is a duty on the plaintiff to mitigate losses flowing from the defendant's wrong.[275] For example, in a personal injury claim the plaintiff may have refused medical treatment which would have alleviated the harm. If such refusal is unreasonable the breach of the duty to mitigate loss is not actionable, nor does it lead to a finding of contributory negligence, but the court may reduce the damages payable. The onus of proving that the plaintiff has failed to attempt reasonable mitigation is on the defendant,[276] who should plead this

---

271. (2004) 216 CLR 515; [2004] HCA 16 at [25] per Gleeson CJ, Gummow, Hayne and Heydon JJ.

272. [2009] NSWCA 258 at [102]–[105].

273. [2009] NSWCA 412 at [20]–[21].

274. As noted by McHugh J (in dissent) in *Hill v Van Erp* (1997) 188 CLR 159 at 210 in relation to proximity; and see *Perre* (1999) 198 CLR 180 at [70]–[74] per McHugh J.

275. See also s 136(1) of the Motor Accidents Compensation Act 1999 (NSW); compare Civil Liability Act 2003 (Qld) s 53.

276. See 2.6; see also *Watts v Rake* (1960) 108 CLR 158 at 159 per Dixon CJ and 163 per Menzies J; *Purkess v Crittenden* (1965) 114 CLR 164; *Munce v Vinidex* [1974] 2 NSWLR 235 (CA); *Glavonjic v Foster* [1979] VR 536.

in defence or give notice to the plaintiff before the trial.[277] Where the plaintiff has attempted reasonable mitigation the cost of so doing is recoverable as damages, even if the attempt increased the loss.[278]

2.54 In assessing *reasonable* mitigation, the court considers what a reasonable person in the plaintiff's circumstances would have done. In *Glavonjic v Foster*[279] the plaintiff suffered a brain injury in a car accident and refused to undergo surgery. Gobbo J said:

> I am of the view that if the matter is to be judged entirely objectively without regard to the plaintiff's knowledge, circumstances and mental condition, refusal of the operation was not a reasonable one. I am of the opinion however that upon analysis of the authorities I am not constrained to apply such a strict and technical test. It seems to me more appropriate to have regard to the circumstances of the plaintiff. That is not to say that one simply applies a subjective test and considers whether the plaintiff thought it was reasonable for him to refuse surgery. It is however appropriate to adopt a test that asks whether a reasonable man in the circumstances as they existed for the plaintiff and subject to the various factors such as difficulty of understanding and the plaintiff's medical history and condition that affected the plaintiff, would have refused treatment. In my opinion, applying the broader test, I am of the view that the defendants have not discharged the onus which is upon them of showing that it was unreasonable of the plaintiff to refuse the surgery proposed.[280]

This formulation was approved by the Full Victorian Supreme Court in *Karabotsos v Plastex Industries Pty Ltd*.[281] Similar reasoning was applied in *Alcoa Minerals of Jamaica Inc v Broderick*,[282] where emissions from the appellant's smelting plant injured the respondent's health and corroded the galvanised zinc roof on his house. The respondent fixed the roof but when it happened again he could not afford the repairs. The Privy Council found that the respondent's refusal to undertake further repairs was reasonable in light of his own personal circumstances and impecuniosity.

It is also unreasonable in negligent sterilisation and contraception cases to expect a mother to mitigate damages by either abortion or adoption.[283]

2.55 If in mitigating the loss the plaintiff benefits from the defendant's breach this will also be taken into account in the damages assessment. In *Hoad v Scone Motors Pty Ltd*[284] the defendant negligently caused a fire which destroyed the plaintiff's seven-year-old tractor. The plaintiff bought a new

---

277. *Geest plc v Lansiquot* [2002] UKPC 48. See also Civil Liability Act 2003 (Qld) s 53.
278. *Gardner v R* [1933] NZLR 730; compare *Unity Insurance Brokers Pty Ltd v Rocco Pezzano Pty Ltd* (1998) 192 CLR 603 at [3] per Brennan CJ.
279. [1979] VR 536.
280. [1979] VR 536 at 540.
281. [1981] VR 675.
282. [2000] UKPC 9.
283. *McFarlane v Tayside Health Board* [2000] 2 AC 59 (HL); compare *Cattanach v Melchior* (2003) 215 CLR 1; [2003] HCA 38.
284. [1977] 1 NSWLR 88 (CA).

tractor as no secondhand tractors were available. The intention of the plaintiff was to sell this tractor 18 months after its purchase because he wanted to give up farming. After discussing the authorities in contract (see **3.25–3.35**), a majority in the New South Wales Court of Appeal held that damages were to be reduced because of the superior performance of the new tractor and its higher resale value.

2.56   While in most torts the duty to mitigate invariably falls upon the plaintiff, in defamation the *defendant* may mitigate damages flowing from the defamation by an offer of amends,[285] making an apology or publishing a correction.[286] If the defendant makes an apology this is not an admission and it is neither relevant nor admissible on the issue of fault or liability.[287] A defendant may also produce evidence in mitigation showing that the plaintiff has already recovered damages, brought proceedings for damages or received or agreed to receive compensation for the publication of matter having the same meaning or effect as the defamatory matter in issue.[288]

ASSESSMENT

Introduction

2.57   As noted at the beginning of this chapter, the general principle in assessing damages in tort is that the plaintiff should as nearly as possible receive a sum of money which, so far as money can, places him or her in the same position as if the wrong had not been sustained.[289] Once the court has found that more than nominal damages are recoverable it will calculate the quantum. There are several factors affecting this exercise. It has already been discussed under the issue of causation that if the plaintiff is guilty of contributory negligence damages may be apportioned. The tribunal of fact, be it the judge or jury, has a discretion here in determining the percentage of loss which should be borne by the plaintiff: see **2.15–2.20**. Damages may also be apportioned between multiple defendants in some civil liability cases while in others there will be a right of contribution among them: see **2.21–2.24**.

---

285. Defamation Act 2005 (NSW) Pt 3 Div 1; Defamation Act 2006 (NT) Pt 3 Div 1; Defamation Act 2005 (Qld) Pt 3 Div 1; Defamation Act 2005 (SA) Pt 3 Div 1; Defamation Act 2005 (Tas) Pt 3 Div 1; Defamation Act 2005 (Vic) Pt 3 Div 1; Defamation Act 2005 (WA) Pt 3 Div 1.

286. Defamation Act 2005 (NSW) s 38(1); Defamation Act 2006 (NT) s 35(1); Defamation Act 2005 (Qld) s 38(1); Defamation Act 2005 (SA) s 36; Defamation Act 2005 (Tas) s 38(1); Defamation Act 2005 (Vic) s 38(1); Defamation Act 2005 (WA) s 38(1).

287. Defamation Act 2005 (NSW) s 20; Defamation Act 2006 (NT) s 19; Defamation Act 2005 (Qld) s 20; Defamation Act 2005 (SA) s 20; Defamation Act 2005 (Tas) s 20; Defamation Act 2005 (Vic) s 20; Defamation Act 2005 (WA) s 20.

288. Defamation Act 2005 (NSW) s 38(1); Defamation Act 2006 (NT) s 35(1); Defamation Act 2005 (Qld) s 38(1); Defamation Act 2005 (SA) s 36; Defamation Act 2005 (Tas) s 38(1); Defamation Act 2005 (Vic) s 38(1); Defamation Act 2005 (WA) s 38(1).

289. *Livingstone v Rawyards Coal Co* [1880] 5 AC 25 at 39; *Butler v Egg and Egg Pulp Marketing Board* (1966) 114 CLR 185 at 190.

This is subject to the rule against double recovery which bars plaintiffs from recovering their losses more than once.[290]

The courts have also developed principles in relation to the date of assessment, lump sum payments, tax, interest and the various heads of damage.

Date of assessment

2.58   Generally, damages are assessed by reference to the date on which the cause of action arose, but the court has a discretion to fix its own date in order to provide fair compensation. For example, in detinue a plaintiff seeks the restitution of goods wrongfully detained. The defendant is given the choice of either returning the goods or paying their value. If the goods are retained this is a continuing wrong, and the court will then ordinarily assess damages at the date of judgment.[291] Damages for personal injury[292] and defamation are also assessed at the date of judgment. Indeed, the general rule is departed from whenever it is in the interests of justice to do so.[293] In exercising this discretion the court will consider the fundamental principle of providing proper compensation for the loss.[294] So, in *Rentokil Pty Ltd v Channon*,[295] a case concerning a negligent misrepresentation in a termite inspection certificate, it was held that the fundamental principle was best served by ordering that damages be assessed at the date of the trial, rather than the date on which the cause of action accrued.

Once-and-for-all rule

2.59   Although common law damages cover past and future loss, the award itself can only be given once-and-for-all by way of a lump sum.[296] Periodic payments cannot be given[297] and a second claim cannot be made for continuing damage.[298] The policy behind the rule, sometimes known as the 'single action rule', is that litigation should finally decide the dispute between the parties. As observed by Lord Hoffman in *Johnston v NEI International Combustion Ltd*, a 'defendant should not have to answer more than once for the consequences of the same act'.[299] The classic illustration is found in *Fitter v Veal*.[300] The plaintiff recovered damages

---

290. *Baxter v Obacelo Pty Ltd* (2001) 205 CLR 635; [2001] HCA 66; and see Andrew Broadfoot, 'Multiple defendant litigation and the rule against double recovery' (2002) 10 *TLJ* 255.

291. See, for example, *General and Finance Facilities Ltd v Cooks Cars (Romford) Ltd* [1963] 1 WLR 644.

292. See *Johnson v Perez* (1988) 166 CLR 351 at 355–6 per Mason CJ.

293. *Johnson v Perez* (1988) 166 CLR 351 at 355–6 per Mason CJ; see also *O'Brien v McKean* (1968) 118 CLR 540 at 545 per Barwick CJ; and *Alcoa Minerals of Jamaica Inc v Broderick* [2000] UKPC 9.

294. *Butler v Egg and Egg Pulp Marketing Board* (1966) 114 CLR 185.

295. (1990) 19 NSWLR 417.

296. *Lim Poh Choo v Camden and Islington Area Health Authority* [1980] AC 174 at 182–3 per Lord Scarman.

297. *Fournier v Canadian National Railway* [1927] AC 167. Note that in most jurisdictions there are statutory exceptions allowing for structured settlements in negligence and personal injury litigation: see **2.60**.

298. *Todorovic v Walker* (1981) 150 CLR 402.

299. [2007] UKHL 39 at 14.

300. (1701) 12 Mod Rep 542; 88 ER 1506.

for trespass to the person and was later debarred from claiming the cost of an operation because his injuries were more serious than first thought.

2.60 There are four exceptions to the once-and-for-all rule. First, in rare cases an appellate court may substitute its own award after hearing evidence of something which has altered the basis of the award of the court below.[301] Second, if there are different causes of action the once-and-for-all rule does not apply, even if the causes of action arise out of the same event. That was the finding in *Brunsden v Humphrey*[302] where the plaintiff was injured in a collision caused by the defendant's negligence. The plaintiff first obtained compensation for damage to his vehicle. Later, in a separate suit, the plaintiff was awarded £350 damages by a jury for the personal injuries he suffered in the collision. The defendant argued that the plaintiff 'could not sue twice for one and the same cause of action'. Brett MR held:

> The collision with the defendant's van did not give rise to only one cause of action: the plaintiff sustained bodily injuries, he was injured in a distinct right, and he became entitled to sue for a cause of action distinct from the cause of action in respect of the damage to his goods: therefore the plaintiff is at liberty to maintain the present action.[303]

Still, in *Marlborough Harbour Board v Charter Travel Co Ltd*[304] Hope JA, in discussing *Brunsden v Humphrey*, observed:

> The better view would seem to be that, although for pragmatic and possibly historical reasons separate actions can be brought for damages in respect of personal injury and damage to property, if an action has been brought for damage to property, or for both personal injury and damage to property, other actions cannot be brought for damage to other property as a result of the same 'casualty'. There would not be, as has been submitted in the present case, a separate cause of action in respect of each knife and fork lost when the *Mikhail Lermontov* sank.[305]

The third exception to the once-and-for-all rule is where the tort is a continuing one such as a recurrent nuisance or trespass.[306] In such cases, further causes of action lie in the future and the plaintiff cannot recover damages until those future actions are decided.[307] Damages may be recovered, however, up to the time of assessment.[308]

---

301. See *Murphy v Stone-Wallwork (Charlton) Ltd* [1969] 1 WLR 1023; *Mulholland v Mitchell* [1971] 2 WLR 93; *McIntosh v Williams* [1976] 2 NSWLR 237; *Gamser v Nominal Defendant* (1977) 136 CLR 145; *McCann v Sheppard* [1973] 2 All ER 881.

302. (1884) 14 QBD 141 (CA); followed in *Jackson v Goldsmith* (1950) 81 CLR 446 at 467 per Fullagar J; *Effem Foods Pty Ltd v Trawl Industries of Australia Pty Ltd* (1993) 43 FCR 510 at 533 per Burchett J (Full FC).

303. (1884) 14 QBD at 145.

304. (1989) 18 NSWLR 223 (CA).

305. (1989) 18 NSWLR at 231.

306. *Adams v Ascot Iron Foundry Pty Ltd* (1968) 72 SR (NSW) 120; compare *Darley Main Colliery v Mitchell* (1886) 11 AC 127 (land subsidence case).

307. *Mann v Capital Territory Health Commission* (1982) 148 CLR 97.

308. See, for example, Federal Court Rules O 38 r 3; Uniform Civil Procedure Rules 2005 (NSW) Pt 30 r 30.3; and Supreme Court (General Civil Procedure) Rules 1996 (Vic) Pt 51.

Finally, there are many statutory exceptions to the once-and-for-all rule.[309] For example, ss 22–26 of the Civil Liability Act 2002 (NSW) permit a 'structured settlement' if both parties agree. A 'structured settlement' is defined in s 22 as:

> … an agreement that provides for the payment of all or part of an award of damages in the form of periodic payments funded by an annuity or other agreed means.[310]

Special damages

2.61   In assessing damages in tort a distinction is sometimes drawn between special and general damages. The meaning given to this distinction, however, depends on the tort in issue and has varied over time. So, in *Ratcliffe v Evans*, the Court of Appeal observed:

> … the term 'special damage', which is found for centuries in the books, is not always used with reference to similar subject matter, nor in the same context.[311]

In most torts special damage refers to an amount awarded for monetary loss actually suffered and expenditure actually incurred up to the date of judgment.[312] Such damage is not presumed but must be claimed and proved specially and, in most cases, be capable of calculation with a close approximation to accuracy. The plaintiff should warn the defendant of the claim in the pleadings.[313]

Personal injury cases

2.62   Examples of special damage in personal injury cases are out-of-pocket expenses such as medical and surgical fees paid or payable, ambulance and hospital expenses. Loss of income up to the date of the verdict is usually regarded as special damage,[314] although there is authority that it be assessed as part of general damages for lost earning capacity.[315]

2.63   The civil liability statutes apply caps and other limits to personal injury claims, whether the claims are brought 'in tort, in contract, under statute or

---

309. See, for example, Civil Procedure Act 2005 (NSW) s 82; Workers Compensation Act 1987 (NSW) s 151Q; Motor Accidents Act 1988 (NSW) s 81; Motor Accidents Compensation Act 1999 (NSW) s 143; Dust Diseases Tribunal Act 1989 (NSW) s 11A; Motor Vehicle (Third Party Insurance) Act 1943 (WA); Supreme Court Act 1970 (NSW) Pt 5 Div 2; Supreme Court Act 1935 (SA) s 30B.

310. See also Personal Injuries (Liabilities and Damages) Act 2003 (NT) s 31–32 and Personal Injuries (Civil Claims) Act 2003 (NT) s 12; Civil Liability Act 2003 (Qld) s 63; Supreme Court Act 1935 (SA) s 30BA; Civil Liability Act 2002 (Tas) s 8; Wrongs Act 1958 (Vic) s 28M; Civil Liability Act 2002 (WA) s 14. The provision in the Civil Law (Wrongs) Act 2002 (ACT) was repealed by the Justice and Community Safety Legislation Amendment Act 2006 (ACT).

311. [1892] 2 QB 524 at 528.

312. See *Paff v Speed* (1961) 105 CLR 549 at 558–9 per Fullagar J.

313. *Ratcliffe v Evans* [1892] 2 QB 524 at 528.

314. *Paff v Speed* (1961) 105 CLR 549 at 558 per Fullagar J; see also *Blundell v Musgrave* (1956) 96 CLR 73; *Deering v Norton* (1970) 92 WN 438; *Treloar v Wickham* (1961) 105 CLR 102.

315. *Forsberg v Maslin* [1968] SASR 432; *Arthur Robinson (Grafton) Pty Ltd v Carter* (1968) 122 CLR 649; *Mavroyeni v Erle* [1970] VR 769. See also the discussion of lost earning capacity at **2.70–2.71**.

otherwise'.[316] Unlike the parts of the Acts discussed in relation to causation and remoteness, these provisions are not restricted to claims arising from negligence. Loss of income up to the date of the verdict is capped at three times the average weekly earnings in all jurisdictions[317] except South Australia where the cap is a prescribed maximum adjusted by reference to the Consumer Price Index.[318]

2.64   The approach in respect of loss of income up to the date of the verdict is to calculate the plaintiff's loss of pay between the time of the accident and the verdict. An allowance in favour of the plaintiff may be made for overtime pay which would probably have been earned.[319] Deductions are then made for savings that the plaintiff may make; for example, if the plaintiff cannot attend work because of the injury, then a deduction will be made for the saving in transport costs to and from work.[320] Where the plaintiff is in hospital and claims both hospital expenses and loss of wages, a proportion of the hospital expenses must be deducted from the loss of wages claimed on the basis of board and lodging.[321] An amount for income tax should also be deducted.[322] If the final amount is more than the statutory cap, any amount over the cap is to be disregarded.

Malicious falsehood

2.65   Malicious or injurious falsehood[323] is not actionable without proof of special or actual damage. Indeed, the only damages available are special damages.[324] Nonetheless, evidence of a general decline in business is admissible on the issue of special damage, even though no names can be given.[325]

Defamation

2.66   Traditionally a distinction was drawn between libel (publication in a permanent form such as in a film or a newspaper) and slander (publication in a non-permanent form such as spoken words). The importance of the distinction was that libel was actionable without proof of special damage whereas, generally, slander was not. The uniform defamation law abolishes

---

316. See, for example, Civil Liability Act 2002 (NSW) s 11A.
317. Civil Law (Wrongs) Act 2002 (ACT) s 98; Personal Injuries (Liabilities and Damages) Act 2003 (NT) s 20; Civil Liability Act 2002 (NSW) s 12; Civil Liability Act 2003 (Qld) s 54; Civil Liability Act 2002 (Tas) s 26; Wrongs Act 1958 (Vic) s 28F; Civil Liability Act 2002 (WA) s 11.
318. Civil Liability Act 1936 (SA) s 54(2) arw s 3 (definitions).
319. *Revesz v Orchard* [1969] SASR 336.
320. See *Sharman v Evans* (1977) 138 CLR 563.
321. *Sharman v Evans* (1977) 138 CLR 563; 13 ALR 57; *Skelton v Collins* (1966) 115 CLR 94 at 106 and see *Shearman v Folland* [1950] 2 KB 43; compare *Dash v Wauton* [1972] 2 QB 262 at 272.
322. *Cullen v Trappell* (1980) 146 CLR 1.
323. See *Palmer Bruyn & Parker Pty Ltd v Parsons* (2001) 208 CLR 388.
324. See *Ratcliffe v Evans* [1892] 2 QB 524; *Fielding v Variety Inc* [1967] 2 QB 841 (C.A).
325. *Ratcliffe v Evans* [1892] 2 QB 524 at 533; *Palmer Bruyn & Parker Pty Ltd v Parsons* (2001) 208 CLR 388 at [52] per Gummow J.

the distinction between libel and slander and, accordingly, the publication of defamatory matter is actionable without proof of special damage.[326]

General damages

2.67 General damages is a common law term but it is also used in many statutes including the various civil liability statutes. However, the civil liability statutes give the term a more limited meaning than in common law. In common law, general damages differ from special damages in four main ways. First, in some torts, such as defamation, general damages may be presumed to be the direct, natural or probable consequence of the tortious wrong.[327] However, where damage is part of the cause of action itself, as is the case with negligence, the plaintiff must still prove factual and legal causation in order to recover general damages. Second, general damages are not capable of precise mathematical calculation. Third, they are awarded not just for the period before the verdict, but also for the future. Finally, general damages can be given for both monetary and non-monetary loss.

Under the civil liability statutes, the term 'general damages' refers to only four categories of non-monetary loss: pain and suffering, loss of amenities of life, loss of expectation of life and disfigurement. In common law, the approach taken with these types of damage was that the amount awarded had to be decided on the merits of each case; it was inappropriate to refer to a norm or standard derived from previous cases.[328] The civil liability statutes have changed this. Except for the ACT, they all implement caps, thresholds or other restrictions on general damages, but in various different ways. In most, the amount payable for a non-monetary loss is implemented by reference to scales or tables; and they allow reference to previous cases.[329]

Even in jurisdictions that have implemented scale values for personal injury claims, the reasoning and approaches in previous cases will be relevant in deciding on an appropriate point in the scale. For this reason, the main common law principles are discussed in the following sections. The discussion at **2.68–2.75** focuses on general damages for personal injury. General damages for defamation are discussed at **2.76–2.77**, and for passing off at **2.78**.

Personal injury cases

2.68 The main heads of general damages in personal injury cases are: future hospital and medical expenses; economic loss in the future, such as loss of earning capacity; loss of amenities or enjoyment of life; pain and suffering;

---

326. See, for example, Defamation Act 2005 (NSW) s 7.

327. *Ratcliffe v Evans* [1892] 2 QB 524 (CA); compare *Domsalla v Barr* [1969] 1 WLR 630 (CA).

328. *Planet Fisheries Pty Ltd v La Rosa* [1968] HCA 62.

329. The differences between the various Acts make it impractical to examine the detail here, but see Personal Injuries (Liabilities and Damages) Act 2003 (NT) ss 24 and 28; Civil Liability Act 2002 (NSW) ss 16–17A; Civil Liability Act 2003 (Qld) ss 61 and 62 and Civil Liability Regulation 2003; Civil Liability Act 1936 (SA) s 52; Civil Liability Act 2002 (Tas) ss 27 and 28. The Civil Liability Act 2002 (WA) ss 9, 10 and 10A and Wrongs Act 1958 (Vic) ss 28G and 28H take slightly different approaches.

and loss of expectation of life. Each head of damage should be itemised by the trial judge and reasons given for the award made.[330] Still, the heads are only meant to be a 'convenient reminder of matters that ought not to be forgotten', and thus it is not always appropriate 'to consider them as if they were distinct items in a balance sheet; for one may overlap and impinge upon another'.[331]

In determining the amount of general damages for future hospital and medical expenses and future loss of earning capacity, the High Court announced the following rule of practice[332] in *Todorovic v Waller*:

> In an action for damages for personal injuries, evidence as to the likely course of inflation, or of possible future changes in rates of wages or of prices, is inadmissible. Where there has been a loss of earning capacity which is likely to lead to financial loss in the future, or where the plaintiff's injuries will make it necessary to expend in the future money to provide medical or other services, or goods necessary for the plaintiff's health or comfort, the present value of the future loss ought to be quantified by adopting a discount rate of 3 per cent in all cases, subject, of course to any relevant statutory provision. This rate is intended to make the appropriate allowance for inflation, for future changes in rates of wages generally or of prices, and for tax (either actual or notional) upon income from investment of the sum awarded. No further allowance should be made for these matters.[333]

Most jurisdictions have made statutory variations increasing the 3 per cent discount rate to at least 5 per cent.[334] Also, in personal injury claims, statutory caps have been placed on the amount that can be awarded as general damages under the civil liability,[335] motor accident[336] and workers' compensation[337] legislation.

2.69   Future medical expenses and gratuitous services   The plaintiff is entitled to recover as general damages the future costs of hospital, medical, nursing

---

330.   *Sharman v Evans* (1977) 138 CLR 563; *Gamser v Nominal Defendant* (1977) 136 CLR 145; *Dessent v Commonwealth* (1977) 51 ALJR 482. Note the cap under ss 16 and 17 of the Civil Liability Act 2002 (NSW).

331.   *Teubner v Humble* (1963) 108 CLR 491 at 505 per Windeyer J.

332.   As described in *Commonwealth v Blackwell* (1987) 163 CLR 428.

333.   (1981) 150 CLR 402 at 409.

334.   Civil Liability Act 2002 (NSW) s 14 (5%); Civil Liability Act 1936 (SA) Pt 8 (5%); Civil Liability Act 2003 (Qld) s 57 (5%); Common Law (Miscellaneous Actions) Act 1986 (Tas) s 4 (7%); Law Reform (Miscellaneous Provisions) Act 1941 (WA) s 5 (6%); Workers Compensation Act 1987 (NSW) s 151J (5%); Motor Accidents Act 1988 (NSW) s 71 (5%); Motor Accidents Compensation Act 1999 (NSW) s 127 (5%); Transport Accident Act 1986 (Vic) (6%).

335.   Civil Law (Wrongs) Act 2002 (ACT); Personal Injuries (Liabilities and Damages) Act 2003 (NT); Civil Liability Act 2002 (NSW); Civil Liability Act 2003 (Qld); Civil Liability Act 1936 (SA) Pt 8; Civil Liability Act 2002 (Tas); Wrongs Act 1958 (Vic); Civil Liability Act 2002 (WA).

336.   Motor Accidents Acts 1988 (NSW); Motor Accidents Compensation Act 1999 (NSW); Transport Accident Act 1986 (Vic).

337.   Commonwealth Employees' Rehabilitation and Compensation Act 1988 (Cth); Workers Compensation Act 1987 (NSW); Workers Rehabilitation and Compensation Act 1986 (SA); Accident Compensation Act 1985 (Vic).

services and home care.[338] An award will be made even if some of these services, such as nursing services and home care, are gratuitously provided by a relative, spouse or other person,[339] and even if that relative or spouse is a defendant.[340] At common law such damages will be calculated by reference to the market cost of such services and not by reference to the income forgone by the care provider.[341] The court will, in its discretion, reduce the amount by taking into account the contingencies of life.

Except in the Australian Capital Territory, the civil liability statutes impose various caps and thresholds on claims for the cost of gratuitous care, but there is little uniformity.[342] For example, New South Wales, the Northern Territory, Queensland and Victoria require a reasonable need for care that arose solely because of the injury; and allow damages only if the services would not have been provided but for the injury. South Australia and Western Australia require the services to be provided by someone in a pre-existing close relationship with the injured person. New South Wales, the Northern Territory and Victoria cap the amount at average weekly earnings, but Queensland does not. New South Wales, Queensland and Victoria had an inelegantly worded threshold prohibiting the award of damages if the services were provided '(a) for less than 6 hours per week; and (b) for less than 6 months'. Decisions in all three jurisdictions[343] interpreted this to mean that both (a) and (b) had to be satisfied before the prohibition applied—so damages could be awarded for less than 6 hours per week of care if it lasted for longer than 6 months (and vice versa). New South Wales and Queensland, but not Victoria, amended their provisions to be more consistent with the slightly clearer Northern Territory provision, but even this has caused difficulty.

The Northern Territory provision says damages cannot be awarded unless services are provided '(a) for 6 hours or more per week; and (b) for 6 months or more'.[344] It more clearly requires both subsections to be satisfied, but deeper complexities were exposed by the New South Wales Court of

---

338. See *Sharman v Evans* (1977) 138 CLR 563; *Todorovic v Waller* (1981) 150 CLR 402.

339. *Griffiths v Kerkemeyer* (1977) 139 CLR 161; *Nguyen v Nguyen* (1990) 169 CLR 245; *Van Gervan v Fenton* (1992) 175 CLR 327; Civil Law (Wrongs) Act 2002 (ACT) s 100; Personal Injuries (Liabilities and Damages) Act 2003 (NT) s 23; Civil Liability Act 2002 (NSW) s 15; Civil Liability Act 2003 (Qld) s 59; Civil Liability Act 1936 (SA) s 58; Wrongs Act 1958 (Vic) s 28IA; Civil Liability Act 2002 (WA) s 12; Motor Accident Insurance Act 1994 (Qld) s 55D; Common Law (Miscellaneous Actions) Act 1986 (Tas) s 5; Transport Accident Act 1986 (Vic) ss 60, 93(10)(c) and 174.

340. *Kars v Kars* (1996) 187 CLR 354.

341. *Van Gervan v Fenton* (1992) 175 CLR 327 at 333–4 per Mason CJ, Toohey and McHugh JJ.

342. Personal Injuries (Liabilities and Damages) Act 2003 (NT) s 23; Civil Liability Act 2002 (NSW) s 15; Civil Liability Act 2003 (Qld) s 59; Civil Liability Act 1936 (SA) s 58; Wrongs Act 1958 (Vic) s 28IA; Civil Liability Act 2002 (WA) s 12.

343. *Harrison v Melhem* [2008] NSWCA 67; *Grice v State of Qld* [2005] QCA 272; *Alcoa Portland Aluminium Pty Ltd v Victorian WorkCover Authority* [2007] VSCA 210.

344. Personal Injuries (Liabilities and Damages) Act 2003 (NT) s 23(2). The wording of the Qld provision is 'at least 6 hours per week' and 'at least 6 months' — Civil Liability Act 2003 (Qld) s 59(1)(c); and the NSW provision is 'at least 6 hours per week' and 'a period of at least 6 consecutive months' — Civil Liability Act 2002 (NSW) s 15(3).

Appeal in *Hill v Forrester*.[345] The court (Tobias JA, Handley AJA and Sackville AJA) held that the '6 hours per week' was a continuing requirement—so even if the services had been for more than 6 hours per week at some stage, once they dropped below 6 hours per week, damages could not be awarded for those times no matter for how long the services continued.[346] But there was a divergence of opinion over a how to calculate the duration requirement of 6 months. Sackville AJA and Tobias JA, for example, felt that the duration requirement only had to be satisfied once,[347] so separate periods of service for less than 6 months before or after satisfaction of the 6 consecutive month duration requirement could also be the subject of an award. On the other hand, Tobias JA could not agree with Sackville AJA's tentative view that the two requirements in (a) and (b) were expressed separately and thus did not have to operate concurrently. On Sackville AJA's view, as long as the duration requirement of 6 months was satisfied, even if partially by periods of less than 6 hours per week, any periods of more than 6 hours per week were claimable.[348] Understandably, all three judges suggested the provision still required 'urgent legislative attention'.

2.70 Future economic loss and lost earning capacity A plaintiff who has lost wages or salary *before* the verdict is entitled to be reimbursed for that loss, and, as discussed at **2.62**, this usually falls to be determined under the head of special damages. If the plaintiff will continue to lose wages or salary *after* the trial, then a sum will be awarded for his or her future loss of earning capacity. Lost earning capacity is a head of general damages because it cannot be easily quantified.[349]

The prerequisites to be proved by the plaintiff in order to obtain a sum for lost earning capacity were discussed by the High Court in *Medlin v State Government Insurance Commission*, where Deane, Dawson, Toohey and Gaudron JJ in a joint judgment held:

> A plaintiff in an action in negligence is not entitled to recover damages for loss of earning capacity unless he or she establishes that two distinct but related requirements are satisfied. The first of those requirements is the predictable one that the plaintiff's earning capacity has in fact been diminished by reason of the negligence-caused injury. The second requirement is also predictable once it is appreciated that damages for loss of earning capacity constitute a head of damages for economic loss awarded in addition to general damages for pain, suffering and loss of enjoyment of life. It is that 'the diminution of … earning capacity is or may be productive of financial loss'.[350]

---

345. [2010] NSWCA 170.
346. [2010] NSWCA 170 per Tobias JA at [1]; Handley AJA at [26]; and Sackville AJA at [96]–[98].
347. [2010] NSWCA 170 per Tobias JA at [3]; Sackville AJA at [100]–[105].
348. [2010] NSWCA 170 per Tobias JA at [8]–[11]; Sackville AJA at [106]–[108].
349. *Skelton v Collins* (1966) 115 CLR 94.
350. (1995) 182 CLR 1 at 3, citing *Graham v Baker* (1961) 106 CLR 340 at 347 per Dixon CJ, Kitto and Taylor JJ.

Their Honours went on to emphasise that, in order to recover an amount for lost earning capacity, the plaintiff must suffer an actual economic loss or an actual loss of earnings.[351] That was found to be the case in *Medlin*, where the plaintiff, a philosophy professor at Flinders University, was injured by the defendant's negligence in a motor vehicle accident. The plaintiff obtained early retirement from the university and claimed that one of the reasons for doing this was that he was prevented from performing to the best of his ability due to the pain and suffering caused by the injury. However, the university still considered the plaintiff a competent employee and was prepared to employ him until normal retirement age. The High Court held the plaintiff was entitled to recover an amount for lost earning capacity because his decision to retire early was in fact caused by the defendant's negligence and, as a result, he actually suffered economic loss or a loss of earning capacity.[352] McHugh J, in a separate judgment, observed:

> Even if the plaintiff was capable of retaining his position as head of the Discipline of Philosophy until he reached the normal retiring age of 65 years, he still had a reduced capacity to do his work. The evidence showed that it was more difficult for him to do his work after the accident while in a state of constant pain and fatigue than it was before the accident. If for any reason he left the University, he would almost certainly have found it difficult to secure a comparable position elsewhere.[353]

2.71   Even though lost earning capacity is not the same as loss of earnings,[354] the usual way of calculating lost earning capacity is to determine the amount of wages or salary the plaintiff is losing after income tax (that is, the net value per week at the date of trial) and then to apply that figure to the period for which the wage or salary loss is likely to continue.[355] If, however, this method does not reflect the plaintiff's lost earning capacity, it may be varied to suit the case.[356] In personal injury claims that fall under the various civil liability statutes, the court is required to 'disregard' earning capacity above a limit fixed at three times average weekly earnings (AWE) in all jurisdictions[357] except South Australia where the cap is a prescribed maximum adjusted by reference to the Consumer Price Index.[358] Some of these statutes also allow plaintiffs to claim a fixed

---

351. (1995) 182 CLR 1 at 4.
352. (1995) 182 CLR 1 at 9 per Deane, Dawson, Toohey and Gaudron JJ, and 17 per McHugh J.
353. (1995) 182 CLR 1 at 17–18 per McHugh J.
354. (1995) 182 CLR 1 at 16 per McHugh J.
355. This may extend past retirement age, depending on the plaintiff's personal circumstances: see (1995) 182 CLR 1 at 24 per McHugh J.
356. In *Husher v Husher* (1999) 197 CLR 138 the plaintiff generated all the income in a business partnership with his wife, but the profit was split equally between them. The High Court overturned the initial finding that in calculating the plaintiff's future economic loss only half the profits could be used in the assessment.
357. Civil Law (Wrongs) Act 2002 (ACT) s 98; Personal Injuries (Liabilities and Damages) Act 2003 (NT) s 20; Civil Liability Act 2002 (NSW) s 12; Civil Liability Act 2003 (Qld) s 54; Civil Liability Act 2002 (Tas) s 26; Wrongs Act 1958 (Vic) s 28F; Civil Liability Act 2002 (WA) s 11.
358. Civil Liability Act 1936 (SA) s 54(2) arw s 3 (definitions).

amount of damages for the loss of employer superannuation entitlements based on the plaintiff's deprivation or impairment of earning capacity.[359]

Where the plaintiff's life is shortened by reason of the injury, the plaintiff may claim loss of earning capacity for those years as well.[360] Where the negligently inflicted injury causes death then those who were dependent on the deceased, such as a spouse or children, can claim for the 'loss of a reasonable expectation of pecuniary benefit'.[361]

After calculating the sum, the court then makes two further deductions. First, where the plaintiff receives a windfall by obtaining a lump sum, the High Court in *Todorovic v Waller*[362] held that it must be discounted by 3 per cent at the date of verdict. In most jurisdictions this has now been increased to 5 per cent:[363] See **2.68**. Second, the court will also reduce the sum, usually by about 5–20 per cent, to take account of the vicissitudes of life, including possible periods of unemployment, leave, illness and accidents.[364]

2.72 Loss of amenities and enjoyment of life In *Skelton v Collins* Taylor J observed:

> The expression 'loss of the amenities of life' is a loose expression but as a head of damages in personal injuries cases it is intended to denote a loss of the capacity of the injured person consciously to enjoy life to the full as, apart from his injury, he might have done. It may be said, of course, that a person who is completely incapacitated as a result of his injuries suffers such a loss whether or not his injuries are of such a character to render him insensible to his loss. But, in my opinion, a proper assessment can be made only upon a comparison of the condition which has been substituted for the victim's previously existing capacity to enjoy life and where the mind is, as it were, willing and the body incapable there is, in my view, a much higher degree of loss than where the victim is completely insensible to his lost capacity.[365]

Damages for loss of amenities and enjoyment of life are awarded both objectively for the actual loss suffered, and subjectively for the plaintiff's sense of the loss.[366] Thus, where the plaintiff is likely to be unconscious until

---

359. Civil Liability Act 2002 (NSW) s 15A; Civil Liability Act 2003 (Qld) s 56; Civil Liability Act 2002 (Tas) s 25.

360. *Skelton v Collins* (1966) 115 CLR 94; *Pickett v British Rail Engineering Ltd* [1980] AC 136.

361. *De Sales v Ingrilli* (2002) 212 CLR 338; [2002] HCA 52.

362. (1981) 150 CLR 402 at 409; Civil Liability Act 2002 (NSW) s 14(1).

363. See also Civil Liability Act 2002 (NSW) s 14(2)(b) (5%); Civil Liability Act 2003 (Qld) s 57 (5%); Civil Liability Act 1936 (SA) Pt 8 (5%); Common Law (Miscellaneous Actions) Act 1986 (Tas) s 4 (7%); Law Reform (Miscellaneous Provisions) Act 1941 (WA) s 5 (6%); Workers Compensation Act 1987 (NSW) s 151J (5%); Motor Accidents Act 1988 (NSW) s 71; Motor Accidents Compensation Act 1999 (NSW) s 127 (5%); Transport Accident Act 1986 (Vic) (6%).

364. See *Todorovic v Waller* (1981) 150 CLR 402; *Arthur Robinson (Grafton) Pty Ltd v Carter* (1968) 122 CLR 649 at 659 per Barwick CJ; *Wynn v NSW Insurance Ministerial Corporation* (1995) 184 CLR 485. See also Personal Injuries (Liabilities and Damages) Act 2003 (NT) s 21; Civil Liability Act 2002 (NSW) s 13; Civil Liability Act 2003 (Qld) s 55.

365. (1966) 115 CLR 94 at 113.

366. Note the cap under ss 3, 16 and 17 of the Civil Liability Act 2002 (NSW).

death, the amount awarded will be small in view of the lack of understanding of the loss.[367]

As discussed at **2.67**, most of the civil liability statutes place a cap or other restriction on the amount that can be awarded for 'non-economic loss' which is defined to include 'loss of amenities of life'.

2.73 Pain and suffering: past and future The plaintiff is entitled to be compensated for pain and suffering caused by the injuries. By pain and suffering the courts mean actual physical or mental pain. Thus, in *Skelton v Collins*[368] the plaintiff, who was 17 at the date of the accident, was allowed nothing for pain and suffering because he was rendered unconscious by the collision and was likely to remain in that state. In *O'Brien v Dunsdon*[369] it was observed that it was 'impossible precisely to translate pain and suffering and the loss of enjoyment of life into money values'. Nonetheless, an attempt must be made and in doing so regard should be had to 'the general standards prevailing in the community'. Where the plaintiff is disfigured (such as facial scarring, loss of an eye, ear or limb) an amount may be awarded for 'disfigurement' even if the 'pain and suffering' of the original injury has been forgotten.[370] As discussed at **2.67**, most of the civil liability statutes place a cap or other restriction on the amount that can be awarded for 'non-economic loss' which is defined to include both 'pain and suffering' and 'disfigurement'.

2.74 Loss of expectation of life Where a plaintiff's life span is shortened as a result of the injury there is an entitlement to compensation for this loss. The plaintiff's life expectancy is calculated by reference to the 'prospective' rather the 'historical' tables published by the Australian Bureau of Statistics.[371] Such damages are awarded for the loss of prospective happiness in the period by which the injured person's life has been shortened. Damages under this head tend to be relatively small.[372] As discussed at **2.67**, most of the civil liability statutes cap or otherwise restrict the amount that can be awarded for 'non-economic loss', which is defined to include 'loss of expectation of life'.

Loss of an opportunity or chance

2.75 As discussed at **2.30**, it is unclear whether the High Court's view in *Tabet v Gett* (of the requirement for proof on the balance of probabilities in loss of chance cases) will only apply to medical negligence, or to all personal injuries, or to a broader category of negligence claims. But the court was

---

367. *Skelton v Collins* (1966) 115 CLR 94; compare *H West and Son Ltd v Shephard* [1964] AC 326 and *Wise v Kay* [1962] 1 QB 638; see also *Sharman v Evans* (1977) 138 CLR 563; *Hawkins v Lindsley* (1974) 4 ALR 697 at 703.

368. (1966) 115 CLR 94.

369. (1965) 39 ALJR 78.

370. See Luntz, *Assessment of Damages for Personal Injury and Death*, 4th ed, LexisNexis Butterworths, Sydney, 2002, pp 245–6.

371. *Golden Eagle International Trading Pty Ltd v Zhang* [2007] HCA 15.

372. See, for example, *Skelton v Collins* (1966) 115 CLR 94, where $3000 was awarded to a young adult.

comfortable recognising that the loss of a contemplated commercial benefit should be treated differently.[373] Where the defendant's tort deprives the plaintiff of a claimable chance or opportunity, the courts' approach to assessing the quantum is the same as that applicable in contract cases. General damages for the loss may be available,[374] provided the chance was not 'negligible'[375] or 'speculative'.[376] In *Malec v J C Hutton Pty Ltd* Deane, Gaudron and McHugh JJ observed:

> If the law is to take account of future or hypothetical events in assessing damages, it can only do so in terms of the degree of probability of those events occurring … But unless the chance is so low as to be regarded as speculative — say less than 1% — or so high as to be practically certain — say over 99% — the court will take that chance into account in assessing damages. Where proof is necessarily unattainable, it would be unfair to treat as certain a prediction which has a 51% probability of occurring, but to ignore altogether a prediction which has a 49% probability of occurring. Thus, the court assesses the degree of probability that an event would have occurred, or might occur, and adjusts its award of damages to reflect the degree of probability.[377]

Each case depends on its own facts.[378] Future chances and contingencies, both positive and negative, such as promotions, illness, leave and periods of unemployment, are also commonly taken into account when considering the 'vicissitudes' of life.[379]

Defamation

2.76   In defamation the plaintiff need not show actual damage to their reputation as damage is presumed to flow from the publication of defamatory matter.[380] Thus damages are said to be 'at large'.[381] The meaning of this phrase was explained by Lord Hailsham in *Broome v Cassell & Co Ltd*:

> The expression 'at large' should be used in general to cover all cases where awards of damages may include elements for loss of reputation, injured feelings, bad or good conduct by either party, or punishment, and where in consequence no precise limit can be set in extent.[382]

373. See, for example, *Tabet v Gett* [2010] HCA 12 at [124] per Kiefel J.
374. See *Sellars v Adelaide Petroleum NL* (1994) 179 CLR 332; *Mallet v McMonagle* [1970] AC 166; *Davies v Taylor* [1974] AC 207; compare *Hotson v East Berkshire Area Health Authority* [1987] AC 750; *Gregg v Scott* [2005] UKHL 2 and *Tabet v Gett* [2010] HCA 12 discussed at **2.28–2.30**.
375. *Sellars v Adelaide Petroleum NL* (1994) 179 CLR 332 at 355 per Mason CJ, Dawson, Toohey and Gaudron JJ.
376. *Fink v Fink* (1946) 74 CLR 127 at 134–5 per Latham CJ and Williams J; *Chappel v Hart* (1998) 195 CLR 232 at [82] per Gummow J.
377. (1990) 169 CLR 638 at 643.
378. *Fink v Fink* (1946) 74 CLR 127 at 135 per Latham CJ and Williams J.
379. See **2.71**; compare *Caddaju Pty Ltd v Taserski* [2003] VSCA 19.
380. *Ratcliffe v Evans* [1892] 2 QB 524 at 528.
381. *Uren v John Fairfax & Sons Pty Ltd* (1966) 117 CLR 118 at 151 per Windeyer J; *Andrews v John Fairfax & Sons Ltd* [1980] 2 NSWLR 225 (CA) at 255 per Mahoney JA.
382. [1972] AC 1027 at 1073.

Traditionally, such damages were decided by a jury, and in this regard McHugh J (in dissent) in *Carson v John Fairfax & Sons Ltd* observed:

> No doubt the rough-and-ready process by which juries assess damages in a defamation action is not one which appeals to the many sophisticated minds of the spreadsheet generation. It does not … purport to be a scientific, or even pseudo-scientific process. There are no columns and rows into which the components of the verdict can be conveniently placed, no relationships which can be made the subject of mathematical formulas. The assessment depends upon nothing more than the good sense and sound instincts of jurors as to what is a fair and reasonable award, having regard to all the circumstances of the case. That is why damages are said to be 'at large'.[383]

It has been observed, however, that some jurors may have misunderstood the meaning of 'at large' as being a substitute for 'large' damages.[384] In *Carson*, for example, a jury awarded a solicitor $600,000 in damages for the publication of two defamatory articles in the *Sydney Morning Herald*. This was overturned by the New South Wales Court of Appeal as being excessive and this was further upheld by a bare 4:3 majority in the High Court. A new trial was ordered but this time the jury, who were not aware of the earlier trial, awarded $1.3 million in damages.

2.77   Following *Carson* in 1994 the New South Wales legislature removed juries from the assessment of damages in favour of the trial judge.[385] This has now been adopted in all jurisdictions under the uniform defamation laws enacted in 2005 and 2006.[386] While the common law is preserved in the sense that damages are still 'at large', this is always subject to the statutory cap on the amount that can be awarded for non-economic loss and the other qualifications found in the sections corresponding with ss 34–37 in the Defamation Act 2005 (NSW):

34   Damages to bear rational relationship to harm

In determining the amount of damages to be awarded in any defamation proceedings, the court is to ensure that there is an appropriate and rational relationship between the harm sustained by the plaintiff and the amount of damages awarded.

35   Damages for non-economic loss limited

(1)   Unless the court orders otherwise under subsection (2), the maximum amount of damages for non-economic loss that may be awarded in defamation proceedings is $250,000 or any other amount adjusted in accordance with this section from time to time (the 'maximum damages amount') that is applicable at the time damages are awarded.

(2)   A court may order a defendant in defamation proceedings to pay damages for non-economic loss that exceed the maximum damages amount applicable at the time the order is made if, and only if, the court

383.   (1993) 178 CLR 44 at 115.

384.   P George, *Defamation Law in Australia*, LexisNexis Butterworths, Sydney, 2006, p 372.

385.   See Defamation Act 1974 (Cth) s 7A inserted in 1994 (now repealed).

386.   See, for example, Defamation Act 2005 (NSW) s 22 (3).

is satisfied that the circumstances of the publication of the defamatory matter to which the proceedings relate are such as to warrant an award of aggravated damages.

(3) The Minister is, on or before 1 July 2006 and on or before 1 July in each succeeding year, to declare, by order published in the *Gazette*, the amount that is to apply, as from the date specified in the order, for the purposes of subsection (1).

> For orders under this subsection, see *Gazettes* No 84 of 30.6.2006, p 5043 (amount declared: $259,500) and No 80 of 15.6.2007, p 3793 (amount declared: $267,500); No 72 of 20.6.2008, p 5482 (amount declared $280,500); No 90 of 19.6.2009, p 3137 (amount declared: $294,500); No 79 of 18.6.2010, p 2452 (amount declared: $311,000) and No 62 of 24.6.2011, p 4588 (amount declared: $324,000).

(4) The amount declared is to be the amount applicable under subsection (1) (or that amount as last adjusted under this section) adjusted by the percentage change in the amount estimated by the Australian Statistician of the average weekly total earnings of full-time adults in Australia over the 4 quarters preceding the date of the declaration for which those estimates are, at that date, available.

(5) An amount declared for the time being under this section applies to the exclusion of the amount of $250,000 or an amount previously adjusted under this section.

(6) If the Australian Statistician fails or ceases to estimate the amount referred to in subsection (4), the amount declared is to be determined in accordance with the regulations.

(7) In adjusting an amount to be declared for the purposes of subsection (1), the amount determined in accordance with subsection (4) is to be rounded to the nearest $500.

(8) A declaration made or published in the Gazette after 1 July in a year and specifying a date that is before the date it is made or published as the date from which the amount declared by the order is to apply has effect as from that specified date.

36 State of mind of defendant generally not relevant to awarding damages

In awarding damages for defamation, the court is to disregard the malice or other state of mind of the defendant at the time of the publication of the defamatory matter to which the proceedings relate or at any other time except to the extent that the malice or other state of mind affects the harm sustained by the plaintiff.

37 Exemplary or punitive damages cannot be awarded

A plaintiff cannot be awarded exemplary or punitive damages for defamation.

The statutory cap on non-economic loss under s 35 provides 'a presumptive outer limit'[387] on the amount that can be awarded under the uniform defamation law. Despite this limit, damages for defamation under

---

387. (2003) 216 CLR 327 at [78]; *Attrill v Christie* [2007] NSWSC 1386 at [43]–[44] per Bell J.

the legislation still serve the same purposes as those at common law. In *Rogers v Nationwide News Pty Ltd*[388] a prominent eye surgeon was defamed on the front page of the *Daily Telegraph*. In restoring the trial judge's award of $250,000 Hayne J explained that the three purposes to be served by an award of damages for defamation are:

(i)   consolation for the personal distress and hurt caused to the appellant by the publication;

(ii) reparation for harm done to the appellant's personal, and in this case, professional reputation; and

(iii) the vindication of the appellant's reputation. … [T]he first two purposes are frequently considered together and constitute consolation for the wrong done to the appellant; vindication looks to the attitudes of others.[389]

Typically the plaintiff will adduce evidence at the trial addressing each purpose. However, all three overlap and if liability is established the trial judge will award a lump sum rather than separate awards because, as observed by Windeyer J in *Uren v John Fairfax & Sons Pty Ltd*, 'the amount of the verdict is the product of inextricable considerations'.[390]

While exemplary damages are prohibited under s 37, it is also clear under s 35(2) that an award for non-economic loss in excess of the cap may be awarded as aggravated damages: see **2.84–2.87**.

Passing off

2.78   In order to obtain common law damages for passing off the plaintiff must show that the defendant's conduct was fraudulent. Fraud in passing off, however, is a term of art because the plaintiff need only show that the defendant has persisted or continued the passing off after notice of the plaintiff's rights.[391] As observed by Gummow J in *ConAgra Inc v McCain Foods (Aust) Pty Ltd*:

A defendant originally may have adopted a mark honestly and innocently, either in ignorance of the existence of the plaintiff's mark or in the belief that his mark was so different from that of the plaintiff as not to be calculated to mislead purchasers. But the authorities establish that in such a case, the continuing use of the mark after awareness that its use does cause the goods of the defendants to be mistaken for those of the plaintiff, is no less fraudulent in the eye of the court than user with an original fraudulent intent … It has been said that this concept of fraud as constituted by persistence after notice is not necessarily such as would support an action of deceit … It may be that even after notice of the plaintiff's rights the defendant does not intend to deceive purchasers of his goods by representing those goods to

---

388. (2003) 216 CLR 327.

389. (2003) 216 CLR 327 at [60], Gleeson CJ and Gummow J agreeing at [35].

390. (1966) 117 CLR 118 at 150.

391. *Turner v General Motors (Australia) Pty Ltd* (1929) 42 CLR 352 at 362; *Star Micronics Pty Ltd v Five Star Computers Pty Ltd (trading as Computerfair)* (1991) 22 IPR 473 at 479 per Davies J (FCA); *Carlton and United Breweries Ltd v Hahn Brewing Co Pty Ltd* (1994) 28 IPR 545 (FCA).

be the goods of the plaintiff. Nevertheless, if the defendant shuts his eyes as to the reasonable consequences, upon facts known to him, of what he is doing, then there would be grounds upon which a jury might make a finding of fraud in the full sense.[392]

While 'the giving of notice has been thought to be a touchstone of an award of damages'[393] in passing off, a warning or communication from the plaintiff is not required if the defendant 'knew or ought to have known' of the plaintiff's rights.[394] So, if the defendant had a 'closed mind' and was 'careless' about the existence of the plaintiff's brand name or indicia then there is no need to prove conscious dishonesty.[395] In a passing off action arising out of the use by the defendant of a registered trade mark, the defendant can rely on the presumption found in s 230 of the Trade Marks Act 1995 (Cth):

230 Passing off actions

(1) Except as provided in subsection (2), this Act does not affect the law relating to passing off.

(2) In an action for passing off arising out of the use by the defendant of a registered trade mark:

    (a) of which he or she is the registered owner or an authorised user; and

    (b) that is substantially identical with, or deceptively similar to, the trade mark of the plaintiff;

damages may not be awarded against the defendant if the defendant satisfies the court:

    (c) that, at the time when the defendant began to use the trade mark, he or she was unaware, and had no reasonable means of finding out, that the trade mark of the plaintiff was in use; and

    (d) that, when the defendant became aware of the existence and nature of the plaintiff's trade mark, he or she immediately ceased to use the trade mark in relation to the goods or services in relation to which it was used by the plaintiff.[396]

Where fraud is established and the goods or services passed off by the defendant are inferior, then, even if there is no evidence of actual or special damage, the plaintiff may be awarded an amount in general damages for injury to reputation.[397] While this is the oldest recognised head of damage in passing off,[398] the major head is ordinarily a direct loss or diversion of sales.

---

392. (1992) 33 FCR 302; 23 IPR 193 at 254.

393. *Star Micronics* (1991) 22 IPR 473 at 479 per Davies J.

394. *Star Micronics* (1991) 22 IPR 473 at 479 per Davies J.

395. *Star Micronics* (1991) 22 IPR 473 at 479 per Davies J.

396. Section 75(2) of the Designs Act 2003 (Cth) and s 123(1) of the Patents Act 1990 (Cth) are in similar terms but also extend to an account of profits; compare Trade Marks Act 1994 (UK) s 2; and see *British Telecommunications plc v One In A Million Ltd* (1998) 42 IPR 289 (CA(UK)) where it was held that merely registering a domain name may amount to passing off.

397. *Prince Manufacturing Inc v ABAC Corp Australia Pty Ltd* (1984) 4 FCR 288 at 294; 4 IPR 104 at 111 per Beaumont J (FCA); *Star Micronics Pty Ltd v Five Star Computers Pty Ltd (trading as Computerfair)* (1991) 22 IPR 473 at 483 per Davies J (Fed C of A).

398. *Singer v Loog* (1882) 8 App Cas 15.

The parties need not be engaged in a 'common field of activity' in order to recover such damage.[399] If there is evidence that persons believe there is 'some association' between the plaintiffs and defendant's businesses then 'that belief gives rise to the inference of likelihood of damage being caused … by diversion of trade'.[400] Similarly, if the defendant's use of the plaintiff's mark or other indicia has eroded its distinctiveness this is recoverable as a head of damage.[401] In character merchandising and celebrity endorsement cases, lost earning capacity is also a relevant head of damage. In *Irvine v Talksport Ltd*,[402] the defendant doctored a photo of the racing driver Eddie Irvine in an advertising brochure to look as if he was holding a portable radio bearing the defendant's brand. Irvine's claim that this was false endorsement was upheld. Damages were assessed initially at £2000, but on appeal this was increased to £25,000 as this was the minimum fee that Irvine could have reasonably earned for such an endorsement.

As discussed in **Chapter 6**, the plaintiff cannot claim both damages and an account of profits in a passing off action as these are alternative and inconsistent remedies. Prior to final judgment the plaintiff must elect which remedy to pursue.[403]

Collateral benefits and set-offs

2.79   In personal injury claims the plaintiff will also often receive benefits from another source, for example, workers' compensation, sickness benefits and insurance benefits. The question arises whether such sums should be set-offs in assessing damages. As discussed below, the answer varies according to the benefit in issue.[404]

Workers' compensation

2.80   If an employee is tortiously injured at work it is usual for compensation to be paid under a statutory workers' compensation scheme. If the employee also sues in tort[405] and thereby obtains an award of damages, then the workers' compensation payments usually have to be either repaid or credited to the employer. The amount to be repaid or credited includes amounts paid in tax, but the employee does not lose out here because, in calculating the damages

---

399. *Campomar Sociedad, Limitada v Nike International Ltd* (2000) 202 CLR 45 at [109].

400. *Geoffrey Inc v Luik* (1997) 38 IPR 555.

401. *Irvine v Talksport Ltd* (2002) 57 IPR 261 (Ch D) at [34]–[38] per Laddie J; compare [2003] 2 All ER 881 (UKCA).

402. *Irvine v Talksport Ltd* [2003] 2 All ER 881 (UKCA).

403. *Dr Martens Australia Pty Ltd v Bata Shoe Company of Australia Pty Ltd* (1997) 38 IPR 163.

404. See *National Insurance Co of NZ v Espagne* (1961) 105 CLR 569; *Manser v Spry* (1994) 181 CLR 428 at 434–7.

405. In New South Wales, injured workers have to elect between suing at common law and obtaining workers' compensation: see s 151A of the Workers Compensation Act 1987 (NSW). In some jurisdictions the right to sue at common law is either abolished or severely restricted: see, for example, the Work Health Act 1986 (NT); Workers Rehabilitation and Compensation Act 1986 (SA) (the effect of payments under this Act on the calculation of damages was considered in *Manser v Spry* (1994) 181 CLR 428); Accident Compensation Act 1985 (Vic).

payable, the amount paid in tax will be returned.[406] Where, in the tort action, the employee's damages are reduced due to contributory negligence, the refund by the employee to the employer must be reduced to the same extent as the contributory negligence apportionment.[407] This is a proportionate reduction, not the actual amount; and it also applies where the tort action is settled out of court.[408]

Other benefits

2.81 The court *will* reduce the amount of damages to take account of sick pay received as part of the plaintiff's ordinary wages.[409] However, the reduction may prove negligible because the loss of sick pay credits is a loss for which damages may be awarded.[410] In personal injury motor vehicle claims there is legislation obliging third party insurers to make payments for out-of-pocket expenses once the insurer admits liability.[411] These advance payments should be removed from the final assessment of damages.[412] Further, if the plaintiff has been guilty of contributory negligence the whole damages award, including the advance payment, should be apportioned and then the advance payment should be deducted.[413]

The court *will not* reduce the award of damages in order to take account of voluntary payments by an employer,[414] gifts[415] and private insurance benefits.[416] Finally, social security benefits paid under the Social Security Act 1991 (Cth) *will not* lead to a reduction in the amount of damages because usually the benefits will either be discontinued or discounted in order to take account of the award of damages.[417]

Interest

2.82 Damages invariably appear to be paid late because, while in theory the plaintiff is entitled to payment as soon as the cause of action arises,[418] in practice the plaintiff will not receive payment until after the court decision. Historically, the loss caused by this late payment was irrecoverable because it was regarded as being too remote.[419] But it is now recognised that such loss is

406. *Fox v Wood* (1981) 148 CLR 438.

407. See, for example, Law Reform (Miscellaneous Provisions) Act 1965 (NSW) s 10(2).

408. *Hickson v Goodman Fielder Ltd* [2009] HCA 11 per Bell J at [45]–[50].

409. *Graham v Baker* (1961) 106 CLR 340.

410. *Graham v Baker* (1961) 106 CLR 340 at 351; *Paff v Speed* (1961) 105 CLR 549 at 566.

411. See, eg, Motor Accidents Act 1988 (NSW) s 45.

412. *Golden Eagle International Trading Pty Ltd v Zhang* [2007] HCA 15.

413. *Golden Eagle International Trading Pty Ltd v Zhang* [2007] HCA 15.

414. *Zheng v Cai* [2009] HCA 52; *Alley v Minister of Works and Helgeson* (1974) 9 SASR 306; compare *Hobbelen v Nunn* [1965] Qd R 105.

415. *National Insurance Co of NZ v Espagne* (1961) 105 CLR 569; *Nguyen v Nguyen* (1990) 169 CLR 245.

416. *Espagne* (1961) 105 CLR 569; *Parry v Cleaver* [1970] AC 1.

417. See ss 17 and 1163–1170; compare s 1184.

418. *Thompson v Faraonio* (1979) 54 ALJR 231 at 233 (PC); *Haines v Bendall* (1991) 172 CLR 60.

419. *Hungerfords v Walker* (1989) 171 CLR 125 at 139 per Mason CJ and Wilson J.

not invariably too remote and, therefore, interest on damages can be awarded at common law because it represents part of the plaintiff's foreseeable loss.[420] Apart from the common law, all jurisdictions have statutory power to award interest on the late payment of damages.[421] Statutory interest usually runs from the date on which the loss accrues until 'the date when the judgment takes effect'. The court retains a discretion to vary this but 'the discretion must be exercised in conformity with the general principles governing the award of damages'.[422]

The function of an award of interest both at common law and under statute, as observed by the High Court in *MBP (SA) Pty Ltd v Gogic*:

> ... is to compensate a plaintiff for the loss or detriment which he or she has suffered by being kept out of his or her money during the relevant period.[423]

This means that interest will not automatically be awarded on all heads of damage,[424] because some of these heads represent the plaintiff's loss after the date of judgment[425] and, therefore, the plaintiff has not been kept out of his or her money in respect of such loss. Also, the civil liability reforms in several jurisdictions prohibit the award of interest on some heads of damage in personal injury cases. For example, s 18 of the Civil Liability Act 2002 (NSW) provides:

18   Interest on damages

(1) A court cannot order the payment of interest on damages awarded for non-economic loss or gratuitous attendant care services (as defined in section 15).[426]

Under s 3, 'non-economic loss' means 'any one or more of' pain and suffering, loss of amenities of life, loss of expectation of life and disfigurement.

Taxation

2.83   In deciding the effect of taxation on an award of damages, it must first be determined whether or not the award itself will be subject to taxation. If the award of damages is to be taxed, then generally the court will award the plaintiff the entire or gross profit of income without deducting an amount

---

420. *Hungerfords v Walker* (1989) 171 CLR 125 at 142–9 per Mason CJ and Wilson J; J Edelman and D Cassidy, *Interest Awards in Australia*, LexisNexis Butterworths, Sydney, 2002. In personal injury claims, note the restrictions under s 18 of the Civil Liability Act 2002 (NSW).

421. See, for example, Supreme Court Act 1933 (ACT) s 53A(1); Supreme Court Act 1970 (NSW) s 94; Civil Procedure Act 2005 (NSW) ss 100 and 101; Supreme Court Act 1935 (SA) s 30C; Supreme Court Act 1986 (Vic) s 60.

422. *Haines v Bendall* (1991) 172 CLR 60 at 67 per Mason CJ, Dawson, Toohey and Gaudron JJ.

423. (1991) 171 CLR 657 at 663.

424. See also s 18(1) of the Civil Liability Act 2002 (NSW), which provides that a 'court cannot order the payment of interest on damages awarded for non-economic loss or gratuitous attendant care services'; compare *Grincelis v House* (2000) 201 CLR 321.

425. *Fire & All Risks Insurance Co Ltd v Callinan* (1978) 140 CLR 427; compare *John Fairfax & Sons Ltd v Kelly* (1987) 8 NSWLR 131 (CA). See also the Federal Court of Australia Act 1976 s 51A(3)(c).

426. See also Personal Injuries (Liabilities and Damages) Act 2003 (NT) ss 29 and 30; Civil Liability Act 2003 (Qld) s 60; Civil Liability Act 1936 (SA) s 56; Supreme Court Act 1935 (WA) s 32.

for taxation.[427] But if the award of damages is *not* to be taxed, which is the usual position in personal injury cases, then the effect of tax will be taken into account in calculating the lump sum. This follows from *Cullen v Trappell*,[428] where the High Court overruled its earlier decision in *Atlas Tiles Ltd v Briers*[429] and held that in calculating the plaintiff's future and past economic loss only his or her net earnings after tax are to be considered: see **2.71**. Finally, it should be noted that the discount rate, mentioned at **2.68**, 'is intended to make the appropriate allowance … for tax (either actual or notional) upon income from investment of the sum awarded' and thus '[n]o further allowance should be made' in respect thereof.[430]

Aggravated damages

2.84   In most torts, including assault,[431] defamation,[432] conspiracy,[433] false imprisonment,[434] intimidation,[435] trespass to land,[436] interference with contract,[437] malicious prosecution[438] and negligence[439] an amount[440] may be awarded under the head of aggravated damages. For example, suppose that the plaintiff sues for damages for an assault occasioned by the defendant spitting in the plaintiff's face. Although the actual physical injury to the plaintiff may in fact be insignificant, nonetheless aggravated damages can be awarded for the injury to the plaintiff's feelings or dignity. As discussed at **2.86** aggravated damages are not awarded in addition to compensatory damages but, rather, as a head of compensatory damages. Even so, such damages should be specifically pleaded[441] and, if they are awarded, they should be separately identified in the judgment.

2.85   While the ordinary rule is that each joint tortfeasor is jointly and severally liable for compensatory damages (see **2.21**), an award of aggravated damages may lead to differential assessments. So in *Konstantinidis v Foreign*

---

427. Compare *Gill v Australian Wheat Board* [1980] 2 NSWLR 795.

428. (1980) 146 CLR 1.

429. (1978) 144 CLR 202.

430. (1981) 150 CLR 402 at 409.

431. *Henry v Thompson* [1989] 2 Qd R 412; *Johnstone v Stewart* [1968] SASR 142.

432. *Carson v John Fairfax & Sons Ltd* (1993) 178 CLR 44; *Uren v John Fairfax & Sons Pty Ltd* (1966) 117 CLR 118; see also s 35(2) Defamation Act 2005 (NSW) and cognate provisions under the uniform defamation law.

433. *Williams v Hursey* (1959) 103 CLR 30.

434. *McFadzean v Construction, Forestry, Mining and Energy Union* [2004] VSC 289.

435. *Rookes v Barnard* [1964] AC 1129.

436. *TCN Channel Nine Pty Ltd v Anning* (2002) 54 NSWLR 333 at 365 (CA).

437. *Zhu v Sydney Organising Committee for the Olympic Games* [2001] NSWSC 989 ($95,000 awarded as aggravated damages); affirmed *Zhu v Treasurer of the State of New South Wales* (2004) 211 ALR 159; [2004] HCA 56.

438. *Commonwealth Life Assurance Society Ltd v Brain* (1935) 53 CLR 343; *A v New South Wales* [2007] HCA 10.

439. See *De Reus v Gray* [2003] VSCA 84 at [29]; compare *Kralj v McGrath* [1986] 1 All ER 54 at 61. However, note the exclusion in the Civil Liability Act 2002 (NSW) s 21 and Civil Liability Act 2003 (Qld) s 52.

440. See *Sutcliffe v Pressdram Ltd* [1990] 2 WLR 271 on assessment of aggravated damages.

441. See, for example, Uniform Civil Procedure Rules 2005 (NSW) Pt 6 r 6.12(5).

Media Pty Ltd,[442] where only some of the joint tortfeasors had engaged in aggravated defamatory conduct, Buddin J held that this reduced the liability of the fourth defendant who had not so engaged. His Honour cited *Bateman v Shepherd*[443] where general compensatory damages for the same amount were awarded against all three joint tortfeasors, but because one of the three had apologised for its defamatory conduct a separate sum was awarded against the other two under aggravated damages. *Bateman* was approved by Winneke P in the Victorian Court of Appeal in *De Reus v Gray*,[444] who also cited with approval the following passage from Cory J in the Supreme Court of Canada in *Manning v Hill*:

> It is a well established principle that all persons who are involved in the commission of a joint tort are jointly and severally liable for the damages caused by that tort. ... It would thus be inappropriate and wrong in law to have a jury attempt to apportion liability either for general or special damages between the joint tortfeasors ... However this comment does not apply to aggravated damages which are assessed on the basis of the particular malice of each joint tortfeasor.[445]

In *De Reus* the respondent, Corrine Gray, aged 30 and the mother of four young boys, was separated from her husband. Before 1994 she had incurred several parking fines and was required to either pay approximately $400 or be imprisoned for two days. She failed to pay and in May 1994 warrants were issued for her imprisonment and on 18 May the sheriff's officers arrived at her house to execute the warrants. They told her that she would be required to go to a police 'lock-up' for 'about two hours' and would then be released to do community work. She explained that she had children in school and was unwell following a recent medical procedure. The officers returned on 20 May and on that day two officers apprehended Ms Gray and took her and another woman in similar circumstances to the Narre Warren Police Station. There they were confronted by Mr Ray De Reus, the police officer in charge of the station. He told a female officer, Ms Pike, that 'he wanted these girls strip-searched' and also said 'Can you teach this constable (Hatch) how to do a strip search?' Even though Ms Gray was shocked she was silent because otherwise she thought she would be forced to comply. No one asked her why she was there. Ms Gray was then escorted to the end of a corridor by two female officers, Pike and Hatch, and ordered by Pike to remove all her clothes, which she did. She was naked and felt embarrassed and humiliated while her clothes were taken and searched. As she waited she had a vaginal discharge due to her recent medical procedure. Ms Gray was detained at the station for three to four hours and the next morning she performed two hours of community work. Ms Gray sued De Reus, Pike, Hatch, and the state

---

442. [2004] NSWSC 835 at [61]–[62] citing Tobin and Sexton, *Australian Defamation Law and Practice*, looseleaf, LexisNexis Butterworths, Sydney, at [22,105].

443. (1997) Aust Torts Reports 81–417.

444. [2003] VSCA 84 at [32] per Winneke P; *McFadzean v Construction, Forestry, Mining and Energy Union* [2004] VSC 289 at [116] and [141]–[142] per Ashley J.

445. (1995) 126 DLR (4th) 129 at 179.

of Victoria for assault and De Reus and Hatch were also sued for negligently authorising the strip-search. She claimed damages for 'distress, anxiety, depression and post-traumatic stress disorder'.[446]

At the trial the jury found in favour of Ms Gray and awarded a total of $337,000. This was made up of $62,000 in compensatory damages including aggravated damages and $265,000 in exemplary damages. Under these heads different amounts were awarded against De Reus, Pike and Hatch. An appeal to the Victorian Court of Appeal to set aside the award was allowed both on the ground that the exemplary damages were excessive and because differing amounts should not have been awarded as aggravated damages against each joint tortfeasor. President Winneke explained the court's decision on the latter point as follows:

> Accepting, as I am content to do for the purposes of the argument, that it is permissible for a judge to have a jury assess and to enter judgment for different awards of aggravated compensatory damages against individual joint tortfeasors, it is my view that it should only be done in those cases where the circumstances clearly warrant it. The circumstances of this case did not warrant such separate awards. Each of the individual defendants — as the plaintiff alleged and as the jury found — acted together to have the respondent strip-searched. As I read the transcript of evidence, there was nothing put to the jury (or, indeed to be found in the evidence) which would have entitled the jury to make a finding that the aggravation of the harm done, and the humiliation caused to the respondent was — from her point of view — to be attributed differentially as between the tortfeasors. Each was content that the strip-search should be conducted and to participate in carrying it out or having it carried out. Nor was there anything to differentiate in the conduct of the defendants down to and during the trial. They were represented by the same counsel; they maintained that the strip-search was authorized; they jointly persisted in the contention that the respondent was wrongly suggesting that it was Pike, and not Hatch, who conducted the search; and none of them apologized notwithstanding that both Hatch and De Reus were compelled, in the end, to concede that they had no authority to carry out strip-searches as a matter of routine. These were all circumstances which told in favour of a single award of aggravated compensatory damages, rather than separate awards against individual tortfeasors.[447]

By consent, the parties requested that the Court of Appeal reassess damages. The President, Ormiston and Charles JJA concurring, then awarded a total of $135,000 consisting of $60,000 for aggravated compensatory damages against the defendants who had jointly assaulted Ms Gray, and $50,000 and $25,000 in exemplary damages against De Reus and Pike respectively.

2.86   Aggravated damages are still compensatory in nature and, in that sense, they need to be distinguished from exemplary or punitive damages even though, as we have just seen, they are often awarded for the same tort. Windeyer J in *Uren v John Fairfax & Sons Pty Ltd* observed:

---

446.   [2003] VSCA 84 at [6] per Winneke P.
447.   [2003] VSCA 84 at [32].

... aggravated damages are given to compensate the plaintiff when the harm done to him by a wrongful act was aggravated by the manner in which the act was done: exemplary damages, on the other hand, are intended to punish the defendant, and presumably to serve one or more of the objects of punishment — moral retribution or deterrence.[448]

The High Court in *Carson v John Fairfax & Sons Ltd* [449] held that no component of aggravated damages should be designed to punish the defendant and, if that has in fact happened, the appellate court may disturb the trial judge's or the jury's finding.[450] The difficulty with this reasoning in defamation cases, however, was noted by Windeyer J in *Uren v John Fairfax & Sons Pty Ltd*, when he observed:

> It seems to me that in truth a punitive or vindictive element does lurk in many cases in which the damages were aggravated by the defendant's conduct.[451]

2.87   The distinction between aggravated and exemplary damages was also in issue in *Zhu v Treasurer of the State of New South Wales*,[452] where the High Court affirmed Bergin J's decision to award both types of damages for the tort of intentional interference with contract. The unanimous decision of Gleeson CJ, Gummow, Kirby, Callinan and Heydon JJ begins with:

> It is a truth almost universally acknowledged — a truth unpatriotic to question — that the period from 15 September 2000–1 October 2000, when the Olympic Games were held in Sydney, was one of the happiest in the history of that city. The evidence in this case, however, reveals that the preparations for that event had a darker side.[453]

The plaintiff, Peter Zhu, was born in China in 1962, migrated to Australia in 1989 and became an Australian citizen in 1997. In March 1999, Zhu agreed with the second defendant, TOC, to act as an exclusive agent to market memberships in an 'Olympic Club' to residents of China wishing to attend the 2000 Olympic Games. TOC provided Zhu with letters of authority and merchandise to sell club memberships. A licence agreement between TOC and the Sydney Organising Committee for the Olympic Games (SOCOG) allowed TOC to use various Olympic Games trade marks and logos and to licence others to use them. By July 1999 TOC was encountering serious financial difficulties and one of the 'few things keeping it alive'[454] was Zhu's payment of $260,000 for his agency rights. Pressure was placed on Zhu to sell as many memberships as possible so as to ease TOC's pressing financial burden, although the latter fact was hidden from Zhu. In July 1999 SOCOG was advised that TOC should be placed into administration immediately and by August 1999 SOCOG assumed sole control of TOC. This was announced

---

448. (1966) 117 CLR 118 at 149.

449. (1993) 178 CLR 44.

450. See also *Sutcliffe v Pressdram Ltd* [1990] 2 WLR 271.

451. (1966) 117 CLR 118 at 151–2; see also *New South Wales v Ibbett* [2006] HCA 57 at [33]–[37].

452. (2004) 211 ALR 159; [2004] HCA 56.

453. (2004) 211 ALR 159; [2004] HCA 56 at [1].

454. (2004) 211 ALR 159; [2004] HCA 56 at [22].

in a press release containing 'some terminological inexactitudes, such as saying that the purpose of the transfer was to achieve "synergistic benefits"'.[455] The process was overseen by Mr Reading and Ms Ford of SOCOG. Mr Reading described Mr Zhu as a 'loose cannon' and in September 1999 instructed TOC managing director Mr Wyness to terminate the agency agreement between TOC and Zhu. In October 1999 Wyness met with Zhu and told him that he had committed various breaches of the agreement (later found to be incorrect and immaterial) and that they wished to terminate the agency. In early November a letter was sent to Zhu purporting to terminate the agreement. Zhu disputed the termination and maintained that the agency agreement was still on foot. After a visit to China in early December 1999 Zhu was arrested and detained by police for 12 hours on arrival at Kingsford Smith Airport, Sydney. His house was searched and his passport and documents relating to the agency agreement were seized. When released he immediately sued SOCOG, TOC and Wyness. In April 2000 police charged Zhu with obtaining and attempting to obtain money by deception. Zhu settled with Wyness and his case against TOC was stayed when a liquidator was appointed to TOC in August 2000. In October 2000, shortly after the Games, the Director of Public Prosecutions dropped the charges and the only remaining defendant by the time of the trial was SOCOG.

At the trial in the New South Wales Supreme Court, Zhu proved that SOCOG had committed the tort of interference with contract by: first, preventing TOC from performing the agency agreement; second, persuading TOC to invalidly terminate (or repudiate) the agreement; and third, by causing his arrest.[456] Bergin J found that SOCOG had failed to make a full disclosure of all relevant facts to the police and its behaviour in relation to the arrest was 'quite extraordinary', 'reprehensible', 'high handed and disgraceful'. In awarding Zhu more than $4.2 million in damages (including $95,000 in aggravated damages and $200,000 in exemplary damages)[457] her Honour explained:

> The plaintiff gave evidence of the hurt to his feelings. He said that he was deeply shocked and humiliated by his arrest. I accept his evidence that he felt he had never had such a horrifying or humiliating experience in his life. SOCOG attempted to suggest that he did not feel hurt by his arrest but I am of the view that such a suggestion was wholly unwarranted. The plaintiff also impressed me as a resilient man with the fortitude to argue for what he believed to be his entitlements. This is evidenced in his conversations with Wyness and his dealings with the arresting officer. That is not to say he was not hurt or did not feel humiliated. It is however a factor I have taken into account in deciding on the quantum by which his damages should be increased by way of this award.
>
> In fixing an amount it is important to ensure that there is no double counting or overlapping with the award of exemplary damages I have made. I have focused

455.	(2004) 211 ALR 159; [2004] HCA 56 at [24].
456.	(2004) 211 ALR 159; [2004] HCA 56 at [3].
457.	(2004) 211 ALR 159; [2004] HCA 56 at [4] and [39].

only on the plaintiff's hurt to feelings and humiliation and have excluded any element of punishment or deterrence or expression of curial disapprobation. I am satisfied that the plaintiff is entitled to an additional amount by way of an award of aggravated damages in the amount of $95,000.[458]

SOCOG successfully appealed to the New South Wales Court of Appeal relying on the defence of justification. While the court strongly criticised Zhu's arrest, it accepted that he had made unauthorised use of various Olympic trade marks and thus SOCOG had a superior statutory right and duty[459] to interfere with the agency contract. Zhu appealed to the High Court and won. In rejecting the justification defence, the court observed that SOCOG attempted to vindicate its concerns 'independently of any concern for legality' and that in its 'view of the world, the whole human scheme was acrawl with requirements for its prior written consent, without which not a sparrow could fall'.[460] Gleeson CJ, Gummow, Kirby, Callinan and Heydon JJ concluded:

> … a course of action was embarked upon which was precipitous, high-handed and oppressive in its consequences. SOCOG was a statutory body created by the Parliament of New South Wales. Its conduct in the present case fell far short of the conduct conventionally expected of bodies exercising powers granted by an Australian Parliament. Its conduct was so unsatisfactory that it may have been acting beyond its statutory power. However, the plaintiff did not challenge the conduct of SOCOG on this ground, and it is unnecessary to take this matter further.[461]

The Court of Appeal's decision was reversed and Bergin J's award of damages, including aggravated and exemplary damages, was affirmed.

EXEMPLARY DAMAGES

2.88   Punishment is the domain of criminal rather than civil law[462] with one main exception: exemplary or punitive damages. Their purpose is to punish the defendant, deter others from like conduct, 'assuage any urge for revenge felt by victims and to discourage any temptation to engage in self-help likely to endanger the peace'.[463] The defendant's conduct must have been fraudulent, violent, cruel, 'high-handed, insolent, vindictive or malicious',[464] amounting to or exhibiting 'a conscious and contumelious disregard for the plaintiff's rights'.[465] Exemplary damages must be specifically pleaded and particularised

458. *Zhu v Sydney Organising Committee for the Olympic Games* [2001] NSWSC 989 at [458]–[459].

459. Under the Sydney 2000 Games (Indicia and Images) Protection Act 1996 (Cth) and the Sydney Organising Committee for the Olympic Games Act 1993 (NSW).

460. (2004) 211 ALR 159; [2004] HCA 56 at [77].

461. (2004) 211 ALR 159; [2004] HCA 56 at [164].

462. See *Fatimi Pty Ltd v Bryant* (2004) 52 NSWLR 678; [2004] NSWCA 140 at [76] per Giles JA.

463. *Lamb v Cotogno* (1987) 164 CLR 1 at 9–10.

464. *Uren v John Fairfax & Sons Pty Ltd* (1966) 117 CLR 118 at 129 per Taylor J.

465. *Uren v John Fairfax & Sons Pty Ltd* (1966) 117 CLR at 129 per Taylor J and at 154 per Windeyer J; *XL Petroleum (NSW) Pty Ltd v Caltex Oil (Australia) Pty Ltd* (1985) 155 CLR 448.

in the plaintiff's statement of claim[466] but while they are often claimed they are rarely awarded. Where exemplary damages have been awarded they are given in addition to either compensatory or nominal[467] damages and 'in that sense, will be a windfall in the hands' of the plaintiff.[468]

If proof of loss is an ingredient in the cause of action, exemplary damages cannot be given in isolation.[469] As observed by Brennan J in *XL Petroleum (NSW) Pty Ltd v Caltex Oil (Australia) Pty Ltd*:

> Exemplary damages are parasitic on compensatory damages, the plaintiff being unable to recover exemplary damages if he is not the victim of the behaviour which attracts the exemplary damages … A single cause of action provides the foundation of a judgment awarding, in an appropriate case, exemplary damages as well as compensatory damages.[470]

In *Fatimi Pty Ltd v Bryant*[471] a claim for exemplary damages based on the tort of conspiracy failed because the 'host' claim for compensatory damages was not made out. After referring to *XL Petroleum* Giles JA explained:

> If exemplary damages can not be obtained when a plaintiff's claim for compensatory damages has been satisfied in full, despite the single cause of action under which exemplary damages could also be awarded, they equally can not be obtained when the plaintiff's claim for compensatory damages has failed. If there is no host, there can not be a parasite.[472]

Apart from satisfying the 'host' claim there are two additional elements to be proved. First, the defendant must have acted in contumelious disregard of the plaintiff's rights. Second, the award must be capable of fulfilling its objectives, namely, punishment, deterrence and assuaging the plaintiff's urge for revenge.[473] While many cases refer to the court's 'discretion' to award exemplary damages, in *Gray* the High Court found this description to be of 'little assistance'.[474] If, for example, the defendant has already been substantially punished this is a complete bar to recovery and such a 'decision is not one that is reached as a matter of discretion dependent upon the facts and circumstances in each particular case'.[475] Further, equitable discretionary defences such as the plaintiff's 'unclean hands'[476] are irrelevant.[477]

---

466. *Hepburn v TCN Channel Nine Pty Ltd* [1983] 2 NSWLR 682 at 692; *Vasta v Queensland Newspapers Pty Ltd* [1991] 2 Qd R 354; Federal Court Rules O 4 r 3(4); Uniform Civil Procedure Rules 2005 (NSW) r 6.12(5).

467. See *Fatimi Pty Ltd v Bryant* (2004) 52 NSWLR 678; [2004] NSWCA 140 at [71] per Giles JA.

468. *Gray v Motor Accident Commission* (1998) 196 CLR 1 at [15].

469. *Amalgamated Television Services Pty Ltd v Marsden (No 2)* (2003) 57 NSWLR 338 at 345.

470. (1985) 155 CLR 448; 57 ALR 639 at 653.

471. (2004) 52 NSWLR 678; [2004] NSWCA 140.

472. (2004) 52 NSWLR 678; [2004] NSWCA 140 at [73].

473. See *James v Hill* [2004] NSWCA 301 at [69] per Tobias JA.

474. (1998) 196 CLR 1 at [25].

475. *Gray v Motor Accident Commission* (1998) 196 CLR 1 at [40] per Gleeson CJ, McHugh, Gummow and Hayne JJ and [510] per Kirby J.

476. For the meaning of 'unclean hands', see **8.35**.

477. *James v Hill* [2004] NSWCA 301 at [74] per Tobias JA.

2.89 There is no fixed list of torts where exemplary damages are available[478] but they have been awarded in assault,[479] battery,[480] false imprisonment,[481] trespass to land,[482] trespass to goods and conversion,[483] conspiracy,[484] nuisance,[485] abuse of process,[486] inducing a breach of contract,[487] interference with contract,[488] malicious prosecution[489] and misfeasance in public office.[490] Exemplary damages have not been awarded in Australia for passing off but their availability was accepted by French J in *Paramount Pictures Corporation v Hasluck*[491] and Wilcox J observed in *Flamingo Park Pty Ltd v Dolly Dolly Creations Pty Ltd*:

> The argument for the award of exemplary damages in a passing off action is perhaps easier to make than is the argument in respect of a breach of contract. Passing off is a tort and it is not difficult to think of circumstances in which a passing off may be in contumelious disregard of a plaintiff's rights.[492]

There is doubt in the United Kingdom about the availability of exemplary damages in deceit,[493] but they are available in Australia.[494] There is also doubt in the United Kingdom about their availability in negligence,[495] but in *Gray v Motor Accident Commission*[496] the High Court held they are available in Australia provided the tortfeasor is guilty of 'conscious wrongdoing'. Gleeson CJ, McHugh, Gummow and Hayne JJ observed:

> … exemplary damages could not properly be awarded in a case of alleged negligence in which there was no conscious wrongdoing by the defendant. Ordinarily, then, questions of exemplary damages will not *arise in most negligence*

---

478. *Kuddus v Chief Constable of Leicester Constabulary* [2002] 2 AC 122.

479. *New South Wales v Ibbett* [2006] HCA 57.

480. *Lamb v Cotogno* (1987) 164 CLR 1; *Pearce v Hallett* [1969] SASR 423; *Henry v Thompson* [1989] 2 Qd R 412.

481. *McFadzean v Construction, Forestry, Mining and Energy Union* [2004] VSC 289.

482. *New South Wales v Ibbett* [2006] HCA 57; *XL Petroleum (NSW) Pty Ltd v Caltex Oil (Australia) Pty Ltd* (1985) 155 CLR 448.

483. *Healing Sales Pty Ltd v Inglis Electrix Pty Ltd* (1968) 121 CLR 584.

484. *Williams v Hursey* (1959) 103 CLR 30; see also *Fatimi Pty Ltd v Bryant* (2004) 52 NSWLR 678; [2004] NSWCA 140 at [70] per Handley JA.

485. *Willoughby Municipal Council v Halstead* (1916) 22 CLR 352.

486. J Delany, *Security for Costs*, Law Book Company, Sydney, 1989, pp 14–16.

487. *Whitfield v De Lauret & Co Ltd* (1920) 29 CLR 71; compare *Hospitality Group Pty Ltd v Australian Rugby Union* [2001] FCA 1040.

488. *Zhu v Sydney Organising Committee for the Olympic Games* [2001] NSWSC 989 ($200,000 awarded as exemplary damages); affirmed *Zhu v Treasurer of the State of New South Wales* (2004) 211 ALR 159; [2004] HCA 56.

489. *A v New South Wales* [2007] HCA 10.

490. Compare *Kuddus v Chief Constable of Leicestershire Constabulary* [2002] 2 AC 122.

491. (2006) 70 IPR 293; [2006] FCA 1431 at [35].

492. (1986) 6 IPR 431 at 457 (FCA).

493. See *Rookes v Barnard* [1964] AC 1129; *Mafo v Adams* [1970] 1 QB 548; *Broome v Cassell & Co Ltd* [1972] AC 1027 at 1078–9 per Lord Hailsham LC and at 1130–1 per Lord Diplock; compare *Archer v Brown* [1985] QB 401.

494. *Musca v Astle Corp Pty Ltd* (1988) 80 ALR 251 (FCA); *James v Hill* [2004] NSWCA 301.

495. *Broome v Cassell & Co Ltd* [1972] AC 1027.

496. (1998) 196 CLR 1.

cases be they motor accident or other kinds of case. But there can be cases, framed in
negligence, in which the defendant can be shown to have acted consciously
in contumelious disregard of the rights of the plaintiff or persons in the
position of the plaintiff. Cases of an employer's failure to provide a safe
system of work for employees in which it is demonstrated that the employer,
well knowing of an extreme danger thus created, persisted in employing the
unsafe system might, perhaps, be of that latter kind[497] … No doubt other
examples can be found.[498]

The High Court also held that if the tortfeasor is insured under a compulsory
scheme of insurance against any liability for exemplary damages this 'would
not bar the award of such damages'.[499] But, if the defendant has already been
punished — as was the case in *Gray* where the tortfeasor had been imprisoned
for a substantial term — exemplary damages will be refused.[500]

2.90   Exemplary damages are awarded in addition to compensatory damages
and must be separately identified in the judgment.[501] Further, there is no
'necessary proportionality' between the two. In *XL Petroleum (NSW) Pty Ltd
v Caltex Oil (Australia) Pty Ltd* Brennan J observed:

> As an award of exemplary damages is intended to punish the defendant for
> conduct showing conscious and contumelious disregard for the plaintiff's
> rights and to deter him from committing like conduct again, the considerations
> that enter into the assessment of exemplary damages are quite different from
> the considerations that govern the assessment of compensatory damages.
> There is no necessary proportionality between the assessment of the two
> categories.[502]

In *Harris v Digital Pulse Pty Ltd* Heydon J observed:

> If exemplary damages are to fulfil their threefold purpose, they must
> not merely irritate, they must sting. It is the gravity and character of the
> defendants' conduct which guides the Court's discretion as to the proper
> amount to award by way of exemplary damages. That is why there is 'no
> necessary proportionality' between the amount awarded as compensation for
> the damage suffered by the plaintiff and the amount of exemplary damages
> awarded against the defendant. A minimal amount of damage inflicted on a
> plaintiff may, if the wrongdoing was outrageous, nevertheless require heavy
> exemplary damages to be visited upon the defendant.[503]

497. Citing in support *Midalco Pty Ltd v Rabenalt* [1989] VR 461 (FC); *Coloca v BP Australia Ltd* [1992] 2 VR 441; *Trend Management Ltd v Borg* (1996) 40 NSWLR 500.

498. (1998) 196 CLR 1 at [22]; compare *A v Bottrill* [2003] 1 AC 449, a medical negligence case where the Privy Council overruled the New Zealand Court of Appeal and, by a majority, found that intentional wrongdoing or conscious recklessness was not a prerequisite for exemplary damages.

499. (1998) 196 CLR at [34]–[35].

500. Compare *James v Hill* [2004] NSWCA 301 at [81]–[82] per Tobias JA.

501. *TCN Channel Nine Pty Ltd v Anning* (2002) 54 NSWLR 333 (CA).

502. (1985) 155 CLR 448 at 471.

503. (2003) 56 NSWLR 298 at [23] (citations omitted); see also *James v Hill* [2004] NSWCA 301.

Unlike some of the heads of compensatory damages (see **2.82**), exemplary damages do not bear interest up to judgment.[504]

Ordinarily, each joint tortfeasor is jointly and severally liable for compensatory damages: see **2.21**. An award of exemplary damages, however, may lead to differential assessments depending on whether the tortfeasor's conduct merits punishment. If it does, then 'a person may be liable for exemplary damages even though their liability for the contumelious act is vicarious'.[505] By contrast, in *XL Petroleum* the jury awarded $400,000 in exemplary damages against Caltex which was one of three joint tortfeasors. On appeal, the amount was reduced to $150,000 by a majority in the New South Wales Court of Appeal (Hutley and Glass JJA; Mahoney JA dissenting), but the court approved the making of a separate judgment against Caltex. This was upheld by the High Court where Gibbs CJ held that the court may 'give separate judgments against two defendants, where one is liable for exemplary damages and the other is not'.[506]

2.91 Under the uniform defamation law exemplary damages are not available for the publication of defamatory matter.[507] Legislation in most jurisdictions also prohibits an award of exemplary damages in survival actions.[508] South Australia provides a limited exception where the defendant is guilty of an 'unreasonable delay' in the resolution of the claim.[509] In New South Wales, in addition to the prohibition on exemplary damages in survival actions and defamation, they are also prohibited in motor accident claims,[510] industrial accident claims[511] and negligently inflicted personal injury claims.[512] In Queensland exemplary damages are prohibited in negligently inflicted personal injury claims.[513] Victorian legislation prohibits an award of exemplary damages in motor accident claims for personal injury and death.[514]

2.92 Not all legislative intervention has been aimed at restricting exemplary damages. In Victoria the Whistleblowers Protection Act 2001 provides that where a person takes 'detrimental action against a person in reprisal for a protected disclosure' there is a criminal sanction, a right to compensatory damages and under s 19(3) '[a]ny remedy that may be granted by a court with

---

504. See, for example, Federal Court of Australia Act 1976 s 51A(3)(c); *TCN Channel Nine Pty Ltd v Anning* (2002) 54 NSWLR 333 at [166] (CA).

505. *Nationwide News Pty Ltd v Naidu* [2007] NSWCA 377 at [275] per Beazley JA.

506. (1985) 155 CLR 448 at 460 and see *De Reus v Gray* [2003] VSCA 84.

507. See, for example, Defamation Act 2005 (NSW) s 37.

508. Law Reform (Miscellaneous Provisions) Act 1944 (NSW) s 2(2)(a)(i); Succession Act 1981 (Qld) s 66(2)(b); Survival of Causes of Action Act 1940 (SA) s 2; Administration and Probate Act 1935 (Tas) s 27; Administration and Probate Act 1958 (Vic) s 29(2)(a); Law Reform (Miscellaneous Provisions) Act 1941 (WA) s 4.

509. Civil Liability Act 1936 (SA) s 70.

510. Motor Accidents Act 1988 (NSW) s 81A; Motor Accidents Compensation Act 1999 (NSW) s 144.

511. Workers Compensation Act 1987 (NSW) s 151R.

512. Civil Liability Act 2002 (NSW) s 21.

513. Civil Liability Act 2003 (Qld) s 52.

514. Transport Accident Act 1986 (Vic) s 93(7).

respect to a tort, including exemplary damages, may be granted by a court in proceedings under this section'. In New Zealand, despite a comprehensive no-fault accident compensation scheme, exemplary damages have been preserved for tortiously inflicted personal injuries.[515] Also, s 115(4) of the Copyright Act 1968 (Cth), s 27(4) of the Circuit Layouts Act 1989 (Cth), s 75(3) of the Designs Act 2003 (Cth) and s 122(1A) of the Patents Act 1990 (Cth) allow for 'additional damages' to be awarded for infringement of the intellectual property rights granted under those Acts 'upon principles which correspond to those governing awards of aggravated and exemplary damages at common law'.[516] As there is no express provision for 'additional' or exemplary damages in the Trade Marks Act 1995 (Cth) French J held in *Paramount Pictures Corporation v Hasluck* that they are not available for trade mark infringement, although in theory they are available for the tort of passing off.[517] At the time of writing it is proposed that the Intellectual Property Laws Amendment (Raising the Bar) Bill 2011(Cth) will amend the Trade Marks Act 1995 (Cth) by allowing for the award of exemplary damages in trade mark infringement cases.

---

515. Injury Prevention, Rehabilitation and Compensation Act 2001 (NZ) s 319.

516. *Polygram Pty Ltd v Golden Editions Pty Ltd* (1997) 148 ALR 4 at 16 per Lockhart J in relation to s 115(4) of the Copyright Act 1968 (Cth); see also *Sullivan v FNH Investments Pty Ltd* (2003) 57 IPR 63; *Aristocrat Technologies Australia Pty Ltd v DAP Services (Kempsey) Pty Ltd (in liq)* (2007) 71 IPR 437; [2007] FCAFC 40 at [42] per Black CJ, Jacobson J and at [113] per Rares J.

517. (2006) 70 IPR 293; [2006] FCA 1431 at [35]–[36] and see **2.89**.

CHAPTER

Damages in Contract

INTRODUCTION

3.1   Contracts 'are made to be performed, not broken'.[1] But when a contract is broken the usual remedy at common law is compensatory damages. The equitable remedies of specific performance and injunction may also be available, but as discussed in Chapters 7 and 8, these are only awarded in the court's discretion.

Damages for a broken contract serve the same function as in tort: an award of money by the court compensating the plaintiff for the defendant's wrong. When it comes to assessing the amount of compensation, however, there is an important difference between contract and tort. For breach of contract, the general principle was stated by Parke B in *Robinson v Harman*:

> The rule of common law is, that where a party sustains a loss by reason of a breach of contract, he is, so far as money can do it, to be placed in the same situation, with respect to damages, as if the contract had been performed.[2]

This can be contrasted with the aim in tort, which is to place a plaintiff in the position they would have been in if the tort had not been committed. The effect of this difference is discussed at 3.42.

3.2   The layout of this chapter is similar to the previous one because the underlying ingredients or elements that lead to a successful common law claim for compensatory damages in tort and contract are identical. Still, there are many differences in how those elements are applied to each cause of action. Notable examples include:

a)   there are different tests of remoteness in contract (see 3.14–3.24) and tort (see 2.37–2.42);

b)   there are several different heads of damage (see 2.57–2.87 and 3.41–3.54);

c)   claims for damages that arise from a lost chance or opportunity are treated differently (see 2.28–2.30 and 3.46);

d)   while the restitutionary remedy of account of profits (see Chapter 6) is an alternative remedy to damages for some torts, it is not an alternative for breach of contract,[3] although the position is different in the UK as a result of the decision of the House of Lords in *Attorney-General v Blake*;[4]

e)   while exemplary damages are available (subject to statute) for all torts (see 2.88–2.92) they have always been denied in contract: see 3.53;

1.   *Golden Strait Corporation v Nippon Yusen Kubishka Karsha* [2007] UKHL 12 at 22 per Lord Bingham (in dissent).

2.   (1848) 1 Ex 850 at 855; 154 ER 363 at 365. For Australian approval of this principle, see, for example, *Commonwealth v Amann Aviation Pty Ltd* (1991) 174 CLR 64 at 80 per Mason CJ and Dawson J; and *Tabcorp Holdings Ltd v Bowen Investments Pty Ltd* (2009) 236 CLR 272 at 286 [13]; [2009] HCA 8 at [13] per French CJ, Gummow, Heydon, Crennan and Kiefel JJ.

3.   *Hospitality Group Pty Ltd v Australian Rugby Union Ltd* (2001) 110 FCR 157; *Biscayne Partners Pty Ltd v Valance Corp Pty Ltd* [2003] NSWSC 874.

4.   [2001] 1 AC 268.

f) claims for negligent breaches of contract may be governed by the Civil Liability Acts (see **Chapter 2** generally for more detailed discussion of the changes these statutory amendments make to claims resulting from negligence).

Equitable compensation is dealt with in **Chapter 11** and damages under the Australian Consumer Law in **Chapter 16**. Restitutionary claims in contract are considered in **Chapter 4**; and rescission of contracts in **Chapter 5**.

ELEMENTS

3.3   In order for the court to award the plaintiff compensatory damages in contract, it must find that:

a) the plaintiff has *a cause of action in contract* — namely, a breach of contract;

b) the defendant's breach of contract has in fact injured or caused a loss to the plaintiff — the element of *causation*;

c) the loss suffered by the plaintiff *is not too remote*; and

d) the plaintiff has not breached his or her 'duty' to *mitigate* unnecessary loss.

3.4   The onus of proving the first three elements rests on the plaintiff.[5] Generally, the plaintiff's case or cause of action, including causation, must be proven on the balance of probabilities.[6] With the last element, mitigation, the principles are the same as those in tort (see **2.53–2.56**). The burden is on the defendant to show that the plaintiff has failed to take reasonable steps to avoid unnecessary loss.[7] In other words, the plaintiff is presumed to have taken reasonable steps towards mitigation unless the defendant proves otherwise. As with tort, the word 'duty' in this context should be treated with caution, since, unlike other duties, if breached, it does not result in a cause of action, nor is the plaintiff regarded as being contributorily negligent. Breach of the duty merely reduces the amount of damages payable — see **3.26**.

The Civil Liability Acts in each of the States and Territories (except for the Northern Territory) have modified the elements of causation and remoteness for any claim for damages resulting from negligence.[8] These modifications, which apply 'regardless of whether the claim is brought in tort, in contract, under statute or otherwise',[9] are discussed at **2.12–2.13** and **2.41–2.42**. Some

---

5.   See, for example, *Erie County Natural Gas & Fuel Co Ltd v Samuel S Carroll* [1911] AC 105; *Commonwealth v Amann Aviation Pty Ltd* (1991) 174 CLR 64 at 80 per Mason CJ and Dawson J.

6.   *Sellars v Adelaide Petroleum NL* (1994) 179 CLR 332 at 355 per Mason CJ, Dawson, Toohey and Gaudron JJ.

7.   *Banco de Portugal v Waterlow* [1932] AC 452; *TCN Channel 9 Pty Ltd v Hayden Enterprises Pty Ltd* (1989) 16 NSWLR 130 at 158 per Hope JA (CA); *Wenkart v Pitman* (1998) 46 NSWLR 502 at 523 per Powell JA (CA).

8.   Civil Law (Wrongs) Act 2002 (ACT) s 45; Civil Liability Act 2002 (NSW) s 5D; Civil Liability Act 2003 (Qld) s 11; Civil Liability Act 1936 (SA) s 34; Civil Liability Act 2002 (Tas) s 13; Wrongs Act 1958 (Vic) s 51; Civil Liability Act 2002 (WA) s 5C. The Personal Injuries (Liabilities and Damages) Act 2003 (NT) does not have similar provisions dealing with causation.

9.   Civil Liability Act 2002 (NSW) s 5A. Similar wording appears in all the other Civil Liability Acts.

contractual claims might also be affected by the limits in some of the Civil Liability Acts on certain claims for personal injury damages or mental harm. These limits are dealt with generally in the chapter dealing with tort damages (at **2.45–2.92**) but are also discussed in relation to contract claims for mental distress at **3.49**.

CAUSE OF ACTION

3.5 While in tort there are many causes of action that support a claim for damages, in contract there is only one: a breach of contract. Even so, there are many types of contracts and numerous ways of breaching them.

Subject to the restriction on an agreed or liquidated damages clause,[10] there is a common law right to damages in all contracts in the event of a breach.[11] Unlike negligence, the breach in itself allows the innocent party to claim nominal damages.[12] As the name suggests, such damages are insignificant;[13] although, for a successful plaintiff, the normal award of costs may be of some value. If the plaintiff is to receive full compensatory damages then actual loss must be proved.[14]

Termination[15] of the contract is usually not required in order for the plaintiff to claim damages.[16] There are two exceptions: cases of anticipatory breach[17] and claims for 'expectation' or 'loss of bargain' damages.[18] In *Sunbird Plaza Ltd v Maloney* Mason CJ held:

> Loss of bargain damages are recoverable only if the contract is at an end. Once termination due to the defendant's wrongful conduct is established the plaintiff is entitled to damages for loss of bargain ... Barwick CJ suggested in *Ogle*[19] ... that termination is not an essential element in an action for loss of bargain damages, except in the case of anticipatory breach, but the preponderant opinion in Australia and in England is against his view.[20]

---

10. Such a clause must not operate as a penalty: *AMEV-UDC Finance Ltd v Austin* (1986) 162 CLR 170 at 186–92 per Mason and Wilson JJ, and 212 per Dawson J; *Esanda Finance Corp v Plessnig* (1989) 166 CLR 131 at 138–43 per Wilson and Toohey JJ, 143–9 per Brennan J, 153–4 per Deane J, and 157 per Gaudron J.

11. *Photo Production Ltd v Securicor Transport Ltd* [1980] AC 827 at 849 per Lord Diplock, extracted at **1.5**.

12. *O'Connor v SP Bray Ltd* (1936) 36 SR (NSW) 248 at 260; *Bowen v Blair* [1933] VLR 398 at 402; *Luna Park (NSW) Ltd v Tramways Advertising Pty Ltd* (1938) 61 CLR 286.

13. Compare *Owner of Steamship 'Mediana' v Owner, Master and Crew of Lightship 'Comet'* [1900] AC 113 at 116 per Lord Halsbury.

14. *Erie County Natural Gas & Fuel Co Ltd v Samuel S Carroll* [1911] AC 105.

15. The meaning of termination is discussed at **5.2**.

16. *Luna Park (NSW) Ltd v Tramways Advertising Pty Ltd* (1938) 61 CLR 286 at 300; *Ogle v Comboyuro Investments Pty Ltd* (1976) 136 CLR 444 at 450.

17. *Ogle v Comboyuro Investments Pty Ltd* (1976) 136 CLR 444 at 450. Anticipatory breach and damages are discussed at **3.31–3.35** and **3.39**.

18. *Sunbird Plaza Ltd v Maloney* (1988) 166 CLR 245 at 260 per Mason CJ. This head of damages is discussed at **3.42**.

19. *Ogle v Comboyuro Investments Pty Ltd* (1976) 136 CLR 444 at 450.

20. (1988) 166 CLR 245 at 260–1.

In order to claim damages for the defendant's breach the plaintiff should be ready and willing to perform their side of the contract.[21] But, where the plaintiff terminates the contract following an anticipatory breach, the plaintiff need only show that this intention existed prior to termination.[22]

CAUSATION

Introduction

3.6   The plaintiff must show that the loss suffered was in fact caused by the defendant's breach. The traditional view of causation is that the court asks: 'but for' the defendant's wrong, would the plaintiff have suffered the loss or damage complained of? So, if the loss or damage would have been suffered anyway — or, as some say, 'just the same' — no award for damages beyond nominal damages can be made. The test should only be used, however, as a rule of thumb.[23] As discussed at **3.9–3.13**, it is difficult to apply where there are intervening or contributing causes.

3.7   An uncomplicated illustration of how the 'but for' test is applied in contract is found in *Reg Glass Pty Ltd v Rivers Locking Systems Pty Ltd*.[24] The defendant agreed to supply the plaintiff with a security door and locking system. The defendant breached the contract by installing a door not reasonably fit for its purpose. The plaintiff's property was subsequently burgled. The High Court said the breach did not necessarily imply that the defendant was liable to compensate the plaintiff for the loss caused by the burglary. If the defendant had proved that the burglars would have gained entry even if a reasonably fit door had been installed, there would have been no liability on the defendant's part beyond nominal damages. However, the court was satisfied that had such a door been installed, the burglary would not have occurred. Thus, 'but for' the defendant's breach, the loss would not have been suffered.

3.8   The courts now recognise that, when considering multiple causes or intervening events, the 'but for' test is 'inadequate or troublesome' and that it is not the exclusive test of causation.[25] In these cases, the courts frequently refer to the chain of causation between the wrong complained of and the loss or damage suffered. Thus, if something intervenes between the wrong and the loss to 'break the chain', the defendant will not be responsible or will only be held partly responsible. But this figurative test is just as problematic as the 'but for' test. What is certain is that there are some events which in the view of the court lessen or even remove the defendant's responsibility for the damage.

---

21. *Foran v Wight* (1989) 168 CLR 385 at 408 per Mason CJ and 451–2 per Dawson J.

22. *Foran v Wight* (1989) 168 CLR at 452 per Dawson J.

23. See *Wenham v Ella* (1972) 127 CLR 454 at 466 per Walsh J; *Alexander v Cambridge Credit Corp Ltd* (1987) 9 NSWLR 310 at 368.

24. (1968) 120 CLR 516.

25. See **Chapter 2** and, in particular, *March v E & M H Stramare Pty Ltd* (1991) 171 CLR 506 at 516 per Mason CJ and 523–4 per Deane J; *Chappel v Hart* (1998) 195 CLR 232.

This was recognised by the High Court in *March v E & M H Stramare Pty Ltd*,[26] where it accepted a commonsense-based analysis of causation, as opposed to philosophical or scientific theories. In this regard, the types of events most likely to persuade the judicial mind that the plaintiff should not receive the full amount claimed in damages is where the plaintiff is guilty of contributory negligence or where there is a new intervening act (*novus actus interveniens*).

Contributory negligence

3.9 If the plaintiff is negligent this may satisfy the court that the 'chain of causation' between the defendant's breach of contract and the plaintiff's loss has been broken. Or, in other words, it may establish that the plaintiff's loss was not in fact caused by the defendant's breach. In *Lexmead (Basingstoke) Ltd v Lewis*[27] the plaintiff purchased a towing hitch to connect his four-wheel drive to a trailer. After the plaintiff used the towing hitch he noticed that it was broken but continued to use it. A serious accident occurred when the trailer became detached. The plaintiff claimed damages by arguing that the defendant supplier was in breach of contract because of a design defect in the towing hitch. The House of Lords rejected this argument and decided that the plaintiff's negligence, in continuing to use the towing hitch in the knowledge that it was unsafe, 'broke the chain' of causation between the defendant's breach and the damage suffered.

3.10 As just discussed, the plaintiff's negligence may sever the chain of causation. But what if the defendant's breach is still causally relevant, despite the plaintiff's negligence? Or, in other words, what if the plaintiff's negligence does not sever the chain of causation, but is merely a contributing cause in conjunction with the defendant's breach? Prior to *Astley v Austrust Ltd*[28] there was a line of authority that the apportionment legislation,[29] usually confined to actions in negligence, could also apply to actions for breach of contract. While no apportionment was available in actions purely concerned with contract,[30] if the action could have been brought in tort or contract (that is, there was concurrent liability in tort and contract) apportionment would apply. As a result, the court could reduce the defendant's liability in both tort *and* contract if the negligence or 'fault' of the plaintiff contributed to the loss or damage.[31] But this approach was rejected by the High Court in *Astley v Austrust Ltd*,[32] which found that the apportionment legislation did not allow for a reduction

26.   (1991) 171 CLR 506.

27.   [1982] AC 225.

28.   (1999) 197 CLR 1.

29.   See the discussion at **2.15-2.24**.

30.   *Harper v Ashton's Circus Pty Ltd* [1972] 2 NSWLR 395 at 404 per Hope JA (CA); compare *Simonius Fisher & Co v Holt & Thompson* [1979] 2 NSWLR 322 at 351-5 per Samuels JA (CA).

31.   *Queen's Bridge Motors v Edwards* [1964] Tas SR 93; *Forsikringsaktieselskapet Vesta v Butcher* [1989] 1 AC 852; *Bains Harding Construction & Roofing (Aust) Pty Ltd v McCredie Richmond & Partners Pty Ltd* (1988) 13 NSWLR 437; compare *AS James Pty Ltd v Duncan* [1970] VR 705.

32.   (1999) 197 CLR 1; see also *Townsend v BBC Hardware Ltd* [2003] QSC 15.

in damages in *any* contract case. *Astley*, however, 'was followed by almost universal initiatives … to prevent the recurrence of the unfair results to which the non-application of the existing apportionment legislation led there'.[33] In all Australian jurisdictions, revised apportionment legislation reversed *Astley*. For example, s 8 of the Law Reform (Miscellaneous Provisions) Act 1965 (NSW) now defines 'wrong' as 'an act or omission' that:

(a) gives rise to a liability in tort in respect of which a defence of contributory negligence is available at common law, or

(b) amounts to a breach of a contractual duty of care that is concurrent and co-extensive with a duty of care in tort.[34]

Section 9(1) provides:

If a person (the claimant) suffers damage as the result partly of the claimant's failure to take reasonable care (contributory negligence) and partly of the wrong of any other person:

(a) a claim in respect of the damage is not defeated by reason of the contributory negligence of the claimant, and

(b) the damages recoverable in respect of the wrong are to be reduced to such extent as the court thinks just and equitable having regard to the claimant's share in the responsibility for the damage.[35]

A common example of a 'concurrent and co-extensive' duty of care in contract and tort is a contract for the performance of professional services. The contract usually contains a term (express or implied) that the services will be performed with reasonable care and skill; and there is a tortious duty to take reasonable care. If the professional fails to take reasonable care, the plaintiff may elect which cause of action to pursue — although there is nothing to prevent a claim in the alternative.[36] The effect of the revised apportionment legislation is that, whether the claim is made in contract or tort if the plaintiff's negligence contributed as a cause of the loss, the court will reduce the plaintiff's damages 'to such extent as the court thinks just and equitable': see **2.15–2.20**. However, there will be no apportionment where there is only

---

33. *I & L Securities Pty Ltd v HTW Valuers (Brisbane) Pty Ltd* (2002) 210 CLR 109 at [211] per Callinan J.

34. See also Law Reform (Miscellaneous Provisions) Act 1955 (ACT) s 14; Law Reform (Miscellaneous Provisions) Act (NT) s 15; Law Reform Act 1995 (Qld) s 5; Wrongs Act 1954 (Tas) s 2; Wrongs Act 1958 (Vic) s 25; Law Reform (Contributory Negligence and Tortfeasors' Contribution) Act 1947 (WA) s 3A. Note that the Law Reform (Contributory Negligence and Apportionment of Liability) Act 2001 (SA) does not use the concept of a 'concurrent and co-extensive' breach of duty, but it appears to be to the same effect — see s 3 as read with s 7.

35. See also Law Reform (Miscellaneous Provisions) Act 1955 (ACT) s 15(1); Law Reform (Miscellaneous Provisions) Act (NT) s 16; Law Reform Act 1995 (Qld) s 10(1); Law Reform (Contributory Negligence and Apportionment of Liability) Act 2001 (SA) s 7; Wrongs Act 1954 (Tas) s 4; Wrongs Act 1958 (Vic) s 26(1); Law Reform (Contributory Negligence and Tortfeasors' Contribution) Act 1947 (WA) ss 3A and 4(1)(a).

36. *Astley v Austrust Ltd* (1999) 197 CLR 1 at 22 [46]. There may also be a cause of action under statute. See, for example, comments made by the High Court in *HTW Valuers (Central Qld) Pty Ltd v Astonland Pty Ltd* [2004] HCA 54;(2004) 217 CLR 640; 211 ALR 79; 79 ALJR 190 at [9] and [13]–[14]; and the discussion of statutory claims for damages or other remedial orders under the Australian Consumer Law in **Chapter 16**.

a duty in contract; or where the claim is made in contract and the duties in contract and tort are not 'concurrent and co-extensive'.[37]

Intervening events

3.11   It may be alleged that the defendant's breach is no longer a cause because of an intervening event or a superseding cause other than contributory negligence. This issue is often discussed as part of the doctrine of *novus actus interveniens* (a new intervening event). Whether an intervening event will break the chain of causation or merely diminish the effect of the defendant's breach as a cause has been held to be determined by a consideration of whether the event was 'reasonably foreseeable' by the defendant.[38]

3.12   In *Monarch Steamship Co Ltd v Karlshamns Oljefabriker A/b*[39] the appellant breached its contract with the defendant to provide a seaworthy ship for the carriage of cargo from Manchuria to Sweden. The breach resulted in the vessel being delayed so that it could not reach Sweden before the outbreak of World War II. On the outbreak of war, the British Admiralty directed the ship to unload at Glasgow. The respondent then had to make new arrangements for the cargo to be shipped to Sweden, and claimed the cost of doing this as damages. The appellant argued that the intervention of the war had caused the damage, but this was rejected by the House of Lords. Their Lordships found that when the contract was made, in April 1939, the appellants 'ought to have foreseen that war might shortly break out and that any prolongation of the voyage might cause the loss of or diversion of the ship'. Consequently, the respondent was entitled to recover the cost of reshipping the cargo as damages.

3.13   The issue of intervening events breaking the chain of causation between the defendant's breach of contract and the plaintiff's loss was considered by the New South Wales Court of Appeal in *Alexander v Cambridge Credit Corp Ltd*.[40] Cambridge Credit argued that its auditors were in breach of contract because of their failure to demand an adjustment to its balance sheet for the end of the 1971 financial year. Had that adjustment been made, a receiver would have been appointed in September 1971 to wind up Cambridge Credit. But the receiver was not appointed until September 1974, and by then Cambridge Credit's debts had soared to $145 million. The

---

37.   Law Reform (Miscellaneous Provisions) Act 1965 (NSW) s 9(2); and see Law Reform (Miscellaneous Provisions) Act 1955 (ACT) s 15(4); Law Reform (Miscellaneous Provisions) Act (NT) s 16(2); Law Reform Act 1995 (Qld) s 10(2); Wrongs Act 1954 (Tas) s 4(1)(a); Wrongs Act 1958 (Vic) s 26(1); Law Reform (Contributory Negligence and Tortfeasors' Contribution) Act 1947 (WA) s 4(1)(a); or, in the case of the Law Reform (Contributory Negligence and Apportionment of Liability) Act 2001 (SA) s 7(3), the harm was not caused by negligent wrongdoing.

38.   *Monarch Steamship Co Ltd v Karlshamns Oljefabriker A/b* [1949] AC 196; *Alexander v Cambridge Credit Corp Ltd* (1987) 9 NSWLR 310 at 354–5 per McHugh JA (CA) (compare Glass JA, at 315, who prefers the contemplation test as propounded in *C Czarnikow Ltd v Koufos* [1969] 1 AC 350).

39.   [1949] AC 196.

40.   (1987) 9 NSWLR 310. See also the discussion of intervening events in tort claims and under statute at **2.14** and **16.14** respectively.

auditors' defence was that Cambridge Credit's plight was brought about by the Federal Government's budgetary measures of 1972–73, so any prior breaches of contract or negligence on their part were no longer causally relevant.

Rogers J rejected the auditors' defence and awarded $145 million in damages to Cambridge Credit. However, the auditors' appeal to the New South Wales Court of Appeal was successful by a 2:1 majority. The majority, Mahoney and McHugh JJA, in separate judgments, found that the continuing existence of Cambridge Credit was not of itself a cause of the loss, but their Honours then gave differing opinions on the applicable law. Mahoney JA, after rejecting the 'but for' test as the definitive test of causality in law,[41] reasoned that there was insufficient evidence to establish an actual link between the auditors' breach and Cambridge Credit's losses.[42] McHugh JA held that, in order to establish a causal connection between a breach of contract and the damage suffered, the plaintiff only needs to show that the breach was *a cause* of the loss; it need not be the *exclusive* cause, it need only have 'causally contributed' to the loss.[43] In this regard, his Honour accepted the 'but for' test as the 'leading test',[44] but in those cases where a number of factors combined to produce the loss or damage it is only a 'guide' and 'the ultimate question is whether, as a matter of common sense, the relevant act or omission was a cause'.[45] Causation was not satisfied in this case because the mere 'existence of a company ... cannot be a cause of its trading losses or profits'.[46] McHugh JA also held that a later event may be so potent as to overwhelm the original wrong, and in this case the economic change did overwhelm the auditors' breach.[47]

Glass JA, in dissent, agreed with McHugh JA that the 'but for' test was to be applied in a 'practical common sense way'[48] but, after applying it in that manner, his Honour found that the auditors' breach did in fact cause Cambridge Credit's loss.[49]

Divergences of opinion as to how to express the role of value judgments in the test of causation continue to trouble Australian courts.[50]

---

41. (1987) 9 NSWLR 310 at 335.
42. (1987) 9 NSWLR 310 at 334–5.
43. (1987) 9 NSWLR 310 at 350.
44. (1987) 9 NSWLR 310 at 352.
45. (1987) 9 NSWLR 310 at 358; compare *March v E & M H Stramare Pty Ltd* (1991) 171 CLR 506 at 532 per McHugh J.
46. (1987) 9 NSWLR 310 at 359.
47. (1987) 9 NSWLR 310 at 362–3.
48. (1987) 9 NSWLR 310 at 315.
49. (1987) 9 NSWLR 310 at 315–16.
50. Compare, for example, the separate judgments given in *Travel Compensation Fund v Robert Tambree t/as R Tambree and Associates* (2005) 224 CLR 627; 222 ALR 263; [2005] HCA 69.

REMOTENESS

Introduction

3.14 Even if the court finds that the damage was caused by the defendant's breach, it must not be too remote in law.[51] The classic test of remoteness in contract was stated by Baron Alderson in *Hadley v Baxendale*:

> Where two parties have made a contract which one of them has broken, the damages which the other party ought to receive in respect of such breach of contract should be such as may fairly and reasonably be considered either arising naturally, ie according to the usual course of things, from such breach of contract itself, or such as may be reasonably supposed to have been in the contemplation of both parties, at the time they made the contract, as the probable result of the breach of it.[52]

Usually it is only this part that is cited as the test of remoteness in contract,[53] but it is worth adding the explanation that follows:

> Now, if the special circumstances under which the contract was actually made were communicated by the plaintiffs to the defendants, and thus known to both parties, the damages resulting from the breach of such a contract which they would reasonably contemplate would be the amount of injury which would ordinarily follow from a breach of contract under these special circumstances so known and communicated. But, on the other hand, if these special circumstances were wholly unknown to the party breaking the contract, he, at the most, could only be supposed to have had in his contemplation the amount of injury which would arise generally, and in the great multitude of cases not affected by any special circumstances, from such a breach of contract. For, had the special circumstances been known, the parties might have specially provided for the breach of contract by special terms as to damages in that case, and of this advantage it would be very unjust to deprive them. Now the above principles are those by which we think the jury ought to be guided in estimating the damages arising out of any breach of contract.[54]

3.15 Baron Alderson's test of remoteness in *Hadley v Baxendale* entails two 'limbs'.[55] The first limb is where loss arises 'naturally' in the *usual* course of things 'as the probable result of the breach'. This is often characterised as a 'direct' loss. The resulting damage is presumed to have been within the contemplation of the parties. The defendant is prima facie liable for such loss; and the plaintiff does not need to adduce evidence that the defendant was aware of the risk of such damages. The second limb is where the loss is of an unusual type, sometimes characterised as an 'indirect' or 'special' loss. Here,

---

51. This also involves a factual investigation: see 3.15 and *Burns v MAN Automotive (Aust) Pty Ltd* (1986) 161 CLR 653 at 675; *Malik v Bank of Credit and Commerce International SA* [1998] AC 20 at 49–50.

52. (1854) 9 Exch 341 at 354; 156 ER 145 at 151.

53. See, for example, *Jackson v Royal Bank of Scotland* [2005] 2 All ER 71; [2005] UKHL 3 at [25] per Lord Hope, at [46] per Lord Walker.

54. (1854) 9 Exch 341 at 354; 156 ER 145 at 151.

55. *Victoria Laundry Ltd v Newman Industries Ltd* [1949] 2 KB 528 (CA).

the plaintiff must prove that the defendant knew or ought to have known that such loss would be 'the probable result of the breach'. Unlike the first limb, there is no presumption. Evidence must be adduced showing that the unusual damage or indirect loss was contemplated at the time the contract was made.[56]

3.16   The approach in *Hadley v Baxendale* is repeated in legislation dealing with the sale of goods.[57] For example, s 54(2) of the Sale of Goods Act 1923 (NSW), provides:

> The measure of damages for breach of warranty is the estimated loss directly and naturally resulting in the ordinary course of events from the breach of warranty.

There are corresponding provisions in other jurisdictions.[58] The second limb is preserved by s 55 of the Sale of Goods Act 1923 (NSW):

> Nothing in this Act shall affect the right of the buyer or seller to recover interest or special damages in any case where by law interest or special damages may be recoverable, or to recover money paid where the consideration for the payment of it has failed.

Again, there are corresponding provisions in other jurisdictions.[59]

3.17   The test for remoteness was analysed by the House of Lords in *C Czarnikow Ltd v Koufos*. Lord Reid concluded that:

> The crucial question is whether, on the information available to the defendant when the contract was made, he should, or the reasonable man in his position would, have realised that such loss was sufficiently likely to result from the breach of contract to make it proper to hold that the loss flowed naturally from the breach or that loss of that kind should have been within his contemplation.[60]

Lord Reid's statement has been cited with approval by the High Court on a number of occasions.[61] It is worth noting that, whereas Baron Alderson's formulation of the rule in *Hadley v Baxendale* refers to the contemplation of *both* parties, the focus of Lord Reid's statement is whether the *defendant* ought to have contemplated the loss. It is also worth noting that Lord Reid's reference to 'a loss of that kind' raises a similar principle to that discussed

---

56.   *Jackson v Royal Bank of Scotland* [2005] 2 All ER 71; [2005] UKHL 3 at [36] per Lord Hope; *Kollman v Watts* [1963] VR 396 at 400–1 per Lowe, Dean and Pape JJ (FC); compare *Unity Insurance Brokers Pty Ltd v Rocco Pezzano Pty Ltd* (1998) 192 CLR 603 at [24] per McHugh J.

57.   See, for example, acknowledgement of this in *Motium Pty Ltd v Arrow Electronics Australia Pty Ltd* [2011] WASCA 65 at [4]–[5] and [71].

58.   Sale of Goods Act 1954 (ACT) s 56; Sale of Goods Act 1972 (NT) s 54; Sale of Goods Act 1896 (Qld) s 54; Sale of Goods Act 1895 (SA) s 52; Sale of Goods Act 1896 (Tas) s 57; Goods Act 1958 (Vic) s 57; Sale of Goods Act 1895 (WA) s 52.

59.   Sale of Goods Act 1954 (ACT) s 57; Sale of Goods Act 1972 (NT) s 55; Sale of Goods Act 1896 (Qld) s 55; Sale of Goods Act 1895 (SA) s 53; Sale of Goods Act 1896 (Tas) s 58; Goods Act 1958 (Vic) s 60; Sale of Goods Act 1895 (WA) s 53.

60.   [1969] 1 AC 350 at 385.

61.   *Wenham v Ella* (1972) 127 CLR 454 at 471–2; *Burns v MAN Automotive* (1986) 161 CLR 653 at 667; *Commonwealth v Amann Aviation* (1991) 174 CKR 64 at 92; *Baltic Shipping v Dillon* (1993) 176 CLR 344 at 368.

at **2.40** in relation to tort damages — it is not the full extent of the loss that needs to have been contemplated, but merely the kind of loss.[62]

3.18   There is 'common ground between the two limbs' because, as explained by Lord Walker in *Jackson v Royal Bank of Scotland*, both are concerned with 'what the contract-breaker knew or must be taken to have known, so as to bring the loss within the reasonable contemplation of the parties'.[63] Lord Reid's restatement in *C Czarnikow Ltd v Koufos* of the *Hadley v Baxendale* rule indicates that the test really only involves a single question: whether, on the information available to the defendant when the contract was made, a reasonable person in the defendant's position would have had a loss of that kind within their contemplation as a likely consequence of the breach. The single question approach has been accepted by the High Court.[64] The benefit of continuing to identify the two limbs is that they highlight how the onus of proof might be discharged. A defendant is prima facie liable for direct losses or losses 'arising naturally' as a 'probable result of the breach'. The plaintiff need not adduce evidence that the defendant was aware of the risk of such damages. With the second limb, on the other hand, it will be up to the plaintiff to show that the defendant contemplated, or ought to have contemplated, the loss.

3.19   The case of *Victoria Laundry Ltd v Newman Industries Ltd*[65] illustrates how both limbs of the rule in *Hadley v Baxendale* operate.[66] In *Victoria Laundry* the defendant engineering company agreed to supply the plaintiff with a boiler by June to assist the plaintiff in its laundry business. In breach of contract the defendant delivered the boiler in November, some 20 weeks late. The plaintiff sued both for loss of normal business profits and loss of a lucrative dyeing contract for the government.

The Court of Appeal held that the plaintiff was entitled to recover, under the first limb of *Hadley v Baxendale*, normal business profits, that is, losses arising 'naturally' from the breach. But the claim for the dyeing contract or extra profits was unusual in that it was work not normally undertaken by the laundry, and therefore it was disallowed. For such a claim to succeed the plaintiff needed to show that the defendant knew of this potential extra loss and knew that such loss was likely to occur.[67]

---

62. *C Czarnikow Ltd v Koufos* [1969] 1 AC 350; *Alexander v Cambridge Credit Corp Ltd* (1987) 9 NSWLR 310; *National Australia Bank Pty Ltd v Nemur Varity Pty Ltd* [2002] VSCA 18; (2002) 4 VR 252, 269–270 [44] and 273–275 [49]–[55].

63. [2005] 2 All ER 71; [2005] UKHL 3 at [48]. See also *C Czarnikow Ltd v Koufos* [1969] 1 AC 350 per Lord Reid at 385.

64. *Commonwealth v Amann Aviation Pty Ltd* (1991) 174 CLR 64 at 92 per Mason CJ and Dawson J; cited with apparent approval in a unanimous judgment by French CJ, Gummow, Hayne, Heydon, and Kiefel JJ in *European Bank Limited v Robb Evans of Robb Evans & Associates* [2010] HCA 6 at [13].

65. [1949] 2 KB 528 (CA).

66. Although the House of Lords in *C Czarnikow Ltd v Koufos* [1969] 1 AC 350 cast doubt on the accuracy of Asquith LJ's interpretation of the rule in so far as it introduces the language of foreseeability; see also *Alexander v Cambridge Credit Corp Ltd* (1987) 9 NSWLR 310 at 363–6 per McHugh JA (CA).

67. [1949] 2 KB 528 at 540.

Contemplation compared with reasonable foreseeability

3.20   In *C Czarnikow Ltd v Koufos*,[68] when expanding on the degree of contemplation required, the House of Lords suggested asking whether the defendant ought to have known that, as a consequence of the breach, the loss was 'liable to result', 'not unlikely', 'a serious possibility' or 'a real danger'. Their Lordships did not favour the suggestion in *Victoria Laundry Ltd v Newman Industries Ltd*[69] that the test for remoteness in contract was the same as the torts test of 'reasonable foreseeability'.

The result of this difference is that remoteness is easier to satisfy in tort than in contract. This is because 'a great many extremely unlikely results'[70] that would not be within the contemplation of the parties as a *likely* consequence of the breach are reasonably foreseeable and would give rise to liability in torts. A wider scope is seen as justified for torts because parties to a contract are free to negotiate terms that manage or even exclude liability for breach; whereas there is no such opportunity in a tortious context.[71]

3.21   The application of different tests of remoteness in tort and contract was challenged by the English Court of Appeal in *H Parsons (Livestock) Ltd v Uttley Ingham & Co.*[72] In that case, the defendant agreed to make and supply a metal, bulk-feed storage hopper for the plaintiff to use on its farm for feeding pignuts to pigs. The defendant negligently installed the hopper by failing to leave a ventilator lid open. Unaware of this, the plaintiff stored the pignuts in the hopper and the nuts went mouldy. The pigs were fed the mouldy nuts from the hopper, became ill, and many died from a rare infection.

The plaintiff sued in contract and claimed damages including a substantial loss of profits. The trial judge found that neither party could 'reasonably have contemplated' a 'real danger' 'or serious possibility' that the pigs would become ill and die from eating mouldy nuts. Thus, in contract, the defendant was not liable. The trial judge also found that the illness was reasonably foreseeable under the tort test, but unfortunately the plaintiff had not sued in tort.

The plaintiff appealed and succeeded. Lord Denning MR said he could not see a distinction between the tests of contemplation and foreseeability and he would not 'swim in this sea of semantic exercises', especially where the causes of action could be in both tort and contract.[73] Instead of distinguishing the causes of action, Lord Denning drew a distinction between economic and physical loss. In his Lordship's view, the more-difficult-to-satisfy contemplation test only applied to economic loss, such as loss of profits, but when dealing with physical loss, the broader 'reasonable foreseeability' tort test applied.

68.   [1969] 1 AC 350.

69.   [1949] 2 KB 528 (CA).

70.   *C Czarnikow Ltd v Koufos* [1969] 1 AC 350 at 385.

71.   *C Czarnikow Ltd v Koufos* [1969] 1 AC 350 per Lord Reid at 385–386; and per Lord Pearce at 413.

72.   [1978] QB 791 (CA).

73.   [1978] QB 791 at 802.

Thus, in Lord Denning's view, the tort test applied if physical loss could be shown, even though no action in tort may have been pleaded. Applying this to the facts, he found that the physical damage suffered by the plaintiff (that is, the death of the pigs and veterinary expenses) was reasonably foreseeable, but the lost profit on future sales was not.[74]

Scarman and Orr LJJ in *H Parsons (Livestock) Ltd v Uttley Ingham & Co* agreed with Lord Denning that the distinction between the contract and tort tests might be absurd but, nonetheless, they rejected his distinction between economic and physical loss.[75] Scarman and Orr LJJ found in favour of the plaintiff by referring to the trial judge's finding that the 'natural result' of feeding toxic food to animals is illness, and perhaps death. This, they thought, brought the facts within the first limb of *Hadley v Baxendale* because there was a 'real danger' or 'serious possibility' of damage.[76]

3.22   In *Commonwealth v Amann Aviation Pty Ltd* Deane J referred to 'the gradual assimilation of the tests of 'within the contemplation of the parties' (in contract) and "reasonably foreseeable" (in tort)',[77] and then cited *H Parsons (Livestock) Ltd v Uttley Ingham & Co* as an example. But his Honour did not speculate on the future course of this so-called 'gradual assimilation'.[78] For the time being, the difference between the tests appears to be well-established in Australian courts. For example, in *Burns v MAN Automotive*, Wilson, Deane and Dawson JJ accepted that *Koufos* was correct.[79] More recently, the High Court acknowledged that '[a]nalysis of the tests for remoteness of damage in contract, in tort and under s 82 [of the Trade Practices Act 1974 (Cth)] may make a difference on the particular facts of some cases'.[80]

Contemplation under the second limb in *Hadley v Baxendale*

3.23   The second limb is concerned with damage of an unusual type, sometimes characterised as a 'special' or 'indirect' loss. The innocent party must prove that the guilty party knew, or ought to have known, that that type of damage would be the 'probable result of the breach'. However, merely to show knowledge on the part of the defendant is insufficient; the defendant must have accepted the risk of the unusual loss. It need not be a term in the

---

74.   [1978] QB 791 at 802–4.

75.   [1978] QB 791 at 806–7.

76.   [1978] QB 791 at 812–3.

77.   (1991) 174 CLR 64 at 116.

78.   See also *Kenny & Good Pty Ltd v MGICA (1992) Ltd* (1999) 199 CLR 413 at [44]–[46] per McHugh J; *National Australia Bank Ltd v Nemur Varity Pty Ltd* (2002) 4 VR 252 at 268–70 per Batt JA (CA).

79.   (1986) 161 CLR 653 at 667. See also *Alexander v Cambridge Credit Corporation Ltd* (1987) 9 NSWLR 310 at 364–6 (CA) and *Kenny & Good Pty Ltd v MGICA (1992) Ltd* (1999) 199 CLR 413 at [46] per McHugh J; *National Australia Bank Ltd v Nemur Varity Pty Ltd* (2002) 4 VR 252 at 270; [2002] VSCA 18 at [43]–[45]; per Batt JA.

80.   *HTW Valuers (Central Qld) Pty Ltd v Astonland Pty Ltd* (2004) 217 CLR 640; 211 ALR 79; 79 ALJR 190 at [14]; [2004] HCA 54.

contract[81] and an oral undertaking may be sufficient.[82] In *Panalpina International Transport Ltd v Densil Underwear Ltd*[83] the plaintiff agreed to arrange for the carriage of the defendant's goods from London to Nigeria. The defendant made it clear that it was important that the goods arrive in Nigeria in time for the Christmas trade, but there was no provision in the parties' contract to that effect. The plaintiff delayed in sending the goods and they did not arrive in Nigeria until 21 December. It was held liable for the increased losses arising from the fact that the goods could not be sold at the higher prices prevailing during December.

3.24 The undertaking to bear the extra loss may be implied.[84] In deciding whether it is implied the court examines the defendant's actual knowledge up until the time the contract was made.[85] It will also consider the nature of the contract, for example, whether it is between business people, the price and so on. If, for example, the defendant received something extra as part of the price for performance, it will be easier to draw the inference that the defendant has accepted the risk for unusual losses because the risk is reflected in the price.

In 2008 the House of Lords revisited remoteness.[86] Three judges felt it necessary to restate the test in an attempt to incorporate this aspect, but they gave separate judgments with slightly different formulations. Lord Hoffmann suggested liability should be limited by 'what would reasonably have been regarded by the contracting party as significant for the purposes of the risk he was undertaking'.[87] Lord Hope said 'the question is whether the loss was a type of loss for which the party can be reasonably assumed to have assumed responsibility';[88] and Lord Walker felt that 'what is most important is the common expectation, objectively assessed, on the basis of which the parties are entering into their contract'.[89] It remains to be seen to what extent these formulations of remoteness influence Australian courts.

MITIGATION

Introduction

3.25 The damages to be awarded to the plaintiff may be reduced either where there has been a failure by the plaintiff to take reasonable steps to

---

81. *C Czarnikow Ltd v Koufos* [1969] 1 AC 350 at 421–2 per Lord Upjohn.
82. *Wright v Langlands Foundry Co* (1874) 5 AJR 113; *Panalpina International Transport Ltd v Densil Underwear Ltd* [1981] 1 Lloyd's Rep 187.
83. [1981] 1 Lloyd's Rep 187.
84. *Robophone Finance Facilities Ltd v Blank* [1966] 1 WLR 1428 at 1448.
85. *Kollman v Watts* [1963] VR 396 (FC). See also *Jackson v Royal Bank of Scotland* [2005] 2 All ER 71; [2005] UKHL 3 at [36]–[37] per Lord Hope.
86. *Transfield Shipping Inc v Mercator Shipping Inc (The Achilleas)* [2008] UKHL 48; [2009] 1 AC 61.
87. [2008] UKHL 48 at [22].
88. [2008] UKHL 48 at [32].
89. [2008] UKHL 48 at [78].

reduce loss or where steps have been taken which have in fact reduced the loss. Conversely, where the plaintiff does attempt reasonable mitigation and this increases the loss, that increased loss is recoverable as damages. Where reasonable steps at mitigation are taken, then irrespective of the success of those steps, the cost of discharging the 'duty' is recoverable as damages.

'Duty' to mitigate

3.26 The plaintiff always bears a legal responsibility or 'duty' to avoid unnecessary losses. Viscount Haldane LC in *British Westinghouse Electric and Manufacturing Co Ltd v Underground Electric Railways Co of London Ltd* observed that the principle of mitigation imposes on a plaintiff:

> … the duty of taking all reasonable steps to mitigate the loss consequent on the breach, and debars him from claiming any part of the damage which is due to his neglect to take such steps.[90]

Similarly, O'Connor J in *Hasell v Bagot, Shakes and Lewis Ltd* said:

> There is no question that it is one of the principles on which damages are assessed that a party to an agreement suffering injury from the other party's breach of its terms is bound to exercise reasonable care in mitigating the injurious consequences of the breach, and is not entitled to recover from the party in default any damage which the exercise of reasonable care on his part would have prevented from arising.[91]

The 'duty' of the plaintiff to mitigate loss is of a special type. A breach of the 'duty' is not actionable, it merely reduces the damages payable by the defendant. Further, if the plaintiff obtains a benefit through mitigation the defendant obtains a credit for this as well.

3.27 The plaintiff's attempt to mitigate or minimise loss caused by the defendant's breach should be 'reasonable'.[92] But what is meant by 'reasonable'? Is it reasonable, for example, to accept an offer of help from the defendant such as alternative performance or another contract? In *Payzu Ltd v Saunders*[93] the defendant agreed to sell 400 pieces of silk, to be delivered in monthly instalments to the plaintiff for a certain price and upon one month's credit. Due to a bona fide mistake about the plaintiff's solvency, the defendant refused further deliveries unless paid in cash. Thus, there was a repudiation of the contract and an offer of a new one. The plaintiff accepted the defendant's repudiation but refused the new offer. But, in a rising market, the plaintiff was unable to buy silk elsewhere for the same price, so he sued the defendant for breach of contract and claimed damages on the basis of the difference between the market price and the contract price. The English Court of Appeal

---

90. [1912] AC 673 at 689.

91. (1911) 13 CLR 374 at 388; see also *Frost v Knight* (1872) LR 7 Ex 111 at 115 per Cockburn CJ; *Jamal v Moolla Dawood Sons and Co* [1916] 1 AC 175 at 179; *Wenham v Ella* (1972) 127 CLR 454 at 463-4 per Menzies J.

92. *Unity Insurance Brokers Pty Ltd v Rocco Pezzano Pty Ltd* (1998) 192 CLR 603 at [3] per Brennan CJ; *Wenkart v Pitman* (1998) 46 NSWLR 502 at 523 per Powell JA (CA).

93. [1919] 2 KB 581.

held that the defendant, by his refusal to deliver, had repudiated the contract; nonetheless, it would have been reasonable for the plaintiff to have accepted the defendant's offer to continue to deliver if paid in cash. Thus, the plaintiff's damages were limited to the loss of value of the credit facility.

3.28   Offers of help from the defendant are common in employment cases and service contracts. The plaintiff, however, will not be required to accept a new offer of employment from the defendant if the new job is at a lower status, even if at the same pay. In *TCN Channel 9 v Hayden Enterprises Pty Ltd*[94] the appellant dismissed a television celebrity and offered him new employment, but on the condition that he release the appellant from any claims arising out of the dismissal. It was held[95] that it was reasonable for the celebrity to reject this offer and, in so doing, there was no breach of his duty to mitigate.[96]

Credit for benefits

3.29   If the defendant's breach enables the plaintiff to obtain benefits not otherwise available, the plaintiff's gain reduces the defendant's liability. This is illustrated in *British Westinghouse Electric & Manufacture Co Ltd v Underground Electric Railways Co of London*.[97] British Westinghouse supplied the Underground with electric turbines which, in breach of the contract, were deficient in power. The Underground discovered the breach after using the turbines. It replaced them with more efficient turbines and it sued British Westinghouse for damages for breach of contract in order to recover the cost of the new machines. The claim was disallowed by the House of Lords. Their Lordships found that the efficiency of the new turbines meant that over the time period of the expected life of the British Westinghouse machines, the Underground would have saved that cost, and more, by reason of the lesser amount of fuel required by the newer machines. The subsequent purchase of the new machines was one in which 'the person whose contract was broken took a reasonable and prudent course quite naturally arising out of the circumstances in which he was placed by the breach'.[98] The Underground's benefit in taking this reasonable course was to be taken into account in determining the measure of damages. Thus the House of Lords held that the Underground was only able to obtain damages for the loss suffered when using the British Westinghouse machines. It was not able to recover anything for the period after acquisition of the new machines.

---

94.   (1989) 16 NSWLR 130 (CA).

95.   (1989) 16 NSWLR 130 at 158 per Hope JA.

96.   It is also unreasonable to expect a plaintiff to mitigate loss through an act injurious to the plaintiff's reputation: see *James Finlay & Co Ltd v NV Kwik Hoo Tong Handel Maatschappij* [1929] 1 KB 400 and *Metal Fabrications (Vic) Pty Ltd v Kelcey* [1986] VR 507.

97.   [1912] AC 673.

98.   [1912] AC 673 at 691 per Viscount Haldane LC.

Cost of mitigation and increasing the loss

3.30   The plaintiff can recover the cost of reasonable mitigation even if it increases the loss.[99] The plaintiff is not obliged, however, to do what he or she cannot afford to do, especially where the financial difficulty is due to the defendant's breach.[100] In *Newmarket Corp Pty Ltd v Kee-vee Properties Pty Ltd* McLure J held:

> … an injured party is only obliged to take such steps as are reasonable and need not resort to measures that are costly, complex or extravagant as where the expenditure in mitigation would exceed the loss.[101]

Anticipatory breach

3.31   Mitigation and anticipatory breach raise special issues. An anticipatory breach occurs where, prior to the date set by the contract for its performance, one of the parties makes it clear that its obligations will not be performed. This will amount to a repudiation or renunciation of its contractual obligations. An anticipatory breach may also be constituted by an 'inability to perform' the contract.[102]

Where there is an anticipatory breach, the innocent party has to choose between either affirming the contract or accepting the repudiation and terminating the contract. Affirming the contract allows the innocent party to ignore the anticipated breach and hold the other party to the contract. Here, there is no duty to mitigate because the contract remains on foot until the time for performance arrives.[103] However, if the plaintiff accepts the repudiation and terminates the contract prior to the time for performance, a duty to mitigate arises immediately. The plaintiff is able to seek immediate damages, although the date for assessment will still be the date set for performance: see **3.39**.

3.32   The choice between affirmation and accepting repudiation can have important practical consequences. First, the quantum of damages may differ. For example, if a buyer accepts a seller's anticipatory breach or repudiation and terminates the contract, the buyer may, in an attempt to mitigate the loss, buy substitute goods in the marketplace. If the goods drop in value by the date of performance, the buyer will still recover as damages the higher cost, so long as the buyer's attempt at mitigation was reasonable. The second practical consequence to consider in cases of anticipatory breach is that because affirmation does not place a 'duty' on the plaintiff to mitigate, the plaintiff need not consider offers of alternative performance or alternative contracts.

---

99.   *Simonius Vischer & Co v Holt & Thompson* [1979] 2 NSWLR 322 at 355–6 per Samuels JA (CA).

100.   *Burns v MAN Automotive* (1986) 161 CLR 653 at 659 per Gibbs CJ and 677 per Brennan J.

101.   [2003] WASC 157 at [172].

102.   *Sunbird Plaza Ltd v Maloney* (1988) 166 CLR 245 at 260–1 per Mason CJ.

103.   *Huppert v Stock Options of Australia Pty Ltd* (1965) 112 CLR 414.

This is illustrated in *Shindler v Northern Raincoat Co Ltd*.[104] An employer purported to repudiate an employment contract with an employee, then offered the employee substitute employment. However, the employee was not actually dismissed until some months later. Diplock J (as he then was) held that in this period the duty to mitigate had not been activated and therefore the alternative employment offer could be ignored. Further, even if there had been a duty to mitigate, the court found it reasonable for the employee to refuse the alternative contract. *Shindler* may be compared with *Brace v Calder*,[105] where Rigby LJ held that an offer of substitute employment 'on the same terms' serving two partners instead of four was a reasonable offer which should have been accepted.[106]

3.33   As mentioned above, the general principle is that where a contract is affirmed there is no duty to mitigate. The breadth of that principle, however, was qualified by the House of Lords in *White & Carter Ltd v McGregor*.[107] White and Carter agreed to a three-year contract to advertise McGregor's garage business by displaying advertising plates on rubbish bins in the area. The contract required McGregor to pay a weekly sum and to contribute towards the cost of the plates. But on the same day the agreement was reached the contract was repudiated by McGregor. White and Carter refused to accept the repudiation and affirmed the contract by displaying the unwanted advertising for the full three years. It then sued in contract for the price, claiming that it had been under no obligation to mitigate its losses since it had not terminated the contract. The House of Lords accepted White and Carter's argument by a bare majority. Lords Hodson and Tucker accepted the argument without qualification, but Lord Reid, also in the majority, noted two limitations. First, if the defendant's cooperation is necessary in order for the plaintiff to perform the contract, then the defendant's failure to cooperate will prevent the plaintiff from earning the contract price. This qualification was applied in *Hounslow London Borough Council v Twickenham Garden Developments Ltd*[108] by Megarry J, who distinguished the facts in *White & Carter*.[109]

3.34   The second restriction referred to by Lord Reid in *White & Carter* was:

> It may well be that, if it can be shown that a person has no legitimate interest, financial or otherwise, in performing the contract rather than claiming damages he ought not to be allowed to saddle the other party with an additional burden with no benefit to himself. If a party has no interest to enforce a stipulation, he cannot in general enforce it: so it might be said that, if a party has no interest to insist on a particular remedy, he ought not to be allowed to insist on it.[110]

---

104. [1960] 2 All ER 239.
105. [1895] 2 QB 253 (CA).
106. [1895] 2 QB 253 at 263–4.
107. [1962] AC 413.
108. [1971] Ch 233.
109. See also *Shevill v Builders' Licensing Board* (1982) 149 CLR 621; *Progressive Mailing House Pty Ltd v Tabali Pty Ltd* (1985) 157 CLR 17 at 44–8 per Brennan J.
110. [1962] AC 413 at 431.

This limitation has been applied in a number of charter-party cases. In *Clea Shipping Corp v Bulk Oil International Ltd (the Alaskan Trader) (No 2)* [111] the owners let their vessel to a charterer for a two-year period. However, 10 months after delivery the vessel was off-hire for six months because it needed extensive repairs. During that time the market cost of hiring such vessels dropped substantially. Before the repairs were finished the charterer indicated to the owners that it would not further employ the vessel. The owners, however, refused to accept this repudiation and, for the remaining eight months of the charter, maintained the vessel ready to sail in accordance with the charterer's original orders. The dispute first went to arbitration on the issue of whether the owners of the vessel were entitled to the hire charges during those eight months or whether they should have accepted the repudiation and recovered damages. The arbitrator decided in favour of the charterer. The owners appealed. Lloyd J considered the previous decisions, including *White & Carter*, and summed them up by observing:

> … there comes a point at which the court will cease, on general equitable principles, to allow the innocent party to enforce his contract according to its strict legal terms. How one defines that point is obviously a matter of some difficulty, for it involves drawing a line between conduct which is merely unreasonable (see per Lord Reid in *White and Carter v McGregor* [112] criticising the Lord President in *Langford Co Ltd v Dutch*) [113] and conduct which is *wholly* unreasonable (see per Kerr J in *The Odenfeld*) [114] … The court is not exercising a dispensing power; nor is it rewriting an improvident contract. It is simply refusing a certain kind of relief. [115]

In dismissing the appeal brought by the owners, Lloyd J said the question of whether the owners' action had been wholly unreasonable was one for the arbitrator, who had correctly applied the relevant principles and found that the owners' conduct had been wholly unreasonable. Lloyd J also pointed out that in the United States the courts take an uncomplicated view by insisting that the duty to mitigate damages arises irrespective of the plaintiff's election to affirm the contract or accept repudiation.

Anticipatory breach and specific performance

3.35 The innocent party may affirm the contract by seeking specific performance (see Chapter 7) instead of accepting the repudiation by terminating the contract. This does not preclude a later termination where there are further breaches of the contract. [116]

---

111. [1984] 1 All ER 129; [1983] 2 Lloyd's Rep 645.

112. [1962] AC 413 at 429–30.

113. 1952 SC 15.

114. [1978] 2 Lloyd's Rep 357 at 374.

115. [1984] 1 All ER 129 at 136–7; [1983] 2 Lloyd's Rep 645 at 651.

116. *Ogle v Comboyuro Investments Pty Ltd* (1976) 136 CLR 444; compare *Sunbird Plaza Ltd v Maloney* (1988) 166 CLR 245 at 260 per Mason CJ.

ASSESSMENT

Date of assessment

3.36 The general principle is that damages are assessed at the date of breach. The principle is not, however, applied rigidly, as noted by Mason CJ in *Johnson v Perez*:

> There is a general rule that damages for torts or breach of contract are assessed at the date of breach or when the cause of action arises. But this rule is not universal; it must give way in particular cases to solutions best adapted to giving an injured plaintiff that amount in damages which will most fairly compensate him for the wrong he has suffered … The general rule that damages are assessed as at the date of breach or when the cause of action arose has been applied more uniformly in contract than in tort and for good reason. But even in contract cases courts depart from the general rule whenever it is necessary to do so in the interests of justice.[117]

3.37 In *Johnson v Perez* the majority of the High Court endorsed the approach of the House of Lords in *Johnson v Agnew*.[118] In the latter case the purchaser of land was in default of the contract where the market price was falling. Title to the land then passed to a third party on a mortgagee sale. The vendor sought damages both at common law and in equity in lieu of specific performance. In a unanimous decision, the House of Lords fixed the date of assessment as that on which specific performance was lost to the vendor. The date of that loss was the date the mortgagees contracted to sell the property. Lord Wilberforce noted that although the general rule was to look to the date of breach, this was not an absolute rule if to follow it would give rise to an injustice.[119]

3.38 The general rule under sale of goods legislation both in Australia and the United Kingdom reflects the common law; that is, damages are assessed at the date of breach.[120] But this may be varied both in the assessment of damages in equity and at common law in order to do justice. So, in *Millstream Pty Ltd v Schultz*[121] damages were assessed at the date of the trial. The defendant failed to deliver a herd of fallow deer by the contract date. Initially, the plaintiff sought specific performance, but at the trial an election was made to terminate the contract.

3.39 In cases of anticipatory breach the innocent party has a right to terminate or affirm. Where there is an affirmation the date of performance is also the relevant date for the assessment of damages. The same date applies where there is a termination; that is, damages are to be assessed at the date

---

117. (1989) 166 CLR 351 at 355–6.
118. [1980] AC 367.
119. [1980] AC at 400–1. See also *Burger King Corporation v Hungry Jack's Pty Ltd* [2001] NSWCA 187 at [643] and [738].
120. See, for example, ss 52 and 53 of the Sale of Goods Act 1923 (NSW), s 51(3) Sale of Goods Act 1979 (UK).
121. [1980] 1 NSWLR 547.

of performance and not the date of the election to terminate.[122] As noted by Atkin LJ in *Millet v Van Heck & Co*:

> … damages are to be fixed in reference to the time for performance of the contract subject to questions of mitigation.[123]

The principle of mitigation may require the plaintiff to consider purchasing substitutes or alternative modes of performance prior to the performance date. Provided the plaintiff acts reasonably, the cost of such mitigation is recoverable even if it increases the loss: see **3.30**.

In the case of an anticipatory breach where the damages claim is brought prior to the date for performance, the court must assess the market price 'as best it can'.[124] Difficulties arise, however, because the court will not shut its eyes to known facts at the trial date. That was in issue in *Golden Strait Corporation v Nippon Yusen Kubishka Kaisha*.[125] On 10 July 1998 the owners of the ship known as the *Golden Victory* agreed to a charter to the respondents until 6 December 2005. Either party was allowed to cancel if war or hostilities broke out between two or more named countries which included the United States, the United Kingdom and Iraq. On 14 December 2001, when the charter still had almost four years to run, the respondents breached the charter by repudiation. On 17 December 2001 the shipowners accepted the repudiation and claimed damages. The owners' claim was successful, but before the arbitrator could assess the damages the Second Gulf War erupted in March 2003. The respondents argued that had the charter still been on foot at that time, it would have exercised its contractual right to cancel. Thus, it submitted, the damages should only be awarded for the period between the date that repudiation was accepted on 17 December 2001 and the outbreak of war in March 2003. The owners disputed this and submitted that damages should be assessed at the date of breach or by reference to what was lost on 17 December 2001. At that time war was a mere possibility to be considered, but was not probable and therefore under the owner's calculation the damages should have been awarded until 6 December 2005. The arbitrator, Langley J and the Court of Appeal all found in favour of the respondents. The House of Lords also found in favour of the respondents by a 3:2 majority. In the majority Lord Scott said:

> If a contract for performance over a period has come to an end by reason of a repudiatory breach but might, if it had remained on foot, have terminated early on the occurrence of a particular event, the chance of that event happening must … be taken into account in an assessment of the damages payable for

122. *Millet v Van Heck & Co* [1921] 2 KB 369; *Tai Hing Cotton Mill Ltd v Kamsing Knitting Factory* [1979] AC 91 at 102 (PC); *Hoffman v Cali* [1985] 1 Qd R 253 at 257 per Campbell J and 261–4 per McPherson J (FC).
123. [1921] 2 KB 369 at 377.
124. *Melachrino v Nickoll* [1920] 1 KB 693 at 699; *Hoffman v Cali* [1985] 1 Qd R 253 (Full Court).
125. [2007] UKHL 12.

the breach. And if it is certain that the event will happen, the damages must be assessed on that footing.[126]

Once-and-for-all rule

3.40   An award of damages is an award 'once and for all'. That is, it can only be made in a lump sum; periodic payments cannot be given.[127] There are three exceptions. First, as in tort (see **2.60**), where there is more than one cause of action the rule does not apply. An example is an instalment contract. Successive breaches of the instalment give rise to different causes of action, and therefore the once-and-for-all rule applies to each cause of action and not generally. Second, and in a similar vein, the once-and-for-all rule does not apply if there is a 'continuing breach'. Whether a breach is a 'continuing breach' will depend on the contract's construction and, in particular, whether it requires the maintenance of a 'state or condition of affairs'. In *Larking v Great Western (Nepean) Gravel Ltd* Dixon J observed:

> If a covenantor undertakes that he will do a definite act and omits to do it within the time allowed for the purpose, he has broken his covenant finally and his continued failure to do the act is nothing but a failure to remedy his past breach and not the commission of any further breach of his covenant. His duty is not considered as persisting and, so to speak, being forever renewed until he actually does that which he promised. On the other hand, if his covenant is to maintain a state or condition of affairs, as, for instance, maintaining a building in repair, keeping the insurance of a life on foot, or affording a particular kind of lateral or vertical support to a tenement, then a further breach arises in every successive moment of time during which the state or condition is not as promised, during which, to pursue the examples, the building is out of repair, the life uninsured, or the particular support unprovided.[128]

The effect of a continuing breach is that damages will only be recoverable for past loss accrued by the date of assessment.[129] The court will not try to anticipate the damage which may be caused by the defendant's future breaches. Third, there are statutory exceptions such as those contained in Pt 6 Div 5 (Interim Payments) of the Civil Procedure Act 2005 (NSW).

Heads of damage

3.41   There are various heads of damage under which the plaintiff may recover depending on the type of contract and breach in issue. In *Commonwealth v Amann Aviation Pty Ltd* Mason CJ and Dawson J observed:

> … the expressions 'expectation damages', 'damages for loss of profits', 'reliance damages' and 'damages for wasted expenditure' are simply manifestations of the central principle enunciated in *Robinson v Harman* rather

---

126. [2007] UKHL 12 at [30].
127. See *Todorovic v Waller* (1981) 150 CLR 402; and see **2.59**.
128. (1940) 64 CLR 221 at 236.
129. See, for example, Uniform Civil Procedure Rules 2005 (NSW) Pt 30 r 30.3.

than discrete and truly alternative measures of damages which a party not in breach may elect to claim.[130]

So, the plaintiff need not choose between the various heads; if applicable they are, subject to the rule against allowing 'double recovery',[131] cumulative.[132] The onus of proof is on the plaintiff.[133]

Expectation damages[134]

3.42   This head of damages, sometimes referred to as 'damage for loss of profits' or 'the loss of a bargain', is the most common in breach of contract cases. Even if the 'contract is not susceptible of specific performance, the other party is legally entitled to expect its performance';[135] and should be compensated for the failure to perform at least in so far as money can achieve this. The court will objectively assess[136] what the plaintiff has lost by comparing the position the plaintiff would have been in if the contract had been performed properly with the actual position created by the breach. As explained by Mason CJ and Dawson J in *Commonwealth v Amann Aviation Pty Ltd*:

> In the ordinary course of commercial dealings, a party supplying goods or rendering services will enter a contract with a view to securing a profit, that is to say, that a party will expect a certain margin of gain to be achieved in addition to the recouping of any expenses reasonably incurred by it in the discharge of its contractual obligations. It is for this reason that expectation damages are often described as damages for loss of profits. Damages recoverable as lost profits are constituted by the combination of expenses justifiably incurred by a plaintiff in the discharge of contractual obligations and any amount by which gross receipts would have exceeded those expenses. This second amount is net profit.[137]

Their Honours went on to explain that even if no net profit would have been generated for the plaintiff, it could still recover damages for wasted expenditure or reliance damages.[138] To claim expectation damages the contract will usually have to be terminated.[139]

Under common law, expectation damages were generally not available to a purchaser of real estate if the vendor, without fraud, was incapable of

---

130.   (1991) 174 CLR 64 at 82.

131.   See *TC Industrial Plant Pty Ltd v Roberts Queensland Ltd* (1963) 180 CLR 130.

132.   (1991) 174 CLR 64 at 161 per McHugh J.

133.   (1991) 174 CLR 64 at 80 per Mason CJ and Dawson J.

134.   Three types of damage are often identified using the terminology made famous when Fuller & Purdue named three 'interests' a plaintiff might have when quantifying contract damages: the 'expectation' interest, the 'reliance' interest and the 'restitution' interest. See 'The Reliance Interest in Contract Damages' (1936) 46 *Yale LJ* 52 and 373.

135.   *Marks v GIO Australia Holdings Ltd* (1998) 196 CLR 494 at 502 per Gaudron J.

136.   *Commonwealth v Amann Aviation Pty Ltd* (1991) 174 CLR 64 at 80 per Mason CJ and Dawson J.

137.   (1991) 174 CLR 64 at 81.

138.   (1991) 174 CLR 64 at 81.

139.   *Sunbird Plaza Pty Ltd v Maloney* (1988) 166 CLR 245 at 260–1 per Mason CJ; and see 3.5.

delivering a good title. This is known as the rule in *Bain v Fothergill*.[140] However, doubts have been expressed about its continued relevance;[141] and it has been abolished by statute in some jurisdictions.[142]

The ability to claim damages to cover an expected profit is a significant difference between contract and tort. While damages in contract and tort are both compensatory in nature, the compensation is for slightly different things. The aim in contract is to place the plaintiff in the position they would have been in if the contract had been performed properly; whereas in tort, the aim is to place the plaintiff in the position they would have been in if the tort had not been committed.[143] If, for example, the seller of a business warrants that the disclosed turnover figures are correct, while fraudulently knowing this to be untrue, it will make a difference as to whether the buyer's claim for damages is made in contract or tort. If suing in contract, the buyer will be able to claim lost profits on the basis of the promised turnover figures being true; whereas if suing in tort, the buyer would not have bought the business if the fraud had not taken place, so the measure of damages would not include the expectation loss.

Reliance damages

3.43   Reliance damages represent the plaintiff's actual costs or wasted expenditure as a result of relying on the defendant's contractual promise. Such damages have been awarded to cover the costs of equipping a salvage operation contemplated by the contract,[144] the costs of supplying a team of men ready to work[145] and the costs or damages associated with employing a subcontractor.[146]

Subject to the rule against allowing 'double recovery',[147] the plaintiff may claim both expectation and reliance damages.[148] Usually, the plaintiff's major head of damage is expectation damages — unless, of course, they are not available or difficult to prove. This was the case in *McRae v Commonwealth Disposals Commission*,[149] where the plaintiff's major head of damage was reliance damages which represented their large costs thrown away in organising a

---

140. (1874) LR 7 HL 158. See discussion of the rule and its origin by Stephen J in *Godfrey Constructions Pty Ltd v Kanangra Park Pty Ltd* [1972] HCA 36; (1972) 128 CLR 529 at 548–549.

141. See *Holmark Construction Co Pty Ltd v Tsoukris* (1988) NSW ConvR 55,397 at 57,679–80 per Priestley JA; *Government Employee Superannuation Board v Martin* (1997) 19 WAR 224 at 253–256 per Ipp J; compare apparent acceptance of the rule in *IGA Distribution Pty Ltd v King & Taylor Pty Ltd* [2002] VSC 440 at [253]–[254] per Nettle J (*obiter*).

142. The rule has been abolished in NSW, Qld and NT. See the Conveyancing Act 1919 (NSW) s 54B; Property Law Act 1974 (Qld) s 68(1); and Law of Property Act 2000 (NT) s 70 respectively.

143. See the principles discussed at **3.1** for contract and **2.1** for torts.

144. *McRae v Commonwealth* (1951) 84 CLR 377 at 419.

145. *Carr v J A Berriman Pty Ltd* (1953) 89 CLR 327.

146. *Carr v J A Berriman Pty Ltd* (1953) 89 CLR 327.

147. See *T C Industrial Plant Pty Ltd v Roberts Queensland Ltd* (1963) 180 CLR 130.

148. *Commonwealth v Amann Aviation Pty Ltd* (1991) 174 CLR 64 at 84–5; compare *Anglia Television Ltd v Reed* [1972] 1 QB 60 at 63–4 per Lord Denning MR.

149. (1951) 84 CLR 377.

salvage expedition from Melbourne to New Guinea searching for a non-existent oil tanker. Expectation damages were not available because it was 'impossible to value a non-existent thing'.[150]

Reliance damages were also the major head of damage in *Commonwealth v Amann Aviation Pty Ltd*.[151] In that case the Commonwealth maintained regular aerial surveillance of Australia's northern coastline for various purposes including quarantine. Skywest Airlines Pty Ltd agreed to perform this aerial surveillance until March 1987. Prior to that date the Commonwealth decided against renewing the Skywest contract and invited tenders for the provision of the service for three years. Amann's tender was accepted and it arranged for the acquisition and fitting out of 14 specially equipped aircraft. The costs were substantial and delays occurred. Meanwhile, Skywest pressed the Commonwealth to terminate the Amann contract and reinstate Skywest before it disposed of its planes. In September 1987 Amann commenced coast watch flights, but not all of its aircraft were ready. The Commonwealth gave notice that it regarded the contract as terminated. Later it was accepted that this notice was invalid and that, as result of the Commonwealth's repudiation of the contract, Amann had a right to terminate and claim damages for breach. Amann's suit included a substantial claim for reliance damages and this was upheld by the High Court. The court accepted that the assessment of expectation damages was not impossible; nonetheless, their assessment was difficult. Mason CJ and Dawson JJ held:

> The present case differs from *McRae* in that it was not impossible, as a matter of theory, for Amann to establish what its profits (if any) would have been had the Commonwealth not repudiated the contract. Indeed, the trial judge's assessment of damages proceeded on that footing, although, significantly, he did not take into account the value to Amann of the prospects of renewal of the contract. But the difficulties attending that undertaking were legion … Not the least of those difficulties were the problems of assessing what were the prospects of early termination of the contract by the Commonwealth had the contract proceeded and, more importantly, the prospects of Amann securing a renewal of the contract. Add to those uncertainties the fact that, on any view, the most substantial part of Amann's damages flowing from the Commonwealth's breach of the original contract was represented by the wasted expenditure.[152]

If the court finds that the plaintiff has made a bad bargain, in the sense that had the contract been performed the plaintiff would not have recouped all the claimed expenditure, then:

> … the plaintiff is only entitled to damages for an amount equivalent to that which would have been earned had the contract been fully performed.[153]

---

150. (1951) 84 CLR 377 at 414 per Dixon and Fullagar JJ.
151. (1991) 174 CLR 64.
152. (1991) 174 CLR 64 at 89.
153. (1991) 174 CLR 64 at 84 per Mason CJ and Dawson J.

This is based on the principle that a plaintiff is not entitled to be placed in a superior position due to the breach.[154] However, the plaintiff does have the benefit of a presumption, albeit rebuttable, that the contract would not have been entered into unless his or her costs were recoverable.[155] This means that in order to recover reliance damages, the plaintiff need only prove that the expenditure was incurred and that it was reasonable.[156] The onus of proof then shifts to the defendant, who must show that the wasted expenditure would not have been recouped under the contract had it been performed.[157]

Restitution damages

3.44   Courts are sometimes prepared to order a refund of payments that the plaintiff made to the defendant under the contract. This can be characterised as a type of reliance damage recoverable in a contractual damages claim.[158] Thus in *McRae v Commonwealth Disposals Commission*,[159] the court awarded a refund of the salvage price paid, since the ship to be salvaged did not exist and the plaintiff received no benefit from payment of the price. The term 'restitution damages' should be treated with caution, however, since it entails a contradiction between the aim of damages (to compensate for a loss) and restitution (to disgorge an unjust gain). Where there is a total failure of consideration, a claim for the return of the contract price would more properly be made as a claim for money had and received, that is, in restitution law itself rather than for contract damages.[160]

Related personal injury or property damage

3.45   Consistently with the general aim of contract damages,[161] a claim may include compensation for expenses that are not directly related to the primary object of the contractual promises, but are incurred as a result of the breach or in recovering from the consequences of the breach.[162] Common examples include personal injuries and damage to other property. Thus where a potentially dangerous item, such as a gas barbeque, is defective when sold and explodes, causing personal injury, the damages claim may include medical expenses.

Personal injury claims are more likely to be made in tort and are discussed at **2.62–2.64**. The discussion there includes the effect of the Civil Liability

---

154. (1991) 174 CLR 64 at 83 per Mason CJ and Dawson J.
155. (1991) 174 CLR 64 at 87 per Mason CJ and Dawson J.
156. (1991) 174 CLR 64 at 87–8 per Mason CJ and Dawson J.
157. (1991) 174 CLR 64 at 87–8 per Mason CJ and Dawson J.
158. Per Mason CJ in *Baltic Shipping v Dillon* (1993) 176 CLR 344 at [30].
159. (1951) 84 CLR 377.
160. See *Baltic Shipping v Dillon* (1993) 176 CLR 344 and the discussion at **4.23**.
161. *Robinson v Harman* (1848) 1 Ex 850 at 855; 154 ER 363 discussed at **3.1**.
162. See for example *Harper v Ashton's Circus Pty Ltd* [1972] 2 NSWLR 395; *Baltic Shipping Co v Dillon* (1993) 176 CLR 344. While this head is sometimes described as the 'indemnity interest' or a 'consequential loss', these terms are not used consistently in the same sense.

Acts. It should be noted, however, that while the main focus of the Acts is on negligence claims, some provisions also apply to personal injury claims which are not the result of negligence, that is, where the cause of action is in contract, under statute or otherwise.[163] Thus, to name a few examples, under the New South Wales Act, the cap on loss of earnings (s 12), the method for determining the amount of damages for non-economic loss (s 16)[164] and the structured settlements provisions (s 22–26) also apply to contract claims for personal injury, whether or not they involve negligence.

Loss of an opportunity or chance

3.46   Damages for the loss of an opportunity or chance raise difficult issues for causation, remoteness and quantum.[165] How the issue is characterised can be critical to the plaintiff's case. If such loss is treated entirely as an issue in causation, it will only be recoverable if, on the balance of probabilities, the loss was more likely to occur than not. To show this, the plaintiff must prove that there was a better than 50 per cent chance that the loss would have occurred. This is the approach adopted in medical negligence cases.[166] As discussed at 2.28–2.29, it results in an 'all or nothing' approach.

If, on the other hand, the problem is treated as raising separate causation and assessment questions, then such loss is recoverable even if it had a less than 50 per cent chance of occurring; and even though the calculation of the loss is 'not only difficult but incapable of being carried out with certainty or precision'.[167] This is the approach taken in contract and trade practices cases.[168] The separate causation question is simply whether the breach caused the loss of an opportunity or chance. While this has to be proven on a balance of probabilities, it is the *existence* of the lost chance, not its likelihood of bearing fruit, which has to be proven. As long as the lost chance is not negligible, at this stage of the enquiry it does not matter how small the chance might have been, as long as it was within the contemplation of the parties (that is, not too remote). Even the existence of a small chance, such as the chance of winning a prize in a beauty competition,[169] could be shown on a balance of probabilities to have been contemplated by the parties and lost as a result of the breach.

---

163. See Pt 2 of the Civil Liability Act 2002 (NSW); etc.

164. See the discussion at 3.49 for the effect this has on claims for feelings, disappointment and mental distress.

165. See the discussions by Brennan J in *Norwest Refrigeration Services Pty Ltd v Bain Dawes (WA) Pty Ltd* (1984) 157 CLR 149 at 172–3 and *Sellars v Adelaide Petroleum NL* (1994) 179 CLR 332 at 360–8.

166. See *Tabet v Gett* [2010] HCA 12; *Gregg v Scott* [2005] UKHL 2 and see 2.30.

167. *Chaplin v Hicks* [1911] 2 KB 786 at 791 per Vaughan Williams LJ; cited with approval in *Luna Park (NSW) Ltd v Tramways Advertising Pty Ltd* (1938) 61 CLR 286 at 301 per Latham CJ. See also *Commonwealth v Amann Aviation Pty Ltd* (1991) 174 CLR 64; *Jackson v Royal Bank of Scotland* [2005] 2 All ER 71; [2005] UKHL 3.

168. *Commonwealth v Amann Aviation Pty Ltd* (1991) 174 CLR 64; *Sellars v Adelaide Petroleum NL* (1994) 179 CLR 332.

169. *Chaplin v Hicks* [1911] 2 KB 786.

It is only once the existence of the lost chance is proven that the likelihood of the chance bearing fruit becomes relevant. The question is: what is the value of the lost chance (that is, how much money would put the plaintiff in the position they would have been in if they had had the opportunity contemplated by the contract)? It is not the full value of the prize in the beauty competition that has been lost, but merely the chance of winning it. In valuing lost chances, courts have tended to ask what the full value would be if the chance came to fruition; and then to discount that value by a percentage figure representing the chance of the event happening.[170] According to Deane, Gaudron & McHugh JJ in *Malec v JC Hutton Pty Ltd*:

> The probability may be very high — 99.9 per cent — or very low — 0.1 per cent. But unless the chance is so low as to be regarded as speculative — say less than 1 per cent — or so high as to be practically certain — say over 99 per cent — the court will take that chance into account in assessing the damages.[171]

Using a percentage to discount the full value of the lost chance is not the only acceptable approach. The aim is merely to value the lost chance. Courts may take a global approach and award a lump sum,[172] but the amount should not be 'plucked from the air'.[173]

The classic contract illustration is found in *Chaplin v Hicks*,[174] where the defendant's breach denied the plaintiff a one in four chance of winning a prize in the defendant's beauty competition. Despite the plaintiff not being able to prove with certainty that she would have won the competition, £100 in damages was awarded for the loss of the chance. This loss was not, in the view of Vaughan Williams LJ, 'of such a nature as to be impossible of assessment'.[175] This reasoning was applied in *Howe v Teefy*[176] where, in September 1926, the defendant bought a racehorse, 'Sankip', and leased it for three years to the plaintiff, a racehorse trainer. In January 1927 the defendant breached the contract by taking the horse away from the trainer. The trainer sued for damages including prospective winnings from bets and stable commissions. The jury assessed damages at £250 and this was upheld on appeal. After referring to *Chaplin v Hicks*, Street CJ summed up the position as follows:

> The question in every case is: has there been any assessable loss resulting from the breach of contract complained of? There may be cases where it

---

170. *Commonwealth v Amann Aviation Pty Ltd* (1991) 174 CLR 64; *Sellars v Adelaide Petroleum NL* (1994) 179 CLR 332.

171. [1990] HCA 20; (1990) 169 CLR 638 at 643; cited with approval in *Sellars v Adelaide Petroleum NL* (1994) 179 CLR 332 at [23]–[24].

172. Brennan & Dawson JJ discouraged the percentage approach in *Malec v JC Hutton Pty Ltd* [1990] HCA 20; (1990) 169 CLR 638 at 640; see also *Tszyu v Fightvision Pty Ltd; Fightvision Pty Ltd v Onisforou* [1999] NSWCA 323; [1999] NSWCA 323; (1999) 47 NSWLR 473 at [141]; *Burger King Corporation v Hungry Jack's Pty Ltd* [2001] NSWCA 187 at [590]–[596].

173. *Sensis Pty Ltd v McMaster-Fay* [2005] NSWCA 163 at [57].

174. [1911] 2 KB 786. See also *Talbot v General TV Corp Pty Ltd* [1980] VR 224.

175. *Chaplin v Hicks* [1911] 2 KB 786 at 791.

176. (1927) 27 SR (NSW) 301 (FC).

would be impossible to say that any assessable loss had resulted from a breach of contract, but, short of that, if a plaintiff has been deprived of something which has a monetary value, a jury is not relieved from the duty of assessing the loss merely because the calculation is a difficult one or because the circumstances do not admit of the damages being assessed with certainty…

The test in every case is … whether the plaintiff was possessed of something which had a monetary value, and of which he was deprived by the defendant's breach of contract.[177]

One ground of appeal in *Howe v Teefy* was that 'the prospective winnings of the plaintiff from bets and stable commissions were too remote and too contingent to be recovered as damages'. In rejecting this ground, Street CJ explained:

Assuming that the damages claimed are capable of assessment, I do not think that it can be said that they are too remote. The determination of that question depends upon whether they were within the contemplation of both parties, that is whether both parties were aware of the circumstances with a view to which the plaintiff was leasing the horse.[178]

In *Sellars v Adelaide Petroleum NL*,[179] an action for damages under the Trade Practices Act 1974 (Cth), the majority in the High Court confirmed that damages for the loss of a chance are capable of assessment in a breach of contract action where the contract deprives the plaintiff of an opportunity of entering into an alternative contract. This is so even if the alternative contract only had a 40 per cent chance of being completed.[180]

Substantial damages for the loss of an opportunity were also awarded in *Burger King Corporation v Hungry Jack's Pty Ltd*.[181] The appellant, Burger King, was the franchisor of the second-largest fast-food chain in the world (after McDonald's) with nearly 9000 restaurants worldwide. The first formal franchise agreement between Burger King and the respondent, Hungry Jack's, was entered into in 1973, after the latter informally opened 14 restaurants in Australia under the Hungry Jack's name using the Burger King system and trade marks. The 1973 agreement permitted the continued operation of the system under the Hungry Jack's banner. A franchise agreement was then required for each store opened by Hungry Jack's. By the 1990s Hungry Jack's was Burger King's largest franchisee in Australia and, indeed, up until the mid-1980s it had been its sole franchisee. A new agreement was reached by the parties in 1990, but Burger King 'was seriously reviewing its role in the Australian market with an eye to increasing its own direct participation' and maintaining 'overall control'.[182] There were continuing disputes about

---

177. (1927) 27 SR (NSW) 301 at 306.

178. (1927) 27 SR (NSW) 301 at 303. Similar reasoning was adopted by the House of Lords in *Jackson v Royal Bank of Scotland plc* [2005] 2 All ER 71; [2005] UKHL 3.

179. (1994) 179 CLR 332.

180. (1994) 179 CLR 332 at 349 per Mason CJ, Dawson, Toohey and Gaudron JJ.

181. [2001] NSWCA 187.

182. [2001] NSWCA 187 at [32].

signage, trade marks, operational issues, new stores, third-party franchisees and promotions. In 1994 Burger King set up its own Australian company and pursued setting up its own outlets in Shell service stations. In 1995 it imposed a freeze on Hungry Jack's recruiting of third-party franchisees and it withdrew financial and operational approval. In 1996 Burger King sent two notices purporting to terminate the agreement between the parties. Hungry Jack's sued for, inter alia, breach of contract and breach of fiduciary duty. At the time the notices of termination were given, Hungry Jack's was operating 148 restaurants and two service station sites and between 1990 and 1996 it had paid in excess of $20 million in royalties to Burger King.

At first instance, Rolfe J found that the agreement was subject to an implied duty of reasonableness and good faith. Burger King's conduct in terminating the agreement breached this duty because it deliberately set out to prevent Hungry Jack's from expanding, so that Burger King could develop in the Australian market 'unhindered by its contractual arrangements'.[183] His Honour awarded more than $70 million in damages under four heads. First, about $43.5 million for the delay in opening company-owned restaurants. This was based on an expert report submitted by Hungry Jack's which showed a loss of more than $96 million. His Honour then discounted this amount by 55 per cent for vicissitudes.[184] Second, almost $24 million in damages for the loss of the opportunity to introduce third-party franchisees. Third, about $1.5 million for equitable compensation for the loss of service royalties for restaurants opened at seven Shell service stations. Finally, almost $2 million for 'cannibalisation' claims based on Burger King authorising Shell to open three restaurants in breach of its agreement with Hungry Jack's.

Burger King's appeal to the New South Wales Court of Appeal (Sheller, Beazley and Stein JJA) was for the most part unsuccessful. The parties had already agreed that the calculation under the first head should have been reduced to about $38 million. The second head was reduced by a small amount to take account of higher overheads; the third was increased to about $2.6 million and the fourth head or the 'cannibalisation' claim was not allowed. Special leave to appeal to the High Court was granted, but the case settled.

Gratuitous benefits

3.47   As noted in *New South Wales Cancer Council v Sarfaty* by Gleeson CJ and Handley JA:

> In an action for breach of contract a plaintiff is not entitled to damages for the loss of benefits which the defendant was not bound under the contract to provide.[185]

---

183. [2001] NSWCA 187 at [310].

184. See also *Mobile Innovations Ltd v Vodafone Pacific Ltd* [2003] NSWSC 166 at [754].

185. (1992) 28 NSWLR 68 at 78 (CA); see also *Commonwealth v Amann Aviation Pty Ltd* (1991) 174 CLR 64 at 91 per Mason CJ and Dawson J, and 102 per Brennan J.

Still, in order to determine what the plaintiff has lost as a result of the defendant's breach, the court looks not only to the express terms of the contract but also to any implied term.[186] Thus, in a suit for wrongful dismissal, a hairdresser's assistant obtained damages not only for lost wages but also for tips that would have been received because the tips were part of an implied promise given by the employer.[187]

Feelings, disappointment and mental distress

3.48   The general rule in breach of contract actions is that no damages can be awarded for mental distress and disappointment.[188] Although in *Baltic Shipping Co v Dillon*, Mason CJ, with whom Toohey J agreed, concluded that this rule was based on 'flimsy policy foundations' and had been 'undermined' by the exceptions 'engrafted upon it',[189] the Chief Justice was not prepared to discard the general rule because:

> … as a matter of ordinary experience, it is evident that, while the innocent party to a contract will generally be disappointed if the defendant does not perform the contract, the innocent party's disappointment and distress are seldom so significant as to attract an award of damages on that score. For that reason, if for no other, it is preferable to adopt the rule that damages for disappointment and distress are not recoverable unless they proceed from physical inconvenience caused by the breach or unless the contract is one the object of which is to provide enjoyment, relaxation or freedom from molestation.[190]

Thus, in line with the exception just quoted, damages for distress, disappointment and loss of enjoyment *have* been awarded where the defendant's breach of contract injured the plaintiff both physically and mentally;[191] where there were contracts to provide a skiing holiday,[192] a holiday cruise on a ship[193] and a swimming pool of a certain design and depth;[194] and where the plaintiff's solicitors failed, in breach of their retainer, to obtain an injunction which would have restrained a man from molesting her.[195] And, in *Farley v Skinner*,[196] a buyer of land was awarded £10,000 for loss of its 'enjoyment' after a surveyor

---

186.   (1991) 174 CLR 64 at 102 per Brennan J.

187.   *Manubens v Leon* [1919] 1 KB 208, cited with approval in *Commonwealth v Amann Aviation Pty Ltd* (1991) 174 CLR 64 at 102–3 per Brennan J.

188.   *Hobbs v London and South Western Railway Co* (1875) LR 10 QB 111 at 122 per Mellor J; *Baltic Shipping Co v Dillon* (1993) 176 CLR 344 at 394 per McHugh J.

189.   (1993) 176 CLR 344 at 362.

190.   (1993) 176 CLR 344 at 365.

191.   See the cases cited by Mason CJ in *Baltic Shipping Co v Dillon* (1993) 176 CLR 344 at 362, fn 95.

192.   *Athens MacDonald Travel Service Pty Ltd v Kazis* [1970] SASR 264; *Jarvis v Swan Tours Ltd* [1973] 1 QB 233; applied by the High Court in *Baltic Shipping Co v Dillon* (1993) 176 CLR 344.

193.   *Baltic Shipping Co v Dillon* (1993) 176 CLR 344.

194.   *Ruxley Electronics and Construction Ltd v Forsyth* [1996] AC 344.

195.   *Heywood v Wellers* [1976] QB 446.

196.   [2001] UKHL 49.

in breach of contract erroneously reported that the land would not be affected by aircraft noise.

By contrast, in *Johnson v Unisys*[197] the House of Lords refused to award damages to an employee who suffered a 'mental breakdown' or psychiatric injuries following a wrongful dismissal. In order to recover, it was noted that the plaintiff would have to overcome *Addis v Gramophone Co Ltd*,[198] where a majority in the House of Lords held that an employee could not recover damages for injured feelings, mental distress or damage to his or her reputation caused by the manner of the dismissal. Another obstacle to recovery in *Johnson* was the statutory regime dealing with wrongful dismissal. As explained by Lord Hoffmann:

> … judges, in developing the law, must have regard to the policies expressed by Parliament in legislation. Employment law requires a balancing of the interests of employers and employees, with proper regard not only to the individual dignity and worth of the employees but also to the general economic interest. Subject to observance of fundamental human rights, the point at which this balance should be struck is a matter for democratic decision. The development of the common law by the judges plays a subsidiary role. Their traditional function is to adapt and modernise the common law. But such developments must be consistent with legislative policy as expressed in statutes. The courts may proceed in harmony with Parliament but there should be no discord.[199]

Johnson was cited with approval in *New South Wales v Paige*[200] by Spigelman CJ, who held:

> Similar considerations apply to the Australian industrial relations context, and similar purposes as those imputed to the UK Parliament are discernible in the legislation governing unfair dismissals in Australia … These arrangements[201] are directed to the efficient handling of unfair dismissal claims and would be thwarted by the creation of a parallel remedy of unlimited scope.[202]

Despite the authority of *Addis* it has been doubted on many occasions and is increasingly being confined to wrongful dismissal actions. It has not been followed in Canada and New Zealand.[203] Lord Steyn in a dissenting speech in *Johnson v Unisys*[204] declined to follow *Addis*. And while Lord Hoffmann in the majority was not prepared to overrule *Addis* so far as wrongful dismissal claims were concerned, his Lordship was prepared to restrict its ambit:

> On the other hand, if such damage is loss flowing from a breach of another implied term of the contract, *Addis's* case does not stand in the way. That

---

197. [2003] 1 AC 518; compare *Mahmud v Bank of Credit and Commerce International SA* [1998] AC 20.

198. [1909] AC 488.

199. [2003] 1 AC 518 at [37].

200. (2002) 60 NSWLR 371; [2002] NSWCA 235 at [135].

201. Industrial Relations Act 1996 (NSW) and the Workplace Relations Act 1996 (Cth).

202. (2002) 60 NSWLR 371; [2002] NSWCA 235 at [147] and [150].

203. See *Re McIntyre; Ex parte Stannard* (2004) 212 ALR 531 at [30] per Finkelstein J.

204. [2003] 1 AC 518.

is why in *Mahmud's* case[205] itself, damages were recoverable for financial loss flowing from damage to reputation caused by a breach of the implied term of trust and confidence.[206]

3.49 The leading High Court case on mental distress[207] was decided several years before the introduction of the various Civil Liability Acts. Do the Acts limit claims for mental distress arising from breaches of contract? Two limitations might apply. First, if mental distress falls under the definition of a personal injury, then (as pointed out in **3.4**) there are provisions that apply to 'an award of personal injury damages … whether … in tort, in contract, under statute or otherwise'.[208] Secondly, some of the Acts have provisions limiting claims for pure mental harm if the harm is a result of negligence.[209]

Two New South Wales cases have considered these issues. In *Insight Vacations Pty Ltd v Young*,[210] Mrs Young was injured while on a coach tour in Slovakia. She sued the defendant company from whom she had purchased the tour. At trial, the defendant was held to be liable for the breach of a contractual warranty imposed by the Trade Practices Act 1974 (Cth) to render services 'with due care and skill'. The court limited Mrs Young's personal injury claim to $11,500 as required by the Civil Liability Act 2002 (NSW). But it also awarded $8,000 for 'disappointment' and 'loss of enjoyment' arising from the breach of contract, holding this was not to be regarded as a personal injury under the Civil Liability Act. On appeal, the New South Wales Court of Appeal held that a claim for disappointment was no different from a claim for mental distress; that a claim for mental distress, at least when made as a consequence of a claim for physical injuries, was within the definition of 'personal injury damages'; that it was therefore not appropriate to separate a contractual 'disappointment' claim from the other personal injuries — they were all subject to the Civil Liability Act; and that mental distress was a type of non-economic loss, either because it was a category of pain and suffering (per Spigelman CJ and Basten J) or because it was a loss of amenity of life (per Sackville J).[211]

Shortly after this judgment, a single judge in the New South Wales Supreme Court held that even where a contractual mental distress claim is made on its own and not as a consequence of other personal injuries, it is still regulated by Pt 2 of the Civil Liability Act; and that if the claim is a result of negligence, the requirement that it be a recognised psychiatric illness also applies.[212]

---

205. *Mahmud v Bank of Credit and Commerce International SA* [1998] AC 20.
206. [2003] 1 AC 518 at [44].
207. *Baltic Shipping v Dillon* (1993) 176 CLR 344.
208. See, for example, Civil Liability Act 2002 (NSW) s 28(1).
209. See, for example, Civil Liability Act 2002 (NSW) s 31.
210. [2010] NSWCA 137.
211. The case was taken on appeal to the High Court, but not on these issues; see *Insight Vacations Pty Ltd v Young* [2011] HCA 16.
212. *Flight Centre v Louw* [2011] NSWSC 132.

Loss of reputation

3.50   Based on *Addis*,[213] the traditional view is that damages for a loss of reputation caused by a breach of contract are not available. Damages for the wrongful dismissal claim in *Addis* were refused both for the injured feelings of the plaintiff and the fact that this would make 'it more difficult for him to obtain fresh employment'.[214] One of the main reasons given was that loss of reputation is a head of damage in tort (in particular, defamation), and therefore it was not a proper head of damage in contract.[215]

However, *Addis* does not apply to all breaches of contract. As noted in the previous paragraph, there are cases where damages have been awarded for the plaintiff's disappointment and injured feelings. There are also cases where damages have been awarded for a loss of publicity[216] and a loss of goodwill.[217] The preferable view to that in *Addis* is that, where the breach of contract injures the plaintiff's reputation, damages for this loss are recoverable, otherwise 'the award of damages will fail to fulfil the objective of compensating the plaintiff for the harm which he or she has suffered as the result of the defendant's breach'.[218]

An example of an award of damages for a loss of reputation caused by the defendant's breach of contract is found in *Flamingo Park Pty Ltd v Dolly Dolly Creations Pty Ltd*.[219] Flamingo Park was controlled by one of Australia's leading fashion designers, Jenny Kee. Mercedes Textiles Pty Ltd agreed with Flamingo Park that it would print onto fabric a design by Jenny Kee and that it would not print the design for anyone else. In breach of the agreement, Mercedes Textiles printed the design on inferior fabric for third parties without Flamingo Park's consent. Wilcox J ordered Mercedes Textiles to pay $30,000 in damages to Flamingo Park for the injury caused to Flamingo Park's reputation by the breach. In so deciding his Honour said:

> Although, no doubt, *Addis* remains authoritative in relation to the precise question there decided and arising out of wrongful dismissal, there appears to be no reason why, in other situations, reputation should not be treated in the same manner as mental distress.[220]

---

213.   [1909] AC 488.

214.   [1909] AC 488 at 491 per Lord Loreburn; and see *Fink v Fink* (1946) 74 CLR 127 at 144, where Dixon and McTiernan JJ held that 'loss of esteem of friends' is not a 'proper element' in a breach of contract action.

215.   *Addis v Gramophone Co Ltd* [1909] AC 488.

216.   See *Marbe v George Edwardes (Daly's Theatre) Ltd* [1928] 1 KB 269 at 281; *Herbert Clayton and Jack Waller Ltd v Oliver* [1930] AC 209; *Withers v General Theatre Corp Ltd* [1933] 2 KB 536; *White v Australian and New Zealand Theatres Ltd* (1943) 67 CLR 266. The latter three cases were cited with approval by Brennan J in *Commonwealth v Amann Aviation Pty Ltd* (1991) 174 CLR 64 at 102.

217.   See *Flamingo Park Pty Ltd v Dolly Dolly Creations Pty Ltd* (1986) 6 IPR 431 (FCA).

218.   As noted by McHugh J in *Baltic Shipping Co v Dillon* (1993) 176 CLR 344 at 396 in relation to damages for distress and disappointment. It should be noted that despite such reasoning, later in his judgment, at 404–5, his Honour accepted that the general rule stated in *Addis* [1909] AC 488 was still good law.

219.   (1986) 6 IPR 431 (FCA).

220.   (1986) 6 IPR 431 at 455.

The importance of protecting reputation was also a major consideration in the High Court case of *White v Australian and New Zealand Theatres Ltd.*[221] The plaintiffs, Eric and Clem White, were revue and pantomime artists who produced their own material. They agreed to provide to the respondent theatre company their 'sole professional services' in staging a revue known as 'Thumbs Up'. After the revue opened the respondent engaged another producer to run the revue. The plaintiffs refused to work for the new producer and sued for £400 in damages. The theatre company cross-claimed. In upholding the plaintiffs' claim for damages and denying the cross-claim, Starke J held:

> The company might control the times and places of performance, the run of the revue, and do many other things in the way of management. But it was not entitled to say that the artist should not act as the producer of the revue known as 'Thumbs Up' and to substitute another producer to whose directions the artist should conform. It was a breach of contract on the part of the company and so important from the point of view of the artist's reputation that it went to the root of the contract, and entitled the artist to treat the contract at an end and to refuse to perform it further on their part and to sue the company for damages for the breach.[222]

Interest

3.51   As mentioned in the previous chapter (see **2.82**), damages are invariably paid late because, in theory, the plaintiff is entitled to payment as soon as the cause of action arises.[223] In order to provide fair compensation, interest on damages can be awarded both at common law and under statute.[224] Interest is awarded for the period between the date on which the loss accrued and 'the date when the judgment takes effect'. The function of such awards is to compensate plaintiffs for their losses caused 'by being kept out' of their money during the relevant period.[225] Thus, interest will not be awarded on all heads of damage because some of these heads represent loss after the date of judgment[226] and, therefore, the plaintiff has not been 'kept out' of this money. Finally, as an alternative[227] to statutory and common law interest payments, the parties may agree to the payment of interest where there is a delay in paying damages for a breach of contract.

Taxation

3.52   In deciding the effect of taxation on an award of damages in a breach of contract case, the court first determines whether or not the award itself will

221. (1943) 67 CLR 266.

222. (1943) 67 CLR 266 at 275.

223. *Thompson v Faraonio* (1979) 54 ALJR 231 at 233 (PC); *Haines v Bendall* (1991) 172 CLR 60.

224. See, for example, Supreme Court Act 1933 (ACT) s 53A(1); Supreme Court Act 1970 (NSW) s 94; Supreme Court Act 1935 (SA) s 30C; Supreme Court Act 1986 (Vic) s 60.

225. *MBP (SA) Pty Ltd v Gogic* (1991) 171 CLR 657 at 663.

226. *Fire & All Risks Insurance Co Ltd v Callinan* (1978) 140 CLR 427; compare *John Fairfax & Sons Ltd v Kelly* (1987) 8 NSWLR 131 (CA).

227. See *Degmam Pty Ltd v Wright* [1983] 2 NSWLR 348.

be subject to taxation in the hands of the plaintiff. If it is subject to taxation, which is the usual position in contract where the award represents lost income or profit, the court *will not* take into account the effect of taxation in making its assessment.[228] But in those rare cases where the award itself is not taxable, the court will take into account the effect of taxation in making its assessment if the award or part of the award represents income or profit which would have been taxable had it been received under the contract.[229]

EXEMPLARY DAMAGES

3.53 Exemplary or punitive damages, as the name suggests, are designed to punish the defendant rather than compensate the plaintiff. While such damages are available in tort (see **2.88–2.92**), they cannot be awarded in contract.[230] This is so 'even in cases of intentional or malicious breach of contract'.[231] In *Butler v Fairclough* Griffith CJ observed:

> The motive or state of mind of a person who is guilty of a breach of contract is not relevant to the question of damages for the breach, although if the contract itself were fraudulent the question of fraud might be material … A breach of contract may be innocent, even accidental or unconscious. Or it may arise from a wrong view of the obligations created by the contract. Or it may be wilful, and even malicious and committed with the express intention of injuring the other party. But the measure of damages is not affected by any such considerations.[232]

The High Court cited this passage with approval in *Gray v Motor Accident Commission*,[233] and noted that 'the position is put somewhat differently' in *Restatement (Second) of Contracts* (US):

> Punitive damages are not recoverable for a breach of contract unless the conduct constituting the breach is also a tort for which punitive damages are recoverable.[234]

This last statement reflects the decision reached by the Supreme Court of Canada in the wrongful dismissal action *Vorvis v Insurance Corporation of British Columbia*,[235] which held that exemplary damages are available in contract

---

228. See, for example, *FCT v Wade* (1951) 84 CLR 105 at 115; *New South Wales Cancer Council v Sarfaty* (1992) 28 NSWLR 68 at 80 (CA) per Gleeson CJ and Handley JA.

229. *Cullen v Trappell* (1980) 146 CLR 1.

230. *Addis v Gramophone Co Ltd* [1909] AC 488; *Butler v Fairclough* (1917) 23 CLR 78 at 89; *Whitfield v De Lauret & Co Ltd* (1920) 29 CLR 71 at 80; *Gray v Motor Accident Commission* (1998) 196 CLR 1; *Moss v Sun Alliance Australia Ltd* (1990) 99 FLR 77; *Hospitality Group Pty Ltd v Australian Rugby Union Ltd* (2001) 110 FCR 157; compare *Flamingo Park Pty Ltd v Dolly Dolly Creations Pty Ltd* (1986) 6 IPR 431 at 456–7 per Wilcox J (FCA).

231. *Gray v Motor Accident Commission* (1998) 196 CLR 1 at [13] per Gleeson CJ, McHugh, Gummow and Hayne JJ.

232. (1917) 23 CLR 78 at 89.

233. (1998) 196 CLR 1 at [13] per Gleeson CJ, McHugh, Gummow and Hayne JJ.

234. 1979 at §355; (1998) 196 CLR 1 at [13].

235. [1989] 1 SCR 1085 at [1106] per McIntyre J.

where there is a concurrent claim in tort. The practical difference, however, between *Vorvis* and the Australian approach is slight. If the conduct that constitutes the breach of contract also amounts to a tort, where exemplary damages are available then such damages may be awarded for the tortious conduct in both jurisdictions. The additional action for exemplary damages in contract recognised in *Vorvis* is an 'extraordinary remedy'[236] allowed only in 'very rare'[237] cases and, in any event, it does not permit double punishment.

Clearly there will be cases where the defendant's breach of contract will amount to tortious conduct. The torts of deceit, inducement of breach of contract and interference with contract are obvious examples here. In *Flamingo Park Pty Ltd v Dolly Dolly Creations Pty Ltd* Wilcox J observed:

> It is not impossible to conceive of circumstances in which a defendant's conduct, in relation to a breach of contract, will be conduct of the type attracting exemplary damages in tort. However, that would probably be a rare event; and if it arose it would be a matter of policy for the courts to determine whether it was appropriate to extend what some see as an anomaly — punishment in a civil action — from tort into contract law.[238]

While this observation has been criticised,[239] the High Court in *Zhu v Treasurer of the State of New South Wales*[240] did uphold an award of exemplary damages where there had been a tortious interference with a contract by a third party.

3.54 In Victoria s 53(2)(b)(ii) of the Domestic Building Contracts Act 1995 allows for the award of exemplary damages in disputes concerning domestic building contracts.

---

236. *Royal Bank of Canada v W Got & Associates Electric Ltd* [1999] 3 SCR 408.
237. [1989] 1 SCR 1085 at [1107] per McIntyre J.
238. (1986) 6 IPR 431 at 456 (FCA).
239. *Hospitality Group Pty Ltd v Australian Rugby Union Ltd* (2001) 110 FCR 157 at [143] per Hill and Finkelstein JJ.
240. (2004) 211 ALR 159; [2004] HCA 56, considered at **2.87**.

Part 3

RESTITUTION

CHAPTER **4**

Restitution

NATURE AND THEORETICAL BASIS

The legal concept of restitution

4.1 The legal concept of restitution is the converse of the concept of compensation, which has been examined in **Chapters 2** and **3**. While compensation seeks to reverse the plaintiff's loss, restitution seeks to reverse the defendant's gain. Because of this difference in nature, monetary awards of restitution are not generally called damages.[1] Goff and Jones have described the law of restitution as:

> ... the law relating to all claims, quasi-contractual or otherwise, which are founded upon the principle of unjust enrichment. Restitutionary claims are to be found in equity as well as at law.[2]

In *BP Exploration Co (Libya) Ltd v Hunt (No 2)* Robert Goff J (as he then was) formulated the principle of unjust enrichment as follows:

> ... the principle of unjust enrichment, presupposes three things: (1) receipt by the defendant of a benefit, (2) at the plaintiff's expense, (3) in such circumstances that it would be unjust to allow the defendant to retain the benefit.[3]

The orthodox view has been that the 'law of restitution' is the same body of law as the 'law of unjust enrichment'. However, that has given way to the 'multicausalist' view that restitution is a secondary right (see **1.2**) that responds to a multiplicity of causative events, not only unjust enrichment. In Professor Birks' words:

> Restitution, like compensation, is a category of response, not a category of causative event. The causative event is not always unjust enrichment. It follows that the law of unjust enrichment is a sub-set of the law of restitution, when rights to restitution are divided according to their causative events.[4]

Restitution and quasi-contract

4.2 Restitutionary personal claims that fall outside of contract, tort and equity have historically been known as the law of 'quasi-contract'. The law of quasi-contract consists of four actions, which are often referred to as the 'common counts' or 'money counts'. By the action for 'money had and received to the use of the plaintiff', the plaintiff seeks restitution of money paid to the defendant on grounds such as mistake, illegality, or failure of consideration. By the actions for *quantum meruit* and *quantum valebat*, the plaintiff seeks restitution for the reasonable value of services (in the case of *quantum meruit*) or restitution for the reasonable value of goods (in the case of

---

1.   H. McGregor, *McGregor on Damages,* 18th ed, Sweet & Maxwell, London, 2009, at [1–006]. The exception, at [12–001], is 'restitutionary damages' in tort and contract.

2.   Lord Goff of Chieveley and G Jones, *The Law of Restitution,* 7th ed, Sweet & Maxwell, London, 2007, [1–001].

3.   [1979] 1 WLR 783 at 839.

4.   P Birks, *Unjust Enrichment,* 2nd ed, Oxford University Press, Oxford, 2005, p 17.

quantum valebat) supplied by the plaintiff to the defendant, at the defendant's request. The action for 'money paid to the use of the defendant', by which the plaintiff seeks restitution for the payment of the defendant's debt, will not be considered in this chapter. A meaningful treatment requires an exposition of the related equitable doctrines of subrogation and contribution. The High Court has recently rejected the unjust enrichment principle as the basis for subrogation in *Bofinger v Kingsway Group Ltd*[5] and for contribution in *Friend v Brooker*.[6]

While the old law of quasi-contract has now been subsumed in the wider modern conception of the law of restitution that embraces both the common law and equity, an understanding of quasi-contract remains relevant for at least three reasons. First, because the historical origins of the modern law lie in quasi-contract; second, because the law of quasi-contract accounts for the majority of the case law that now comprises the law of restitution; and third, because the principle of unjust enrichment has not been accepted as an independent cause of action in Australian law.

The implied contract theory

4.3   Quasi-contract was a creature of the common law.[7] As the name suggests, quasi-contract shared common historical origins with the law of contract. Both contract and quasi-contract developed from the common law action in *assumpsit* (meaning 'he promised'). Initially, the distinction between contract and quasi-contract turned upon the nature of the alleged promise. While contractual obligations were based upon express promises, quasi-contractual obligations were based upon implied promises. However, the implied promises in quasi-contractual actions in *indebitatus assumpsit* were often fictions imposed by the common law. The need to imply fictitious contracts is explained by the old forms of action at common law. Under these forms of action, obligations at common law originated either in contract or in tort. In the United Kingdom, the forms of action were abolished by the Common Law Procedure Act 1852,[8] but the implied contract theory was perpetuated by the House of Lords into the twentieth century.[9] As Mason CJ explained in *Baltic Shipping Co v Dillon*:

> The abolition of the forms of action inspired an analysis of the sources of obligation in the common law in terms of a rigid dichotomy between contract and tort. In that context, there was little room for restitutionary obligation imposed by law except as a 'quasi-contractual' appendix to the law of contract.[10]

---

5.   (2009) 239 CLR 269; [2009] HCA 44. Compare with the judgment of the House of Lords to the contrary in *Banque Financière de la Cité v Parc (Battersea) Ltd* [1999] AC 221.

6.   (2009) 239 CLR 129; [2009] HCA 21.

7.   See S J Stoljar, *The Law of Quasi Contract*, 2nd ed, Law Book Company, Sydney, 1989, pp 10–17.

8.   15 & 16 Vict c 76.

9.   *Sinclair v Brougham* [1914] AC 398; overruled in *Westdeutsche Landesbank Girozentrale v Islington London Borough Council* [1996] AC 669.

10.   (1993) 176 CLR 344 at 356–7.

Reception of the principle of unjust enrichment

4.4   In the United Kingdom and Australia, the alternative explanation of quasi-contractual obligations in terms of unjust enrichment, and the formulation of a wider concept of the law of restitution, owes much to the scholarship of Lord Goff of Chieveley, Professor Gareth Jones[11] and the late Professor Peter Birks.[12] In Australia, the High Court rejected the implied contract theory and accepted unjust enrichment as the basis of the action for *quantum meruit* in *Pavey & Matthews Pty Ltd v Paul.*[13] Subsequently, in *Australia and New Zealand Banking Group Ltd v Westpac Banking Corp,*[14] *David Securities Pty Ltd v Commonwealth Bank of Australia*[15] and *Baltic Shipping Co v Dillon,*[16] the High Court also accepted unjust enrichment as the basis of the action for money had and received.

4.5   In the United Kingdom, the House of Lords did not reject the implied contract theory until *Lipkin Gorman v Karpnale Ltd,*[17] where their Lordships acknowledged unjust enrichment as the basis of the action for money had and received. The House of Lords affirmed that view in a line of authorities starting with *Woolwich Building Society v Inland Revenue Commissioners,*[18] *Westdeutsche Landesbank Girozentrale v Islington London Borough Council*[19] and *Kleinwort Benson Ltd v Lincoln City Council.*[20]

4.6   While unjust enrichment has been identified as the underlying rationale for a number of restitutionary claims, the Australian authorities have not recognised unjust enrichment as an independent cause of action that can be directly applied to the facts of a case.[21] Hence, unjust enrichment should be 'seen as a concept rather than a definitive legal principle'.[22] In *Pavey & Matthews Pty Ltd v Paul,* Deane J warned against treating the principle of unjust enrichment as conferring 'a judicial discretion to do whatever idiosyncratic notions of what is fair and just might dictate'.[23] Instead, the true relevance of the principle of unjust enrichment in Australian law was identified by Deane J as follows:

11.   R Goff and G Jones, *The Law of Restitution,* 1st ed, Sweet & Maxwell, London, 1966.
12.   P Birks, *An Introduction to the Law of Restitution,* Clarendon Press, Oxford, 1985.
13.   (1987) 162 CLR 221.
14.   (1988) 164 CLR 662.
15.   (1992) 175 CLR 353.
16.   (1993) 176 CLR 344.
17.   [1991] 2 AC 548.
18.   [1993] AC 70.
19.   [1996] AC 669.
20.   [1999] 2 AC 349.
21.   *Pavey & Matthews v Paul* (1987) 162 CLR 221 at 256 per Deane J; *David Securities Pty Ltd v Commonwealth Bank of Australia* (1992) 175 CLR 353 at 378 per Mason CJ, Wilson, Deane, Toohey and Gaudron JJ; *Hill v Van Erp* (1997) 188 CLR 159 at 239 per Gummow J.
22.   *Roxborough v Rothmans of Pall Mall Australia Ltd* (2001) 208 CLR 516 at 545 per Gummow J.
23.   (1987) 162 CLR 221 at 256.

It constitutes a unifying legal concept which explains why the law recognises, in a variety of distinct categories of case, an obligation on the part of a defendant to make fair and just restitution for a benefit derived at the expense of a plaintiff and which assists in the determination, by the ordinary processes of legal reasoning, of the question whether the law should, in justice, recognise such an obligation in a new or developing category of case.[24]

4.7   The unjust enrichment principle was considered again by the differently constituted High Court in *Roxborough v Rothmans of Pall Mall Australia Ltd*.[25] In that case, Gummow J urged 'caution in judicial acceptance of any all-embracing theory of restitutionary rights and remedies founded upon a notion of "unjust enrichment"'.[26] His Honour criticised such 'top-down' reasoning whereby 'a theory about an area of law is invented or adopted and then applied to existing decisions to make them conform to the theory and to dictate the outcome in new cases'.[27] Instead of the unjust enrichment principle, his Honour looked to equity. His Honour acknowledged the common law nature of the old action for money had and received,[28] but explained how 'notions derived from equity have been worked into and in that sense have become part of the fabric of the common law'.[29] His Honour cited *Moses v Macferlan*,[30] where Lord Mansfield, speaking of the action for money had and received, said that 'the gist of this kind of action is, that the defendant, upon the circumstances of the case, is obliged by the ties of natural justice and equity to refund the money'.[31] Applying Lord Mansfield's dictum, his Honour identified the equitable concept of 'unconscientious retention' as the basis for restitution in these cases.[32]

The rejection of the unjust enrichment principle by Gummow J in *Roxborough* marks a turning point in the Australian law of restitution. As a matter of precedent, it was not supported by the High Court's own judgments in *Australia and New Zealand Banking Group Ltd v Westpac Banking Corp*,[33] *David Securities Pty Ltd v Commonwealth Bank of Australia*[34] and *Baltic Shipping Co v Dillon*.[35] In these cases, the unjust enrichment principle was unambiguously

---

24.   (1987) 162 CLR 221 at 256–7.

25.   (2001) 208 CLR 516.

26.   (2001) 208 CLR 516 at 544.

27.   (2001) 208 CLR 516 at 544.

28.   (2001) 208 CLR 516 at 553, citing *Miller v Atlee* (1849) 13 Jur 431 at 431 per Pollock CB, *arguendo*; and *Sinclair v Brougham* [1914] AC 398 at 455–6 per Lord Sumner.

29.   (2001) 208 CLR 516 at 554.

30.   (1760) 2 Burr 1005; 97 ER 676. See The Hon Mr Justice WMC Gummow, 'Moses v Macferlan: 250 Years On' (2010) 84 *ALJ* 756.

31.   (1760) 2 Burr 1005 at 1012; 97 ER 676 at 681. Gummow J was unconvinced (at 548) by Birks' argument that Lord Mansfield's reference to 'equity' in the context of 'natural justice and equity' was a reference to the *jus naturale* of Roman law, not the doctrines of the Court of Chancery. See P Birks, 'English and Roman Learning in *Moses v Macferlan*' (1984) 37 *Current Legal Problems* 1 at 21.

32.   (2001) 208 CLR 516 at 551, 557.

33.   (1988) 164 CLR 662.

34.   (1992) 175 CLR 353.

35.   (1993) 176 CLR 344.

identified by the High Court, as it was then constituted, as the basis of the common law action for money had and received. The only basis for reconciliation is provided by *dicta* in *ANZ v Westpac* that 'contemporary legal principles of restitution or unjust enrichment can be equated with seminal equitable notions of good conscience.'[36]

4.8   However, the shift in the High Court's jurisprudence in *Roxborough* was apparent in its overruling of the New South Wales Court of Appeal in *Farah Constructions Pty Ltd v Say-Dee Pty Ltd*.[37] One of the issues in contention in this case was the personal liability of third parties who receive property that was disposed of in breach of trust or fiduciary duty. This is the equitable doctrine known as the 'first limb' of the rule in *Barnes v Addy*,[38] or 'knowing receipt'. The traditional view, which is supported by *obiter dicta* from the High Court in *Consul Development Pty Ltd v DPC Estates Pty Ltd*, is that recipient liability is based upon the recipient's actual or constructive notice of the wrongdoing,[39] thus making retention of the property unconscionable. The difficulty lies in defining the requisite degree of notice, which remains controversial.[40] However, in this case the New South Wales Court of Appeal re-interpreted the first limb of *Barnes v Addy* and held that recipient liability is based upon the recipient's unjust enrichment at the expense of the beneficiary, without the need to establish any notice of the wrongdoing.[41] In support of this view, the Court of Appeal cited *obiter dicta* from the Privy Council in *Royal Brunei Airlines Sdn Bhd v Tan*, where Lord Nicholls said that 'recipient liability is restitution-based'.[42]

4.9   On appeal, the Full High Court held unanimously that the Court of Appeal had fallen into 'grave error'.[43] By abandoning the notice test, the Court of Appeal was 'flying in the face not only of the received view of the first limb of *Barnes v Addy*, but also of statements by members of this court in *Consul Development Pty Ltd v DPC Estates Pty Ltd*'.[44] Expressed in terms similar to the judgment of Gummow J in *Roxborough,* the joint judgment of the Full High Court vehemently rejected the 'restitution basis' adopted by the Court of Appeal, saying variously that:

> [T]he restitution basis is unhistorical. There is no sign of it in clear terms in any but the most recent authorities … The restitution basis reflects a mentality

---

36.   (1988) 164 CLR 662 at 673, cited in *Equuscorp Pty Ltd v Haxton* [2012] HCA 7 at [32].

37.   [2007] HCA 22; (2007) 236 ALR 209.

38.   (1874) LR 9 Ch App 244.

39.   (1975) 132 CLR 373 at 410 per Stephen J (Barwick CJ agreeing).

40.   See J D Heydon and M J Leeming, *Jacobs' Law of Trusts in Australia*, 7th ed, LexisNexis Butterworths, Sydney, 2006, [1333]–[1337].

41.   *Say-Dee Pty Ltd v Farah Constructions Pty Ltd* [2005] NSWCA 309 at [234] per Tobias JA (Mason P and Giles JA agreeing).

42.   [1995] 2 AC 378 at 386 (Lords Goff, Ackner, Steyn, and Sir John May agreeing).

43.   [2007] HCA 22 at [131]; (2007) 236 ALR 209 at 250 per Gleeson CJ, Gummow, Callinan, Heydon and Crennan JJ.

44.   [2007] HCA 22 at [134]; (2007) 236 ALR 209 at 251.

in which considerations of ideal taxonomy prevail over a pragmatic approach to legal development … The restitution basis was imposed as a supposedly inevitable offshoot of an all-embracing theory. To do that was to bring about an abrupt and violent collision with received principles without any assigned justification.[45]

On the particular facts in *Farah Constructions v Say-Dee*, the High Court held that recipient liability did not arise because 'there was no relevant receipt of property, and no relevant notice'.[46]

As in *Farah Constructions v Say-Dee*, the High Court's next examinations of the unjust enrichment principle in *Bofinger v Kingsway Group Ltd*,[47] on the doctrine of subrogation, and in *Friend v Brooker*,[48] on the doctrine of contribution, all fell within the exclusive jurisdiction of equity, where the High Court's expressions of disapproval have been the strongest. In *Friend v Brooker*, the High Court expressed its approval that the plaintiff had 'disavowed any reliance upon a cause of action framed as a case of unjust enrichment.'[49] In both cases, the High Court rejected an unjust enrichment analysis where 'the principles of equity which govern the outcome are well developed and have the vitality to permit further development in an orthodox fashion'.[50]

The joint judgment of the Full High Court in *Bofinger v Kingsway Group Ltd* reiterates, under the heading of 'Unjust Enrichment and the English Decisions', the recurring themes in the High Court's treatment of the unjust enrichment principle.[51] In summary, these are: First, that 'the concept of unjust enrichment [is] not a principle supplying a sufficient premise for direct application to a particular case'. Second, that 'the concept of unjust enrichment may provide a means for comparing and contrasting various categories of liability'. Third, that 'the concept of unjust enrichment may also assist in the determination by the ordinary processes of legal reasoning of the recognition of obligations in a new or developing category of case'. As we have seen, these first three points are taken from the judgment of Deane J in *Pavey & Matthews Pty Ltd v Paul*.[52] Fourth, that the High Court rejects 'the imposition of the 'top-down' reasoning which is a characteristic of some all-embracing theories of unjust enrichment'. This fourth point was made by Gummow J in *Roxborough v Rothmans of Pall Mall Australia Ltd*[53] that 'top-down' reasoning conflicts with the traditional common law method of case-by-case evolution of the law. Finally, the point that was made in *Farah Constructions*

45. [2007] HCA 22 at [130]–[158]; (2007) 236 ALR 209 at 250–9.

46. [2007] HCA 22 at [115]; (2007) 236 ALR 209 at 245.

47. [2009] HCA 44; (2009) 239 CLR 269.

48. [2009] HCA 21; (2009) 239 CLR 129.

49. [2009] HCA 21 at [8]; (2009) 239 CLR 129 at 141 per French CJ, Gummow, Hayne and Bell JJ.

50. *Bofinger v Kingsway Group Ltd* [2009] HCA 44 at [89]; (2009) 239 CLR 269 at 300, per Gummow, Hayne, Heydon, Kiefel and Bell JJ.

51. [2009] HCA 44 at [85] [94]; (2009) 239 CLR 269 at 299–301.

52. (1987) 162 CLR 221 256–7.

53. (2001) 208 CLR 221 at 544.

v Say-Dee: 'such all-embracing theories [of unjust enrichment] may conflict in a fundamental way with well-settled equitable doctrines and remedies'.

Since *Bofinger,* the High Court has most recently handed down its judgment in *Equuscorp Pty Ltd v Haxton,* on restitution for illegal contracts.[54] In a joint majority judgment, French CJ, Crennan and Kiefel JJ repudiated the fourth point made Gummow J above, holding that:

> Unjust enrichment …has a taxonomical function referring to categories of cases in which the law allows recovery by one person of a benefit retained by another. In that aspect, it does not found or reflect any 'all-embracing theory of restitutionary rights and remedies'. It does not, however, exclude the emergence of novel occasions of unjust enrichment supporting claims for restitutionary relief.[55]

Restitution and contract

4.10   To appreciate the circumstances in which a restitutionary claim may arise, the general relationship between restitution and contract needs to be examined. At least three points can be made. First, since the law of restitution exists independently of contract, many restitutionary claims arise where there has never been a contract between the parties. Second, the law of restitution is generally subordinate to the law of contract. As the New South Wales Court of Appeal affirmed in *Coshott v Lenin,* 'no action can be brought for restitution while an inconsistent contractual promise subsists between the parties in relation to the subject matter of the claim'.[56] As we will see, the point arose in *Lumbers v W Cook Builders Pty Ltd (in liq),* where the High Court emphasised that 'It is essential to consider how the claim [in restitution] fits with contracts the parties have made'.[57] The third point, which is subject to the second point, is that there may be scope for a claim in restitution where the contract has been discharged for breach or repudiation,[58] or frustration;[59] or where the contract is void[60] or unenforceable.[61] However, in response to the House of

---

54.   [2012] HCA 7.

55.   [2012] HCA 7 at [30]. The joint judgment of Gummow and Bell JJ did not refer to unjust enrichment.

56.   [2007] NSWCA 153 at [11] per Mason P, quoting from *Trimis v Mina* [1999] NSWCA 140 at [54]. See also *Pavey & Matthews Pty Ltd v Paul* (1987) 162 CLR 221 at 256 per Deane J; *Update Constructions Pty Ltd v Rozelle Child Care Centre Ltd* (1990) 20 NSWLR 251 at 275 per Priestley JA; *Brenner v First Artists' Management Pty Ltd* [1993] 2 VR 221 at 257 per Byrne J; *Pan Ocean Shipping Co Ltd v Creditcorp Ltd (The Trident Beauty)* [1994] 1 All ER 470 at 473 per Lord Goff.

57.   (2008) 232 CLR 635 at 663 per Gummow, Hayne, Crennan and Kiefel JJ. See A. O'Brien, 'The Relationship Between the Laws of Unjust Enrichment and Contract: Unpacking *Lumbers v Cook*' (2011) 32 *Adelaide Law Review* 83.

58.   *Sumpter v Hedges* (1898) 1 QB 673; *Renard Constructions (ME) Pty Ltd v Minister for Public Works* (1992) 26 NSWLR 234 at 277 per Meagher JA (CA).

59.   *Fibrosa Spolka Akcyjna v Fairbairn Lawson Combe Barbour Ltd* [1943] AC 32; *BP Exploration Co (Libya) Ltd v Hunt (No 2)* [1979] 1 WLR 783 (on the Law Reform (Frustrated Contracts) Act 1943 (UK)). See: Frustrated Contracts Act 1978 (NSW); Frustrated Contracts Act 1988 (SA); Frustrated Contracts Act 1959 (Vic).

60.   *Craven-Ellis v Canons Ltd* [1936] 2 KB 403 (CA); *Rover International Ltd v Cannon Film Sales (No 3) Ltd* [1989] 1 WLR 912 (CA); *David Securities Pty Ltd v Commonwealth Bank of Australia* (1992) 175 CLR 353.

61.   *Pavey & Matthews Pty Ltd v Paul* (1987) 162 CLR 221 at 256 per Deane J.

Lords' unprecedented decision to the contrary in *Attorney-General v Blake*,[62] Australian courts have maintained the traditional exclusion of restitutionary damages and accounting for profits as remedies for breach of contract.[63] See **6.18**.

The underlying rationale for these rules is to avoid overlap and conflict between the contractual and restitutionary regimes of liability. While the law of restitution seeks to reverse the defendant's gain, the law of contract seeks to compensate for the plaintiff's loss. To claim both compensation and restitution would result in a double award to the plaintiff, which the law deems to be an unjust result. This view was affirmed by the High Court in *Baltic Shipping Co v Dillon*,[64] where it was held that full compensatory damages in contract and complete restitution cannot be awarded for the same breach of contract.

For practicality, we have organised the cases according to the traditional forms of action. While the law is no longer bound by these forms of action, the archaic terminology continues in active usage by the highest appellate courts.

ACTIONS FOR MONEY HAD AND RECEIVED

Introduction

4.11   In *Equuscorp Pty Ltd v Haxton*, the High Court explained the role of the unjust enrichment principle in actions for money had and received in the following terms:

- recovery depends upon enrichment of the defendant by reason of one or more recognised classes of 'qualifying or vitiating' factors;

- the category of case must involve a qualifying or vitiating factor such as mistake, duress, illegality or failure of consideration, by reason of which the enrichment of the defendant is treated by the law as unjust;

- unjust enrichment so identified gives rise to a prima facie obligation to make restitution;

- the prima facie liability can be displaced by circumstances which the law recognises would make an order for restitution unjust.[65]

This section will examine four categories of cases where an action in restitution, in the form of an action for money had and received, will lie:

---

62.   [2001] 1 AC 268.

63.   *Hospitality Group Pty Ltd v Australian Rugby Union Ltd* (2001) 110 FCR 157 at 196 per Hill and Finkelstein JJ. See also *Multigroup Distribution Services Pty Ltd v TNT Australia Pty Ltd* (2001) 191 ALR 402 at 418 per Gyles J; *Mainland Holdings Ltd v Szady* [2002] NSWSC 699 at [64] per Gzell J; *Biscayne Partners Pty Ltd v Valance Corp Pty Ltd* [2003] NSWSC 874.

64.   (1993) 176 CLR 344.

65.   [2012] HCA 7 at [30] per French CJ, Crennan and Kiefel JJ.

a)   to recover money paid under a mistake;

b)   to recover money paid upon a consideration that has failed;

c)   to recover money paid under an illegal contract; and

d)   to claim the proceeds of a tort (known as 'waiver of tort').

Recovery of money paid under a mistake

4.12   In *Australia and New Zealand Banking Group Ltd v Westpac Banking Corp*, Mason CJ and Wilson, Deane, Toohey and Gaudron JJ stated the principle that:

> ... receipt of a payment which has been made under a mistake is one of the categories of case in which the facts give rise to a prima facie obligation to make restitution, in the sense of compensation for the benefit of unjust enrichment, to the person who has sustained the countervailing detriment.[66]

In *ANZ v Westpac*, ANZ had telegraphically transferred to Westpac an overpayment of money. The overpayment was due to a clerical error by ANZ. Because each of the parties conceded that the clerical error was a mistake of fact which gave ANZ a prima facie right of recovery, the only questions in dispute before the High Court were matters of defence. That aspect of the case will be considered under the topic of defences to restitutionary claims: see **4.82**. The importance of *ANZ v Westpac* for present purposes is the High Court's recognition of unjust enrichment as the true basis of the action for money had and received in circumstances where a payment has been made under a mistake of fact.

4.13   The question of what types of mistake will support a restitutionary claim was taken up by the High Court in *David Securities Pty Ltd v Commonwealth Bank of Australia*.[67] That litigation arose from payments made by David Securities to the Commonwealth Bank in accordance with a contractual provision that was held to be void by statute. The remainder of the contract was valid and enforceable. In the Federal Court, David Securities had failed in its claim for restitution of payments made under the void contractual provision because the relevant mistake was characterised as a mistake of law.

Mistakes of fact and mistakes of law

4.14   Historically, the case law on mistaken payments has distinguished between payments made under mistakes of fact and payments made under mistakes of law. Consistently with the old maxim that *ignorantia juris non exusat* (meaning 'ignorance of the law does not excuse'), the traditional rule, which follows the supposed authority of *Bilbie v Lumley*,[68] has precluded restitution based upon mistakes of law. But the unsatisfactory distinction between mistakes of fact and law was apparent even in the early cases. In *Kelly*

---

66.   (1988) 164 CLR 662 at 673.

67.   (1992) 175 CLR 353.

68.   (1802) 2 East 469; 102 ER 448.

v Solari[69] an insurer paid money under a life insurance policy to the widow of the insured, without realising that the policy had lapsed before the death of the insured, thereby relieving the insurer of liability. The mistake of the payer in that instance was characterised as a mistake of fact, thereby allowing restitution. But the relevant mistake could easily have been characterised as one of legal obligation under the insurance policy.

4.15   In *Bilbie v Lumley* an underwriter claimed restitution of money paid under an insurance policy in circumstances where the insured had failed to disclose material facts when the policy was made, thereby relieving the underwriter of liability. In this case, the underwriter was aware of the non-disclosure at the time when he made the payment to the assured, but had not realised the legal consequences of the non-disclosure. Characterising the underwriter's mistake as one of law, Lord Ellenborough CJ refused relief because 'every man must be taken to be cognisant of the law; otherwise there is no saying to what extent the excuse of ignorance might not be carried'.[70]

4.16   In *David Securities*,[71] the High Court overturned the traditional rule precluding restitution based on mistakes of law.[72] The majority judges reinterpreted *Bilbie v Lumley* as authority for a more narrow rule that a voluntary payment made in satisfaction of an honest claim is irrecoverable. This rule is 'founded firmly on the policy that the law wishes to uphold bargains and enforce compromises freely entered into'.[73] Mason CJ and Deane, Toohey, Gaudron and McHugh JJ held that a payment will be characterised as 'voluntary' for these purposes:

> ... if the plaintiff chooses to make the payment even though he or she believes a particular law or contractual provision requiring the payment is, or may be, invalid, or is not concerned to query whether the payment is legally required; he or she is prepared to assume the validity of the obligation, or is prepared to make the payment irrespective of the validity or invalidity of the obligation, rather than contest the claim for payment.[74]

The principle concerning 'voluntary' payments does no more than preclude restitution where the payer's mistake does not cause the payment. Accordingly, whether the mistake is one of fact or law, the essential criterion for recovery is causation. The High Court stated the new principle as follows:

> ... the payer will be entitled prima facie to recover moneys paid under a mistake if it appears that the moneys were paid by the payer in the mistaken

---

69.   (1841) 9 M & W 54; 152 ER 24.

70.   (1802) 2 East 469 at 472; 102 ER 448 at 449.

71.   (1992) 175 CLR 353.

72.   In Western Australia, the rule precluding restitution based upon mistakes of law was abolished by s 23 of the Law Reform (Property, Perpetuities and Succession) Act 1962 (WA), subsequently re-enacted as s 124 of the Property Law Act 1969 (WA).

73.   (1992) 175 CLR 353 at 374 per Mason CJ, Deane, Toohey, Gaudron and McHugh JJ.

74.   (1992) 175 CLR 353 at 373–4. A payment is also voluntary if it is made *in anticipation* of an honest claim: *Re Magarey Farlam Lawyers Trust Accounts (No 3)* [2007] SASC 9 at [169]; (2007) 96 SASR 337 at 386 per Debelle J.

belief that he or she was under a legal obligation to pay the moneys or that the payee was legally entitled to payment of the moneys. Such a mistake would be causative of the payment.[75]

In the United Kingdom, the traditional rule against recovery of money paid under a mistake of law remained standing until the judgment of the House of Lords in *Kleinwort Benson Ltd v Lincoln City Council*,[76] where the reasoning of the majority judgments in *David Securities* was cited with approval.

4.17   A claim for money paid under a mistake of law was upheld by the Victorian Court of Appeal in *Hookway v Racing Victoria Ltd*.[77] The dispute arose from a horse race where the first-placed horse was disqualified by the results of a subsequent drug test. After the prize money was then paid to the appellant who owned the second-placed horse, the disqualification of the first horse was reversed on appeal by the race officials. In these circumstances, Racing Victoria successfully claimed for restitution of the prize money from the appellant. The Victorian Court of Appeal identified the relevant mistake of law as that of the Racing Victoria officer who paid the money 'in ignorance of the first placegetter's legal rights of appeal and thus in ignorance of the potentiality for a lawful change in the placings for the race'.[78] Contrary to the view of Lord Ellenborough in *Bilbie v Lumley*, 'sheer ignorance' of the law is a sufficient mistake.[79] The Court of Appeal further held that the payment was not 'voluntary' and therefore irrecoverable within the meaning of *David Securities*, because 'there was no bargain involved in the making of the payment nor compromise freely entered into, nor any payment made "in satisfaction of an honest claim"'.[80] The sufficiency of a bank's 'sheer ignorance of something relevant to the transaction at hand' was upheld by the Victorian Court of Appeal as a causative mistake of law in *Hilliard v Westpac Banking Corporation*.[81]

The effect of carelessness

4.18   Provided that the criterion of causation is satisfied, carelessness on the part of the payer is not a bar to restitution.[82] This proposition was established early in *Kelly v Solari*[83] in which the mistaken insurer had the means

---

75.   (1992) 175 CLR 353 at 378. See also *Hollis v Atherton Shire Council* [2003] QSC 147; (2003) 128 LGERA 348.

76.   [1999] 2 AC 349. See now *Deutsche Morgan Grenfell Group plc v Inland Revenue Commissioners* [2006] UKHL 49; [2007] 1 AC 558.

77.   [2005] VSCA 310; (2005) 13 VR 444.

78.   [2005] VSCA 310 at [45]; (2005) 13 VR 444 at 463 per Ormiston JA (Warren CJ agreeing).

79.   *David Securities Pty Ltd v Commonwealth Bank of Australia* (1992) 175 CLR 353 at 369 and 474 per Mason CJ, Deane, Toohey, Gaudron and McHugh JJ; *Commissioner of State Revenue (Vic) v Royal Insurance Australia Ltd* (1994) 182 CLR 51.

80.   [2005] VSCA 310 at [45]; (2005) 13 VR 444 at 463–4 per Ormiston JA (Warren CJ agreeing).

81.   [2009] VSCA 211 at [76]; (2009) 25 VR 139 at 158 per Maxwell P, Osborn AJA.

82.   *David Securities Pty Ltd v Commonwealth Bank of Australia* (1992) 175 CLR 353 at 374 per Mason CJ, Mason CJ, Deane, Toohey, Gaudron and McHugh JJ; *Kleinwort Benson Ltd v Lincoln City Council* [1999] 2 AC 349 at 399 per Lord Hoffmann and at 410 per Lord Hope.

83.   (1841) 9 M&W 54; 152 ER 24.

of knowing, and arguably should have known, that the relevant insurance policy had lapsed. The distinction between careless mistaken payments, where restitution is allowed, and voluntary payments, where restitution is precluded, is that voluntary payments are not caused by the payer's mistake.

Recovery of money upon a failure of consideration

4.19   Where a plaintiff has paid money under a contract that he or she has elected to terminate for breach or repudiation, the plaintiff may be entitled to restitution of that payment if the consideration for the payment has totally failed. In such circumstances, unless the contract provides otherwise, a restitutionary action for money had and received is an alternative remedy to compensatory damages for breach of contract. In *Baltic Shipping Co v Dillon*,[84] Deane and Dawson JJ identified the 'modern substantive categorisation' of such a claim as 'an action in unjust enrichment'.[85] In sale of goods contracts, the buyer's right to restitution for failure of consideration is recognised by legislation.[86] Section 55 of the Sale of Goods Act 1923 (NSW) provides that:

> Nothing in this Act shall affect the right of the buyer … to recover money paid where the consideration for the payment of it has failed.

The concept of consideration

4.20   When the cases refer to a 'total failure of consideration' in the contractual context, 'it is the performance of the defendant's promise, not the promise itself, which is the relevant consideration'.[87] As Viscount Simon LC explained in *Fibrosa Spolka Akcyjna v Fairbairn Lawson Combe Barbour Ltd*:

> … in the law relating to the formation of contract, the promise to do a thing may often be the consideration, but when one is considering the law of failure of consideration and of the quasi-contractual right to recover money on that ground, it is, generally speaking, not the promise which is referred to as the consideration, but the performance of the promise. The money was paid to secure performance and, if performance fails the inducement which brought about the payment is not fulfilled.[88]

4.21   However, for the purposes of the action for money had and received, the High Court has recognised that failure of consideration is not confined to failure of contractual performance. In *Roxborough v Rothmans of Pall Mall Australia Ltd*,[89] the respondent wholesaler had supplied tobacco products to the appellant retailer. A 'distinct and separate element' of the consideration for each purchase of goods was an amount of tax levied under the Business

---

84.   (1993) 176 CLR 344.

85.   (1993) 176 CLR 344 at 375.

86.   Sale of Goods Act 1954 (ACT) s 57; Sale of Goods Act 1972 (NT) s 55; Sale of Goods Act 1896 (Qld) s 55; Sale of Goods Act 1895 (SA) s 53; Sale of Goods Act 1896 (Tas) s 58; Goods Act 1958 (Vic) s 60; Sale of Goods Act 1895 (WA) s 53.

87.   *Baltic Shipping Co v Dillon* (1993) 176 CLR 344 at 350–1 per Mason CJ.

88.   [1943] AC 32 at 48.

89.   (2001) 208 CLR 516.

Franchise Licences (Tobacco) Act 1987 (NSW). When the Act was later declared invalid on constitutional grounds, the retailer demanded a refund of the tax payments that the wholesaler had retained, but was no longer required to pay over to the revenue authority. Significantly, the wholesaler's refusal to refund the payments was not a breach of contract. Since the contract had been fully performed by both parties, there was arguably no occasion for a claim in restitution at all.[90] Neither was there any causative mistake of fact or law. Nevertheless, the High Court held that the retailer was entitled to restitution of the payments because the consideration for these payments had totally failed. Gleeson CJ, Gaudron and Hayne JJ said that:

> Failure of consideration is not limited to non-performance of a contractual obligation, although it may include that. The authorities referred to by Deane J in his discussion of the common law count for money had and received in *Muschinski v Dodds*,[91] show that the concept embraces payment for a purpose which has failed as, for example, where a condition has not been fulfilled, or a contemplated state of affairs has disappeared.[92]

Similarly, Gummow J said that 'failure of consideration' in this context 'identifies the failure to sustain itself of the state of affairs contemplated as a basis for the payments the appellants seek to recover'.[93] Birks called this a 'failure of basis'.[94] In these circumstances, it was held that the wholesaler had been unjustly enriched at the expense of the retailer, even though the retailer had already 'passed-on' or recouped the invalid tax payments by charging higher prices to consumers.[95]

Total failure distinguished from partial failure of consideration

4.22   The main limitation upon the action for money had and received is that the failure of consideration must be total. There is generally no right to restitution where the failure of consideration is partial. In *Hunt v Silk*,[96] Silk agreed to lease a property to Hunt, to carry out certain repairs, and to execute a lease within 10 days, all for a consideration of £10. Hunt paid the money and took immediate possession of the property but Silk failed to carry out the repairs or to execute the lease within 10 days. Hunt stayed in possession for a few more days before terminating the agreement, vacating the property and claiming restitution of the £10. Hunt's action for money had and received

---

90.   See J W Carter and G J Tolhurst, '*Roxborough v Rothmans of Pall Mall*' (2003) 19 *JCL* 287 at 297.

91.   (1985) 160 CLR 583 at 619–20.

92.   (2001) 208 CLR 516 at 525.

93.   (2001) 208 CLR 516 at 557. See also *Ideas Plus Investments Ltd v National Australia Bank Ltd* [2006] WASCA 215 at [68]–[74] per Steytler P; *Spangaro v Corporate Investment Australia Funds Management Ltd* [2003] FCA 1025; (2003) 47 ACSR 285 at 301–2 per Finkelstein J; P Birks, *An Introduction to the Law of Restitution*, revised ed, Clarendon Press, Oxford, 1989, p 223.

94.   P Birks, 'Failure of Consideration and its Place on the Map' (2002) 2 *Oxford University Commonwealth Law Journal*, 1 at 3–4.

95.   (2001) 208 CLR 516 at 528–30 per Gleeson CJ, Gaudron and Hayne JJ, at 542 per Gummow J, and at 567–70 per Kirby J. See also *Commissioner of State Revenue (Vic) v Royal Insurance Australia Ltd* (1994) 182 CLR 51.

96.   (1804) 5 East 449; 102 ER 1142.

failed because he had received the benefit of intermediate enjoyment of the property.

The strict nature of the traditional rule was affirmed by the High Court in *Baltic Shipping Co v Dillon*.[97] In that case, Dillon was a passenger aboard the appellant's cruise ship, the *Mikhail Lermontov*, which ran aground and sank on the eighth day of a 14-day holiday cruise in the South Pacific. Dillon had fully paid the fare in advance. It was held that Dillon's claim in restitution for a full refund of the fare, based upon a total failure of consideration, was defeated by the fact that she had enjoyed the benefit of eight days cruising aboard the appellant's ship before the sinking occurred. The High Court rejected Dillon's argument that any benefit had been 'entirely negated' by the subsequent catastrophe. The issue of fault by the appellant and its agents in causing the catastrophe was irrelevant to Dillon's claim in restitution.

4.23 The relationship between restitutionary claims for money had and received upon a total failure of consideration and compensatory damages for breach of contract was also considered by the High Court in *Baltic Shipping Co v Dillon*. Dillon's claim in restitution for a refund of the fare was held to be inconsistent with her further claim for damages in contract for disappointment and distress. Each of the majority justices held that full damages and complete restitution cannot be awarded for the same breach of contract.[98] The remedies are alternative and inconsistent. As Gaudron J explained, if Dillon 'were to receive damages and a refund of her fare as well, she would, in effect, take the benefit of the contract without an obligation to give consideration for it'.[99]

4.24 The critical question in the contractual context is 'whether the promisor has performed any part of the contractual duties in respect of which the payment is due'.[100] If the promisor conferred a benefit that was different in kind from that which the promisee contracted for, there may still be a total failure of consideration. In *Rowland v Divall*,[101] the relevant facts were that the plaintiff had bought a car from the defendant, who had no right to sell it. Although the plaintiff had used the car for months before it was identified as stolen property and returned to the true owner, the English Court of Appeal found a total failure of consideration that entitled the plaintiff to restitution of the purchase price. As Atkin LJ said:

> … the buyer has not received any part of that which he contracted to receive — namely, the property and right to possession — and, that being so, there has been a total failure of consideration.[102]

---

97. (1993) 176 CLR 344.

98. (1993) 176 CLR 344 at 359 per Mason CJ, at 379–80 per Deane and Dawson JJ, at 383 per Toohey J, and at 387 per Gaudron J.

99. (1993) 176 CLR 344 at 387.

100. *Stocznia Gdanska SA v Latvian Shipping Co* [1998] 1 All ER 883 at 896 per Lord Goff (HL).

101. [1923] 2 KB 500.

102. [1923] 2 KB 500 at 507, cited with approval in *David Securities Pty Ltd v Commonwealth Bank of Australia* (1992) 175 CLR 353 at 382; *Baltic Shipping Co v Dillon* (1993) 176 CLR 344 at 351.

Severability of consideration

4.25   The requirement of a total failure of consideration has also been ameliorated by the doctrine of severability of consideration. In *Roxborough v Rothmans of Pall Mall Australia Ltd*, the High Court affirmed the principle that 'where the consideration is severable, complete failure of part may form a ground for recovering a proportionate part of the money paid for it'.[103] That may be so even if the whole of the consideration has not failed. On the particular facts in *Roxborough*, the majority justices held that the invalid tax was treated by the parties as a 'distinct and separate element' of the consideration for each purchase of goods, and so 'the failure of the tax involved the failure of a severable part of the consideration'.[104] Kirby J, dissenting, characterised the consideration for each purchase as 'a single aggregate amount' that 'subsumed, and included within it, various components'.[105] Because the invalid tax was only one of these components, Kirby J held that any failure of consideration was only partial.

4.26   The High Court had earlier applied the severability doctrine in *David Securities Pty Ltd v Commonwealth Bank of Australia*, where the court recognised that a mistaken payer may be denied restitution where the payer has received 'good consideration' for the mistaken payment.[106] Once again, 'consideration' in this context means actual performance by the promissor. On the facts in *David Securities*, this 'defence' of good consideration was not available to the payee bank for two related reasons. First, the respective obligations of the parties under the loan contract were severable into their component parts. Second, although the loan contract as a whole did not fail for a lack of consideration, there was a total failure of consideration for the mistaken payments in question.[107] Although the High Court specifically left the point open, the recognition of a defence of good consideration necessarily implies that failure of consideration is the ultimate basis for the restitution of mistaken payments.[108] In both circumstances, there is a 'failure to sustain itself of the state of affairs contemplated as a basis for the payments the [plaintiffs] seek to recover'.[109]

Recovery of money by the defaulting party

4.27   In each of the cases considered so far on contracts discharged for breach or repudiation, the party seeking restitution of payments made under

---

103. (2001) 208 CLR 516 at 525 per Gleeson CJ, Gaudron and Hayne JJ, quoting from the 1868 edition of Bullen and Leake's *Precedents of Pleadings*. See also *Goss v Chilcott* [1996] AC 788 at 798 per Lord Goff (PC).

104. (2001) 208 CLR 516 at 527 per Gleeson CJ, Gaudron and Hayne JJ, and at 587 per Callinan J.

105. (2001) 208 CLR 516 at 577.

106. (1992) 175 CLR 353 at 380 per Mason CJ, Deane, Toohey, Gaudron and McHugh JJ. See **4.88**.

107. (1992) 175 CLR 353 at 383 per Mason CJ, Deane, Toohey, Gaudron and McHugh JJ.

108. See P A Butler, 'Mistaken Payments, Change of Position and Restitution' in P D Finn (ed), *Essays on Restitution*, Law Book Company, Sydney, 1990, p 87.

109. *Roxborough v Rothmans of Pall Mall Australia Ltd* (2001) 208 CLR 516 at 557 per Gummow J.

the contract has been the terminating party. Once the contract has been discharged by the terminating party, the defaulting party may also be entitled to an action for money had and received where the consideration for payments made under the contract has totally failed.

In the case of a defaulting purchaser under a contract for the sale of land, Dixon J said in *McDonald v Dennys Lascelles Ltd*:[110]

> … it is now beyond question that instalments already paid may be recovered by a defaulting purchaser when the vendor elects to discharge the contract.[111] Although the parties might by express agreement give the vendor an absolute right at law to retain the instalments in the event of the contact going off, yet in equity such a contract is considered to involve a forfeiture from which the purchaser is entitled to be relieved.[112]

4.28 The authorities have drawn a distinction in this context between 'part payments' and 'deposits'. When the payments were intended by the contracting parties to form part of the total purchase price, as Dixon J held in *McDonald v Dennys Lascelles Ltd*, these part payments or instalments are generally recoverable by the purchaser upon discharge of the contract, even if the discharge was in response to the purchaser's own breach. That is because the vendor's 'title to retain the money has been considered not to be absolute but conditional upon the subsequent completion of the contract'.[113] While it is debatable whether this reasoning is based upon contract or the discredited implied contract theory of restitution,[114] Dixon J did not attribute any significance to fault. As always in these cases, the defaulting purchaser's claim is subject to any cross-claim by the vendor seeking damages for breach of contract.

4.29 By contrast with part payments, payments in the nature of deposits are generally 'forfeited' to the vendor at common law if the contract is discharged in response to the purchaser's breach. This is a matter for construction of the contract.[115] Certainly, forfeited deposits are different in nature from damages for breach of contract.[116] The nature of a deposit was explained by Cotton LJ in *Howe v Smith*:

> The deposit, as I understand it, … is a guarantee that the contract shall be performed. If the sale goes on, of course, not only in accordance with the

110. (1933) 48 CLR 457 at 478.

111. *Mayson v Clouet* [1924] AC 980.

112. *Pitt v Curotta* (1931) 31 SR (NSW) 477 at 480–1 per Long Innes J. On the jurisdiction of equity to relieve against penalties and forfeitures, see R P Meagher, J D Heydon and M J Leeming, *Meagher, Gummow and Lehane's Equity: Doctrines and Remedies*, 4th ed, LexisNexis Butterworths, Sydney, 2002, Chapter 18.

113. (1933) 48 CLR 457 at 477.

114. See J W Carter and G J Tolhurst, 'Conditional Payments and Failure of Consideration: Contract or Restitution?' (2001) 9 *Asia Pacific Law Review* 1.

115. *Palmer v Temple* (1839) 9 Ad & El 508; 112 ER 1304.

116. *Commissioner of Taxation v Reliance Carpet Co Pty Ltd* [2008] HCA 22 at [22]–[27] per Gleeson CJ, Gummow, Heydon, Crennan and Kiefel JJ.

words of the contract, but in accordance with the intention of the parties in making the contract, it goes in part payment of the purchase-money for which it is deposited; but if on the default of the purchaser the contract goes off, that is to say, if he repudiates the contract, then, ... he can have no right to recover the deposit.[117]

However, the amount of the deposit must be 'reasonable' in the circumstances. At least in sale of land cases, this generally means 10 per cent or less of the contract price. A deposit which exceeds that amount is likely to constitute a penalty in equity.[118] There is also a statutory jurisdiction in some states to relieve against forfeiture of deposits.[119]

4.30   These principles that were developed in sale of land cases were applied to a sale of goods contract by Stable J in *Dies v British and International Mining and Finance Corporation Ltd*.[120] In that case, the vendor contracted to sell certain rifles and ammunition to the purchaser. After making a part-payment of £100,000 towards the contract price of £135,000, the purchaser repudiated the contract and refused to take delivery of the goods. The vendor elected to accept the repudiation and discharged the contract. The significance of the case is that the defaulting purchaser then succeeded in proceedings to recover the payment from the vendor. Stable J said:

> ... where the language used in the contract is neutral, the general rule is that the law confers on the purchaser the right to recover his money, and that to enable the seller to keep it he must be able to point to some language in the contract from which the inference to be drawn is that the parties intended and agreed that he should.[121]

While the facts and result of the case are consistent with a total failure of consideration, regardless of the purchaser's breach, Stable J specifically held that an action for money had and received would not lie at the suit of the defaulting purchaser in this case because 'there was no failure of consideration, total or partial. It was not the consideration that failed but the party to the contract'.[122] However, Stable J did not explain why the consideration had not failed, either totally or partially.

4.31   There are different views about the relevance, if any, of fault by the party in breach seeking restitution for a total failure of consideration. In *Baltic Shipping Co v Dillon*, where there was no question of any default by Dillon in paying the fare, Mason CJ said:

---

117. (1884) 27 Ch D 89 at 95.

118. *Workers Trust and Merchant Bank Ltd v Dojap Investments Ltd* [1993] 2 All ER 370 (PC), where the forfeited deposit was 25 per cent. See PW Young, C Croft and M Smith, *On Equity,* Law Book Co, Sydney, 2009, [5.1050]–[5.1060].

119. Conveyancing Act 1919 (NSW) s 55(2A); Property Law Act 1974 (Qld) s 69(1); Property Law Act 1958 (Vic) s 49(2).

120. [1939] 1 KB 724.

121. [1939] 1 KB 724 at 743.

122. [1939] 1 KB 724 at 744.

... there can, of course, be no such failure [of consideration] when the plaintiff's unwillingness or refusal to perform the contract on his or her part is the cause of the defendant's non-performance.[123]

Similarly, there are dicta by Lord Wright in *Fibrosa Spolka Akcyjna v Fairbairn Lawson Combe Barbour Ltd* that a total failure of consideration requires failure for a 'reason not involving fault by the plaintiff'.[124] The problem with this view is that it conflicts with the actual result in *Dies,* where the defaulting purchaser succeeded regardless.

In *Baltic Shipping Co v Dillon*, Mason CJ preferred to explain the result in *Dies* as a contractual case of conditional payment where the condition had failed, as in *McDonald v Dennys Lascelles Ltd*.[125] Gaudron J also took that view of *Dies*.[126]

Taking a different path to the same result, McHugh J did not regard fault as a disqualification for restitution in *Baltic Shipping Co v Dillon*. Instead, McHugh J concurred with Birks that the result in *Dies* is best explained as a total failure of consideration, irrespective of the purchaser's breach of contract:[127]

> Once the seller elected to accept the buyer's repudiation and terminate the contract, the consideration for the advance payment had wholly failed because the seller retained the guns and ammunition.[128]

The balance of authority supports this view of *Dies*,[129] putting aside the cryptic reasoning of Stable J in the actual case. McHugh J endorsed Birks' argument that 'once it does appear that the condition for retaining the money has failed the fact that it failed in response to the payer's own breach does not matter'.[130] It therefore seems that both the restitutionary and contractual explanations of *Dies* are based upon the concept of conditional payment, where liability is independent of fault.

Recovery of money paid under an illegal contract

4.32   The action for money had and received based upon a total failure of consideration is not confined to contracts discharged for breach or repudiation. In *Equuscorp Pty Ltd v Haxton*,[131] the High Court considered

---

123. (1993) 176 CLR 344 at 352.

124. [1943] AC 32 at 64. See also *Intertransport International Private Ltd v Donaldson* [2005] VSCA 303 at [29] per Chernov JA (Eames JA agreeing).

125. (1993) 176 CLR 344 at 352.

126. (1993) 176 CLR 344 at 385-6.

127. P Birks, *An Introduction to the Law of Restitution*, revised ed, Clarendon Press, Oxford, 1989, p 237.

128. (1993) 176 CLR 344 at 390.

129. *Rover International Ltd v Cannon Film Sales (No 3) Ltd* [1989] 1 WLR 912 at 931-2 per Kerr LJ; at 936 per Dillon LJ (Nicholls LJ agreeing); *Hyundai Heavy Industries Co Ltd v Papadopoulos* [1980] 1 WLR 1129 at 1147-8 per Lord Fraser; *Shaw v Ball* (1963) 63 SR (NSW) 910 at 915 per Sugerman J. Contrast *Mozynia Gdanska SA v Latvian Shipping Co* [1998] 1 All ER 883 at 897, per Lord Goff.

130. P Birks, *An Introduction to the Law of Restitution*, revised ed, Clarendon Press, Oxford, 1989, p 238. See also P Birks, *Unjust Enrichment*, 2nd ed, Oxford University Press, Oxford, 2005, pp 141-2.

131. [2012] HCA 7.

the availability of an action in restitution to recover money advanced under certain loan agreements that were 'unenforceable' for illegality. The appellant, Equuscorp, was the assignee of the original lender, Rural. The respondents were the borrowers. The loan agreements were illegal in this case because they had been made 'in furtherance of an illegal purpose'. The illegal purpose was an agricultural investment scheme for which the invitations to invest had been issued without a registered prospectus, in contravention of the Companies Code. The High Court held that the statutory obligation to register a prospectus was intended for the benefit of potential investors, such as the respondents, by requiring the disclosure of information about the investment scheme. The majority of the High Court adopted the criterion proposed by Professor Birks for the grant or refusal of restitutionary relief in relation to illegal contracts: 'Would allowing that cause of action to be maintained make nonsense of the refusal to enforce the contract?'[132]. The majority of the High Court endorsed Birks' characterisation of the issue as one of 'self-stultification of the law'. This is consistent with the approach that the High Court has taken to other species of unenforceable contracts: see 4.51. In the present case, the High Court concluded:

> The failure of consideration invoked by Equuscorp was the product of Rural's own conduct in offering the loan agreements in furtherance of an illegal purpose. This is a clear case in which the coherence of the law, and the avoidance of stultification of the statutory purpose by the common law, lead to the conclusion that Rural did not have a right to claim recovery of money advanced under the loan agreements as money had and received.[133]

This reasoning supports the view that fault by the party seeking restitution is relevant where the ground for restitution is a total failure of consideration.

Waiver of tort

4.33　'Waiver of tort' or 'waiving the tort' is an old quasi-contractual doctrine by which the victim of a tort may claim an identified gain in the hands of the tortfeasor. The plaintiff's claim takes the form of an action in restitution for money had and received. In these circumstances, a claim in restitution is an alternative to, and inconsistent with, an action in tort for compensatory damages. The waiver of tort doctrine is exceptional because most torts, especially negligence, only result in a loss to the plaintiff, without any gain to the tortfeasor.

The waiver of tort doctrine has most commonly been applied in cases of conversion or detinue, where the defendant has wrongfully sold the plaintiff's goods to a third party. In these cases an action for money had and received will allow the plaintiff to claim the proceeds of sale from the tortfeasor. In *Lamine v Dorrell*, where the defendant wrongfully sold the plaintiff's debentures to a third party, Powell J explained the basis of the action as follows:

---

132. P Birks, 'Recovering Value Transferred Under an Illegal Contract,' (2000) 1 *Theoretical Inquiries in Law* 155 at 203.

133. [2012] HCA 7 at [45] per French CJ, Crennan and Kiefel JJ.

... the plaintiff may dispense with the wrong, and suppose the sale made by his consent, and bring an action for the money they were sold for, as money received to his use.[134]

Theory of extinctive ratification

4.34   Birks labelled the explanation given in *Lamine v Dorrell* as the theory of 'extinctive ratification'.[135] The theory supposes, by means of a legal fiction, that the tortfeasor is an agent of the plaintiff. By ratifying the act of the tortfeasor, and thereby extinguishing the tort, the plaintiff becomes entitled to claim the proceeds of sale under the principles of agency. While the fiction of extinctive ratification may have been historically justifiable by the constraints of the old forms of action, it was rejected by the House of Lords in *United Australia Ltd v Barclays Bank Ltd*,[136] which involved the conversion of a cheque.

In that case, a cheque payable to the appellant was wrongfully converted by MFG Trust Ltd, and collected for that company by its bankers, Barclay's Bank. The appellant commenced an action in restitution for money had and received against MFG Trust for the amount of the cheque, but discontinued those proceedings before judgment. The issue before the House of Lords in this case was to determine whether the appellant could maintain a subsequent action in tort against Barclay's Bank for wrongful conversion of the cheque, arising from the same transaction. Barclays Bank argued, on the basis of extinctive ratification, that commencement of the earlier action in restitution against MFG Trust had necessarily extinguished the tort by ratification, thereby making the present action against Barclays Bank impossible to maintain. The House of Lords rejected the ratification argument and identified election rather than waiver as the basis upon which recovery in restitution is allowed. Quoting from the American Law Institute's *Restatement of the Law of Restitution*, Viscount Simon LC identified the correct principle as follows:

> A person upon whom a tort has been committed and who brings an action for the benefits received by the tortfeasor is sometimes said to 'waive the tort'. The election to bring an action of *assumpsit* is not, however, a waiver of tort but is the choice of one of two alternative remedies.[137]

Accordingly, the plaintiff's election is not irrevocable until judgment is entered in one of the two alternative causes of action.[138] Since the appellant had discontinued its earlier action in restitution against MFG Trust before judgment, an action in tort against Barclays Bank was not precluded.

---

134.   (1701) 2 Ld Raym 1216 at 1216; 92 ER 303 at 303; affirmed in *Attorney General v Blake* [2001] 1 AC 268 at 280 per Lord Nicholls.

135.   P Birks, *An Introduction to the Law of Restitution*, revised ed, Clarendon Press, Oxford, 1989, p 315.

136.   [1941] AC 1.

137.   [1941] AC 1 at 18. See also *Suttons Motors Pty Ltd v Campbell* (1956) 56 SR (NSW) 304; *Halifax Building Society v Thomas* [1996] 1 Ch 217 at 227 per Peter Gibson LJ; *Attorney General v Blake* [2001] 1 AC 268 at 280 per Lord Nicholls.

138.   [1941] AC 1 at 21 per Viscount Simon LC. See also *Tang Man Sit v Capacious Investments Ltd* [1996] 1 AC 514 (PC).

Which torts can support an alternative analysis in restitution?

4.35 As well as other cases of conversion and detinue,[139] the waiver of tort doctrine has been applied in cases of trespass to goods,[140] deceit,[141] trespass to land,[142] and actions for the loss of services.[143] What of other torts? Many torts do not result in an identifiable sum of money in the hands of the tortfeasor, so the question does not arise. In the *United Australia* case, Viscount Simon LC said that defamation and assault were excluded from the doctrine because these torts 'could not be dressed up into a claim in *assumpsit*.'[144] However, as his Lordship pointed out, any procedural advantages to claiming in *assumpsit* became historical with the abolition of the old forms of action. For similar pragmatic reasons, claims for money had and received have sometimes been advantaged over claims in tort because of the survival of actions after death, and different limitation periods.[145]

One supposed restriction upon the waiver of tort doctrine arises from the judgment of the English Court of Appeal in *Phillips v Homfray*.[146] This case was concerned with the trespassing use of passage ways under the plaintiff's land to transport coal, whereby the defendants had saved for themselves the expense of using alternative means. The judgment has been interpreted to confine the quasi-contractual action to those torts in which property belonging to the plaintiff, or the proceeds of such property, has been appropriated by the defendant. However, the better view is that *Phillips v Homfray* does not support any such proposition,[147] and the case has not been followed in Australia.

Restitutionary damages in tort

4.36 The most direct path to achieving restitution for torts would be for damages in tort to be assessed upon a restitution basis as an alternative to damages assessed upon a compensation basis. Such a claim would not take the form of an action for money had and received, so the archaic waiver of tort doctrine could be abandoned entirely. However, the authorities do not support any general right to restitutionary damages in tort. So far, the authorities have only recognised limited exceptions to the general principle that damages in tort are compensatory in nature. Subject to these exceptions, the general rule

---

139. *Hambly v Trott* (1776) 1 Cowp 371; 98 ER 1136; *Chesworth v Farrar* [1967] 1 QB 407.

140. *Oughton v Seppings* (1830) 1 B & Ad 241; 109 ER 776; *Neate v Harding* (1801) 6 Exch 349; 155 ER 577

141. *Hill v Perrott* (1810) 3 Taunt 274; 128 ER 109; *Abbots v Barry.* (1820) 2 Brod & Bing 369; 129 ER 1009.

142. *Powell v Rees* (1837) 7 Ad & E 426; 112 ER 530.

143. *Lightly v Clouston* (1808) 1 Taunt 112; 127 ER 774; *Foster v Stewart* (1814) 3 M & S 191; 105 ER 582.

144. [1941] AC 1 at 13. Query where the defendant has been paid a sum of money to assault the plaintiff.

145. *Chesworth v Farrar* [1967] 1 QB 407. On the limitation of actions in restitution, see: K Mason, J W Carter and G J Tolhurst, *Mason and Carter's Restitution Law in Australia,* 2nd ed, LexisNexis Butterworths, Australia, 2008, [943]–[968].

146. (1883) 24 Ch D 439.

147. The Hon Mr Justice W M C Gummow, 'Unjust Enrichment, Restitution and Proprietary Remedies' in P D Finn (ed), *Essays on Restitution*, Law Book Company, Sydney, 1990, pp 60–7.

therefore remains that only nominal damages may be awarded to a plaintiff in tort who has suffered no loss: see **2.7**.

What are the exceptions? In *Attorney-General v Blake*, Lord Nicholls affirmed that restitutionary damages are available for torts which involve an 'interference with rights of property'.[148] Detinue and trespass to land are two cases, although nuisance has anomalously been excluded.[149] In *Devenish Nutrition Ltd v Sanofi-Aventis SA (France)*, which involved the tort of breach of statutory duty, the English Court of Appeal affirmed the converse proposition that restitutionary damages are not available for so called 'non-proprietary torts'.[150] Apart from precedent, however, the Court of Appeal offered no justification in principle for maintaining the distinction.[151] Passing-off and the intellectual property torts are *sui generis*, where restitution has historically taken the form of an account of profits in equity: see **6.5**.

Trespass to land

4.37 The availability of restitutionary damages for trespass to land was affirmed by the English Court of Appeal in *Ministry of Defence v Ashman*, where Hoffmann LJ (as he then was) rationalised the authorities into the following principles:

> A person entitled to possession of land can make a claim against a person who has been in occupation without his consent on two alternative bases. The first is for the loss which he has suffered in consequence of the defendant's trespass. This is the normal measure of damages in the law of tort. The second is the value of the benefit which the occupier has received. This is a claim for restitution. The two bases of claim are mutually exclusive and the plaintiff must elect before judgment which of them he wishes to pursue.[152]

Because the plaintiff landlord in *Ashman* had proven no loss, the Court of Appeal assessed the landlord's claim for damages (or 'mesne profits') by the value of the premises to the defendant tenant.[153] This approach has been called the 'user principle', an expression that was adopted by Nicholls LJ (as he then was) in *Stoke-on-Trent City Council v W & J Wass Ltd*.[154] In *Ashman*, both Hoffmann and Kennedy LJJ explicitly acknowledged the restitutionary nature of the principle.[155] It was accepted by the Court of Appeal that the value of the premises to the tenant would ordinarily have been the equivalent

---

148. [2001] 1 AC 268 at 278.

149. *Stoke on Trent City Council v W & J Wass Ltd* [1988] 1 WLR 1406; *Forsyth Grant v Allen* [2008] EWCA Civ 505. Contrast *Penarth Dock Engineering Co Ltd v Pounds* [1963] 1 Lloyd's Rep 359.

150. [2008] EWCA Civ 1086, [2009] Ch 390.

151. See C Rotherham, 'Gain-Based Relief in Tort After *Attorney-General v Blake*' (2010) 126 *LQR* 102.

152. [1993] 2 EGLR 102 at 105 per Hoffmann LJ. See also *Whitwham v Westminster Brymbo Coal & Coke Co* [1896] 2 Ch 538; *Penarth Dock Engineering Co Ltd v Pounds* [1963] 1 Lloyd's Rep 359; *Swordheath Properties Ltd v Tabet* [1979] 1 WLR 285; *Inverugie Investments Ltd v Hackett* [1995] 3 All ER 841.

153. See E Cooke, 'Trespass, Mesne Profits and Restitution' (1994) 110 *LQR* 421.

154. [1988] 1 WLR 1406 at 1413 at 1416.

155. [1993] 2 EGLR 102 at 104 per Kennedy LJ and 105 per Hoffmann LJ. See also *Lollis v Loulatzis* [2007] VSC 547 at [219], [228] per Kaye J.

of market rent for the period of trespassing occupation, as the landlord had claimed. However, on the particular facts of the case, the Court of Appeal held that the value of the premises to this particular tenant was less than the market rate, because she was eligible and waiting for subsidised housing.[156] As Lord Nicholls explained in *Sempra Metals Ltd v Commissioners of Inland Revenue*:[157]

> A benefit is not always worth its market value to a particular defendant. When it is not it may be unjust to treat the defendant as having received a benefit possessing the value it has to others. In Professor Birks' language, a benefit received by a defendant may sometimes be subject to 'subjective devaluation'.[158] An application of this approach is to be found in the Court of Appeal decision in *Ministry of Defence v Ashman*.

4.38   In Australia, the user principle has similarly been applied in cases of trespass to land.[159] In *LJP Investments Pty Ltd v Howard Chia Investments Pty Ltd*,[160] restitutionary damages were awarded for the trespass of the defendant's scaffolding into the plaintiff's airspace. The defendant, which was the adjacent landowner, had thereby enhanced the value of its property by building up to the boundary, and had saved paying the licence fee that the plaintiff demanded. Rejecting the defendant's submission that the measure of damages was simply the market value of what was used, Hodgson J of the New South Wales Supreme Court held that:

> ... in my view, if what is used has peculiar value for a defendant, then damages under this head should reflect that value, rather than the general value.[161]

Detinue

4.39   The user principle derived from the authorities on trespass to land was applied to wrongful detention of goods by the English Court of Appeal in *Strand Electric & Engineering Co Ltd v Brisford Entertainments Ltd*.[162] In that case, the defendant had detained and used for its own commercial purposes the plaintiff's portable switchboards, which the plaintiff otherwise hired out for profit. The Court of Appeal held that the defendant was liable to pay the market hiring charge for the whole 43 weeks of detention, without any deduction for the probability that the goods would otherwise have been left unhired for part of that time. As Denning LJ (as he then was) explained:

> The claim for a hiring charge is ... not based on the loss to the plaintiff, but on the fact that the defendant has used the goods for his own purposes. It is an

---

156. See also *Ministry of Defence v Thompson* [1993] 2 EGLR 107 (CA); *Bloor (Measham) Ltd v Calcott* [2001] EWHC Ch 467.

157. [2007] UKHL 34 at [119]; [2007] 4 All ER 657 at 690.

158. P Birks, *An Introduction to the Law of Restitution*, revised ed, Clarendon Press, Oxford, 1989, p 413.

159. *Yakamia Dairy Pty Ltd v Wood* [1976] WAR 57; *Bilambil-Terranora v Tweed Shire Council* [1980] 1 NSWLR 465; *Lamru Pty Ltd v Kation Pty Ltd* (1998) 44 NSWLR 432. See also *Finesky Holdings Pty Ltd v Minister for Transport for Western Australia* [2002] WASCA 206; (2002) 26 WAR 368.

160. (1989) 24 NSWLR 499.

161. (1989) 24 NSWLR 499 at 507.

162. [1952] 2 QB 246.

action against him because he has had the benefit of the goods. It resembles, therefore, an action for restitution rather than an action of tort.[163]

Each of Somervell and Romer LJJ delivered concurring judgments, but neither spoke of restitution. While each of their Lordships expressed their reasoning differently, they were consistent on the fundamental points that the Court was awarding compensation for the plaintiff's loss; that the nature and measure of the plaintiff's loss was the market hiring charge for the whole period of detention, and that the plaintiff was not required to prove the actual loss. The Court of Appeal was therefore divided on whether it was awarding compensation or restitution, with the majority favouring the former.

The judgment in *Strand Electric* was approved and applied to similar facts by the New South Wales Supreme Court in *Gaba Formwork Contractors Pty Ltd v Turner Corporation Ltd*.[164] In this case, the defendants had wrongfully detained, and used for their own commercial purposes, building formwork materials that the plaintiff owner had hired out to them. In awarding a 'reasonable hiring fee' for the entire period of detention, Giles J (as he then was) relied upon *Strand Electric* as authority that it was unnecessary to show an available market in which the plaintiff would have hired out the goods. In other words, the plaintiff was not required to prove the actual loss. His Honour acknowledged 'a degree of departure' from the compensation principle in this respect,[165] but held that it was permissible on these particular facts, as it had been in *Strand Electric*, because the defendants had used the materials for their own commercial purposes during the period of detention. His Honour also acknowledged that 'the influences which inform the law of unjust enrichment are not without effect in our law', citing the High Court judgment in *Pavey and Matthews Pty Ltd v Paul*.[166]

The New South Wales Court of Appeal recently approved and applied *Strand Electric* and *Gaba Formwork* in *Bunnings Group Ltd v CHEP Australia Ltd*.[167] In similar circumstances, the respondent Chep was in the business of hiring out pallets for the carriage, storage and display of manufactured goods. The appellant Bunnings operated a national chain of retail warehouses. Although the appellant had never hired the respondent's pallets, the appellant had the possession and use of approximately 64,690 of them that the appellant had accumulated from suppliers of goods over many years. Nevertheless, the Court of Appeal held that the respondent remained the owner of the pallets at all times, and had the immediate right to possession of them. After a series of demands by the respondent over a period of years, the appellant ultimately returned all of the pallets. These proceedings were about the liability of the appellant in tort for detinue and conversion during the period of wrongful detention, when the appellant had failed to make the pallets available for

163. [1952] 2 QB 246 at 254.
164. (1993) 32 NSWLR 175.
165. (1993) 32 NSWLR 175 at 188.
166. (1987) 162 CLR 221.
167. [2011] NSWCA 342.

return upon the respondent's demand. The award of $9,375,798 made by the trial judge by reference to lost hiring fees was upheld by the Court of Appeal. Allsop P, with whom Giles and Macfarlan JJA concurred, held that:[168]

> The legitimacy of assessing compensation or damages in conversion and detinue for interference with proprietary or possessory rights by use of property that earns or is capable of earning a profit, by reference to a hiring fee that is appropriate in all of the circumstances, was confirmed by the Privy Council in *Inverugie Investments Ltd v Hackett*[169] and by the House of Lords in *Attorney-General v Blake*.[170]

However, as in *Strand Electric*, the Court of Appeal was divided on whether it was awarding compensation or restitution. Citing the need for stability of approach in commercial matters, Allsop P, with whom Macfarlan JA concurred on this point, said:

> It is entirely logical and in accordance with justice and commonsense that a wrongdoer should pay a price for using the goods of another as a matter of compensation for the denial of the right concerned. I do not see this as contrary to, or undermining of, the principle of compensation.[171]

The most authoritative statement of the opposing view, although it was not cited on this point, was given by Lord Nicholls in *Attorney-General v Blake*. Referring to the awards in *Strand Electric* and *Ministry of Defence v Ashman*, his Lordship said:

> … these awards cannot be regarded as conforming to the strictly compensatory measure of damage for the injured person's loss unless loss is given a strained and artificial meaning. The reality is that the injured person's rights were invaded but, in financial terms, he suffered no loss. Nevertheless the common law has found a means to award him a sensibly calculated amount of money.[172]

In *Bunnings v Chep*, Giles JA, who was the judge in *Gaba Formwork*, also preferred to acknowledge explicitly the element of restitution in the award:

> Once there is departure from strict compensation principles in some circumstances, as the law undoubtedly permits, a restitutionary element for conversion or detinue in damages representing what the defendant would have had to pay for the use of the chattel can readily enough be accepted.
>
> I respectfully prefer that view of *Strand Electric*. On strict compensation principles, the tortfeasor's use of the chattel once conversion or detinue has been found would not matter for damages.[173]

168. [2011] NSWCA 342 at [173].
169. [1995] 1 WLR 713 at 717–8.
170. [2000] UKHL 45; [2001] AC 268 at 278–9.
171. [2011] NSWCA 342 at [175].
172. [2001] 1 AC 268 at 279. See also *Kuwait Airways Corp v Iraqi Airways Co (Nos 4 and 5)* [2002] UKHL 19 at [87]–[88]; [2002] 2 AC 883 at 1094–5 per Lord Nicholls; *Sempra Metals Ltd v Commissioners of Inland Revenue* [2007] UKHL 34 at [116]; [2007] 3 All ER 657 at 689 per Lord Nicholls.
173. [2011] NSWCA 342 at [198]–[199].

This seems to be the better view. As Lord Lloyd said in *Inverugie Investments Ltd v Hackett*, the user principle 'need not be characterised as exclusively compensatory, or exclusively restitutionary; it combines elements of both.'[174]

Restitution and exemplary damages in tort

4.40   A further exception to the compensation principle in tort is exemplary damages. The purpose of exemplary damages is 'to punish the defendant for conduct showing a conscious and contumelious disregard for the plaintiff's rights and to deter him from committing like conduct again.': see **2.90**. Exemplary damages are awarded in addition to compensatory damages, but nominal damages can suffice as a basis 'where the plaintiff has a complete cause of action without proof of loss'.[175] Consistently with their punitive nature, exemplary damages can be awarded for the purpose of stripping the defendant of a wrongful gain. In *Rookes v Barnard*, Lord Devlin said that one of the occasions for awarding exemplary damages is where 'the defendant's conduct has been calculated by him to make a profit for himself which may well exceed the compensation payable to the plaintiff'.[176] An award of exemplary damages in these circumstances was made by the House of Lords for a defamatory publication in *Broome v Cassell & Co Ltd*.[177] In Australia, however, exemplary and punitive damages for defamation have been abolished by the uniform defamation law.[178] Nevertheless, the same principles could be applied to other torts where exemplary damages are available: see **2.89**.

The restitutionary nature of such awards was recognised in *Kuddus v Chief Constable of Leicestershire Constabulary*, where the House of Lords affirmed the availability of exemplary damages in English law for the tort of misfeasance in public office.[179] Lords Nicholls and Scott each expressed the view that the function of exemplary damages as a gain-stripping remedy in tort should be a matter for the law of restitution. Lord Scott said:

> Restitutionary damages are available now in many tort actions … The profit made by a wrongdoer can be extracted from him without the need to rely on the anomaly of exemplary damages.[180]

In actions for infringement under the Copyright Act 1968 (Cth), the Patents Act 1990 (Cth), the Circuit Layouts Act 1989 (Cth), and the Designs Act 2003 (Cth) the court has a statutory discretion to award 'additional'

174. [1995] 3 All ER 841 at 845. See P Jaffey, 'Licence Fee Damages' [2011] *Restitution Law Review*, 95.
175. *Fatimi Pty Ltd v Bryant* (2004) 59 NSWLR 678 at 690; [2004] NSWCA 140 at [71] per Giles JA. Exemplary damages are available for trespass to land, which is actionable *per se*: *New South Wales v Ibbett* [2005] NSWCA 445, (2005) 65 NSWLR 168; affirmed [2006] HCA 57, (2006) 229 CLR 638.
176. [1964] AC 1129 at 1226.
177. [1972] AC 1027.
178. Civil Law (Wrongs) Act 2002 (ACT) s 139H; Defamation Act 2005 (NSW) s 37; Defamation Act 2006 (NT) s 34; Defamation Act 2005 (Qld) s 37; Defamation Act 2005 (SA) s 35; Defamation Act 2005 (Tas) s 37; Defamation Act 2005 (Vic) s 37; Defamation Act 2005 (WA) s 37
179. [2002] 2 AC 122, applied in *Rowan v Cornwall (No 5)* (2002) 82 SASR 152 at [712] per Debelle J.
180. [2002] 2 AC 122 at 157 per Lord Scott; at 145 per Lord Nicholls.

damages,[181] which are in the nature of exemplary damages at common law,[182] having regard to matters that include 'any benefit shown to have accrued to the defendant by reason of the infringement'.

ACTIONS FOR *QUANTUM MERUIT* AND *QUANTUM VALEBAT*

Introduction

4.41   In an action for *quantum meruit* (meaning, 'as much as he has earned'), the plaintiff claims reasonable remuneration for services rendered, or money spent, for and at the defendant's request, where there is no effective contract between them. In *Pavey & Matthews Pty Ltd v Paul*, Mason CJ and Wilson J identified the action for *quantum meruit* as 'one based upon unjust enrichment'.[183] The related action for *quantum valebat* (meaning, 'as much as they were worth') lies to recover a reasonable price for goods supplied by the plaintiff at the defendant's request. The action for *quantum valebat* has largely been superseded by the sale of goods legislation and by statutory provisions regulating liability for unsolicited goods. The rule against restitution for unsolicited services is reflected in s 40(2) of the Australian Consumer Law,[184] which provides:

> A person must not, in trade or commerce, assert a right to payment from another person for unsolicited services unless the person has reasonable cause to believe that there is a right to payment.

Request for services

4.42   Under the old forms of action at common law, the plaintiff claiming *quantum meruit* was required to plead that 'the defendant, in consideration of some service rendered [by] the plaintiff at [the defendant's] request, promised to pay to the plaintiff the reasonable value of that service'. If there was not an express request for the services or a promise to pay, these elements could be implied from the surrounding circumstances.[185]

4.43   The High Court re-asserted the traditional requirement of a request for the plaintiff's services in *Lumbers v W Cook Builders Pty Ltd (in liq)*.[186] In that case, the defendant owners had made an oral contract with W Cook

---

181. Copyright Act 1968 (Cth) s 115(4)(b)(iii); Patents Act 1990 (Cth) s 122(1A)(d); Circuit Layouts Act 1989 (Cth) s 27(4)(b)(ii); Designs Act 2003 (Cth) s 75(3). See also the Intellectual Property Laws Amendment (Raising the Bar) Bill, 2011 (Cth) Sch 5, pt 3.

182. See *Polygram Pty Ltd v Golden Editions Pty Ltd* (1997) 148 ALR 4 at 14–16 per Lockhart J; *FNH Investments Pty Ltd v Sullivan* [2003] FCAFC 246; (2003) 59 IPR 121 at 125–7 per Whitlam, Moore and Kiefel JJ; *Facton Ltd v Rifai Fashions Pty Ltd* [2012] FCAFC 9 at [30]–[37] per Lander and Gordon JJ.

183. (1987) 162 CLR 221 at 227.

184. Competition and Consumer Act 2010 (Cth) Sch 2.

185. D J Ibbetson, *An Historical Introduction to the Law of Obligations*, Oxford University Press, Oxford, 1999, p 269–270.

186. (2008) 232 CLR 635.

and Sons Pty Ltd ('Sons') to build a house on the defendants' land, according to the defendants' own distinctive design. However, without the knowledge or consent of the defendants, the greater part of the building work was carried out by the plaintiff, W Cook Builders Pty Ltd. The two companies were under common ownership and control at the time, but Sons was a licensed builder and the plaintiff was not, contrary to the Builders Licensing Act 1986 (SA). In the absence of any contract for the plaintiff to enforce against the defendants, the plaintiff claimed in restitution against the defendants for the payment of certain disputed amounts after the house was completed. Sons was not an active party to the proceedings.

4.44   The Full Court of the Supreme Court of South Australia upheld the plaintiff's claim in restitution for *quantum meruit*. The Full Court held that the defendants had been unjustly enriched because the plaintiff's building services had conferred upon the defendants the 'incontrovertible benefit' of the completed house, which the defendants had 'freely accepted' without making full payment.[187]

4.45   The principle of 'free acceptance' was formulated by Goff and Jones to operate where a defendant has been unjustly enriched by the unrequested services of the plaintiff, without making payment. In the absence of a request, Goff and Jones say that free acceptance occurs where:

> [The defendant], as a reasonable man, should have known that the claimant who rendered the services expected to be paid for them, and yet he [the defendant] did not take a reasonable opportunity open to him to reject the proffered services. Moreover, in such a case, he cannot deny that he has been unjustly enriched.[188]

4.46   Applying this principle to the facts, the majority of the Full Court held that the defendants had freely accepted the plaintiff's services, because the defendants had acquiesced to the building work on their land, they had known that the work was not being carried out gratuitously, and they had accepted the benefit of the work by taking up occupation of the completed house.[189] It was further held that the defendants' ignorance or mistake about the identity of the company that actually carried out the building work did not vitiate the defendants' free acceptance of the plaintiff's work.[190]

The decision of the High Court

4.47   On appeal, the majority of the High Court said that the underlying principle of a claim for *quantum meruit* can be expressed in the following terms:

187.   [2007] SASC 20 at [100], (2007) SASR 406 at 426 per Sulan and Layton JJ.

188.   Lord Goff of Chieveley and G Jones, *The Law of Restitution*, 7th ed, Sweet & Maxwell, London, 2007 [1-019].

189.   [2007] SASC 20 at [82], (2007) SASR 406 at 423 per Sulan and Layton JJ.

190.   [2007] SASC 20 at [84], (2007) SASR 406 at 423. Compare with the position in contract: *Cundy v Lindsay* [1878] 3 App Cas 459; *Lewis v Averay* [1972] 1 QB 198.

The doing of work, or the payment of money, for and at the request of another, are archetypal cases in which it may be said that a person receives a 'benefit' at the 'expense' of another which the recipient 'accepts', and which it would be unconscionable for the recipient to retain without payment.[191]

However, the High Court added a crucial qualification, which applied in this case:[192]

> It is essential to consider how the claim fits with contracts the parties have made because, as Lord Goff rightly warned in *Pan Ocean Shipping Co Ltd v Creditcorp*, 'serious difficulties arise if the law seeks to expand the law of restitution to redistribute risks for which provision has been made under an applicable contract.'[193]

4.48   On the particular facts of this case, the High Court upheld the finding of the trial judge that the plaintiff had carried out the work in performance of a separate 'subcontract' between itself and its related entity, Sons. This subcontract was separate and distinct from the 'head contract' between the defendants and Sons. In these circumstances, the High Court held that the plaintiff's remedies, if any, resided in its subcontract with Sons, without recourse to the defendants by an action in restitution. In this respect, the plaintiff was in the same position as any subcontractor. The High Court concluded that the majority of the Supreme Court had failed to take sufficient account of this subcontract in its reasoning, except in the dissenting judgment of Vanstone J.[194] The High Court's reasoning about the contractual allocation of risks has been approved and applied by the English Court of Appeal in *Costello v MacDonald*:

> ... the policy considerations articulated by Lord Goff in *Pan Ocean* and by the majority of the High Court of Australia in *Lumbers*...clearly support the general policy of refusing restitutionary relief for unjust enrichment against a defendant who has benefited from the plaintiff's services rendered pursuant to a contract to which the defendant was not a party.[195]

Although this point was sufficient to dispose of the appeal, the High Court turned to the plaintiff's claim for *quantum meruit*.[196] Gleeson CJ, in a separate concurring judgment, acknowledged the free acceptance principle, but held that the defendants had not freely accepted the plaintiff's work in this case because the defendants had no option but to 'take the benefit' of the

---

191. (2008) 232 CLR 635 at 663 per Gummow, Hayne, Crennan and Kiefel JJ.

192. (2008) 232 CLR 635 at 663.

193. [1994] 1 WLR 161 at 166.

194. [2007] SASC 20 at [125], (2007) SASR 406 at 430.

195. [2011] EWCA Civ 930 at [30] per Etherton LJ (Pill and Patten LJJ concurring). See also *Henderson's Automotive Technologies Pty Ltd (in liq) v Flaton Management Pty Ltd* [2011] VSCA 167 at [56] per Tate JA (Ashley and Neave JJA concurring).

196. In *Farah Constructions Pty Ltd v Say-Dee Pty Ltd*, the High Court held, as a general matter of precedent, that intermediate courts of appeal in Australia are bound by 'seriously considered dicta of a majority of this Court.' (2007) 230 CLR 89 at 151 per Gleeson CJ, Gummow, Callinan, Heydon and Crennan JJ.

building work because it was annexed to their land.[197] Neither was there any acquiescence because the defendants were ignorant of the plaintiff's existence and its role.

4.49   However, the majority of the High Court denied the plaintiff's claim for a different reason. Implicitly rejecting the free acceptance principle, the majority held that the plaintiff's claim for *quantum meruit* failed because the plaintiff's work had not been carried out for, and at the request of, the defendants. The High Court acknowledged that 'It would matter not at all whether the request was made expressly, or its making was to be implied from the actions of the parties in the circumstances of the case'.[198] However, in the particular circumstances of this case, the defendants' requests for work and their progress payments had been made to Sons, not the plaintiff, in performance of the defendants' 'head contract' with Sons. Mistake was not an issue. The subsequent accounting between Sons and the plaintiff was irrelevant to the defendants, who knew nothing of it.

Acceptance of services

4.50   As the result of *Lumbers v Cook*, the 'free acceptance' principle, at least as formulated by Goff and Jones, is not part of Australian law, although it had been approved and applied in a number of Australian cases as a test of enrichment and an 'unjust factor'.[199] In this respect, *Lumbers v Cook* marks a point of departure from the English cases.[200] The plaintiff's submission that acceptance of a benefit, without a request, suffices to found an action for *quantum meruit* was rejected by the majority of the High Court because it was 'inconsistent with long-established principles governing actions for work and labour done or money paid'.[201] The earlier decision of the Full Court of the Supreme Court of South Australia in *Angelopoulos v Sabatino*[202] was overruled to the extent that it relied upon acceptance of a benefit in its reasoning. The High Court's decision has been criticised, with some force, for having 'taken us

---

197.   (2008) 232 CLR 635 at 656, citing *Sumpter v Hedges* [1898] 1 QB 673 at 676 per Collins LJ.

198.   (2008) 232 CLR 635 at 666 per Gummow, Hayne, Crennan and Kiefel JJ.

199.   *Brenner v First Artists' Management Pty Ltd* [1993] 2 VR 221 at 260 per Byrne J; *Angelopoulos v Sabatino* (1995) 65 SASR 1 at 8–11 per Doyle CJ; *ABB Power Generation Ltd v Chapple* [2001] WASCA 412 at [33], (2001) 25 WAR 158 at 166 per Murray J; *Damberg v Damberg* [2001] NSWCA 87 at [187]–[194], (2001) 52 NSWLR 492 at 528–530 per Heydon JA; *Andrew Shelton & Co Pty Ltd v Alpha Healthcare Ltd* [2002] VSC 248 at [96]–[117], (2002) 5 VR 577 at 599–605 per Warren J; *Concrete Constructions Group v Litevale Pty Ltd (No 2)* [2003] NSWSC 411 at [15]–[18] per Mason P; *Oliver v Lakeside Property Pty Ltd* [2005] NSWSC 1040 at [77]–[89] per Barrett J (affirmed [2006] NSWCA 285); *Alma Hill Constructions Pty Ltd v Onal* [2007] VSC 86 at [57]–[64]; (2007) 16 VR 190 at 208–210 per Kaye J.

200.   *Bridgewater v Griffiths* [2000] 1 WLR 524 at 532 per Burton J; *Rowe v Vale of White Horse District Council* [2003] EWHC 388 (Admin) at [12]–[14], [2003] 1 Lloyd's Rep 418 at 421–22 per Lightman J; *Cressman v Coys of Kensington (Sales) Ltd* [2004] EWCA Civ 47 at [28]–[32], [2004] 1 WLR 2775 at 2787–89 per Mance LJ (Thorpe LJ and Wilson J agreeing); *Greater Manchester Police v Wigan Athletic AFC Ltd* [2008] EWCA Civ 1449 at [38]–[47], [66], [2009] 1 WLR 1580 at 1594–97 per Sir Andrew Morritt C, at 1601 per Maurice Kay LJ.

201.   (2008) 232 CLR 635 at 665–6 per Gummow, Hayne, Crennan and Kiefel JJ.

202.   (1995) 65 SASR 1.

back into the blind alley of the forms of action.'[203] The sufficiency of 'implied requests' suggests a revival of the old implied contract theory of restitution. It remains to be seen how far *Lumbers v Cook* unsettles the substantial body of authority which supports acceptance as a basis for restitution,[204] including the High Court's own decisions in *Pavey & Matthews Pty Ltd v Paul*[205] and *Steele v Tardiani*.[206]

Unenforceable contracts

4.51 In *Pavey & Matthews Pty Ltd v Paul*[207] the High Court considered a claim for *quantum meruit* in the context of an unenforceable contract. Under the terms of an oral contract between the parties, the appellant builder had carried out renovations on the respondent's cottage. She had agreed to pay 'a reasonable remuneration for that work, calculated by reference to prevailing rates of payment in the building industry.' Both parties were ignorant that the contract was 'not enforceable' for lack of writing under s 45 of the Builders' Licensing Act 1971 (NSW). After the building work was completed and the respondent had accepted the benefit of it by taking up occupation of the renovated cottage, she refused to pay the whole amount that the builder claimed as reasonable remuneration. Allowing for the amount that the respondent had paid to the builder already, the question on appeal to the High Court was to determine if the builder's action in restitution for the balance owing was precluded by the statute.

Relying upon the implied contract theory, the respondent argued that to allow an action in restitution would amount to an indirect enforcement of the unenforceable contract. A majority of the High Court rejected that argument and upheld the builder's claim. Mason and Wilson JJ concurred with Deane J that:

> … an action on a *quantum meruit*, such as that brought by the appellant, rests, not on implied contract, but on a claim to restitution or one based on unjust enrichment, arising from the respondent's acceptance of the benefits accruing to the respondent from the appellant's performance of the unenforceable oral contract.[208]

4.52 In *Lumbers v Cook*, the Full Court of the Supreme Court of South Australia quoted this passage from *Pavey* with approval in upholding the plaintiff builder's claim for restitution, based upon the acceptance of a benefit by the defendants.[209] Although the decision of the Full Court seemed to be a direct application of the reasoning in *Pavey*, as we have seen, the plaintiff's

---

203. A. Burrows, 'The Australian Law of Restitution: Has the High Court Lost its Way?' in E Bant and M Harding (eds), *Exploring Private Law*, Cambridge University Press, Cambridge, 2010, p 67 at 84.

204. See G J Tolhurst and J W Carter 'Acceptance of Benefit as a Basis for Restitution' (2002) 18 *JCL* 1.

205. (1987) 162 CLR 221.

206. (1946) 72 CLR 386.

207. (1987) 162 CLR 221.

208. (1987) 162 CLR 221 at 227 per Mason and Wilson JJ.

209. [2007] SASC 20 at [49], (2007) SASR 406 at 417 per Sulan and Layton JJ.

claim failed on appeal in the High Court for the lack of a request. In *Lumbers v Cook*, the High Court distinguished *Pavey*, in part, by holding that:

> …there was no issue in that case about whether the plaintiff, a builder, had a claim for work and labour done and materials supplied. … the issue was whether the builder's action on a *quantum meruit* was a direct or indirect enforcement of the oral contract the parties had made.[210]

The High Court endorsed *Pavey* as an authority on the interpretation of statutes based upon the Statute of Frauds 1677 (UK), which made certain contracts 'unenforceable' for lack of writing.[211] As in *Pavey*, these statutes have generally been interpreted to permit independent actions in restitution that do not enforce the contract.[212] However, as Deane J pointed out in *Pavey*, a distinction needs to be drawn in this context between unenforceable and illegal transactions. The statute in *Pavey*, as interpreted by Deane J, did 'not make an agreement to which it applies illegal or void'.[213] It is a matter of identifying the intention of the invalidating statute. In *Nelson v Nelson* McHugh J explained that one category of 'illegal' transactions is where 'the statute discloses an intention that those rights should be unenforceable in all circumstances'.[214] Applying this reasoning, the Queensland Court of Appeal distinguished *Pavey* in *Marshall v Marshall*[215] and in *Sutton v Zullo Enterprises Pty Ltd*,[216] where the relevant statute prohibited unlicensed building work and provided that 'a person who carries out building work in contravention of this section is not entitled to any monetary or other consideration for doing so.'[217] In both of these cases, the statute was interpreted to preclude an action in restitution for *quantum meruit* as well as any action to enforce the contract.[218]

In *Lumbers v Cook*, the Builders Licensing Act 1986 (SA) was drafted in similar terms. It provided that an unlicensed builder, as the plaintiff was in that case, 'shall not be entitled to recover any fee or other consideration in respect of the building work unless … the person's failure to be licensed resulted from inadvertence only.'[219] However, the High Court declined to decide the point because the plaintiff's claim in restitution failed for other reasons, as we have seen.

---

210. (2008) 232 CLR 635 at 664–665 per Gummow, Hayne, Crennan and Kiefel JJ.

211. (2008) 232 CLR 635 at 665 per Gummow, Hayne, Crennan and Kiefel JJ.

212. *Mostia Constructions Pty Ltd v Cox* [1994] 2 Qd R 55; *O'Connor v LEATHF Pty Ltd* (1997) 42 NSWLR 285; *Nunkuwarrin Yunti v AL Seeley Constructions Pty Ltd* (1998) 72 SASR 21; *Great City Pty Ltd v Kemayan Management Services (Australia) Pty Ltd* (1999) 21 WAR 44; *Corradini v Lorrimor Crafter Pty Ltd* (2000) 77 SASR 125. Compare *Sevastopoulos v Spanos* [1991] 2 VR 194.

213. (1997) 162 CLR 221 at 262. On the recovery of money paid under an illegal contract, see 4.32.

214. (1995) 184 CLR 538 at 613. See also *Fitzgerald v FJ Leonhardt Pty Ltd* (1997) 189 CLR 215 at 230–1 per McHugh and Gummow JJ.

215. [1999] 1 Qd R 173.

216. [2000] 2 Qd R 196. See also *Investmentsource Corp Pty Ltd v Knox Street Apartments Pty Ltd* [2002] NSWSC 710, (2002) 56 NSWLR 27.

217. Queensland Building Services Authority Act 1991 (Qld), s 42. See also *Cook's Constructions Pty Ltd v SFS 007.298.633 Pty Ltd* [2009] QCA 75.

218. See also, for example, *Equuscorp Pty Ltd v Wilmoth Field Warne* [2007] VSCA 280, (2007) 18 VR 250, where *quantum meruit* was precluded under a 'void' solicitor's costs agreement.

219. Builders Licensing Act 1986 (SA), s 39.

Contracts discharged for breach

Position of the terminating party

4.53   In cases of non-monetary benefits conferred under contracts discharged for breach or repudiation, the authorities distinguish between the position of the terminating party and the position of the defaulting party. The terminating party may elect between an action for breach of contract and an action in restitution. This principle was stated by Meagher JA of the New South Wales Court of Appeal in *Renard Constructions (ME) Pty Ltd v Minister for Public Works*:

> … an innocent party who accepts the defaulting party's repudiation of a contract has the option of either suing for damages for breach of contract or suing on a *quantum meruit* for work done.[220]

4.54   In *Renard* the plaintiff construction company agreed to construct two pumping stations for the defendant. Before completion of the work, the defendant repudiated the contract. The plaintiff accepted the repudiation, terminated the contract, and made a restitutionary claim for *quantum meruit*. The claim in restitution related to that portion of the work that the plaintiff had carried out and for which the plaintiff remained unpaid. It was established in *Pavey & Matthews Pty Ltd v Paul* that the ordinary measure of restitution in *quantum meruit* claims will be 'the fair value of the benefit provided (eg: remuneration calculated at a reasonable rate for work actually done or the fair market value of materials supplied)'.[221] If it is customary in an industry for services to be remunerated on a commission basis, the court may award a reasonable commission.[222] The date for assessment is 'when the benefit was received'.[223] Because the restitutionary claim arises independently of the contract, the measure of restitution is not governed by the contract, but the terms of the ineffective contract may be used as evidence of fair market value.[224] Accordingly, an action in restitution for *quantum meruit* is to be distinguished from a contractual action for *quantum meruit*, which is governed by the contract.

4.55   The issue on appeal in *Renard* was to determine if the total contract price should be the upper limit of the plaintiff's claim in restitution. The Court of Appeal rejected any such limitation. Referring to the plaintiff's right of election between a claim for damages arising from the repudiation of the contract and a restitutionary claim for *quantum meruit* for work carried out

---

220. (1992) 26 NSWLR 234 at 277.

221. (1987) 162 CLR 221 at 263 per Deane J.

222. *Way v Latilla* [1937] 3 All ER 759 at 764 per Lord Atkin; *Brenner v First Artists' Management Pty Ltd* [1993] 2 VR 221 at 264 per Byrne J; *Upjay Pty Ltd v MJK Pty Ltd* (2001) 79 SASR 32 at 49 per Wicks J.

223. *Flett v Deniliquin Publishing Co Ltd* [1964–65] NSWR 383 at 386 per Herron CJ.

224. *Pavey & Matthews Pty Ltd v Paul* (1987) 162 CLR 221 at 257 per Deane J; *Flett v Deniliquin Publishing Co Ltd* [1964–65] NSWR 383 at 386 per Herron CJ and 388 per Asprey J.

at the defendant's request, Meagher JA (with whom Priestley JA[225] and Handley JA[226] agreed on this point) said:

> There is nothing anomalous in the notion that two different remedies, proceeding on entirely different principles, might yield different results. Nor is there anything anomalous in the fact that either remedy may yield a higher monetary figure than the other. Nor is there anything anomalous in the prospect that a figure arrived at on a *quantum meruit* might exceed, or even far exceed, the profit which would have been made if the contract had been fully performed. Such a result would only be anomalous if there were some rule of law that the remuneration arrived at contractually was the greatest possible remuneration available, or that it was a reasonable remuneration for all work requiring to be performed. There is no such rule of law … The most one can say is that the amount contractually agreed is evidence of the reasonableness of the remuneration claimed on a *quantum meruit*; strong evidence perhaps, but certainly not conclusive evidence. On the other hand, it would be extremely anomalous if the defaulting party when sued on a *quantum meruit* could invoke the contract which he has repudiated in order to impose a ceiling on amounts otherwise recoverable.[227]

4.56   The result in *Renard*, where the plaintiff was awarded substantially more than the contract price, remains controversial. In the context of contracts discharged for breach, Goff and Jones consider that the contract price should be the ceiling to a claim in restitution.[228] Similarly, Birks' final view was that the valuation of incomplete contractual performance 'must be made in the light of the contract price, even though the contract is defunct.'[229] Carter says that the result 'seems erroneous'.[230] However, in terms of authority, *Renard* is consistent with the judgment of the Privy Council (on appeal from the Supreme Court of New Zealand) in *Lodder v Slowey*.[231] In Australia, *Renard* was approved and applied to similar facts by the Queensland Court of Appeal in *Iezzi Constructions Pty Ltd v Watkins Pacific (Qld) Pty Ltd*[232] and by the Victorian Court of Appeal in *Sopov v Kane Constructions Pty Ltd (No 2)*.[233]

In *Renard* and the cases applying it, there was no dispute that the defendant had benefited from the plaintiff's incomplete construction work. It seems, however, that a restitutionary claim for *quantum meruit* may succeed even where the part performance by the terminating party confers no apparent benefit

225. (1992) 26 NSWLR 234 at 271.
226. (1992) 26 NSWLR 234 at 283.
227. (1992) 26 NSWLR 234 at 277–8.
228. Lord Goff of Chieveley and G Jones, *The Law of Restitution*, 7th ed, Sweet & Maxwell, London, 2007 [20-022]–[20-023], citing *Taylor v Motability Finance Ltd* [2004] EWHC 2619 (Comm) at [26] per Cooke J.
229. P Birks, *Unjust Enrichment*, 2nd ed, Oxford University Press, Oxford, 2005, p 59.
230. J W Carter, *Carter's Breach of Contract*, LexisNexis Butterworths, Australia, 2011, [13-55].
231. [1904] AC 442.
232. [1995] 2 Qd R 350. See also *Len Lichtnauer Developments Pty Ltd v James Trowse Constructions Pty Ltd* [2005] QCA 214.
233. [2009] VSCA 141; (2009) 24 VR 510.

upon the defaulting party. This was so in the problematic case of *Planché v Colburn*,[234] where the plaintiff author had partly completed a manuscript for publication that was never delivered to the defendant publisher because the defendant repudiated the publishing contract. In terms of the unjust enrichment principle, the result is difficult to explain. Nevertheless, on equivalent facts, the Full Court of the Supreme Court of Victoria allowed a restitutionary *quantum meruit* claim in *Brooks Robinson Pty Ltd v Rothfield*.[235] The result in both cases might be better explained by a request-based analysis.

Position of the defaulting party

4.57   Where a contract has been discharged for breach or repudiation, a restitutionary claim for *quantum meruit* is not generally available to the defaulting party in respect of non-monetary benefits conferred under the contract, unless there has been an acceptance of those benefits by the terminating party. An action in restitution for *quantum meruit* is to be distinguished from a contractual action for *quantum meruit*, based upon the doctrine of substantial performance by the defaulting party.[236]

4.58   In *Sumpter v Hedges*,[237] Sumpter contracted to build two houses and stables on Hedges' land in consideration of a lump sum payable upon completion. Sumpter abandoned the contract when the building work was only partly completed, and left additional unused building materials on Hedges' land. Hedges later used these building materials to complete the buildings. Sumpter's claim for *quantum valebat* in respect of the unused building materials was successful, but his claim for *quantum meruit* in relation to the incomplete building work was rejected both at first instance and by the English Court of Appeal.

4.59   In terms of the unjust enrichment principle, both aspects of *Sumpter v Hedges* can be explained by reference to the concepts of request and acceptance. If the incomplete building work was a benefit at all, there could be no acceptance of that benefit because, as Collins LJ pointed out, 'the circumstances are such as to give the defendant no option whether he will take the benefit of the work or not'.[238] Furthermore, because of the incomplete nature of the building work, any benefit received by Hedges was substantially different from that which he had requested. To translate the same proposition into contractual language, Sumpter's obligations under the contract were 'entire' in so far as Hedges had only bargained for completed buildings, not

---

234. (1831) 8 Bing 14; 131 ER 305.

235. [1951] VLR 405.

236. *Hoenig v Isaacs* [1952] 2 All ER 176 (CA). See also *Eminent Forms Pty Ltd v Formosa* [2004] SASC 192 at [46]–[70] per Besanko J; *Firepat Pty Ltd v Clydebank Pty Ltd* [2007] WASCA 13 at [66]–[71] per Martin CJ (Roberts-Smith and Buss JJA agreeing).

237. [1898] 1 QB 673. See B McFarlane and R Stevens, 'In Defence of *Sumpter v Hedges*' (2002) 118 *LQR* 569.

238. [1898] 1 QB 673 at 676. This passage was quoted with approval by Gleeson CJ in *Lumbers v Cook* (2008) 232 CLR 635 at 656.

for partly completed buildings, as the condition precedent to payment. There was no question of substantial performance on the facts. Accordingly, neither a contractual claim nor a restitutionary claim for *quantum meruit* was available in respect of the building work. By contrast, there was acceptance of the unused building materials left by Sumpter on Hedges' land because Hedges had the option of returning those materials, but chose not to do so. The claim in respect of these building materials was purely restitutionary in nature.

4.60 The judgment in *Sumpter v Hedges* was approved by the High Court in *Steele v Tardiani*.[239] In that case, the plaintiff labourers had contracted to cut the defendant's timber into firewood of a certain width, in consideration of an agreed payment per ton. The plaintiffs cut 1500 tons of timber, but most of it was not cut to the required width. Unlike *Sumpter v Hedges*, the contract here was 'divisible' in nature, and so the plaintiffs were entitled to contractual *quantum meruit* for 'each divisible application' of the contract that had been fully or substantially performed. For the remaining balance, Dixon J denied any right to remuneration unless the plaintiffs could 'show circumstances removing their right to remuneration from the exact conditions of the special contract'.[240] Dixon J held that such circumstances were established by the evidence. The defendant's conduct in accepting the defective firewood without protest, and later selling it, amounted to 'a taking of the benefit of the work and so, as involving either a dispensation from precise performance or an implication at law of a new obligation to pay the value of the work done'.[241] Accordingly, the defendant had accepted the benefit of the plaintiffs' work.

4.61 The crucial role of acceptance in *Steele v Tardiani* and *Sumpter v Hedges* is difficult to reconcile with the reasoning in *Lumbers v Cook*, where the High Court denied acceptance as a basis for restitution. *Steele v Tardiani* was not overlooked in *Lumbers v Cook*. The High Court cited *Steele v Tardiani* as an authority on the primacy of contract over restitution.[242]

Necessitous intervention

4.62 In each of the *quantum meruit* claims considered so far, the obligation to make restitution for services has depended upon a request or, debatably, acceptance by the defendant of the plaintiff's services. Outside of these circumstances, the general position at common law remains that the bare fact of supply of goods or services by the plaintiff to the defendant is not, in itself, sufficient to impose an obligation to pay reasonable remuneration. In *Lumbers v Cook*,[243] the High Court quoted with approval the famous dictum by Bowen LJ in *Falcke v Scottish Imperial Insurance Co*:

239. (1946) 72 CLR 386.
240. (1946) 72 CLR 386 at 402.
241. (1946) 72 CLR 386 at 405.
242. (2008) 232 CLR 635 at 663.
243. (2008) 232 CLR 635 at 663.

The general principle is, beyond all question, that work and labour done or money expended by one man to preserve or benefit the property of another do not according to English law create any lien upon the property saved or benefitted, nor, even if standing alone, create any obligation to repay the expenditure. Liabilities are not to be forced upon people behind their backs any more than you can confer a benefit upon a man against his will.[244]

However, the High Court went on to say:

The principle is not unqualified. Bowen LJ identified salvage in maritime law as one qualification. Other cases, including other cases of necessitous intervention, may now be seen as further qualifications to the principle but it is not necessary to examine in this case how extensive are those further qualifications or what is their content.[245]

4.63 While the law of maritime salvage is too voluminous to consider here, it is an early instance of what the common law has called an 'agency of necessity', which is the historical basis for any general principle of restitution for necessitous intervention. Bowstead and Reynolds define agency of necessity in the following terms:

A person may have authority to act on behalf of another in certain cases where he is faced with an emergency in which the property or interests of that other are in imminent jeopardy and it becomes necessary, in order to preserve the property or interests, so to act.[246]

4.64 In these circumstances, the 'agent' under this doctrine may have an action in restitution for *quantum meruit* against the principal for reimbursement of the expenses of having so acted. In *Falcke*, Bowen LJ had insisted that 'no similar doctrine applies to things lost upon land, nor to anything except ships or goods in peril at sea.'[247] However, the maritime doctrine was extended to the carriage of goods by land by the Court of Exchequer in *Great Northern Railway Co v Swaffield*.[248] In that case, the plaintiff railway company had transported the defendant's horse to the station of destination. On arrival there late at night, there was no one to claim the horse. Since the plaintiff's station master had no accommodation for the horse, it was sent to a nearby livery stable. When the defendant's servant arrived soon after and demanded the horse, he was referred to the livery stable keeper, who refused to release the horse until payment of his reasonable charges. The defendant refused to pay any charges and intransigently left the horse at the stable for four months, until the plaintiff ultimately paid the accrued livery charges and delivered the horse to the defendant. The plaintiff was held entitled to reimbursement in restitution of the charges from the defendant. Kelly CB said:

244. (1886) 34 Ch D 234 at 248.

245. (2008) 232 CLR 635 at 663–4.

246. P Watts and F M B Reynolds, *Bowstead and Reynolds on Agency*, 19th ed, Sweet and Maxwell, London, 2010, at [4–002].

247. (1886) 34 Ch D 234 at 249.

248. (1874) LR 9 Ex 132.

...it has been held that a ship owner who, through some accidental circumstance, finds it necessary for the safety of the cargo to incur expenditure, is justified in doing so, and can maintain a claim for reimbursement against the owner of the cargo. That is exactly the present case. The plaintiffs were put into much the same position as the shipowner occupies under the circumstances I have described. They had no choice, unless they would leave the horse at the station or in the high road to his own danger and the danger of other people, but to place him in the care of a livery stable keeper, and as they are bound by their implied contract with the livery stable keeper to satisfy his charges, a right arises in them against the defendant which they have incurred for his benefit.[249]

4.65 *Swaffield* was approved and applied in *Prager v Blatspiel, Stamp and Heacock Ltd*,[250] where McCardie J identified three essential elements of an agency of necessity. Firstly, the alleged agent must have been unable to communicate with the principal in order to seek instructions. However, with advances in telecommunications since the older cases, it is now sufficient if the principal fails to give instructions once notified.[251] Secondly, the alleged agent 'must prove an actual and definite commercial necessity,' for his actions. Thirdly, the alleged agent 'must satisfy the court that he was acting *bona fide* in the interests of the parties concerned.'[252]

4.66 The phrase 'agency of necessity' is misleading because the so-called 'agency' arises by operation of law, and lacks the usual incidents of agency at common law and in equity. Bowstead and Reynolds say that the agency of necessity doctrine 'should nowadays ... be considered against the background not of agency but of a possible general principle of necessitous intervention within the law of restitution.'[253] In so far as the authorities have recognized that an agent of necessity is entitled, by operation of law, to reimbursement of expenses for having so acted, it is unclear whether that right can only arise within an existing legal relationship between the parties, such as contract, bailment, or a 'true' but limited agency. A wide view of agency of necessity was taken by Latham CJ, dissenting, in *Burns Philp and Co Limited v Gillespie Brothers Pty Limited*:

> ... the phrase 'agent of necessity' is, in my opinion, only a convenient expression used in rationalizing to some extent the rights and obligations which are created in certain circumstances of emergency. It is a 'shorthand' method of saying that such circumstances may create an authority to act in relation to the property of another person or to impose a liability upon him

---

249. (1874) LR 9 Ex 132 at 136. See also *J Gadsden Pty Ltd v Strider 1 (The AES Express)* (1990) 20 NSWLR 57.

250. [1924] 1 KB 566.

251. *China Pacific SA v Food Corporation of India (The Winson)* [1982] AC 939 at 962 per Lord Diplock.

252. [1924] 1 KB 566 at 571–2. *Prager* was an action in conversion against an agent who sold his principal's goods without instructions. The agent pleaded agency of necessity in defence, but the plea failed on the facts because there was insufficient necessity to sell the goods and the agent had not acted *bona fide* in the interests of the principal.

253. *Bowstead and Reynolds on Agency* at [4-006].

which would not exist in ordinary circumstances. Thus in some circumstances a wife may be an agent of necessity to pledge her husband's credit for necessaries. ...Agency of necessity arises from action in circumstances of necessity and not from any real or presumed agreement between the person who becomes an 'agent of necessity' and the person in whose interest he has acted. In the case of masters of ships, the rule is, as stated by their Lordships in *Cargo ex Argos*[254], that in circumstances where the cargo will be lost or destroyed unless some exceptional action is taken, there is not merely a power given but a duty is cast on the master to act for the safety of the cargo in such manner as may be best under the circumstances. If he does so act, then the shipowner entitled to be paid [by the cargo owner] a reasonable remuneration for the services rendered.[255]

4.67   It remains an open point whether a stranger acting in an emergency to save another's property would have an independent claim in restitution for reimbursement of expenses against the person who benefited from the stranger's actions.[256]

4.68   Apart from the authorities on preserving another's property, there is another line of authorities, referred to by Latham CJ above in *Gillespie*, on preserving human life and health in circumstances of necessity, but not necessarily of emergency.[257] These authorities are concerned with reimbursement in restitution for the cost of providing 'necessaries' to persons who were known in law as lunatics, drunkards, and minors.[258] Unlike the property cases, the concept of 'necessaries' in this context is flexible,[259] depending upon the condition in life of the particular person in need. In these cases of policy-based restitution, an unjust enrichment analysis has limited relevance.

4.69   The leading case is the judgment of the English Court of Appeal in *Re Rhodes*.[260] That case was a claim for reimbursement against the estate of Eliza Rhodes, who had lived for the last 25 years of her life in the care of a private 'lunatic asylum'. Over two generations, her family had made a practice, unknown to her, of supplementing her income in order to pay for the costs of her care. It was considered relevant that Miss Rhodes was in the 'social position of a lady'. Although no records of the expenses had been kept by her family, and no claim had been made during her lifetime, certain family members made a claim in restitution against her estate for reimbursement of the costs of providing these 'necessaries'. Cotton LJ said:

---

254. (1873) LR 5 PC 134.

255. (1947) 74 CLR 148 at 175.

256. For an unsuccessful claim involving a tow truck, see *Suburban Towing & Equipment Pty Ltd v Suttons Motor Finance Pty Ltd* [2008] NSWSC 1346.

257. *Re F (Mental Patient: Sterilisation)* [1990] 2 AC 1 at 75 per Lord Goff.

258. In New South Wales, see the Minors (Property and Contracts) Act, 1970.

259. In *McLaughlin v Freehill* (1908) 5 CLR 858, the respondent's legal services were a 'necessary' for the mentally incapacitated appellant.

260. (1890) 44 Ch D 94.

I have no difficulty as to the question of the expenditure being for necessaries, for the law is well established that when the necessaries supplied are suitable to the position in life of the lunatic an implied obligation to pay for them out of his property will arise. But then the provision of money or necessaries must be made under circumstances which would justify the Court in implying an obligation.[261]

4.70 The claim failed in this case because, as Lindley LJ said, 'in order to raise an obligation to repay, the money must have been expended with the intention on the part of the person providing it that it should be repaid.'[262] The Court of Appeal held that the payments in this case were intended as gifts by the family, with no expectation of being repaid. While the particular claim in *Re Rhodes* failed, the general principles about the supply of necessaries to the legally incapacitated are reflected in s 7 of the Sale of Goods Act 1923 (NSW). The equivalent legislation in other states includes 'infants or minors'.[263] Section 7 provides:

> Capacity to buy and sell is regulated by the general law concerning capacity to contract and to transfer and acquire property:
>
> Provided that where necessaries are sold and delivered to a person who, by reason of mental incapacity or drunkenness, is incompetent to contract, the person must pay a reasonable price therefor.
>
> Necessaries in this section mean goods suitable to the condition in life of such person, and to the person's actual requirements at the time of the sale and delivery.

4.71 As *Re Rhodes* illustrates, there is a general principle against restitution for benefits conferred as gifts, gratuities or acts of charity or benevolence. A stranger who merely finds another's property and takes care of it for the owner, has no claim in restitution for any expenses incurred.[264] Restitution is also denied where a person has acted 'officiously' in conferring a benefit. Birks gave the example of someone who cleans another's car while the other is away.[265] The intervener in these circumstances is a 'risk-taker'. Similarly, Goff and Jones say that such a person 'takes the risk that the defendant will pay him for the benefit which he conferred on him. The risk is on his head. He has no cause to complain if his hope is disappointed.'[266] The doctrine of necessitous intervention operates as an exception to these general principles.

4.72 The most extreme circumstances of necessitous intervention are professional medical services rendered to save a human life in an emergency.

---

261. (1890) 44 Ch D 94 at 105.

262. (1890) 44 Ch D 94 at 107.

263. Sale of Goods Act 1954 (ACT) s 7; Sale of Goods Act 1972 (NT) s 7; Sale of Goods Act 1896 (Qld) s 5; Sale of Goods Act 1895 (SA) s 2; Sale of Goods Act 1896 (Tas) s 7; Goods Act 1958 (Vic) s 7; Sale of Goods Act 1895 (WA) s 2.

264. *Nicholson v Chapman* (1793) 2 H Bl 254; 126 ER 536.

265. P Birks, *An Introduction to the Law of Restitution*, revised ed, Clarendon Press, Oxford, 1989, pp 102–3.

266. Lord Goff of Chieveley and G Jones, *The Law of Restitution*, 7th ed, Sweet & Maxwell, London, 2007 [1—080]. See *Damburg v Damburg* (2001) 52 NSWLR 492 at 530 per Heydon JA.

The leading case is the judgment of the Manitoba Court of Appeal in *Matheson v Smiley*.[267] In that case, friends of Smiley had discovered him alive, but in a very serious condition, after he had apparently attempted to commit suicide by shooting himself at home. A doctor was summoned immediately, who arranged for Smiley to be taken to hospital and operated upon by the plaintiff surgeon, but without success. The surgeon subsequently claimed *quantum meruit* for his professional fee from Smiley's estate. In defence, it was argued on behalf of the estate that there was 'no request to [the] plaintiff binding upon the defendant'. Although the point was not made, it might even have been inferred from the circumstances that Smiley did not want the plaintiff's services. Whether the services were requested or not, Robson JA considered *Re Rhodes*, along with the Canadian authorities, and concluded that 'I look upon the surgeon's service here as a necessity for Smiley even though the effort was unavailing.'[268] Accordingly the surgeon's claim for *quantum meruit* was upheld.

Mistakenly rendered services

4.73 While restitution for mistaken payments is commonplace, the common law has yet to recognise any general principle of restitution for mistakenly rendered services. No such claim for *quantum meruit* was known under the old forms of action at common law, which is better explained by history than principle.[269] Until recent times, there was also the traditional rule against restitution for mistakes of law.[270] Since the High Court judgment in *Lumbers v Cook,* there is the particular difficulty that restitution for mistakenly rendered services may be defeated by the re-invigorated principle against restitution for unrequested or unsolicited services. As stated by Bowen LJ in *Falcke v Scottish Imperial Insurance Co,* the general principle remains that 'liabilities are not to be forced upon people behind their backs any more than you can confer a benefit upon a man against his will.'[271] However, as we have seen, the High Court acknowledged in *Lumbers v Cook* that the general exclusionary principle 'is not unqualified'.[272]

Mistaken improvements to chattels

4.74 There is a line of authority to support a claim in restitution for mistaken improvements to chattels.[273] In the leading case of *Greenwood v Bennett*,[274] the second claimant, Harper, was the *bona fide* purchaser of a Jaguar motor car,

267. [1932] 2 DLR 787.
268. [1932] 2 DLR 787 at 791.
269. S J Stoljar, *The Law of Quasi-Contract,* 2nd ed, Law Book Company, Sydney, 1989, pp 52–58.
270. See **4.14**.
271. (1886) 34 Ch D 234 at 248.
272. (2008) 232 CLR 635 at 663–4, per Gummow, Hayne, Crennan and Kiefel JJ.
273. See R J Sutton, 'What Should be Done for Mistaken Improvers?' in P D Finn (ed) *Essays on Restitution,* Law Book Company, Sydney, 1990.
274. [1973] 1 QB 195.

without notice that the car had been stolen from Bennett. During the time of his possession, Harper paid for the cost of carrying out necessary repairs to the car, in the mistaken belief that he was the owner. The police then seized the stolen car. In interpleader proceedings that were brought by the police to determine the competing claims to the car, the court at first instance upheld Bennett's claim of ownership of the car, which Harper conceded, but the court rejected Harper's claim against Bennett for an allowance for the cost of improvements to the car.

4.75 Harper's claim succeeded in the English Court of Appeal. Since specific recovery of chattels (whether in detinue or in equity) is a discretionary remedy, it can be argued that *Greenwood v Bennett* simply illustrates the uncontroversial proposition that specific recovery of chattels may be ordered on terms.[275] However, in the leading judgment, Lord Denning M R recognised an independent claim in restitution for the mistaken improver:

> There is a principle at hand to meet the case. It derives from the law of restitution. The plaintiffs should not be allowed unjustly to enrich themselves at his expense. The court will order the plaintiffs, if they recover the car, or its improved value, to recompense the innocent purchaser for the work he has done on it. No matter whether the plaintiffs recover it with the aid of the courts, or without it, the innocent purchaser will recover the value of the improvements he has done to it.[276]

Both Phillimore and Cairns LJJ concurred that an allowance should be made for the cost of improvements to the car, but neither of their Lordships expressed their reasons in terms of an action in restitution.

4.76 Goff and Jones cite *Greenwood v Bennett* in support of their proposition that 'a restitutionary claim grounded on mistake, may lie, even in the absence of free acceptance,[277] if it can be shown that the defendant has been incontrovertibly benefited by the services which have been rendered.'[278] The concept and terminology of 'incontrovertible benefit' were formulated by Goff and Jones as a test of enrichment by non-monetary benefits. According to Goff and Jones:

> … a person has been incontrovertibly benefited if a reasonable person would conclude that he has been saved an expense which he otherwise would necessarily have incurred or where he has made, in consequence of the plaintiff's acts, a realisable financial gain.[279]

275. *Peruvian Guano Co Ltd v Dreyfus Brothers & Co* [1892] AC 166 at 176 per Lord Macnaghten.
276. [1973] 1 QB 195 at 202.
277. In Australia, the 'free acceptance' principle was rejected by the High Court in *Lumbers v Cook*. See **4.50**.
278. Lord Goff of Chieveley and G Jones, *The Law of Restitution*, 7th ed, Sweet & Maxwell, London, 2007 [6-001].
279. Lord Goff of Chieveley and G Jones, *The Law of Restitution*, 7th ed, Sweet & Maxwell, London, 2007 [1-023]. In *Lumbers v Cook*, the Supreme Court of South Australia held that the completed house was an 'incontrovertible benefit' to the defendants: [2007] SASC 20 at [69]-[76], (2007) 96 SASR 406 at 421-22.

4.77 In other words, these are circumstances where no reasonable person can deny being enriched by the plaintiff's services. Enrichment is, of course, a fundamental element in an unjust enrichment analysis, though not necessarily in a request-based analysis. On the facts in *Greenwood v Bennett*, Bennett was enriched because he was saved a necessary expense by Harper. The enrichment was unjust because of Harper's honest mistake. In the United Kingdom, an allowance for a mistaken but honest improver of goods is now statutory.[280]

4.78 The reasoning in *Greenwood v Bennett* and the concept of incontrovertible benefit were applied to similar facts by Young J (as he then was) in *McKeown v Cavalier Yachts Pty Ltd*.[281] In that case, the mistaken improver had completed the building of a yacht that was successfully claimed by the plaintiff in proceedings for specific restitution of the yacht in equity. Applying *Greenwood v Bennett*, Young J reasoned that 'the plaintiff must pay compensation as a prerequisite to obtaining an order for specific recovery of the chattel and the measure of that compensation is the amount of incontrovertible benefit'.[282] The quantum of the incontrovertible benefit in this case was 'the increased value in the yacht as a result of the second defendant's [the improver's] work rather than the cost of providing such work which cost presumably includes profit margins'.[283] Robert Goff J (as he then was) had drawn the same distinction in *BP Exploration Co (Libya) Ltd v Hunt (No 2)*:

> [Where] the benefit has been requested by the defendant, the basic measure of recovery in restitution is the reasonable value of the plaintiff's performance — in a case of services, a quantum meruit or reasonable remuneration, … Such cases are to be contrasted with cases where such a benefit has not been requested by the defendant. In the latter class of case, recovery in restitution is rare; but if the sole basis for recovery was that the defendant had been incontrovertibly benefited, it might be legitimate to limit recovery to the defendant's actual benefit. …[284]

4.79 Similarly, Deane J acknowledged in *Pavey & Matthews Pty Ltd v Paul* that a less onerous measure of restitution should apply where 'unsolicited but subsequently accepted work is done in improving property in circumstances where remuneration for the unsolicited work calculated at what was a reasonable rate would far exceed the enhanced value of the property.'[285] This must now be read in the light of *Lumbers v Cook*, where the High Court rejected the acceptance of an unrequested or unsolicited benefit as a basis for restitution. However, the appeal in *Lumbers v Cook* was not argued before the High Court as a case of mistaken improvement. In both *Greenwood v Bennett* and *McKeown v Cavalier Yachts Pty Ltd*, the mistaken improvements were made to chattels, not land. Mistaken improvements to land have traditionally been

---

280. Torts (Interference With Goods) Act, 1977 (UK) s 6(1). There is no equivalent legislation in Australia.
281. (1988) 13 NSWLR 303.
282. (1988) 13 NSWLR 303 at 313.
283. (1988) 13 NSWLR 303 at 314.
284. [1979] 1 WLR 783 at 805.
285. (1987) 162 CLR 221 at 263.

treated as matters of estoppel by acquiescence or proprietary estoppel in equity.[286] Under the line of authorities following *Ramsden v Dyson*,[287] a mistaken improver of land will be denied relief unless, amongst other requirements, the defendant knows of the plaintiff's mistaken belief and has 'encouraged the plaintiff in his expenditure of money or in the other acts which he has done, either directly or by abstaining from asserting his legal right.'[288] This rationale is broadly consistent with the concept of free acceptance in the law of restitution.[289]

DEFENCES

Introduction

4.80 It is arguably unnecessary to speak of 'defences' to restitutionary claims. Since the principle of unjust enrichment requires that the retention of the benefit by the defendant is unjust, circumstances which are relevant to the element of 'unjustness' might be the same circumstances that would otherwise be called a defence.

Change of position

4.81 The 'change of position' defence is unique to the law of restitution for unjust enrichment.[290] It arises where the defendant has received a benefit and 'has acted to his or her detriment on the faith of the receipt'.[291] Derived from the older and more limited defence of estoppel by representation,[292] the change of position defence has its most common application in cases of mistaken payments.

4.82 The change of position defence was first recognised by the High Court in *Australia and New Zealand Banking Group Ltd v Westpac Banking Corp*.[293] Westpac, acting as the agent of its customer, had received a mistaken overpayment of money from ANZ. Before receiving notice of the mistake, and acting within the scope of its agency, Westpac had applied part of the

---

286. R P Meagher, J D Heydon and M J Leeming, *Meagher, Gummow and Lehane's Equity: Doctrines and Remedies*, 4th ed, Butterworths LexisNexis, Sydney, 2002 [17-075]-[17-115].

287. (1866) LR 1 HL 129. See *Willmott v Barber* (1880) 15 Ch D 96; *Inwards v Baker* [1965] 2 QB 29; *Taylor Fashions Ltd v Liverpool Victoria Trustees Co Ltd* [1982] QB 133.

288. *Willmott v Barber* (1880) 15 Ch D 96 at 105-6 per Fry J.

289. See *Cooke v Dunn* (1998) 9 BPR 16,489.

290. See, generally, E Bant, *The Change of Position Defence*, Hart Publishing, Oxford, 2009.

291. *David Securities Pty Ltd v Commonwealth Bank of Australia* (1992) 175 CLR 353 at 385 per Mason CJ, Deane, Toohey, Gaudron and McHugh JJ.

292. See the analysis in *TRA Global Pty Ltd v Kebakoska* [2011] VSC 480.

293. (1988) 164 CLR 662. In Western Australia, the change of position defence in relation to mistaken payments was introduced by s 24 of the Law Reform (Property, Perpetuities and Succession) Act 1962 (WA), subsequently re-enacted as s 125(1) of the Property Law Act 1969 (WA). The change of position defence for trustees was introduced by s 65(8) of the Trustees Act 1962 (WA). In Queensland, the change of position defence for trustees was introduced by s 109(3) of the Trusts Act 1973 (Qld).

overpayment in reduction of its customer's overdraft account. The overdraft account was a debt payable by the customer to Westpac. In the High Court, both parties conceded that if ANZ had demanded restitution of the mistaken payment before Westpac had applied the payment to its customer's overdraft account, Westpac would have been liable to make restitution of the entire mistaken payment. The issue in dispute before the High Court was the liability of Westpac to make restitution of that portion of the mistaken payment which Westpac had appropriated to itself in reduction of its customer's overdraft account.

Assuming a relationship of agency between Westpac and its customer, Mason CJ, Wilson, Deane, Toohey and Gaudron JJ in a joint judgment held that:

> … an agent who has received money on his principal's behalf will, without more, have a good defence if, before learning that the money was paid under fundamental mistake, he has 'paid it to the principal or done something equivalent' thereto.[294]

Treating the payment by Westpac to itself as a payment by an agent (being Westpac) to a third party (also being Westpac) on behalf of its principal (being the customer), the High Court held that Westpac was not liable to make restitution of the amount which it had applied to the customer's overdraft account. Recognising that the agency defence is a specific example of a more general principle, the High Court went on to say:

> If the matter needs to be expressed in terms of detriment or change of position, the payment by the agent to the principal of the money which he has received on the principal's behalf, of itself constitutes the relevant detriment or change of position. In that regard, no relevant distinction can be drawn between payment to the principal or payment to another or others on behalf of the principal.[295]

4.83   While it can be said that *ANZ v Westpac* was decided by an application of established agency principles, that was not so in *David Securities Pty Ltd v Commonwealth Bank of Australia*.[296] In that case, the Commonwealth Bank argued that it had incurred a liability for withholding tax, which it would not otherwise have incurred, in the genuine belief that David Securities could be and was contractually obliged to reimburse the bank for that tax liability. In truth, the relevant contractual obligation was illegal and void. While declining to decide the issue for a lack of evidence, the High Court accepted that a change of position by the Commonwealth Bank would defeat a claim for restitution based upon David Securities' mistake of law.

---

294. (1988) 164 CLR 662 at 681–2. See also *Port of Brisbane Corporation v ANZ Securities Ltd (No 2)* [2003] 2 Qd R 661 (CA), where the defence was allowed to a stockbroker that had bought and sold shares in good faith, as the unknowing agent of a fraudulent client. Alternatively, the stockbroker had never been enriched by money received as the agent and trustee of its client: *NIML Ltd v Man Financial Australia Ltd* [2004] VSC 449 at [98] per Harper J.

295. (1988) 164 CLR 662 at 682.

296. (1992) 175 CLR 353.

Citing with approval a passage from Birks,[297] the High Court identified the 'central element' of the defence as the defendant having 'acted to his or her detriment on the *faith of the receipt*'.[298] This incorporates two related requirements that the High Court had earlier identified in *ANZ v Westpac*. First, that the defendant acted in good faith.[299] Mere negligence does not suffice to show a lack of good faith.[300] The defence is not available to a 'wrongdoer',[301] or where the defendant acted with knowledge of the payer's mistake.[302] Short of actual knowledge, having 'good reason to believe that the payment was made by mistake' was sufficient for the English Court of Appeal to reject the defence in *Niru Battery Manufacturing Co v Milestone Trading Ltd*.[303] Clarke LJ (as he then was) quoted with approval from the judgment of Moore-Bick J at first instance, who referred to:

> ... cases where the payee has grounds for believing that the payment may have been made by mistake, but cannot be sure. In such cases good faith may well dictate that an enquiry be made of the payer. The nature and extent of the enquiry called for will, of course, depend on the circumstances of the case, but I do not think that a person who has, or thinks he has, good reason to believe that the payment was made by mistake will often be found to have acted in good faith if he pays the money away without first making enquiries of the person from whom he received it.[304]

Conversely, in *Heperu Pty Ltd v Belle*, the New South Wales Court of Appeal took *Niru* to mean that having the 'mere means of knowledge' does not disqualify for the defence.[305] As Clarke LJ said in *Niru*, 'the question is whether it would be inequitable or unconscionable to deny restitution' to the mistaken payer.[306]

4.84 The second requirement identified by the High Court in *ANZ v Westpac* is that the defendant acted 'in reliance on the payment'.[307] In *David Securities*, the High Court endorsed the requirement found in the Canadian and United States authorities that 'the defendant point to expenditure or financial commitment which can be ascribed to the mistaken payment'. The change of position defence is not available where the defendant has 'simply spent the

---

297. P Birks, *An Introduction to the Law of Restitution*, revised ed, Clarendon Press, Oxford, 1989, p 410.

298. (1992) 175 CLR 353 at 385 per Mason CJ, Deane, Toohey, Gaudron and McHugh JJ (original emphasis).

299. (1988) 164 CLR 662 at 673 per Mason CJ, Wilson, Deane, Toohey and Gaudron JJ.

300. *Port of Brisbane Corporation v ANZ Securities Ltd (No 2)* [2003] 2 Qd R 661 at 674–5 per McPherson JA.

301. *Lipkin Gorman v Karpnale Ltd* [1991] 2 AC 548 at 580 per Lord Goff. See also *Barros Mattos Jnr v MacDaniels Ltd* [2004] EWHC 1188 (Ch); [2004] 3 All ER 299.

302. *Lipkin Gorman v Karpnale Ltd* [1991] 2 AC 548 at 580 per Lord Goff.

303. [2003] EWCA Civ 1446 at [164]; [2004] QB 985 at 1004 per Clarke LJ.

304. [2002] EWHC 1425 (Comm) at [135]; [2002] 2 All ER (Comm) 705 at 741, quoted with approval in *Abou Rahmah v Abacha* [2006] EWCA Civ 1492 at [48]; [2007] 1 All ER 827 at 840 per Rix LJ.

305. [2009] NSWCA 252 at [75]; (2009) 76 NSWLR 230 at 249 per Allsop P.

306. [2003] EWCA Civ 1446 at [152]; [2004] QB 985 at 1000–1 per Clarke LJ.

307. (1988) 164 CLR 662 at 673.

money received on ordinary living expenses'.[308] It is not a change of position to repay an existing debt that would have needed to be repaid in any event, whether sooner or later.[309] Similarly, Lord Goff has stressed that 'the mere fact that the defendant has spent the money, in whole or in part, does not of itself render it inequitable that he should be called upon to repay'.[310]

4.85 The question of what constitutes acting 'on the faith of the receipt' by a bank was considered by the New South Wales Court of Appeal in *State Bank of New South Wales v Swiss Bank Corp*.[311] The Swiss Bank, acting at the instigation of a fraudulent employee, mistakenly made a payment of $20 million to the State Bank. Before the fraud was revealed, the State Bank disbursed the payment according to the instructions of a customer. Crucially, the mistaken payment had been made by the Swiss Bank without reference to any customer of the State Bank,[312] and the State Bank had relied upon its own inquiries as to the destination of the funds. In these circumstances, the Court of Appeal held that the State Bank had not changed its position 'on the faith of the receipt':

> A bank which receives a mistaken payment and disburses it can only bring itself within the change of position defence if it shows that at the time of the disbursement it knew or thought it knew more than the fact of receipt standing alone. This must be information which, if true, would entitle the payee to deal with the receipt as it did and that information must have come from the payer.[313]

This requirement that the 'information must come from the payer' was clarified by the Court of Appeal in *Perpetual Trustees Australia Ltd v Heperu Pty Ltd*.[314] Speaking of its decision in *Swiss Bank*, the Court of Appeal said:

> Care should be taken not to overextend the application of what was said by the Court beyond the facts. … True it is that a payee must know more than the fact of mere receipt. It must have information that entitles it (on the basis of the information) to deal with the receipt. The requirement that the information came from the 'payer' can be seen as no more than a requirement that the change of position must be on the faith of the receipt and its attendant circumstances. … There needs to be a foundation of information obtained in connection with the receipt to justify acting on the basis of the receipt. That was absent in *Swiss Bank*.[315]

---

308. (1992) 175 CLR 353 at 385–6.
309. *Scottish Equitable plc v Derby* [2001] 3 All ER 818, about the early repayment of a mortgage debt.
310. *Lipkin Gorman v Karpnale Ltd* [1991] 2 AC 548 at 580.
311. (1995) 39 NSWLR 350.
312. Accordingly, the funds were received by the defendant bank as a principal, and not as an agent. Compare *Australia and New Zealand Banking Group Ltd v Westpac Banking Corp* (1988) 164 CLR 662.
313. (1995) 39 NSWLR 350 at 356.
314. (2009) 76 NSWLR 195; [2009] NSWCA 84.
315. (2009) 76 NSWLR 195 at 224; [2009] NSWCA 84 at [139] per Allsop P and Handley JA (Campbell JA agreeing).

On the facts in *Heperu*, the appellant bank successfully claimed the change of position defence, even though the false information about the payments came primarily from a fraudulent agent of the payers, not the payers themselves. The Court of Appeal separately held that the bank had not acted negligently.

4.86   The concept of acting 'on the faith of the receipt' also requires a causal link between the defendant receiving the payment and the defendant incurring the detriment, normally in that order of events. The English authorities have considered whether the change of position defence extends to cases of 'anticipatory reliance' where the defendant changed position *before* receiving the anticipated payment. In *South Tyneside Metropolitan Borough Council v Svenska International plc*, Clarke J (as he then was) said that 'save perhaps in exceptional circumstances, the defence of change of position is in principle confined to changes which take place after receipt of the money'.[316] However, in *Dextra Bank & Trust Co Ltd v Bank of Jamaica*,[317] the Privy Council took the opposite view. Lords Goff and Bingham said:

> … it is difficult to see what relevant distinction can be drawn between (1) a case in which the defendant expends on some extraordinary expenditure all or part of a sum of money which he has received from the plaintiff, and (2) one in which the defendant incurs such expenditure in the expectation that he will receive the sum of money from the plaintiff, which he does in fact receive … It is surely no abuse of language to say, in the second case as in the first, that the defendant has incurred the expenditure in reliance on the plaintiff's payment or, as is sometimes said, on the faith of the payment.[318]

4.87   In all of the cases considered so far, the relevant 'detriment' or 'change of position' by the defendant has been a payment away or expenditure of money by the defendant. However, benefits that were foregone or given up by the defendant, acting on the faith of the receipt, may also qualify as a change of position for the purposes of the defence. In *Palmer v Blue Circle Southern Cement Ltd*,[319] the appellant pleaded the defence to an action for the recovery of workers' compensation payments that the respondent had made under a mistake of law. Applying the rule in *David Securities Pty Ltd v Commonwealth Bank of Australia*, Palmer's expenditure of the payments on ordinary living expenses did not qualify for the defence. Instead, Bell J of the New South Wales Supreme Court identified the relevant detriment as Palmer having irrevocably foregone his entitlement to receive social security benefits for the period in question. Because Palmer had done so on the faith of the receipt of the mistaken workers' compensation payments, the defence was allowed. The same conclusion on equivalent facts was reached by the Victorian

---

316. [1995] 1 All ER 545 at 565.
317. [2001] UKPC 50; [2002] 1 All ER (Comm) 193.
318. [2001] UKPC 50 at [38]; [2002] 1 All ER (Comm) 193 at 204, followed by the English Court of Appeal in *Commerzbank Ag v Price Jones* [2003] EWCA Civ 1663.
319. (1999) 48 NSWLR 318.

Supreme Court in *TRA Global Pty Ltd v Kebakoska*.[320] In *Gertsch v Atsas*,[321] Foster AJ held that giving up paid employment to pursue unpaid full-time study was a sufficient detriment to qualify for the defence, in circumstances where the defendant had acted upon the faith of the mistaken payments.

Good consideration

4.88 In both *Australia and New Zealand Banking Group Ltd v Westpac Banking Corp*[322] and *David Securities Pty Ltd v Commonwealth Bank of Australia*,[323] the High Court recognised that an action for money had and received for the restitution of a mistaken payment may be defeated to the extent that the mistaken payer has received 'good consideration' for the mistaken payment. Similarly, it has been explained that a claim based upon a total failure of consideration will be defeated completely if the plaintiff has received any part of the consideration for which the plaintiff had bargained: see **4.22**. In each of these contexts, 'consideration' means 'the performance of the defendant's promise, not the promise itself'.[324]

4.89 The receipt of good consideration was allowed by the Victorian Court of Appeal as a complete defence to the mistaken payer's claim in *Ovidio Carrideo Nominees Pty Ltd v Dog Depot Pty Ltd*.[325] In that case, the plaintiff tenant claimed against the defendant landlord to recover all of the rent that the plaintiff had paid over a period of years in ignorance of the Retail Tenancies Reform Act 1998 (Vic). The Act relevantly provided that the tenant was 'not liable to pay rent' until the landlord had given the tenant a disclosure statement as required by the Act. In this case, the landlord had neglected to do so. Nevertheless, the Court of Appeal rejected the tenant's claim in restitution because the tenant had received the consideration for which it had bargained, being the exclusive use and occupation of the landlord's premises for the duration of the tenancy.

---

320. [2011] VSC 480.

321. [1999] NSWSC 898; (1999) 10 BPR 18,431 at 18,451–2.

322. (1988) 164 CLR 662 at 673 per Mason CJ, Wilson, Deane, Toohey and Gaudron JJ, referring to 'valuable consideration'.

323. (1992) 175 CLR 353 at 379–80 per Mason CJ, Deane, Toohey, Gaudron and McHugh JJ.

324. *Baltic Shipping Co v Dillon* (1993) 176 CLR 344 at 350–1 per Mason CJ.

325. [2006] VSCA 6.

Part 4

EQUITY

CHAPTER

Rescission

NATURE OF THE REMEDY

5.1   Rescission is the reversal of a transaction so that each party is restored to its original position. Rescission is a remedy of both the common law and equity. Common law rescission is confined to contracts, but rescission in equity extends to gifts and other transactions. This chapter will concentrate on contracts.

Rescission and termination

5.2   In the case law, the terms 'rescission' and 'termination' are sometimes used interchangeably as if they both refer to the same concept. They are different concepts. 'Termination' refers to the position where there has been a breach of a contractual condition, and the promisee has elected to terminate further performance of the contract. The differences between rescission and termination were explained by Dixon J in *McDonald v Dennys Lascelles Ltd*:

When a party to a simple contract, upon a breach by the other contracting party of a condition of the contract, elects to treat the contract as no longer binding upon him, the contract is not rescinded as from the beginning. Both parties are discharged from the further performance of the contract, but rights are not divested or discharged which have already been unconditionally acquired. Rights and obligations which arise from the partial execution of the contract and causes of action which have accrued from its breach alike continue unaffected. When a contract is rescinded because of matters which affect its formation, as in the case of fraud, the parties are to be rehabilitated and restored, so far as may be, to the position they occupied before the contract was made. But when a contract, which is not void or voidable at law, or liable to be set aside in equity, is dissolved at the election of one party because the other has not observed an essential condition or has committed a breach going to its root, the contract is determined so far as it is executory only and the party in default is liable for damages for its breach.[1]

Contracts that are liable to rescission are described as 'voidable' rather than 'void'. Voidable contracts are effective unless and until there is an election to rescind or 'avoid' the contract. By contrast, if a contract is void, there is nothing to rescind. Because rescission operates *ab initio*,[2] an election to rescind a voidable contract extinguishes the right to enforce the contract according to its terms, including any accrued right to damages in contract or specific performance. Accordingly, rescission and damages in contract are mutually exclusive remedies. Rescission may, however, be combined with other remedies that do not involve the enforcement of the avoided contract. For example, rescission for fraudulent misrepresentation may be combined with a claim for damages in tort for deceit.[3] Alternatively, payments made under the avoided contract may be recoverable by an action in restitution for money had and received: see **Chapter 4**.

ELEMENTS

5.3   The remedy of rescission requires three elements to be satisfied:

a)   the presence of a *vitiating factor* in the formation of the contract;

b)   an *election* to rescind the contract; and

c)   *restitutio in integrum*, the restoration of both parties to their respective precontractual positions.

VITIATING FACTORS

5.4   At common law, contracts can be rescinded for fraudulent misrepresentation and duress. In equity, contracts can be rescinded for innocent and fraudulent misrepresentation, mistake, duress, undue influence, unconscionable dealing and breach of fiduciary duty.

---

1.   (1933) 48 CLR 457 at 476–7.
2.   *Alati v Kruger* (1955) 94 CLR 216 at 224 per Dixon CJ, Webb, Kitto and Taylor JJ; *Vadasz v Pioneer Concrete (SA) Pty Ltd* (1995) 184 CLR 102 at 111 per Deane, Dawson, Toohey, Gaudron and McHugh JJ.
3.   *Newbigging v Adam* (1886) 34 Ch D 589 at 592 per Bowen LJ.

Misrepresentation

5.5   A contract can be voidable for misrepresentation if the representor has made a misrepresentation of fact that induced the representee to enter into the contract. Each element of this proposition will be considered in turn.

There must be a representation of fact

5.6   Representations or statements of fact may be express or implied. They may be inferred from 'a single word, or … a nod or a wink, or a shake of the head, or a smile'.[4] Except in contracts of 'utmost good faith', such as insurance contracts, where there is a duty to disclose all relevant matters,[5] the traditional rule is that mere silence is not actionable at common law.[6] Hence, the doctrine of *caveat emptor*. However, silence in the form of a partial truth may be misleading because 'concealment of a fact may cause the true representation of another fact to be misleading, and may thus become a substantive misrepresentation'.[7]

5.7   Statements of fact have been distinguished from mere words of 'puffery'. In *Mitchell v Valherie*,[8] the Supreme Court of South Australia held that the words 'Nothing to Spend — Perfect Presentation' in a sales brochure did not amount to a representation of fact, either true or false, about the structural integrity of a house.

The authorities have drawn a similar distinction between statements of fact and statements of opinion or belief. Statements of opinion or belief generally provide no grounds for rescission if the opinion or belief is honestly held. In *Bisset v Wilkinson*[9] a statement by the vendor of a farm as to the sheep-carrying capacity of the farm was held to be a statement of opinion, thereby denying the purchaser rescission of the contract when the statement proved to be untrue. The vendor had believed in the truth of his statement when he made it. In concluding that the vendor's statement was one of opinion, the Privy Council (on appeal from the New Zealand Court of Appeal) emphasised that the land in question had never been used as a sheep farm to the knowledge of both the vendor and the purchaser. Accordingly, the distinction between statements of fact and statements of opinion or belief may turn upon the relative knowledge of the parties. In *Smith v Land and House Property Corp*[10] the vendors of a property misrepresented the existing tenant to the purchasers as 'a most desirable tenant'. In truth, the vendors knew that the tenant was chronically in arrears of rent. Bowen LJ of the English Court of Appeal said:

---

4.   *Walters v Morgan* (1861) 3 De GF & J 718 at 724; 45 ER 1056 at 1059 per Lord Campbell LC.
5.   Insurance Contracts Act 1984 (Cth) ss 13 and 21.
6.   *W Scott Fell & Co v Lloyd* (1906) 4 CLR 572; *United Dominions Corporation Ltd v Brian Pty Ltd* (1985) 157 CLR 1 at 6 per Gibbs CJ.
7.   *Curwen v Yan Yean Land Co Ltd* (1891) 17 VLR 745 at 751 per Higinbotham CJ; applied in *Krakowski v Eurolynx Properties Ltd* (1995) 183 CLR 563 at 575 per Brennan, Deane, Gaudron and McHugh JJ.
8.   [2005] SASC 350; (2005) 93 SASR 76.
9.   [1927] AC 177.
10.   (1884) 28 Ch D 7.

In a case where the facts are equally well known to both parties, what one of them says to the other is frequently nothing but an expression of opinion. The statement of such opinion is in a sense a statement of fact, about the condition of the man's own mind, but only of an irrelevant fact, for it is of no consequence what the opinion is. But if the facts are not equally known to both sides, then a statement of opinion by the one who knows the facts best involves very often a statement of a material fact, for he impliedly states that he knows facts which justify his opinion.[11]

In the particular circumstances of the case, Bowen LJ held that the vendors' statement was 'an assertion of a specific fact' that 'nothing has occurred in the relations between the landlords and the tenant which can be considered to make the tenant an unsatisfactory one'.[12] Accordingly, the contract was set aside for misrepresentation.

5.8   The same principles apply to statements of intention. In *Edgington v Fitzmaurice*,[13] a subscriber to an issue of debentures successfully claimed damages in tort for deceit on the basis of a fraudulent statement of intention in the prospectus. The statement concerned the purpose for which the money raised by the issue of debentures would be used. Treating the statement in the prospectus as a fraudulent statement of fact as to the directors' present intentions, Bowen LJ said:

A mere suggestion of possible purposes to which a portion of the money might be applied would not have formed a basis for an action of deceit. There must be a misstatement of an existing fact: but the state of a man's mind is as much a fact as the state of his digestion. It is true that it is very difficult to prove what the state of a man's mind at a particular time is, but if it can be ascertained it is as much a fact as anything else. A misrepresentation as to the state of a man's mind is, therefore, a misstatement of fact.[14]

5.9   Statements of law have also been treated as statements of opinion. Accordingly, an honestly stated opinion on a matter of law provides no basis for rescission.[15] But a fraudulently stated opinion on a matter of law is treated as a statement of fact because it implies that the representor honestly holds that opinion. Rescission is therefore allowed in cases of fraudulently stated opinions on matters of law.[16] By contrast, statements of foreign law are always treated as statements of fact.[17]

---

11. (1884) 28 Ch D 7 at 15. See *RAIA Insurance Brokers Ltd v FAI General Insurance Co Ltd* (1993) 112 ALR 511 at 519–20 per Beaumont and Spender JJ; *Middleton v AON Risk Services Australia Ltd* [2008] WASCA 239. Compare *Economides v Commercial Insurance Co plc* [1998] QB 587.
12. (1884) 28 Ch D 7 at 15.
13. (1885) 29 Ch D 459.
14. (1885) 29 Ch D 459 at 483.
15. *Eaglesfield v Marquis of Londonderry* (1876) 4 Ch D 693.
16. *West London Commercial Bank Ltd v Kitson* (1884) 13 QBD 360 at 362–3 per Bowen LJ; *Public Trustee v Taylor* [1978] VR 289 at 299 per Kaye J.
17. *Andre & Cie SA v Ets Michel Blanc & Fils* [1979] 2 Lloyd's Rep 427.

The representation must be false when acted upon

5.10   Whether a representation is true or false is a question of fact that is normally judged when the representation was made. But a representation that was true when made may subsequently become false before the representee acts upon it. Where the representation is a continuing representation that has become false to the knowledge of the representor, a duty arises to inform the representee of the changed circumstances before the representation is acted upon. In *With v O'Flanagan*,[18] the vendor of a medical practice made precontractual representations to the purchaser about the income of the practice. Although the representations were true when they were made, the income of the practice had declined substantially by the time the contract was made. Because the vendor knew of this changed circumstance and had neglected to inform the purchaser, the English Court of Appeal set aside the contract for misrepresentation. In deciding whether the vendor's initial representations continued down to the making of the contract, Lord Wright MR observed that 'a representation made as a matter of inducement to enter into a contract is to be treated as a continuing representation'.[19]

Inducement

5.11   The principles governing inducement were restated by Wilson J of the High Court in *Gould v Vaggelas*:

1.   Notwithstanding that a representation is both false and fraudulent, if the representee does not rely upon it he has no case.

2.   If a material representation is made which is calculated to induce the representee to enter into a contract and that person in fact enters into the contract there arises a fair inference of fact that he was induced to do so by the representation.

3.   The inference may be rebutted, for example, by showing that the representee, before he entered into the contract, either was possessed of actual knowledge of the true facts and knew them to be true or alternatively made it plain that whether he knew the true facts or not he did not rely on the representation.

4.   The representation need not be the sole inducement. It is sufficient so long as it plays some part even if only a minor part in contributing to the formation of the contract.[20]

Rescission at common law: the concept of fraud

5.12   Historically, the remedies for misrepresentation have turned upon whether the misrepresentation was fraudulently or innocently made. The common law has only afforded relief for fraudulent misrepresentation, and

18.   [1936] Ch 575. See also *Jones v Dumbrell* [1981] VR 199.
19.   [1936] Ch 575 at 584. Compare *Macquarie Generation v Peabody Resources Ltd* (2001) Aust Contract R 90-121 (NSWCA).
20.   (1985) 157 CLR 215 at 236. See also: *Thomson v STX Pan Ocean Co Ltd* [2012] FCAFC 15 at [23] per Greenwood, McKerracher and Reeves JJ.

not for innocent misrepresentation. The principal remedies at common law for fraudulent misrepresentation are rescission and damages in tort for deceit.

The meaning of fraud at common law was settled by the House of Lords in *Derry v Peek*.[21] Although the case was an action in deceit, it has been accepted by the High Court[22] and elsewhere as the authority defining fraud for the purposes of rescission at common law. The litigation in *Derry v Peek* arose from a prospectus issued on behalf of the Plymouth, Devonport and District Tramways Company. The company was incorporated by an Act of Parliament which provided that the tramways could be operated by animal power and, with the consent of the Board of Trade, by steam power. In the prospectus issued on behalf of the company, the directors made an unqualified representation that the company was allowed to use steam power. The plaintiff subscribed for shares in the company in reliance upon this representation, which the directors had honestly believed. When the Board of Trade later refused permission for the company to use steam power, the company was wound up and the plaintiff claimed damages against the directors for deceit. The House of Lords held that the directors were not liable in deceit because the directors had honestly believed in the truth of their statement. Lord Herschell said:

> I think the authorities establish the following propositions: First, in order to sustain an action of deceit, there must be proof of fraud, and nothing short of that will suffice. Secondly, fraud is proved when it is shewn that a false representation has been made (1) knowingly, or (2) without belief in its truth, or (3) recklessly, careless whether it be true or false. Although I have treated the second and third as distinct cases, I think the third is but an instance of the second, for one who makes a statement under such circumstances can have no real belief in the truth of what he states. To prevent a false statement being fraudulent, there must, I think, always be an honest belief in its truth.[23]

5.13 In the absence of common law fraud, there is no remedy of damages for innocent misrepresentation at common law. However, that gap has been filled to an extent by the tort of negligent misstatement[24] and statutory liability for misleading or deceptive conduct in trade or commerce: see **5.18**. Damages for innocent misrepresentation are available under the misrepresentation legislation in the United Kingdom, the Australian Capital Territory and South Australia.[25]

---

21. (1889) 14 App Cas 337.
22. *Civil Service Co-Operative Society of Victoria Ltd v Blyth* (1914) 17 CLR 601 at 609 per Barton J; *Krakowski v Eurolynx Properties Ltd* (1995) 183 CLR 563 at 579–80 per Brennan, Deane, Gaudron and McHugh JJ.
23. (1889) 14 App Cas 337 at 374.
24. See *Hedley Byrne & Co Ltd v Heller & Partners Ltd* [1964] AC 465; *L Shaddock & Associates Pty Ltd v Parramatta City Council* (1981) 150 CLR 225; *San Sebastian Pty Ltd v Minister Administering the Environmental Planning and Assessment Act 1979* (1986) 162 CLR 340.
25. Misrepresentation Act 1967 (UK) s 2(1); Civil Law (Wrongs) Act 2002 (ACT) s 174(2); Misrepresentation Act 1972 (SA) s 7(1).

Rescission in equity for innocent misrepresentation

5.14   The expression 'innocent misrepresentation' is a residual category comprising all misrepresentations that are not fraudulent in the common law sense. Equity has always taken a much wider view of fraud than the common law. In particular, fraud in equity does not require 'an actual intention to cheat'.[26] Equity exercises a concurrent jurisdiction with the common law to rescind contracts induced by misrepresentations that are fraudulent in the common law sense. Based upon the equitable concept of fraud, equity exercises an auxiliary jurisdiction to rescind contracts induced by innocent misrepresentation. The equitable jurisdiction to rescind contracts for innocent misrepresentation was explained by Sir George Jessel MR in *Redgrave v Hurd*:

> According to the decisions of Courts of Equity it was not necessary, in order to set aside a contract obtained by material false representation, to prove that the party who obtained it knew at the time when the representation was made that it was false. It was put in two ways, either of which was sufficient. One way of putting the case was, "A man is not to be allowed to get a benefit from a statement which he now admits to be false. He is not to be allowed to say, for the purpose of civil jurisdiction, that when he made it he did not know it to be false; he ought to have found that out before he made it". The other way of putting it was this: "Even assuming that moral fraud must be shewn in order to set aside a contract, you have it where a man, having obtained a beneficial contract by a statement which he now knows to be false, insists upon keeping that contract. To do so is a moral delinquency: no man ought to seek to take advantage of his own false statements".[27]

Misrepresentations incorporated as contractual terms

5.15   Where a misrepresentation has been incorporated as a term of the contract, there is English authority that the right to rescind in equity for innocent misrepresentation is lost.[28] The rationale is that the representee is entitled to contractual remedies for breach. The better view, taken in the Australian authorities,[29] is that the representee may elect between rescission and contractual remedies. The supposed restriction upon rescission has been removed by the misrepresentation legislation in the United Kingdom, the Australian Capital Territory and South Australia.[30] In sale of goods transactions, the restriction has also been removed in New South Wales and, for consumer sales, in Victoria.[31]

---

26.   *Nocton v Lord Ashburton* [1914] AC 932 at 934 per Lord Haldane LC.
27.   (1881) 20 Ch D 1 at 12–13.
28.   *Pennsylvania Shipping Co v Compagnie Nationale de Navigation* [1936] 2 All ER 1167 at 1171 per Branson J.
29.   *Simons v Zartom Investments Pty Ltd* [1975] 2 NSWLR 30 at 36 per Holland J; *Academy of Health and Fitness Pty Ltd v Power* [1973] VR 254 at 264–7 per Crockett J. Compare *Svanosio v McNamara* (1956) 96 CLR 186 at 205 per McTiernan, Williams and Webb JJ.
30.   Misrepresentation Act 1967 (UK) s 1(a); Civil Law (Wrongs) Act 2002 (ACT) s 173; Misrepresentation Act 1972 (SA) s 6(1).
31.   Sale of Goods Act 1923 (NSW) s 4(2A)(a); Fair Trading Act 1999 (Vic) s 32OA(2).

Rescission after completion: the rule in Seddon's case

5.16   When a contract has been completed, in the sense that each party has fully executed its obligations and any property has passed, there is authority that the right to rescind for innocent misrepresentation is lost. The rule derives from *Seddon v North East Salt Co Ltd*,[32] where Joyce J refused rescission of an executed contract for the sale of shares that had been induced by innocent misrepresentation. In *Angel v Jay*[33] the rule was applied in the case of a lease induced by innocent misrepresentation. Although the rule in *Seddon's* case has been heavily criticised,[34] the High Court left the point open in *Svanosio v McNamara*,[35] and cited the rule with apparent approval in *Krakowski v Eurolynx Properties Ltd*.[36] Otherwise, the rule has been reversed by the misrepresentation legislation in the United Kingdom, the Australian Capital Territory and South Australia.[37] In sale of goods transactions, the rule has also been reversed in New South Wales and, for consumer sales, in Victoria.[38]

Exclusion of liability clauses

5.17   As a matter of public policy, the right to rescind a contract for fraudulent misrepresentation cannot be excluded by a contractual term.[39] The parties to a contract may, by means of a contractual term, exclude rescission of the contract in equity for any innocent misrepresentation that induced the contract.[40] However, the freedom to contract out of liability for innocent misrepresentation has been restricted by the misrepresentation legislation in the United Kingdom, the Australian Capital Territory and South Australia.[41] In each of these jurisdictions, the effectiveness of the exclusion of liability is dependent upon a statutory test of reasonableness.

Misleading or deceptive conduct under the Australian Consumer Law

5.18   Irrespective of whether the misrepresentation was made fraudulently or innocently, s 18(1) of the Australian Consumer Law provides:

> A person shall not, in trade or commerce, engage in conduct that is misleading or deceptive or is likely to mislead or deceive.

---

32.   [1905] 1 Ch 326.
33.   [1911] 1 KB 666.
34.   See, for example, *Baird v BCE Holdings Pty Ltd* (1996) 40 NSWLR 374 at 379–80 per Young J. Compare *Akron Securities Ltd v Iliffe* (1997) 41 NSWLR 353 at 369 per Mason P.
35.   (1956) 96 CLR 186 at 198 per Dixon CJ and Fullagar J, and at 209 per McTiernan, Williams and Webb JJ.
36.   (1995) 183 CLR 563 at 585 per Brennan, Deane, Gaudron and McHugh JJ.
37.   Misrepresentation Act 1967 (UK) s 1(b); Civil Law (Wrongs) Act 2002 (ACT) s 173; Misrepresentation Act 1972 (SA) s 6(1).
38.   Sale of Goods Act 1923 (NSW) s 4(2A)(b); Fair Trading Act 1999 (Vic) s 32OA(1).
39.   *S Pearson & Son Ltd v Dublin Corp* [1907] AC 351; *Commercial Banking Co of Sydney Ltd v RH Brown & Co* (1972) 126 CLR 337.
40.   *Life Insurance Co of Australia Ltd v Phillips* (1925) 36 CLR 60 at 82 per Isaacs J and at 87 per Starke J; *Dorotea Pty Ltd v Christos Doufas Nominees Pty Ltd* [1986] 2 Qd R 91.
41.   Misrepresentation Act 1967 (UK) s 3; Civil Law (Wrongs) Act 2002 (ACT) s 176; Misrepresentation Act 1972 (SA) s 8.

This section replaces s 52(1) of the former Trade Practices Act 1974 (Cth). The major restriction is that the relevant conduct must have occurred 'in trade or commerce'.[42] The significance of s 18(1) is that it expands the scope of actionable misrepresentations and makes available the range of remedies under the Australian Consumer Law, where 'rescission is not the only or inevitable remedy' for infringing conduct.[43] Remedies under the Australian Consumer Law are discussed in Chapter 16.

Mistake

5.19 The orthodox approach to rescission of contracts for mistake is to consider the law in terms of three categories: common mistake, mutual mistake and unilateral mistake. Common mistake refers to the situation where both parties share the same mistake. Mutual mistake refers to the situation where both parties are mistaken, but their respective mistakes are not the same. Unilateral mistake refers to the situation where only one of the parties is mistaken. Traditionally, an operative mistake must be one of fact rather than law, but that rule has been abolished, at least in cases of common mistake.[44] The doctrine of mistake may operate in any of three possible ways. First, mistake may prevent the formation of a contract. Second, mistake may render a contract void at common law, in which case no question of rescission can arise. Third, mistake may render a contract voidable in equity.

Contracts void at law for common mistake

5.20 The leading authority supporting the view that contracts can be void at law for common mistake is the House of Lords' judgment in *Bell v Lever Brothers Ltd*.[45] In that case, Lever Brothers mistakenly paid compensation to Bell and Snelling for the early termination of their service contracts. The payments were made under termination agreements with each of them. At the time, Lever Brothers was not aware that Bell and Snelling had each engaged in misconduct that would have entitled Lever Brothers to terminate the service contracts without compensation. After learning the truth, Lever Brothers sought to recover the payments by arguing that the termination agreements were void at common law for mistake. Because of the jury's finding that neither Bell nor Snelling had in mind their respective misconduct at the time when the compensation payments and termination agreements were negotiated, the case was treated as one of common mistake (although called 'mutual' mistake). In these circumstances, a majority of the House of Lords held that Lever Brothers' claim failed because the common mistake related not to the 'subject matter' of the termination agreements, but to the 'quality' of the agreements. Lord Atkin, with whom Lord Thankerton agreed, said:

42. See *Concrete Constructions (NSW) Pty Ltd v Nelson* (1990) 169 CLR 594.
43. *Akron Securities Ltd v Iliffe* (1997) 41 NSWLR 353 at 368 per Mason P.
44. *Clasic International Pty Ltd v Lagos* (2002) 60 NSWLR 241.
45. [1932] AC 161.

> Mistake as to the quality of the thing contracted for … will not affect assent unless it is the mistake of both parties, and is as to the existence of some quality which makes the thing without the quality essentially different from the thing as it was believed to be.[46]

Applying this principle to the facts of the case, Lord Atkin identified the relevant question as whether 'an agreement to terminate a broken contract [is] different in kind from an agreement to terminate an unbroken contract'? Lord Atkin thought not, because in both cases 'the party paying for release gets exactly what he bargains for'.[47]

5.21   In Australian law, the authority of *Bell v Lever Brothers Ltd* on common mistake has been doubted after the High Court judgment in *McRae v Commonwealth Disposals Commission*.[48] In *McRae*, the plaintiff purchased from the defendant a submerged oil tanker that, unknown to both parties, had never existed. In defending an action for breach of contract, the defendant argued that the contract was void at law for common mistake. The High Court rejected the defendant's argument and awarded damages for breach of contract. Dixon and Fullagar JJ (with whom McTiernan J agreed) approached the issue of mistake in terms of contractual promises, by asking:

> … whether the contract was subject to an implied condition precedent that the goods were in existence. Prima facie, one would think, there would be no such implied condition precedent, the position being simply that the vendor *promised* that the goods *were* in existence.[49]

In cases where an implied condition precedent of the type referred to by Dixon and Fullagar JJ can be found on the facts, no contract comes into existence. Where, as in *McRae*, no such implied condition precedent can be found, the contract is effective and the promisee will be entitled to contractual remedies for breach. While the High Court did not reject the reasoning in *Bell v Lever Brothers Ltd* in terms, Meagher, Heydon and Leeming cite *McRae* as authority for their view that there is no doctrine of common mistake at law in Australia.[50] Nevertheless, the doctrine of common mistake has limited statutory force under s 11 of the Sale of Goods Act 1923 (NSW) and equivalent legislation in other states.[51] Section 11 provides that:

> Where there is a contract for the sale of specific goods, and the goods without the knowledge of the seller have perished at the time when the contract is made, the contract is void.

---

46.   [1932] AC 161 at 218.
47.   [1932] AC 161 at 223–4.
48.   (1951) 84 CLR 377.
49.   (1951) 84 CLR 377 at 407.
50.   R P Meagher, J D Heydon and M J Leeming, *Meagher, Gummow and Lehane's Equity: Doctrines and Remedies*, 4th ed, LexisNexis Butterworths, Sydney, 2002, [14–130].
51.   Sale of Goods Act 1954 (ACT) s 11; Sale of Goods Act 1972 (NT) s 11; Sale of Goods Act 1896 (Qld) s 9; Sale of Goods Act 1895 (SA) s 6; Sale of Goods Act 1896 (Tas) s 11; Goods Act 1958 (Vic) s 11; Sale of Goods Act 1895 (WA) s 6.

In *McRae*, the High Court distinguished an equivalent statutory provision, because 'Here the goods never existed, and the seller ought to have known that they did not exist'.[52]

5.22   The effect of common mistake on contracts at law was considered by the English Court of Appeal in *Great Peace Shipping Ltd v Tsavliris Salvage (International) Ltd*.[53] In that case, the defendants were providing salvage services to the owners of a damaged vessel at sea. Fearing for the safety of the crew, the defendants sought to hire the nearest merchant vessel for assistance. The defendants contracted to hire the claimants' vessel, *The Great Peace*, under the common mistake that it was only 35 miles away from the damaged vessel. Unknown to the parties, *The Great Peace* was 410 miles away. When the mistake was discovered, the defendants hired another vessel and cancelled the contract with the claimants, but refused to pay the cancellation fee under the contract. When the claimants sought to enforce the contract, the defendants argued that the contract was void at law, or voidable in equity, for common mistake.

Applying the authority of *Bell v Lever Brothers Ltd*, the Court of Appeal held that 'the issue in relation to common mistake turns on the question of whether the mistake as to the distance apart of the two vessels had the effect that the services that *The Great Peace* was in a position to provide were something essentially different from that to which the parties had agreed'.[54] The Court of Appeal thought not. Lord Phillips, giving the judgment of the court, identified five elements that must be present for a contract to be void at law for common mistake:

> (i) there must be a common assumption as to the existence of a state of affairs; (ii) there must be no warranty by either party that that state of affairs exists; (iii) the non-existence of the state of affairs must not be attributable to the fault of either party; (iv) the non-existence of the state of affairs must render performance of the contract impossible; (v) the state of affairs may be the existence, or a vital attribute, of the consideration to be provided or circumstances which must subsist if performance of the contractual adventure is to be possible.[55]

Lord Phillips said that the second and third of these elements were 'well exemplified' in *McRae v Commonwealth Disposals Commission*, which his Lordship cited with approval.[56]

In *Australia Estates Pty Ltd v Cairns City Council*,[57] the Queensland Court of Appeal held that the test to be applied in cases of common mistake at law is the five elements set out by Lord Phillips in *Great Peace v Tsavliris*.

---

52.   (1951) 84 CLR 377 at 410 per Dixon and Fullagar JJ.
53.   [2003] QB 679.
54.   [2003] QB 679 at 708 per Lord Phillips.
55.   [2003] QB 679 at 703.
56.   [2003] QB 679 at 703–4.
57.   [2005] QCA 328 at [51]–[62] per Atkinson J (Jerrard JA agreeing, McMurdo P not deciding).

Rescission in equity for common mistake

5.23 The existence of a modern equitable jurisdiction to rescind contracts for common mistake largely depends upon the judgment of the English Court of Appeal in *Solle v Butcher*.[58] In that case, the parties had entered into a lease of premises under the common mistake that rent-restriction legislation did not apply to the premises. The rent specified in the lease was more than that allowed under the legislation. Having discovered the mistake, the lessee sought to recover the excess rent that he had paid, and the lessor cross-claimed for rescission of the lease. On the question of rescission, the majority of the Court of Appeal held that the lease could be rescinded in equity for common mistake. According to Denning LJ (as he then was):

> A contract is … liable in equity to be set aside if the parties were under a common misapprehension either as to facts or as to their relative and respective rights, provided that the misapprehension was fundamental and that the party seeking to set it aside was not himself at fault.[59]

However, in *Great Peace Shipping Ltd v Tsavliris Salvage (International) Ltd*, the English Court of Appeal overruled its own judgment in *Solle v Butcher*, and declared that 'there is no jurisdiction [in equity] to grant rescission of a contract on the ground of common mistake where that contract is valid and enforceable on ordinary principles of contract law'.[60] The Court of Appeal gave two primary reasons for its conclusion. First, because *Solle v Butcher* is irreconcilable with the binding authority (in England) of the House of Lords in *Bell v Lever Brothers Ltd*, where no such jurisdiction in equity was adverted to. Second, because the authorities relied upon by Denning LJ in *Solle v Butcher*, especially *Cooper v Phibbs*,[61] do not support the existence of an equitable jurisdiction to rescind contracts for common mistake.[62]

5.24 In Australian law, the status of *Solle v Butcher* is unsettled. In *Svanosio v McNamara*,[63] the appellant purchaser sought a declaration that a completed conveyance of land was void for common mistake. The mistake was that a portion of the land that the respondent vendor purported to sell was, unknown to both parties, owned by the Crown. Having concluded that the contract was effective at common law, Dixon CJ and Fullagar J of the High Court considered the question of rescission in equity for common mistake:

> "Mistake" might, of course, afford a ground on which equity would refuse specific performance of a contract, and there may be cases of "mistake" in which it would be so inequitable that a party should be held to his contract that equity would set it aside … But we would agree … that it is difficult to conceive any circumstances in which equity could properly give relief by

---

58. [1950] 1 KB 671.
59. [1950] 1 KB 671 at 693.
60. [2003] QB 679 at 725 per Lord Phillips.
61. (1867) LR 2 HL 149.
62. The Court of Appeal approved the analysis which now appears in: R P Meagher, J D Heydon and M J Leeming, *Meagher, Gummow and Lehane's Equity: Doctrines and Remedies*, 4th ed, LexisNexis Butterworths, Sydney, 2002, [14–095]–[14–120].
63. (1956) 96 CLR 186.

setting aside the contract unless there has been fraud or misrepresentation or a condition can be found express or implied in the contract.[64]

Because there was no such 'fraud or misrepresentation' in *Svanosio v McNamara*, the purchaser was left without a remedy at common law or in equity. However, the reference to 'fraud' in this context has been considered ambiguous. Referring to the above passage in *Svanosio v McNamara*, a majority of the High Court said in *Taylor v Johnson*:

> Presumably, their Honours were referring to "fraud" in the wide equitable sense which includes unconscionable dealing. If they were not, we do not share the difficulty to which they referred. To the contrary, it seems to us that the reported cases, including *Solle v Butcher* itself, readily provide concrete examples of such circumstances.[65]

Although *Taylor v Johnson* was a case of unilateral mistake, these dicta gave some support to the existence of an equitable jurisdiction to rescind contracts for common mistake in Australian law.

In *Australia Estates Pty Ltd v Cairns City Council*,[66] the Queensland Court of Appeal reviewed 'the somewhat qualified approach taken to *Solle v Butcher* by the High Court' and preferred to apply the reasoning in *Great Peace v Tsavliris*. The Court of Appeal adopted the proposition that 'There is no equitable jurisdiction to set aside, on the ground of common mistake, an agreement, which is valid and enforceable at common law'.[67]

The effect of mutual mistake at law

5.25 The effect of mutual mistake at common law is best understood by reference to the rules concerning offer and acceptance in the formation of contracts. Where the parties are at such cross-purposes that offer and acceptance do not correspond, no contract comes into existence. However, the correspondence of offer and acceptance is judged objectively, according to the external manifestations of the parties' intentions.[68] When analysed in terms of offer and acceptance, there is no separate doctrine of mutual mistake at law.[69]

Rescission in equity for mutual mistake

5.26 Where the common law rules concerning offer and acceptance prevent the formation of a contract, no question of rescission arises. There is no

64.   (1956) 96 CLR 186 at 196. See also *McRae v Commonwealth Disposals Commission* (1951) 84 CLR 377 at 407 per Dixon and Fullagar JJ.
65.   (1983) 151 CLR 422 at 431 per Mason ACJ, Murphy and Deane JJ.
66.   [2005] QCA 328 at [51]–[62] per Atkinson J (Jerrard JA agreeing, McMurdo P not deciding).
67.   [2005] QCA 328 at [64] per Atkinson J. See also *Errichetti Nominees Pty Ltd v Paterson Group Architects Pty Ltd* [2007] WASC 77.
68.   *Goldsbrough Mort & Co Ltd v Quinn* (1910) 10 CLR 674 at 695 per Isaacs J; *Taylor v Johnson* (1983) 151 CLR 422 at 429 per Mason ACJ, Murphy and Deane JJ; *Toll (FGCT) Pty Ltd v Alphapharm Pty Ltd* (2004) 211 ALR 342 at 351–2 per Gleeson CJ, Gummow, Hayne, Callinan and Heydon JJ.
69.   See J W Carter, E Peden, and G J Tolhurst, *Contract Law in Australia*, 5th ed, LexisNexis Butterworths, Australia, 2007, [20-33]–[20-34].

authority to support the existence of an equitable jurisdiction to rescind contracts for mutual mistake. That view is consistent with the reasoning of the English Court of Appeal in *Riverlate Properties Ltd v Paul*.[70]

The effect of unilateral mistake at law

5.27   The unilateral mistake of a contracting party does not generally render a contract void at common law. In a passage that has been cited with approval on three occasions by the High Court,[71] Denning LJ summarised the position at common law in *Solle v Butcher*:

> … once a contract has been made, that is to say, once the parties, whatever their inmost states of mind, have to all outward appearances agreed with sufficient certainty in the same terms on the same subject matter, then the contract is good unless and until it is set aside for failure of some condition on which the existence of the contract depends, or for fraud, or on some equitable ground. Neither party can rely on his own mistake to say it was a nullity from the beginning, no matter that it was a mistake which to his mind was fundamental, and no matter that the other party knew that he was under a mistake.[72]

5.28   In *Taylor v Johnson*,[73] the High Court identified three possible exceptions at common law to the principles stated by Denning LJ. First, in cases of certain 'informal' contracts;[74] second, in cases 'where there is a mistake as to the identity of the other party';[75] and third, in cases 'where the mistake is as to the nature of the contract'. The third exception is the common law doctrine of *non est factum* (meaning 'it is not my deed') by which contracts may be void at common law for unilateral mistake. The doctrine was formulated in the following terms by the High Court in *Petelin v Cullen*:

> The class of persons who can avail themselves of the defence is limited. It is available to those who are unable to read owing to blindness or illiteracy and who must rely on others for advice as to what they are signing; it is also available to those who through no fault of their own are unable to have any understanding of the purport of a particular document. To make out the defence a defendant must show that he signed the document in the belief that it was radically different from what it was in fact and that, at least as against innocent persons, his failure to read and understand it was not due to carelessness on his part.[76]

---

70.   [1975] Ch 133.
71.   *McRae v Commonwealth Disposals Commission* (1951) 84 CLR 377 at 408 per Dixon and Fullagar JJ; *Svanosio v McNamara* (1956) 96 CLR 186 at 195–6 per Dixon CJ and Fullagar J; *Taylor v Johnson* (1983) 151 CLR 422 at 430 per Mason ACJ, Murphy and Deane JJ.
72.   [1950] 1 KB 671 at 691.
73.   (1983) 151 CLR 422 at 430 per Mason ACJ, Murphy and Deane JJ.
74.   See *Hartog v Colin & Shields* [1939] 3 All ER 566.
75.   See *Ingram v Little* [1961] 1 QB 31, since disapproved by the House of Lords in *Shogun Finance Ltd v Hudson* [2004] 1 AC 919. See also *Lewis v Averay* [1972] 1 QB 198.
76.   (1975) 132 CLR 355 at 359–60 per Barwick CJ, McTiernan, Gibbs, Stephen and Mason JJ. See also *Ford v Perpetual Trustees Victoria Ltd* (2009) 75 NSWLR 42; [2009] NSWCA 186.

Rescission in equity for unilateral mistake

5.29 The question of rescission in equity for unilateral mistake was considered by the High Court in *Taylor v Johnson*.[77] This case involved a contract for the sale of land made between the plaintiff purchaser and the defendant vendor. Although the purchase price was stated in the contract as $15,000, the vendor mistakenly believed that the purchase price was $15,000 per acre. Crucially, the purchaser was aware of the vendor's mistake and had deliberately set out to ensure that the vendor was not disabused of her mistake. When the vendor ultimately refused to complete the conveyance for $15,000, the purchaser sought specific performance of the contract, and the vendor cross-claimed for rescission of the contract in equity for unilateral mistake. The vendor succeeded in the High Court. In setting aside the contract, Mason ACJ, Murphy and Deane JJ stated the following principle:

> … a party who has entered into a written contract under a serious mistake about its contents in relation to a fundamental term will be entitled in equity to an order rescinding the contract if the other party is aware that circumstances exist which indicate that the first party is entering the contract under some serious mistake or misapprehension about either the content or subject matter of that term and deliberately sets out to ensure that the first party does not become aware of the existence of his mistake or misapprehension.[78]

The High Court identified the basis for relief in such cases of unilateral mistake as being the jurisdiction of equity to set aside 'any instrument or other transaction "in which the Court is of [the] opinion that it is unconscientious for a person to avail himself of the legal advantage which he has obtained"'.[79]

Duress

5.30 A transaction is voidable for duress if it was induced by the application of illegitimate pressure. In historical terms, the development of the law of duress has been a process of identifying those categories of pressure that the law considers to be illegitimate. Although duress was a doctrine originally developed by the common law, equity has long exercised a concurrent jurisdiction.[80] In this section, the law will be considered according to the established categories: duress to the person, duress of goods and economic duress.

'Overborne will' theory

5.31 The basis for legal intervention in cases of duress is that the application of illegitimate pressure affects the quality of assent of the victim. Some cases contain statements to the effect that assent must entirely be negated. In *Occidental Worldwide Investment Corp v Skibs A/S Avanti (The Siboen and The Sibotre)*, Kerr J said that the court must 'be satisfied that the consent of the other party was

---

77. (1983) 151 CLR 422.
78. (1983) 151 CLR 422 at 432. See also *Tutt v Doyle* (1997) 42 NSWLR 10; *Clarion Ltd v National Provident Institution* [2000] 2 All ER 265 at 283–4 per Rimer J.
79. (1983) 151 CLR 422 at 431, quoting from *Torrance v Bolton* (1872) LR 8 Ch App 118 at 124 per James LJ.
80. *Barton v Armstrong* [1976] AC 104 at 118 per Lord Cross.

overborne by compulsion so as to deprive him of any *animus contrahendi*.[81] That view is known as the 'overborne will' theory. However, the overborne will theory has largely been discredited for two reasons. First, it is inconsistent with the prevailing view that duress renders contracts voidable, rather than void.[82] If contractual assent were entirely absent, no contract would come into existence, and there would be nothing to rescind. Second, in terms of authority, the overborne will theory was rejected by the Privy Council (on appeal from the New South Wales Court of Appeal) in *Barton v Armstrong*,[83] by the New South Wales Court of Appeal in *Crescendo Management Pty Ltd v Westpac Banking Corp*,[84] and by the House of Lords in *Dimskal Shipping Co SA v International Transport Workers' Federation (The Evia Luck)*.[85] As McHugh JA observed in *Crescendo*, 'a person who is the subject of duress usually knows only too well what he is doing'.[86]

Duress to the person

5.32   The oldest category of duress is actual or threatened physical harm to the person, including false imprisonment. Threats to a person's family will suffice.[87]

A modern application of the doctrine of duress to the person is the advice of the Privy Council (on appeal from the New South Wales Court of Appeal) in *Barton v Armstrong*.[88] The plaintiff Barton and the defendant Armstrong were both directors and major shareholders of a public company. After arm's length negotiations, Barton executed a deed whereby he purchased Armstrong's interests in the company. There were significant commercial advantages to Barton in doing so. Barton subsequently sought to rescind the deed because he was induced to execute it partly by death threats made by or on behalf of Armstrong. The Privy Council upheld Barton's case for rescission of the deed.

The advice of the Privy Council in *Barton v Armstrong* establishes two propositions that apply generally to the law of duress. First, there is no requirement for the transaction to be improvident or disadvantageous to the rescinding party. Second, there is no requirement that the illegitimate pressure be the sole or predominant reason for that party entering into the transaction. Having rejected the overborne will theory, Lord Cross said that 'if Armstrong's threats were "a" reason for Barton's executing the deed he is entitled to relief even though he might well have entered into the contract if Armstrong had uttered no threats to induce him to do so'.[89] In *Dimskal Shipping Co SA v International Transport Workers' Federation (The Evia Luck)*, Lord Goff cited

---

81.   [1976] 1 Lloyd's Rep 293 at 336. See also *Pao On v Lau Yiu Long* [1980] AC 614 at 635–6 per Lord Scarman.
82.   *Universe Tankships Inc of Monrovia v International Transport Workers' Federation (The Universe Sentinel)* [1983] 1 AC 366 at 384 per Lord Diplock.
83.   [1976] AC 104 at 119 per Lord Cross.
84.   (1988) 19 NSWLR 40 at 45–6 per McHugh JA (Samuels and Mahoney JJA agreeing).
85.   [1992] 2 AC 152 at 165–6 per Lord Goff (Lords Keith, Ackner and Lowry agreeing).
86.   (1988) 19 NSWLR 40 at 45–6.
87.   *Williams v Bayley* (1866) LR 1 HL 200.
88.   [1976] AC 104.
89.   [1976] AC 104 at 119.

both *Barton v Armstrong* and *Crescendo Management Pty Ltd v Westpac Banking Corp*
with approval, and held that the illegitimate pressure must have 'constituted a
significant cause inducing the plaintiff to enter into the relevant contract'.[90]

Duress of goods

5.33   The second category of duress is duress of goods, which involves an
actual or threatened detention, damage or destruction of a person's goods
without a lawful excuse. While there is old authority to suggest that duress
of goods does not operate in the same manner as duress to the person by
vitiating contractual assent,[91] that view has since been rejected in modern
English and Australian authority.[92] Payments induced by duress of goods, as
distinct from *contracts to pay*, were always recoverable at the suit of the payer by
means of an action in restitution for money had and received.[93]

Economic duress

5.34   Given that the law has recognised duress of goods as illegitimate pressure,
it is logical to grant relief on the basis of other forms of illegitimate economic
pressure. The modern doctrine of economic duress was recognised by the House
of Lords in *Universe Tankships Inc of Monrovia v International Transport Workers'
Federation (The Universe Sentinel)*.[94] In *The Universe Sentinel* a contract was made by
the plaintiff shipowner to make a payment into a welfare fund conducted by the
defendant trade union. The contract and payment were made under a threat
of industrial action by the trade union. Carrying out the threatened industrial
action would have been tortious and would have caused 'catastrophic' economic
consequences for the shipowner. In these circumstances, a majority of the
House of Lords held that the pressure was illegitimate and that the shipowner
was entitled to rescind the contract and recover the payment by an action in
restitution for money had and received. Lord Diplock explained the doctrine of
economic duress in the following terms:

> The rationale is that his apparent consent was induced by pressure exercised
> upon him by that other party which the law does not regard as legitimate,
> with the consequence that the consent is treated in law as revocable unless
> approbated either expressly or by implication after the illegitimate pressure has
> ceased to operate on his mind. It is a rationale similar to that which underlies
> the avoidability of contracts entered into and the recovery of money exacted
> under … undue influence or in consequence of threats of physical duress.[95]

5.35   The leading Australian authority on economic duress is the judgment
of the New South Wales Court of Appeal in *Crescendo Management Pty Ltd*

90.   [1992] 2 AC 152 at 165 (Lords Keith, Ackner and Lowry agreeing).
91.   *Skeate v Beale* (1841) 11 Ad & E 983; 113 ER 688.
92.   *Occidental Worldwide Investment Corp v Skibs A/S Avanti (The Siboen and The Sibotre)* [1976] 1 Lloyd's Rep
      293 at 335 per Kerr J; *J & S Holdings Pty Ltd v NRMA Insurance Ltd* (1982) 41 ALR 539 at 557 per
      Blackburn, Deane and Ellicott JJ.
93.   *Astley v Reynolds* (1731) 2 Str 915; 93 ER 939.
94.   [1983] 1 AC 366.
95.   [1983] 1 AC 366 at 384.

v Westpac Banking Corp.[96] McHugh JA, with whom Samuels and Mahoney JJA agreed, proposed a two step approach:

> The proper approach in my opinion is to ask whether any applied pressure induced the victim to enter into the contract and then ask whether that pressure went beyond what the law is prepared to countenance as legitimate? Pressure will be illegitimate if it consists of unlawful threats or amounts to unconscionable conduct. But the categories are not closed. Even over-whelming pressure, not amounting to unconscionable or unlawful conduct, however, will not necessarily constitute economic duress.[97]

His Honour's reference to 'unconscionable conduct' in this context has been considered ambiguous. In *Westpac Banking Corp v Cockerill*, Kiefel J did not think that McHugh JA was referring to the equitable doctrine of unconscionable dealing because that is 'an independent ground on which a court exercising equitable jurisdiction can relieve from a contract'.[98] Otherwise, 'unconscionable conduct' has various shades of meaning, as the High Court has acknowledged.[99]

5.36 On the meaning of 'unlawful conduct', acts or threats of criminal or tortious conduct are clearly included. The authorities have also long-recognised that a threatened breach of contract can be a species of illegitimate pressure.[100] In *North Ocean Shipping Co Ltd v Hyundai Construction Co Ltd (The Atlantic Baron)*,[101] the defendant shipbuilders agreed to build a tanker for the plaintiff shipowners for a fixed price in United States currency. Payment was to be made by instalments during construction of the tanker. As security for repayment of the instalments in the event of default by the shipbuilders, the shipbuilders opened a letter of credit in favour of the shipowners. After payment of the first instalment by the shipowners, the United States currency was devalued and the shipbuilders demanded a corresponding increase in the future instalments. Although there was no legal basis for this demand, the shipowners made a further contract to pay the additional amounts under a threat by the shipbuilders to breach the existing contract. If the tanker were not delivered on time, the shipowners would have forfeited a lucrative contract

---

96.   (1988) 19 NSWLR 40.
97.   (1988) 19 NSWLR 40 at 46, cited with approval in *Dimskal Shipping Co SA v International Transport Workers' Federation (The Evia Luck)* [1992] 2 AC 152 at 165–6 per Lord Goff; *Scolio Pty Ltd v Cote* (1992) 6 WAR 475 at 480–1 per Rowland J; *Equiticorp Finance Ltd (in liq) v Bank of New Zealand* (1993) 32 NSWLR 50 at 149 per Clarke and Cripps JJA; *Caratti v Deputy Federal Commissioner of Taxation* (1993) 27 ATR 448 at 454 per Ipp J; *Deemcope Pty Ltd v Cantown Pty Ltd* [1995] 2 VR 44 at 48 per Coldrey J; *Westpac Banking Corp v Cockerill* (1998) 152 ALR 267 at 289 per Kiefel J; *Huyton SV v Peter Cremer GmbH & Co* [1999] 1 Lloyd's Rep 620 at 637 per Mance J; *Ford Motor Co of Australia Ltd v Arrowcrest Group Pty Ltd* (2003) 134 FCR 522 at 545 per Lander J; *Mitchell v Pacific Dawn Pty Ltd* [2011] QCA 98 at [51] per Frazer JA.
98.   (1998) 152 ALR 267 at 289.
99.   *Tanwar Enterprises Pty Ltd v Cauchi* (2003) 201 ALR 359 at 364–66 per Gleeson CJ, McHugh, Gummow, Hayne and Heydon JJ.
100. *Nixon v Furphy* (1925) 25 SR (NSW) 151; *T A Sundell & Sons Pty Ltd v Emm Yannoulatos (Overseas) Pty Ltd* (1956) 56 SR (NSW) 323.
101. [1979] 1 QB 705. See also *B & S Contracts and Design Ltd v Victor Green Publications Ltd* [1984] ICR 419; *Vantage Navigation Corp v Suhail & Saud Bahwan Building Materials LLC (The Alev)* [1989] 1 Lloyd's Rep 138.

for the charter of the tanker. The shipbuilders provided consideration for the further contract by increasing the amount of the letter of credit. Mocatta J accepted that the conduct of the shipbuilders amounted to economic duress that rendered the further contract voidable. However, subsequent conduct by the shipowners had affirmed the contract, so the right to rescind was lost.

In cases such as *The Atlantic Baron*, where the pressure is a threatened breach of contract, the more recent cases have recognised that good or bad faith in making the threat is relevant to the legitimacy of the pressure. In *Mitchell v Pacific Dawn Pty Ltd*, the Queensland Court of Appeal said:

> In deciding whether a threatened breach of contract involves illegitimate pressure or merely part of the "rough and tumble of the pressures of normal commercial bargaining" it is necessary also to take into account whether the persons allegedly exerting such pressure have acted in good or bad faith.[102]

The issue in that case was the setting aside, for economic duress, of a settlement agreement between the parties to a complex and long-running contractual dispute. Although the terms of settlement were disadvantageous to one party, the Court of Appeal upheld the settlement agreement because it was 'a genuine compromise of legitimate contending claims.'[103]

5.37 A different approach to economic duress was taken by the New South Wales Court of Appeal in *Australia and New Zealand Banking Group Ltd v Karam*,[104] where the Court departed from existing authority and rejected the terminology of 'economic duress' and 'illegitimate pressure'. The Court said:[105]

> The vagueness in the terms "economic duress" and "illegitimate pressure" can be avoided by treating the concept of "duress" as limited to threatened or actual unlawful conduct. The threat or conduct in question need not be directed to the person or the property of the victim, narrowly defined, but can be to the legitimate commercial and financial interests of the party ... if the conduct or threat is not unlawful, the resulting agreement may nevertheless set aside where the weaker party establishes undue influence (actual or presumptive) or unconscionable conduct based on an unconscientious taking advantage of his or her special disability or special disadvantage, in the sense identified in *Commercial Bank of Australia Ltd v Amadio*.[106]

In *ANZ v Karam*, the respondents were the directors of a family trading company that was in financial difficulties. As a condition of the appellant bank extending further credit to the company, the bank required personal guarantees from the respondent directors. When the company subsequently failed and the bank called upon the guarantees, the respondents sought to have the guarantees set aside because they had been procured by economic duress. However, as the Court of Appeal said:

---

102. [2011] QCA 98 at [52] per Frazer JA (Chesterman JA and Lyons J agreeing), quoting from *DSND Subsea Ltd v Petroleum Geo Services ASA* [2000] EWHC 185 (TCC) at [131] per Dyson J. See also *Carillion Construction Ltd v Felix* [2000] All ER (D) 1696.
103. [2011] QCA 98 at [52] per Frazer JA (Chesterman JA and Lyons J agreeing).
104. [2005] NSWCA 344; (2005) 64 NSWLR 149.
105. [2005] NSWCA 344 at [66]; (2005) 64 NSWLR 149 at 168 per Beazley, Ipp and Basten JJA.
106. (1983) 151 CLR 447. See 5.51.

Once it is accepted, correctly, that the perilous financial circumstances of the Company were "not the Bank's doing", there is no basis for saying that the Bank, in a legal sense, subjected the Karams to pressure.[107]

Apart from the absence of causation by the bank, there was no duress because the bank had not acted unlawfully in procuring the guarantees. Moreover, in the absence of any undue influence or any special disadvantage of the respondents in dealing with the bank, they were left without a remedy, outside of statute.

Lawful act duress

5.38 Contrary to the view expressed in *ANZ v Karam*, the weight of authority supports the proposition that acts or threats of lawful conduct can amount to duress, so-called 'lawful act duress'.[108] That is the case where an act or threat of lawful conduct is made in support of an unlawful demand. Bad faith is inherent in these cases. As Lord Scarman pointed out in *Universe Tankships Inc of Monrovia v International Transport Workers' Federation (The Universe Sentinel)*, 'blackmail is often a demand supported by a threat to do what is lawful, eg to report criminal conduct to the police'.[109] This passage was cited with approval by the Privy Council (on appeal from the New Zealand Court of Appeal) in *R v Attorney-General for England and Wales*, where Lord Hoffmann said:

> Generally speaking, the threat of any form of unlawful action will be regarded as illegitimate. On the other hand, the fact that the threat is lawful does not necessarily make the pressure legitimate.[110]

5.39 Commencing or threatening to commence legal proceedings can amount to duress where the act or threat is made in support of an unlawful demand. In *J & S Holdings Pty Ltd v NRMA Insurance Ltd*,[111] the mortgagee threatened to commence winding-up proceedings against the mortgagor to enforce the terms of the mortgage. However, the threat was made in support of the mortgagee's wrongful refusal to discharge the mortgage unless it was paid more than it was entitled to demand. In these circumstances, the Full Federal Court held that the mortgagee's conduct was illegitimate pressure.[112] The Court further held that the mortgagor had been induced to pay the additional amount 'involuntarily under compulsion'.[113] Accordingly, the elements of economic duress were established. Even if, as required in *ANZ v Karam*, unlawful conduct by the defendant is necessary to constitute

---

107. [2005] NSWCA 344 at [95]; (2005) 64 NSWLR 149 at 171–2 per Beazley, Ipp and Basten JJA.
108. *Universe Tankships Inc of Monrovia v International Transport Workers' Federation (The Universe Sentinel)* [1983] 1 AC 366 at 401 per Lord Scarman; *Caratti v Deputy Federal Commissioner of Taxation* (1993) 27 ATR 448 at 457 per Ipp J; *CTN Cash and Carry Ltd v Gallaher Ltd* [1994] 4 All ER 714; *Westpac Banking Corp v Cockerill* (1998) 152 ALR 267 at 289 per Kiefel J; *McKay v National Australia Bank Ltd* [1998] 4 VR 677 at 690 per Tadgell JA; *Huyton SV v Peter Cremer GmbH & Co* [1999] 1 Lloyd's Rep 620 at 637 per Mance J.
109. [1983] 1 AC 366 at 401, citing *Thorne v Motor Trade Association* [1937] AC 797 at 806 per Lord Atkin.
110. [2003] UKPC 22 at [16]; [2004] 2 NZLR 577 at 583.
111. (1982) 41 ALR 539.
112. (1982) 41 ALR 539 at 555–6 per Blackburn, Deane and Ellicott JJ.
113. (1982) 41 ALR 539 at 556.

duress, the High Court confirmed in *Williams v Spautz* that commencing legal proceedings 'for a purpose or to effect an object beyond that which the legal process offers' constitutes the tort of 'collateral abuse of process'.[114]

Undue influence

5.40   Undue influence 'arises out of a relationship between two persons where one has acquired over another a measure of influence, or ascendancy, of which the ascendant person then takes unfair advantage'.[115] The doctrine of undue influence comprises two elements. First, there must be a relationship of influence; and second, there must be an abuse or undue exercise of that influence by the stronger party. The effect of undue influence is to render a transaction voidable in equity at the election of the weaker party. The doctrine of undue influence shares common origins with the doctrine of duress. Both doctrines look to 'the quality of the consent or assent of the weaker party'.[116]

Relationships of influence

5.41   Despite a lack of uniform terminology in the case law, it is broadly accepted that relationships of influence may be divided into two classes, which are not mutually exclusive. These classes are, first, presumptive relationships of influence; and second, proven relationships of influence. As the name implies, the distinctive feature of presumptive relationships is a rebuttable presumption of law that a relationship of influence exists between the parties. That presumption gives a significant procedural advantage to the weaker party in seeking to rescind a transaction. By contrast, in cases where a relationship of influence is not presumed, the weaker party must prove by evidence that a relationship of influence exists. These are proven relationships of influence. In either case, the essential characteristic of all relationships of influence is that 'one party occupies or assumes towards another a position naturally involving an ascendancy or influence over that other, or a dependence or trust on his part'.[117]

Presumptive relationships of influence

5.42   Equity presumes a relationship of influence between certain persons. While some of the presumptive relationships are fiduciary relationships in the general equitable sense, others are not. Relationships of influence and fiduciary relationships are not coextensive categories. The main presumptive relationships are: parent and child; guardian and ward;[118] priest and penitent;[119]

---

114. (1992) 174 CLR 509 at 523 per Mason CJ, Dawson, Toohey and McHugh JJ.
115. *Royal Bank of Scotland plc v Etridge (No 2)* [2002] 2 AC 773 at 795 per Lord Nicholls.
116. *Commercial Bank of Australia Ltd v Amadio* (1983) 151 CLR 457 at 474 per Deane J.
117. *Johnson v Buttress* (1936) 56 CLR 113 at 134–5 per Dixon J.
118. *Kerr v West Australian Trustee Executor & Agency Co Ltd* (1937) 39 WALR 34; *Lamotte v Lamotte* (1942) 42 SR (NSW) 99; *West v Public Trustee* [1942] SASR 109; *Phillips v Hutchison* [1946] VLR 270; *Bullock v Lloyds Bank Ltd* [1955] Ch 317; *Webber v New South Wales* (2004) 31 Fam LR 425.
119. *Huguenin v Baseley* (1807) 14 Ves 273; 33 ER 526; *Allcard v Skinner* (1887) 36 Ch D 145.

solicitor and client;[120] physician and patient;[121] and express trustee and beneficiary.[122] The categories of presumptive relationships are not immutable, and may change as society changes. For example, in *Yerkey v Jones*,[123] Dixon J said that a presumption of influence arises between a man and his fiancée. But in *Zamet v Hyman*,[124] Lord Evershed MR referred to changed social conditions and doubted any presumption of influence in such cases. Brennan J expressed similar doubts in *Louth v Diprose*.[125] By contrast, husbands and wives have not been included in the presumptive relationships since the nineteenth century.[126] Nevertheless, the High Court has affirmed in *Garcia v National Australia Bank Ltd* that special considerations apply where a wife gives a guarantee of her husband's debts, based upon 'trust and confidence, in the ordinary sense of those words, between marriage partners'.[127]

Proven relationships of influence

5.43　Where a relationship of influence is not presumed in equity, the party seeking rescission may prove a relationship of influence by evidence. A proven relationship of influence was found by the High Court in *Johnson v Buttress*.[128] In that case, the donor was a 67-year-old man who was described as illiterate, unintelligent, inexperienced in business matters, and habitually dependent upon others for advice and assistance. Shortly after the death of his wife, the donor made a gratuitous transfer of his home to the donee, in appreciation of the 'kindness' shown by the donee to the donor and his wife. The donor's home was his only substantial asset. In making the transfer, the donee's solicitor had acted for both parties. In these circumstances, the High Court found that the onus was upon the donee to justify the transaction and she had failed to do so. Accordingly, the transfer was set aside. Similarly, in *Watkins v Combes*,[129] the High Court set aside a transfer of property by a 69-year-old woman to relatives upon whom she depended for advice and assistance. Although the transfer was made in consideration of a promise to maintain her for life, the transaction was shown to be 'highly disadvantageous' to her. Neither had she received independent advice.

---

120. *Dowsett v Reid* (1912) 15 CLR 695 at 707 per Barton J; *Haywood v Roadknight* [1927] VLR 512 at 520 per Lowe J.
121. *Johnson v Buttress* (1936) 56 CLR 113 at 119 per Latham CJ and 134 per Dixon J; *Breen v Williams* (1996) 186 CLR 71 at 92 per Dawson and Toohey JJ.
122. *Jenyns v Public Curator* (Qld) (1953) 90 CLR 113 at 133 per Dixon CJ, McTiernan and Kitto JJ; *Union Fidelity Trustee Co of Australia Ltd v Gibson* [1971] VR 573 at 577 per Gillard J; *Whereat v Duff* [1972] 2 NSWLR 147 at 154 per Sugerman P.
123. (1940) 63 CLR 649 at 675.
124. [1961] 3 All ER 933 at 938.
125. (1992) 175 CLR 621 at 630.
126. *Yerkey v Jones* (1940) 63 CLR 649 at 675 per Dixon J; *Barclays Bank plc v O'Brien* [1994] 1 AC 180 at 190 per Lord Browne-Wilkinson; *Garcia v National Australia Bank Ltd* (1998) 194 CLR 395 at 425 per Kirby J; *Royal Bank of Scotland plc v Etridge (No 2)* [2002] 2 AC 773 at 797 per Lord Nicholls.
127. (1998) 194 CLR 395 at 404 per Gaudron, McHugh, Gummow and Hayne JJ. See **5.50**.
128. (1936) 56 CLR 113.
129. (1922) 30 CLR 180.

Abuse or undue exercise of influence

5.44 Not all transactions between parties to a relationship of influence, whether proven or presumed, fall within the doctrine of undue influence. A gift of small value, for example, will be excluded where the gift can be explained by 'friendship, relationship, charity, or other ordinary motives on which ordinary men act'.[130] For the doctrine of undue influence to apply, there must be an abuse or undue exercise of influence, whether actual or presumed. There will be an undue exercise of influence if 'the person in a position of domination has used that position to obtain unfair advantage for himself, and so to cause injury to the person relying upon his authority or aid'.[131] In *Allcard v Skinner*, Cotton LJ of the English Court of Appeal classified cases of undue influence into two categories as follows:

> First, where the court has been satisfied that the gift was the result of influence expressly used by the donee for the purpose; second, where the relations between the donor and donee have at or shortly before the execution of the gift been such as to raise a presumption that the donee had influence over the donor. In such a case the court sets aside the voluntary gift, unless it is proved that in fact the gift was the spontaneous act of the donor acting under circumstances which enabled him to exercise an independent will and which justifies the court in holding that the gift was the result of a free exercise of the donor's will. The first class of cases may be considered as depending on the principle that no one shall be allowed to retain any benefit arising from his own fraud or wrongful act. In the second category of cases the court interferes, not on the ground that any wrongful act has in fact been committed by the donee, but on the ground of public policy, and to prevent the relations which existed between the parties and the influence arising therefrom being abused.[132]

5.45 *Allcard v Skinner* involved gifts of property made by the plaintiff to the defendant, who was the superior of the religious sisterhood to which they both belonged. In the absence of affirmative proof that the gifts were 'the result of influence expressly used' by the defendant for that purpose (within the meaning of the first category of cases referred to by Cotton LJ) the Court of Appeal presumed an undue exercise of influence by the defendant (within the meaning of the second category of cases). The first category has become known as cases of 'actual undue influence'. In these cases, 'it is necessary for the claimant to prove affirmatively that the wrongdoer exerted undue influence on the complainant to enter into the particular transaction which is impugned'.[133] The second category has become known as cases of 'presumed undue influence'. Lord Browne-Wilkinson explained this category in *Barclays Bank plc v O'Brien*:

---

130. *Allcard v Skinner* (1887) 36 Ch D 145 at 185 per Lindley LJ.
131. *Watkins v Combes* (1922) 30 CLR 180 at 194 per Isaacs J.
132. (1887) 36 Ch D 145 at 171.
133. *Barclays Bank plc v O'Brien* [1994] 1 AC 180 at 189 per Lord Browne-Wilkinson (Lords Templeman and Lowry agreeing).

In these cases the complainant only has to show, in the first instance, that there was a relationship of trust and confidence between the complainant and the wrongdoer of such a nature that it is fair to presume that the wrongdoer abused the relationship in procuring the complainant to enter into the impugned transaction. In ... [these] cases therefore there is no need to produce evidence that actual undue influence was exerted in relation to the particular transaction impugned: once a confidential relationship has been proved, the burden then shifts to the wrongdoer to prove that the complainant entered into the impugned transaction freely, for example by showing that the complainant had independent advice.[134]

There has been some confusion about the concept of 'presumed undue influence' because the judgment in *Allcard v Skinner* involved two levels of presumption. First, there was the presumption of a relationship of influence between the parties, based upon the existing cases involving priests and penitents, such as *Huguenin v Baseley*.[135] Second, there was the presumption of an abuse or undue exercise of influence. The first presumption was of law, and the second presumption was of fact. Although the plaintiff in *Allcard v Skinner* ultimately failed in seeking equitable relief because of laches and acquiescence, the Court of Appeal made the crucial point that an undue exercise of influence need not affirmatively be proven by the weaker party in every case. Once a relationship of influence is either proven by evidence or presumed as a matter of law, the onus of proof is cast upon the stronger party to justify the transaction by proving that the actions of the weaker party were carried out free from the influence of the stronger party. That view is consistent with the approach taken by the High Court in *Johnson v Buttress*[136] and in *Watkins v Combes*.[137] The onus of proof cast upon the stronger party in such circumstances is often referred to as the 'presumption of undue influence'. Unfortunately, the cases have not been consistent in using that phrase. As Meagher, Heydon, and Leeming point out:

> ... the phrase "presumption of undue influence" really refers to the taking of a benefit by or at the suggestion of a person in a position of influence (presumed or proved) who will be taken unless the contrary is proved to have procured the benefit by undue exercise of that influence.[138]

Rebutting a presumption of undue influence

5.46   In order to rebut a presumption of undue influence, the stronger party must prove that the transaction was 'the independent and well-understood act of a man in a position to exercise a free judgment based on information as full as that of the donee'.[139] In practice, rebuttal normally involves a consideration

---

134. [1994] 1 AC 180 at 189. See also *Royal Bank of Scotland plc v Etridge (No 2)* [2002] 2 AC 773 at 797 per Lord Nicholls.
135. (1807) 14 Ves 273; 33 ER 526.
136. (1936) 56 CLR 113.
137. (1922) 30 CLR 180.
138. R P Meagher, J D Heydon and M J Leeming, *Meagher, Gummow and Lehane's Equity: Doctrines and Remedies*, 4th ed, LexisNexis Butterworths, Sydney, 2002, [15–030].
139. *Johnson v Buttress* (1936) 56 CLR 113 at 134 per Dixon J.

of two factors: the presence of independent advice and the adequacy of consideration. Since gifts, by definition, involve no consideration, it is sometimes observed that gifts of substantial value are more readily set aside for undue influence than other transactions.[140]

5.47 Independent advice A recurring feature of the cases on rescission for undue influence is the absence of independent advice being received by the weaker party before entering into the transaction. *Allcard v Skinner*, *Johnson v Buttress* and *Watkins v Combes*, discussed above, are all examples. The cases contemplate that the advice should be given by a lawyer. While the presence of independent advice will be an important factor in rebutting the presumption of undue influence, the presence of independent advice is not essential.[141] The courts also take into account the quality of advice. In *Bester v Perpetual Trustee Co Ltd*,[142] the advice consisted of a verbatim reading by an independent solicitor of the deed of settlement to be executed by the 21-year-old plaintiff. Although the solicitor invited questions from the plaintiff, no advice was given upon the 'general topic of whether a settlement should be entered into at all, and, if so, the general nature of the settlement'.[143] Street J held that the advice was insufficient in the circumstances.

5.48 Adequacy of consideration Where the transaction is not intended as a gift, the evidentiary relevance of inadequate consideration was stated by Street J in *Bester v Perpetual Trustee Co Ltd*:

> If it can be demonstrated that the transaction is, so far as the settlor is concerned, improvident, then that will be a powerful consideration pointing towards success on the part of a settlor seeking to set aside a settlement upon the ground that it was not thoroughly comprehended, and deliberately and of the settlor's own free will carried out.[144]

However, the presence of adequate consideration is not a complete defence. In the context of unconscionable dealing, Deane J explained why in *Commercial Bank of Australia Ltd v Amadio* that:

> Notwithstanding that adequate consideration may have moved from the stronger party, a transaction may be unfair, unreasonable and unjust from the view point of the party under the disability. An obvious instance of circumstances in which that may be so is the case where the benefit of the consideration does not move to the party under the disability but moves to some third party involved in the transaction.[145]

140. *Watkins v Combes* (1922) 30 CLR 180 at 193 per Isaacs J.
141. *Inche Noriah v Shaik Allie bin Omar* [1929] AC 127; *Watkins v Combes* (1922) 30 CLR 180 at 196 per Isaacs J.
142. [1970] 3 NSWR 30.
143. [1970] 3 NSWR 30 at 35.
144. [1970] 3 NSWR 30 at 35.
145. (1983) 151 CLR 447 at 475.

Guarantees: the Yerkey *and* Garcia *principles*

5.49   The position in Australian law of wives who guarantee their husbands' debts was stated by Dixon J in *Yerkey v Jones* as follows:

> Although the relation of husband to wife is not one of influence, yet the opportunities it gives are such that if the husband procures his wife to become surety for his debt a creditor who accepts her suretyship obtained through her husband has been treated as taking it subject to any invalidating tendency on the part of her husband even if the creditor be not actually privy to such conduct.[146]

His Honour went on to distinguish between two categories of cases where the wife may be entitled to rescind a guarantee or suretyship of her husband's debts (or the debts of a company controlled by him) to a third-party creditor: first, in cases where 'a wife, alive to the nature and effect of the obligation she is undertaking, is procured to become her husband's surety by the exertion by him upon her of undue influence, affirmatively established'; second, in cases where there is no undue influence, but the wife 'does not understand the effect of the document or the nature of the transaction of suretyship'.[147]

The second category of case was considered by the High Court in *Garcia v National Australia Bank Ltd*,[148] where the court affirmed the judgment of Dixon J in *Yerkey v Jones*. The appellant wife in *Garcia* was described as 'an intelligent articulate lady with a professional position'. She had been a willing party to the transaction, but had not taken any independent advice. The majority justices held that it was 'unconscionable' of the respondent bank to enforce the transaction against her because of the circumstances that:

> (a) in fact the surety did not understand the purport and effect of the transaction; (b) the transaction was voluntary (in the sense that the surety obtained no gain from the contract the performance of which was guaranteed); (c) the lender is to be taken to have understood that, as a wife, the surety may repose trust and confidence in her husband in matters of business and therefore to have understood that the husband may not fully and accurately explain the purport and effect of the transaction to his wife; and yet (d) the lender did not itself take steps to explain the transaction to the wife or find out that a stranger had explained it to her.[149]

Rejecting the approach taken by the House of Lords in *Barclays Bank plc v O'Brien*,[150] the majority of the High Court in *Garcia v National Australia Bank Ltd* denied that the wife's equity against the creditor bank depended upon 'the creditor having, at the time the guarantee is taken, notice of some unconscionable dealing between the husband as borrower and the wife as

---

146.   (1939) 63 CLR 649 at 678.

147.   (1939) 63 CLR 649 at 684.

148.   (1998) 194 CLR 395.

149.   (1998) 194 CLR 395 at 409 per Gaudron, McHugh, Gummow and Hayne JJ.

150.   [1994] 1 AC 180. See also *Royal Bank of Scotland plc v Etridge (No 2)* [2002] 2 AC 773.

surety'.[151] The only question of notice was 'whether the creditor knew at the time of the taking of the guarantee that the surety was then married' to the borrower.[152]

5.50   In *Garcia v National Australia Bank Ltd*, the High Court left open the extension of these principles to 'long term and publicly declared relationships short of marriage between members of the same or of opposite sex'.[153] However, the Victorian Court of Appeal and the Queensland Court of Appeal have extended the *Garcia* principles even further to include non-domestic relationships of 'trust and confidence, in the ordinary sense of those words',[154] irrespective of gender, where the guarantor is a volunteer who claims not to have understood the transaction. In *Kranz v National Australia Bank Ltd*,[155] the guarantor and debtor were brothers-in-law, as well as the debtor being the accountant and business adviser of the guarantor. In *ANZ Banking Group Ltd v Alirezai*,[156] the guarantor was a trusted friend of the debtor, whom he felt morally obliged to assist. However, in neither case was it 'unconscionable' for the bank to enforce the transaction because, among other reasons, the bank did not know, and was not put on inquiry, that the relationship between the debtor and guarantor was one of 'trust and confidence', so as to attract the *Garcia* principles. In *Kranz v National Australia Bank Ltd*, Charles JA, with whom Winneke P and Eames JA agreed, re-formulated the *Garcia* principles in the following terms:

> The principle stated by the High Court in *Garcia* would make it unconscionable for a bank to enforce a guarantee given by a volunteer if it has not explained the situation to the guarantor, and does not know that an independent person has done so, if the bank knows that there was a relationship of trust and confidence between the guarantor and debtor whose debt has been guaranteed.[157]

However, the cases have been inconsistent. In *Watt v State Bank of New South Wales*,[158] the Australian Capital Territory Court of Appeal held that the High Court's reasoning in *Garcia v National Australia Bank Ltd* did not support the extension of those principles to parents who guarantee their children's debts. Their Honours pointed out that 'the principle in *Yerkey v Jones* was based upon the need to protect married women from the consequences of improvident transactions entered into at the request of their husbands'.[159] In parent and child relationships, their Honours observed, 'parents do not

---

151. (1998) 194 CLR 395 at 408, 410–11.
152. (1998) 194 CLR 395 at 411.
153. (1998) 194 CLR 395 at 404 per Gaudron, McHugh, Gummow and Hayne JJ. See *Liu v Adamson* [2003] NSWSC 74; (2004) NSW ConvR 56-074. Contrast *State Bank of New South Wales Ltd v Hibbert* [2000] NSWSC 628; (2000) 9 BPR 17,543 (de facto relationships).
154. (1998) 194 CLR 395 at 404.
155. (2003) 8 VR 310.
156. [2004] QCA 006; [2004] ANZ ConvR 132.
157. (2003) 8 VR 310 at 322, cited with approval in *ANZ Banking Group Ltd v Alirezai* [2004] QCA 006 at [82]; [2004] ANZ ConvR 132 at 135–6 per Jerrard JA. Special leave to appeal in *Kranz* was refused by the High Court: [2004] HCATrans 211.
158. [2003] ACTCA 7.
159. [2003] ACTCA 7 at [20] per Higgins CJ and Crispin P.

normally leave business decisions to their children or rely unquestioningly on their judgment',[160] even though some parents may do so:[161]

> Hence, in our opinion, it cannot be said that the relationship of parent to child or parent to son or daughter-in-law is of such a character that any potential lender who is aware that the debtor is a child or the partner of a child of the surety must by reason of that fact alone be taken to have appreciated that the surety "may well receive from the debtor no sufficient explanation of the transaction's purport and effect".[162]

In the interests of certainty in future transactions, the High Court explained in *Garcia v National Australia Bank Ltd* how banks 'may readily avoid the possibility that the surety will later claim not to have understood' the proposed transaction:

> If the creditor itself explains the transaction sufficiently, or knows that the surety has received "competent, independent and disinterested"[163] advice from a third party, it would not be unconscionable for the creditor to enforce it against the surety even though the surety is a volunteer and it later emerges that the surety claims to have been mistaken.[164]

Unconscionable dealing

5.51   In *Commercial Bank of Australia Ltd v Amadio*, Deane J said:

> The jurisdiction of courts of equity to relieve against unconscionable dealing … is long established as extending generally to circumstances in which (i) a party to a transaction was under a special disability in dealing with the other party with the consequence that there was an absence of any reasonable degree of equality between them and (ii) that disability was sufficiently evident to the stronger party to make it prima facie unfair or "unconscientious" that he procure, or accept, the weaker party's assent to the impugned transaction in the circumstances in which he procured or accepted it. Where such circumstances are shown to have existed, an onus is cast upon the stronger party to show that the transaction was fair, just and reasonable.[165]

Special disadvantage

5.52   In *Amadio's* case, the plaintiffs were two elderly migrants who were unfamiliar with written English. The plaintiffs were asked by their son to execute a guarantee and mortgage in favour of the defendant bank in order to secure the liabilities of a company controlled by their son. The documents were presented to the plaintiffs for immediate execution in their home by an officer of the bank. Having been misled by their son, the plaintiffs were mistaken about the nature and contents of the documents. The plaintiffs had not received independent advice. By reason of the age of the plaintiffs,

---

160. [2003] ACTCA 7 at [21] per Higgins CJ and Crispin P.
161. Such as the elderly widowed mother in *Siglin v Choules* [2002] WASCA 9.
162. [2003] ACTCA 7 at [21], quoting from *Garcia v National Australia Bank Ltd* (1998) 194 CLR 395 at 409 per Gaudron, McHugh, Gummow and Hayne JJ.
163. *Yerkey v Jones* (1939) 63 CLR 649 at 686 per Dixon J.
164. (1998) 194 CLR 395 at 411 per Gaudron, McHugh, Gummow and Hayne JJ.
165. (1983) 151 CLR 447 at 474.

their lack of familiarity with written English, the circumstances in which the documents were presented to the plaintiffs for execution and the plaintiffs' lack of understanding of the documents, the plaintiffs were held to be in a position of special disadvantage in relation to the bank. Moreover, this position of special disadvantage was held to be sufficiently apparent to the officer of the bank. Accordingly, the High Court set aside the guarantee and mortgage. The requirement of a *special* disadvantage was explained by Mason J:

> I qualify the word "disadvantage" by the adjective "special" in order to disavow any suggestion that the principle applies whenever there is some difference in the bargaining power of the parties and in order to emphasize that the disabling condition or circumstance is one which seriously affects the ability of the innocent party to make a judgment as to his own interests, when the other party knows or ought to know of the existence of that condition or circumstance and of its effect on the innocent party.[166]

In *Australian Competition and Consumer Commission v C G Berbatis Holdings Pty Ltd*,[167] the High Court reiterated that a person is not subject to a special disadvantage 'simply because of inequality of bargaining power'.[168]

5.53 The factors that may constitute a special disadvantage or disability for the purposes of unconscionable dealing are not fixed. In *Blomley v Ryan* Fullagar J listed as examples:

> ... poverty or need of any kind, sickness, age, sex, infirmity of body or mind, drunkenness, illiteracy or lack of education, lack of assistance or explanation where assistance or explanation is necessary. The common characteristic seems to be that they have the effect of placing one party at a serious disadvantage vis-à-vis the other.[169]

Blomley v Ryan was a suit for specific performance of a contract for the sale of land by the purchaser, and a counter-claim for rescission of the contract by the administrator of the deceased vendor's estate. The 78-year-old vendor, who was 'in worse than his normal poor state of mental and bodily health by reason of drinking excesses and irregular living', made a contract for the sale of his grazing property at a considerable under-value. The negotiations for the sale were conducted over a bottle of rum that was supplied by the purchaser's agent, and the vendor had not received independent advice. In these circumstances, the High Court set aside the contract.

In circumstances that were far removed from those in *Blomley v Ryan*, the plaintiff in *Louth v Diprose*[170] was an experienced solicitor who made a gift of $58,000 to the defendant for the purpose of buying a house for herself and her children to live in. The plaintiff's special disadvantage was his strong emotional dependence upon the defendant. In circumstances where the defendant had

---

166.   (1983) 151 CLR 447 at 462.
167.   (2003) 214 CLR 51.
168.   (2003) 214 CLR 51 at 64 per Gleeson CJ (Gummow and Hayne JJ agreeing at 76–7).
169.   (1956) 99 CLR 362 at 405. See also *Kakavas v Crown Melbourne Ltd* [2009] VSC 559, where the plaintiff's 'pathological gambling' was recognised as a special disability in his dealings with the defendant casino operator.
170.   (1992) 175 CLR 621.

misled the plaintiff to believe that she was facing eviction, and had threatened suicide unless the plaintiff provided the money, the High Court held that the defendant had acted unconscionably in procuring and retaining the gift. The relevance of emotional dependence as a basis for special disadvantage was affirmed by the High Court in *Bridgewater v Leahy*:

> The position of disadvantage which renders one party subject to exploitation by another such that an improvident disposition by the disadvantaged party may not in good conscience be retained may stem from a strong emotional dependence or attachment.[171]

Bridgewater v Leahy involved a transfer of grazing land from an 84-year-old uncle to his nephew for a price of $696,811. At the same time the parties executed a deed of forgiveness, which reduced the price to $150,000. The nephew had initiated the transaction, and the same solicitor had acted for both parties. Although the (now deceased) uncle was found to be 'of sound mind and capable of making decisions about his personal affairs',[172] the majority of the High Court held that the uncle's 'emotional attachment to and dependency upon' the nephew was a sufficient special disadvantage for the deed of forgiveness to be set aside as unconscionable.[173] In a strong dissenting judgment, Gleeson CJ and Callinan J upheld the findings of fact by the lower courts that the uncle was not subject to any special disadvantage.[174]

The reasoning in *Louth v Diprose* and *Bridgewater v Leahy* was taken a step further by the New South Wales Court of Appeal in *Lopwell Pty Ltd v Clarke*.[175] The respondents in that case had entered into certain guarantees, upon the advice of their 'long-standing and trusted' accountant, who had an undisclosed personal interest in the transactions. There was no benefit for the respondents in the transactions, and they did not read the documents before signing them. In setting aside the guarantees for unconscionable dealing, the Court held that 'complete dependence upon a trusted adviser for financial advice can be just as much a disability for this purpose as the emotional dependence in *Louth v Diprose* and *Bridgewater v Leahy*.'[176]

Adequacy of consideration

5.54   In *Blomley v Ryan*, Fullagar J made the following observations about adequacy of consideration:

> It does not appear to be essential in all cases that the party at a disadvantage should suffer loss or detriment by the bargain … But inadequacy of consideration, while never of itself a ground for resisting enforcement, will often be a specially important element in cases of this type. It may be important in either or both of two ways — firstly as supporting the inference

---

171.   (1998) 194 CLR 457 at 490 per Gaudron, Gummow and Kirby JJ.
172.   (1998) 194 CLR 457 at 491.
173.   (1998) 194 CLR 457 at 493 per Gaudron, Gummow and Kirby JJ.
174.   (1998) 194 CLR 457 at 469–72.
175.   [2009] NSWCA 165.
176.   [2009] NSWCA 165 at [47] per Ipp, Campbell and Macfarlan JJA. Special leave to appeal was refused by the High Court: [2010] HCATrans 17.

that a position of disadvantage existed, and secondly as tending to show that an unfair use was made of the occasion. Where, as here, intoxication is the main element relied upon as creating the position of disadvantage, the question of adequacy or inadequacy of consideration is, I think, likely to be a matter of major, and perhaps decisive, importance.[177]

These observations of Fullagar J in *Blomley v Ryan* were cited with approval by Deane J in *Amadio's* case.[178] *Amadio's* case is authority that a transaction may be rescinded for unconscionable dealing even where there is adequate consideration. In *Amadio's* case, the consideration for the plaintiffs' guarantee was the provision of finance by the bank to the company controlled by the plaintiffs' son. However, there was no benefit for the plaintiffs personally in the transaction. Similarly, in *Garcia v National Australia Bank Ltd*, the High Court described the wife's guarantee of her husband's debts as 'voluntary' because she 'obtained no gain from the contract the performance of which was guaranteed'.[179]

Unconscientious conduct of the defendant

5.55 It is insufficient to prove that one party was subject to a special disadvantage, unless the other party was sufficiently aware of the disadvantage. In *Hart v O'Connor*,[180] the Privy Council (on appeal from the New Zealand Court of Appeal) upheld a contract for the sale of land that was made by a vendor 'of unsound mind', whose disadvantage was not apparent. Because the purchaser had no knowledge of the vendor's disadvantage, the purchaser had therefore not taken any unconscientious advantage of the vendor. But actual knowledge of the special disadvantage is not a requirement. In *Amadio's* case, Mason J said it is sufficient that the other contracting party 'is aware of the possibility that that situation may exist or is aware of facts that would raise that possibility in the mind of any reasonable person'.[181]

Where the defendant has sufficient knowledge of the special disadvantage, the Privy Council said in *Hart v O'Connor* that unconscientious conduct 'can consist either of the active extortion of a benefit or the passive acceptance of a benefit in unconscionable circumstances'.[182] This principle was affirmed by a majority of the High Court in *Bridgewater v Leahy*, where it was held that 'the equity to set aside the deed may be enlivened not only by the active pursuit of the benefit it conferred but by the passive acceptance of that benefit'.[183]

177. (1956) 99 CLR 362 at 405.
178. (1983) 151 CLR 447 at 475.
179. (1998) 194 CLR 395 at 409 per Gaudron, McHugh, Gummow and Hayne JJ.
180. [1985] AC 1000.
181. (1983) 151 CLR 447 at 467. See also *Jedda Investments Pty Ltd v Krambousanos* (1997) 72 FCR 138; *Micarone v Perpetual Trustees Australia Ltd* (1999) 75 SASR 1.
182. [1985] AC 1000 at 1024 per Lord Brightman.
183. (1998) 194 CLR 457 at 493 per Gaudron, Gummow and Kirby JJ. See also *Turner v Windever* [2005] NSWCA 73 at [72] where it was held that 'mere unawareness of a matter material to the interests of a party to a transaction is not a special disadvantage'.

Distinguishing unconscionable dealing from undue influence

5.56   It was observed by the High Court in *Bridgewater v Leahy* that the doctrines of unconscionable dealing and undue influence may each 'be seen as a species of that genus of equitable intervention to refuse enforcement of or to set aside transactions which, if allowed to stand, would offend equity and good conscience'.[184] Although the categories are not mutually exclusive, the two doctrines remain distinct, at least in theory. In a passage that was adopted by the High Court in both *Louth v Diprose* and *Bridgewater v Leahy*, Deane J explained the distinction in *Amadio's* case:

> Undue influence, like common law duress, looks to the quality of the consent or assent of the weaker party … Unconscionable dealing looks to the conduct of the stronger party in attempting to enforce, or retain the benefit of, a dealing with a person under a special disability in circumstances where it is not consistent with equity or good conscience that he should do so.[185]

Unconscionable conduct under the Australian Consumer Law

5.57   The equitable concept of unconscionable dealing is imported into the Australian Consumer Law[186] by s 20(1), which provides that:

> A person must not, in trade or commerce, engage in conduct that is unconscionable, within the meaning of the unwritten law from time to time.[187]

The 'unwritten law' means the law expounded in the cases, as distinct from statute. Section 20(1) replaces s 51AA(1) of the former Trade Practices Act, 1974 (Cth).[188] The legislative intent of the former s 51AA was expressed in the Explanatory Memorandum to the legislation as follows:

> The provision embodies the equitable concept of unconscionable conduct as recognised by the High Court in *Blomley v Ryan* (1956) 99 CLR 362 and *Commercial Bank of Australia v Amadio* (1983) 151 CLR 447 …
>
> Section 51AA is not intended to extend the principles of unconscionable conduct beyond those recognised by the courts of this country under the laws of equity. The advantages of providing a statutory prohibition for conduct which is already dealt with by equity lie in the availability of remedies under the Principal Act …

In addition to s 20(1), the Australian Consumer Law contains further prohibitions against unconscionable conduct in consumer transactions in s 21(1) (which replaces s 51AB of the Trade Practices Act), and unconscionable conduct in business transactions in s 22(1) (which replaces s 51AC of the Trade Practices Act). Neither of these sections contains a definition of

---

184. (1998) 194 CLR 457 at 478 per Gaudron, Gummow and Kirby JJ.
185. (1983) 151 CLR 447 at 474.
186. Competition and Consumer Act 2010 (Cth) Sch 2.
187. Section 12CA(1) of the Australian Securities and Investments Commission Act 2001 (Cth) creates a specific prohibition in relation to financial services: 'A person must not, in trade or commerce, engage in conduct in relation to financial services if the conduct is unconscionable within the meaning of the unwritten law, from time to time, of the States and Territories.'
188. The legislative history of s 51AA is outlined by Kirby J in *Australian Competition and Consumer Commission v C G Berbatis Holdings Pty Ltd* (2003) 214 CLR 51 at 81–4.

unconscionable conduct. Instead, there is a non-exhaustive list of matters, drafted in similar terms for each section, to which the Court may have regard in determining whether a person has engaged in 'conduct that is, in all the circumstances, unconscionable.' In consumer transactions, these are:

(a) the relative strengths of the bargaining positions of the supplier and the consumer; and

(b) whether, as a result of conduct engaged in by the person, the consumer was required to comply with conditions that were not reasonably necessary for the protection of the legitimate interests of the supplier; and

(c) whether the consumer was able to understand any documents relating to the supply or possible supply of the goods or services; and

(d) whether any undue influence or pressure was exerted on, or any unfair tactics were used against, the consumer or a person acting on behalf of the consumer by the supplier or a person acting on behalf of the supplier in relation to the supply or possible supply of the goods or services; and

(e) the amount for which, and the circumstances under which, the consumer could have acquired identical or equivalent goods or services from a person other than the supplier.[189]

The cases have recognised that unconscionable conduct under these provisions is not confined by equivalent equitable doctrines.[190] The provisions expand the concept of unconscionable conduct and the remedies that are available for it. Remedies under the Australian Consumer Law are discussed in Chapter 16.

ELECTION

5.58 It was explained at 5.2 that contacts liable to rescission are voidable and not void. A voidable contract is effective unless and until it is rescinded. The innocent party must therefore elect either to affirm or to rescind a voidable contract. An election to affirm a voidable contract extinguishes the right to rescind. Conversely, an election to rescind a voidable contract extinguishes the right to enforce the contract according to its terms, including any accrued right to damages or specific performance of the contract. These propositions are illustrations of the general doctrine of election, which applies whenever a party is faced with alternative and inconsistent rights or remedies.[191] An election, once made, is irrevocable.

189. Australian Consumer Law, s 21(2), which replaces s 51AB of the Trade Practices Act.
190. Australian Competition and Consumer Commission v Berbatis Holdings Pty Ltd, (2000) 169 ALR 324 at 335; [2000] FCA 2 at [24] per French J; Australian Competition and Consumer Commission v Simply No Knead (Franchising) Pty Ltd (2000) 178 ALR 304; [2000] FCA 1365; Australian Securities and Investments Commission v National Exchange Pty Ltd [2005] FCAFC 226 at [30] per Tamberlin, Finn and Conti JJ.
191. See, generally, K R Handley, Estoppel by Conduct and Election, Sweet and Maxwell, London, 2006.

In *Sargent v ASL Developments Ltd*, Stephen J said:

> The words or conduct ordinarily required to constitute an election must be unequivocal in the sense that it is consistent only with the exercise of one of the two sets of rights and inconsistent with the exercise of the other.[192]

No question of election can arise before the innocent party at least becomes aware of the facts which entitle that party to rescind.[193] An election is not required immediately. The innocent party 'might keep the question open, so long as it did nothing to affirm the contract and so long as the respondents' position was not prejudiced in consequence of the delay'.[194] It is unsettled whether the innocent party must also be aware of its legal entitlement to rescind.[195] In the context of rescission for fraudulent misrepresentation, the Victorian Supreme Court held in *Coastal Estates Pty Ltd v Melevende*[196] that an election can only arise if there is knowledge of both the falsity of the representation and of the legal right to rescind. As Adam J said:

> Because the making of an election necessarily presupposes a knowledge that a choice between alternative courses is open, in general, no question of affirmation can arise in the absence of such knowledge.[197]

However, outside the context of rescission for misrepresentation, the High Court held in *Khoury v Government Insurance Office of NSW* that 'at least where the alternative rights arise under the terms of one contract, a party may be held to have elected to affirm it notwithstanding that he was unaware of the actual right to avoid it'.[198]

In *Hawker Pacific Pty Ltd v Helicopter Charter Pty Ltd*, Priestley JA of the New South Wales Court of Appeal said that the concept of affirmation:

> … covers situations governed by two particular legal theories, election and estoppel … to make a case of affirmation the appellant here needs to show either that the respondent elected not to avoid the contract or became estopped from asserting its right to avoid the contract.[199]

---

192. (1974) 131 CLR 634 at 646; *Khoury v Government Insurance Office of NSW* (1984) 165 CLR 622 at 633 per Mason, Brennan, Deane and Dawson JJ; *Immer (No 145) Pty Ltd v Uniting Church in Australia Property Trust (NSW)* (1993) 182 CLR 26 at 40 per Deane, Toohey, Gaudron and McHugh JJ. See also *Christiansen v Klepac* (2001) 10 BPR 18,955 at 18,958 per Young J (NSW SC).

193. *Sargent v ASL Developments Ltd* (1974) 131 CLR 634 at 642 per Stephen J and 658 per Mason J; *Khoury v Government Insurance Office of NSW* (1984) 165 CLR 622 at 633–4 per Mason, Brennan, Deane and Dawson JJ; *Immer (No 145) Pty Ltd v Uniting Church in Australia Property Trust (NSW)* (1993) 182 CLR 26 at 30 per Brennan J, and at 40 per Deane, Toohey, Gaudron and McHugh JJ.

194. *Tropical Traders Ltd v Goonan* (1964) 111 CLR 41 at 55 per Kitto J; *Sargent v ASL Developments Ltd* (1974) 131 CLR 634 at 656 per Mason J; *Immer (No 145) Pty Ltd v Uniting Church in Australia Property Trust (NSW)* (1993) 182 CLR 26 at 39 per Deane, Toohey, Gaudron and McHugh JJ. See also *GEC Marconi Systems Pty Ltd v BHP Information Technology Pty Ltd* (2003) 128 FCR 1 at 89–92 per Finn J.

195. See the discussion of authorities in *Sargent v ASL Developments Ltd* (1974) 131 CLR 634 at 643–6 per Stephen J and at 656–8 per Mason J.

196. [1965] VR 433.

197. [1965] VR 433 at 453.

198. (1984) 165 CLR 622 at 633–4 per Mason, Brennan, Deane and Dawson JJ. See also *Immer (No 145) Pty Ltd v Uniting Church in Australia Property Trust (NSW)* (1993) 182 CLR 26 at 40 per Deane, Toohey, Gaudron and McHugh JJ; *Ellison v Lutre Pty Ltd* (1999) 88 FCR 116 at 125–30 per von Doussa, Mansfield and Goldberg JJ.

199. (1991) 22 NSWLR 298 at 304. See also *Helicopters Pty Ltd v Bankstown Airport Ltd* [2010] NSWCA 178.

RESTITUTIO IN INTEGRUM

5.59 The principal restriction upon the availability of rescission is the requirement of 'putting the parties in the position they were in before the contract'.[200] This is known as the requirement of *restitutio in integrum*. The concept of 'restitution' in this context means 'restoration'. Questions of restitution only arise in relation to executed or partially executed contracts, and not where a contract is wholly executory. In practical terms, the main reasons for impossibility of *restitutio in integrum* are the destruction or deterioration of property that has passed under the voidable contract, or the subsequent acquisition by a bona fide third-party purchaser of property that has passed under the voidable contract. If complete restitution is not possible, the court may exercise its discretion to order partial rescission or rescission subject to terms.[201]

5.60 The requirement of restitution applies whether the contract is being rescinded at common law or in equity, but the standard of restitution differs between the two jurisdictions. The common law takes a strict view of restitution. Historically, the common law attitude is justified because of the limited range of ancillary remedies that are available at common law to make adjustments between the parties. By contrast, the availability of ancillary remedies in equity to make adjustments between the parties has always been less restricted. Accordingly, equity merely requires substantial restitution to achieve effective rescission.

5.61 The possibility of restitution was at issue in *Alati v Kruger*.[202] The litigation in *Alati v Kruger* arose from the sale of a fruit business by the appellant vendor to the respondent purchaser. The sale of the business included a transfer of goodwill, stock-in-trade and the assignment of a lease. The purchaser later sought to rescind the transaction on the basis of fraudulent misrepresentations made by the vendor as to the income of the business. By the time that judgment was given, the purchaser had allowed the business to close down, the goodwill had dissipated and the lessor had retaken possession of the leased premises. In these circumstances, the vendor argued that *restitutio in integrum* was impossible. The High Court rejected the vendor's argument and ordered rescission of the contract in equity and the return of the purchase price, subject to deductions for stock-in-trade not returned by the purchaser and reasonable compensation to the vendor for use of the property comprised in the contract. The purchaser was not considered responsible for loss of the goodwill. Dixon CJ, Webb, Kitto and Taylor JJ explained the differences between common law and equitable rescission as follows:

---

200. *Brown v Smitt* (1924) 34 CLR 160 at 165 per Knox CJ, Gavan Duffy and Starke JJ.
201. *Vadasz v Pioneer Concrete (SA) Pty Ltd* (1995) 184 CLR 102 at 115 per Deane, Dawson, Toohey, Gaudron and McHugh JJ.
202. (1955) 94 CLR 216.

If the case had to be decided according to the principles of the common law, it might have been argued that at the date when the respondent issued his writ he was not entitled to rescind the purchase, because he was not then in a position to return to the appellant *in specie* that which he had received under the contract, in the same plight as that in which he had received it … But it is necessary here to apply the doctrines of equity, and equity has always regarded as valid the disaffirmance of a contract induced by fraud even though precise *restitutio in integrum* is not possible, if the situation is such that, by the exercise of its powers, including the power to take accounts of profits and to direct inquiries as to allowances proper to be made for deterioration, it can do what is practically just between the parties, and by so doing restore them substantially to the *status quo* … The difference between the legal and the equitable rules on the subject simply was that equity, having means which the common law lacked to ascertain and provide for the adjustments necessary to be made between the parties in cases where a simple handing back of property or repayment of money would not put them in as good a position as before they entered into their transaction, was able to see the possibility of *restitutio in integrum*, and therefore to concede the right of a defrauded party to rescind, in a much wider variety of cases than those which the common law could recognise as admitting of rescission.[203]

Since equity exercises a concurrent jurisdiction in every case where the common law allows rescission, under the judicature system, the equitable standard of restitution has prevailed.

Doing equity

5.62   Applying the maxim that 'he who seeks equity must do equity', a court may order partial rescission of the transaction, or rescission subject to terms, where that is necessary to achieve 'what is practically just' for all parties.[204] In *Vadasz v Pioneer Concrete (SA) Pty Ltd*,[205] the appellant was a company director who gave a personal guarantee of the company's past and future indebtedness to the respondent. The respondent had required the guarantee as a condition of continuing to supply goods to the company, which later defaulted. The appellant sought rescission of the guarantee because it was induced by the misrepresentation that his liability was confined to the company's future indebtedness. The misrepresentation was assumed to be fraudulent. The High Court allowed rescission, but in respect of the company's past indebtedness only. The court said that 'to enforce the guarantee to the extent of future indebtedness is to do no more than hold the appellant to what he was prepared to undertake independently of any misrepresentation'.[206] In reaching that conclusion, the High Court rejected dicta by Lord Browne-Wilkinson in *Barclays Bank plc v O'Brien* that rescission is 'an all or nothing process', and that

---

203.   (1955) 94 CLR 216 at 223–4.
204.   *Bridgewater v Leahy* (1998) 194 CLR 457 at 473 per Gleeson CJ and Callinan J.
205.   (1995) 184 CLR 102.
206.   (1995) 184 CLR 102 at 115 per Deane, Dawson, Toohey, Gaudron and McHugh JJ.

rescission for misrepresentation 'does not involve reforming the transaction to accord with the representation'.[207]

The importance of 'doing equity' as a condition of rescission is further illustrated by the High Court judgment in *Maguire v Makaronis*.[208] The case involved a claim for rescission of a mortgage that secured a loan between the appellant solicitors and the respondent clients. The appellants had taken the mortgage in breach of fiduciary duty by failing to disclose their identity as the mortgagees. The respondents were in default of the loan. The High Court set aside the mortgage, but conditionally upon repayment of the loan, with interest. Without that condition of relief, 'the respondents would be left with the fruits of the transaction of which they complain'.[209]

207. [1994] 1 AC 180 at 199, cited in *TSB Bank plc v Camfield* [1995] 1 WLR 430 at 435–7 per Nourse LJ.
208. (1997) 188 CLR 449.
209. (1997) 188 CLR 449 at 475 per Brennan CJ, Gaudron, McHugh, and Gummow JJ. See also *Wilby v St George Bank* (2001) 80 SASR 404 (CA); *Westpac Banking Corporation v Paterson* (2001) 187 ALR 168 at 176 per Branson, Mansfield and Katz JJ (Full Federal Court); *Elkofairi v Permanent Trustee Co Ltd* [2002] NSWCA 413 at [98]–[100]; (2003) 11 BPR 20,841 at 20,859–61 per Santow JA.

CHAPTER

Account of Profits

NATURE OF THE REMEDY

6.1 An account of profits is an order that requires the defendant, under the supervision of the court, to account to the plaintiff for the profits of a wrong. The modern remedy is a species of the equitable action of account. Although the wrongs giving rise to an account of profits have never been stated exhaustively, the principal applications of the remedy are for breaches of trust and fiduciary duty in the exclusive jurisdiction of equity, and for infringements of intellectual property rights in the auxiliary jurisdiction of equity, where equity acts in aid of common law rights. Unlike an award of compensatory damages (see **Chapters 2** and **3**), an account of profits is a restitutionary remedy because it seeks to disgorge the defendant of a profit. The plaintiff need not have suffered any loss.[1] Accordingly, damages and accounting for profits are alternative and inconsistent remedies between which the plaintiff must elect.[2] The difference between the remedies was explained by Windeyer J of the High Court in *Colbeam Palmer Ltd v Stock Affiliates Pty Ltd*:

> The distinction between an account of profits and damages is that by the former the infringer is required to give up his ill-gotten gains to the party whose rights he has infringed: by the latter he is required to compensate the party wronged for the loss he has suffered. The two computations can obviously yield different results, for a plaintiff's loss is not to be measured by the defendant's gain, nor a defendant's gain by the plaintiff's loss. Either may be greater, or less, than the other.[3]

6.2   In *Dart Industries Inc v Decor Corp Pty Ltd*, the High Court said that 'the purpose of an account of profits is not to punish the defendant but to prevent its unjust enrichment'.[4] Although *Dart* was a case of intellectual property infringement, the High Court appeared to be stating a principle of general application. However, in *Warman International Ltd v Dwyer*, the High Court subsequently differentiated between the purpose of an account of profits for intellectual property infringement and the purpose of an account of profits for breach of fiduciary duty, in the following terms:

> In the context of patent infringement, the purpose of ordering an account is not to punish the defendant, but to prevent the defendant's unjust enrichment. But the liability of a fiduciary to account differs from that of an infringer in an intellectual property case. It has been suggested that the liability of a fiduciary to account for a profit made in breach of the fiduciary duty should be determined by reference to the concept of unjust enrichment, namely, whether the profit is made at the expense of the person to whom the fiduciary duty is owed, and to the honesty and bona fides of the fiduciary. But the authorities in Australia and England deny that liability of a fiduciary to account depends upon detriment to the plaintiff or the dishonesty and lack of bona fides of the fiduciary … The objectives which the rule seeks to achieve are to preclude the fiduciary from being swayed by considerations of personal interest and from accordingly misusing the fiduciary position for personal advantage.[5]

---

1.   *Consul Development Pty Ltd v DPC Estates Pty Ltd* (1975) 132 CLR 373 at 394 per Gibbs J; *Warman International Ltd v Dwyer* (1995) 182 CLR 544 at 557 per Mason CJ, Brennan, Deane, Dawson and Gaudron JJ; *Attorney-General v Blake* [2001] 1 AC 268 at 280 per Lord Nicholls.

2.   *Neilson v Betts* (1871) LR 5 HL 1 at 22 per Lord Westbury; *De Vitre v Betts* (1873) LR 6 HL 319 at 321 per Lord Chelmsford; *Warman International Ltd v Dwyer* (1995) 182 CLR 544 at 559 per Mason CJ, Brennan, Deane, Dawson and Gaudron JJ; *Tang Man Sit v Capacious Investments Ltd* [1996] 1 AC 514 (PC).

3.   (1968) 122 CLR 25 at 32. See: M J Leeming, 'When Should a Plaintiff Take an Account of Profits?' (1996) 7 AIPJ 127.

4.   (1993) 179 CLR 101 at 114 per Mason CJ, Deane, Dawson and Toohey JJ.

5.   (1995) 182 CLR 544 at 557–8 per Mason CJ, Brennan, Deane, Dawson and Gaudron JJ.

Grounds for awarding an account of profits

Breach of trust and fiduciary duty

6.3   The award of an account of profits for breaches of trust and fiduciary duty is an exercise of the exclusive jurisdiction of equity in respect of purely equitable obligations. Where the defaulting trustee or fiduciary has caused a loss, the appropriate remedy is an award of equitable compensation: see Chapter 11. Where the trustee or fiduciary has made a gain, he or she must account for all profits made 'by reason of' the breach of trust or fiduciary duty. No element of penalty is involved.[6] In *Warman International Ltd v Dwyer*, which involved the exploitation of a business opportunity by a senior manager of the plaintiff's business, the High Court formulated the authorities into the following principles:

> A fiduciary must account for a profit or benefit if it was obtained either (1) when there was a conflict or possible conflict between his fiduciary duty and his personal interest, or (2) by reason of his fiduciary position or by reason of his taking advantage of opportunity or knowledge derived from his fiduciary position.[7]

An account of profits is always a personal remedy, whether it is awarded in the exclusive jurisdiction or the auxiliary jurisdiction of equity.[8] But, in cases of defaulting trustees or fiduciaries, an account may be secured by the imposition of a constructive trust[9] or an equitable lien[10] over the fund constituting the profit. In such cases, the plaintiff has the benefit of personal remedies against the trustee or fiduciary and an equitable proprietary interest in the fund.

Breach of confidence

6.4   An account of profits may be awarded for a breach of confidence in the exclusive jurisdiction of equity where the obligation of confidence is purely equitable in nature.[11] In *Australian Broadcasting Corporation v Lenah Game Meats Pty Ltd*, Gleeson CJ identified the elements of an action for breach of confidence in the following terms:

> ... first, that the information is confidential, secondly, that it was originally imparted in circumstances importing an obligation of confidence and thirdly,

---

6.   *Harris v Digital Pulse Pty Ltd* (2003) 56 NSWLR 298 at 369–70 per Heydon JA.

7.   (1995) 182 CLR 544 at 557 per Mason CJ, Brennan, Deane, Dawson and Gaudron JJ. See also *Hospital Products Ltd v United States Surgical Corp* (1984) 156 CLR 41 at 107 per Mason J; *Consul Development Pty Ltd v DPC Estates Pty Ltd* (1975) 132 CLR 373 at 393 per Gibbs J; *Chan v Zacharia* (1984) 154 CLR 178 at 198–9 per Deane J.

8.   *Warman International Ltd v Dwyer* (1995) 182 CLR 544 at 557 per Mason CJ, Brennan, Deane, Dawson and Gaudron JJ; *Consul Development Pty Ltd v DPC Estates Pty Ltd* (1975) 132 CLR 373 at 395 per Gibbs J.

9.   *Chan v Zacharia* (1984) 154 CLR 178 at 199 per Deane J.

10. *Scott v Scott* (1963) 109 CLR 649.

11. *Attorney-General v Guardian Newspapers Ltd (No 2)* [1990] 1 AC 109.

that there has been, or is threatened, an unauthorized use of the information to the detriment of the party communicating it.[12]

Where the obligation of confidence arises from the express or implied terms of a contract, the parties are entitled to their contractual remedies for breach. In Australia, an account of profits is not available as a remedy for breach of contract.[13] Two further points arise in this context. First, it has been recognized since the earliest cases that equitable and contractual obligations of confidence can exist concurrently in relation to the same confidential subject matter.[14] The second, more difficult, issue is whether a plaintiff in these circumstances can elect for an account of profits in the exclusive jurisdiction of equity, as an alternative to the common law remedy of damages for breach of contract. Gurry cites *Peter Pan Manufacturing Corp v Corsets Silhouette Ltd*[15] as authority that 'the independent jurisdiction in equity may be exercised as an alternative to the contractual jurisdiction when there may be an express obligation of confidence in the contract.'[16]

Much depends upon the terms of the contract. In *Deta Nominees Pty Ltd v Viscount Plastic Products Pty Ltd*, Fullagar J held that equity would withhold further remedies for breach of confidence where adequate remedies were available at law.[17] More recently, in *Coles Supermarkets Australia Pty Ltd v FKP Ltd*,[18] Gordon J followed the view expressed by Campbell JA in *Del Casale v Artedomus (Aust) Pty Ltd* that 'if there was a contractual obligation that covered the topic, there would, of course, be no occasion for equity to intervene to impose its own obligation.'[19] Campbell JA relied upon the following passage from the judgment of Megarry J in *Coco v AN Clark (Engineers) Ltd*:

> I think it is quite plain ... that the obligation of confidence may exist where, as in this case, there is no contractual relationship between the parties. In cases of contract, the primary question is no doubt that of construing the contract and any terms implied in it.[20]

Both *Deta Nominees* and *Coles* were distinguished by the Full Federal Court in *Optus Networks Pty Ltd v Telstra Corp Ltd*, where the court held that the plaintiff could elect for an account of profits in that case because the equitable remedy was not excluded by the terms of the relevant contract.[21] The court

12. [2001] HCA 63 at [30]; (2001) 208 CLR 199 at 222, citing *Coco v A N Clark (Engineers) Ltd* [1969] RPC 41 at 47 per Megarry J.

13. *Hospitality Group Pty Ltd v Australian Rugby Union Ltd* (2001) 110 FCR 157. See 6.21.

14. *Morison v Moat* (1851) 9 Hare 241, 68 ER 492; *Robb v Green* [1895] 2 QB 315. Contrast *Coles Supermarkets Australia Pty Ltd v FKP Ltd* [2008] FCA 1915 at [63]–[64] per Gordon J.

15. [1963] RPC 45.

16. F Gurry, *Breach of Confidence*, Clarendon Press, Oxford, 1984, p 44.

17. [1979] VR 167 at 191.

18. [2008] FCA 1915 at [63].

19. [2007] NSWCA 172 at [118].

20. [1969] RPC 41 at 47.

21. [2010] FCAFC 21 at [29] per Finn, Sundberg and Jacobson JJ.

made the final point that, if the plaintiff elected for an account, 'the grant of that relief remains a matter for the court.'[22]

Infringement of intellectual property rights

6.5   An account of profits may be awarded in the auxiliary jurisdiction of equity against the infringer of an intellectual property right, subject to three considerations:

1. an account will normally be awarded as ancillary relief to an injunction, but not otherwise;

2. the account is limited to the profits derived from the defendant's *knowing* infringement of the plaintiff's rights; and

3. an account is a discretionary remedy that is subject to equitable defences.

Historical background: the requirement of an injunction

6.6   Before the enactment of the statutory antecedents of the present intellectual property regime, equity had long exercised an auxiliary jurisdiction to award an account of profits for the infringement of patents,[23] copyright[24] and common law trade marks.[25]

It is a reflection of the equitable origins of the remedy that an account of profits in the auxiliary jurisdiction will not normally be awarded in intellectual property cases unless the account is ancillary to an injunction restraining infringement.[26] Accordingly, where an injunction cannot be awarded, neither can an account of profits be awarded. The original justification for the rule lies in the period before the judicature system. In *Smith v London & South Western Railway Co*,[27] Page Wood V-C cited with approval the following passage from *Baily v Taylor*:[28]

> This Court has no jurisdiction to give to a Plaintiff a remedy for an alleged piracy, unless he can make out that he is entitled to the equitable interposition of this Court by injunction; and in such case, the Court will also give him an account, that his remedy here may be complete. If this Court do not interfere by injunction, then his remedy, as in the case of any other injury to his property, must be at law.

In breach of confidence cases, the rule in *Smith v London & South Western Railway Co*[29] should, according to general principles, apply where the obligation

---

22. [2010] FCAFC 21 at [41], citing *Australian Medic-Care Co Ltd v Hamilton Pharmaceuticals Pty Ltd* (2009) 261 ALR 501 at [628]–[629] per Finn J.

23. *Smith v London & South Western Railway Co* (1854) Kay 408; 69 ER 173.

24. *Baily v Taylor* (1829) 1 Russ & My 73; 39 ER 28.

25. *Edelsten v Edelsten* (1863) 1 De GJ & S 185; 46 ER 72.

26. *Smith v London & South Western Railway Co* (1854) Kay 408; 69 ER 173; *Price's Patent Candle Co Ltd v Bauwen's Patent Candle Co Ltd* (1858) 4 K & J 727; 70 ER 302. See also *Delpin Pty Ltd v Nargol Holdings Pty Ltd* (2002) Aust Contracts Reports 90–147 at 92,072 per Windeyer J (NSW SC).

27. (1854) Kay 408 at 415; 69 ER 173 at 176.

28. (1829) 1 Russ & My 73; 39 ER 28 per Leach MR.

29. (1854) Kay 408; 69 ER 173.

of confidence is contractual. Where the obligation of confidence is purely equitable, an account of profits may be awarded in the exclusive jurisdiction of equity without an injunction.[30]

Statutory jurisdiction

6.7   The jurisdiction to award an account of profits is now based upon statute in cases of registered trade mark infringement,[31] patent infringement,[32] copyright infringement,[33] infringement of the monopoly in a registered design,[34] infringement of an eligible layout right[35] and infringement of a plant breeder's right.[36] However, the statutory remedy 'retains its equitable characteristics'.[37]

The statutory jurisdiction to award an account of profits in cases of registered trade mark infringement was considered by the High Court in *Colbeam Palmer Ltd v Stock Affiliates Pty Ltd*.[38] That case was concerned with the operation of s 65 of the Trade Marks Act 1955 (Cth), which is the equivalent of s 126 of the Trade Marks Act 1995 (Cth). The section was relevantly drafted as follows:

> The relief which a court may grant in an action or proceeding for infringement of a registered trade mark includes an injunction (subject to such terms, if any, as the court thinks fit) and ... at the option of the plaintiff, either damages or an account of profits.

At first glance, the section did no more than state the equitable principles governing the award of an account of profits for passing off in the auxiliary jurisdiction. Windeyer J appeared to confirm that view by observing that:

> On general principles, and as I read s 65, damages or an account of profits are forms of relief which *ordinarily* are to be had in a trade mark case only as ancillary to an injunction.[39]

However, the facts in *Colbeam* were unusual for two reasons. First, the plaintiff had assigned the relevant trade mark during the pendency of the infringement litigation, and had not joined the assignee as a party. Second, the registration of the trade mark had expired during the pendency of the litigation. In these circumstances, Windeyer J held:

> Although I think that an injunction cannot now be granted at the suit of the plaintiff, it could have been when the action was commenced. The plaintiff asks for an account of profits which, as an alternative to damages, was sought

---

30.   *Attorney-General v Guardian Newspapers Ltd (No 2)* [1990] 1 AC 109.

31.   Trade Marks Act 1995 (Cth) s 126.

32.   Patents Act 1990 (Cth) s 122(1).

33.   Copyright Act 1968 (Cth) s 115(2).

34.   Designs Act 2003 (Cth) s 75(1).

35.   Circuit Layouts Act 1989 (Cth) s 27(2).

36.   Plant Breeder's Rights Act 1994 (Cth) s 56(3).

37.   *Dart Industries Inc v Decor Corp Pty Ltd* (1993) 179 CLR 101 at 111 per Mason CJ, Deane, Dawson and Toohey JJ.

38.   (1968) 122 CLR 25.

39.   (1968) 122 CLR 25 at 31 (emphasis added).

when the action was commenced. I am prepared, therefore, to order an account for such period as the facts warrant.[40]

Colbeam is at least authority that the grant of an injunction is not an absolute prerequisite for the award of an account of profits in cases of registered trade mark infringement. In reaching that conclusion, Windeyer J rejected the argument that s 65 of the Trade Marks Act 1955 had enlarged the auxiliary jurisdiction of equity to award an account of profits. His Honour held:

> The effect of s 65 is to make expressly available in the case of the infringement of a registered trade mark the same remedies and relief as can be had in a passing-off action in the case of a common law trade mark.[41]

Because an injunction was not, therefore, an absolute prerequisite for the award of an account of profits in the auxiliary jurisdiction of equity (at least in cases of passing off), and because of the similar drafting used in the relevant provisions of the trade marks, copyright, patents, registered designs, circuit layouts and plant breeder's rights legislation, the availability of an injunction at the commencement of infringement proceedings, but not necessarily at judgment, is arguably sufficient for the award of an account of profits in all of these cases. Accordingly, the loss of entitlement to injunctive relief during the pendency of the litigation may not necessarily foreclose the award of an account of profits.[42]

Innocent infringement in the auxiliary jurisdiction of equity

6.8 In the auxiliary jurisdiction of equity, an account of profits is limited to the profits made from the defendant's knowing infringement of the plaintiff's rights. The defendant is not, therefore, obliged to account for profits made from 'innocent' (meaning 'ignorant') infringement of the plaintiff's rights. Windeyer J in *Colbeam* explained the rationale for that rule in the following terms:

> … the account of profits retains the characteristics of its origin in the Court of Chancery. By it a defendant is made to account for, and is then stripped of, profits he has made which it would be unconscionable that he retain. These are profits made by him dishonestly, that is by his knowingly infringing the rights of the proprietor of the trade mark. This explains why the liability to account is still not necessarily coextensive with acts of infringement. The account is limited to the profits made by the defendant during the period when he knew of the plaintiff's rights.[43]

Because the defence of innocent infringement has not been affected by the trade marks legislation, the same equitable principles apply both in cases of registered trade mark infringement and passing off.[44] In *Colbeam*, the defendant had been infringing the plaintiff's registered trade mark for four years. Windeyer J accepted the defendant's evidence that he was genuinely

---

40.   (1968) 122 CLR 25 at 31.
41.   (1968) 122 CLR 25 at 32.
42.   See also D Browne, *Ashburner's Principles of Equity*, 2nd ed, Butterworths, London, 1933, p 349.
43.   (1968) 122 CLR 25 at 34.
44.   (1968) 122 CLR 25 at 34–5 per Windeyer J.

ignorant of the plaintiff's rights until the plaintiff's trade mark attorney issued a letter of demand to the defendant. While acknowledging that the defendant had been 'remiss' in failing to 'make all the inquiries that a more prudent person in his position might have made', Windeyer J nevertheless limited the account of profits to the period after which the defendant had received actual notice of the plaintiff's rights. In doing so, his Honour observed:

> … a lack of diligence in inquiry does not turn ignorance into knowledge. Dishonesty is not to be inferred from lack of care. This is not a case of "wilful blindness", the expression used in another context to describe a deliberate abstaining from inquiry from fear of what inquiry might reveal.[45]

6.9 The difference between lack of diligence and wilful blindness is one of degree. One such case of wilful blindness is *Edward Young & Co Ltd v Holt*,[46] a passing off case. In *Young* it was accepted that the defendant lacked actual notice of the plaintiff's common law trade mark when the defendant commenced using the infringing mark. Nevertheless, Wynn Parry J held that the innocent infringement defence was not available to the defendant on the facts of the case.[47] First, the defendant, who was described as having 'long experience' in the trade, had taken no 'step by way of enquiry' before commencing to use the infringing mark. Second, the defendant had continued using the infringing mark and had refrained from making any investigation of the plaintiff's rights even after the defendant was 'most clearly and expressly put on enquiry' by a letter from a confused customer.

Innocent breach of confidence

6.10 It is unsettled whether 'innocent' defendants are liable to account for profits in breach of confidence cases within the exclusive jurisdiction of equity. Part of the uncertainty arises from the judgment of the English Court of Appeal in *Seager v Copydex Ltd*.[48] In that case, the defendant breached its obligation of confidence by the 'unconscious' use of the plaintiff's invention. Because there was no contract between the parties, an account of profits could only have been awarded in the exclusive jurisdiction of equity. Lord Denning MR said that the case 'may not be a case for injunction or even for an account, but only for damages'.[49] Unfortunately, Lord Denning did not state why. Nevertheless, the case suggests that accounting for profits is confined to cases of 'knowing' breach.[50]

Innocent infringement in the statutory jurisdiction

6.11 Except for the Trade Marks Act 1995 (Cth), each of the current intellectual property statutes contains provisions which regulate the defence

---

45.   (1968) 122 CLR 25 at 32–3.
46.   (1948) 65 RPC 25.
47.   (1948) 65 RPC 25 at 31.
48.   [1967] RPC 349.
49.   [1967] RPC 349 at 368.
50.   See Lord Goff of Chieveley and G Jones, *The Law of Restitution*, 7th ed, Sweet & Maxwell, London, 2007, [34-021].

of innocent infringement in actions for an account of profits. However, the provisions are not drafted in the same terms.

6.12　Patents and plant breeder's rights　Section 123(1) of the Patents Act 1990 (Cth) provides as follows:

> A court may refuse to award damages, or make an order for an account of profits, in respect of an infringement of a patent if the defendant satisfies the court that, at the date of the infringement, the defendant was not aware, and had no reason to believe, that a patent for the invention existed.

Section 57(1) of the Plant Breeder's Rights Act 1994 (Cth) is drafted in similar terms. The innocent infringement defence under both statutes differs from the position in equity because the defendant is not only required to prove the absence of *actual* notice of the plaintiff's rights, but is also required to prove the absence of *constructive* notice of the plaintiff's rights. In the Patents Act, the concept of constructive notice is imported by the words 'and had no reason to believe, that a patent for the invention existed'. Similar drafting is used in s 57(1) of the Plant Breeder's Rights Act. Both statutes provide for one non-exhaustive instance of constructive notice. Section 123(2) of the Patents Act provides:

> If patented products, marked so as to indicate that they are patented in Australia, were sold or used in the patent area to a substantial extent before the date of the infringement, the defendant is to be taken to have been aware of the existence of the patent unless the contrary is established.

6.13　Section 57(2) of the Plant Breeder's Rights Act is drafted in similar terms. Aside from these provisions, there is no statutory guidance as to the meaning of constructive notice. In particular, neither the Patents Act nor the Plant Breeder's Rights Act indicates whether registration in the Register of Patents or the Register of Plant Varieties constitutes constructive notice to the world, despite the fact that both registers are, by statute, open to public search. In *Colbeam*, the defendant's failure to search the Register of Trade Marks did not preclude the defence of innocent infringement. However, the drafting of the Trade Marks Act 1995 differs from that of the Patents Act and the Plant Breeder's Rights Act because the Trade Marks Act makes no provision for constructive notice in cases of registered trade mark infringement.

6.14　Registered designs　The Designs Act 2003 (Cth) requires separate discussion because the innocent infringement defence provided for in s 75(2) differs from the equivalent provisions in both the Patents Act and the Plant Breeder's Rights Act. Section 75(2) of the Designs Act provides:

> The court may refuse to award damages, reduce the damages that would otherwise be awarded, or refuse to make an order for an account of profits, if the defendant satisfies the court:
>
> (a)　in the case of primary infringement:
>
> 　　(i)　that at the time of the infringement, the defendant was not aware that the design was registered; and
>
> 　　(ii)　that before that time, the defendant had taken all reasonable steps to ascertain whether the design was registered; or

(b) in the case of secondary infringement — that at the time of the infringement, the defendant was not aware, and could not reasonably have been expected to be aware, that the design was registered.

The section is notable because it applies a more stringent test of innocence to 'primary infringement' (which is the making of infringing products under s 71(1)(a) of the Act) than the Act applies to 'secondary infringement' (which includes the importing, selling or hiring of infringing products under s 71(1)(b), (c), (d) or (e) of the Act). The Designs Act also contains a constructive notice provision that is drafted in similar terms to s 123(2) of the Patents Act. Section 75(4) of the Designs Act provides:

> It is prima facie evidence that the defendant was aware that the design was registered if the product embodying the registered design to which the infringement proceedings relate, or the packaging of the product, is marked so as to indicate registration of the design.

6.15   Copyright and eligible layout rights   Section 115(3) of the Copyright Act 1968 (Cth) provides as follows:

> Where, in an action for infringement of copyright, it is established that an infringement was committed but it is also established that, at the time of the infringement, the defendant was not aware, and had no reasonable grounds for suspecting, that the act constituting the infringement was an infringement of the copyright, the plaintiff is not entitled under this section to any damages against the defendant in respect of the infringement, but is entitled to an account of profits in respect of the infringement whether any other relief is granted under this section or not.

Section 27(3) of the Circuit Layouts Act 1989 (Cth) is drafted in similar terms. Both sections literally provide that a plaintiff is 'entitled' to an account of profits (but not damages) in cases of innocent infringement. Despite the language of entitlement, the provisions do not exclude the discretion of the court to refuse the remedy upon other grounds.[51]

Discretionary defences: delay

6.16   In both the exclusive and auxiliary jurisdictions of equity, the award of an account of profits is discretionary, and may be 'defeated by equitable defences such as estoppel, laches, acquiescence and delay'.[52] The most common discretionary defence in intellectual property cases is unreasonable delay by the plaintiff between first knowing of the defendant's infringement and commencing infringement proceedings. In particular, the plaintiff does not have the option of waiting for a profit to accrue and then claiming the proceeds of the defendant's efforts. In *Lever Brothers, Port Sunlight Ltd v Sunniwite Products Ltd*,[53] a registered trade mark case, the plaintiff allowed nine months

---

51. *Robert J Zupanovich Pty Ltd v B & N Beale Nominees Pty Ltd* (1995) 32 IPR 339 at 356 per Carr J.

52. *Warman International Ltd v Dwyer* (1995) 182 CLR 544 at 559 per Mason CJ, Brennan, Deane, Dawson and Gaudron JJ.

53. (1949) 66 RPC 84; applied in *Kalamazoo (Aust) Pty Ltd v Compact Business Systems Pty Ltd* (1985) 5 IPR 213 at 242 per Thomas J (copyright infringement).

to elapse between first knowing of the infringement and issuing a letter of demand. The plaintiff then commenced proceedings six weeks later. The account of profits awarded to the plaintiff was confined to the period after the letter of demand. Similarly, in the context of breach of fiduciary duty, the High Court affirmed in *Warman International Ltd v Dwyer* that:

> … the conduct of the plaintiff may be such as to make it inequitable to order an account. Thus a plaintiff may not stand by and permit the defendant to make profits and then claim entitlement to those profits.[54]

Other grounds

6.17   The categories of cases in which an account of profits may be awarded are not closed. In the exclusive jurisdiction, an account of profits can be awarded for any species of equitable wrong. In the auxiliary jurisdiction, Lord Cottenham LC said in *North-Eastern Railway Co v Martin* that it was 'impossible with precision to lay down rules or establish definitions as to the cases in which it may be proper for this Court to exercise this jurisdiction'.[55] However, gains-based relief in the auxiliary jurisdiction, in the form of an account of profits, has largely been confined to the intellectual property torts and other torts which involve interferences with rights of property:[56] see **4.36**.

Breach of contract

6.18   As a matter of precedent, accounting for profits has not traditionally been available as a remedy for breach of contract because it is inconsistent with the compensatory nature of damages in contract.[57] However, in *Attorney-General v Blake*,[58] the House of Lords rejected the traditional view and ruled that an account of profits can be awarded for breach of contract, but only in exceptional circumstances. The facts in *Attorney-General v Blake* were that Blake had formerly been employed as an intelligence officer by the British Government from 1944 until 1961, during the Cold War era. In 1951 he became an agent of the Soviet Union. In 1961 he was convicted of offences under the Official Secrets Act 1911 (UK), and sentenced to 42 years' imprisonment. After escaping from prison and fleeing to Moscow in 1966, Blake wrote his autobiography in later years. It was published in the United Kingdom in 1990.

6.19   In civil proceedings that were brought against Blake and his publisher for breach of a fiduciary duty owed to the Crown, the lower courts held that the information disclosed in the book was no longer confidential, and

---

54.   (1995) 182 CLR 544 at 559 per Mason CJ, Brennan, Deane, Dawson and Gaudron JJ.

55.   (1848) 2 Ph 758 at 762; 41 ER 1136 at 1138. See also *Rapid Metal Developments (Australia) Pty Ltd v Rosato* [1971] Qd R 82 at 86–8 per Wanstall J.

56.   *Stoke-on-Trent City Council v W & J Wass Ltd* [1988] 1 WLR 1406; *Forsyth-Grant v Allen* [2008] EWCA Civ 505.

57.   *Teacher v Calder* [1899] AC 451 at 467–8 per Lord Davey.

58.   [2001] 1 AC 268.

that Blake no longer owed any fiduciary duty to the Crown. However, it was held that Blake had breached a surviving contractual duty 'not to divulge any official information gained by me as a result of my employment, either in the press or in book form'. The duty was expressed to apply beyond the period of his employment. In these circumstances, where Blake and his publisher had profited from Blake's breach of contract, but the Crown had suffered no compensable loss, the House of Lords ordered Blake and his publisher to account to the Crown for all sums that were payable to Blake under his publishing agreement. Lord Nicholls (with whom Lords Goff, Browne-Wilkinson and Steyn agreed) delivered the leading judgment:

> Normally the remedies of damages, specific performance and injunction, coupled with the characterization of some contractual obligations as fiduciary, will provide an adequate response to a breach of contract. It will be only in exceptional circumstances, where those remedies are inadequate, that any question of accounting for profits will arise. No fixed rules can be prescribed. The court will have regard to all the circumstances, including the subject matter of the contract, the purpose of the contractual provision which has been breached, the circumstances in which the breach occurred, the consequences of the breach and the circumstances in which relief is being sought. A useful general guide, although not exhaustive, is whether the plaintiff had a legitimate interest in preventing the defendant's profit-making activity and, hence, in depriving him of his profit.[59]

In *Hospitality Group Pty Ltd v Australian Rugby Union Ltd*, the Full Federal Court refused to follow *Attorney-General v Blake* because 'it would be inconsistent with the current principles laid down by the High Court to confer a windfall on a plaintiff under the guise of damages for breach of contract'.[60] Although the case was not cited, the High Court held in *Commonwealth v Amann Aviation Pty Ltd* that 'a plaintiff is not entitled, by the award of damages upon breach, to be placed in a superior position to that which he or she would have been in had the contract been performed.'[61] In *Hospitality Group Pty Ltd v Australian Rugby Union Ltd* and the cases following it, the High Court has been taken to mean that gains-based relief in the form of an account of profits or restitutionary damages are not available as remedies for breach of contract in Australian law. The High Court refused special leave to appeal against the decision.[62]

59. [2001] 1 AC 268 at 285. See also *Esso Petroleum Co Ltd v Niad Ltd* [2001] EWHC Ch 458; *Experience Hendrix Ltd v PPX Enterprises Inc* [2003] EWCA 323; [2003] 1 All ER (Comm) 830; *World Wide Fund for Nature v World Wrestling Federation Entertainment Inc* [2007] EWCA Civ 286.

60. (2001) 110 FCR 157 at 196 per Hill and Finkelstein JJ. See also *Multigroup Distribution Services Pty Ltd v TNT Australia Pty Ltd* (2001) 191 ALR 402 at 418 per Gyles J; *Mainland Holdings Ltd v Szady* [2002] NSWSC 699 at [64] per Gzell J; *Biscayne Partners Pty Ltd v Valance Corp Pty Ltd* [2003] NSWSC 874 at [228]-[237] per Einstein J. Distinguished in *Dalecoast Pty Ltd v Guardian International Pty Ltd* [2003] WASCA 142 at [105]-[107] per Murray J; *Finesky Holdings Pty Ltd v Minister for Transport for Western Australia* (2002) 26 WAR 368 at 382 per Steytler J; *Town & Country Property Management Services Pty Ltd v Kaltoum* [2002] NSWSC 166 at [83] per Campbell J. See 3.2.

61. (1991) 174 CLR 64 at 82 per Mason CJ and Dawson J, citing the compensation principle in *Robinson v Harman* (1848) 1 Ex 850 at 855; 154 ER 363 at 365.

62. (2002) 23(11) Leg Rep SL4.

ASSESSMENT

Breach of trust and fiduciary duty

6.20   In the exclusive jurisdiction of equity, the general rule is that a trustee or fiduciary must account for the entire profit made 'by reason of' the breach of trust or fiduciary duty.[63] At least six subsidiary points can be made about the application of that rule. First, an account of profits is not penal in nature, therefore a trustee or fiduciary will not be required to account for more than he or she has received from the breach of duty.[64] Second, where a trustee or fiduciary has acted without dishonesty in making a profit, he or she may be granted an equitable allowance from the profit as remuneration for his or her 'work and skill'.[65] But the exercise of the jurisdiction is confined to 'those cases where it cannot have the effect of encouraging trustees in any way to put themselves in a position where their interests conflict with their duties as trustees'.[66] Third, where a trustee makes a profit entirely by the misapplication of trust money, the beneficiary will be entitled to the entire profit. Fourth, where a trustee makes a profit by the misapplication of trust money mixed with other money, the beneficiary will generally be entitled to a proportionate share of the profit. Fifth, where property has been purchased entirely or partly by the misapplication of trust money, the trustee's obligation to account is not postponed until the trustee chooses to sell the property and realise the profit. The third, fourth and fifth principles were all reaffirmed by the High Court in *Scott v Scott*.[67] Finally, where a business, as distinct from a specific asset, is acquired and operated in breach of fiduciary duty, the High Court said in *Warman International Ltd v Dwyer*:

> … it may well be inappropriate and inequitable to compel the errant fiduciary to account for the whole of the profit of his conduct of the business or his exploitation of the principal's goodwill over an indefinite period of time. In such a case, it may be appropriate to allow the fiduciary a proportion of the profits, depending upon the particular circumstances. That may well be the case when it appears that a significant proportion of an increase in profits has been generated by the skill, efforts, property and resources of the fiduciary, the capital which he has introduced and the risks he has taken, so long as they are not risks to which the principal's property has been exposed. Then it may be said that the relevant proportion of the increased profits is not the product or consequence of the plaintiff's property but the product of the fiduciary's skill, efforts, property and resources.[68]

---

63.   *Consul Development Pty Ltd v DPC Estates Pty Ltd* (1975) 132 CLR 373 at 393 per Gibbs J; *Visnic v Sywak* [2009] NSWCA 173.

64.   *Vyse v Foster* (1872) LR 8 Ch App 309 at 333 per James LJ; *Hospital Products Ltd v United States Surgical Corp* (1984) 156 CLR 41 at 109 per Mason J; *Harris v Digital Pulse Pty Ltd* (2003) 56 NSWLR 298 at 369–70 per Heydon JA.

65.   *Boardman v Phipps* [1967] 2 AC 46 at 104 per Lord Cohen and at 112 per Lord Hodson.

66.   *Guinness plc v Saunders* [1990] 2 AC 663 at 701 per Lord Goff.

67.   (1963) 109 CLR 649. See also *Hagan v Waterhouse* (1991) 34 NSWLR 308 at 354–6 per Kearney J.

68.   (1995) 182 CLR 544 at 561 per Mason CJ, Brennan, Deane, Dawson and Gaudron JJ.

Infringement of intellectual property rights

6.21   The High Court acknowledged in *Dart Industries Inc v Decor Corp Pty Ltd*[69] that the assessment of profits in intellectual property cases is 'notoriously difficult' and that 'mathematical exactitude is generally impossible'. However, difficulty of assessment is not in itself a sufficient reason for refusing the remedy.

The concept of profit for present purposes was neatly summarised by Pennycuick J in *Peter Pan Manufacturing Corp v Corsets Silhouette Ltd*, a breach of confidence case:

> ... what has the plaintiff expended upon manufacturing the goods? What is the price which he has received on their sale? and the difference is profit.[70]

Two issues of general importance arise in assessing profit in intellectual property cases. First, identifying the defendant's costs attributable to the manufacture and sale of the infringing goods. Second, making an apportionment of the resulting profit between that part of the profit that is attributable to the defendant's infringement, and that part of the profit that the defendant is entitled to keep. Both issues are considered below.

Deductions

6.22   The onus of proof is upon the defendant to establish which costs are attributable to the manufacture and sale of the infringing goods. It has long been accepted that the defendant may deduct 'costs of material', 'costs of wages' and any other costs that are 'solely referable' to the manufacture and sale of the infringing goods. However, 'under no circumstances' can the defendant 'claim any remuneration to himself.'[71]

6.23   The further question has arisen of whether the defendant may also deduct any part of its general overhead expenses, such as rent, electricity and office expenses. The question was considered by the High Court in *Dart Industries Inc v Decor Corp Pty Ltd*,[72] where a majority of the court distinguished between two sets of factual circumstances.

First, where the infringing goods were a 'side line' of the defendant's business, meaning that the making and selling of those goods took up 'unused capacity in the defendant's business in the form of overheads which would have been incurred whether or not the articles had been sold and delivered'.[73] In these cases of unused capacity, no deduction is allowed, because the expenses would have been incurred in any event. *Colbeam Palmer Ltd v Stock*

69.   (1993) 179 CLR 101 at 111 per Mason CJ, Deane, Dawson and Toohey JJ.

70.   [1963] RPC 45 at 60.

71.   *Leplastrier & Co Ltd v Armstrong Holland Ltd* (1926) 26 SR (NSW) 585 at 593 per Harvey CJ (in Eq). See also *Tenderwatch Pty Ltd v Reed Business Information Pty Ltd* [2008] FCA 934 (copyright infringement).

72.   (1993) 179 CLR 101.

73.   (1993) 179 CLR 101 at 113 per Mason CJ, Deane, Dawson and Toohey JJ.

Affiliates Pty Ltd[74] was identified as one such 'side line' case, where Windeyer J had refused any deduction for general overhead expenses.

By contrast, in cases such as the present case, where there was no unused capacity, and 'the defendant has forgone the opportunity to manufacture and sell alternative [non-infringing] products', the High Court held that 'it will ordinarily be appropriate' to allow a proportional deduction for general overhead expenses:

> In calculating an account of profits, the defendant may not deduct the opportunity cost, that is, the profit forgone on the alternative products. But there would be real inequity if a defendant were denied a deduction for the opportunity cost as well as being denied a deduction for the cost of the overheads which sustained the capacity that would have been utilized by an alternative product and that was in fact utilized by the infringing product. If both were denied, the defendant would be in a worse position than if it had made no use of the patented invention.[75]

In these circumstances, the High Court upheld the judgment of the Full Court of the Federal Court that the defendants 'are at liberty to show that various categories of overhead [are attributable] to the obtaining of the relevant profit, and to show how and in what proportion they should be allocated in the taking of the account of profits'.[76]

Apportionment

6.24 Windeyer J in *Colbeam* stated the principle governing the apportionment of profits between owners and infringers:

> The true rule, I consider, is that a person who wrongly uses another man's industrial property — patent, copyright, trade mark — is accountable for any profits which he makes which are attributable to his use of the property which was not his.[77]

The apportionment of profit in *Colbeam* was achieved by a two-stage process. The first stage was to calculate the entire profit made from sales of goods bearing the mark. The second stage was to isolate that part of the profit that was attributable to the infringing use of the mark. As Windeyer J explained:

> … infringement consists in the unauthorised use of the mark in the course of trade in relation to goods in respect of which it is registered. The profit for which the infringer of a trade mark must account is thus not the profit he made from selling the article itself but … the profit made in selling it under the trade mark.[78]

---

74. (1968) 122 CLR 25.
75. (1993) 179 CLR 101 at 113.
76. (1993) 179 CLR 101 at 119–20. See also *Apand Pty Ltd v Kettle Chip Co Pty Ltd* (1999) 43 IPR 225; *LED Builders Pty Ltd v Eagle Homes Pty Ltd* (1999) 44 IPR 24; (1999) 46 IPR 375.
77. (1968) 122 CLR 25 at 42–3.
78. (1968) 122 CLR 25 at 37.

6.25 The position is different, however, where sales of an article can be attributed entirely to the infringing use of the plaintiff's intellectual property. That was so in *Dart Industries Inc v Decor Corp Pty Ltd.*[79] Decor manufactured and sold plastic kitchen canisters incorporating a press button seal that infringed Dart's patent. Apart from the press button seal, the body of the canisters was non-infringing. Notwithstanding the composite nature of the goods, King J of the Supreme Court (Vic) at first instance[80] held as an issue of fact that all sales of the canisters were attributable entirely to the use of the patented invention. Accordingly, Decor was directed to account for the entire profit. The Full Court of the Federal Court upheld the award of the entire profit to Dart.[81] In the High Court, Decor made an application for special leave to reopen the apportionment issue. After stating that both the trial judge and the Full Court had applied the correct apportionment principle as stated in *Colbeam*, the High Court unanimously dismissed Decor's application for special leave because apportionment is an issue of fact.[82] It is apparent from the judgment in *Dart* that the apportionment principle stated in *Colbeam* applies generally in cases of intellectual property infringement.[83]

---

79.   (1993) 179 CLR 101.

80.   (1990) 20 IPR 144 at 154.

81.   (1991) 104 ALR 621 at 631–2.

82.   (1993) 179 CLR 101 at 121.

83.   See *Robert J Zupanovich Pty Ltd v B & N Beale Nominees Pty Ltd* (1995) 32 IPR 339 at 357–9 per Carr J.

CHAPTER

7

Specific Performance

NATURE OF THE REMEDY

7.1 Specific performance directs a party to an agreement to perform the agreement. The remedy is usually applied to breaches or threatened[1] breaches of contract. The aim is to 'place the parties in the positions actually contemplated by contract performance.'[2] It owes its development to the fact that damages may be an inadequate remedy for the breach. This is especially true of contracts for the sale of rare and unique items such as land, works of art and intellectual property. Damages are inadequate because substitutes cannot be readily found.

In *Zhu v Treasurer of the State of New South Wales* the High Court explained the role of specific performance as follows:

> ... subject to the established limits on the grant of specific performance and injunctions, in Australian law each contracting party may be said to have a right to the performance of the contract by the other. It is not true here to say: "The duty to keep a contract at common law means a prediction that you must pay damages if you do not keep it, — and nothing else."[3]

Similarly, in *Seven Network (Operations) Ltd v Warburton (No 2)* Pembroke J observed:

> One of the abiding principles of a civilised system of law such as ours is that contracts are meant to be observed. Lawyers sometimes use the Latin phrase pacta sunt servanda to describe the principle. We make decisions on the assumption that contractual obligations will generally be performed and solemn commitments will not be ignored. The general policy of the law is that people should honour their contracts[4] ... If there were not adherence to such a principle, the conduct of private and commercial affairs would become an uncertain jumble. And certainty is what the law of contracts strives to achieve.[5]

---

1.   See *Turner v Bladin* (1951) 82 CLR 463 at 472. If the time for performance has not arrived the order may be postponed until it has: see *Hasham v Zenab* [1960] AC 316.

2.   *Jaddcal Pty Ltd v Minson [No 3]* [2011] WASC 362 at [171] per Le Miere J.

3.   (2004) 211 ALR 159; [2004] HCA 56 at [128] per Gleeson CJ, Gummow, Kirby, Callinan and Heydon JJ citing Oliver Wendell Holmes, 'The Path of the Law' (1897) 10 *Harvard Law Review* 457 at 462; see also *Tabcorp Holdings Ltd v Bowen Investments Pty Ltd* (2009) 236 CLR 272; [2009] HCA 8 at [13] per French CJ, Gummow, Heydon, Crennan and Kiefel JJ.

4.   *Baltic Shipping Co v Dillon* (1991) 22 NSWLR 1 at 9 (Gleeson CJ).

5.   [2011] NSWSC 386 at [3].

While specific performance is usually granted in aid of a legal right it does extend to cases where there is no remedy at common law provided the doctrine of part performance can be satisfied: see **7.6–7.11**.

7.2   Traditionally, a distinction is drawn between specific performance in the 'proper sense' and specific performance in the wide sense. As explained by Dixon J in *J C Williamson Ltd v Lukey & Mulholland*:

> Specific performance, in the proper sense, is a remedy to compel the execution in specie of a contract which requires some definite thing to be done before the transaction is complete and the parties' rights are settled and defined in the manner intended. Moreover, the remedy is not available unless complete relief can be given, and the contract carried into full and final execution so that the parties are put in the relation contemplated by their agreement.[6]

In the strict or 'proper sense' specific performance compels a party to execute a final instrument, such as a transfer of land or deed, to give effect to an earlier agreement. Such contracts are known as executory contracts. They require the performance of a specific obligation, such as the execution of a document or delivery of a chattel.

Specific performance in the wide sense, sometimes referred to as relief 'analogous' or 'approximate' to specific performance, is where the contract is already on foot (that is, it has already been executed as a 'final expression of obligation'[7] for the parties), but one party is ordered to perform its obligations under the contract according to its terms. For the most part, the principles to be applied to specific performance of executory and executed contracts are the same,[8] but the distinction remains important as observed by Beazley JA in *Waterways Authority of New South Wales v Coal and Allied (Operations) Pty Ltd*:

> The distinction between specific performance in the true sense and an order that a contractual obligation be performed in specie, was acknowledged in *Pakenham Upper Fruit Co Ltd v Crosby*[9], where the Court observed that the relevance of the distinction lay in the underlying basis that attracted the intervention in equity. In the case of true specific performance, the equity that gave rise to the remedy was the need to place the parties in the relative legal positions contemplated by the contract. In the case of an executed agreement, some other basis for the intervention of equity must be established 'appropriate to the *actual* legal relative situations of the parties' (emphasis added) having regard to the terms of the contract. It is apparent that when their Honours referred to the 'actual relative legal situations of the parties', they were referring to those obligations which, under the terms of the contract, remained to be performed. Otherwise, there would [be] no obligation of which performance could be ordered.

---

6.   (1931) 45 CLR 282 at 297.

7.   *J C Williamson Ltd v Lukey & Mulholland* (1931) 45 CLR 282 at 297 per Dixon J.

8.   *Australian Hardwoods Pty Ltd v Commissioner for Railways* [1961] 1 WLR 425 at 434; [1961] 1 All ER 737 at 743 (PC); *Opie v Collum* [1999] SASC 376 [279]–[286]; affirmed *Collum v Opie* (2000) 76 SASR 588; *BHP Petroleum v Oil Basins Ltd* [1985] VR 725; compare *Hewett v Court* (1983) 149 CLR 639.

9.   (1924) 35 CLR 386; [1924] HCA 55.

The distinction between specific performance in its strict sense and an order made requiring performance of a term of a contract has continued to be drawn ... In *Bridge Wholesale Acceptance Corporation (Australia) Ltd v Burnard*[10] Clarke JA ... stated ... that where the applicant has carried out its part of the bargain, the contract is not executory and the relief sought is analogous to specific performance, in the sense that 'a party seeks the aid of the court to compel the other party to perform its obligations according to the terms of the contract'.

It follows from these principles, that where a contract has come to an end, in the sense that all the obligations under it have been performed, or, in the case of a lease, the term of the lease has expired, specific performance of obligations that were to be performed during the term is not available. A straightforward example is to be found in *McMahon v Ambrose*,[11] where it was held ... that the Court did not have jurisdiction to grant specific performance, or equitable damages in lieu thereof, in respect of an oral agreement for lease where the term of the lease had expired at that time when proceedings were commenced.[12]

ELEMENTS

7.3   The prerequisites in order for specific performance to be granted are:

a)   an agreement;

b)   a breach or threatened breach of the agreement by the defendant;

c)   common law damages would be an inadequate remedy for the breach; and

d)   there is no discretionary defence or denial disentitling relief.

Generally, 'the plaintiff has the onus of establishing that it is entitled to an order for specific performance'.[13] For practical purposes, a distinction is drawn between the three jurisdictional prerequisites in (a), (b) and (c) and the court's discretion in (d).[14] Such a distinction is not, however, free of difficulty: 7.34 and 11.10. Each jurisdictional element is discussed below, followed by a discussion of the various discretionary defences and denials.

AGREEMENT

Introduction

7.4   The first jurisdictional prerequisite is that there must be a contract or an agreement. So, if the contract is uncertain or if no contract has been

---

10.   (1992) 27 NSWLR 415 at 423 (Mahoney and Meagher JJA agreeing); see also 7.41.

11.   [1987] VR 817 at 819 per Murray J and at 849–50 per Marks J.

12.   [2007] NSWCA 276 at [62]–[64].

13.   *Perpetual Trustee Company Ltd v Meriton Property Management Pty Ltd* [2004] NSWSC 1258 at [78] per Bergin J.

14.   See, for example, *McMahon v Ambrose* [1987] VR 817 at 842 per Marks J.

formed[15] or the contract has been rescinded or terminated, the remedy will not be available.[16] The High Court refused specific performance in *Tanwar Enterprises Pty Ltd v Cauchi* where the vendors terminated contracts for the sale of three adjoining parcels of land at Glenwood, Sydney following the purchaser's breach of a 'time is of the essence' clause.[17] Similarly, in a case heard consecutively with *Tanwar, Romanos v Pentagold Investments Pty Ltd,*[18] specific performance of contracts for the sale of three adjoining properties at Harris Park, Sydney, was refused following the purchaser's breach to pay the deposit in a timely manner. Importantly, in both *Tanwar* and *Romanos*, there was no 'unconscionability',[19] 'fraud, accident, mistake or surprise'[20] accompanying the vendors' termination and they had not in any way contributed to the purchasers' breach.

Oral contracts that should have been in writing may be specifically enforced if the doctrine of part performance is satisfied: see **7.6–7.10**.

7.5   The general principle is that only the parties to the contract may be the proper parties in a suit for specific performance.[21] The rule is not absolute, however, because a third party or a stranger to the contract can be made a defendant in a suit for specific performance where he or she 'is in possession of the subject matter of the contract with notice of the contract'.[22]

Doctrine of part performance

7.6   A transaction unenforceable at law or under a statute may be specifically enforced if the equitable doctrine of part performance has been satisfied. The object of the doctrine 'is always to enlarge part performance into complete performance'.[23] The doctrine is usually applied to oral contracts which fail to comply with a statutory requirement that they must be in writing or executed in a formal manner. For example, s 54A(1) of the Conveyancing Act 1919 (NSW) provides:

---

15. On uncertainty and mistake, see *Wily v Thomson Media Group Pty Ltd* (SC(NSW), Young J, 4 December 1997, unreported).

16. See **Chapter 5** for a discussion of rescission.

17. (2003) 201 ALR 359.

18. (2003) 201 ALR 399.

19. *Romanos* (2003) 201 ALR 399 at [25], [52] and [64]; compare *Lam v Nguyen* [2003] NSWSC 1119.

20. Tanwar (2003) 201 ALR 359 at [58] per Gleeson CJ, McHugh, Gummow, Hayne and Heydon JJ.

21. See *Tasker v Small* (1837) 3 My & Cr 63; 40 ER 848; *Howard v Miller* [1915] AC 318; *Thomson v Richardson* (1928) 29 SR (NSW) 221 at 222–3 per Harvey CJ (in Eq); *Duncombe v New York Properties Pty Ltd* [1986] 1 Qd R 16 (FC); and compare *Trident General Insurance Co Ltd v McNiece Bros Pty Ltd* (1988) 165 CLR 107 at 119 per Mason CJ and Wilson J.

22. *Moonking Gee v Tahos* (1963) 63 SR (NSW) 935 at 941–2 per Else-Mitchell J. There is also legislation allowing third-party beneficiaries to sue on the contract, as noted in *Trident General Insurance Co Ltd v McNiece Bros Pty Ltd* (1988) 165 CLR 107 at 117–18 by Mason CJ and Wilson J, citing in support s 55 of the Property Law Act 1974 (Qld), s 11 of the Property Law Act 1969 (WA), and the Contracts (Privity) Act 1982 (NZ).

23. *J C Williamson Ltd v Lukey & Mulholland* (1931) 45 CLR 282 at 310 per Evatt J.

No action or proceedings may be brought upon any contract for the sale or other disposition of land or any interest in land, unless the agreement upon which such action or proceedings is brought, or some memorandum or note thereof, is in writing, and signed by the party to be charged or by some other person thereunto lawfully authorised by the party to be charged.[24]

This section was derived from the Statute of Frauds 1677 (UK). But, contrary to the purpose of such provisions, they are occasionally used as a cloak for fraud: the defendant orally promises to do something and then seeks to avoid the promise on the basis that it was not in writing. There are several possible remedies here — estoppel, constructive trust and restitution: see 7.11. There is also the doctrine of part performance. As explained in *Jones v Baker* by Young CJ in Eq, this doctrine permits:

> … a court to grant specific performance where there has been a non-compliance with the Statute of Frauds or its modern equivalent. The Court does so by salving the defendant's conscience by ordering him or her to bring into being a formal contract which complies with the Statute and then order specific performance of it. The Court does not ignore the Statute, but enforces a personal equity against the defendant …[25]

The doctrine is preserved in s 54A(2) of the Conveyancing Act 1919 (NSW), which provides (among other things) that '[t]his section … does not affect the law relating to part performance'.

7.7 The main application of the doctrine of part performance has been in relation to land, but it is not confined to land[26] (nor is it confined to specific performance).[27] In each case, the contract must be otherwise specifically enforceable,[28] in the sense that the other elements of the remedy must be satisfied and the court must, in its discretion, be in favour of the order. So, if damages would be adequate, the contract requires the constant supervision of the court, or if the contract is for personal services, the remedy may be refused.[29] Of course, in cases of part performance, damages at law will be totally inadequate because they are not available.[30]

7.8 There are two lines of authority as to what has to be proved in order to satisfy the doctrine of part performance. The traditional view is found in *Maddison v Alderson*.[31] Alderson orally agreed with his housekeeper, Maddison,

---

24. See also Property Law Act 1974 (Qld) s 59; Law of Property Act 1936 (SA) s 26; Conveyancing and Law of Property Act 1884 (Tas) s 36(1); Instruments Act 1958 (Vic) s 126; Law Reform (Statute of Frauds) Act 1962 (WA) s 2; Property Law Act 1969 (WA) s 34.

25. (2002) 10 BPR 19,115 at [40].

26. *J C Williamson Ltd v Lukey & Mulholland* (1931) 45 CLR 282; *Actionstrength Ltd v International Glass Engineering* [2003] UKHL 17.

27. It may apply to other equitable remedies such as a mandatory injunction to enforce a provision in a contract: see *Jones v Baker* (2002) 10 BPR 19,115.

28. *J C Williamson Ltd v Lukey & Mulholland* (1931) 45 CLR 282; *Commonwealth Oil Refineries Ltd v Hollins* [1956] VLR 169.

29. *Britain v Rossiter* (1879) 11 QBD 123; *Elliott v Roberts* (1912) 28 TLR 436.

30. See, for example, *McMahon v Ambrose* [1987] VR 817 at 828.

31. (1883) 8 App Cas 467.

to leave her a life estate in his farm in return for her unpaid services as a housekeeper. The agreement was embodied in a will, but due to incorrect attestation was ineffective. Alderson's heir successfully resisted Maddison's claim based on part performance. The House of Lords found the agreement to be unenforceable for lack of writing under the Statute of Frauds, and because Maddison's services were not 'unequivocally' referable to an agreement. Lord Selborne LC held:

> … the acts relied upon as part performance must be unequivocally, and in their own nature referable to some such agreement as that alleged.[32]

Their Lordships found that merely because Maddison had continued to work for Alderson without payment was not of itself sufficient to prove part performance of the alleged contract.

7.9   *Maddison v Alderson* was approved by the High Court in *McBride v Sandiland*,[33] *Cooney v Byrnes*[34] and *JC Williamson Ltd v Lukey & Mulholland*.[35] However, in *Steadman v Steadman*,[36] a majority in the House of Lords refused to apply the narrow *Maddison v Alderson* test and held that the appropriate test was to ask whether it was more probable than not that a contract has been entered into. Lord Simon observed:

> It may be questionable whether it was direct respect for the statute which led to such confinement of the doctrine, or whether it was not rather because part performance seems sometimes to have been regarded as an alternative way of proving an oral agreement; for Equity allowed a person to prove by parol evidence that land conveyed to another was so conveyed on trust for himself, notwithstanding s 7 of the Statute of Frauds: *Rochefoucauld v Boustead*;[37] *Bannister v Bannister*[38] — the passages show here, too, the guiding rule was that the court would not allow the statute to be used as a cloak for fraud. However that may be, the speech of Earl of Selborne LC has always been regarded as authoritative, notwithstanding that what he said about part performance was, strictly, obiter.[39]

In *Ogilvie v Ryan*, Holland J said that in *Steadman*:

> The court held that the alleged acts of part performance had to be considered in their surrounding circumstances, and, if they pointed on a balance of probabilities to some contract between the parties, and either showed the nature of, or were consistent with, the oral agreement alleged, then there was sufficient part performance of the agreement for the purpose of enforcing the contract.[40]

---

32.   (1883) 8 App Cas 467 at 479.

33.   (1918) 25 CLR 69 at 78 per Isaacs and Rich JJ.

34.   (1922) 30 CLR 216 at 222.

35.   (1931) 45 CLR 282 at 297 per Dixon J.

36.   [1976] AC 536.

37.   [1897] 1 Ch 196 at 206.

38.   [1948] 2 All ER 133 at 136.

39.   [1976] AC 536 at 559.

40.   [1976] 2 NSWLR 504 at 521.

7.10 Generally, Australian courts have rejected the more liberal test in *Steadman*. On the basis of earlier High Court authority, Glass JA in *Millett v Regent*[41] was of the view that the New South Wales Court of Appeal was not at liberty to apply the *Steadman* test. On appeal, the High Court[42] found it unnecessary to finally decide the questions raised by *Steadman*. Holland J clearly preferred *Steadman* in *Ogilvie v Ryan*,[43] but felt bound to follow Glass JA in *Millett v Regent*. In *Australian and New Zealand Banking Group Ltd v Widin* the Full Federal Court followed *Maddison v Alderson* and Hill J concluded:

> It may be possible to reconcile what is said in *Steadman* with the orthodox approach taken by the High Court to date and while there is much to be said for the adoption in Australia of *Steadman*, these are matters for the High Court rather than an intermediate Court of Appeal.[44]

In *Khoury v Khouri*[45] the New South Wales Court of Appeal were of a similar view. Bryson JA (Handley and Hodgson JJA concurring) held:

> Consideration of part performance in the High Court of Australia has not produced any relaxation or departure from *Maddison v Alderson*.[46]

In *Khoury*, Marina, Peter and Bechara were three of seven brothers and sisters. Marina and Peter bought a house for $130,000 at Johnston Road, Bass Hill in Sydney in 1988 as tenants in common in equal shares. They lived in the house with their parents, who had contributed part of the purchase price. In 1992 Peter moved out after buying another property at Glenfield. In 1996 the parents also moved out leaving Marina in occupation. Bechara never occupied the house but claimed he was entitled to a half-share due to a 1992 oral agreement between him and Peter. Under this agreement Bechara was to pay Peter both $30,000 and Peter's share of instalments under a Commonwealth Bank loan. In return Peter was to hold his half-share in the house for the benefit of Bechara despite Peter's name being on the register. The facts surrounding this agreement were further complicated by other oral agreements with a personal friend of the Khoury family, Bishop Gibran Rimlawi, who had lent money to Marina.

The trial judge, Barrett J, found that Bechara had performed his obligations under the oral agreement with Peter by paying him $30,000 and paying $70,000 to the Bishop who then discharged Peter's share of the Commonwealth Bank loan. Barrett J also declared that since 1992 Peter had held his half-share *on trust* for Bechara. Although the trial judge did not find it necessary to rely on the doctrine of part performance, his Honour expressed the view that the

41.   [1975] 1 NSWLR 62.
42.   *Regent v Millett* (1976) 133 CLR 679.
43.   [1976] 2 NSWLR 504; see also *Fleming v Beevers* [1994] 1 NZLR 385; *Richardson v Armistead* [2000] VSC 551; *Marminta Pty Ltd v French* [2002] QSC 423.
44.   (1990) 26 FCR 21 at 37.
45.   (2006) 66 NSWLR 241.
46.   (2006) 66 NSWLR 241 at [80]; see also *Lighting By Design (Aust) Pty Ltd v Cannington Nominees Pty Ltd* [2008] WASCA 23 at [73]-[77] per Buss JA; at [168] per Le Miere AJA; at [49] per Pullin JA (dissenting).

doctrine had been satisfied by Bechara's payments of money. However, Peter and Marina's appeal to the Court of Appeal was successful. It was critical of the declaration of trust as this represented a disposition of an interest in land which must be in writing. It preferred to focus on whether there were sufficient acts of part performance by Bechara to support the oral agreement. However, Bryson JA held:

> In the present case there are no acts of ownership such as taking possession, paying rates or paying for the upkeep or improvement of the property, or receipt of rent or profits, or any other act at all. Acts of part performance have been almost universally closely related to possession and use or tenure of the land itself, such as where a purchaser is put into possession by the vendor, or allowed to take possession by the vendor, or where the purchaser carries out improvements. They have not necessarily been acts which the contract requires to be done. Acts on the land can much more readily be seen as unequivocally referable to the contract than payments of money.[47]

Alternatives to part performance

7.11   The difficulties of applying a strict part performance test in order to obtain specific performance has to some extent been ameliorated by other remedies and actions such as equitable estoppel,[48] restitution[49] and constructive trusts.[50]

NON-PERFORMANCE

7.12   The plaintiff must prove that the defendant has not performed the contract according to its terms; for example, non-delivery of a chattel or the refusal to execute a transfer of land. Thus, there must be a breach of contract or a threatened[51] breach. In cases of anticipatory breach, the innocent party may seek specific performance instead of accepting the repudiation by terminating the contract. However, the order for specific performance may be postponed until the time for performance arrives.[52]

7.13   A specific jurisdictional denial that can be raised by the defendant on the issue of breach is to assert that performance is impossible. If that assertion turns out to be true, the court will refuse the remedy.[53] This is so even if the defendant caused the impossibility.[54] Performance may be impossible because of illegality[55] or because the necessary consent of a third person,

---

47.   (2006) 66 NSWLR 241 at [89]; see also Hodgson JA at [21].

48.   See *Walton Stores (Interstate) Ltd v Maher* (1988) 164 CLR 387; *Collin v Holden* [1989] VR 510.

49.   See, for example, *Pavey & Mathews Pty Ltd v Paul* (1987) 162 CLR 221; and see **4.47**.

50.   See *Ogilvie v Ryan* [1976] 2 NSWLR 504 at 519 per Holland J.

51.   *Turner v Bladin* (1951) 82 CLR 463 at 472.

52.   See *Hasham v Zenab* [1960] AC 316.

53.   *Ferguson v Wilson* (1866) LR 2 Ch App 77; *Holland v Goltrans Pty Ltd* [1984] 1 Qd R 18.

54.   *Kennedy v Vercoe* (1960) 106 CLR 521; *Brown v Heffer* (1967) 116 CLR 344.

55.   *Norton v Angus* (1926) 38 CLR 523 at 534; *Renowden v Hurley* [1951] VLR 13; *Warmington v Miller* [1973] QB 877; compare *SDS Corp Ltd v Pasdonnay Pty Ltd* [2004] WASC 26 at [392], affirmed in *Pasdonnay Pty Ltd v SDS Corp Ltd* [2005] WASCA 9.

such as a minister of government, is not forthcoming.[56] However, pending the determination of the third party's consent the court may make a conditional order, as noted by Jenkins J in *Avenue (WA) Pty Ltd v Plazaline Pty Ltd*:

> … the fact that a contract is subject to the consent of a third party does not automatically mean that a contract is impossible to perform. Where the consent of a third party is required, courts have ordered the parties to take all reasonable or necessary steps to obtain such consent and, if it is obtained, to specifically perform the contract …[57]

7.14 Impossibility of performance is usually treated as a jurisdictional issue,[58] while futility of performance has usually been treated as a discretionary defence: see **7.43**. There is no obvious reason why one should be treated as a matter of jurisdiction and the other as a matter of discretion. Refusing relief for either impossibility or futility of performance is based upon the maxim that equity does nothing in vain.

INADEQUACY OF DAMAGES

Introduction

7.15 Equity follows the law, so it will not provide a remedy where there is an adequate common law remedy. As observed by Sir John Leach V-C in *Adderley v Dixon*:

> Courts of Equity decree the specific performance of a contract, not upon any distinction between realty and personalty, but because damages at law may not, in the particular case, afford a complete remedy.[59]

A different approach appears to be developing in the United Kingdom. For example, in *Beswick v Beswick* Lord Upjohn held:

> Equity will grant specific performance when damages are inadequate to meet the justice of the case.[60]

But in Australia the 'adequacy of damages as a jurisdictional limitation' has not been 'replaced with the discretionary approach as to whether it would be more just to grant specific performance rather than damages'.[61]

7.16 There are a number of types of contracts where common law damages are clearly inadequate or inadequate to meet the justice of the case. Indeed,

---

56. *Dougan v Ley* (1945) 71 CLR 142; *Dillon v Nash* [1950] VLR 293; *Kennedy v Vercoe* (1960) 106 CLR 521; *Brown v Heffer* (1967) 116 CLR 344.

57. [2007] WASC 173 at [80]; see also *Liu v Nguyen* [2011] NSWSC 1369 at [110]–[113] per Slattery J.

58. *McMahon v Ambrose* [1987] VR 817 at 849 per Marks J; see also **11.11**.

59. (1824) 1 Sim & St 607 (Ch).

60. [1968] AC 58 at 102; cited with approval by Mason CJ and Wilson J in *Trident General Insurance Co Ltd v McNiece Bros Pty Ltd* (1988) 165 CLR 107 at 119; compare *Hewett v Court* (1983) 149 CLR 639 at 665 per Deane J.

61. *Waterways Authority of New South Wales v Coal and Allied (Operations) Pty Ltd* [2007] NSWCA 276 at [95]–[96] per Beazley JA.

one approach is to determine whether a contract falls in a particular category where specific performance has usually been available. But, as observed by Windeyer J, in dissent, in *Coulls v Bagot's Executor and Trustee Co Ltd*:

> There is no reason today for limiting by particular categories, rather than by general principle, the cases in which orders for specific performance will be made.[62]

Accordingly, specific performance has been found to be available in respect of contracts for the sale of a racehorse[63] as well as a thoroughbred stallion[64], a contract to publish an apology[65] and a contract to settle litigation.[66] Despite this approach it is still worth examining the traditional categories, as they shed light on the test of whether damages will be adequate. Broadly speaking, contracts for the sale of land, works of art and intellectual property are regarded as specifically enforceable, whereas contracts for the sale of goods, animals, stocks, shares, securities, the payment of money, and the provision of personal services are usually not specifically enforceable. In examining these categories, however, it must always be remembered that there will be exceptions based on the general principle that 'damages are inadequate if they cannot satisfy the demands of justice, and that justice to a promisee might well require that a promisor perform the promise'.[67] Damages are obviously inadequate where they are not available, such as in cases of part performance: see **7.6–7.10**.

Land

7.17   Equity has always ordered specific performance of contracts for the sale of land. Damages are inadequate because substitutes cannot be readily found.[68] As observed by Sir John Leach V-C in *Adderley v Dixon*:

> ... a Court of Equity decrees performance of a contract for land, not because of the real nature of land, but because damages at law, which must be calculated upon the general money value of land, may not be a complete remedy to the purchaser, to whom the land may have a peculiar and special value.[69]

---

62. (1967) 119 CLR 460 at 503; cited with approval in *Zhu v Treasurer of the State of New South Wales* (2004) 211 ALR 159; [2004] HCA 56 at [128] per Gleeson CJ, Gummow, Kirby, Callinan and Heydon JJ.

63. *Borg v Howlett* (SC(NSW), Young J, 24 May 1996, unreported).

64. *Austin Bloodstock Pty Ltd v Massey* [2011] VSC 421.

65. See *Summertime Holidays Pty Ltd v Environmental Defender's Office Ltd* (1998) 45 NSWLR 291, where a defamation apology was found to be specifically enforceable but refused in the court's discretion.

66. *NSW v Karibian* [2005] NSWSC 1357; *Wily v Thomson Media Group Pty Ltd* (SC(NSW), Young J, 4 December 1997, unreported); *SDS Corp Ltd v Pasdonnay Pty Ltd* [2004] WASC 26; affirmed in *Pasdonnay Pty Ltd v SDS Corp Ltd* [2005] WASCA 9; *We Two Pty Ltd v Shorrock (No 2)* [2005] FCA 934 at [13] and [15] per Finkelstein J.

67. *Zhu v Treasurer of the State of New South Wales* (2004) 211 ALR 159; [2004] HCA 56 at [128] per Gleeson CJ, Gummow, Kirby, Callinan and Heydon JJ.

68. *McIntosh v Dalwood (No 4)* (1930) 30 SR (NSW) 415 at 418; *Pianta v National Finance & Trustees Ltd* (1964) 38 ALJR 232.

69. (1824) 1 Sim & St 607 at 610 (Ch).

The same principle applies to the airspace above land.[70] Damages are also inadequate where land has been misdescribed.[71]

7.18   The remedy is mutually available to the purchaser and the vendor, as observed in *Turner v Bladin* by Williams, Fullagar and Kitto JJ:

> … that where the contract is of such a kind that the purchaser can sue for specific performance, the vendor can also sue for specific performance, although the claim is to merely recover a sum of money and that he can do so although at the date of the writ the contract has been fully performed except for the payment of the purchase money or some part thereof.[72]

Money

7.19   Generally, specific performance of a contract to pay money will not be ordered because damages will be adequate.[73] Indeed, damages are a payment of money, albeit pursuant to a court order. There are two exceptions: first, if a purchaser can obtain specific performance then the vendor can also obtain specific performance, even if it is merely to obtain the payment of a sum of money;[74] second, consistent with the general principle, specific performance is available if damages will be an inadequate remedy for the breach.[75] Examples here are some indemnity contracts,[76] a contract to execute a mortgage,[77] security contracts[78] and contracts involving both the payment of money and land. *Loan Investment Corp v Bonner*[79] involved a contract of the latter type. Bonner sold land to the Loan Investment Corporation (LIC), which wanted to develop the land. The purchase price was £13,300, but in selling the land Bonner also agreed to lend LIC £11,000, without security, for 10 years at 7.5 per cent interest. Later, Bonner repudiated the agreement and LIC sought specific performance of the contract. LIC succeeded at first instance, but lost on appeal in both the New Zealand Court of Appeal and the Privy Council. Lord Pearson noted the contract was a 'composite' contract containing two transactions. One was the sale of land at £13,300 and the other was the loan transaction. However, his Lordship noted that the intention of the parties was that the contract was entire and indivisible, each part could not be separated

---

70.   *Uniting Church in Australia Property Trust (NSW) v Immer (No 145) Pty Ltd* (1991) 24 NSWLR 510 at 511 per Meagher JA (CA); reversed on the issue of election, *Immer (No 145) Pty Ltd v Uniting Church in Australia Property Trust (NSW)* (1993) 182 CLR 26.

71.   *Mortlock v Buller* (1804) 10 Ves Jun 292; 32 ER 857.

72.   (1951) 82 CLR 463 at 473.

73.   *McIntosh v Dalwood (No 4)* (1930) 30 SR (NSW) 415 at 418; *Loan Investment Corp v Bonner* [1970] NZLR 724. Compare *Beswick v Beswick* [1968] AC 58 at 81 per Lord Hodson.

74.   *Tambic Pty Ltd v Northwind Holdings Pty Ltd* [2001] WASC 44 at [3].

75.   *Coulls v Bagot's Executor and Trustee Co Ltd* (1967) 119 CLR 460 at 503 Windeyer J.

76.   See *McIntosh v Dalwood (No 4)* (1930) 30 SR (NSW) 415, where Street CJ held that the essential question to ask was whether damages were an adequate remedy; compare *Sydney Consumers' Milk Ltd v Hawkesbury Dairy Ltd* (1931) 31 SR (NSW) 458.

77.   *Takemura v National Australia Bank Ltd* [2003] NSWSC 339.

78.   See, for example, *Swiss Bank Corp v Lloyds Bank Ltd* [1982] AC 584 at 595 per Buckley LJ.

79.   [1970] NZLR 724 (PC).

and, therefore, specific performance could not be awarded, because such contracts in their entirety were not suitable for specific performance.

7.20   The more enduring approach is that of Sir Garfield Barwick, in dissent, in *Loan Investment Corporation v Bonner*.[80] In his view, the real issue is whether damages would be adequate or not.[81] There was a general assumption that breach of a mere promise to lend money can ordinarily be compensated for by an award of damages. But that assumption was one of fact rather than law and therefore it was not of universal application. In particular, this assumption had to yield where damages were inadequate, as was the situation in this case, where the agreement also involved the transfer of land.[82] The view of Sir Garfield Barwick was applied in *Wight v Haberden Pty Ltd*[83] and cited with apparent approval by Mason CJ and Wilson J in *Trident General Insurance Co Ltd v McNiece Bros Pty Ltd*.[84]

7.21   Agreements to pay money to a third party create special problems because of the doctrine of privity. This means, in most cases, that if the defendant refuses performance, the third-party beneficiary cannot obtain a remedy because it is not a contracting party.[85] However, the plaintiff may seek specific performance even though the beneficiary is a third party. In *Coulls v Bagot's Executor and Trustee Co Ltd*[86] Mr Coulls agreed to grant O'Neil Construction Pty Ltd (O'Neil) the right to quarry and remove stone from his land for £5. O'Neil also agreed to pay an amount of 3d for each ton of stone quarried and removed, with a fixed minimum royalty of £12 per week. The final clause provided that all moneys due under the agreement were payable to Mr and Mrs Coulls. The contract was signed by both Mr and Mrs Coulls and by a representative of O'Neil. Later, Mr Coulls died and his executors, Bagot's, asked the court for guidance on whether O'Neil had to pay the royalties to Bagot's or to Mrs Coulls.

    The majority, McTiernan, Taylor and Owen JJ, held that the wife was a third-party beneficiary who would not be able to specifically enforce the contract because she was not party to it. In their view, the only person who could enforce the agreement was Mr Coulls. The dissenting judges, Barwick CJ and Windeyer J, held that the agreement was between the company and both Mr and Mrs Coulls, and thus Mrs Coulls could sue for specific performance. Barwick CJ observed:

> It must be accepted that according to our law a person not a party to a contract may not himself sue upon it so as to directly enforce its obligations. For my part I find no difficulty or embarrassment in this conclusion. Indeed, I would

---

80.   [1970] NZLR 724 (PC).

81.   [1970] NZLR 724 at 741–2.

82.   [1970] NZLR 724 at 744–6.

83.   [1984] 2 NSWLR 280.

84.   (1988) 165 CLR 107 at 119–20.

85.   *Tasker v Small* (1837) 3 My & Cr 63, 440 ER 848; *Hood v Cullen* (1885) 6 NSWR 22.

86.   (1967) 119 CLR 460.

find it odd that a person to whom no promise was made could himself in his own right enforce a promise made to another. But that does not mean that it is not possible for that person to obtain the benefit of a promise made with another for his benefit by steps other than enforcement by himself in his own right ... Where A promises B for consideration supplied by B to pay C then B may obtain specific performance of A's promise, at least where the nature of the consideration given would have allowed the debtor to have obtained specific performance. I can see no reason whatever why A in those circumstances should not be bound to perform his promise. That C provided no part of the consideration seems to me irrelevant.[87]

Barwick CJ's view, however, still means that a party to the contract must seek the remedy, and not the third party who is to receive the benefit. Mrs Coulls was found by both Barwick CJ and Windeyer J to be a party to the contract and, therefore, was able to obtain specific performance in her own right.

7.22 Shortly after *Coulls*, the House of Lords in *Beswick v Beswick*[88] also considered the issue of specifically enforcing a contract to pay money to a third party. Peter Beswick was a coal merchant who sold his business to his nephew. In return, the nephew was to pay Peter Beswick £6 10s a week for the rest of his life; if Mr Beswick's wife survived him, the nephew was also to pay £5 a week to her for the rest of her life. Peter Beswick died and the nephew paid the widow one payment and refused further payments. The widow sued for specific performance and unpaid arrears. An important issue in the case was that the widow sued in her capacity as the administrator of her husband's estate (that is, as a successor to a party to the contract), rather than suing in her personal capacity as a third party to the contract. The House of Lords held that as an administrator of her husband's estate she was entitled to sue on the contract. However, only nominal damages for the breach were available because the injury to the estate was nil since the beneficiary was not the estate but a 'third party'. This meant that damages were 'inadequate to meet the justice of the case'[89] and therefore the House of Lords ordered the specific performance of the contract.

Beswick v Beswick[90] was applied in *Baig v Baig*[91] and both *Beswick* and the dissenting judgments in *Coulls* were cited with apparent approval by the High Court in *Trident General Insurance Co Ltd v McNiece Bros Pty Ltd*.[92]

---

87.   (1967) 119 CLR 460 at 478.
88.   [1968] AC 58.
89.   [1968] AC at 102 per Lord Upjohn.
90.   [1968] AC 58.
91.   [1970] VR 833.
92.   (1988) 165 CLR 107 at 114 and 118–19 per Mason CJ and Wilson J, and at 142–4 per Deane J.

Goods

7.23　The general principle is that contracts for the sale of goods are not specifically enforceable.[93] As observed by Sir John Leach V-C in *Adderley v Dixon*:

> … a Court of Equity will not, generally, decree performance of a contract for the sale of stock or goods, not because of their personal nature, but because damages at law, calculated upon the market price of the stock or goods, are as complete a remedy to the purchaser as the delivery of the stock or goods contracted for; inasmuch as, with the damages, he may purchase the same quantity of the like stock or goods.[94]

According to the same principle, if the article is of unusual beauty, rarity and distinction — say an original painting or a vintage aircraft[95] — then damages may be inadequate.[96] The authorities discussed below also suggest damages will be inadequate where:

a)　supply of the chattel is severely interrupted; and

b)　the chattel is necessary for the plaintiff's business.

Restricted supply

7.24　The mere fact that supply is temporarily low will not be sufficient to attract equity's jurisdiction.[97] The case of *Cook v Rodgers*[98] concerned a suit for specific performance of a car immediately after World War II. The evidence showed that if the car was not supplied under the contract the plaintiff would have considerable difficulty in obtaining a substitute. Nonetheless, specific performance was refused. Roper J held:

> Normally the wrongful detention of goods gives no equity to the person entitled to possession. His remedy will be at common law. Where the goods have a peculiar value and damages at law would not be an adequate remedy, an equity does arise. The article in question here is a motor vehicle of no peculiar value other than that attaching to motor cars generally. Six or more years ago it would have been clear that the circumstances of this case gave rise to no equity. It has been put, however, that as the demand for motor cars now exceeds supply (of which there is no evidence strictly before me), and as prices are fixed, damages in this case would not be an adequate remedy and the plaintiff therefore has a remedy in equity. I do not agree with this proposition. There would be an extraordinary extension of the jurisdiction in equity if it were attracted to cases in which it would otherwise be absent merely by the fact that the goods were temporarily in short supply and difficult to obtain, or by that fact together with the additional fact that the prices of the goods were fixed

93.　*Dougan v Ley* (1945) 71 CLR 142.
94.　(1824) 1 Sim & St 607 at 610 (Ch).
95.　*Smythe v Thomas* [2007] NSWSC 844.
96.　*Falcke v Gray* (1859) 4 Drew 651 at 658; *Aristoc Industries Pty Ltd v R A Wenham (Builders) Pty Ltd* [1965] NSWR 581 at 588 per Jacobs J.
97.　*Cook v Rodgers* (1946) 46 SR (NSW) 229; compare *Howard E Perry & Co Ltd v British Railways Board* [1980] 1 WLR 1375.
98.　(1946) 46 SR (NSW) 229.

by law. If this were so the remedies of injunction and specific performance would at the present time presumably be available in a very large number of ordinary mercantile contracts. In my opinion, the existence of market difficulties of an apparently temporary nature does not give a jurisdiction to this court which it would not otherwise have, even though it might be difficult to predict when the difficulties will disappear.[99]

Necessary for the plaintiff's business

7.25 In *Dougan v Ley*,[100] Dougan agreed to sell his taxi cab and the licence to operate it to Ley for £1850. Dougan later refused to perform his side of the contract. The number of licensed taxi cabs in New South Wales at that time was severely limited and diminishing. Ley sought specific performance and persisted with this action even after he managed to obtain another taxi cab and licence for £1900 prior to the hearing. Roper J granted specific performance of the contract at first instance.[101] Dougan's appeal to the High Court was dismissed. Dixon J observed:

> The subject matter, it is said, is the sale of a chattel and, in general, a suit for specific performance on an agreement to sell and deliver chattels will not be entertained. But, when the substance of the matter is considered, the agreement is not of this simple character ... The subject of the sale is ... a special right attached to a chattel, transferable only with it, and numerically restricted ...
>
> In the present case I think that we should have no difficulty in concluding that, because of the limited number of vehicles registered and licensed as taxi-cabs, because of the extent to which the price represents the value of the licence, and because of the essentiality to the purchasers' calling of the chattel and the licence annexed thereto, we should treat the contract as within the scope of the remedy of specific performance.[102]

7.26 The principle in *Dougan v Ley*[103] has also been applied in relation to a mandatory injunction: see 8.63–8.67. In *Doulton Potteries Ltd v Bronotte*[104] the plaintiffs used a die to manufacture pipes for use in industry. It sent the die to the defendant manufacturer for repairs. The defendant repaired the die but wrongfully refused to return it because of a dispute about the cost of the repairs. The die was essentially irreplaceable because it could only be made by the defendant, who had access to the necessary confidential information. Hope J ordered the specific restitution of the die by granting a mandatory injunction. After referring, inter alia, to *Dougan v Ley*, his Honour observed:

> These authorities establish that the jurisdiction of the Court of Equity to intervene in respect of chattels arises, inter alia, where those chattels are of special value to a person in the carrying on of his business, and where its

99. (1946) 46 SR (NSW) 229 at 232–3.
100. (1945) 71 CLR 142.
101. *Ley v Dougan* (1945) 63 WN (NSW) 224.
102. (1945) 71 CLR 142 at 149–51.
103. (1945) 71 CLR 142.
104. [1971] 1 NSWLR 591.

jurisdiction is attracted by the nature of the relevant chattels, the court can give whatever relief be appropriate, including an order for the specific return of the particular chattel.

> It is clear that the subject die and flexible core are chattels which have a special value to the plaintiffs in the carrying on of their business … It is equally clear that damages would be an entirely inadequate remedy for the wrongful detention of the die, and accordingly the jurisdiction of this Court is attracted.[105]

7.27   The equitable rules governing specific performance are not displaced by the sale of goods legislation. In New South Wales, s 56 of the Sale of Goods Act 1923 provides:

> Nothing in this Act shall affect any remedy in equity of the buyer or the seller in respect of any breach of a contract of sale or any breach of warranty.

In the other Australian jurisdictions[106] and New Zealand,[107] there are provisions corresponding with s 52 of the Sale of Goods Act 1979 (UK), which provides:

> In any action for breach of contract to deliver specific or ascertained goods the court may, if it thinks fit … direct that the contract shall be performed specifically, without giving the defendant the option of retaining the goods on payment of damages.[108]

The effect of this section is that the equitable rules governing specific performance still apply.[109]

Intellectual property

7.28   Intellectual property rights are unique, and thus contracts concerning patents, designs, copyright or trade marks are specifically enforceable if damages are inadequate. Williams, Fullagar and Kitto JJ in *Turner v Bladin*[110] cited with approval the case of *Cogent v Gibson*[111] concerning a contract for the sale of a patent.[112] The contract was specifically enforceable at the suit of the vendor, although the vendor only required the purchase money. A patentee can also sue a proposed exclusive licensee for specific performance if the licence is for a definite period and on clear terms.[113]

---

105. [1971] 1 NSWLR at 598–9.
106. Sale of Goods Act 1954 (ACT) s 55; Sale of Goods Act 1972 (NT) s 56; Sale of Goods Act 1896 (Qld) s 53; Sale of Goods Act 1895 (SA) s 51; Sale of Goods Act 1896 (Tas) s 56; Goods Act 1958 (Vic) s 58; Sale of Goods Act 1895 (WA) s 51.
107. Sale of Goods Act 1908 (NZ) s 53.
108. This corresponds with its repealed predecessor, Sale of Goods Act 1893 (UK) s 52.
109. See, for example, *Whiteley v Hilt* [1918] 2 KB 808 (specific performance of a piano refused); *Cohen v Roche* [1927] 1 KB 169 (specific performance of a set of ordinary chairs refused); *Behnke v Bede Shipping Co Ltd* [1927] 1 KB 649; *Re Wait* [1927] 1 Ch 606.
110. (1951) 82 CLR 463 at 473.
111. (1864) 33 Beav 557; 55 ER 485.
112. See also *SDS Corp Ltd v Pasdonnay Pty Ltd* [2004] WASC 26; affirmed in *Pasdonnay Pty Ltd v SDS Corp Ltd* [2005] WASCA 9.
113. *Brake v Radermacher* (1903) 20 RPC 631; compare *Stocker v Wedderburn* (1857) 3 K & J 393; 69 ER 1162.

7.29 Agreements to assign copyright are specifically enforceable.[114] But if the agreement contains 'unnecessary' or 'oppressive' terms, 'they must be justified before they can be enforced'.[115] If they are not justified, the contract may be rescinded (see Chapter 5), and thus the first element of specific performance will not have been established; that is, there will be no contract or relevant term to specifically enforce: see **7.4** and **7.39**. Agreements to publish material may also be specifically enforced where there is certainty as to the subject matter to be published.[116]

7.30 A contract assigning or licensing the right to use a trade name, trade mark or other indicia is specifically enforceable. In an interlocutory injunction application, *Jabuna Pty Ltd v Hartley*,[117] Beazley J accepted that there was a serious question to be tried[118] as to whether specific performance should be ordered of a contract granting an exclusive right to use the trade name Wholesome Bake. Likewise, in *Wily v Thomson Media Group Pty Ltd*,[119] Young J declared that a contract settling litigation by transferring two publication mastheads, *Australian Horse News* and *Sire's Guide*, was specifically enforceable.

Goodwill and business assets

7.31 As discussed at **7.25–7.26**, where a chattel is of special value to the plaintiff in carrying on his or her business then a contract for its sale may be specifically enforced. Similarly, a contract for the sale of the goodwill of a business may be specifically enforced if, consistent with the general principle, damages will be inadequate.[120] For example, in *Pasdonnay Pty Ltd v SDS Corp Ltd* the merger of mining, oil, gas and construction corporations (which also involved the transfer of patent rights) was found to be specifically enforceable.[121]

Personal services and employment

7.32 Traditionally courts would not order specific performance of contracts for personal services or employment.[122] This absolute rule was said to be justified because such an order would involve the court's constant supervision, might compel unwilling parties to maintain personal cooperative relations and would be difficult to enforce because performance of personal service

---

114. *Erskine Macdonald Ltd v Eyles* [1921] 1 Ch 631.
115. *A Schroeder Music Publishing Co Ltd v Macaulay* [1974] 3 All ER 616 at 622 per Lord Reid (HL).
116. *Barrow v Chappell & Co Ltd* [1976] RPC 355; compare *Joseph v National Magazine Co Ltd* [1959] Ch 14.
117. (FCA, Beazley J, 18 April 1994, unreported).
118. For the meaning of 'serious question to be tried', see **8.48–8.54**.
119. (SC (NSW), Young J, 4 December 1997, unreported).
120. *Beswick v Beswick* [1968] AC 58 at 89 per Lord Pearce; compare *Kennedy v Vercoe* (1960) 105 CLR 521 at 529; *International Advisor Systems Pty Ltd v XYYX Pty Ltd* [2008] NSWSC 2.
121. [2005] WASCA 9 affirming *SDS Corp Ltd v Pasdonnay Pty Ltd* [2004] WASC 26.
122. See the discussion in *Maiden v Maiden* (1909) 7 CLR 727; *J C Williamson Ltd v Lukey & Mulholland* (1931) 45 CLR 282 at 298 per Dixon J; *Coulls v Bagot's Executor and Trustee Co Ltd* (1967) 119 CLR 460 at 503 per Windeyer J; see also **8.38–8.44**.

contracts involve matters of personal opinion and taste. But Megarry J in *C H Giles & Co Ltd v Morris*[123] rejected the existence of an absolute rule and preferred to say that the court was merely reluctant to make such an order.[124] In *Tito v Waddell (No 2)* Megarry V-C held:

> The real question is whether there is a sufficient definition to what has to be done in order to comply with the order of the court. That definition may be provided by the contract itself, or it may be supplied by the terms of the order, in which case there is the further question whether the court considers that the terms of the contract sufficiently support, by implication or otherwise, the terms of the proposed order.[125]

Megarry V-C's reasoning in *Tito v Waddell* was approved both in Australia in *Patrick Stevedores Operations No 2 Pty Ltd v Maritime Union of Australia*[126] and England in *Posner v Scott-Lewis*.[127] In the latter case, Mervyn Davies J ordered specific performance of a covenant in a lease to provide a resident porter. While the courts have been willing to grant injunctions to restrain breaches of 'special service' contracts,[128] relief is usually refused where the parties are required to maintain obligations of trust and confidence as is the case with partnership and agency agreements.[129] In summary, the courts remain reluctant to order specific performance of personal service contracts 'save for exceptional cases'.[130] Nonetheless, in *Quinn v Overland* Bromberg J granted an interlocutory injunction restraining the suspension of an employee and held:

> There ought not be and there is no longer a fixed rule against specific performance of an employment contract ...

> Furthermore, the appropriateness of specific performance as a remedy is strengthened by a growing acceptance at common law of the right of an employee to perform work. That recognition has arisen out of changed social attitudes. There is now a greater recognition than ever that employment is important to an employee not simply because it provides economic sustenance. Workplaces are a hub of important human exchanges which are vital to the wellbeing of individual workers. Work provides employees with purpose, dignity, pride, enjoyment, social acceptance and many social connections. As well, the performance of work allows for skill enhancement and advances career opportunities. These non pecuniary attributes of work are important

---

123. [1972] 1 All ER 960 (Ch).
124. See also *Turner v Australasian Coal and Shale Employees Federation* (1984) 6 FCR 177 at 192–3; and see Chapter 8.
125. [1977] Ch 106 at 321.
126. (1998) 195 CLR 1 at [78]–[80] per Brennan CJ, McHugh, Gummow, Kirby and Hayne JJ.
127. [1987] 1 Ch 25.
128. See, for example, *Curro v Beyond Productions Pty Ltd* (1993) 30 NSWLR 337 at 346–8 per Meagher JA (CA), discussed at 8.41.
129. *Cannavo v FCD (Holdings) Pty Ltd* [2000] NSWSC 304.
130. *Zhu v Treasurer of the State of New South Wales* (2004) 211 ALR 159; [2004] HCA 56 at [128] per Gleeson CJ, Gummow, Kirby, Callinan and Heydon JJ. For an example of exceptional circumstances see *Mezey v South West London & St George's Mental Health NHS Trust* [2007] EWCA Civ 106.

and their denial can be devastating to the legitimate interests of any worker, either skilled or unskilled.[131]

Stocks, shares and securities

7.33 In *Dougan v Ley* Dixon J observed:

In the case of goods or securities obtainable upon the market, damages at law place the disappointed buyer or seller in as good a position as delivery of the articles or receipt of the price because it enables him to go upon the market.[132]

But consistent with the general principle, a contract for the sale of stocks, shares or securities will be specifically enforceable if damages will be an inadequate remedy.[133] Damages will be inadequate, for example, if the shares are in a private company,[134] if the shares should have been issued under an agreement implementing a court-approved scheme of arrangement,[135] if the vendor owns all the shares in the company and is 'anxious to retain them'[136] or if they are not otherwise readily available on the market.[137] In such cases, the remedy is mutually available to both the vendor and purchaser despite the former merely requiring the payment of money.[138]

COURT'S DISCRETION AND DEFENCES

Introduction

7.34 Even if the above elements are satisfied, the court may refuse specific performance in its discretion.[139] This usually involves a consideration of the defendant's various defences and denials discussed below, but it may also involve a consideration of the public interest in the order being granted.[140]

A distinction is often drawn between jurisdictional elements (or ingredients) and discretionary defences.[141] The practical importance of this distinction is that proof of the jurisdictional element will allow the plaintiff to claim damages in equity even if specific performance would be

---

131. [2010] FCA 799 at [100]–[101]; see also *Construction, Forestry, Mining and Energy Union v BHP Coal Pty Ltd* [2011] FCA 971.
132. (1945) 71 CLR 142 at 150.
133. *Dougan v Ley* (1946) 71 CLR at 151 per Dixon J; *Loan Investment Corp v Bonner* [1970] NZLR 724 at 742 and 749 per Sir Garfield Barwick (in dissent) (PC); see also *SDS Corp Ltd v Pasdonnay Pty Ltd* [2004] WASC 26; affirmed in *Pasdonnay Pty Ltd v SDS Corp Ltd* [2005] WASCA 9.
134. *Iambic Pty Ltd v Northwind Holdings Pty Ltd* [2001] WASC 44.
135. *Toal v Aquarius Platinum Ltd* [2004] FCA 550.
136. *ANZ Executors and Trustees Ltd v Humes Ltd* [1990] VR 615 at 629 per Brooking J; affirmed in *Humes Ltd v PS (Enterprises) Nominees Pty Ltd* (1989) 7 ACLC 992.
137. *Dougan v Ley* (1945) 71 CLR 142 at 151 per Dixon J.
138. *Iambic Pty Ltd v Northwind Holdings Pty Ltd* [2001] WASC 44 at [3] per Bredmeyer M.
139. *Dowsett v Reid* (1912) 15 CLR 695 at 705–6 per Griffiths CJ; *Loan Investment Corp v Bonner* [1970] NZLR 724 at 746–8 per Sir Garfield Barwick (in dissent).
140. *Toal v Aquarius Platinum Ltd* [2004] FCA 550 at [61]–[64] per French J.
141. See, for example, *McMahon v Ambrose* [1987] VR 817 at 842 per Marks J.

defeated by a discretionary defence: see **Chapter 9**. It must be noted, however, that the distinction is awkward because, undoubtedly, the court also exercises a discretion in deciding what is a matter of jurisdiction and what is a matter of discretion. There is no obvious or logical distinction between the two. Nevertheless, the matters discussed below have been treated by the courts as discretionary defences and denials where the defendant, for the most part, bears the onus of proof.

Ready and willing

7.35   At all material times, including at the trial[142] and at judgment,[143] the party seeking specific performance should be ready and willing to perform the substance of the contract.[144] This is a discretionary matter, though, because failure to plead it is not fatal to the plaintiff's case.[145] Further, if the defendant ignores the matter, the plaintiff need not adduce evidence to show that he or she is ready and willing.[146] In *Mulkearns v Chandos Developments Pty Ltd* Young CJ in Eq explained the principle as follows:

> … traditionally equity only assisted a party in specific performance if that party had shown himself or herself at all material times ready, willing and able to complete the contract. In early days, this requirement was very strict as can be seen from the case discussed during argument of *Benedict v Lynch*,[147] a decision of Chancellor Kent. In more modern times, equity has been more merciful and even though a party seeking specific performance may have been in breach of contract at some time during the contract period of the contractual regime, if at present time it has cleared all breaches and is demonstrably ready, willing and able to complete, then relief is given.[148]

7.36   The usual way of proving the plaintiff is not ready and willing to perform the contract is to show that he or she is in breach of contract. However, as explained by Barwick CJ in *Mehmet v Benson*, only a breach of an 'essential term' will suffice:

> The question as to whether or not the plaintiff has been and is ready and willing to perform the contract is one of substance not to be resolved in any technical or narrow sense. It is important to bear in mind what is the substantial thing for which the parties contract and what on the part of the plaintiff in a suit for specific performance are his essential obligations. Here the substantial thing for which the defendant bargained was the payment of

---

142. *SDS Corp Ltd v Pasdonnay Pty Ltd* [2004] WASC 26 at [455]–[456] per Roberts-Smith J; affirmed in *Pasdonnay Pty Ltd v SDS Corp Ltd* [2005] WASCA 9.
143. *Norgard v Abco Holding Pty Ltd* [2001] WASC 324.
144. See, for example, *Mehmet v Benson* (1965) 113 CLR 295; *Baird v Magripilis* (1925) 37 CLR 321.
145. *Bahr v Nicolay (No 2)* (1988) 164 CLR 604 at 640 per Wilson and Toohey JJ; *Darter Pty Ltd v Malloy* [1993] 2 Qd R 615 (FC); *Tranchita v Danehill Nominees Pty Ltd* [2004] WASC 154 at [31]; *Dalswinton Pastoral Company Pty Ltd v Cole* [2006] NSWSC 570.
146. *Nobleza v Lamp* (1986) 85 FLR 147.
147. (1815) 1 Johns Ch 370; 7 Am Dec 484.
148. (2003) 11 BPR 21,277; [2003] NSWSC 1132 at [67]; affirmed *Chandos Developments Pty Ltd v Mulkearns* [2008] NSWCA 62.

the price: and, unless time be and remain of the essence, he obtains what he bargained for if by the decree he obtains his price with such ancillary orders as recompense him for the delay in its receipt. To order specific performance in this case would not involve the court in dispensing with anything for which the vendor essentially contracted.

Of course, the plaintiff must not by his unreadiness or unwillingness to perform have disowned his obligation to do so, or abandoned his rights to the benefit of the contract. But it is the essential terms of the contract which he must be ready and willing to perform.[149]

In *Mehmet* the plaintiff agreed to pay £16,000 in instalments plus interest on the unpaid balance over several years in order to purchase land in Wollongong. The plaintiff paid the first two instalments of £3000 each but then fell into arrears. Specific performance was granted despite the plaintiff's default because he had not abandoned or disowned his obligations under the contract. By contrast, in *Mulkearns* the plaintiff was denied specific performance of a contract for the sale of land at Dural in Sydney because the 'whole history' of the purchaser:

> … did not show a person ready willing and able to complete. It did not pay the deposit in full. It did not pay the occupation fee until after the proceedings were commenced and it was virtually forced on it as a term of obtaining an interlocutory injunction. Moreover, the plaintiffs are … willing to take any technicality believed open to him in order to postpone the time of settlement.[150]

In exceptional cases, such as unconscionable or unconscientious conduct on the part of the defendant, the plaintiff's breach may not disentitle the application for specific performance.[151] The plaintiff should, nonetheless, be ready and willing to perform the substance of the contract.[152]

Mutuality

7.37   The court is reluctant to order specific performance unless it is available to both parties.[153] So, as we have already seen, specific performance is available in contracts for the sale of land to both the purchaser and vendor, even though damages for the latter may be adequate.[154] Mutuality, however, is a 'somewhat elusive doctrine'[155] because the court has a discretion to grant the plaintiff specific performance even though it is not available to the defendant;[156] the

149. (1965) 113 CLR 295 at 307–8.

150. (2003) 11 BPR 21,277; [2003] NSWSC 1132 at [68] per Young CJ in Eq; affirmed *Chandos Developments Pty Ltd v Mulkearns* [2008] NSWCA 62.

151. See *Legione v Hateley* (1983) 152 CLR 406 (specific performance granted to the purchaser despite a breach of a 'time is of the essence' clause); *Stern v McArthur* (1988) 165 CLR 489 at 525–6 per Deane and Dawson JJ, and 530 per Gaudron J; compare *Ciaverella v Balmer* (1983) 153 CLR 438.

152. *Thors v Weekes* (1990) 92 ALR 131 at 144 per Gummow J.

153. *J C Williamson v Lukey & Mulholland* (1931) 45 CLR 282 at 298 per Dixon J.

154. *Turner v Bladin* (1951) 82 CLR 463.

155. *Attwells v Campbell* [2000] NSWCA 132 at [8] per Meagher JA.

156. See *Price v Strange* [1978] Ch 337 at 357 per Goff LJ (CA).

same is true for injunctions.[157] After noting that specific performance may be ordered, notwithstanding a lack of mutuality, Santow J observed in *Cannavo v FCD (Holdings) Pty Ltd*:

> The real basis of any notion of mutuality … is that it points to the weighing up process that a court necessarily carries out in order to determine whether granting specific performance at the behest of the plaintiff would, by reason of the plaintiff being unable to be required to carry out his obligations in specie, produce such hardship to the defendant that to compel specific performance would be inequitable.[158]

Specific performance may not be available to the defendant, for example, where:

a)   the plaintiff has already performed his or her obligations;[159]

b)   the plaintiff has not performed his or her obligations but the court is satisfied this breach can be adequately compensated for in damages;[160] or

c)   the defendant is guilty of fraud or unconscionable conduct.

7.38   A common example of a lack of mutuality is a contract with a minor. Such a contract is ordinarily void or voidable, and thus the minor cannot be asked to specifically perform the contract; nor can the other party.[161] However, mutuality need not exist at the date of making the contract.[162] So, in the example just given, specific performance would be allowed if the minor had attained the age of majority and ratified the contract before the suit.[163]

Hardship

7.39   The court is reluctant to order specific performance if it will cause undue hardship or unfairness to the defendant.[164] Examples include:

a)   an unfair or low purchase price for the defendant vendor;[165]

b)   an erroneous valuation fixed the price of the contract;[166]

---

157. *Warren v Mendy* [1989] 3 All ER 103 at 113; *Curro v Beyond Productions Pty Ltd* (1993) 30 NSWLR 337 at 348 per Meagher JA (CA).

158. [2000] NSWSC 304 at [64].

159. *Price v Strange* [1978] Ch 337 at 357 and 365.

160. Compare *Sutton v Sutton* [1984] Ch 184.

161. *Boyd v Ryan* (1947) 48 SR (NSW) 163.

162. See, for example, *Macaulay v Greater Paramount Theatres Ltd* (1921) 22 SR (NSW) 66; *Dougan v Ley* (1945) 71 CLR 142 at 154 per Williams J; *Price v Strange* [1978] Ch 337.

163. *Kell v Harris* (1915) 15 SR (NSW) 473.

164. *Norton v Angus* (1926) 38 CLR 523; *Patel v Ali* [1984] Ch 283.

165. *Farrell v Bussell* [1960] NSWR 398 at 401 per McLelland CJ (in Eq). Inadequate consideration, however, would normally have to be either grossly inadequate (*Jacobs v Bills* [1967] NZLR 249 at 253) or coupled with unconscionable conduct: see 5.49 and 5.54.

166. *Legal & General Life of Australia Ltd v A Hudson Pty Ltd* (1985) 1 NSWLR 314 at 331–6 per McHugh JA.

c) enforced removal of a physically disabled defendant vendor with children from property where she was able to receive help from relatives and friends who lived close by;[167]

d) the land purchased by the defendant would be subject to forfeiture;[168]

e) the order would expose the defendant to prosecution;[169]

f) the defendant lessor of a hotel would be required to undertake many costly repairs and pay taxes without receiving rent or profit for many months while the plaintiff retained possession;[170]

g) the defendant would be required to run a business at a loss;[171]

h) the defendant would be forced to become the reluctant proprietor of a brothel;[172]

i) the defendant would be required to maintain a joint venture after an 'irretrievable breakdown of relations';[173] and

j) *semble*, the order would cause the defendant to suffer 'loss or liability' under the Competition and Consumer Act 2010 (Cth).[174]

However, the defence is not established if there is merely an increase in the value of land since the date of the contract[175] or if the defendant is experiencing financial difficulties.[176]

Unclean hands

7.40 If the plaintiff has unclean hands then the remedy may be refused in the court's discretion. But not all unmeritorious conduct will disentitle the plaintiff to relief. As observed by Gleeson CJ in *Official Trustee in Bankruptcy v Tooheys Ltd*:

> The unmeritorious conduct which debars relief is not 'general depravity'; it must be conduct which 'has an immediate and necessary relation to the equity suited for'.[177]

It will have an immediate and necessary relation to the equity sued for if, for example, the plaintiff is guilty of unconscionable conduct such as fraud or undue influence: see Chapter 5. But if the plaintiff is merely guilty of sharp

167. *Patel v Ali* [1984] Ch 283.
168. *Norton v Angus* (1926) 38 CLR 523.
169. See *Pottinger v Genge* (1967) 116 CLR 328 at 337 per Barwick CJ, McTiernan and Taylor JJ.
170. *Dowsett v Reid* (1912) 15 CLR 695.
171. *Co-operative Insurance Society v Argyll Stores (Holdings) Ltd* [1998] AC 1.
172. *Hope v Walters* [1900] 1 Ch 257.
173. *Cannavo v FCD (Holdings) Pty Ltd* [2000] NSWSC 304 at [67] per Santow J.
174. *Demagogue Pty Ltd v Ramensky* (1992) 110 ALR 608 (FCA) per Gummow J.
175. *Fitzgerald v Masters* (1956) 95 CLR 420 at 433.
176. *Pasadina (Holdings) Pty Ltd v Khouri* (1977) 1 BPR 9460; *Longtom Pty Ltd v Oberon Shire Council* (1996) 7 BPR 14,799; *Jambu Pty Ltd v Northwind Holdings Pty Ltd* [2001] WASC 44 at [6] per Bredmeyer M; *Boyarsky v Taylor* [2008] NSWSC 1415.
177. (1993) 29 NSWLR 641 at 650 (CA) citing in support *Dering v Earl of Winchelsea* (1787) 1 Cox 318 at 319; 29 ER 1184 at 1184-5; see also *Keystone Driller Co v General Excavator Co* 290 US 240 (1933).

practice, not amounting to unconscionability, this will not have an immediate and necessary relation to the equity sued for.[178] Also, not all innocent misrepresentations by the plaintiff have an immediate and necessary relation to the equity sued for: see **8.35**.[179] The same point can be made where the plaintiff has breached the contract: see **7.35–7.36**.

Whole contract should be enforced

7.41   The whole contract should be specifically enforceable.[180] In this regard Clarke JA observed in *Bridge Wholesale Acceptance Corp (Australia) Ltd v Burnard*:

> The distinction [between executory and executed contracts] is important because of the general rule applicable in cases of the first class, that an order for specific performance is an order that the whole of the contract, not individual obligations under it, be carried into effect. In the present case the contract is an executed one and the appellant seeks an order compelling the respondent to carry out his bargain in an important respect and the rule to which I have just referred does not apply.[181]

Still, the part to be enforced must be severable or divisible from the whole contract;[182] for example, the sale of several lots of land referred to in one contract.[183] It will not be severable and specifically enforceable if the obligations of the parties are 'interdependent'.[184]

Continuing supervision

7.42   Specific performance may be refused if the court is required to continually supervise its order.[185] The court will not, for example, order that a defendant 'carry on an activity, such as running a business over a more or less extended period of time'.[186] The court's reluctance to make such orders stems from the concern that a breach exposes the defendant to penalties for

---

178. *ANZ Executors and Trustees Ltd v Humes Ltd* [1990] VR 615.

179. *Coghlan v Pyoanee Pty Ltd* [2003] 2 Qd R 636 (CA).

180. *Ryan v Mutual Tontine Westminster Chambers Association* [1893] 1 Ch 116 at 123 per Lord Esher MR; *J C Williamson Ltd v Lukey & Mulholland* (1931) 45 CLR 282 at 294 and 314; *Loan Investment Corp v Bonner* [1970] NZLR 724.

181. (1992) 27 NSWLR 415 at 423–4 (CA); see also *Waterways Authority of New South Wales v Coal and Allied (Operations) Pty Ltd* [2007] NSWCA 276.

182. *Ryan v Mutual Tontine Westminster Chambers Association* [1893] 1 Ch 116 at 124 per Lord Esher MR; *J C Williamson Ltd v Lukey and Mulholland* (1931) 45 CLR 282 at 294; *Bridge Wholesale Acceptance Corp (Australia) Ltd v Burnard Clark* (1992) 27 NSWLR 415 at 423; see also *Cannavo v FCD (Holdings) Pty Ltd* [2000] NSWSC 304 at [61]–[65] per Santow J.

183. *Lewin v Guest* (1826) 1 Russ 325, 38 ER 126; compare *Roffey v Shallcross* (1819) 4 Madd 227.

184. *Sugar Australia Ltd v Conneq* [2011] NSWSC 805 at [20] per McDougall J.

185. *J C Williamson Ltd v Lukey and Mulholland* (1931) 45 CLR 282 at 293 per Starke J and 297–8 per Dixon J.

186. *Co-operative Insurance Society v Argyll Stores (Holding) Ltd* [1998] AC 1 at 13 per Lord Hoffman; *Waste Recycling & Processing Corp v Global Renewables Eastern Creek Pty Ltd* [2009] NSWSC 453 at [153] per Einstein J.

contempt.[187] But the 'continuing supervision' defence is not absolute.[188] In *Patrick Stevedores Operations No 2 Pty Ltd v Maritime Union of Australia* a majority in the High Court observed:

> We see in the orders no defect which sometimes is expressed as the involvement of the court in "constant supervision" of continued conduct. Reservations of that nature have been expressed in decisions of this Court … However, questions of degree rather than absolute restrictions upon the scope of curial relief are involved …

> Reference to constant court applications should not be misunderstood. The courts are well accustomed to the exercise of supervisory jurisdiction upon applications by trustees, receivers, provisional liquidators and others with the responsibility for the conduct of administrations.[189]

Examples are also found in building and repair cases where the courts grant the remedy despite the need for supervision,[190] provided the terms of the order particularising the work to be done are clear and precise.[191] Still, such orders are 'exceptional'[192] and 'extraordinary'[193] rather than the rule.

Futility

7.43   If specific performance would be futile it may be refused in the court's discretion. Thus, the court will not order specific performance if the defendant can terminate the contract at will.[194] By contrast, in *Iambic Pty Ltd v Northwind Holdings Pty Ltd* it was held that it was not futile to order specific performance of a contract to sell shares in a private company where the purchaser could no longer afford the agreed price.[195]

If the defendant can establish that performance of the contract is impossible, as a matter of jurisdiction the order will be refused: see **7.13**.

---

187. *Waste Recycling & Processing Corp v Global Renewables Eastern Creek Pty Ltd* [2009] NSWSC 453 at [158] [161].

188. See *Shiloh Spinners Ltd v Harding* [1973] AC 691 at 724 per Lord Wilberforce; *Tito v Waddell (No 2)* [1977] Ch 106 at 321 per Megarry V-C; *C H Giles & Co Ltd v Morris* [1972] 1 All ER 960 (Ch).

189. (1998) 195 CLR 1 at [78]–[80] per Brennan CJ, McHugh, Gummow, Kirby and Hayne JJ (citations omitted).

190. See *Wolverhampton Corp v Emmons* [1901] 1 KB 515; *York House Pty Ltd v Federal Commissioner of Taxation* (1930) 43 CLR 427; *Thomas v Harper* (1935) 36 SR (NSW) 142 at 147–8 per Long Innes CJ (in Eq).

191. *Co-operative Insurance Society v Argyll Stores (Holding) Ltd* [1998] AC 1 at 13–14 per Lord Hoffman.

192. *Crouch Developments Pty Ltd v D & M (Australia) Pty Ltd* [2008] WASC 151 at [21] per Martin CJ.

193. *Sugar Australia Ltd v Conneq* [2011] NSWSC 805 at [19] per McDougall J.

194. See *Heppingstone v Stewart* (1910) 12 CLR 126 at 129 and 138; *Tito v Waddell (No 2)* [1977] Ch 106 at 325–7.

195. [2001] WASC 44 at [7] per Bredmeyer M.

Delay, acquiescence and laches

7.44   Mere delay will not bar relief unless it amounts to acquiescence or laches,[196] that is, where it would result in the defendant or a third party being prejudiced. In *Lamshed v Lamshed* Kitto J held:

> ... the special remedy of specific performance is available to those only who are prompt to claim it. The degree of promptness required depends on the nature of the case and all its circumstances ... Accordingly there is little point in citing cases for the purpose of comparing the period of delay in the present case with the delay which has been considered fatal to claims for specific performance in the circumstances of other cases. The bare fact of delay is not enough. Where there is nothing at all in the circumstances to justify either a conclusion that the delay has been to the prejudice of the defendant or of any third party, or a conclusion that the plaintiff ought to be regarded as having abandoned any rights he ever had, specific performance is not ordinarily refused ...[197]

So, in *Fitzgerald v Masters*,[198] specific performance was granted despite a 26-year delay because laches was absent and because the court was prepared to order that compensation be paid to the defendant for any disadvantage caused by the order. But in *Lamshed v Lamshed* an order for specific performance was refused after a six-year delay because the defendant had agreed to sell the property to an innocent third-party purchaser.[199] It will also be refused if the defendant denies being bound by the contract and the plaintiff fails to explain the delay in approaching the court.[200]

---

196. For a discussion on the distinction between acquiescence and laches, see **8.36–8.37** and see *Orr v Ford* (1989) 167 CLR 316 at 337–9 per Deane J.

197. (1963) 109 CLR 440 at 452–3.

198. (1956) 95 CLR 420.

199. See also *Carter v Hyde* (1923) 33 CLR 115; *Pearson v Arcadia Stores* (1935) 53 CLR 571; *Mehmet v Benson* (1965) 113 CLR 295; *Boyns v Lackey* [1958] SR (NSW) 395; *Hughes v Schofield* [1975] 1 NSWLR 8; *Hoon v Westpoint Management Ltd* [2011] WASC 239 at [68]–[69] per Corboy J.

200. *Holland v Roperti* [2009] VSC 378 at [88]–[91] per Hansen J.

CHAPTER

Injunctions

NATURE OF THE REMEDY

8.1 One of the law's most potent and frequently used remedies is the injunction. It orders a person to do an act *or* not to do an act. The typical injunction is the negative or prohibitory injunction. It restrains or forbids the defendant from engaging in a wrongful act such as breaching a trust, trespassing on land, passing off goods or services as those of another, infringing a right (such as copyright, a patent, a design or a trade mark) or breaching a contract. Less common, but nonetheless extremely useful, is the mandatory or positive injunction: see **8.63**. It directs the defendant to perform an act, such as performing an agreement, transferring control of a domain name and website,[1] surrendering and cancelling a business or company name, reducing the height of a boundary wall built in breach of contract[2] or demolishing a house built in contravention of the law.[3] A further distinction is drawn between final and interlocutory injunctions. Final injunctions are granted only after a full determination of the rights of the parties, while interlocutory injunctions are temporary and preserve the status quo until the final hearing: see **8.45–8.62**. Despite the apparent transient nature of interlocutory injunctions their power is not to be underestimated. Many cases settle following the early determination of the rights of the parties: see **8.53**. Another potent variant is the *quia timet* injunction, which is granted because a person fears and the court finds that a wrong may occur: see **8.13**.

Irrespective of whether an injunction is granted in equity's exclusive or auxiliary jurisdiction or under statute, it is still an order to do something or not do something. But not all such orders are necessarily injunctions. While the leading modern authority on the definition and nature of equitable injunctions is the High Court decision in *Cardile v LED Builders*,[4] it actually did not concern an injunction at all but, rather, the granting of a Mareva *order*. Such orders, also known as freezing orders, prohibit the defendant from disposing of their assets. Conversely, they require the defendant to take positive steps to preserve their assets. Prior to *Cardile*, they were often referred to as Mareva *injunctions* and considered as a form of equitable injunction. But the High Court said the courts have 'developed doctrines and remedies, outside the injunction as understood in courts of equity, to protect the integrity of its processes once set in motion'.[5] The Mareva order was such a development. There are also numerous statutory remedies that use the term 'injunction'[6] and these should

---

1. *Body Technology Pty Ltd v Babak Moini* [2010] NSWSC 1414.
2. *Collum v Opie* (2000) 76 SASR 588; [2000] SASC 107 (FC).
3. See *Shire of Hornsby v Danglade* (1929) 29 SR (NSW) 118.
4. (1999) 198 CLR 380.
5. (1999) 198 CLR 380 at [40] per Gaudron, McHugh, Gummow and Callinan JJ.
6. Citing various legislation including s 80 of the Trade Practices Act 1974 (Cth) (repealed and replaced with s 80, Competition and Consumer Act 2010) and s 114 of the Family Law Act 1975 (Cth).

take their 'content from the provisions of the particular statute in question'.[7] Such provisions 'empower courts to give a remedy in many cases where none would have been available in a court of equity.'[8] But the High Court said there is a 'strain placed upon' the traditional equitable injunction 'by its use to identify new statutory remedies and to its misapplication to identify either the nature of or the juridical foundation for the Mareva order'.[9] That 'strain' was also evident with search orders which were originally known as Anton Piller injunctions. Such orders preserve the evidence the subject matter of the trial and, in common with Mareva orders, they are both negative and prohibitory in form. It is now accepted that Anton Piller orders are not a form of equitable injunction.

Part of the reason for this doctrinal confusion is that interlocutory injunctions, freezing orders and search orders are all remedies that protect the integrity of the court's processes pending the trial. Interlocutory injunctions preserve the *status quo*, freezing orders preserve the defendant's *assets* and search orders preserve the *evidence*. The confusion is likely to continue with the recent use of the terms 'super' and 'anonymised' injunctions. These are also designed to protect the integrity of the court's processes by preserving *confidential information* pending the trial: see **8.68–8.74**.

8.2   Principles applicable to all injunctions are:

a)   the injunction must enforce a legal or an equitable cause of action;[10]

b)   injunctions are always granted in the discretion of the court;[11]

c)   the 'injunction ought to make clear what it is that the defendant is required to do or not do'.[12]

Traditionally injunctions are granted in both the exclusive and auxiliary jurisdictions of equity The distinction between these jurisdictions is important[13] because when the court exercises its discretion the principles to be applied are not the same. The differences between the jurisdictions are discussed later in this chapter.

The last element, namely 'the injunction ought to make clear what it is that the defendant is required to do or not do'[14] is sometimes treated as an element in its own right and sometimes as a discretionary matter. It is important because the defendant will be guilty of contempt of court and face heavy penalties if the order is breached. In one of the leading cases on mandatory

---

7.   (1999) 198 CLR 380 at [29] per Gaudron, McHugh, Gummow and Callinan JJ.

8.   (1999) 198 CLR 380 at [28] per Gaudron, McHugh, Gummow and Callinan JJ.

9.   (1999) 198 CLR 380 at [27] per Gaudron, McHugh, Gummow and Callinan JJ.

10.   *Cardile v LED Builders Pty Ltd* (1999) 198 CLR 380 at 395–6; *Australian Broadcasting Corp v Lenah Game Meats Pty Ltd* (2001) 208 CLR 199 at 216, 231–2, 241.

11.   Specific discretionary defences are considered at **8.10** and **8.34–8.44**.

12.   See *Curro v Beyond Productions Pty Ltd* (1993) 30 NSWLR 337 at 348 (CA); *Redland Bricks Ltd v Morris* [1970] AC 652 at 666 (HL).

13.   For a further discussion on the practical importance of the distinction, see **Chapter 11**.

14.   *Curro v Beyond Productions Pty Ltd* (1993) 30 NSWLR 337 at 348 (CA).

injunctions, *Morris v Redland Bricks Ltd*, Lord Upjohn said that 'the court must be careful to see that the defendant knows exactly in fact what he has to do and this means not as a matter of law but as a matter of fact.'[15] Similarly, in *Attorney-General v Punch Ltd*, a case concerning confidential information and an editor's contempt of court in disclosing that information, Lord Hope said:

> I take as my starting point for an examination of this issue the principle that an injunction must always be expressed with precision and with clarity. As Lord Deas put it in a Scottish case, if an injunction is to be granted at all, it must be in terms so plain that he who runs may read[16] … This is because of the penal consequences that will follow if it is breached. Then there is another important principle. The prohibition must extend no further than is necessary to serve the purpose for which the order is to be made.'[17]

While precision and clarity are important it has been noted by Callinan J (in dissent on the result) in *Maggbury Pty Ltd v Hafele Australia Pty Ltd* that '[e]xcessively narrow formalism in framing the injunction may wreak its own injustice'.[18] This was cited with approval by Giles JA in the New South Wales Court of Appeal in *Orleans Investments Pty Ltd v Mindshare Communications Ltd*. His Honour observed that:

> Injunctions are practical tools in the administration of justice. There are limits to the precision and clarity which can be attained … [the plaintiff] should not suffer an injustice through undue insistence on precise statement of what the appellants must do or not do. Orders are often made in the terms that the defendant must not do certain things "so as to cause a nuisance", … and … an order relevantly restraining engaging in the practice of resale price maintenance in the manner alleged in the statement of claim "or in any similar manner" … an order that the defendant not publish any "imputation of and concerning [a person] which is calculated to expose her to hatred, ridicule and contempt". In *Maggbury Pty Ltd v Hafele Australia Pty Ltd*[19] Callinan J said that the "potential for embarrassment for want of certainty" was no greater than in cases where courts had restrained defendants from using confidential information or know-how despite the long recognition "that the boundary between know-how and personal skills can be hard to draw".[20]

In *Orleans Investments* the court had to consider the enforcement of a negative contractual promise to not engage in conduct which might harm or injure the name or reputation of the plaintiff, Mindshare, or a 'Related Body Corporate'. Giles JA held the framing of the injunction was a 'discretionary

---

15. [1970] AC 652 at 666 (HL).
16. *Kelso School Board v Hunter* (1874) 2 R 228 at 230.
17. [2003] 1 AC 1046 at [111].
18. (2001) 210 CLR 181 at 220.
19. (2001) 210 CLR 181 at [106].
20. [2009] NSWCA 40 at [105].

consideration' and not 'a bar to relief if there were less than complete clarity for the appellants' future conduct.'[21]

EXCLUSIVE JURISDICTION

Introduction

8.3 When an injunction is granted in equity's exclusive jurisdiction, a common law remedy, usually damages, cannot be awarded for the obvious reason that the court is dealing with the infringement of a purely equitable right. This means that one of the key criteria in deciding whether an injunction is available in equity's auxiliary jurisdiction — namely, whether the common law will provide an adequate remedy — is irrelevant in deciding whether an injunction is available in the exclusive jurisdiction. This is so despite the fact that equitable compensation may be available under Lord Cairns' Act: see Chapter 11.

Elements

8.4 In order to obtain an injunction in equity's exclusive jurisdiction, the plaintiff must:

a) have an equitable cause of action; and

b) satisfy the court that in its discretion it should grant the injunction.

Generally, the onus is on the plaintiff to establish both elements, although in the second the defendant bears the burden of establishing any equitable defence raised.

Equitable cause of action

8.5 In the exclusive jurisdiction, injunctions issue to restrain infractions or apprehended infractions (see 8.13) of purely equitable rights and obligations. There is no requirement that the right needs to be proprietary in nature, although property may be incidentally protected: see 8.14–8.16. An injunction will lie to restrain a breach of a fiduciary obligation or a breach of a trust.[22] An injunction may also issue against third parties who deal with the trust property.[23] Two areas, discussed below, which have attracted controversy as to whether they are legal or equitable rights are confidential information and a person's so-called right to work.

Confidential information

8.6 Subject to available defences,[24] an injunction will lie against a person who receives confidential information, such as a trade secret, and is threatening to

---

21. [2009] NSWCA 40 at [97].

22. *Park v Dawson* [1965] NSWR 298; *Wylde v Attorney General for New South Wales* (1948) 78 CLR 224.

23. *Ackerley v Palmer* [1910] VLR 339.

24. See, for example, *Cream Holdings Ltd v Banerjee* [2004] UKHL 44 which considered public interest and free speech defences under the Human Rights Act 1998 s 12 (UK).

disclose the information. But is confidential information a legal or equitable right? The answer is that it can be both. If there is a contract (or statute[25]) prohibiting disclosure, then a breach will be a breach of a legal right.[26] If an injunction is to be obtained here, it will be in equity's auxiliary jurisdiction. In contract cases the plaintiff will need to show that common law damages are an inadequate remedy for the breach of the legal right.[27]

But not all confidential information cases concern a contract between the parties or a statutory obligation. There is also a purely equitable obligation of confidence.[28] Indeed, the lack of a common law tort of invasion of privacy has enlivened this area of equity.[29] The inadequacy of damages at common law is an irrelevant element in deciding whether an injunction should be granted to protect a purely equitable obligation. Nonetheless, in addition to or in lieu of the injunction, the plaintiff may be able to claim equitable damages under Lord Cairns' Act or equitable compensation in the exclusive jurisdiction of equity.[30]

It is also possible that both equitable and contractual duties of confidence will exist concurrently in relation to the same subject matter.[31] For the most part these concurrent duties do not cause any problems in relation to the granting and framing of the injunction. But, it does raise the difficult issue of whether the plaintiff may elect between common law damages for breach of contract and an account of profits in equity's exclusive jurisdiction.[32]

The equitable jurisdiction to grant an injunction preserving confidential information has played a key role in the development of new procedural remedies. Search orders, originally known as Anton Piller injunctions, were created in 1975 in relation to preserving and seizing confidential information: see **10.4**. More recently, the equitable obligation of confidence has played a key role in the development of super and anonymised injunctions: see **8.68–8.74**.

---

25. See, for example, Charter of Human Rights and Responsibilities Act 2006 s 13(a) (Vic); Human Rights Act 2004 s 12 (ACT); European Convention for the Protection of Human Rights and Fundamental Freedoms (1950), Art 8(1).

26. Compare *Maggbury Pty Ltd v Hafele Australia Pty Ltd* (2001) 210 CLR 181 at [49].

27. See **8.30–8.33**.

28. See *Moorgate Tobacco Co Ltd v Philip Morris Ltd (No 2)* (1984) 156 CLR 414 at 437–8 per Deane J; *Best Australia Ltd v Aquagas Marketing Pty Ltd* (1989) 13 IPR 600; *Argyll v Argyll* [1967] Ch 302.

29. See, for example, *Campbell v MGN Ltd* [2004] UKHL 22, [2004] 2 AC 457; *OBG Ltd v Allan; Douglas v Hello! Ltd; Mainstream Properties Ltd v Young* [2008] 1 AC 1; *Giller v Procopets* [2008] VSCA 236, (2008) 24 VR 1 discussed at **11.21**.

30. See **Chapter 11**.

31. See **6.18**.

32. See **6.19**.

Person's right to work

8.7   Although at common law a contract, including an employment contract, is void if it imposes an unreasonable restraint of trade,[33] this doctrine only applies to the parties to the contract. But last century equity developed a doctrine protecting a person's right to work, irrespective of whether that person was a party to the contract which threatened or curtailed that right. The leading United Kingdom case is *Nagle v Fielden*.[34] In order to train horses for racing at jockey-club meetings, a person had to be licensed by the club stewards. However, their policy was to refuse licences to women. Nagle, a woman, had been repeatedly refused a licence even though her employees had not. She sought a declaration that the stewards' practice was void as against public policy, together with a mandatory injunction compelling the stewards to grant her a licence. At first instance, the statement of claim was struck out by a Master of the Court on the basis that it disclosed no cause of action. This was affirmed by Stephenson J, but the United Kingdom Court of Appeal allowed the appeal. Lord Denning MR said:

> We live in days when many trading or professional associations operate "closed shops". No person can work at his trade or profession except by their permission. They can deprive him of his livelihood. When a man is wrongly ejected or ousted by one of these associations, has he no remedy? I think that he may well have, even though he can show no contract. The courts have power to grant him a declaration that his rejection and ouster was invalid and an injunction requiring the association to rectify their error. He may not be able to get damages unless he can show a contract or tort; but he may get a declaration and injunction ...
>
> The true ground of jurisdiction in all these cases is a man's right to work. I have said before, and I repeat it now, that a man's right to work at his trade or profession is just as important, if not more important than his rights of property. Just as the courts will intervene to protect his rights of property, so they will also intervene to protect his right to work.[35]

8.8   The High Court applied *Nagle* in *Buckley v Tutty*.[36] *Buckley* arose out of the rules of the New South Wales Rugby Football League (NSWRFL), which permitted clubs to place players on a 'retain list' if they wanted to transfer to another club. The club losing the player could then demand a transfer fee. Tutty had a contract to play for the Balmain District Rugby League Football Club (Balmain) and it provided that he was bound by the NSWRFL rules, including the retainer list and transfer rules. Tutty wished to transfer and was placed on the retainer list by Balmain. He then sought a declaration against both the NSWRFL and Balmain that the transfer rules were not binding on

33.   See *Curro v Beyond Productions Pty Ltd* (1993) 30 NSWLR 337 at 341–6 per Meagher JA (CA). In New South Wales, the common law is modified by s 4(1) of the Restraints of Trade Act 1976 (NSW) which provides a 'restraint of trade is valid to the extent to which it is not against public policy, whether it is in severable terms or not'.

34.   [1966] 2 QB 633.

35.   [1966] 2 QB 633 at 646.

36.   (1971) 125 CLR 353.

him because they were an unreasonable restraint of trade. The difficulty was that there was no contract between Tutty and the NSWRFL. Further, the NSWRFL had never sought to enforce the rules by suing Tutty. Nonetheless, the New South Wales Supreme Court in Equity granted the declaration and the injunction restraining the NSWRFL and Balmain from enforcing the rules against Tutty. In dismissing an appeal by the NSWRFL, the High Court approved the declarations and injunctions granted by the Supreme Court. Barwick CJ, McTiernan, Windeyer, Owen and Gibbs JJ found that the rules were an unreasonable restraint of trade. The court did not expressly mention equity, but held, following *Nagle*, that it had the power to intervene in order to protect a person's right to work, despite there being no contract between the parties.[37]

8.9   In *Curro v Beyond Productions Pty Ltd*,[38] Meagher JA observed that a person's 'right to work' is not a 'right in the strict sense', it is 'merely a liberty'.[39] His Honour then cited in support the following passage from Barwick CJ's judgment in *Forbes v NSW Trotting Club*:[40]

> To convert the doctrine that … there should be no unreasonable restraint on employment into a doctrine that every man has a "right to work", is, in my opinion, to depart radically from … the common law … It is in the public interest that a man should be able to exercise his capacity to work. The law does not enforce a right to exercise that capacity: it does no more than remove the unreasonable impediment upon its exercise.[41]

Meagher JA also noted that this passage was approved in *Hepples v Federal Commissioner of Taxation*.[42]

Court's discretion

8.10   Not only must the court be satisfied that the plaintiff has an equitable cause of action, it must also be satisfied that in its discretion the injunction should be granted. So, if the plaintiff has 'unclean hands' (see **8.35**), if there is delay, laches or acquiescence (see **8.36**) or if justice will be best served by granting alternative relief, such as an account of profits (see **Chapter 6**), the injunction may be refused.

---

37.   Compare *Avellino v All Australia Netball Association Ltd* [2004] SASC 56 at [63]–[73] per Bleby J.

38.   (1993) 30 NSWLR 337.

39.   (1993) 30 NSWLR 337 at 346.

40.   (1979) 143 CLR 242.

41.   (1979) 143 CLR 242 at 260–1; and see *Peters (WA) Ltd v Petersville Ltd* (2001) 205 CLR 126 at [14]; *Automotive, Food, Metals, Engineering, Printing and Kindred Industries Union v Noack* [2004] NSWSC 347.

42.   (1992) 173 CLR 492 at 502, 527 and 549; compare *Hughes v Western Australian Cricket Association (Inc)* (1988) 19 FCR 10 (FCA) per Toohey J; *Quinn v Overland* [2010] FCA 799.

Auxiliary jurisdiction

Introduction and elements

8.11   The purpose of injunctions in the auxiliary or concurrent jurisdiction is to protect common law rights and, in some cases, statutory rights: see **8.29**. To obtain an injunction in this jurisdiction, the plaintiff must show:

a)   a cause of action;

b)   that damages would be an inadequate remedy; and

c)   that the court in its discretion should grant the injunction.

   Generally, the onus is on the plaintiff to establish these elements, although in (c) the defendant bears the burden of establishing any equitable defence raised.

Cause of action

Introduction

8.12   Objectionable conduct which does not sound in law is insufficient, so the threshold requirement is that the plaintiff must have a recognised cause of action.[43] As observed by Meagher JA in *Curro v Beyond Productions Pty Ltd*,[44] injunctions 'are granted to enforce existing rights' and they 'are not a mechanism for creating new rights'. For the most part, the cause of action is found at common law, but equity will grant an injunction in aid of a statutory right: see **8.29**.

   As discussed below, in an application for a *quia timet* injunction the absence of a complete cause of action may be excused if the action is likely to crystallise in the near future. Another qualification to the need to show a cause of action was recognised by Hoffmann J in *Associated Newspapers Group plc v Insert Media Ltd*, namely, where there is an application for an 'anti-suit' injunction to restrain proceedings being brought in a foreign court.[45] The anti-suit injunction, however, does 'not involve the exercise of power deriving from the Court of Chancery', but rather it is 'an exercise of the power of the court to protect the integrity of its processes once set in motion'.[46]

Quia timet injunctions

8.13   *Quia timet* injunctions lie to restrain threatened or apprehended legal wrongs. It is not necessary to prove that the common law action

---

43.   *Associated Newspapers Group plc v Insert Media Ltd* [1988] 2 All ER 420 at 424–5 (Ch D); *Australian Broadcasting Corporation v Lenah Game Meats Pty Ltd* (2001) 208 CLR 199; 185 ALR 1.

44.   (1993) 30 NSWLR 337 at 350 (CA).

45.   [1988] 2 All ER 420 at 424–5.

46.   *Australian Broadcasting Corporation v Lenah Game Meats Pty Ltd* (2001) 208 CLR 199; 185 ALR 1 at [94] per Gummow and Hayne JJ; see also *CSR Ltd v Cigna Insurance Australia Ltd* (1997) 189 CLR 345 at 391–92 and 395–96; *QBE Insurance (Australia) Ltd v Hotchin* [2011] NSWSC 681 at [15] and [25] per Bergin CJ in Eq.

has crystallised.[47] In New South Wales this principle has statutory force. Section 66(1) of the Supreme Court Act 1970 (NSW) provides:

> The court may, at any stage of proceedings, by interlocutory or other injunction, restrain any threatened or apprehended breach of contract or other injury.[48]

Proprietary rights

8.14 It is sometimes put that, in order for an injunction to lie, the plaintiff's right must be in the nature of property. But this is controversial and, as Windeyer J observed in relation to common law trade marks in *Colbeam Palmer Ltd v Stock Affiliates Pty Ltd*:

> There is, no doubt, some circuity in saying that the protection which the Court of Chancery gave by injunctions to plaintiffs who had acquired trade marks by use and reputation made such trade marks a form of property — and then saying that the intervention of the court in such cases was based upon the protection of an equitable proprietary interest.[49]

8.15 The better view is that a right which constitutes or will constitute a cause of action is sufficient irrespective of whether property is protected.[50] The point is illustrated by *Victoria Park Racing v Taylor*.[51] The defendant set up a tower next to a racecourse and broadcast the races on radio. When attendances began to fall, the racecourse owners sought an injunction restraining the defendant from making the broadcasts. The High Court refused the injunction. Dixon J observed:

> If English law had followed the course of development that has recently taken place in the United States, the "broadcasting rights" in respect of the races might have been protected as part of the quasi-property created by the enterprise, organisation and labour of the plaintiff in establishing and equipping a racecourse and doing all that is necessary to conduct race meetings. But courts of equity have not in British jurisdictions thrown the protection of an injunction around all the intangible elements of value, that is, value in exchange, which may flow from the exercise by an individual of his powers or resources whether in the organisation of a business or undertaking or the use of ingenuity, knowledge, skill or labour. This is sufficiently evidenced by the history of the law of copyright and by the fact that the exclusive rights to invention, trade marks, designs, trade name and reputation are dealt with in English law as special heads of protected interests and not under a wide generalisation.
>
> … it is not because the individual has by his efforts put himself in a position to obtain value for what he can give that his right to give it becomes protected

---

47. See *Associated Newspapers plc v Insert Media Ltd* (1989) 18 IPR 345 at 358 per Mummery J (Ch D).

48. See *Magic Menu Systems Pty Ltd v AFA Facilitation Pty Ltd* (1997) 72 FCR 261 (Full FC); *Corvisy v Corvisy* [1982] 2 NSWLR 557; *Swimsure (Laboratories) Pty Ltd v McDonald* [1979] 2 NSWLR 796 at 802 per Hunt J; *Church of Scientology of California Inc v Reader's Digest Services Pty Ltd* [1980] 1 NSWLR 344 at 358 per Hunt J.

49. (1968) 122 CLR 25 at 34.

50. *Cardile v LED Builders Pty Ltd* (1999) 198 CLR 380; *Australian Broadcasting Corporation v Lenah Game Meats Pty Ltd* (2001) 208 CLR 199; 185 ALR 1.

51. (1937) 58 CLR 479.

by law and so assumes the exclusiveness of the property, but because the intangible or incorporeal right he claims falls within a recognised category to which legal or equitable protection attaches.[52]

8.16   As Dixon J concludes in *Victoria Park*, not all injuries to property are forbidden by law. This reasoning was applied by Deane J in the High Court in *Moorgate Tobacco Co Ltd v Philip Morris Ltd (No 2)*,[53] when it rejected a new tort of unfair competition even though this would have protected the plaintiff's property. Examples can also be found in defamation and injurious falsehood. In both causes of action a published comment may have caused injury to a business reputation — a recognised form of property in intellectual property law — yet the damage to property is allowed, and an injunction will be refused, if the statement is protected by defences such as justification and free speech.

Dixon J's requirement for a 'recognised category', however, does not necessarily prevent the development of new torts. In *Australian Broadcasting Corporation v Lenah Game Meats Pty Ltd*[54] the slaughter of brush-tail possums had been secretly filmed by a trespasser on the respondent's abattoir. The film innocently fell into the hands of ABC Television which, on appeal to the High Court, successfully dissolved the injunction restraining its broadcast. While the abattoir's novel claim to a tortious right to privacy for *corporations* was rejected, the High Court left the door open on the tort's development for *individuals*.[55] By contrast, the House of Lords in *Wainwright v Home Office*[56] rejected the notion that there is a common law tort of invasion of privacy. This has not, however, diminished the development of the equitable obligation of confidence in Australia and England.[57]

Various causes of action which have supported injunctions in the auxiliary jurisdiction are considered below.

Defamation

8.17   It has often been held that injunctions, particularly interlocutory injunctions (see **8.45**), restraining the publication of defamatory material should only be granted in 'exceptional' or 'very clear cases'.[58] In a passage

---

52.   (1937) 58 CLR 479 at 508–9.

53.   (1984) 156 CLR 414.

54.   (2001) 208 CLR 199; 185 ALR 1.

55.   Justice McHugh, 'The Strengths of the Weakest Arm' (2004) 25 *Aust Bar Rev* 181 at 190; see also *Campbell v MGN Ltd* [2004] UKHL 22, [2004] 2 AC 457; *Grosse v Purvis* (2003) Aust Torts Reps 81–706; [2003] QDC 151; *Hosking v Runting* (2004) 7 HRNZ 301; compare *Giller v Procopets* (2008) 24 VR 1 at [167]–[168]; [2008] VSCA 236 per Ashley JA, discussed at **11.21**.; *Kalaba v Commonwealth* [2004] FCA 763.

56.   [2004] 2 AC 406; *OBG Ltd v Allan* [2008] 1 All ER 1 at [272] per Lord Walker (dissenting).

57.   See **8.6** and **8.68** to **8.74**.

58.   *Chappell v TCN Channel Nine Pty Ltd* (1988) 14 NSWLR 153 at 158, 163 and 172 per Hunt J; see also *Stocker v McIlhinney (No 2)* (1961) 79 WN (NSW) 541 at 543–4 per Walsh J; *Shiel v Transmedia Productions Pty Ltd* [1987] 1 Qd R 199 (FC); *National Mutual Life Association v GIO Corp Pty Ltd* [1989] VR 747 (FC).

approved by the High Court in *Australian Broadcasting Corporation v O'Neill*[59] Lord Coleridge CJ in *Bonnard v Perryman* said:

> ... it is obvious that the subject-matter of an action for defamation is so special as to require *exceptional caution* in exercising the jurisdiction to interfere by injunction before the trial of an action to prevent an anticipated wrong. The right of free speech is one which it is for the public interest that individuals should possess, and, indeed, that they should exercise without impediment, so long as no wrongful act is done; and, unless an alleged libel is untrue, there is no wrong committed; but, on the contrary, often a very wholesome act is performed in the publication and repetition of an alleged libel. Until it is clear that an alleged libel is untrue, it is not clear that any right at all has been infringed; and the importance of leaving free speech unfettered is a strong reason in cases of libel for dealing most cautiously and warily with the granting of interim injunctions.[60] [italics added]

The reason for 'exceptional caution' in deciding whether to restrain the publication of alleged defamatory matter was further explained by Hunt J in *Chappell v TCN Channel Nine Pty Ltd*:

> ... in most cases the grant of [an interlocutory] injunction before the rights of the parties have been finally determined at a trial involves an interference with an important right of the defendant, that of his freedom of speech, which is necessarily interfered with if its exercise is delayed or prevented. In many cases, the grant of such an injunction before those rights have been finally determined involves an interference with an even more important right, the right of the community in general to discuss in public matters of public interest and concern and to be informed of the different views held by others. This is ... the independent and overriding principle ... A free and general discussion of public matters is fundamental to a democratic society.[61]

If the defendant is able to rely on the defence of justification, the injunction is likely to be refused.[62] In order for an interlocutory injunction to be granted, the plaintiff should establish 'that a jury's verdict of no libel would be set aside as unreasonable', although this is not an absolute rule.[63]

8.18   In *Australian Broadcasting Corporation v O'Neill* Mr O'Neill had abducted and murdered a nine-year-old boy in Tasmania in February 1975. In May 1975 he confessed to police that he had also killed another nine-year-old boy. After the conviction for the first murder O'Neill was sentenced to life imprisonment and the prosecutors dropped the charges in relation to the second murder. Since 1999 a former Victorian detective, Gordon Davie, had been investigating Mr O'Neill. Mr Davie and Roar Film Pty Ltd produced a documentary titled *The Fisherman*, in which it was alleged that Mr O'Neill was linked with the abduction of more children, including the notorious disappearance of the

---

59.   (2006) 227 CLR 57 at [16]–[18] per Gleeson CJ and Crennan J; at [73] per Gummow and Hayne JJ.

60.   [1891] 2 Ch 269 at 284, Lord Esher MR, Lindley, Bowen and Lopes LJJ concurring.

61.   (1988) 14 NSWLR 153 at 163–4.

62.   (1988) 14 NSWLR at 158 and 160–1 per Hunt J; *Ron West Motors Ltd v Broadcasting Corporation of New Zealand* [1989] 3 NZLR 433 and, on appeal, [1989] 3 NZLR 520.

63.   *Chappell v TCN Channel Nine Pty Ltd* (1988) 14 NSWLR 153 at 163 per Hunt J.

three Beaumont children, aged nine, seven and four, from Glenelg beach in Adelaide on Australia Day 1966. These allegations were reported in the Tasmanian media and there was intense political attention following the January 2005 screening of the documentary at the Hobart Summer Film Festival. It was also due to be broadcast on ABC Television on 28 April 2005. But on 15 April 2005, Mr O'Neill sued the ABC, Mr Davie and Roar Film for defamation, including a claim for damages. He also applied for a *quia timet* interlocutory injunction restraining the ABC from televising the documentary. There were no current or contemplated criminal proceedings against Mr O'Neill nor was there any 'intention on the part of any prosecuting authority to charge the respondent with offences in relation to the Beaumont children, or any other children'.[64] Mr O'Neill claimed that this made his position all the worse because he would 'face trial by media, with all the unfairness and injustice that entails'.[65]

At the interlocutory hearing the ABC conceded that *The Fisherman* conveyed the imputations that Mr O'Neill was a multiple killer of children and that he was a suspect in the disappearance and murder of the Beaumont children. As the alleged defamatory matter was published prior to the uniform defamation law, truth alone was not a defence. But the ABC submitted that the imputations conveyed in the documentary were justified because they were both true and in the public interest. While Crawford J in the Tasmanian Supreme Court found that the ABC could probably establish truth, the interlocutory injunction was, nonetheless, granted because it could not establish that the publication was also in the public interest. This was upheld by a majority on appeal to the Full Court. But the ABC's further appeal to the High Court was successful, the injunction was quashed by a 4:2 majority and the program was eventually televised in October 2006.

In a joint judgment Gleeson CJ and Crennan J in the majority said that a foremost consideration in the defamation context is the public interest in free speech. Further, where justification is an issue this is a matter for the jury and 'the plaintiff's general character may be found to be such that, even if the publication is defamatory, only nominal damages will be awarded'.[66] Their Honours held that the publication of the material was in the public interest:

> The unsolved mystery of the disappearance of the Beaumont children, the presence within the Tasmanian prison system of a convicted murderer who is suspected of responsibility, the respondent's confession to another murder with which he has never been charged, and the political controversies concerning release on licence or parole of serious offenders are all matters of public interest in the relevant sense. It would have been open to a tribunal of fact to find that the public discussion of those matters, with particular reference to the respondent, is for the public benefit. What might be thought

---

64.   (2006) 227 CLR 57 at [8] per Gleeson CJ and Crennan J.
65.   (2006) 227 CLR 57 at [8] per Gleeson CJ and Crennan J.
66.   (2006) 227 CLR 57 at [19].

to stand in need of explanation is how suppression of public discussion of those matters could serve the public interest.[67]

Gleeson CJ and Crennan J were critical of the primary judge and the majority in the Full Court that had decided in favour of the interlocutory injunction:

> It is difficult to resist the conclusion that, in their natural and proper concern for fairness to the respondent, the judges who decided the case in [Mr O'Neill's] favour have fallen into the error of treating the criminal trial process as the only proper context in which matters of the kind presently in question may be ventilated. More fundamentally, however, it is apparent that they failed to take proper account of the public interest in free communication of information and opinion, which is basic to the caution with which courts have approached the topic of prior restraint of allegedly defamatory matter.
>
> … It is one thing for the law to impose consequences, civil or criminal, in the case of an abuse of the right of free speech. It is another matter for a court to interfere with the right of free speech by prior restraint. In working out the consequences of abuse of such freedom, the law strikes a balance between competing interests, which include an individual's interest in his or her reputation. When, however, a court is asked to intervene in advance of publication wider considerations are involved. This is the main reason for the "exceptional caution" with which the power to grant an interlocutory injunction in a case of defamation is approached.[68]

In the minority Kirby and Heydon JJ wrote separate judgments dismissing the ABC's appeal. Heydon J observed:

> In truth, only one proposition of any importance flows from the appeal. That is that as a practical matter no plaintiff is ever likely to succeed in an application against a mass media defendant for an interlocutory injunction to restrain publication of defamatory material on a matter of public interest, however strong that plaintiff's case, however feeble the defences, and however damaging the defamation.[69]

Despite this conclusion, plaintiffs in England have been successful in obtaining interlocutory injunctions against mass media defendants if the publication also breaches privacy and an equitable obligation of confidence: see **8.68–8.72**.

Malicious falsehood

8.19 In *Swimsure (Laboratories) Pty Ltd v McDonald*[70] Hunt J granted an application to continue an ex parte interlocutory injunction restraining a threatened malicious falsehood. The plaintiff had just launched a pool cleaning product known as *Hydrophane 7*. For many years the second defendant had sold a similar product known as *HTH Chlorine*. The first defendant was the

---

67. (2006) 227 CLR 57 at [24].
68. (2006) 227 CLR 57 at [30] and [32].
69. (2006) 227 CLR 57 at [170].
70. [1979] 2 NSWLR 796.

marketing manager for the second defendant. Within a few weeks of the launch of the plaintiff's product he told distributors and retailers that it was not suitable for its purpose, that it had not been passed for sale by the New South Wales Health Commission and that the plaintiff's claims about its safety and effectiveness were completely untrue. The plaintiff was initially granted a short term ex parte injunction restraining the defendants from further publishing such statements. Following the grant of the injunction the defendants were willing, without admissions, to give undertakings in similar terms 'but preserving their right to put material before any regulatory body which may have the effect of the statements in question.'[71] The plaintiff rejected this and applied to the New South Wales Supreme Court to continue the injunction. The plaintiff relied upon both defamation and slander of goods (alternatively referred to as injurious or malicious falsehood or trade libel).

Hunt J would not grant an interlocutory injunction based on defamation as such relief 'must be exercised with great caution, and only in very clear cases'.[72] However, this exceptional test — which helps protect the public interest in free speech as well as the liberty of the press — does not necessarily apply to interlocutory applications for injurious falsehood.[73] While the plaintiff cannot avoid the exception by merely framing a defamation action as injurious falsehood, if the matter consists of disparaging a product it is 'difficult, if not impossible, to see how these concepts of free speech and discussion and the liberty of the press can be involved.'[74] In continuing the injunction Hunt J relied on s 66 of the Supreme Court Act 1970 (NSW), which allows the court to grant an injunction in cases of threatened or apprehended injuries. For the purpose of the interlocutory proceedings it was held that where evidence of actual damage is absent (an essential ingredient in injurious falsehood) this is not fatal to the application if malice in the publication is established and 'there is a reasonable probability that actual damage will result to the plaintiff.'[75]

Hunt J's reasoning was applied by White J in *Kaplan v Go Daddy Group*.[76] In that case, the second defendant, Mr English left his car to be serviced by Hunter Holden at St Leonards, Sydney. The car was stolen from the premises and Hunter Holden put the matter in the hands of its insurers and arranged a replacement car. The insurers tried to settle the matter, without admissions, by offering to pay the indemnity value of the car. Mr English rejected this and while the dispute remained unresolved, on 6 June he established a blog website hunterholdensucks.com. This invited anyone to 'Share your comments about Hunter Holden Automotive here'. On 9 June, between 1.49am and 2.07am, six postings were made under various headings including "Car Stolen", "Fraud"

71.   [1979] 2 NSWLR 796 at 799.

72.   [1979] 2 NSWLR 796 at 799.

73.   [1979] 2 NSWLR 796 at 800.

74.   [1979] 2 NSWLR 796 at 801; see also *Australian Broadcasting Corporation v O'Neill* (2006) 227 CLR 57 at [56] per Gummow and Hayne JJ.

75.   [1979] 2 NSWLR 796 at 802.

76.   [2005] NSWSC 636.

and "Overcharging". The director of Hunter Holden discovered the website on 17 June. On the same day he applied for and was granted an ex parte injunction on the basis that Mr English had committed and was threatening to commit the tort of injurious falsehood. At the inter parte hearing an injunction was granted restraining Mr English from maintaining the domain name hunterholdensucks.com, 'or establishing or maintaining an internet website of the same or similar name, and from publishing false statements of or concerning'[77] Hunter Holden. Following *Swimsure*, the injunction was granted despite the fact that no 'special damage' had been demonstrated.[78]

Hunt J's reasoning in *Swimsure* was also applied by Harrison J in *Beechwood Homes (NSW) Pty Ltd v Camenzuli*.[79] An interlocutory injunction was granted restraining the defendant from publishing on his website material about the plaintiff that was misleading and constituted malicious falsehood. His Honour rejected the defendant's argument that the plaintiff's true action was 'one in defamation effectively in the guise of injurious falsehood'.[80] This was because the defendant's statements were 'directed to the products and services provided by the plaintiff and to its methods of doing business'.[81] Following *Swimsure*, there was 'a reasonable probability that actual damage will result to the plaintiff from the continued publication of the statements in question.'[82]

The *Swimsure*, *Kaplan* and *Beechwood* cases are illustrations of Kirby J's observation (in the minority) in *Australian Broadcasting Corporation v O'Neill*:

> Whilst free speech and the free press are important values in Australian law, they must find their expression and operation in a way that is harmonious with other legal values, including the protection of reputation, individual honour, privacy and the fair trial of legal proceedings.[83]

Negligence

8.20 There is no reported case where an injunction has been granted to restrain negligent conduct.[84] In New South Wales it is clear that such injunctions can be granted[85] under s 66 of the Supreme Court Act 1970 (NSW), because it empowers the court to restrain the commission of any tort. Thus, like injurious falsehood, even if damage is the gist of the action and no damage is actually proven, the injunction may be granted.

---

77. [2005] NSWSC 636 at [52].
78. [2005] NSWSC 636 at [27].
79. [2010] NSWSC 521.
80. [2010] NSWSC 521 at [12].
81. [2010] NSWSC 521 at [15].
82. [2010] NSWSC 521 at [52].
83. (2006) 227 CLR 57 at [112].
84. See the observations of Lord Denning in *Miller v Jackson* [1977] 1 QB 966 at 980 (CA) and Gillard J in *Champagne View Pty Ltd v Shearwater Resort Management Pty Ltd* [2000] VSC 214 at [60].
85. R P Meagher, J D Heydon and M J Leeming, *Meagher, Gummow and Lehane's Equity: Doctrines and Remedies*, 4th ed, LexisNexis Butterworths, Sydney, 2002, [21–105].

Nuisance

8.21   An injunction will lie to restrain a threatened or a continued nuisance[86] such as a nuisance caused by noise,[87] flooding,[88] vibration[89] and smell.[90] In *Kennaway v Thompson*[91] an injunction was granted restraining the use of speed boats on a lake beside the plaintiff's property. An injunction will also be issued to restrain nuisances caused by the entry of golf balls on to the plaintiff's land.[92] In *Miller v Jackson*,[93] however, a majority in the Court of Appeal refused an injunction to restrain the playing of cricket on a field beside the plaintiff's property.

Passing off

8.22   An injunction will lie to restrain the tort of passing off. A historical oddity is that injunctions have been granted to restrain a passing off even though the common law action would fail because of an absence of fraud.[94] This raises the question of whether, in granting an injunction to restrain an innocent passing off, equity is acting in its exclusive jurisdiction rather than in its auxiliary jurisdiction. The better view is that it is acting in its auxiliary jurisdiction[95] because, in granting the injunction, the court effectively gives the defendant notice of the plaintiff's rights or confirms the plaintiff's earlier warning; thus, if the defendant ignores the notice, this will amount to fraudulent passing off: see **2.78**.

Conversion, detinue and trespass

8.23   In accordance with general principles an injunction will lie to restrain these torts if the common law remedy, usually damages, will be inadequate. While in most cases common law damages will be an adequate remedy, (see **8.30**) in *Burton v Spragg* an ex parte interlocutory injunction was granted restraining further excavation of land adjoining the plaintiff's boundary as well as subterranean intrusions into the plaintiff's land.[96] There was an imminent

---

86.   R P Meagher, J D Heydon and M J Leeming, *Meagher, Gummow and Lehane's Equity: Doctrines and Remedies*, 4th ed, LexisNexis Butterworths, Sydney, 2002, [21-085].

87.   *Vincent v Peacock* [1973] 1 NSWLR 466 at 468; *Cohen v City of Perth* [2000] WASC 306 (the noise emitted by garbage trucks).

88.   *Bonucci v Ku-ring-gai Municipal Council* [2001] NSWSC 1190; compare *Bankstown City Council v Alamdo Holdings Pty Ltd* (2005) 223 CLR 660 where the council had statutory immunity from liability in relation to flooding.

89.   *Shelfer v City of London Electric Lighting Co* [1895] 1 Ch 287.

90.   *Halsey v Esso Petroleum Co Ltd* [1961] 2 All ER 145.

91.   [1981] 1 QB 88 (CA).

92.   *Champagne View Pty Ltd v Shearwater Resort Management Pty Ltd* [2000] VSC 214.

93.   [1977] 1 QB 966; [1977] 3 All ER 338 (CA).

94.   See *Conagra Inc v McCain Foods (Aust) Pty Ltd* (1992) 106 ALR 465 at 506-7 per Lockhart J, at 519-21 per Gummow J (FC of the Fed C of A).

95.   *Conagra Inc v McCain Foods (Aust) Pty Ltd* (1992) 106 ALR 465 at 521 per Gummow J (FC of the Fed C of A).

96.   [2007] WASC 247.

threat of the plaintiff's house collapsing. It was found that there was a prima facie case that the defendant's actions constituted trespass and an infringement of the plaintiff's common law right to support. An interlocutory mandatory injunction[97] was also granted requiring the defendant to restore support to the plaintiff's land.

Assault

8.24   An injunction will lie to restrain a threatened assault.[98] But, apart from New South Wales where there is a statutory power to award an injunction to restrain the commission of any tort,[99] including an assault,[100] such an injunction will only be granted in 'exceptional circumstances'.[101]

Inducing a breach of contract and interference with contract

8.25   An injunction will lie to restrain the economic tort of inducing a breach of contract, but only if the breach is incomplete.[102] An injunction will also lie to restrain the separate tort of interference with contractual relations.[103] As explained by the High Court in *Zhu v Treasurer of the State of New South Wales*:

> In days when lawyers insisted more commonly than they do now that, negative covenants apart, injunctions could not be granted in the auxiliary jurisdiction of equity unless in aid of a proprietary right, it was common for injunctions, interlocutory and final, to be granted against interferences with contract. Thus in *Woolley v Dunford*[104] Wells J said that an injunction was available not only to protect "proprietary rights or rights in possession, [stricto] sensu", but also to protect "rights created by a concluded contract" which were being tortiously interfered with.[105]

Contract

8.26   An injunction may lie to restrain a breach of contract. Historically this was subject to the rule in *Doherty v Allman* that if the term to be enforced was

---

97.   See **8.67**.

98.   *Egan v Egan* [1975] 1 Ch 218; see also *Daley v Martin* [1982] Qd R 2.

99.   Supreme Court Act 1970 (NSW) s 66.

100.   *Corvisy v Corvisy* [1982] 2 NSWLR 557.

101.   *Parry v Crooks* (1981) 27 SASR 1 at 9 per King CJ (FC).

102.   *Delphic Wholesalers Pty Ltd v Elco Food Co Pty Ltd* (1987) 8 IPR 545 at 554 per McGarvie J (SC(Vic)), citing in support *Williams v Hursey* (1959) 103 CLR 30 at 77; compare *Warren v Mendy* [1989] 3 All ER 103 (CA) and *Australian Liquor, Hospitality & Miscellaneous Workers Union v Liquorland (Aust) Pty Ltd* [2002] FCA 528.

103.   See *Jaddcal Pty Ltd v Minson* [2011] WASC 28 where it was accepted that an injunction is available to restrain a tortious interference with contractual relations but was rejected due to a lack of evidence and delay.

104.   (1972) 3 SASR 243 at 297.

105.   (2004) 211 ALR 159; [2004] HCA 56 at [129] and see [158]. The leading English case on these economic torts is the House of Lords decision in *OBG Ltd v Allan; Douglas v Hello! Ltd; Mainstream Properties Ltd v Young* [2008] 1 AC 1.

negative in substance rather than positive [106] then the court has no discretion to exercise. In that case, Lord Cairns LC said that:

> ... if there had been a negative covenant, I apprehend, according to well-settled practice, a Court of Equity would have had no discretion to exercise. If parties, for valuable consideration, with their eyes open, contract that a particular thing shall not be done, all that a Court of Equity has to do is say, by way of injunction, that which the parties have already said by way of covenant, that the thing shall not be done; and in such case the injunction does nothing more than give the sanction of the process of the court to that which already is the contract between the parties. It is not then a question of the balance of convenience or inconvenience, or of the amount of damage or injury — it is the specific performance, by the court, of that negative bargain which the parties have made, with their eyes open, between themselves.[107]

This absolute approach has been criticised as an 'overstatement'[108] and has not been followed on three grounds. First, proof of a negative stipulation will not relieve the plaintiff of the need to prove that damages are an inadequate remedy (see 8.32–8.33); second, proof of a negative stipulation will not divest the court of its discretion;[109] and, third, the distinction between positive and negative stipulations is awkward because all obligations may be expressed in both positive and negative form.[110] For example, an agreement to supply goods or services may be expressed as an agreement not to prevent the supply of those goods or services. These last two criticisms were raised by Mason J in *Dalgety Wine Estates Pty Ltd v Rizzon*:

> There has been general agreement that Lord Cairns' statement that a court of equity has no discretion to refuse an injunction restraining a breach of a negative covenant is not accurate. In *Doherty v Allman*[111] itself Lord Blackburn, who ... was inclined to repudiate the notion that a distinction should be made between negative and affirmative words, considered that there were cases in which a court of equity would refuse to enforce a negative covenant on discretionary grounds.[112]

His Honour concluded that it was 'impossible to formulate an illuminating statement of principle which is capable of universal application' because the attitude of the courts to enforcing negative contractual terms varies with the nature of the term, the nature of the contract, the effect of the injunction on the parties and the character of the order required to enforce the term.[113]

---

106. See *Atlas Steels (Aust) v Atlas Steels Ltd* (1948) 49 SR (NSW) 157; *Ampol Petroleum Ltd v Mutton* (1952) 53 SR (NSW) 1 at 9–10 per McLelland J; *Administrative and Clerical Officers' Association v Commonwealth* (1979) 26 ALR 497.

107. (1878) 3 App Cas 709 at 719–20.

108. *Dalgety Wine Estates Pty Ltd v Rizzon* (1979) 141 CLR 552 at 560 per Gibbs J; *Cardile v LED Builders Pty Ltd* (1999) 198 CLR 380 at [30] per Gaudron, McHugh, Gummow and Callinan JJ; *Orleans Investments Pty Ltd v MindShare Communications Ltd* (2009) 254 ALR 81 at 107 per Giles JA.

109. See *Curro v Beyond Productions Pty Ltd* (1993) 30 NSWLR 337 at 346–7 per Meagher JA (CA).

110. *Whitwood Chemical Co v Hardman* [1891] 2 Ch 416 at 426 per Lindley LJ.

111. (1878) 3 App Cas 709 at 729–32.

112. (1979) 141 CLR 552 at 573.

113. (1979) 141 CLR 552 at 573–4.

Dalgety was cited with approval by the High Court in *Cardile v LED Builders Pty Ltd* where Gaudron, McHugh, Gummow and Callinan JJ observed:

> … the view once taken that an injunction should issue to restrain breach of a negative stipulation, without weighing the usual discretionary considerations, has been discounted as an overstatement.[114]

8.27   Despite Mason J's refusal to formulate a 'universal principle' in *Dalgety*, he declined to enforce a stipulation which he characterised as positive in substance in *Administrative and Clerical Officers' Association v Commonwealth*.[115] In that case, the Commonwealth agreed with two trade unions, one being the Administrative and Clerical Officers' Association (ACOA), to deduct union dues from the employees' salaries. The Commonwealth initially agreed to deduct the money and pay the union dues to ACOA. The Commonwealth threatened to stop this practice and ACOA sought an injunction to restrain the Commonwealth from ceasing to deduct the dues and pay them over to ACOA. The union argued that the only way the Commonwealth could do this was if the contract was properly terminated, otherwise it would be in breach of contract. Mason J refused the injunction on the ground that ACOA was really trying to enforce a positive covenant. His Honour said:

> … in substance the injunction claimed is to enforce an affirmative stipulation. The stipulation is not negative in substance because mere inactivity on the part of the Commonwealth would not constitute performance, performance requires deduction and payment to the plaintiffs.[116]

Finally, there are ways of avoiding the rule against enforcement of positive stipulations. First, a positive stipulation in an executed contract may be enforced by specific performance: see Chapter 7. Second, a mandatory injunction may be available, although the court is reluctant to order this if specific performance is not available: see 8.67.

Conspiracy

8.28   In *Patrick Stevedores Operations No 2 Pty Ltd v Maritime Union of Australia (No 3)* Brennan CJ, McHugh, Gummow, Kirby and Hayne JJ held:

> A court whose jurisdiction is invoked in a conspiracy case has power to grant an injunction to prevent the completion or effecting of the conspiracy … Where the acts contemplated by the conspirators have all occurred and the tort is complete, the remedy available to an injured plaintiff is ordinarily limited to the recovery of pecuniary damages … But for over a century it has been established that "there is no rule which prevents the court from granting a mandatory injunction[117] where the injury sought to be restrained has been completed before the commencement of the action" … Where the damage caused by tortious conduct is ongoing and is "extreme, or at all events

---

114. (1999) 198 CLR 380 at [30]; see also *Lucas Stuart Pty Ltd v Hemmes Hermitage Pty Ltd* [2010] NSWCA 283 at [5]-[8] per Campbell JA.
115. (1979) 53 *ALJR* 588.
116. (1979) 53 ALJR 588 at 590.
117. Mandatory injunctions are considered at 8.63–8.67.

very serious", a mandatory injunction may issue compelling the wrongdoer to prevent the occurrence of further damage …[118]

Restraining breaches of statute

8.29   Injunctions may lie to enforce or prevent breaches of statutory provisions, but this is subject to the wording in the statute and it may also be affected by a consideration of whether the right is public or private in nature. Some statutes, such as the Copyright Act 1968 (Cth), the Patents Act 1990 (Cth), the Trade Marks Act 1995 (Cth), the Designs Act 2003 (Cth), the Circuit Layouts Act 1989 (Cth) and the Plant Breeder's Rights Act 1994 (Cth), confer express statutory power on prescribed courts to grant an injunction where there is a contravention or infringement of a private or proprietary right granted under the Act. In *Australian Broadcasting Corporation v Lenah Game Meats Pty Ltd* Gummow and Hayne JJ said:

> Where interlocutory injunctive relief is sought in some special statutory jurisdiction which uses the term "injunction" to identify a remedy for which it provides, that term takes its colour from the statutory regime in question …[119]

As a matter of practice, if the statutory regime does not provide 'a complete code of remedies' and there is no express or implied exclusion, the courts will apply the equitable principles.[120]

If the right granted under the statute is a public right, then ordinarily the proper plaintiff is either the Attorney-General or a relator with the approval of the Attorney-General. An individual may commence an action for an injunction protecting a public right subject to the rule in *Boyce v Paddington Borough Council*.[121] By contrast, the public rights conferred under the Australian Consumer Law contained in Sch 2 of the Competition and Consumer Act 2010 (Cth) may be enforced under s 80 by either the Australian Competition and Consumer Commission 'or any other person': see 16.37–16.38.

Equity is not the 'handmaid of the criminal law'[122] and is reluctant to grant an injunction to restrain criminal conduct. But in exceptional cases 'a court of equity may assist … if the likely future conduct at issue is also an infraction against a public right as well as an offence.'[123] Equity may also assist

---

118.   (1998) 195 CLR 1 at [33] (omitting citations).
119.   (2001) 208 CLR 199 at 240 citing *Cardile v LED Builders Pty Ltd* (1999) 198 CLR 380 at 394 per Gaudron, McHugh, Gummow and Callinan JJ.
120.   See *Ramsay v Aberfoyle Manufacturing Co (Aust) Pty Ltd* (1935) 54 CLR 230 at 240–1 per Latham CJ.
121.   [1903] 1 Ch 109; *Bateman's Bay Local Aboriginal Land Council v Aboriginal Community Benefit Fund Pty Ltd* (1998) 194 CLR 247. The rule is discussed at 13.5–13.9.
122.   *Ramsay v Aberfoyle Manufacturing Co (Aust) Pty Ltd* (1935) 54 CLR 230 at 260 per McTiernan J.
123.   *City of Stirling v Duesbury* [2011] WASC 126 at [21] per Kenneth Martin J.

to restrain those who flout the law, to protect public safety[124] or if there is an emergency.[125]

Inadequacy of damages

8.30 The second element in deciding whether an injunction should be granted in the auxiliary jurisdiction is governed by the general principle that if the common law remedies (usually damages) are inadequate, the injunction will be allowed. In *Irving v Emu & Prospect Gravel & Road Metal Co Ltd* Street J observed:

> It is true that in a proper case the court will interfere by injunction to restrain a wrong, but this does not mean that every action in tort can be turned into a suit in equity at the option of the plaintiff by asking for an injunction. "The very first principle of injunction law", says Lindley LJ in *London & Blackwall Railway Co v Cross*,[126] "is that prima facie you do not obtain injunctions to restrain actionable wrongs for which damages are the proper remedy". The equitable remedy by injunction in cases of actionable wrongs was designed to meet the case where there was either no remedy at all at law, or such remedy as there was, was inadequate.[127]

By contrast, in *Evans Marshall & Co Ltd v Bertola SA*, Sachs LJ observed:

> The standard question in relation to the grant of an injunction: "Are damages an adequate remedy?", might perhaps, in light of the authorities of recent years, be rewritten: "Is it just, in all the circumstances, that the plaintiff should be confined to his remedy in damages?"[128]

8.31 One way of proving the inadequacy of damages at law is to show that the defendant's wrong or threatened wrong will cause irreparable harm or injury to the plaintiff, or a third person (see **7.21–7.22**), in the sense that it cannot be reversed by an award of damages. So an injunction will not ordinarily lie to restrain a trespass to or conversion of goods because damages will allow the plaintiff to readily purchase substitutes.[129] Damages may be inadequate and the injury irreparable, however, if the goods have a peculiar value to the plaintiff.[130] Damages will also be inadequate where the defendant is impecunious[131] or where the plaintiff has to commence multiple proceedings in order to obtain complete compensation.[132] In passing off cases,

---

124. *Australian Securities and Investments Commission v HLP Financial Planning (Aust) Pty Ltd* (2007) 164 FCR 487 at [20] Finkelstein J.
125. *Gouriet v Union of Post Office Workers* [1978] AC 435 at 481 per Lord Wilberforce; *Commonwealth v John Fairfax & Sons Ltd* (1980) 147 CLR 39 at 49–50 per Mason J.
126. (1886) 31 Ch D 354 at 369.
127. (1909) 26 WN (NSW) 137 at 137.
128. [1973] 1 All ER 992 at 1005.
129. *Cook v Rodgers* (1946) 46 SR (NSW) 229.
130. *Aristoc Industries Pty Ltd v Wenhman (Builders) Pty Ltd* [1965] NSWR 581 at 588 per Jacobs J; and see *Doulton Potteries Ltd v Bronotte* [1971] 1 NSWLR 591 at 597–9 per Hope J.
131. See, for example, *Franklin International Export Ltd v Wattie Exports Ltd* (1988) 12 IPR 358 at 364–5 per Tompkins J (HC(NZ)).
132. Compare *Gedbury Pty Ltd v Michael David Kennedy Autos* [1986] 1 Qd R 103 at 104 per Thomas J.

it is 'rare for damages to be an adequate remedy' because of the need to prove fraud at common law,[133] and because of the difficulties in assessing the loss of distinctiveness in the relevant indicia.[134]

Contract

8.32 In contract cases the issue of inadequacy of damages in relation to the grant of an injunction is often distorted by the rule in *Doherty v Allman*.[135] The effect of the decision in that case is that a court will enforce negative stipulations irrespective of the issue of whether damages would be an adequate remedy. So, in *Ampol Petroleum v Mutton*, McLelland J held:

> I am of the opinion that a court of equity can enforce by injunction a stipulation which is negative in both form and in substance, even if the contract as a whole is not the subject matter of equitable jurisdiction and the breach complained of may be properly satisfied by damages. In the present case the covenant is, in my opinion, negative in form and in substance. I find nothing, in the circumstances of this case, on which as a matter of discretion, I ought to refuse the injunction.[136]

However, McLelland J then held that even if he was wrong 'damages would not be a sufficient remedy' because the 'task of estimating the damages which the plaintiff would suffer from the breach by the defendants would be most difficult'.[137]

8.33 The contrary view to that of McLelland J in *Ampol Petroleum v Mutton* was expressed by Long Innes J in *Wood v Corrigan*:

> ... even an express negative stipulation will not, or should not, found an injunction to restrain a breach of contract, if the contract as a whole is not the subject matter of equitable jurisdiction, and the breach complained of may be properly satisfied by damages.[138]

This view was expressly endorsed in *JC Williamson Ltd v Lukey and Mulholland* by Evatt J who added:

> In an injunction suit it is not sufficient to prove that a contract involves a substantial negative, where damages would be a complete remedy for the threatened breach and where the contract is of such a nature that it cannot be specifically enforced. This seems to be the principle which is gradually being evolved, and the result seems both just and convenient.[139]

---

133. *Totara Vineyards v Villa Maria* (1986) 8 IPR 51 at 55 per Henry J (HC(NZ)).

134. *Totara Vineyards v Villa Maria* (1986) 8 IPR 51 at 55 per Henry J (HC(NZ)); *Taittinger v Allbev Ltd* (1993) 27 IPR 105 (CA); *Sodastream v Thorn Cascade* [1982] RPC 459 at 471 (CA).

135. (1878) 3 App Cas 709; see 8.26 8.28.

136. (1952) 53 SR (NSW) 1 at 13.

137. (1952) 53 SR (NSW) 1 at 13.

138. (1928) 28 SR (NSW) 492 at 500. See also *Dalgety Wine Estates Pty Ltd v Rizzon* (1979) 141 CLR 552 at 560 per Gibbs J, with whom Barwick CJ agreed at 555; and see 573–4 per Mason J; *Lucas Stuart Pty Ltd v Hemmes Hermitage Pty Ltd* [2010] NSWCA 283 at [5]–[8] per Campbell JA.

139. (1931) 45 CLR 282 at 308.

And in *Curro v Beyond Productions Pty Ltd*,[140] discussed at **8.41**, the New South Wales Court of Appeal restrained a threatened breach of a negative stipulation in a personal service contract, one of the grounds being that damages would have been an inadequate remedy.[141] Arguably in that case, however, the issue was treated as a discretionary matter: see **8.41**.

Court's discretion

8.34   The court must be satisfied that in its discretion the plaintiff is entitled to the injunction. There are many matters which affect this exercise, including the discretionary defences: 'unclean hands', laches, delay and acquiescence. In contract cases, many of the matters which determine the availability of specific performance are also relevant: see **7.34–7.44** and **8.33–8.44**.

Unclean hands

8.35   It is an equitable maxim that someone who comes to equity must have clean hands. It applies to all equitable remedies and 'requires the Court to look at the conduct of the litigant who seeks the assistance of equity, rather than the conduct of the defendant'.[142] So, in *Kettles and Gas Appliances Ltd v Anthony Hordern & Sons Ltd*,[143] Long Innes J refused an injunction where the defendant had innocently passed off its kettles as those of the plaintiff because the latter had, inter alia, misrepresented to the public that its kettles were protected by a patent. Although the plaintiff in *Kettles and Gas Appliances* offered an undertaking to consent to any condition that the court might impose on the future use of the word 'patent', this did not mean that it 'had effectively washed its hands before it came into court'.[144] On this point Long Innes J distinguished *Benedictus v Sullivan, Powell & Co Ltd*,[145] *Mrs Pomeroy Ltd v Scale*[146] and *J H Coles Pty Ltd v Need*.[147] In *Benedictus* 'the misrepresentations had been discontinued for more than a year' before the suit was brought. In *Mrs Pomeroy* the misrepresentation was accidental, and only for a short period, and an undertaking was given one month before the commencement of proceedings. And with regard to *J H Coles Pty Ltd v Need*, Long Innes J observed:

> … it was held that the plaintiff never had any fraudulent intent; but that even if it had, that would constitute no reason why it should not — for the protection of the public as well as itself — maintain the suit which was in that case the only way in which it could wash its hands.[148]

140.   (1993) 30 NSWLR 337.
141.   (1993) 30 NSWLR 337 at 348.
142.   *Black Uhlans Inc v New South Wales Crime Commission* [2002] NSWSC 1060 at [159] per Campbell J.
143.   (1934) 35 SR (NSW) 108.
144.   (1934) 35 SR (NSW) 108 at 129–31.
145.   (1895) 12 RPC 25.
146.   (1904) 24 RPC 177.
147.   [1934] AC 82; (1933) 50 RPC 379.
148.   (1934) 35 SR (NSW) 108 at 130.

In refusing the injunction in *Kettles and Gas Appliances*, however, Long Innes J made it clear that the defendant's innocent passing off would be restrained in the event that the plaintiff managed to 'wash its hands'.[149] His Honour cautioned the defendant:

> In the result I hold that the plaintiff is disentitled to relief in this suit, but in dismissing this suit I do so without prejudice to any suit which it may be advised to bring hereafter in the event of a repetition of the wrong, and when it has cleansed its hands to the necessary extent.[150]

For the plaintiff to be guilty of 'unclean hands' its conduct must have 'an immediate and necessary relation to the equity suited for'.[151] So, for example, in passing off, a misrepresentation by the plaintiff does not amount to 'unclean hands' if the misrepresentation was innocent *and* the 'general public' suffers 'no harm'.[152] A failure to register a business name has also been held not to constitute 'unclean hands'.[153]

Laches and delay

8.36   The doctrine of laches reflects the maxim: equity aids the vigilant, and not those who sleep on their rights. The onus is on the defendant to show that he or she was prejudiced by laches.[154] In *Lindsay Petroleum Co v Hurd*, Lord Selborne LC explained the operation of laches and delay as follows:

> Now the doctrine of *laches* in Courts of Equity is not an arbitrary or a technical doctrine. Where it would be practically unjust to give a remedy, either because a party has, by his conduct, done that which might fairly be regarded as equivalent to a waiver of it, or where by his conduct and neglect he has, though perhaps not waiving that remedy, yet put the other party in a situation in which it would not be reasonable to place him if the remedy afterwards were to be asserted, in either of these cases, lapse of time and delay are most material. But in every case, if an argument against relief, which otherwise would be just, is founded upon mere delay, that delay of course not amounting to a bar by any statute of limitations, the validity of that defence must be tried upon principles substantially equitable. Two circumstances, always important in such cases, are, the length of the delay and the nature of the acts done during the interval, which might affect either party and cause the balance of justice or injustice in taking the one course or the other, so far as relates to the remedy.[155]

---

149. See also *Cadwallader v Bajco Pty Ltd* [2002] NSWCA 328 at [179]–[180] per Heydon J.

150. (1934) 35 SR (NSW) 108 at 131.

151. *Official Trustee in Bankruptcy v Tooheys Ltd* (1993) 29 NSWLR 641 at 650 per Gleeson CJ (CA); *Kyriakou v Salva* [2000] VSC 318 at [33]–[35] per Balmford J; *Argyll v Argyll* [1967] Ch 302 at 332 per Ungoed-Thomas J.

152. *Angelides v James Stedman Hendersons Sweets Ltd* (1927) 40 CLR 43 at 78 per Higgins J.

153. See *The Entrance Red Bus Service Pty Ltd v Transpax Pty Ltd* (SC (NSW), Young J, 24 February 1994, unreported). Further examples are provided in *Black Uhlans Inc v New South Wales Crime Commission* [2002] NSWSC 1060 at [157]–[185] per Campbell J.

154. *Lindsay Petroleum Co v Hurd* (1874) LR 5 PC 221.

155. (1874) LR 5 PC 221 at 239–40.

This passage was cited with approval by the High Court in *Turner v General Motors (Australia) Pty Ltd*[156] and *Orr v Ford* where Deane J (in dissent) held:

> The ultimate test effectively remains that enunciated by Lord Selborne LC … in *Lindsay Petroleum Co v Hurd*, namely, whether the plaintiff has, by his inaction and standing by, placed the defendant or a third party in a situation in which it would be inequitable and unreasonable "to place him if the remedy were afterwards to be asserted".[157]

Acquiescence

8.37 There is an obvious overlap between acquiescence and laches. Classic acquiescence is where the plaintiff knowingly accepts an infringement of his or her rights. But, as explained by Deane J in *Orr v Ford*, it may also refer:

(i) to a representation by silence of a type which may found an estoppel by conduct …; or

(ii) to acceptance of a past wrongful act in circumstances which give rise to an active waiver of rights or a release of liability …; or

(iii) to an election to abandon or not enforce rights.[158]

Discretionary matters in contract cases

8.38 The discretionary factors discussed in the previous chapter affecting the award of specific performance — including mutuality,[159] hardship and futility — are all relevant in considering whether the court will grant an injunction to restrain a breach of contract. Traditionally, the court would be reluctant to order either specific performance or an injunction if the court's constant supervision was required. But this is no longer an absolute restriction but a question of degree.[160]

Likewise, the courts have been reluctant to compel the performance of a contract for personal services and employment contracts. So, in *Warren v Mendy*[161] and *Page One Records v Britton*[162] injunctions were refused which would have compelled performance of personal service contracts involving obligations of mutual trust and confidence of a fiduciary nature over several years. But this too is not an absolute restriction. In *Lumley v Wagner*,[163] *Warner Bros Inc v Nelson*,[164] *Curro v Beyond Productions Pty Ltd*[165] and *Seven Network (Operations) Ltd v Warburton (No 2)*[166] the court granted short-term injunctions

---

156. (1929) 42 CLR 352 at 366 per Isaacs J; and see Dixon J at 369–70.
157. (1989) 167 CLR 316 at 341 (citation omitted).
158. (1989) 167 CLR 316 at 337.
159. See *Curro v Beyond Productions Pty Ltd* (1993) 30 NSWLR 337 at 348 (CA).
160. *Patrick Stevedores Operations No 2 Pty Ltd v Maritime Union of Australia* (1998) 195 CLR 1; and see **7.42**.
161. [1989] 3 All ER 103 (CA).
162. [1967] 3 All ER 822.
163. (1852) 1 De G M & G 604; 42 ER 687.
164. [1937] 1 KB 209.
165. (1993) 30 NSWLR 337 (CA).
166. [2011] NSWSC 386.

of less than 12 months restraining breaches of negative, restraint of trade stipulations in personal 'special service' contracts. These decisions recognise, however, that such orders do not, in effect, compel specific performance of the contract.[167] But, in an employment contract case, *Hill v C A Parsons & Co Ltd*,[168] a majority in the English Court of Appeal went further by granting an injunction restraining the implementation of a notice of termination, even though the effect was to indirectly compel specific performance of a personal services contract which still had two years to run. These cases are discussed further below.

8.39 In *Lumley v Wagner*[169] the plaintiff sought an injunction restraining the famous German opera singer, Wagner, from singing at Covent Garden, because this was in breach of her three-month contract to sing at Her Majesty's Theatre, London. The contract provided that Wagner would not use her talents at any other theatre during the three months without the permission of the plaintiff theatre. Lord St Leonards LC said he was prepared to grant the injunction to restrain her from singing elsewhere because this was a breach of a negative stipulation. But the court would not grant an order akin to specific performance; that is, the court would not order her to sing. *Lumley v Wagner* was expressly approved and applied in *Warner Bros Inc v Nelson*[170] and *Curro v Beyond Productions Pty Ltd*,[171] both of which are discussed below.

8.40 In *Warner Bros Inc v Nelson*[172] the film star Bette Davis agreed with the plaintiff that during the currency of the contract she would not work for another studio. She threatened to breach this stipulation. The plaintiff sought an injunction similar to the one in *Lumley v Wagner*. Counsel for Bette Davis argued that the grant of the injunction would compel her to perform a personal service contract because what she could earn as an actor would far exceed what she would earn in other pursuits and, therefore, she would have to perform the contract rather than go out and clean the streets. Branson J rejected the argument and, in granting the injunction, he followed *Lumley v Wagner*. His Honour's view was that the injunction would not in effect compel specific performance of a contract for personal services. In any event, this was not the test to be applied and, even if it was, Bette Davis would not be driven to perform the contract, although the money she was being offered may have tempted her.[173]

8.41 In *Curro v Beyond Productions Pty Ltd*[174] Curro agreed with the respondent (Beyond) to present and host the television documentary program 'Beyond

167. See, for example, *Curro v Beyond Productions Pty Ltd* (1993) 30 NSWLR 337 at 348 (CA).

168. [1972] Ch 305; [1971] 3 All ER 1345.

169. (1852) 1 De G M & G 604; 42 ER 687.

170. [1937] 1 KB 209.

171. (1993) 30 NSWLR 337 (CA).

172. [1937] 1 KB 209.

173. [1937] 1 KB 209 at 219.

174. (1993) 30 NSWLR 337 (CA).

2000' and 'not to enter into any agreement or carry on any activity which might reasonably be expected to prevent her from rendering to Beyond her services under this agreement'. About six months before the contract was due to expire (although there was an option for further renewal), Curro advised Beyond that she wished to accept an offer from a rival television network to work for a program known as '60 Minutes'. Shortly thereafter, she formally accepted the rival offer. Beyond sought and was granted a *Lumley v Wagner* injunction by Cole J restraining Curro from breaching her agreement with Beyond. In an expedited appeal the injunction was upheld by Meagher, Handley and Cripps JJA, who were of the view:

> ... that the authorities establish that in a *Lumley v Wagner* case, an injunction will still be granted when the balance of discretionary factors is in the plaintiff's favour. In the present case, to grant the injunction sought is not to order specific performance of the service and services contracts. Miss Curro could comply with the injunctions without resuming work for Beyond. She would not be forced to choose between service with Beyond or idleness. Other employments would be open to her. There is no question of her being destitute. Damages would not be an adequate remedy. The final injunctions granted by Cole J only continue until 11 August, a relatively short period. Her breach of contract was flagrant and opportunistic. She sought to justify her behaviour by giving evidence which the judge found was untrue and ... deliberately misleading. The injunctions do no more than oblige Miss Curro to comply with negative promises which are part of a fair and freely negotiated bargain made less than two years ago. We see no reason at all why she should not be ordered to keep her word.[175]

Earlier in the judgment, the Court of Appeal accepted that the *Lumley v Wagner* doctrine applied to contracts for 'special services' which included 'opera singers', 'movie stars', 'actresses', 'rock singers', 'football players' and 'newspaper production managers'.[176] The categories are not closed;[177] and now, of course, it applies to television presenters.[178] The court was untroubled by the fact that 'no satisfactory definition of "special services" could be formulated' because this was 'also true of many other terms of practical utility, both non-legal (for example, beauty, elegance) and legal (for example, reasonableness, unconscionability)'.[179] The Court of Appeal did accept,[180] however, the exception to *Lumley v Wagner* as formulated in *Page One Records v Britton*[181] and followed in *Warren v Mendy*.[182]

---

175.   (1993) 30 NSWLR 337 at 348.

176.   (1993) 30 NSWLR 337 at 347.

177.   (1993) 30 NSWLR 337 at 347.

178.   Compare *Network Ten Ltd v Fulwood* (1995) 62 IR 43, where an injunction was refused where the presenter's two-year contract had fewer than 25 days to run.

179.   (1993) 30 NSWLR 337 at 347.

180.   (1993) 30 NSWLR 337 at 347–8.

181.   [1967] 3 All ER 822.

182.   [1989] 3 All ER 103 (CA).

In *Seven Network (Operations) Ltd v Warburton (No 2)*[183] an injunction was granted restraining a television executive from taking up employment with a rival television network for 10 months. At the time of accepting the rival's offer, the executive's employment contract had a further 7 months to run and he had agreed in a management equity participation deed to a 12 month post-employment restraint.

8.42 In *Page One Records v Britton* [184] the defendants, a popular music group known as The Troggs, were parties to an exclusive five-year management contract and a three-year publishing contract with the plaintiffs. The Troggs tried to terminate these contracts early. The manager and publisher sought an injunction restraining the group from performing and appointing another manager and publisher. Stamp J refused the injunction and said:

> The present case is clearly distinguished, in principle, from *Lumley v Wagner* … for there the only obligation on the part of the plaintiffs seeking to enforce the negative stipulation was an obligation to pay remuneration and an obligation which clearly could be enforced by the defendants. Here, however, the obligations to the first plaintiff, involving personal services, were obligations of trust and confidence and were obligations which, plainly, could not be enforced at the suit of The Troggs. Here, indeed, so it seems to me, the totality of the obligations between the parties are more a joint venture almost approaching the relationship of partners than anything else, involving mutual confidence and reciprocal obligations on all sides.[185]

The plaintiffs submitted, relying on *Warner Bros Inc v Nelson*, that if the injunction was granted The Troggs would not be driven to perform the personal service contract because they could 'continue as a group on their own or seek other employment of a different nature'.[186] But Stamp J doubted that The Troggs could act as their own managers and noted:

> Indeed, it is the plaintiffs' own case that The Troggs are simple persons, of no business experience, and could not survive without the services of a manager. As a practical matter on the evidence before me, I entertain no doubt that they would be compelled, if the injunction were granted on the terms that the plaintiffs seek, to continue to employ the plaintiffs as their manager, and agent.[187]

8.43 The English Court of Appeal applied *Page One* in *Warren v Mendy*[188] in refusing an injunction which would have compelled a professional boxer to perform a three-year service contract. Nourse LJ distinguished *Lumley*

---

183. [2011] NSWSC 386.

184. [1967] 3 All ER 822.

185. [1967] 3 All ER 822 at 826.

186. [1967] 3 All ER 822 at 827.

187. [1967] 3 All ER 822 at 827.

188. [1989] 3 All ER 103 (CA).

v Wagner and *Warner* by noting that in those cases the personal-service contracts were of a short duration, namely, fewer than 20 weeks.[189]

8.44 In *Hill v CA Parsons & Co Ltd*[190] the defendant engineering company agreed in May 1970 with a trade union, the Draftsmen and Allied Technicians' Association (DATA), that after 12 months its technical staff, as a condition of service, should be members of DATA. The plaintiff engineer had been employed by the defendant for many years but was a member of another union. The defendant wrote to the plaintiff in May 1971 giving him one month's notice of the change in his conditions of employment requiring him to join DATA. The plaintiff refused to join. On 30 July 1971 the defendant gave the plaintiff one month's notice of termination. At that time the plaintiff was 63 years old and due to retire in two years. In August 1971 he sought an interlocutory injunction restraining the defendant from implementing the notice. At first instance, Brightman LJ refused relief on the ground that he had no power because the contract was one for personal services. The plaintiff's appeal to the Court of Appeal was successful by a 2:1 majority. Lord Stamp, in dissent, applied the traditional view that the court would not enforce a contract for personal services. Lord Denning MR, Sachs LJ concurring, granted the injunction restraining the defendant from dismissing the plaintiff. Lord Denning was of the view that under the contract the plaintiff was entitled to at least six months' notice. Also, damages were inadequate because the plaintiff's pension depended on his average salary for the last three years and if he had been sacked his entitlement would have been considerably reduced.[191]

INTERLOCUTORY INJUNCTIONS

Introduction

8.45 If the defendant's wrong or threatened wrong will cause irreversible damage then an interlocutory or temporary injunction may lie to preserve the status quo[192] pending the trial. In *American Cyanamid Co v Ethicon Ltd* Lord Diplock observed:

> The object of the interlocutory injunction is to protect the plaintiff against injury by violation of his right for which he could not be adequately compensated in damages recoverable in the action if the uncertainty were resolved in his favour at the trial.[193]

---

189. [1989] 3 All ER 103 at 112. Compare *Curro v Beyond Productions Pty Ltd* (1993) 30 NSWLR 337 (CA), discussed above; *Harrigan v Brown* [1967] 1 NSWR 342; *Evening Standard Co Ltd v Henderson* [1987] ICR 588; *Hawthorn Football Club Ltd v Harding* [1988] VR 49; *Buckenara v Hawthorn Football Club Ltd* [1988] VR 39.

190. [1972] Ch 305; [1971] 3 All ER 1345.

191. See also *Paras v Public Service Body Head of the Department of Infrastructure* [2006] FCA 622 at [38] – [45] per Young J. Compare *Baker v Gough* [1963] NSWR 1345.

192. As to the meaning of 'status quo' in interlocutory injunctions, see *Garden Cottage Foods Ltd v Milk Marketing Board* [1983] 2 All ER 770 at 774–5 per Lord Diplock.

193. [1975] AC 396 at 406.

An incidental but potent effect of the remedy is that it often resolves the dispute by leading to a settlement before the hearing: see 8.53.

8.46 In extremely urgent cases an interlocutory injunction may be granted ex parte. That is usual for Mareva and Anton Piller orders where surprise is critical. Apart from those remedies, the usual course is to apply inter parte with an abridged time for service. However, if the matter is heard ex parte the plaintiff should disclose all material facts relevant to the grant of the injunction.[194] A material non-disclosure by the plaintiff may lead to the dissolution of the injunction, but the court may determine a fresh application on the basis of all relevant facts.[195] An accidental material non-disclosure may be excused in the court's discretion.

Guidelines

8.47 Interlocutory injunctions are available in both mandatory and prohibitory form, and in both the exclusive and auxiliary jurisdictions of equity. The general principles governing injunctions also apply to interlocutory injunctions; that is, the remedy must enforce a recognised legal or an equitable cause of action,[196] it can only be granted in the court's discretion[197] and it 'ought to make clear what it is that the defendant is required to do or not do'.[198] In considering whether to grant an interlocutory injunction, however, the court considers these principles by addressing two main inquiries that were laid down by the High Court in the seminal case *Beecham Group Ltd v Bristol Laboratories*[199] and endorsed in *Australian Broadcasting Corporation v O'Neill*:[200]

> The first is whether the plaintiff has made out a prima facie case, in the sense that if the evidence remains as it is there is a probability that at the trial of the action the plaintiff will be held entitled to relief ... The second inquiry is ... whether the inconvenience or injury which the plaintiff would be likely to suffer if an injunction were refused outweighs or is outweighed by the injury which the defendant would suffer if an injunction were granted.[201]

These two inquiries or guidelines assist the court in the exercise of its discretion but are not to be interpreted as 'rigid formulae'.[202] The guidelines are derived from the fundamental principle 'that the court should take

---

194. *Thomas A Edison Ltd v Bullock* (1913) 15 CLR 679 at 682 per Isaacs J.

195. *Jabuna Pty Ltd v Hartley* (FCA, Beazley J, 18 April 1994, unreported).

196. *Cardile v LED Builders Pty Ltd* (1999) 198 CLR 380 at 395–6; *Australian Broadcasting Corp v Lenah Game Meats Pty Ltd* (2001) 208 CLR 199 at 216, 231–2, 241.

197. Specific discretionary defences are considered at 8.10 and 8.34–8.44.

198. See *Curro v Beyond Productions Pty Ltd* (1993) 30 NSWLR 337 at 348 (CA); *Redland Bricks Ltd v Morris* [1970] AC 652 at 666 (HL).

199. (1968) 118 CLR 618.

200. (2006) 227 CLR 57 at [65] per Gummow and Hayne JJ.

201. (1968) 118 CLR 618 at 622–3 per Kitto, Taylor, Menzies and Owen JJ.

202. *Appleton Papers Inc v Tomasetti Paper Pty Ltd* [1983] 3 NSWLR 208 at 215–16 per McLelland J; see also *Chappell v TCN Channel Nine Pty Ltd* (1988) 14 NSWLR 153 at 160 per Hunt J.

whichever course appears to carry the lower risk of injustice'.[203] Apart from these inquiries it is also essential, as discussed at 8.60, that the plaintiff provide an adequate undertaking as to damages.

Prima facie case

Introduction

8.48 The plaintiff must be able 'to show a sufficient colour of right to final relief to justify the grant of an interlocutory injunction'.[204] In the United Kingdom (and for many years in Australia) the threshold test is to determine whether the plaintiff has a 'serious question to be tried'. This was Lord Diplock's favoured phrase in the patent infringement case, *American Cyanamid Co v Ethicon Ltd*:

> The use of such expressions as "a probability", "a prima facie case", or "a strong prima facie case" in the context of the exercise of a discretionary power to grant an interlocutory injunction leads to confusion as to the object sought to be achieved by this form of temporary relief. The court no doubt must be satisfied that the claim is not frivolous or vexatious; in other words, that there is a serious question to be tried.[205]

However, as discussed below, following the High Court decision in *Australian Broadcasting Corporation v O'Neill*[206] the *Beecham* 'prima facie case' test is the preferred wording in Australia.

8.49 In *Beecham* Kitto, Taylor, Menzies and Owen JJ held that the threshold requirement in interlocutory injunctions is:

> … whether the plaintiff has made out a prima facie case, in the sense that if the evidence remains as it is there is a probability that at the trial of the action the plaintiff will be held entitled to relief.[207]

But for many years after *American Cyanamid* most Australian judges applied Lord Diplock's wording. Substitute expressions, such as 'a triable issue',[208] surfaced, but failed to eclipse the 'serious question to be tried' test.[209] This test was even applied in Australian intellectual property cases[210] despite the

---

203. *Films Rover International Ltd v Cannon Film Sales Ltd* [1986] 3 All ER 772 at 780 per Hoffmann J; cited with approval in *Businessworld Computers Pty Ltd v Australian Telecommunications Commission* (1988) 82 ALR 499 at 502 per Gummow J (FCA); see also *Bradto Pty Ltd v State of Victoria* [2006] VSCA 89 at [32] per Maxwell P and Charles JA.

204. *Australian Broadcasting Corporation v O'Neill* (2006) 227 CLR 57 at [2] per Gleeson CJ and Crennan J; *Australian Broadcasting Corporation v Lenah Game Meats Pty Ltd* (2001) 208 CLR 199 at 217.

205. [1975] AC 396 at 407.

206. (2006) 227 CLR 57 at [65] per Gummow and Hayne JJ.

207. (1968) 118 CLR 618 at 622.

208. See *Murphy v Lush* (1986) 60 ALJR 523.

209. See *Castlemaine Tooheys Ltd v South Australia* (1986) 161 CLR 148; 67 ALR 553, where the High Court accepted that a 'serious question to be tried' meant the same as 'triable issue'.

210. See, for example, in relation to registered trade marks, *New South Wales Dairy Corp v Murray-Goulburn Co-Operative Co Ltd* (1988) 12 IPR 587 at 591–3 per Wilcox J (FCA) and *Digby International (Aust) Pty Ltd v Beyond Imagination Pty Ltd* (1995) 31 IPR 410; in relation to patents, *Martin Engineering Co v Trison Holdings Pty Ltd* (1988) 81 ALR 543; 11 IPR 611 at 615–18 per Gummow J (FCA).

authority of *Beecham*. However, in *O'Neill* (see **8.18**) Gummow and Hayne JJ in the High Court resurrected the *Beecham* prima facie case test and held:

> By using the phrase "prima facie case", their Honours did not mean that the plaintiff must show that it is more probable than not that at trial the plaintiff will succeed; it is sufficient that the plaintiff show a *sufficient likelihood of success* to justify in the circumstances the preservation of the status quo pending the trial.[211] [italics added]

In deciding what is a 'sufficient likelihood of success', Gummow and Hayne JJ further approved the following reasoning in *Beecham*:

> How strong the probability needs to be depends, no doubt, upon the nature of the rights [the plaintiff] asserts and the practical consequences likely to flow from the order he seeks.[212]

Their Honours questioned the 'disparity' between *Beecham* and *American Cyanamid* and noted that both cases dealt with patent infringement and had similar outcomes; that is, interlocutory injunctions were granted in favour of the patentee on appeal after initially being refused because the bar had been set 'too high'.[213] Further, Gummow and Hayne JJ said there was 'no objection' to the use of the 'serious question to be tried' label provided:

> ... it is understood as conveying the notion that the seriousness of the question, like the strength of the probability referred to in *Beecham*, depends upon the considerations emphasised in *Beecham*.[214]

The phrase 'serious question to be tried' continues to be used in Australia,[215] but in the sense that Gummow and Hayne JJ stipulated in *O'Neill*, that is, the plaintiff must show that there is a 'sufficient likelihood of success' at the trial of the proceeding.

8.50   There are certain types of interlocutory injunctions and orders where the courts have adopted wording that is either additional or different to both the 'serious question to be tried' and the 'prima facie case' tests. For example, in defamation proceedings an interlocutory injunction will only be granted in a 'very clear' or 'exceptional' case: see **8.18**. This additional consideration, however, does not alter the 'organising principles' upon which interlocutory injunctions are granted. In *O'Neill* Gleeson CJ and Crennan J held:

> ... in all applications for an interlocutory injunction, a court will ask whether the plaintiff has shown that there is a serious question to be tried as to the plaintiff's entitlement to relief, has shown that the plaintiff is likely to suffer injury for which damages will not be an adequate remedy, and has shown that the balance of convenience favours the granting of an injunction. These are the organising principles, to be applied having regard to the nature and circumstances of the case, under which issues of justice and convenience are

---

211. (2006) 227 CLR 57.
212. (1968) 118 CLR 618 at 622.
213. (2006) 227 CLR 57 at [67].
214. (2006) 227 CLR 57 at [70].
215. See, for example, *Jackel International Ltd v Jackel Pty Ltd* [2011] FCA 1516.

addressed. We agree with the explanation of these organising principles in the reasons of Gummow and Hayne JJ, and their reiteration that the doctrine of the Court established in *Beecham Group Ltd v Bristol Laboratories Pty Ltd* should be followed. In the context of a defamation case, the application of those organising principles will require particular attention to the considerations which courts have identified as dictating caution. Foremost among those considerations is the public interest in free speech. A further consideration is that, in the defamation context, the outcome of a trial is especially likely to turn upon issues that are, by hypothesis, unresolved. Where one such issue is justification, it is commonly an issue for jury decision. In addition, the plaintiff's general character may be found to be such that, even if the publication is defamatory, only nominal damages will be awarded.[216]

8.51   Similarly, in an application for a mandatory interlocutory injunction the plaintiff must establish 'a high degree of assurance' of success at the final trial: see **8.67**. Equity has also developed different threshold tests in relation to Mareva and Anton Piller orders where the plaintiff must establish, respectively, a 'good arguable' case and a '*strong* prima facie' case: see **9.6** and **10.9**. In light of *O'Neill* the need for wording that differs from either the 'serious question to be tried' or the 'prima facie case' tests is greatly diminished because the real issue is how strong the probability of success at the final hearing needs to be in relation to the particular right or cause of action asserted by the plaintiff.[217] That particular right or cause of action, such as defamation, may require a stronger probability of success in order to demonstrate a prima facie case.

Decisions on evidence and law

8.52   In considering whether there is a prima facie case at an inter partes hearing, the court will have regard to the evidence and arguments on both sides. However, as noted by Lord Diplock in *American Cyanamid*:

> It is no part of the court's function at this stage of the litigation to try to resolve conflicts of evidence on affidavit as to facts on which the claims of either party may ultimately depend nor to decide difficult questions of law which call for detailed argument and mature consideration. These are matters to be dealt with at the trial.[218]

So, in *Martin Engineering Co v Trison Holdings Pty Ltd*, an application for an interlocutory injunction to restrain an infringement of a patent, Gummow J refused to express 'detailed views, especially on the question of validity'.[219] In granting the injunction for one of the infringement claims, his Honour said that his 'overall evaluation' at the interlocutory stage was 'that the case for infringement' was 'stronger than that for invalidity'.

---

216. (2006) 227 CLR 57 at [19].
217. (2006) 227 CLR 57 at [65] per Gummow and Hayne JJ.
218. [1975] AC 396 at 407.
219. (1988) 81 ALR 543 at 550–1; 11 IPR 611 at 618–19 (FCA).

Determinative interlocutory relief[220]

8.53 Ordinarily the court will not conduct a preliminary or 'mini' trial of the issues and 'give or withhold interlocutory relief upon a forecast as to the ultimate result in the case'.[221] But if the decision on the interlocutory injunction is likely to determine in a 'practical sense ... the substance of the matter in issue', then in deciding the second element (that is, where the balance of convenience lies), the court may 'evaluate the strength of the plaintiff's case for final relief'.[222] Such a practice is common in patent infringement cases[223] and applications to restrain passing off.[224] If the decision will finally decide the matter then ordinarily there will be a prima facie case for granting leave to appeal.[225]

Defences

8.54 Generally, the onus of proving that a defence is likely to succeed at the trial rests on the defendant.[226] The 'plaintiff does not have to show that the defences available to the defendant are, in effect, so weak that they would be struck out as unarguably bad'.[227]

Although it is not a complete defence to the plaintiff's cause of action, if the defendant's offending conduct is unlikely to be repeated then the injunction will be refused. In *Louis Vuitton Malletier SA v Knierum* Finkelstein J held, in a trade mark infringement case concerning handbags, wallets and an umbrella imported from China:

> The basis for the grant of an injunction in an intellectual property case is in every respect the same as in any other case. The plaintiff must show that there is a risk that the defendant will engage in infringing conduct in the future. If the plaintiff is unable to make good that proposition, he will not obtain an injunction ... On the question of proof of the risk of repetition some judges have been prepared to infer that risk simply from past infringement. But the better view is expressed by Laddie J in *Coflexip SA v Stolt Comex Seaway*

220. See W Sofrinoff, 'Interlocutory Injunctions Having Final Effect' (1987) 61 ALJ 341.

221. *Beecham Group Ltd v Bristol Laboratories* (1968) 118 CLR 618 at 622; and see *Kolback Securities Ltd v Epoch Mining NL* (1987) 8 NSWLR 533 at 536 per McLelland J.

222. *Kolback Securities Ltd v Epoch Mining NL* (1987) 8 NSWLR 533 at 536 per McLelland J; applied in *Hitech Contracting Ltd v Lynn* (SC(NSW), Austin J, 5 June 2001, unreported); see also *Samsung Electronics Co Ltd v Apple Inc* [2011] FCAFC 156 at [71]–[74] per Dowsett, Foster and Yates JJ.

223. See, for example, *Samsung Electronics Co Ltd v Apple Inc* [2011] FCAFC 156 at [70]–[74] per Dowsett, Foster and Yates JJ.

224. See, for example, *Newsweek v BBC* [1979] RPC 441 (CA); *BBC v Talbot Motor Co* [1981] FSR 228 at 233; *The Entrance Red Bus Service Pty Ltd v Transpax Pty Ltd* (SC(NSW), Young J, 24 February 1994, unreported).

225. *Bond v Barry* [2007] FCA 2034 at [27] per Gilmour J; *Samsung Electronics Co Ltd v Apple Inc* [2011] FCAFC 156 at [25]–[37] per Dowsett, Foster and Yates JJ.

226. *Commonwealth v John Fairfax & Sons Ltd* (1980) 147 CLR 39.

227. *Chappell v TCN Channel Nine Pty Ltd* (1988) 14 NSWLR 153 at 159 per Hunt J, citing in support *Commonwealth v John Fairfax & Sons Ltd* (1980) 147 CLR 39 at 57.

MS Ltd[228], where he said[229] that it is simply not right to treat [all intellectual property right] infringers as "bad apples".[230]

Louis Vuitton was distinguished on its facts by Crennan J in *Nokia Corporation v Truong* where in granting a permanent injunction her Honour said there was 'clear evidence that the respondents have continued to sell the infringing products, despite being aware of these proceedings, and the respondents have given no undertakings not to infringe.'[231]

Balance of convenience

Introduction

8.55 In *American Cyanamid Co* Lord Diplock observed:

> … the plaintiff's need for [the] protection [of an interlocutory injunction] must be weighed against the corresponding need of the defendant to be protected against injury resulting from his having been prevented from exercising his own legal rights for which he could not be adequately compensated under the plaintiff's undertaking in the damages if the uncertainty were resolved in the defendant's favour at the trial. The court must weigh one need against the other and determine where 'the balance of convenience' lies.[232]

A similar observation was made by the High Court in *Beecham*. Kitto, Taylor, Menzies and Owen JJ held that the 'second inquiry' in deciding whether an interlocutory injunction should be granted is:

> … whether the inconvenience or injury which the plaintiff would be likely to suffer if an injunction were refused outweighs or is outweighed by the injury which the defendant would suffer if an injunction were granted.[233]

The plaintiff bears the onus of establishing that the balance of convenience favours the grant of the injunction.[234] The factors to be taken into account are numerous and vary from case to case. Recurrent factors are the strength of the plaintiff's case, hardship to either party or even a third party,[235] the risk of irreparable damage or injury to the plaintiff, delay and the sufficiency of the plaintiff's undertaking as to damages.

---

228. [1999] 2 All ER 593.
229. [1999] 2 All ER 593 at 605.
230. [2004] FCA 1584 at [15] and [17].
231. [2005] FCA 1141 at [46]; see also *Solahart Industries Pty Ltd v Solar Shop Pty Ltd (No 2)* (2011) 282 ALR 43; [2011] FCA 780 at [7]–[8] per Perram J.
232. [1975] AC 396 at 406.
233. (1968) 118 CLR 618 at 622–3.
234. *Australian Broadcasting Corporation v O'Neill* (2006) 227 CLR 57 at [71] per Gummow and Hayne JJ.
235. See *Silktone Pty Ltd v Devreal Capital Pty Ltd* (1990) 21 NSWLR 317 (CA); *Patrick Stevedores Operations No 2 Pty Ltd v Maritime Union of Australia (No 3)* (1998) 195 CLR 1 at [65]–[66].

Strength of the plaintiff's case

8.56   The strength of the plaintiff's case and the balance of convenience are not 'separate and independent, but must be examined together.'[236] If the plaintiff has a strong case on the merits, then the balance of convenience is likely to favour the plaintiff.[237] This is particularly true where the balance of convenience is otherwise evenly balanced.[238]

Irreparable harm or damage

8.57   The plaintiff will ordinarily have to demonstrate that irreparable harm, detriment or damage will result if the interlocutory injunction is refused. This is not a separate element but, rather, 'part of the determination of the balance of convenience'. [239]Still, in the auxiliary jurisdiction, if irreparable harm will result this shows that common law damages will be inadequate and, because this is an element to consider in relation to all auxiliary jurisdiction injunctions, failure to establish it may be fatal. In *American Cyanamid* Lord Diplock observed:

> If damages in the measure recoverable at common law would be [an] adequate remedy and the defendant would be in a financial position to pay them, no interlocutory injunction should normally be granted, however strong the plaintiff's claim appeared to be at that stage.[240]

Thus, if the defendant is impecunious, damages will be an inadequate remedy. If damages will be 'very difficult to quantify'[241] then the balance of convenience will favour the plaintiff. For example, in a trade mark matter if the defendant's actions mean that the plaintiff will lose expenditure, reputation and opportunity this may constitute 'unquantifiable detriment'.[242] In deciding where the balance of convenience lies, the court may also consider the adequacy of the plaintiff's undertaking to pay damages to the defendant if the injunction is dissolved.[243]

In the exclusive jurisdiction, the court will not consider whether common law damages will be inadequate, because in this jurisdiction they are not available, but it may consider whether the plaintiff should be confined

---

236. *Australian and International Pilots Association v Qantas Airways Ltd* [2011] FCA 1487 at [70] per Dodds-Streeton J; see also *Samsung Electronics Co Ltd v Apple Inc* [2011] FCAFC 156 at [67] per Dowsett, Foster and Yates JJ.

237. *Castlemaine Tooheys Ltd v South Australia* (1986) 161 CLR 148 at 155; *Trade Practices Commission v Santos Ltd* (1992) 110 ALR 517 at 532 per Hill J; *Jabuna Pty Ltd v Hartley* (FCA, Beazley J, 18 April 1994, unreported).

238. *American Cyanamid Co v Ethicon Ltd* [1975] AC 396 at 409 per Lord Diplock.

239. *Active Leisure (Sports) Pty Ltd v Sportsman's Australia Ltd* [1991] 1 Qd R 301 at 313 per Cooper J (FC); see also *Samsung Electronics Co Ltd v Apple Inc* [2011] FCAFC 156 at [61]–[63] per Dowsett, Foster and Yates JJ.

240. [1975] AC 396 at 408.

241. *Body Technology Pty Ltd v Babak Moini* [2010] NSWSC 1414 at [9] per Ball J.

242. *Jackel International Ltd v Jackel Pty Ltd* [2011] FCA 1516 at [62] per Dodds-Streeton J.

243. *American Cyanamid* [1975] AC 396 at 408 per Lord Diplock; *Franklin International Export Ltd v Wattie Exports Ltd* (1988) 12 IPR 358 at 364–5 per Tompkins J (HC(NZ)).

to an account of profits or equitable compensation: see **Chapters** 6 and 11 respectively.

Delay

8.58 'Delay of itself is not a disentitling factor',[244] but unexplained delay can be fatal to the plaintiff's application for an interlocutory injunction.[245] If the delay has caused substantial detriment[246] or has allowed the defendant to establish a business or an enterprise, the balance of convenience will be against the plaintiff. In *American Cyanamid Co v Ethicon Ltd*, Lord Diplock observed:

> If the defendant is enjoined temporarily from doing something that he has not done before, the only effect of the interlocutory injunction in the event of his succeeding at the trial is to postpone the date at which he is able to embark upon a course of action which he has not previously found it necessary to undertake; whereas to interrupt him in the conduct of an established enterprise would cause much greater inconvenience to him since he would have to start again to establish it in the event of his succeeding at the trial.[247]

8.59 While each case depends on its own facts, it is useful to look at passing off and trade mark infringement cases where interlocutory injunction applications are common. Relief was refused in *Pacific Hotels Pty Ltd v Asian Pacific International Ltd*,[248] where there had been a four-month delay; in *Century Electronics v CVC Enterprises*[249] — a six-month delay; in *Essex Electric (PTE) Ltd v IPC Computers UK Ltd*[250] — an eight-month delay; and in *Wang v Anying Group Pty Ltd*[251] — a 15-month delay. In these cases there was no satisfactory explanation for the delay. By contrast, in *ESPN, Inc v Thomas* a ten–week delay was excused in an ex parte application because the defendant had acted with his 'eyes open' to the plaintiff's objections following several letters of demand.[252] Similarly, in *The Great American Success Co Ltd v Kattaineh*,[253] a five-month delay was excused where it was established that the defendant had notice of the complaint.[254] In *Nintendo Co Ltd v Care* a 14-month delay was excused, but there was both a satisfactory explanation for eight of those months and the delay had not prejudiced the respondents.[255] It is common practice in intellectual

---

244. *Nintendo Co Ltd v Care* (2000) 52 IPR 34 at [26] per Goldberg J.
245. See, for example, *Azbuild Pty Ltd v Fairfax Media Publications* [2010] NSWSC 1080 at [9] per Slattery J.
246. *Gibson v The Minister for Finance, Natural Resources and the Arts* [2011] QSC 401.
247. [1975] AC 396 at 406.
248. (1987) 7 IPR 239 (FCA).
249. [1983] FSR 1.
250. (1991) 19 IPR 639 (Ch D).
251. [2009] FCA 1500.
252. [2010] FCA 1232.
253. [1976] FSR 554.
254. See also *The Entrance Red Bus Services Pty Ltd v Transpax Pty Ltd* (SC(NSW), Young J, 24 February 1994, unreported); *Tavener Rutledge v Trexapalm* [1977] RPC 275; [1975] FSR 479; *J C Penney Co Inc v Penneys Ltd* [1975] FSR 367 (CA); *CPC (UK) v Keenan* [1986] FSR 527 at 534.
255. (2000) 52 IPR 34 at [26]–[27] per Goldberg J.

property matters to seek undertakings from the proposed defendant in a letter of demand and then to commence proceedings if these are not given. Reasonable delay for that purpose may be excused.[256]

If the defendant is guilty of fraud then the plaintiff's delay may not bar relief,[257] particularly where the fraud has concealed the cause of action.

Undertaking as to damages

8.60 In seeking an equitable remedy the plaintiff is required to 'do equity.'[258] This means in most cases the plaintiff will be required to give an undertaking to the court that if the interlocutory injunction is later dissolved the plaintiff will compensate the defendant for any injury or loss caused by the injunction.[259] In *First Netcom Pty Ltd v Telstra Corp Ltd* the Full Federal Court held:

> … the giving of an undertaking is, in general, an essential condition of the grant of an interim injunction. But although an appropriate undertaking may be proffered by the plaintiff, there is no compulsion upon the plaintiff that the undertaking be given. In that sense, as Stephen J observed in *Air Express*,[260] the giving of the undertaking is an entirely voluntary act on the part of the plaintiff. This is illustrated by the traditional form of order by way of injunction. The order is made in these terms: "*Upon* the plaintiff giving the usual undertaking as to damages, the Court orders … (etc) …" In other words, the coming into operation of the injunction is dependent upon the giving of the undertaking. If the undertaking is not forthcoming, the injunction will never come into effect. That is to say, the order is made conditional upon a contingency which, if not satisfied, has the effect that the injunction itself, which is merely inchoate, never comes into effect. The foundation of the practice is the discretionary nature of the grant of an interim injunction. The exercise of the discretion is almost invariably conditional upon the plaintiff's being willing to proffer an undertaking as to damages. The plaintiff can elect to give the undertaking, in which case the injunction will run; or the plaintiff can decline to give the undertaking, in which event the injunction will not run.
>
> There is a "usual" form of undertaking as to damages. However, since its terms are a matter for the discretionary judgment for the court, its provisions will be moulded so as to fit the circumstances of the case at hand. These circumstances may include the likelihood of the plaintiff's insolvency, which might produce an inability to discharge any liability to the party enjoined pending a final hearing that might accrue under the undertaking. In that event, the court is required to exercise its judgment as to what is appropriate

---

256. See *ESPN, Inc v Thomas* [2010] FCA 1232; *Express Newspapers plc v Liverpool Daily Post and Echo plc* [1985] 3 All ER 680; (1985) 5 IPR 193; compare *Pacific Hotels Pty Ltd v Asian Pacific International Ltd* (1987) 7 IPR 239 (FCA).

257. *Gillette v Diamond Edge* (1926) 43 RPC 310.

258. *European Bank Ltd v Evans* (2010) 240 CLR 432 at [17] per French CJ, Gummow, Hayne, Heydon and Kiefel JJ.

259. See *Beecham Group Ltd v Bristol Laboratories* (1968) 118 CLR 618 at 623; *Auto Securities Ltd v Standard Telephones & Cables Ltd* [1965] RPC 92.

260. *Air Express Ltd v Ansett Transport Industries (Operations) Pty Ltd* (1981) 146 CLR 249 at 318–19.

in order to ensure the reality of adequate compensation, and not merely an empty form of compensation, to a party who is ultimately successful.[261]

8.61   If the plaintiff cannot meet or otherwise provide adequate security[262] for the undertaking the injunction will not be granted.[263] The undertaking may extend to pay damages to third parties.[264] For example, the Uniform Civil Procedure Rules provide:

Meaning of "usual undertaking as to damages"

The "usual undertaking as to damages", if given to the court in connection with any interlocutory order or undertaking, is an undertaking to the court to submit to such order (if any) as the court may consider to be just for the payment of compensation (to be assessed by the court or as it may direct) to any person (whether or not a party) affected by the operation of the interlocutory order or undertaking or of any interlocutory continuation (with or without variation) of the interlocutory order or undertaking.[265]

8.62   If the matter affects the public interest the usual undertaking may be dispensed with or modified.[266] The court also has a discretion not to enforce the undertaking if the payment of damages would be 'inequitable'.[267] But once the court decides to award damages their assessment is, according to Lord Diplock in *Hoffmann-La Roche*:

… made upon the same basis as that upon which damages for breach of contract would be assessed if the undertaking had been a contract between the plaintiff and the defendant that the plaintiff would not prevent the defendant from doing that which he was restrained from doing by the terms of the injunction.[268]

This view, however, has been rejected in Australia. In *Air Express Ltd v Ansett Transport Industries (Operations) Pty Ltd* Stephen J held:

Damages awarded under such an undertaking are, therefore, of a rather different nature from those awarded at common law. Their special character appears from the fact that their source lies in the plaintiff's own voluntary undertaking, given as the price of obtaining an injunction.[269]

261. (2000) 101 FCR 77 at [22]–[23].

262. See *Wells Fargo Bank Northwest National Association v Victoria Aircraft Leasing Ltd (No 2)* [2004] VSC 341; *Bayblu Holdings Pty Ltd v Capital Finance Australia Ltd* [2011] NSWCA 39.

263. *Permanent Promotions Pty Ltd v Independent Distillers (Aust) Pty Ltd* [2004] FCA 794.

264. See, for example, Uniform Civil Procedure Rules 2005 (NSW) Pt 25, r 25.8; *Smith Kline French Laboratories (Australia) Ltd v Secretary, Department of Community Services and Health* (1990) 16 IPR 281 at 286 per Gummow J.

265. See, for example, reg 25.8 Uniform Civil Procedure Rules 2005 (NSW).

266. *Century Metals and Mining NL v Yeomans* (1989) 40 FCR 564; 85 ALR 54; see also 16.40–16.41.

267. *F Hoffmann-La Roche & Co AG v Secretary of State for Trade and Industry* [1975] AC 295 at 361 per Lord Diplock.

268. *F Hoffmann-La Roche & Co AG v Secretary of State for Trade and Industry* [1975] AC at 361; compare *Air Express Ltd v Ansett Transport Industries (Operations) Pty Ltd* (1981) 146 CLR 249.

269. (1981) 146 CLR 249 at 318–19.

The High Court observed in *European Bank Ltd v Evans* that the usual undertaking as to damages is given to and enforced by the court. It is not 'a contract between parties or some other cause of action upon which one party can sue the other.'[270] French CJ, Gummow, Hayne, Heydon and Kiefel JJ concluded:

> In *Air Express*, Mason J said that there was little to be gained from an examination of the authorities dealing with causation of damage in contract, tort and other situations; the court was better advised to look to the purpose which the undertaking as to damages is to serve and to identify the causal connection or standard of causal connection which is most appropriate to that purpose.[271]

> A party seeking an equitable remedy is required to "do equity" and this is the origin of the requirement that the party giving an undertaking as to damages submit to such order for payment of compensation as the court may consider to be just. Given its origin and application to varied circumstances in particular cases, the process of assessment of compensation cannot be constrained by a rigid formulation.[272]

Thus, unlike damages in contract, exemplary damages may be awarded on an undertaking as to damages.[273]

MANDATORY INJUNCTIONS

Introduction

8.63 A mandatory injunction orders a person to *do* something; that is, it is a positive injunction, as opposed to the more commonly used negative or prohibitory injunction.[274] A mandatory injunction may be granted in both final and interlocutory form and, for the most part, it is granted on the same principles as prohibitory or negative injunctions.[275] Nonetheless, there are some important qualifications to this statement of principle, arising from the decision of the House of Lords in *Redland Bricks Ltd v Morris*,[276] discussed at 8.65.

8.64 There are two types of mandatory injunctions. First, restorative mandatory injunctions compel the defendant to repair the consequences of his or her own wrongful act; for example, to publish advertisements correcting

---

270. *European Bank Ltd v Evans* (2010) 240 CLR 432 at [14] per French CJ, Gummow, Hayne, Heydon and Kiefel JJ.

271. (1981) 146 CLR 249 at 324.

272. (2010) 240 CLR 432 at [16]–[17].

273. See *Smith v Day* (1882) 21 Ch D 421; *Columbia Picture Industries v Robinson* [1987] Ch 38; *Toga Systems International AB v Shop & Display Equipment Pty Ltd* (SC(Vic), Hayne J, 14 April 1992, unreported).

274. Note that s 65(1) of the Supreme Court Act 1970 (NSW) provides that the 'Court may order any person to fulfil any duty in the fulfilment of which the person seeking the order is personally interested'.

275. *Davies v Gas Light & Coke Co* [1909] 1 Ch 248 at 259.

276. [1970] AC 652.

the effect of conduct in breach of a statute (see **16.44**), demolish a house built in breach of a statute,[277] reduce the height of a boundary wall built in breach of contract,[278] prevent ongoing 'extreme' or 'serious' damage caused by a conspiracy[279] transfer control of a domain name and website[280] or remove scaffolding or advertising signs built on the plaintiff's property.[281] The second type of mandatory injunction is the enforcing kind. It resembles specific performance because it compels the defendant to do something which he or she has promised to do for consideration. The principles governing the grant of these two types of injunction are discussed below.

Restorative

8.65 The restorative injunction requires the defendant to repair the consequence of his or her wrongful act. The leading decision is that of the House of Lords in *Redland Bricks Ltd v Morris*.[282] Redland Bricks excavated a large pit to extract clay from land adjoining the plaintiff's land which was used as a strawberry farm. The farm began to subside towards Redland Bricks and despite remedial work, further subsidence was likely. The plaintiff brought an action against Redland Bricks for damages and injunctions. Redland Bricks consented to an injunction restraining further excavation, but opposed the grant of a restorative injunction compelling the restoration of the plaintiff's land to its former state. To comply with this injunction would have cost £30,000, yet the plaintiff's land was only worth about £12,000. The House of Lords refused the mandatory injunction. Lord Upjohn in delivering the leading speech observed that the grant of such an injunction is 'entirely discretionary' and warned that '[e]very case must depend essentially upon its own particular circumstances'.[283] His Lordship said that generally a mandatory injunction will lie where, first, there is 'a very strong probability on the facts that grave damage will accrue to [the plaintiff] in the future'.[284] Second, 'damages will not be a sufficient or adequate remedy'.[285] Third, the cost of preventing future occurrences must be taken into account.[286] If the defendant has acted 'wantonly' and 'unreasonably' the cost of restoration may be ordered even if it is out of proportion to the advantage accruing to the plaintiff. If the defendant has acted reasonably the cost of complying with the mandatory injunction and the hardship caused to the defendant if the injunction were to be granted needs to be weighed against the anticipated damage to the plaintiff.

---

277. *Shire of Hornsby v Danglade* (1929) 29 SR (NSW) 118.
278. *Collum v Opie* (2000) 76 SASR 588; [2000] SASC 107 (FC).
279. *Patrick Stevedores Operations No 2 Pty Ltd v Maritime Union of Australia (No 3)* (1998) 195 CLR 1 at [33].
280. *Body Technology Pty Ltd v Babak Moini* [2010] NSWSC 1414.
281. See *LJP Investments Pty Ltd v Howard Chia Investments Pty Ltd* (1989) 24 NSWLR 499.
282. [1970] AC 652.
283. [1970] AC 652 at 665.
284. [1970] AC 652 at 665.
285. [1970] AC 652 at 665.
286. [1970] AC 652 at 666.

Finally, if the injunction is granted it must be worded so the defendant knows 'exactly in fact' what he or she has to do.[287]

The approach to restorative mandatory injunctions taken by the House of Lords in *Redland Bricks* was adopted by Gibbs CJ in the High Court in *Queensland v Australian Telecommunications Commission*,[288] and by French J in the Federal Court in *Everdure Pty Ltd v BLE Capital*.[289] It was also cited with approval by the High Court in *Jemena Gas Networks (NSW) Ltd v Mine Subsidence Board*[290] where the majority observed:

> Although the remedy of damages at law is not available until the subsidence has caused injury to a landowner's property, in equity the landowner may apply for a negative injunction (interlocutory or final) against conduct causing subsidence in future, whether or not there has been any subsidence, whether or not there has been any injury caused by subsidence, and indeed whether or not mining has begun. And the landowner may apply for a mandatory injunction (interlocutory or final) of a quia timet kind, compelling the defendant to take positive steps to prevent subsidence-causing injury. It is not necessary to explore the details of the hurdles in the landowner's path in taking those courses: depending on the circumstances, they may be significant but they are not insurmountable.[291]

Enforcing

8.66 The enforcing mandatory injunction is virtually identical to specific performance. In *Businessworld Computers Pty Ltd v Australasian Telecommunications Commission* Gummow J observed[292] that the court is reluctant to grant a mandatory injunction in a case where specific performance would not be available.[293] Thus, a mandatory injunction restraining termination of a contract may be refused in the court's discretion if the plaintiff is not ready and willing to perform their side of the bargain[294] or if it will cause hardship[295] or if it is a building contract requiring the continuing supervision of the court.[296] The attraction of both specific performance and mandatory injunctions is that the rule in *Doherty v Allman*[297] does not apply.[298] But, like all injunctions

287. [1970] AC 652 at 666.
288. (1985) 59 ALR 243.
289. (FCA, French J, 15 August 1991, unreported).
290. (2011) 277 ALR 257; [2011] HCA 19.
291. (2011) 277 ALR 257; [2011] HCA 19 at [33] per French CJ, Gummow, Hayne, Heydon, Crennan, Kiefel and Bell JJ.
292. (1988) 82 ALR 499 at 501 (FCA).
293. See also *Burns Philp Trust Co Pty Ltd v Kwikasair Freightlines Ltd* (1963) 63 SR (NSW) 492 at 498 (FC).
294. *Telstra Corporation Ltd v First Netcom Pty Ltd* (1997) 148 ALR 202 at 206 per Lockhart, Beaumont and Hill JJ (Full FC).
295. Compare *Opie v Collum* [1999] SASC 376; affirmed *Collum v Opie* (2000) 76 SASR 588; [2000] SASC 107 (FC).
296. *Crouch Developments Pty Ltd v D & M (Australia) Pty Ltd* [2008] WASC 151 at [27], [28] per Martin CJ.
297. (1878) 3 App Cas 709. The rule is discussed at 8.26–8.27.
298. *Burns Philp Trust Co Pty Ltd v Kwikasair Freightlines Ltd* (1963) 63 SR (NSW) 492 at 499.

in the auxiliary jurisdiction — and like specific performance — if damages would be an adequate remedy the remedy will be refused.[299] If only a part of the contract is to be enforced, that part must be 'separable and distinct from the rest'.[300] If it is, the court in granting the injunction will leave the parties to pursue their remedies at law as to the balance of the agreement.[301]

Interlocutory mandatory injunctions

8.67   An interlocutory mandatory injunction may be granted by the court,[302] but there are two lines of authority on whether the applicable guidelines are the same or different to those that apply to negative interlocutory injunctions. In *Shepherd Homes Ltd v Sandham* Megarry J held that a different test was applicable to interlocutory mandatory injunctions:

> In a normal case the court must, inter alia, feel a high degree of assurance that at the trial it will appear that the injunction was rightly granted; and this is a higher standard than is required for a prohibitory injunction.[303]

This statement of principle was approved by Gibbs CJ in *Queensland v Australian Telecommunications Commission*[304] and by the Full Court of the Queensland Supreme Court in *Active Leisure (Sports) Pty Ltd v Sportsman's Australia Ltd*.[305] It has been applied in building contract cases where generally 'neither specific performance nor interlocutory injunctions having the effect of specific performance will be granted … in other than exceptional circumstances'.[306] However, in *Businessworld Computers Pty Ltd v Australasian Telecommunications Commission*[307] Gummow J in granting a mandatory interlocutory injunction rejected the need to show 'a high degree of assurance'. His Honour preferred to apply the same principles as apply to the grant of negative interlocutory injunctions, on the basis that the effect of both negative injunctions and mandatory injunctions can, in terms of severity, be the same.[308] The two

---

299. (1963) 63 SR (NSW) at 498.

300. *J C Williamson Ltd v Lukey and Mulholland* (1931) 45 CLR 282 at 294 per Starke J, cited with approval in *Burns Philp Trust Co Pty Ltd v Kwikasair Freightlines Ltd* (1963) 63 SR (NSW) 492 at 497; *Sugar Australia Ltd v Conneq* [2011] NSWSC 805 at [20] per McDougall J.

301. (1931) 45 CLR 282 at 294 per Starke J.

302. See also s 65(2) of the Supreme Court Act 1970 (NSW).

303. [1971] Ch 340 at 351.

304. (1985) 59 ALR 243 at 244.

305. [1991] 1 Qd R 301 at 304 per Shepherdson J and at 315 per Cooper J.

306. *Crouch Developments Pty Ltd v D & M (Australia) Pty Ltd* [2008] WASC 151 at [21] per Martin CJ; *Sugar Australia Ltd v Conneq* [2011] NSWSC 805 at [17] per McDougall J.

307. (1988) 82 ALR 499 at 501–4 (FCA).

308. See also *Tumminello v TAB Ltd* [2011] NSWSC 1639 at [43] per Slattery J; *Adamek v Royal Motor Yacht Club of NSW Ltd* [2007] NSWSC 1043; *ADI v Aerospace Systems Management* [2003] NSWSC 758; *Regent's Pty Ltd v Subaru (Aust) Pty Ltd* (1995) 33 IPR 655; *Carson v Minister for Education of Queensland* (1989) 25 FCR 326 at 338 per Spender J; *MIPS Computer Systems Inc v MIPS Computer Resources Pty Ltd* (1990) 18 IPR 577 at 591 (FCA); *'Q' Promotions Pty Ltd v Queensland Bloodstock Breeders and Sales Pty Ltd* (FCA, Drummond J, 16 July 1993, unreported); *Bates & Partners Pty Ltd v The Law Book Co Ltd* (1994) 29 IPR 11 (SC(NSW)); compare *Everdure Pty Ltd v BLE Capital Ltd* (FCA, French J, 15 August 1991, unreported); and see **8.45–8.60** for a discussion on the principles applying to interlocutory injunctions generally.

alternative approaches were further considered by the Victorian Court of Appeal in *Bradto Pty Ltd v State of Victoria*. In following Gummow J's reasoning in *Businessworld Computers*, Maxwell P and Charles JA held:

> In our view, it is desirable that a single test be applied in all cases where an interlocutory injunction is sought. There is nothing in the body of authority to which we have referred, nor any consideration of principle, which requires a special test to be applied to one subcategory of such injunction applications, namely, those where mandatory relief is sought. On the contrary, as pointed out convincingly by Hoffmann J in *Films Rover*,[309] the grant of a mandatory interlocutory injunction may be justified in a particular case notwithstanding that the court does not feel the requisite "high degree of assurance".[310]

> … the flexibility and adaptability of the remedy of injunction as an instrument of justice will be best served by the adoption of the Hoffmann approach. That is, whether the relief sought is prohibitory or mandatory, the court should take whichever course appears to carry the lower risk of injustice if it should turn out to have been "wrong", in the sense of granting an injunction to a party who fails to establish his right at the trial, or in failing to grant an injunction to a party who succeeds at trial.[311]

The Victorian Court of Appeal's decision in *Bradto* that a single test applies to all interlocutory injunctions, including mandatory interlocutory injunctions, has since been applied and cited with approval in the Federal Court.[312]

SUPER AND ANONYMISED INJUNCTIONS

Introduction

8.68 The interaction between equitable interlocutory injunctions and court procedure is fertile ground for the emergence of new remedies. The aim of the interlocutory injunction is to preserve the status quo pending trial. This purpose has also played a central role in the development of freezing[313] and search orders. These three remedies have some common characteristics: they are all interim procedural orders that protect the integrity of the court's processes pending the trial; they are all granted in the court's discretion; and in each case the plaintiff is usually required to give an undertaking as to damages. Nonetheless, how they protect the integrity of the court's processes is different. The interlocutory injunction preserves the plaintiff's legal or equitable rights, freezing orders preserve the defendant's assets and search orders preserve the evidence. The High Court preferred to focus on the differences in *Cardile v LED Builders* and noted that the equitable injunction jurisdiction has been put under 'strain' by the development of new remedies, such as freezing orders,

309. *Films Rover International Ltd v Cannon Film Sales Ltd* [1987] 1 WLR 670 at [26].
310. (2006) 15 VR 65 at [33].
311. (2006) 15 VR 65 at [35].
312. *Jackel International Ltd v Jackel Pty Ltd* [2011] FCA 1516; *Australian and International Pilots Association v Qantas Airways Ltd* [2011] FCA 1487.
313. *Cardile v LED Builders* (1999) 198 CLR 380 at [51] per Gaudron, McHugh, Gummow and Callinan JJ.

which for many years were treated as a variety of interlocutory injunction.[314] In common with search orders, these are now treated as *sui generis* remedies with an independent jurisdictional basis.

Despite this 'strain,' the interaction between the interlocutory injunction and court procedure has yet again led to the emergence of new remedies or at least old remedies with new names, namely, the 'anonymised' injunction and 'super-injunction'. These are also designed to protect the integrity of the court's processes, but rather than preserving the status quo by freezing assets or seizing evidence, these injunctions carry an order that preserves *confidential information* and *privacy* pending the trial. They are an exception to the common law principle of open justice. As observed by Tugendhat J in *John Terry v Persons Unknown* this is 'one of the oldest principles of English law, going back to before Magna Carta.'[315] It requires hearings to be held in public and parties to be named in judgments and orders.[316] Similarly, in Australia jurisdiction is to be exercised in open court.[317] But this has never been an absolute principle. It must 'yield to privacy or secrecy' if it 'would frustrate the court's ability to administer justice properly.' For example, the Federal Court may, if 'necessary,' forbid the publication of evidence as well as the names of a party or witness.[318] Similar provisions in the United Kingdom have helped create anonymised and super-injunctions as an exception to the open court principle.[319] The genesis of these remedies is that the court's ability to do justice in a confidential information or a trade secret case is 'undermined' if the proceedings are 'entirely public or if the judgment disclosed those trade secrets.'[320] Essentially there is nothing new about super and anonymised injunctions because they are interlocutory injunctions which protect legal, equitable and statutory rights. The only element that distinguishes super and anonymised injunctions are additional orders preserving the plaintiff's anonymity, privacy or confidential information. As observed by Maurice Kay LJ in the English Court of Appeal in *Ntuli v Donald*:

> Superinjunctions attract understandable controversy. Sometimes it is the product of more heat than light. Although the concept carries the nomenclature of novelty, there is much that is simply a reflection of general principles.[321]

---

314. (1999) 198 CLR 380.
315. [2010] 1 FCR 659; [2010] EWHC 119 (QB).
316. *In re Guardian News and Media Ltd* [2010] UKSC1 at [22] per Lord Rodger.
317. See, for example, Federal Court of Australia Act 1976, s 17(1) (Cth).
318. Federal Court of Australia Act 1976, s 50 (Cth).
319. Neuberger, Lord (Master of the Rolls), *Report of the Committee on Super-Injunctions: Super-Injunctions, Anonymised Injunctions and Open Justice* (Judiciary of England and Wales, May 2011 — www.judiciary. gov.uk), p 8.
320. *Report of the Committee on Super-Injunctions*, p 9.
321. [2010] EWCA Civ 1276 at [47].

Definitions

8.69   Anonymised and super-injunctions are often confused because many anonymised injunctions have been incorrectly labelled super-injunctions. This has led to the misconception that super-injunctions are commonplace and a 'fear that a new form of permanently secret justice has arisen'.[322] The more common anonymised injunction is where the identity of one or more parties to the proceeding is confidential. It may also extend to a witness. Essentially it involves an injunction with the addition of an anonymity order. In contrast to super-injunctions, there is no prohibition on disclosing the existence of the proceedings and the nature of the injunction. The term 'super-injunction' was coined by *The Guardian* newspaper in relation to the injunction granted in the *Trafigura* case which protected the plaintiffs' confidential information *and* prohibited the reporting of the existence of the proceedings.[323] Maurice Kay LJ in the English Court of Appeal in *Ntuli v Donald* noted that it is this last element which transforms an injunction into a super-injunction.[324] At the beginning of his judgment Maurice Kay LJ observes:

> … Eady J granted an anonymised claimant an injunction restraining an anonymised defendant from doing specified but unpublishable things *and* further restraining the defendant and others from publishing the fact that the injunction had been sought and obtained. This type of relief has become known as a superinjunction.[325] (emphasis added)

However, the first part of this definition needs to be read with caution. Although a super-injunction may have anonymised parties, 'anonymity by itself does not render an injunction a super-injunction' and 'it is not even a necessary feature of a super-injunction'.[326] An application for a super-injunction is heard in private and is designed to 'facilitate the administration of justice' by preserving confidential and private information pending the trial.[327] It is this latter aspect that is emphasised in the *Report of the Committee on Super-Injunctions: Super-Injunctions, Anonymised Injunctions and Open Justice*.[328] The Committee on Super-Injunctions was set up in April 2010 in response to English media concerns. In May 2011 Lord Neuberger, Master of the Rolls, delivered the Committee's report and the super-injunction was defined as:

> … an interim injunction which restrains a person from: (i) publishing information which concerns the applicant and is said to be confidential or

322.   *Report of the Committee on Super-Injunctions* p 20.
323.   *Report of the Committee on Super-Injunctions*, p 19.
324.   [2010] EWCA Civ 1276 at [43].
325.   [2010] EWCA Civ 1276 at [1].
326.   *Report of the Committee on Super-Injunctions*, p 20 citing *Gray v UVW* [2010] EWHC 2637 (QB) at [19].
327.   *Report of the Committee on Super-Injunctions*, p 17.
328.   Neuberger, Lord (Master of the Rolls), *Report of the Committee on Super-Injunctions: Super-Injunctions, Anonymised Injunctions and Open Justice* (Judiciary of England and Wales, May 2011 — < www.judiciary. gov.uk >).

private; *and* (ii) publicising or informing others of the existence of the order and the proceedings.[329]

The super–injunction is often served on the media, which is then prohibited from disclosing the confidential information including the existence of the proceedings. They are controversial because they are exceptions to both open justice and freedom of speech; and they have often been obtained to protect the privacy of celebrities and wealthy litigants. A further concern, expressed by Tugendhat J in *Terry v Persons Unknown,* was the impression that 'extensive derogations from open justice' had become 'routine in claims for misuse of private information'.[330] The Foreword to the *Report of the Committee on Super-Injunctions* states:

> The Committee on Super-Injunctions was set up ... in order to examine well-publicised issues of concern to Parliament, the judiciary, the media, and the wider public, following the *Trafigura*[331] and *John Terry*[332] cases. These concerns centred round the perceived growth in the use and application of super-injunctions and the increasing frequency with which proceedings were being anonymised ...

The Committee did not consider substantive law reform in relation to confidential information, trade secrets, privacy and defamation but, rather, it focussed on amendments to procedural law with the followings aims:

> The Committee's recommendations, once implemented, are intended to ensure that the proper balance is struck between the interests of claimants and defendants (who are usually media organisations). They should also ensure that exceptions to the principle of open justice will only be allowed when they are strictly necessary in the interests of justice, and that when allowed they will go no further than is strictly necessary. This should mean that super-injunctions will only be granted in very limited circumstances and, at least normally, for very short periods of time.

The *Trafigura* case

8.70 As mentioned above, the *Trafigura* case led to the coining of the term 'super–injunction' by *The Guardian* newspaper. It was also one of the cases that led to the Committee's Report. In 2006 Trafigura, a multinational company, chartered a ship called the *Probo Koala*. It began to unload 'a mixture of petrochemical waste and caustic soda'[333] at Amsterdam port for processing. The processing company raised their price from €12,000 to €250,000[334] when it realised the waste was far more toxic than what had been agreed. Trafigura baulked at the cost, the waste was reloaded on the *Probo Koala* and it eventually sailed to the large African seaport Abidjan, Ivory Coast. More than 400 tons of

---

329. *Report of the Committee on Super-Injunctions,* p iv.
330. [2010] 1 FCR 659 at [107].
331. *RJW & SJW v The Guardian Newspaper & Person or Persons* (claim no. HQ09).
332. *Terry v Persons Unknown* [2010] 1 FCR 659.
333. *New York Times,* October 18, 2009.
334. *New York Times,* October 2, 2006.

the waste was unloaded and given to a local company which illegally dumped it in open landfills.[335] Thousands of Ivory Coast residents became sick through exposure and some died. The residents blamed Trafigura which denied wrongdoing due to its belief that the local company could do the job safely.[336] Trafigura confidentially commissioned a preliminary scientific report, known as the Minton report, which found that the waste was potentially toxic and that disposing of it 'onto landfill sites would be forbidden' in Europe. The report remained confidential while Trafigura was in the process of settling claims for the cleanup and compensation by paying US$250 million to the Ivory Coast.[337] But before the settlement was announced, the report was leaked to *The Guardian* newspaper in England.

On 11 September 2009 Maddison J granted Trafigura an injunction restraining *The Guardian* newspaper and 'a person or persons unknown' from disclosing the existence of the report due to confidentiality and legal professional privilege. The applicants' names were anonymised and listed as RJW and SJW and the injunction included an order prohibiting disclosure of the proceedings. The injunction was continued by Sweeney J on 18 September 2009 who set a hearing down for the week commencing 12 October 2009. On that date and while the injunction was still in force, a member of the British Parliament tabled a question in the House of Commons 'on the alleged dumping of toxic waste in the Ivory Coast, commissioned by Trafigura.' As found in the *Report of the Committee on Super-Injunctions*, the question raised concerns as to whether a super-injunction 'could inhibit Parliamentary debate.' The committee concluded 'that it plainly cannot'[338] and that 'court orders, however framed, cannot interfere with, or inhibit, Parliamentary speech, debate or proceedings'.[339] However, it did raise the difficult question as to whether such an injunction prohibits the reporting of Parliamentary proceedings. The lawyers for Trafigura and *The Guardian* agreed that it did prevent reporting of the question tabled in Parliament. *The Guardian* said that it had been 'gagged from reporting Parliament' which was 'a sacrosanct right since the 18th-century'.[340] These concerns were not tested in court because on 13 October 2009 the Trafigura injunction was amended by the consent of both Trafigura and *The Guardian* to allow the reporting of parliament.[341] The Committee found, however, that 'unfettered reporting of Parliamentary proceedings (in apparent breach of court orders) has not been established as a clear right'.[342] It also stated in the foreword to the *Report of the Committee on Super-Injunctions*:

335. *New York Times*, October 2, 2006.

336. *New York Times*, October 4, 2006.

337. *New York Times*, July 23, 2010.

338. *Report of the Committee on Super-Injunctions*, p 66.

339. *Report of the Committee on Super-Injunctions*, p 68.

340. *Report of the Committee on Super-Injunctions*, p 66.

341. *Report of the Committee on Super-Injunctions*, p 67.

342. *Report of the Committee on Super-Injunctions*, p 76.

The *Trafigura* case demonstrated that where a super-injunction or an anonymised injunction exists, there is no adequate mechanism to enable the relevant Parliamentary authorities (the House authorities) to ascertain whether there are active proceedings in place.[343]

Following the overseas publication of the Minton report, Trafigura agreed to the dissolution of the injunction in its entirety on 16 October 2009.

John Terry case

8.71 In *John Terry v Persons Unknown*[344] the English football captain John Terry had an extra-marital affair with his team-mate's girlfriend. While rumours circulated the captain applied for an injunction restraining publication of the affair on the grounds that it was a breach of confidence and that it infringed his rights to privacy under the Human Rights Act 1998 (UK). Notice was not given to any respondent or other person. Terry said that the order was 'likely to be served on media third parties' and the *News of the World* had been identified in the evidence. Initially orders were made for there to be a private hearing, anonymity and a short term injunction prohibiting publication of the story and any related photographs. But at the first return date one week later, the super-injunction was not continued. Tugendhat J (who was later one of the committee's members that delivered the *Report of the Committee on Super-Injunctions*) found that information about the affair had not been disclosed in confidence and there was neither a breach of confidence nor privacy under the Human Rights Act. The result may have been different if there was a threat to publish 'intrusive details' or photographs about the affair, but there was no such threat.[345] His Honour was critical of the evidence which had been assembled by the captain's 'business partners' and not by his solicitors. This included evidence of a number of high profile sponsorship, endorsement and very well-known brand name deals. It showed that the 'real basis for the concern' was to protect Terry's reputation and 'the impact of any adverse publicity upon the business of earning sponsorship and similar income.'[346] His Honour noted that initially an order was also sought 'prohibiting the disclosure of the fact that an order has been made and providing for sealing the whole court file.' Tugendhat J noted that some newspapers refer to these as 'super injunctions'[347] and said:

> The reason why, on some occasions, applicants wish for there to be an order restricting reports of the fact that an injunction has been granted is in order to prevent the alleged wrongdoer from being tipped off about the proceedings before an injunction could be applied for, or made against him, or before he can be served. In the interval between learning of the intention of the applicant to bring proceedings, and the receipt by the alleged wrongdoer of

343. *Report of the Committee on Super-Injunctions*, p vi.
344. [2010] EWHC 119 (QB).
345. [2010] EWHC 119 (QB) at [69].
346. [2010] EWHC 119 (QB) at [39], [95] and [149].
347. [2010] EWHC 119 (QB) at [24].

an injunction binding upon him, the alleged wrongdoer might consider that he or she could disclose the information, and hope to avoid the risk of being in contempt of court. Alternatively, in some cases, the alleged wrongdoer may destroy any evidence which may be needed in order to identify him as the source of the leak. Tipping off of the alleged wrongdoer can thus defeat the purpose of the order.[348]

His Honour said he would not continue a super-injunction and noted that the plaintiff had already conceded that such an order was unnecessary.[349] The *Report of the Committee on Super-Injunctions* notes[350] that since the *Terry* case the committee knew of only two super-injunctions that had been granted to protect private and confidential information, namely *Ntuli v Donald*[351] and *DFT v TFD*.[352] The injunction granted in *Ntuli* was set aside on appeal and in *DFT* the injunction was only for 7 days and was granted to avoid tipping off.

8.72 In contrast to the rare use of super-injunctions, there has been an increase in the granting of anonymised injunctions. This is where a party's identity or a witness is kept secret but, unlike the super-injunction, there is no prohibition on disclosing the existence of the proceedings and the nature of the injunction. Historically, anonymity orders were not granted in respect of confidential information cases.[353] But they have become commonplace in the United Kingdom due to court procedural rules and the adoption of Art 8 of the European Convention for the Protection of Human Rights and Fundamental Freedoms. This means 'Everyone has the right to respect for his private and family life, his home and his correspondence.'[354] It 'requires public authorities, such as the court, to respect private and family life'.[355]

The increase in anonymised injunctions across a wide variety of proceedings has been subject to judicial criticism. In *re Guardian News and Media Ltd* Lord Rodger in setting aside an anonymous freezing order agreed with counsel that his 'first term docket' read 'like alphabet soup' and said:

> ... until the recent efflorescence of anonymity orders, the general rule both in theory and in practice was that judicial proceedings were held in public and the parties were named in judgments. Their names would also be given in newspaper reports and in the law reports. That is still usually the position – as can be seen from the frequent press reports of, say, employment tribunal hearings and decisions where details of personal and sexual relationships among the warring parties are a common feature.

348. [2010] EWHC 119 (QB) at [138].

349. [2010] EWHC 119 (QB) at [137].

350. *Report of the Committee on Super Injunctions: Super Injunctions, Anonymised Injunctions and Open Justice*, Lord Neuberger MR, p iv (20 May 2011).

351. [2010] EWCA Civ 1276.

352. [2010] EWHC 2335 (QB).

353. *Report of the Committee on Super Injunctions: Super Injunctions, Anonymised Injunctions and Open Justice*, Lord Neuberger MR, p 23 (20 May 2011).

354. *In re Guardian News and Media Ltd* [2010] UKSC1 at [28] per Lord Rodger.

355. [2010] UKSC1 at [28] per Lord Rodger.

In the nineteenth century many couples would doubtless have been only too pleased to agree to have their divorce heard in private. But the court sat in public and reports of the evidence, often recounting high-class intrigues, were published in the newspapers. These reports gave rise to concern in some quarters, especially since they were particularly popular reading-matter among servants. So, during the nineteenth and early twentieth centuries, various attempts were made to introduce legislative controls. The attempts foundered, partly because the unpleasant publicity was thought to act as a welcome deterrent against couples divorcing. Against that background, in *Scott v Scott*[356] the House of Lords affirmed in the strongest possible terms the long-established stance of the English courts that hearings should be held in public. …

Over the years Parliament has gone on to create a considerable number of exceptions to the ordinary rule that proceedings must be held in public …[It] has introduced other statutory restrictions on what may be reported in various kinds of cases, especially those involving children …

In an extreme case, identification of a participant in legal proceedings, whether as a party or (more likely) as a witness, might put that person or his family in peril of their lives or safety because of what he had said about, say, some powerful criminal organization.[357]

Super and anonymised injunctions in Australia

8.73   Australia has many similar laws to the United Kingdom in relation to confidentiality, privacy and procedure which allow the granting of super and anonymised injunctions. The legal and equitable obligations of confidence continue to evolve in Australian courts to protect the private rights of individuals and companies.[358] In addition, Victoria[359] and the Australian Capital Territory[360] have legislation which is similar[361] to the Human Rights Act 1998 (UK) and there is a proposed federal statutory cause of action for a serious invasion of privacy.[362] Further, Australian courts have an inherent jurisdiction to make an order for confidentiality[363] and this is reinforced by statutory provisions for anonymity and suppression orders in various civil, criminal and family law procedure statutes.[364] In relation to the civil law, it

---

356. [1913] AC 417.

357. [2010] UKSC1 at [22]–[26] per Lord Rodger.

358. See, for example, *Giller v Procopets* (2008) 24 VR 1; [2008] VSCA 236 discussed at 11.21.

359. Charter of Human Rights and Responsibilities Act 2006, s 13(a) (Vic); considered in *Momcilovic v R* (2011) 280 ALR 221; [2011] HCA 34 at [522] per Crennan and Kiefell JJ, at [672] per Bell J.

360. Human Rights Act 2004, s 12 (ACT); see *Momcilovic v R* (2011) 280 ALR 221; [2011] HCA 34 at [146] per Gummow J.

361. Compare *Momcilovic v R* [2011] HCA 34 at [146], [148]-[161] per Gummow J where his Honour found that the New Zealand Bill of Rights Act 1990 (NZ) was of 'greater comparative utility' than the Human Rights Act 1998 (UK).

362. *For Your Information: Australian Privacy Law and Practice*, Australian Law Reform Commission (2008).

363. *Deputy Commissioner of Taxation v Karas* [2011] VSC 304 at [3] per Davies J.

364. See *DJL v The Central Authority* (2000) 201 CLR 226 at 240-241; *Central Equity Ltd v Chua* [1999] FCA 1067.

is common practice in relation to freezing[365] and search orders[366] to have temporary secrecy until the first return date so that other wrongdoers are not tipped off. Section 50(1) of the Federal Court of Australia Act 1976 (Cth) allows the court to forbid the publication of evidence, the name of a party or witness 'as appears to the Court to be *necessary* in order to prevent prejudice to the administration of justice or the security of the Commonwealth' (emphasis added). This qualifies the general provision in s 17(1) that the jurisdiction is to be exercised in open court.[367] If a trade secret or confidential information 'is the subject-matter of the proceedings' then it is 'in the interests of justice that the processes for determination of those very proceedings not destroy or seriously depreciate the value of that subject matter'.[368] Still, the power to make a suppression order is exercised with caution because the word 'necessary' in s 50 'is a strong word' and 'suggests Parliament was not dealing with trivialities.'[369] In *Hogan v Australian Crime Commission*[370] the High Court emphasized that the making or continuation of a suppression order does not satisfy the 'necessary' threshold merely because it is 'convenient, reasonable or sensible'. So, if disclosure will merely 'cause embarrassment or damage to reputation' this will be insufficient.[371] The order must, pursuant to s 50, be 'necessary to prevent prejudice to the administration of justice or the security of the Commonwealth.'

8.74   Proposed uniform federal[372] and state legislation[373] on suppression and non-publication orders similar to the Court Suppression and Non–publication Orders Act 2010 (NSW) will allow the granting of remedies that resemble anonymised[374] and super-injunctions.[375] One of the reasons for the legislation is to ensure that 'the privacy and safety of participants in court proceedings is not unduly compromised'.[376] Section 7(a) provides that a suppression or non-publication order may prohibit or restrict disclosure of information that would reveal the identity of 'any party or witness' or 'any person who is related to or otherwise associated with any party to or witness in proceedings

---

365. See Chapter 9.

366. See Chapter 10.

367. *Hogan v Australian Crime Commission* (2010) 240 CLR 651 at [7] per French CJ, Gummow, Hayne, Heydon and Kiefel JJ.

368. *Hogan v Australian Crime Commission* (2010) 240 CLR 651 at [42] per French CJ, Gummow, Hayne, Heydon and Kiefel JJ, citing in support *Australian Broadcasting Commission v Parish* (1980) 29 ALR 228 at 235.

369. *Hogan v Australian Crime Commission* (2010) 240 CLR 651 at [30] per French CJ, Gummow, Hayne, Heydon and Kiefel JJ.

370. (2010) 240 CLR 651.

371. *Deputy Commissioner of Taxation v Karas* [2011] VSC 304 at [10].

372. The Access to Justice (Federal Jurisdiction) Amendment Bill 2011 (Cth).

373. Based on the model suppression order law developed by the Standing Committee of Attorneys-General in 2010.

374. See, Court Suppression and Non-publication Orders Act 2010, s 7(a) (NSW).

375. See, Court Suppression and Non-publication Orders Act 2010, s 7(b) (NSW).

376. New South Wales, Legislative Council, Second Reading speech (*Hansard*) 23 November 2010.

before the court'. In making such orders the court 'must take into account
that a primary objective of the administration of justice is to safeguard the
public interest in open justice'.[377] It must also specify the ground or grounds
on which the order is made[378] as set out in 8(1):

8 Grounds for making an order

(1) A court may make a suppression order or non-publication order on one
or more of the following grounds:

(a) the order is necessary to prevent prejudice to the proper
administration of justice,

(b) the order is necessary to prevent prejudice to the interests of the
Commonwealth or a State or Territory in relation to national or
international security,

(c) the order is necessary to protect the safety of any person,

(d) the order is necessary to avoid causing undue distress or embarrassment
to a party to or witness in criminal proceedings involving an offence
of a sexual nature (including an act of indecency),

(e) it is otherwise necessary in the public interest for the order to be
made and that public interest significantly outweighs the public
interest in open justice.

These grounds, particularly ss 8(1)(a) and (e), are capable of supporting
both anonymised and super-injunctions to preserve confidential information
and trade secrets. However, in common with s 50 of The Federal Court
Act 1976 (Cth), the use of the word 'necessary' in each paragraph 'suggests
Parliament was not dealing with trivialities'[379] and the 'necessary' threshold
test will not be satisfied merely because the order is convenient, reasonable
or sensible.[380] Still, s 8(1) has a potentially wider application than s 50 of
The Federal Court Act 1976 (Cth) because of the extra grounds found in
ss 8(1)(c),[381] (d) and (e).

There are two types of orders that can be made: the 'suppression order'
and the 'non-publication order'. The broader suppression order prohibits
or restricts the disclosure of information 'by publication or otherwise'.[382]
'Information' includes 'any document' and 'publish' means to disseminate or
provide access to the public or a section of the public 'by any means', including
'in a book, newspaper, magazine or other written publication', 'broadcast by
radio or television', 'public exhibition' and 'broadcast or publication by means
of the Internet.'[383] The narrower 'non-publication order' prohibits or restricts
'the publication of information (but that does not otherwise prohibit or

---

377. Court Suppression and Non-publication Orders Act 2010, s 6 (NSW).

378. Court Suppression and Non-publication Orders Act 2010, s 8(2) (NSW).

379. *Hogan v Australian Crime Commission* (2010) 240 CLR 651 at [30] per French CJ, Gummow, Hayne,
Heydon and Kiefel JJ.

380. *Hogan v Australian Crime Commission* (2010) 240 CLR 651.

381. See *Welker v Rinehart (No 5)* [2012] NSWSC 45.

382. Court Suppression and Non-publication Orders Act 2010, s 3 (NSW).

383. Court Suppression and Non-publication Orders Act 2010, s 3 (NSW).

restrict the disclosure of information)'. This allows 'the media and the general public to access information, but not publish it'.[384] Both orders can be made on an interim basis 'without determining the merits of the application,' but the court must then 'determine the application as a matter of urgency'.[385] The order may extend beyond New South Wales if this is 'necessary for achieving the purpose for which the order is made'.[386] The duration of the order is 'decided by the court and specified in the order' but 'the court is to ensure that the order operates for no longer than is reasonably necessary to achieve the purpose for which it is made'.[387] This provision reflects the reasoning in the *Terry* case that super and anonymised injunctions should have return dates so that they cannot become permanent apart from 'very, very rare cases' and even here 'the order should be kept under active and close scrutiny by the court'.[388]

A contravention of the order may be punished as either an offence or a contempt of court.[389] A review of the order can be made by the court on its 'own initiative' or by the applicant for the order, a party to the proceedings, the federal or state governments, a news media organisation and 'any other person who, in the court's opinion, has a sufficient interest in the question of whether a suppression order or non-publication order should have been made or should continue to operate'.[390] A 'news media organisation' is defined broadly to mean 'a commercial enterprise that engages in the business of broadcasting or publishing news or a public broadcasting service that engages in the dissemination of news through a public news medium'.[391]

---

384. New South Wales, Legislative Council, Second Reading speech (*Hansard*) 23 November 2010.

385. Court Suppression and Non-publication Orders Act 2010, s 10 (NSW).

386. Court Suppression and Non-publication Orders Act 2010, s 11 (NSW).

387. Court Suppression and Non-publication Orders Act 2010, s 12 (NSW).

388. *Report of the Committee on Super-Injunctions*, pp 30 and 34; see also *Hogan v Australian Crime Commission* (2010) 240 CLR 651 at [29].

389. Court Suppression and Non-publication Orders Act 2010, s 16 (NSW).

390. Court Suppression and Non-publication Orders Act 2010, s 13 (NSW).

391. Court Suppression and Non-publication Orders Act 2010, s 3 (NSW).

CHAPTER

Mareva or Freezing Orders

INTRODUCTION

9.1 A Mareva or freezing order restrains the defendant or potential defendant from disposing of his or her assets which may be required to satisfy the plaintiff's claim. It is an 'extraordinary' remedy because it restricts 'the right to deal with assets even before judgment, and is commonly granted without notice.'[1] The danger is that if the defendant has notice it may lead to the removal or dissipation of the assets. First used by the English Court Appeal

---

1. Federal Court Practice Note CM 9 para 6 (1 August 2011).

in 1975 in *Nippon Yusen Kaisha v Karageorgis*[2] and *Mareva Compania Naviera SA v International Bulk Carriers SA*,[3] it was originally only available against foreign defendants who were likely to frustrate judgment by transferring assets out of the jurisdiction. It is now available against any defendant who threatens to place his or her assets beyond the reach of the plaintiff. In common with Anton Piller orders discussed in the next chapter, the remedy was described by Donaldson J in the English Court of Appeal as one of 'the law's two nuclear weapons'.[4] But due to its far reaching consequences it has become 'closely regulated'.[5] As explained by Pullin J in *Cadura Investments Ltd v Rototek Pty Ltd*:

> Because a mareva order is an interlocutory order which, if granted, imposes a severe restriction upon a defendant's right to deal with his or her assets, it is necessary to pay close attention to the basis for the claim which is put forward. The purpose of a mareva order is to preserve the status quo, not to change it in favour of the plaintiff. The function of the order is not to provide a plaintiff with security in advance for a judgment it hopes to obtain and which it fears might not be satisfied, and it is not to improve the position of the plaintiff in the event of a defendant's insolvency.[6]

Similarly, in *Fourie v Le Roux* Lord Bingham in the House of Lords observed:

> Mareva (or freezing) injunctions were from the beginning, and continue to be, granted for an important but limited purpose: to prevent a defendant dissipating his assets with the intention or effect of frustrating enforcement of a prospective judgment. They are not a proprietary remedy. They are not granted to give a claimant advance security for his claim, although they may have that effect. They are not an end in themselves. They are a supplementary remedy, granted to protect the efficacy of court proceedings, domestic or foreign ...[7]

History

9.2   The first reported use of a Mareva-type order was in *Nippon Yusen Kaisha v Karageorgis*.[8] Japanese shipowners issued a writ against Greek charterers, who were not in the jurisdiction, claiming money for the unpaid charter of three ships. Shortly after the writ, the shipowners sought an ex parte injunction in the English High Court restraining the charterers from removing from the jurisdiction any funds they had in the jurisdiction. At first instance, the injunction was refused by Donaldson J, but an ex parte appeal to the English Court of Appeal was successful. Lord Denning MR, in the majority, granted the injunction.

---

2.   [1975] 3 All ER 282; [1975] 1 WLR 1093.

3.   [1975] 2 Lloyd's Rep 509.

4.   *Bank Mellat v Nikpour* (1985) FSR 87 (CA) at 92.

5.   *Fourie v Le Roux* [2007] UKHL 1 at 3 per Lord Bingham.

6.   [2003] WASC 255 at [3].

7.   [2007] UKHL 1 at 2.

8.   [1975] 3 All ER 282; [1975] 1 WLR 1093.

The facts in *Mareva Compania Naviera SA v International Bulk Carriers SA*[9] were similar to *Nippon*. In the High Court Donaldson J was again the first instance judge, but this time he granted the injunction for a short period so that the Court of Appeal could consider his view that he lacked the necessary jurisdiction. Lord Denning MR thought differently and confirmed the remedy.

9.3   Since the *Nippon* and *Mareva* cases, the remedy has been extended to apply to all defendants, local and foreign, who dissipate their assets in or out of the jurisdiction. In Australia, the High Court endorsed the availability of Mareva orders in *Jackson v Sterling Industries*[10] and *Cardile v LED Builders Pty Ltd*.[11] The High Court also confirmed in *Pelechowski v Registrar, Court of Appeal*[12] that a Mareva order may be obtained both before and after judgment.

Jurisdiction

9.4   In the *Nippon* and *Mareva* cases, Lord Denning said that the jurisdiction to grant a Mareva 'injunction' was founded on s 45(1) of the Supreme Court of Judicature (Consolidation) Act 1925 (UK), because this provision allowed the court to grant an injunction wherever it was 'just and convenient to do so'.[13] Section 37 of the Supreme Court Act 1981 (UK) provides a statutory 'endorsement' of the remedy.[14] This section did not 'turn the common law *Mareva* injunction into a statutory remedy, but it assumed the remedy existed, and tacitly endorsed its validity.'[15]

In Australia, the jurisdiction to grant Mareva orders is found both in the court's inherent power to prevent an abuse of process and in statutory provisions such as s 23 of the Supreme Court Act 1970 (NSW), which provides:

> The Court shall have all jurisdiction which may be necessary for the administration of justice in New South Wales.[16]

The order has been described as 'the paradigm example of an order to prevent the frustration of a court's process'.[17]

In *Cardile v LED Builders Pty Ltd* the High Court preferred the term 'Mareva order' or 'asset preservation order'[18] to 'Mareva injunction' so as 'to avoid confusion as to its doctrinal basis'.[19] But the majority saw 'no harm in

9.   [1975] 2 Lloyd's Rep 509.

10.   (1987) 162 CLR 623.

11.   (1999) 198 CLR 380.

12.   (1999) 198 CLR 435.

13.   The equivalent in New South Wales is s 66(4) of the Supreme Court Act 1970.

14.   See *A J Bekhor & Co v Bilton* [1981] QB 923.

15.   *Mercedes Benz AG v Leiduck* [1996] AC 284 at 299 (PC) per Lord Mustill.

16.   *See Riley McKay Pty Ltd v McKay* [1982] 1 NSWLR 264 (CA), cited with approval in *Jackson v Sterling Industries* (1987) 162 CLR 612 at 617 per Wilson and Dawson JJ.

17.   *Patrick Stevedores Operations No 2 Pty Ltd v Maritime Union of Australia (No 3)* (1998) 195 CLR 1 at [35].

18.   (1999) 198 CLR 380 at [79] per Kirby J.

19.   (1999) 198 CLR 380 at [42] per Gaudron, McHugh, Gummow and Callinan JJ.

the use of the term Mareva'.[20] In the United Kingdom they are commonly called 'freezing orders'.[21] While the name 'Mareva order' continues to be used in practice,[22] the Australian harmonised court rules use the name 'freezing order.' For example, r 7.32 of the Federal Court Rules 2011 provides:

7.32 Freezing order

(1) The Court may make an order (a *freezing order*), with or without notice to a respondent, for the purpose of preventing the frustration or inhibition of the Court's process by seeking to meet a danger that a judgment or prospective judgment of the Court will be wholly or partly unsatisfied.

(2) A freezing order may be an order restraining a respondent from removing any assets located in or outside Australia or from disposing of, dealing with, or diminishing the value of, those assets.

ELEMENTS

9.5 The elements for granting a Mareva or freezing order may be summarised as follows:

a) the plaintiff has a judgment in their favour *or* a good arguable case;

b) the defendant has assets subject to the jurisdiction of the court;

c) there is a danger that a judgment will be unsatisfied due to the disposition or dissipation of the defendant's assets;

d) the court's discretion and the balance of convenience favours the granting of the remedy; and

e) the plaintiff has provided undertakings to the court including the usual undertaking as to damages.

A judgment or good arguable case

9.6 The traditional threshold test was that the plaintiff required a good arguable case or a prima facie cause of action against the defendant.[23] A good arguable case is 'one which is more than barely capable of serious argument, and yet not necessarily one which the judge believes would have a better than 50 per cent chance of success'.[24] While the test does not require proof on the balance of probabilities it has been held to be more difficult to satisfy than the 'serious question to be tried' test[25] because a Mareva order 'is a drastic remedy

---

20. (1999) 198 CLR 380 at [40] per Gaudron, McHugh, Gummow and Callinan JJ.

21. *Fourie v Le Roux* [2007] UKHL 1.

22. See, for example, Federal Court Practice Note CM 9 – Freezing Orders (also known as 'Mareva Orders' or 'Asset Preservation Orders') (1 August 2011).

23. *Patterson v BTR Engineering (Aust) Ltd* (1989) 18 NSWLR 319 at 321 per Gleeson CJ (CA).

24. *Ninemia Maritime Corp v Trave GmbH & Co KG ("The Niedersachsen")* [1984] 1 All ER 398 at 404 per Mustill J.

25. *Polly Peck International plc v Nadir (No 2)* [1992] 4 All ER 769 at 786 per Lord Donaldson MR; *Derby v Weldon (No 1)* [1990] 1 Ch 48 at 57–8 and 64; Zuckerman, 'Mareva and Interlocutory Injunctions Disentangled' (1992) 108 *LQR* 559; see also **8.48**.

which should not be granted lightly'.[26] In *Fourie v Le Roux* Lord Bingham in the House of Lords observed:

> In recognition of the severe effect which such an injunction may have on a defendant, the procedure for seeking and making Mareva injunctions has over the last three decades become closely regulated. I regard that regulation as beneficial and would not wish to weaken it in any way. The procedure incorporates important safeguards for the defendant. One of those safeguards, by no means the least important, is that the claimant should identify the prospective judgment whose enforcement the defendant is not to be permitted, by dissipating his assets, to frustrate. The claimant cannot of course guarantee that he will recover judgment, nor what the terms of the judgment will be. But he must at least point to proceedings already brought, or proceedings about to be brought, so as to show where and on what basis he expects to recover judgment against the defendant.[27]

9.7   The harmonised rules of court now provide two distinct requirements, namely, that the plaintiff either has a court judgment in their favour *or* a good arguable case on an accrued or prospective cause of action. For example, subrs 7.35(1) to (3) of the Federal Court Rules 2011 provide:

(1) This rule applies if:

   (a) judgment has been given in favour of an applicant by:

     (i)   the Court to which subrule (2) applies — another court; or

   (b) an applicant has a good arguable case on an accrued or prospective cause of action that is justiciable in:

     (i)   the Court; or

     (ii) for a cause of action to which subrule (3) applies — another court.

(2) This subrule applies to a judgment if there is a sufficient prospect that the judgment will be registered in or enforced by the Court.

(3) This subrule applies to a cause of action if:

   (a) there is a sufficient prospect that the other court will give judgment in favour of the applicant; and

   (b) there is a sufficient prospect that the judgment will be registered in or enforced by the Court.

The requirement in the rules for either a judgment or a good arguable case reflects pre-existing law that there are stronger grounds for granting the remedy after judgment rather than before.[28]

9.8   The term 'another court' in r 7.35 of the Federal Court Rules 2011 is defined broadly in r 7.31 to mean 'a court outside Australia or a court in Australia other than the Court' that is hearing the application for the remedy. So a foreign judgment, defined to include an order,[29] may support a freezing order if there is a 'sufficient prospect' that the judgment or order will be

---

26. *Cardile v LED Builders Pty Ltd* (1999) 198 CLR 380 at 409 per Gaudron, McHugh, Gummow and Callinan JJ.

27. [2007] UKHL 1 at 3.

28. See *Babanaft International Co SA v Bassatne* [1989] 2 WLR 232 at 243–244, 254.

29. See, for example, r 7.31 Federal Court Rules 2011.

registered in or enforced by the court hearing the freezing order application. Even a good arguable case or 'prospective' cause of action in a foreign court will support a freezing order if there is a 'sufficient prospect' that *both* the other court will give judgment in favour of the applicant *and* the judgment will be registered in or enforced by the court hearing the freezing order application.

The Federal Court Practice Note CM 9 para 15 states:

> The rules of court confirm that certain restrictions expressed in *The Siskina*[30] do not apply in this jurisdiction. First, the Court may make a freezing order before a cause of action has accrued (a *"prospective"* cause of action). Secondly, the Court may make a free-standing freezing order in aid of foreign proceedings in prescribed circumstances. Thirdly, where there are assets in Australia, service out of Australia is permitted under a new "long arm" service rule.

The 'long arm' service rule is r 7.37 of the Federal Court Rules 2011. It provides that an 'application for a freezing order or an ancillary order may be served on a person who is outside Australia (whether or not the person is domiciled or resident in Australia) if any of the assets to which the order relates are within the jurisdiction of the Court'.

9.9 The harmonised court practice notes on freezing orders also provide guidance on the evidence that should be provided in support. For example, Federal Court Practice Note CM 9 para 20 provides:

> The affidavits relied on in support of an application for a freezing or ancillary order should, if possible, address the following:
>
> (a) information about the judgment that has been obtained, or, if no judgment has been obtained, the following information about the cause of action:
>
>   (i)   the basis of the claim for substantive relief;
>
>   (ii) the amount of the claim; and
>
>   (iii) if the application is made without notice to the respondent, the applicant's knowledge of any possible defence;
>
> (b) the nature and value of the respondent's assets, so far as they are known to the applicant, within and outside Australia;
>
> (c) the matters referred to in Rule 7.35 of the Rules;[31] and
>
> (d) the identity of any person, other than the respondent, who, the applicant believes, may be affected by the order, and how that person may be affected by it.

9.10 Prior to the harmonised court rules it was held that if the cause of action had not accrued at the time of application, but would inevitably do so, was sufficient to establish a prima facie cause of action.[32] The harmonised

---

30.   [1979] AC 210.

31.   See **9.7**.

32.   *Riley McKay Pty Ltd v McKay* [1982] 1 NSWLR 264 (CA).

rules now expressly provide that a good arguable case may be based on a 'prospective cause of action'.[33]

Assets subject to the court's jurisdiction

9.11   The plaintiff must establish that the defendant has assets subject to the jurisdiction of the court. As the freezing order jurisdiction operates *in personam* the defendant's assets need not be in Australia: see [9.14]. The assets could include real estate, money, a bank account, a secured overdraft,[34] a ship's cargo, a car or goodwill.[35] The court may make ancillary asset disclosure orders[36] including orders requiring the defendant to attend court for an oral examination as to his or her assets; [37] to disclose 'the nature and location of particular assets';[38] requiring the delivery of specified assets; directing the defendant's bank to disclose information to the plaintiff; to pay money into court; appointing a receiver to the defendant's assets; and an order transferring assets from one foreign jurisdiction to another.

9.12   Ancillary asset disclosure orders are frequently made against a person who is not a party to the proceedings.[39] In *Winter v Marac Australia*[40] it was held that orders can be made in respect of assets held by third parties if the defendant has some right in respect of the asset or has control over or other access to the asset. In *Cardile v LED Builders Pty Ltd* the High Court held that a Mareva order could even extend to the shared or concurrent goodwill in a trade mark or trading name if its disposition by the third party is likely to affect the value of the defendant's share in the goodwill. In that case LED sued Eagle Homes Pty Ltd in 1993 and 1994 for copyright infringements in building plans. The only shareholders in Eagle Homes Pty Ltd were Mr and Mrs Cardile who received a $400,000 dividend in 1993. In 1995, after the litigation was commenced but before the hearing, a new company, Ultra Modern Developments Pty Ltd was formed and controlled by Mr and Mrs Cardile. Shortly thereafter Ultra Modern Developments became the sole owner of the business name Eagle Homes, although both Ultra Modern Developments and Eagle Homes concurrently used this name in relation to their businesses. The copyright infringement actions were heard in March 1996. Eagle Homes Pty Ltd was facing defeat. But in the same year it declared an $800,000 dividend and some $660,000 of this was paid to the Cardiles. In July 1996 judgment in the copyright infringement

---

33.   See, for example, rule 7.35(1)(b) Federal Court Rules 2011.

34.   *Third Chandris Shipping Corp v Unimarine SA* [1979] QB 645 (CA).

35.   *Cardile v LED Builders Pty Ltd* (1999) 198 CLR 380.

36.   Rule 7.33(2)(a) Federal Court Rules 2011.

37.   See *Pathways Employment Services v West* [2004] NSWSC 903 at [9] per Campbell J; *Universal Music Australia Pty Ltd v Sharman License Holdings Ltd* [2005] FCA 1587; Federal Court Practice Note CM 9 para 14 (1 August 2011).

38.   *Bax Global (Australia) Pty Ltd v Evans* (1999) 47 NSWLR 538 at 544–5 per Austin J; *Kuan Han Pty Ltd v Oceanview Group Holdings Pty Ltd* [2003] FCA 1063 at [44]–[50] per Conti J.

39.   See, for example, rule 7.34 Federal Court Rules 2011.

40.   (1986) 7 NSWLR 11 (CA).

matters were decided in favour of LED and orders were made in August 1996. In December 1996 further orders were made against Eagle Homes Pty Ltd restricting its dealings with realty. In June 1997 Mareva orders were made against Eagle Homes Pty Ltd as well as Ultra Modern Developments Pty Ltd and the Cardiles. The High Court found that even though Ultra Modern Developments Pty Ltd and the Cardiles were not parties they should nonetheless be subject to Mareva orders. The payment of 'the dividends was a non-commercial exercise and was … done with a view to limiting the funds available to meet a judgment in favour of LED.'[41] As the Cardiles had actually received about $1.06 million the Mareva order was restricted to this amount. The order against Ultra Modern Developments was limited to restraining it from disposing of, encumbering or otherwise dealing with the Eagle Homes business name[42] and this extended to the goodwill that attached to the Eagle Homes name[43]. It was held that, subject to the other elements being satisfied, the principles that should guide the courts in determining whether to grant an order against a third party are:

(i) the third party holds, is using, or has exercised or is exercising a power of disposition over, or is otherwise in possession of, assets, including 'claims and expectancies', of the judgment debtor or potential judgment debtor; or

(ii) some process, ultimately enforceable by the courts, is or may be available to the judgment creditor as a consequence of a judgment against that actual or potential judgment debtor, pursuant to which, whether by appointment of a liquidator, trustee in bankruptcy, receiver or otherwise, the third party may be obliged to disgorge property or otherwise contribute to the funds or property of the judgment debtor to help satisfy the judgment against the judgment debtor.[44]

9.13 Based on *Cardile* the harmonized rules of court expressly provide for freezing orders to be made against a person that is not a party to the proceeding[45] and against third parties. For example, r 7.35(5) of the Federal Court Rules 2011 provides:

The Court may make a freezing order or an ancillary order or both against a person other than a judgment debtor or prospective judgment debtor (a ***third party***) if the Court is satisfied, having regard to all the circumstances, that:

(a) there is a danger that a judgment or prospective judgment will be wholly or partly unsatisfied because:

(i) the third party holds or is using, or has exercised or is exercising, a power of disposition over assets (including claims and expectancies) of the judgment debtor or prospective judgment debtor; or

---

41. (1999) 198 CLR 380 at [64] per Gaudron, McHugh, Gummow and Callinan JJ.
42. (1999) 198 CLR 380 at [75] per Gaudron, McHugh, Gummow and Callinan JJ.
43. (1999) 198 CLR 380 at [63] per Gaudron, McHugh, Gummow and Callinan JJ.
44. (1999) 198 CLR 380 at [57] per Gaudron, McHugh, Gummow and Callinan JJ; applied in *Caboche v Southern Equities Corp Ltd* [2001] SASC 55.
45. See, for example, r 7.34 Federal Court Rules 2011.

    (ii) the third party is in possession of, or in a position of control or influence concerning, assets (including claims and expectancies) of the judgment debtor or prospective judgment debtor; or

(b) a process in the Court is or may ultimately be available to the applicant as a result of a judgment or prospective judgment, under which process the third party may be obliged to disgorge assets or contribute toward satisfying the judgment or prospective judgment.

9.14 The freezing order operates *in personam*,[46] that is, the court's jurisdiction is over the defendant as an individual. Accordingly, a freezing order may extend beyond Australia to assets held by the defendant anywhere in the world. The harmonised court practice note provides:

> A freezing or ancillary order may be limited to assets in Australia or in a defined part of Australia, or may extend to assets anywhere in the world, and may cover all assets without limitation, assets of a particular class, or specific assets (such as the amounts standing to the credit of identified bank accounts).[47]

If the order extends to assets outside Australia it 'should provide for the protection of persons outside Australia and third parties.'[48] In *Talacko v Talacko* Kyrou J held that Mareva orders in respect of foreign assets are guided by the following principles:

(a) Provided that the defendant is subject to this court's jurisdiction, this court has power to make a Mareva order in respect of foreign assets and there is no rule of practice against granting such an injunction.

(b) Whether the assets were in the jurisdiction at the time the proceeding was commenced, or indeed have ever been within the jurisdiction, does not affect whether the court has jurisdiction to make a Mareva order or its practice in relation to such orders. However, it may be relevant to the exercise of the discretion.

(c) It has been said that the discretion to make a Mareva order in respect of foreign assets should be exercised with considerable circumspection and care. The suggestion in one Australian case that the jurisdiction should only be exercised in "exceptional cases", which appears to broadly reflect the English position, has not been followed consistently in the Australian cases dealing with the exercise of discretion. With respect, I do not accept that the discretion can only be exercised in exceptional cases. Nevertheless, as discussed shortly, I regard the present case as exceptional.

(d) The discretion will be exercised more readily after judgment.[49] (footnotes omitted)

---

46.   *Cardile v LED Builders Pty Ltd* (1999) 198 CLR 380 at [50] and [55] per Gaudron, McHugh, Gummow and Callinan JJ.

47.   Federal Court Practice Note CM 9 para 8 (1 August 2011).

48.   Federal Court Practice Note CM 9 para 13 (1 August 2011).

49.   [2009] VSC 349 at [35]; see also *Dadourian Group International Inc v Simms* [2006] 1 WLR 2499 at 2502 [25] (UKCA).

Additionally, the 'long arm' service rule provides that 'a freezing order or an ancillary order may be served on a person who is outside Australia (whether or not the person is domiciled or resident in Australia) if any of the assets to which the order relates are within the jurisdiction of the Court.'[50]

Unsatisfied judgment danger

9.15 Traditionally there had to be a 'real risk' or 'danger' that the defendant would frustrate the judgment, either before or after judgment,[51] by absconding or dissipating his or her assets.[52] The harmonised rules of court now provide that there must be 'a danger that a judgment or prospective judgment will be wholly or partly unsatisfied.' For example, subr 7.35(4) of the Federal Court Rules 2011 provides:

> The Court may make a freezing order or an ancillary order or both against a judgment debtor or prospective judgment debtor if the Court is satisfied, having regard to all the circumstances, that there is a danger that a judgment or prospective judgment will be wholly or partly unsatisfied because any of the following might occur:
>
> (a) the judgment debtor, prospective judgment debtor or another person absconds;
>
> (b) the assets of the judgment debtor, prospective judgment debtor or another person are:
>
>   (i) removed from Australia or from a place inside or outside Australia; or
>
>   (ii) disposed of, dealt with or diminished in value.

The term 'judgment' in this rule is defined broadly to extend to an 'order'.[53]

9.16 The plaintiff will need to adduce admissible evidence of the risk or danger. It is not sufficient to have a mere assertion,[54] a prima facie cause of action,[55] an admission in without prejudice or privileged correspondence,[56] an insolvent defendant[57] or merely establish that the defendant intends to leave the jurisdiction.[58] But the danger may be a matter of inference if there is evidence from which 'a prudent, sensible commercial' person could 'properly infer a danger of default.'[59] If the defendant is fraudulent, this will not only

50. Rule 7.37 of the Federal Court Rules 2011.

51. *Pelechowski v Registrar, Court of Appeal* (1999) 198 CLR 435.

52. *Patterson v BTR Engineering (Aust) Ltd* (1989) 18 NSWLR 319 at 326 per Meagher JA (CA).

53. See, for example, r 7.31 Federal Court Rules 2011.

54. *Third Chandris Shipping Corp v Unimarine SA* [1979] QB 645 at 669 per Lord Denning MR; *Curtis v NID Pty Ltd* [2010] FCA 1072.

55. *Patterson v BTR Engineering (Aust) Pty Ltd* (1989) 18 NSWLR 319 at 326 per Meagher JA; *Australian Competition and Consumer Commission v Chaste Corp (No 1)* (2003) 127 FCR 418 at [29] per Spender J.

56. *Frigo v Culhaci* [1998] NSWCA 88.

57. *Hortico (Aust) Pty Ltd v Energy Equipment Co (Aust) Pty Ltd* (1985) 1 NSWLR 545.

58. *Brereton v Milstein* [1988] VR 508; compare *Klein v Botsman* [2003] TASSC 106 at [19] per Blow J (defendant intending to permanently relocate overseas).

59. *Third Chandris Shipping Corporation v Unimarine SA* [1979] QB 645 at 671–672.

assist in establishing a good arguable case but will also allow an inference to be drawn that if the assets are left in the defendant's hands they are not likely to be preserved.[60] Likewise, if the defendant is a persistently bad debtor or has previously removed assets in order to defeat judgment, this will constitute evidence of a danger of dissipation.[61] If the plaintiff has 'made substantial efforts to ascertain the whereabouts of the defendants but to no avail' this may constitute a real risk or danger of dissipation of assets.[62]

Balance of convenience and discretion

9.17   In common with all equitable remedies freezing orders are only available in the court's discretion.[63] The court will weigh in the balance the strength of the plaintiff's case and the risk that the defendant will abscond, dispose of or dissipate his or her assets against other discretionary matters, such as delay, possible defences and lack of full and frank disclosure by the plaintiff. In *Cardile v LED Builders Pty Ltd* the High Court, while considering the effects of Mareva relief on a third party, held that:

> Discretionary considerations generally also should carefully be weighed before an order is made. Has the applicant proceeded diligently and expeditiously? Has a money judgment been recovered in the proceedings? Are proceedings (for example, civil conspiracy proceedings) available against the third party? Why, if some proceedings are available, have they not been taken? Why, if proceedings are available against the third party and have not been taken and the court is still minded to make a Mareva order, should not the grant of the relief be conditioned upon an undertaking by the applicant to commence, and ensure so far as is possible the expedition of, such proceedings? It is difficult to conceive of cases where such an undertaking would not be required. Questions of this kind may be just as relevant to the decision to grant Mareva relief as they are to a decision to dissolve it.[64]

Undertakings

9.18   The granting of a Mareva or freezing order is conditional on the plaintiff or applicant providing various undertakings to the court. The most common is that it 'should, in general, be supported by an undertaking as to damages'[65] or the 'usual undertaking as to damages'. For example, the Federal Court practice note on freezing orders provides the following wording for the usual undertaking as to damages:

> The applicant undertakes to submit to such order (if any) as the Court may consider to be just for the payment of compensation (to be assessed by the

---

60.   *Patterson v BTR Engineering (Aust) Ltd* (1989) 18 NSWLR 319 at 325 per Gleeson CJ; at 326 per Meagher JA (CA).

61.   *The 'Niedersachsen'* [1984] 1 All ER 398 at 406 per Mustill J.

62.   *Huynh v Phan* [2004] VSC 151 at [16] per Cummins J.

63.   *Patterson v BTR Engineering (Aust) Ltd* (1989) 18 NSWLR 319 (CA).

64.   (1999) 198 CLR 380 at [53] per Gaudron, McHugh, Gummow and Callinan JJ.

65.   *Cardile v LED Builders Pty Ltd* (1999) 198 CLR 380 at [43] per Gaudron, McHugh, Gummow and Callinan JJ.

Court or as it may direct) to any person (whether or not a party) affected by
the operation of the order.[66]

The New South Wales Court of Appeal held in *Frigo v Culhaci* that it could
not 'conceive of circumstances where an ex parte mareva [order] should be
granted otherwise than subject to an undertaking as to damages'.[67] Further,
it 'is the duty of the lawyers of the parties to remind the judge of this
prerequisite.'[68]

If the plaintiff has insufficient assets within the court's jurisdiction he or
she may be required to provide security to support the undertaking as to
damages.[69] The court closely scrutinises the undertaking '[b]ecause there may
be difficulties associated with quantification and recovery of damages'[70] if the
order is later discharged. If it is, then ordinarily there will be an inquiry into
damages: see 9.25.

9.19   Apart from the undertaking as to a damages the plaintiff will usually
undertake, as soon as practicable, to file and serve on the defendant copies of
the order, the application for the order, the evidence and written submissions
relied on at the hearing and, if available, the court transcript and originating
process.[71] The plaintiff may also be required to provide an undertaking
to indemnify or pay the reasonable costs of third parties for their costs in
complying with the order. [72] If the order ceases to have effect — because, for
example, the defendant pays money into court or provides security — the
plaintiff usually undertakes to promptly notify in writing affected persons that
the order has ceased to have effect.[73]

FORM

9.20   While the freezing order should be 'framed according to the
circumstances of the case'[74] there are examples attached to the harmonised
court practice notes which provide guidance. Typically the order will exclude
the defendant's legitimate dealings with their assets by allowing them, to pay
for ordinary living expenses, reasonable legal expenses, debts and pursue the
normal conduct of his or her business. [75] Example exception or exclusion
orders found in the harmonised practice notes provide:

---

66.   Federal Court Practice Note CM 9 (1 August 2011) Sch A.
67.   [1998] NSWCA 88 per Mason P, Sheller JA and Sheppard AJA.
68.   *Cardile v LED Builders Pty Ltd* (1999) 198 CLR 380 at [122] per Kirby J.
69.   Federal Court Practice Note CM 9 (1 August 2011); see also *Heartwood Architectural Timber & Joinery Pty Ltd v Redchip Lawyers* [2009] QSC 195.
70.   *Cadura Investments Ltd v Rototek Pty Ltd* [2003] WASC 255 at [4] per Pullin J.
71.   Federal Court Practice Note CM 9 (1 August 2011).
72.   See *Z Ltd v A–Z* [1982] QB 558; *Guinness Peat Aviation (Belgium) NV v Hispania Lineas Aereas SA* [1992] 1 Lloyd's Rep 190; Federal Court Practice Note CM 9 (1 August 2011).
73.   Federal Court Practice Note CM 9 (1 August 2011).
74.   *Zhen v Mo* [2008] VSC 300 at [28] per Forrest J.
75.   *Klein v Botsman* [2003] TASSC 106 at [23] per Blow J.

This order does not prohibit you from:

(a) paying [up to $................. a week/day on] [your ordinary] living expenses;

(b) paying [$....................on] [your reasonable] legal expenses;

(c) dealing with or disposing of any of your assets in the ordinary and proper course of your business, including paying business expenses bona fide and properly incurred; and

(d) in relation to matters not falling within (a), (b) or (c), dealing with or disposing of any of your assets in discharging obligations bona fide and properly incurred under a contract entered into before this order was made, provided that before doing so you give the applicant, if possible, at least two working days written notice of the particulars of the obligation.[76]

9.21 The value of the assets covered by the order 'should not exceed the likely maximum amount of the applicant's claim, including interest and costs'.[77] The plaintiff 'must establish with some precision the value of the prospective judgment' and the order 'should not unnecessarily tie up a party's assets and property'.[78] But precision may not be possible if, for example, an employer discovers that an employee has been making fraudulent misappropriations, but does not know the extent of the misappropriation at the time of the application to the court.[79]

DISSOLUTION AND VARIATION

9.22 A freezing order made without notice will usually be for a limited period and automatically terminate or dissolve on the return date of the application, an event or subject to a condition.[80] The return date should be as 'early as practicable' and 'usually not more than a day or two' after the order is made.[81] Additionally, the order itself will reserve liberty for the defendant to apply to the court on short notice.

9.23 The plaintiff and the defendant may agree in writing to vary the exceptions to the freezing order. A consent order signed by both parties recording the variation should then be filed with the court as soon as practicable and the court 'may order that the exceptions are varied accordingly'.[82] In deciding whether to agree to a variation it is reasonable for

---

76. See, for example, Federal Court Practice Note CM 9 (1 August 2011).
77. Federal Court Practice Note CM 9 para 11 (1 August 2011); *Cardile v LED Builders Pty Ltd* (1999) 198 CLR 380 at 409 [70] per Gaudron, McHugh, Gummow and Callinan JJ; *Fletcher v Fortress Credit Corp (Australia) II Pty Ltd* (2011) 82 ACSR 352.
78. *Zhen v Mo* [2008] VSC 300 at [11] per Forrest J.
79. Federal Court Practice Note CM 9 para 11 (1 August 2011).
80. Such as an application under s 37A of the Conveyancing Act 1919 (NSW) or under s 121 of the Bankruptcy Act 1966 (Cth), see *Tagget v Sexton* (2009) 255 ALR 522, [2009] NSWCA 91 at [67] per Beazley JA.
81. Federal Court Practice Note CM 9 para 9 (1 August 2011).
82. See, for example, Federal Court Practice Note CM 9 (1 August 2011).

the plaintiff to seek information about whether the defendant has access to other sources of funds which are within their direct or indirect control.[83] But this does not 'justify seeking what is, in effect, legal discovery of documents or requesting answers to what are, in effect, legal interrogatories'.[84]

9.24   An application by the defendant to have the order dissolved or varied will 'normally' be treated by the court as urgent.[85] A variation will often be required in order for the sale of an asset to proceed. [86] In *Deputy Commissioner of Taxation v Karas* Bell J observed that the 'experience of the court is that banks and other financial institutions often require the approval of the court or the plaintiff before they will allow particular transactions to take place, even for apparently permitted purposes'.[87] Affected third parties may also apply to have the order varied, [88]and the costs of such an application may have to be borne by the plaintiff.[89]

In order to completely discharge, dissolve or melt the freezing order, the defendant will ordinarily show that one of the elements was not satisfied, for example, deny the existence of a good arguable case or submit evidence showing that there has never been a real risk or danger of dissipation of the defendant's assets. Another ground for dissolution is where the plaintiff has failed to make a full and frank disclosure of material facts at the ex parte hearing.[90] The harmonised court practice note provides:

> An applicant for a freezing order made without notice is under a duty to make full and frank disclosure of all material facts to the Court. This includes disclosure of possible defences known to the applicant and of any information which may cast doubt on the applicant's ability to meet the usual undertaking as to damages from assets within Australia.[91]

The plaintiff's lack of candor means the order 'is liable to be discharged without a hearing on the merits'.[92] The order may also be dissolved if the plaintiff has relied on inadmissible evidence such as confidential without prejudice and privileged communications.[93] The 'continuing absence' of the undertaking as to damages will also lead 'to the dissolution of the ex parte

83.   *Deputy Commissioner of Taxation v Karas* [2011] VSC 673 at [16].

84.   *Deputy Commissioner of Taxation v Karas* [2011] VSC 673 at [16].

85.   See, for example, Federal Court Practice Note CM 9 para 10 (1 August 2011).

86.   *Unconventional Conventions v Accent Oz* [2004] NSWSC 247.

87.   [2011] VSC 673 at [14].

88.   *Z Ltd v A–Z* [1982] QB 558 at 588.

89.   *Project Development Co Ltd SA v KMK Securities Ltd* [1982] 1 WLR 1470.

90.   See *Riley Leisure Products Pty Ltd v Dokeyo Co Ltd* (1986) 7 IPR 464; *Redwin Industries Pty Ltd v Feetsafe Pty Ltd* [2002] VSC 427; *Westpac Banking Corporation v Hilliard* [2001] VSC 187.

91.   See, for example, Federal Court Practice Note CM 9 para 19 (1 August 2011); see also *Lock International plc v Beswick* [1989] 1 WLR 1268.

92.   *Heartwood Architectural Timber & Joinery Pty Ltd v Redchip Lawyers* [2009] QSC 195 at [32] per Applegarth J.

93.   *Frigo v Culbaci* [1998] NSWCA 88.

orders, including those requiring the defendants to file an affidavit disclosing their assets and liabilities'.[94]

9.25   If the freezing order is dissolved on the defendant's application to the court then ordinarily the defendant will be entitled to an inquiry into damages. In *Cardile v LED Builders Pty Ltd* the High Court observed:

> Another reason, unfortunately rarely adverted to in the cases, for care in exercising the power to grant a *Mareva* order is that there may be difficulties associated with the quantification and recovery of damages pursuant to the undertaking if it should turn out that the order should not have been granted. These matters were the subject of discussion by Aickin J in *Air Express Ltd v Ansett Transport Industries (Operations) Pty Ltd*.[95] A further question to which a *Mareva* order gives rise is the identification of the events to trigger its dissolution or an entitlement to damages. So far as this is possible, some attention to that question should be given at the time that the order is framed in the first instance.[96]

The court has a discretion to refuse to enforce the undertaking as to damages[97] or delay its implementation until the result of the principal litigation is known.[98]

---

94.   *Frigo v Culbaci* [1998] NSWCA 88.
95.   [1979] HCA 36; (1979) 146 CLR 249 at 260 et seq; affd (1981) 146 CLR 306.
96.   (1999) 198 CLR 380 at [52] per Gaudron, McHugh, Gummow and Callinan JJ.
97.   *Redwin Industries Pty Ltd v Feetsafe Pty Ltd* [2002] VSC 427 at [45] per Habersberger J who ordered an inquiry as to damages following the discharge of the order.
98.   *Fourie v Le Roux* [2007] UKHL 1 at 42.

CHAPTER 10

Anton Piller Orders

INTRODUCTION

10.1 An Anton Piller or search order directs the defendant to allow the plaintiff's representative to enter the defendant's premises and search for and remove evidence that is in danger of being destroyed or hidden. While the aim of the Mareva order is to preserve the defendant's *assets* to satisfy the plaintiff's claim, the aim of the Anton Piller order is to preserve the *evidence* the subject of the plaintiff's claim. In common with Mareva orders, Anton Piller orders were described by Donaldson J in the English Court of Appeal as one of 'the law's two nuclear weapons'.[1] It is an 'extraordinary remedy'

---

1. *Bank Mellat v Nikpour* (1985) FSR 87 (CA) at 92.

because 'it is intrusive, potentially disruptive, and made *ex parte* and prior to judgment.'[2] The *raison d'etre* is that the defendant may destroy or hide the evidence before trial and avoid justice by denying proper discovery. While the remedy may be granted at any stage of the proceedings it is usually sought prior to the institution of proceedings without notice to the proposed defendant. Surprise is critical in ensuring that the evidence is not destroyed.[3] In *Long v Specifier Publications Pty Ltd* Powell JA explained the order as follows:

> Reduced to its essentials, an Anton Piller order is an order that the defendant to whom, or to which it is directed, should permit the persons specified in the order to enter upon his, or its, premises, and to inspect, take copies of, and remove, specified material or classes of material, indicating, where appropriate, documents, articles or other forms of property. It is an extraordinary remedy, designed to obtain, and to preserve, vital evidence pending the final determination of the plaintiff's claim in the proceedings, in a case in which it can be shown that there is a high risk that, if forewarned, the defendant, would destroy, or hide, the evidence, or cause it to be removed from the jurisdiction of the court. For this reason, such orders are invariably made ex parte.[4]

10.2   The remedy resembles and aids discovery because both require evidence to be preserved and produced to the court. The need for an order beyond discovery, however, is based on the fact that there are dishonest defendants, particularly pirates and counterfeiters, who will not preserve the evidence for production to the court. In common with Mareva orders it operates *in personam* on the defendant who is personally required to permit persons specified in the order to enter the designated premises (including a vehicle or vessel of any kind[5]) and search for, inspect, film, photograph, copy and remove the things described in the order. The defendant or named party will also be required to provide assistance by disclosing the whereabouts of the listed items and enabling the search party to access them by providing keys to locks and passwords for computers. The order is also negative in character, in that the defendant should not, subject to what is said below, frustrate the entry, search, inspection and removal of the things specified in the order. The defendant should not, for example, destroy or hide the relevant documents or goods. The remedy is not, however, a search warrant, because the court lacks jurisdiction to grant such an order in favour of the plaintiff.[6] So, unlike a search warrant, if the defendant refuses access, the specified persons may not lawfully enter the premises. But if the search order has been duly served, the defendant will be liable for contempt.[7] The Canadian Supreme Court noted that the distinction between a criminal search warrant and a civil search order,

---

2.   Federal Court Practice Note CM11 (1 August 2011).

3.   Although it may be more readily granted if the defendant has notice, see *EMI Ltd v Bay Imports Pty Ltd* [1980] FSR 328 at 331 per Waddell J.

4.   (1998) 44 NSWLR 545 at 547.

5.   See, for example, r 7.41 FCR 2011.

6.   *Anton Piller KG v Manufacturing Process Ltd* [1976] Ch 55 (CA); *Long v Specifier Publications Pty Ltd* (1998) 44 NSWLR 545 at 548 per Powell JA (CA).

7.   *Long v Specifier Publications Pty Ltd* (1998) 44 NSWLR 545 at 548 per Powell JA (CA); and see **10.16**.

however, means little to the 'ordinary citizen faced on his or her doorstep with an Anton Piller order.'[8]

10.3 As discussed below, because the order is an extraordinary and draconian remedy only granted in 'exceptional circumstances,'[9] the court will carefully scrutinise its execution in order to avoid abuse.[10] The plaintiff that 'has procured the court to make it must act with prudence and caution in pursuance of it.'[11] Beyond cases that are concerned with pirates and counterfeiters Biscoe J observed in *Jeray v Blue Mountains City Council*:

> Even where there is overwhelming evidence that a respondent has behaved wrongfully, that does not necessarily justify an ex parte search order. Such a person would not necessarily disobey a subpoena or an order of the court requiring them to deliver up or preserve documents. In many cases therefore it will be sufficient to issue a subpoena or make an order that the respondent deliver up or preserve documents pending further order.
>
> Over the years, painful experience of the dangers and potential abuses in the obtaining, form and execution of such orders has shown that it is essential to build safeguards for the respondent into the form of the order.
>
> In all proceedings taken ex parte, but particularly in search order cases, there is a heavy obligation on the applicant to make full and frank disclosure of all relevant facts to the court.[12]

Indeed, both compensatory and exemplary damages may be awarded to the defendant where the execution of the order is faulty or oppressive: see 10.19.

History

10.4 The Anton Piller order derived its name from *Anton Piller KG v Manufacturing Processes Ltd*.[13] This was decided in 1975, but from 1974 such orders were granted in several copyright actions concerning pirated music tapes.[14] The order used in those cases was approved by Lord Denning MR, Ormrod and Shaw LJJ in the English Court of Appeal in the *Anton Piller* case. The case was concerned with industrial espionage and the blatant misuse of confidential information and copyright. The plaintiff, Anton Piller KG, was a reputable German manufacturer of frequency converters for computers. The defendants, Manufacturing Processes Ltd (MPL), was the plaintiff's United Kingdom agent and dealer. The commercial manager and sales manager for MPL discovered that MPL had disclosed to other German manufacturers,

---

8.   *Celanese Canada Inc v Murray Demolition Corp* [2006] 2 SCR 189, 2006 SCC 36 at [28].

9.   *Microsoft Corporation v Goodview Electronics Pty Ltd* (1999) 46 IPR 159; [1999] FCA 754 at [13] per Branson J; *PMSI Group v Wilson* [2003] NSWSC 263 at [1] per Campbell J; *Bugaj v Bates* [2004] FCA 1260 at [10] per Stone J.

10. See the discussion in *Universal Thermosensors Ltd v Hibben* [1992] 1 WLR 840 at 859–61 per Sir Donald Nicholls V-C.

11. *Alanco Australia Pty Ltd v Higgins* [2010] FCA 1484 at [40] per McKerracher J.

12. [2010] NSWLEC 139 at [4], [6].

13. [1976] Ch 55 (CA).

14. See, for example, *EMI Ltd v Pandit* [1975] 1 All ER 418; [1975] 1 WLR 302.

Ferrostaal and Lechmotoren, confidential information about the plaintiff's power units and details of a new frequency converter called the Silent Block. Upset with their findings, the 'defectors,' as they were called by Lord Denning, put themselves in a perilous position by flying to Germany and informing Anton Piller about MPL's damaging disclosures. The defectors were supported by evidence proving that MPL was in regular communication with Ferrostaal and Lechmotoren with a view to Lechmotoren manufacturing a prototype machine copied from Anton Piller. Anton Piller applied ex parte for an interim injunction restraining the defendants from infringing their copyright and disclosing its confidential information together with an order to enter, search, inspect and remove relevant documents into the plaintiff's solicitors' custody. Brightman J granted the injunction but refused to order inspection or removal of documents from MPL's premises. But the remedy was granted on the plaintiff's successful ex parte application to the Court of Appeal. The case remains important, not just because the remedy originally gained its name from the case, but also because the principles announced by Lord Denning MR and Ormrod LJ continue to have a profound effect on the development of the remedy. Ormrod LJ noted that the order is 'at the extremity of this court's powers' and depends on the following three essential conditions:

> First, there must be an extremely strong prima facie case. Secondly, the damage, potential or actual, must be very serious for the applicant. Thirdly, there must be clear evidence that the defendants have in their possession incriminating documents or things, and that there is a real possibility that they may destroy such material before any application inter partes can be made.[15].

These principles have been widely accepted in Commonwealth jurisdictions. In 1982 Ormrod LJ's reasoning was approved by Stephen J in the High Court of Australia in *Simsek v MacPhee*.[16] His Honour noted[17] that in 1962 Dixon CJ had observed that he had never any doubt 'that the incidental power of the Court can preserve any subject matter, human or not, pending a decision.'[18] While Anton Piller orders have long been available in Canada,[19] they are not generally available in the United States. But there are similar statutory remedies available there in relation to copyright infringement such as impounding orders under s 503(a) of the Copyright Act (17 U.S.C, § 503(a)).

Although the name Anton Piller order is still used in practice this has been replaced with 'search order' in the United Kingdom[20] and in the Australian harmonised rules of court. For example, r 7.42 of the Federal Court Rules 2011 provides:

---

15. *Anton Piller KG v Manufacturing Processes Ltd* [1976] Ch 55 at 62.
16. (1982) 148 CLR 636 at [12].
17. (1982) 148 CLR 636 at [12].
18. *Tait v The Queen* (1962) 108 CLR 620 at 623.
19. *Celanese Canada Inc v Murray Demolition Corp* [2006] 2 SCR 189.
20. See s 7 of the Civil Procedure Act 1997 (UK).

Search order

The Court may make an order (a **search order**), in any proceeding or in anticipation of any proceeding in the Court, with or without notice to the respondent, for the purpose of securing or preserving evidence and requiring a respondent to permit persons to enter premises for the purpose of securing the preservation of evidence that is, or may be, relevant to an issue in the proceeding or anticipated proceeding.

10.5 Although the original and still dominant use of the search order is in relation to intellectual property, they are not restricted to such actions: see 10.10. But the increase in the use of the order has not been without criticism. The courts are not inclined to grant the remedy unless stringent safeguards are followed protecting the rights of the defendant.[21] In *Microsoft Corporation v Goodview Electronics Pty Ltd* Branson J observed:

> ... the caution with which courts have entertained applications for Anton Piller orders has increased, rather than diminished, as their experience with such orders has increased. The Court must, in my view, be careful to avoid the extraordinary jurisdiction of the Court to make an Anton Piller order from being subverted to a mere investigatory tool for applicants or indeed, from being used for any purpose other than the preservation of vital evidence pending the hearing and determination of a proceeding.[22]

Representative orders

10.6 A further development is the making of a 'representative', 'roving', or 'John Doe' search order — that is, an order against a named defendant but extending to other unnamed persons who are involved in a 'common enterprise' or 'have close ties of co-ordination' with the defendant.[23] Such orders developed out of those court rules allowing for the representation of concurrent interests in litigation.[24] The order may be available even where no particular defendant is named.[25] But such an order may be dissolved and the action dismissed if the plaintiff knew the defendant's identity when applying for the order.[26] In *Tony Blain Pty Ltd (t/as ACME Merchandising) v Jamison* a representative order was made against several unnamed respondents who were selling counterfeit merchandise at a series of popular music concerts including Paul McCartney and the band Metallica. As held by Burchett J, the orders sought were:

> ... not Anton Piller orders in the normal sense; they do not involve requiring a defendant to consent to entry upon his real estate. But they do have features analogous to Anton Piller orders; they do involve orders requiring persons

21. See 10.8; and see *Universal Thermosensors Ltd v Hibben* [1992] 1 WLR 840 at 859–60 per Sir Donald Nicholls V-C; *Long v Specifier Publications Pty Ltd* (1998) 44 NSWLR 545 (CA).

22. (1999) 46 IPR 159; [1999] FCA 754 at [26].

23. *Tony Blain Pty Ltd (t/as ACME Merchandising) v Jamison* (1993) 26 IPR 8 at 13 per Burchett J (FCA); *EMI Records Ltd v Khudhail* [1985] FSR 36, (1983) 4 IPR 513 (CA); *Columbia Picture Industries Ltd v Robinson* [1987] Ch 38.

24. See, for example, Division 9.2 Representative Proceedings, Federal Court Rules 2011.

25. See, for example, *Billy Joel v Various John Does* 499 F Supp 791 (1980).

26. *Vinod Chopra Films Private Limited v John Doe* [2010] FC 387 per Hughes J Fed C of Canada.

selling merchandise bearing the trade marks, for instance, of an applicant to deliver up such merchandise upon service of the order, and the making of a demand for compliance with it ... I have ... required the applicants to give an undertaking designed to ensure that independent legal advice will be available, on the spot, to persons required by the terms of the order to deliver up what may be, at least in some sense, their own property.[27]

Jurisdiction

10.7   Unlike Mareva orders, search orders have escaped jurisdictional controversy. Three grounds have been recognised. First, equity has long held an inherent jurisdiction to preserve property the subject of the trial. While the remedy may have undergone a name change from the memorable and distinctive 'Anton Piller' order to the generic 'search' order, its equitable origins still loom large. In particular, the equitable principles decided in the *Anton Piller case* still largely govern the availability remedy and, in common with all equitable remedies, it is only granted in the court's discretion.

The second recognised jurisdictional ground is that most courts have the statutory power to issue search orders. An example is found in s 23 of the Federal Court of Australia Act 1976 (Cth) which provides:

> The Court has power, in relation to matters in which it has jurisdiction, to make orders of such kinds, including interlocutory orders, and to issue, or direct the issue of, writs of such kinds, as the Court thinks appropriate.[28]

The breadth of this statutory power with its emphasis on discretion in deciding what is 'appropriate' has, however, supplemented rather than supplanted the remedy's historical links with equity.

Third, the court's inherent and statutory jurisdiction are supported by the rules of court aimed at the interim preservation of property forming the subject matter of the trial.[29] Since 2006 federal and state courts have specific harmonised rules and practice notes for search orders, but these do not diminish the court's inherent, implied or statutory jurisdiction to make a search order.[30] For example, r 7.44 of the Federal Court Rules 2011 provides:

> **Jurisdiction**
>
> Nothing in this Division diminishes the inherent, implied or statutory jurisdiction of the Court to make a search order.

Safeguards

10.8   Despite criticism based on the fact that the defendant risks imprisonment for contempt, a bare majority in the European Court of Human Rights

---

27.   (1993) 26 IPR 8 at 13.

28.   See *Microsoft Corporation v Goodview Electronics Pty Ltd* (1999) 46 IPR 159; [1999] FCA 754 at [10] per Branson J; *Bugaj v Bates* [2004] FCA 1260.

29.   See *Rank Film Distributors Ltd v Video Corp Centre* [1982] AC 380 (HL); compare Laddie and Dockray, 'Piller Problems' (1990) 106 *LQR* 601, cited with approval in *Universal Thermosensors Ltd v Hibben* [1992] 1 WLR 840 at 861 per Sir Donald Nicholls V-C.

30.   See, for example, r 7.44 FCR 2011.

was satisfied in *Chappell v United Kingdom* that the safeguards applied in the United Kingdom courts are adequate.[31] *Chappell* concerned the simultaneous execution of both a police search warrant and the plaintiff's search order at Mr Chappell's business premises in Bath, England which was also his home. The search warrant was based on the police belief that Mr Chappell was illegally distributing pornographic videos and the plaintiff's search order was to remove and preserve video piracy evidence. The English Court of Appeal refused to discharge the search order despite concerns about the simultaneous execution of the search warrant and the search order.

But since *Chappell* further safeguards have been developed and implemented in the United Kingdom and these were 'substantially incorporated' into Australian law.[32] Further, the Australian harmonised rules and practice notes that have been adopted since 2006 now contain several safeguards in favour of the defendant. These include the requirement that the execution of the order be supervised by an independent lawyer[33] who may need to be a woman if the occupant of the premises is likely to be a woman or a child. An independent computer expert may also be required. Both the independent lawyer and the computer expert have specific duties and responsibilities in relation to the defendant, the court and the seized evidence. Ordinarily the order will need to be executed in business hours so that the defendant can obtain the advice of their own lawyer. The order will contain provisions safeguarding the defendant's objections based on confidentiality and the privilege against self-incrimination.[34] Before removing any evidence the independent lawyer must supply a list to the defendant and provide reasonable time for the defendant to check its accuracy. The defendant may apply to the court at any time to vary or discharge the search order and usually a telephone number for the duty judge is provided in the actual order for this purpose. Further, the issue that led to the challenge in *Chappell* is now specifically addressed in the harmonised practice notes, that is, the remedy 'must not be executed at the same time as the execution of a search warrant by the police or by a regulatory authority.'[35]

ELEMENTS

10.9   In order to obtain a search order or Anton Piller order the plaintiff must:

a)   have an extremely strong prima facie case;

b)   prove the damage, potential or actual, must be very serious;

---

31.   [1989] FSR 617.

32.   P Biscoe, *Freezing and Search Orders, Mareva and Anton Piller Orders*, 2nd ed, Lexis Nexis 2008, p 309.

33.   See, for example, r 7.46 Federal Court Rules 2011; see also 10.13.

34.   See 10.17.

35.   Para 14 Federal Court Practice Note CM11 (1 August 2011).

c) have convincing proof that the defendant possesses incriminating documents or goods and there is a likelihood or real possibility that the defendant will destroy them;

d) provide various undertakings to the court including an undertaking as to damages; and

e) convince the court that in its discretion it should grant the order.

The first three elements are based on Ormrod LJ's reasons in the *Anton Piller* case. They are repeated in similar terms in the harmonised rules.[36] The main differences between Ormrod LJ's formulation and the rules is the absence of the words 'extremely' and 'very' from the first and second elements. But this is unlikely to lead to a change in practice as these 'strong adverbs' have never been essential requirements.[37] In common with other interlocutory equitable remedies, the fourth element has always been an essential prerequisite for the granting of the order. The final element, the court's discretion, is preserved in the harmonised rules of court which provide that the court 'may make a search order' if 'satisfied' that the first three requirements are met.[38] These elements are discussed below.

Strong prima facie case

10.10   In *Anton Piller KG v Manufacturing Processes Ltd*, Ormrod LJ observed that, because of the draconian nature of the order, 'there must be an extremely strong prima facie case'.[39] While the harmonised rules of court[40] do not use the word 'extremely' this has not changed practice as it reflects the view that this adverb was never part of the test.[41] The plaintiff should establish a strong cause of action against the defendant. Indeed, the harmonised court rules provide that the plaintiff should have a 'strong prima facie case on an accrued cause of action'.[42] But, this does not mean that the search order should be 'limited to the precise cause of action known' as this would limit the 'utility' of the order.[43] Where the plaintiff can establish that he or she will suffer substantial damage by the defendant's criminal act, proof of this will be sufficient.[44] Due to the obligation to make full and frank disclosure, the plaintiff should inform the court of any known possible defences.[45]

---

36. See, for example, r 7.43 Federal Court Rules 2011.

37. *Brags Electrics Pty Ltd t/as Inscope Building Technologies v Gregory* [2010] NSWSC 1205 at [18] per Brereton J.

38. See r 7.43 of the Federal Court Rules 2011.

39. [1976] Ch 55 at 62 (CA); see also *Cope Allman (Marrickville) Ltd v Farrow* (1984) 3 IPR 567; *Gianitsios v Karagiannis* (1986) 7 IPR 36.

40. See, for example, r 7.43(a) of the Federal Court Rules 2011.

41. See, for example, *Brags Electrics Pty Ltd t/as Inscope Building Technologies v Gregory* [2010] NSWSC 1205 at [18] per Brereton J.

42. See, for example, r 7.43(a) of the Federal Court Rules 2011.

43. *Aristocrat Technologies Australia Pty Ltd v Global Gaming Pty Ltd* [2006] FCA 862 at [6]-[7] per Allsop J.

44. See *Ex parte Island Records Ltd* [1978] Ch 122; *RCA Corp v Pollard* [1982] 1 WLR 979; compare *Carlin Music Corp v Collins* [1979] FSR 548.

45. See 10.17.

Strong prima facie cases have been found in the following intellectual property areas: copyright piracy,[46] trade secrets and confidential information,[47] patent infringement,[48] trade mark infringement[49] and passing off.[50] Strong prima facie cases have also been found in the following areas: assault,[51] family law,[52] restitution[53] and trusts.[54] The categories are not closed although the dominant use of the remedy is still in relation to intellectual property.

Serious damage

10.11   In *Anton Piller KG v Manufacturing Processes Ltd* Ormrod LJ observed that 'the damage, potential or actual, must be very serious for the applicant'.[55] Similarly, the harmonised rules of court, such as r 7.43(b) of the Federal Court Rules 2011 provide 'the potential or actual loss or damage to the applicant will be serious if the search order is not made'. While the rule does not use the word 'very' this has not changed practice as it reflects the view that this adverb was never an essential part of the test.[56]

In cases concerning intellectual property and counterfeit goods the damage can be readily demonstrated by the potential or actual loss of sales and by the inferior quality of the defendant's goods. Serious damage is readily demonstrated in trade secret and misuse of confidential information cases, such as the *Anton Piller* case, by actual or potential disclosure to the plaintiff's trade rivals.

Likely destruction of incriminating evidence

10.12   In *Anton Piller KG v Manufacturing Processes Ltd* Ormrod LJ observed that:

> ... there must be clear evidence that the defendants have in their possession incriminating documents or things, and that there is a real possibility that they may destroy such material before any application *inter partes* can be made.[57]

Similarly, the harmonised rules of court, such as r 7.43(c) of the Federal Court Rules 2011 provide:

---

46.   *EMI Ltd v Pandit* [1975] 1 All ER 418; [1975] 1 WLR 302.

47.   *Anton Piller KG v Manufacturing Process Ltd* [1976] Ch 55 (CA); *Odi Optical Coatings Ltd v Spectron Optical Coatings Ltd* [1980] FSR 227.

48.   *International Electronics Ltd v Weigh Data Ltd* [1980] FSR 423.

49.   *Tony Blain Pty Ltd (t/as ACME Merchandising) v Jamison* (1993) 26 IPR 8 (FCA).

50.   *Sony Corp v Anand* [1981] FSR 398.

51.   *Ex parte Mashini* [1986] FSR 454.

52.   *Emanuel v Emanuel* [1982] 1 WLR 669; *K v K* [1982] 13 Fam Law 46; *Kepa v Kepa* (1982) 4 FLR 515. Regulation 14.04 of the Family Court Rules 2004 (Cth) provides for Anton Piller orders; see also *Zael & Liao* [2008] FamCAFC 127.

53.   *Yousif v Salama* [1980] 1 WLR 1540.

54.   *A v C* [1980] 2 All ER 347; *Bankers Trust Co v Shapira* [1980] 3 All ER 353.

55.   [1976] Ch 55 at 62 (CA).

56.   See, for example, *Brags Electrics Pty Ltd t/as Inscope Building Technologies v Gregory* [2010] NSWSC 1205 at [18] per Brereton J.

57.   [1976] Ch 55 at 62 (CA).

… there is sufficient evidence in relation to a respondent that:

(i)　the respondent possesses important evidentiary material; and

(ii)　there is a real possibility that the respondent might destroy such material or cause it to be unavailable for use in evidence in a proceeding or anticipated proceeding before the Court.

If the defendant does not intend to destroy the evidence but, rather, intends to hide or remove it from the jurisdiction, this is sufficient.[58] But the purpose of the order must not be for a 'fishing expedition' by the plaintiff.[59]

In deciding whether there is a real possibility of destruction of the evidence or causing it to be unavailable, the court is entitled 'to take into account the usual practices of pirates of copyright and the like'.[60] This may mean that it is easier to obtain a search order against a disreputable defendant. As observed by Hoffmann J in discharging an Anton Piller order in *Lock International plc v Beswick*:

… these defendants were no fly-by-night video pirates. They were former long service employees with families and mortgages who had openly said that they were entering into competition and whom the plaintiff knew to be financed by highly respectable institutions.[61]

Plaintiff's undertakings and form of the order

10.13　The plaintiff will need to give several undertakings to the court. In common with injunctions and Mareva orders, the whole order should be subject to an undertaking as to damages.[62] Security for its performance, (such as a bank's irrevocable undertaking for payment into court) may be required if the plaintiff has insufficient assets within the jurisdiction.[63]

There will also be 'a proviso which preserves the privilege against self-incrimination and legal professional privilege of the defendant'.[64] The plaintiff should also give an undertaking that the defendant will be advised of his or her right to obtain prompt legal advice before the order is executed.

To help protect against abuse the plaintiff will be required to give an undertaking to make available and pay the reasonable costs of an independent lawyer to explain the order and provide advice to the defendant.[65] The independent lawyer should be experienced in the execution of search orders

58.　See *Microsoft Corporation v Goodview Electronics Pty Ltd* (1999) 46 IPR 159; [1999] FCA 754 at [24]–[25] per Branson J.

59.　*Hytrac Conveyors v Conveyors International Ltd* [1983] 1 WLR 44 at 47 per Lawton J.

60.　*Busby v Thorn EMI Video Programmes Ltd* [1984] 1 NZLR 461 at 467 per Cooke J.

61.　[1989] 1 WLR 1268 at 1283.

62.　See 10.19 and *Foga Systems International AB v Shop & Display Equipment Pty Ltd* (SC(Vic), Hayne J, 14 April 1992, unreported), where damages were awarded to the defendant.

63.　Federal Court Practice Note CM11 para 18 (1 August 2011).

64.　*PMSI Group v Wilson* [2003] NSWSC 263 at [13] per Campbell J.

65.　*Tony Blain Pty Ltd (t/as ACME Merchandising) v Jamison* (1993) 26 IPR 8 at 13 per Burchett J (FCA); Federal Court Practice Note CM11 (1 August 2011).

and should not be a member or employee of the plaintiff's firm.[66] This lawyer will be required to give a written report to the court concerning the service and execution of the order[67] and should attend the hearing on the return date of the search order.[68] In *PMSI Group v Wilson* Campbell J explained the role of the supervising solicitor as follows:

> The role of the Supervising Solicitor is most important. The Supervising Solicitor must be a solicitor who is independent of the solicitor for the plaintiff, and who has experience in the execution of Anton Piller orders. This particular Supervising Solicitor was a woman, because the premises proposed to be entered were a dwelling house, where it was reasonable to expect that a woman might possibly be alone at the premises at the time the order was executed. It is not appropriate for the Court to make an order on terms which might result in a woman being in her home with no one else present other than men executing the order.

> While in the present case the plaintiff was able to nominate a Supervising Solicitor who is a woman, it would be desirable for the Law Society, if it does not already do so, to maintain a list of solicitors who are experienced in the execution of Anton Piller orders, and willing to receive instructions to act as a Supervising Solicitor. If the courts are going to require the presence of a Supervising Solicitor when an Anton Piller order is executed, it is important, in the interests of there being equal access to justice, that the ability of a plaintiff to obtain such an order should not depend, in practical terms, on whether the plaintiff's solicitor happens to know of someone who is able and willing to act as Supervising Solicitor.

> In the present case I was prepared to make an order on the plaintiff giving an undertaking to the Court to file an affidavit establishing that the Supervising Solicitor had experience in execution of orders like the present order. While that course sometimes needs to be followed when an ex parte order is made in circumstances of urgency, it is preferable, if possible, for the application for the Anton Piller order to be accompanied by evidence of the identity and experience of the Supervising Solicitor.

> The requirement for the Supervising Solicitor to prepare a written report promptly after execution of the order, the requirement to serve the report on the defendant, and the granting of liberty to apply on very short notice, are all designed to ensure that the process of execution of the order is as open and as subject to the control of the Court as is possible under the circumstances. If it is possible for the return of the summons to be before the judge who made the order, that should be done.[69]

The plaintiff's lawyer is usually required to give undertakings not to use any of the documents, information or goods obtained except in connection with the plaintiff's own civil proceedings and not to disclose to the plaintiff, without the court's leave, any information that the plaintiff's lawyer acquires as

---

66.   Federal Court Practice Note CM11 (1 August 2011).
67.   *Tony Blain Pty Ltd (t/as ACMI Merchandising) v Jamison* (1993) 26 IPR 8 at 13 per Burchett J.
68.   Federal Court Practice Note CM11 (1 August 2011).
69.   [2003] NSWSC 263 at [8]–[11].

a result of the search order.[70] In the case of trade rivals 'a very clear case needs to be shown to justify ordering release of the search material at a relatively early stage in the litigation, beyond the professional adviser and independent expert, direct to the trade rival.'[71] A detailed list or inventory of items removed should be prepared[72] and the defendant should also be given an opportunity to check the list.[73]

10.14   The practice notes and harmonised rules of the courts provide examples of the form of the order. Rule 7.45 of the Federal Court Rules 2011 provides:

7.45 Terms of search order

(1) A search order may direct each person who is named or described in the order:

(a) to permit, or arrange to permit, other persons named or described in the order:

(i)   to enter premises specified in the order; and

(ii) to take any steps that are in accordance with the terms of the order; and

(b) to provide, or arrange to provide, other persons named or described in the order with any information, thing or service described in the order; and

(c) to allow other persons named or described in the order to take and retain in their custody any thing described in the order; and

(d) not to disclose any information about the order, for up to 3 days after the date the order was served, except for the purposes of obtaining legal advice or legal representation; and

(e) to do or refrain from doing any act as the Court considers appropriate.

(2) Without limiting the generality of subparagraph (1)(a)(ii), the steps that may be taken in relation to a thing specified in a search order include:

(a) searching for, inspecting or removing the thing; and

(b) making or obtaining a record of the thing or any information it may contain.

(3) A search order may contain other provisions the Court considers appropriate.

(4) In subrule (2):

record includes a copy, photograph, film or sample.

Court's discretion

10.15   The harmonised rules provide that the court 'may make a search order' if the prerequisites are met.[74] Thus in common with all equitable remedies

---

70.   See, for example, Federal Court Practice Note CM 11 (1 August 2011).

71.   *Alanco Australia Pty Ltd v Higgins* [2010] FCA 1484 at [42] per McKerracher J.

72.   *Long v Specifier Publications Pty Ltd* (1998) 44 NSWLR 545 (CA).

73.   *Universal Thermosensors Ltd v Hibben* [1992] 1 WLR 840 at 860 per Sir Donald Nicholls V-C.

74.   See, for example, rr 7.42 and 7.43 of the Federal Court Rules 2011.

the plaintiff must satisfy the court that in its discretion the order should be granted. The court will weigh in the balance equitable matters such as delay,[75] acquiescence and unclean hands. The court expects the plaintiff to give a full and frank disclosure of the relevant matters at the ex parte hearing. [76] Indeed, this is a possible ground for dissolution at the inter partes hearing: see **10.18**.

CONTEMPT

10.16   The Anton Piller or search order is not a search warrant, so forced entry by the search party is not permitted. Still, if the defendant fails to comply with the order, this will expose him or her to proceedings for contempt.[77] The order itself will usually carry a prominent warning that if the defendant or any other person assisting the defendant disobeys the order they will be liable to 'imprisonment, sequestration of property or other punishment.'[78] In *Anton Piller KG v Manufacturing Processes Ltd* Ormrod LJ observed:

> The order is an order on the defendant *in personam* to permit inspection. It is therefore open to him to refuse to comply with such an order, but at his peril either of further proceedings for contempt of court — in which case, of course, the court will have the widest discretion as to how to deal with it, and if it turns out that the order was made improperly in the first place, the contempt will be dealt with accordingly — but more important, of course, the refusal to comply may be the most damning evidence against the defendant at the subsequent trial.[79]

The search party cannot enter the premises without the defendant's consent. The defendant can only refuse entry until he or she has obtained legal advice. Such advice must be obtained promptly, and refusal to allow entry after the advice has been obtained amounts to contempt.[80] The defendant will also be guilty of contempt if he or she destroys relevant documents and articles prior to allowing access by the plaintiff's solicitors.[81] The plaintiff's representatives may also be guilty of contempt if they abandon control of the seized items,[82] or allow the unauthorised removal of documents or goods, or use information for purposes other than the proposed or initiated proceedings.[83] Finally, while the courts have power to imprison those in contempt, this power is rarely exercised in relation to search orders.[84]

---

75.   See P Biscoe, *Freezing and Search Orders*, 2nd ed, LexisNexis, 2008 pp 314–15, 353–54.

76.   See *Dormeuil Freres v Nicolian International (Textiles) Ltd* [1989] FSR 256 (Ch D); *Swedac Ltd v Magnet & Southerns plc* [1989] FSR 243 (Ch D). Federal Court Practice Note CM11 (1 August 2011).

77.   *Long v Specifier Publications Pty Ltd* (1998) 44 NSWLR at 548 per Powell JA (CA).

78.   See the example form of search order attached to Federal Court Practice Note CM11 (1 August 2011).

79.   [1976] Ch 55 at 62 (CA).

80.   *Bhimji v Chatwani* [1991] 1 WLR 989.

81.   *WEA Records Ltd v Visions Channel 4 Ltd* [1983] 1 WLR 721.

82.   *Long v Specifier Publications Pty Ltd* (1998) 44 NSWLR 545 (CA).

83.   See *VDU Installations Ltd v Integrated Computer Systems and Cybernetics Ltd* [1989] FSR 378.

84.   *Fabrics v Myristis* [1984] FSR 263.

Privilege against self-incrimination

10.17   Prior to statutory intervention the defendant had the common law right to raise the defence of self-incrimination where the production of documents to the search party was likely to incriminate the defendant in a crime or expose him or her to a civil penalty.[85] But in most common law jurisdictions this privilege has been abolished or restricted. The privilege was abolished in New Zealand.[86] In the United Kingdom, the defence was restricted by legislation preventing the use of such material against the defendant or the defendant's spouse in a subsequent criminal proceeding.[87] Australian legislation does not abolish the privilege, rather it provides a process by which a witness may claim the privilege but may still be required to give incriminating evidence in return for a certificate granting immunity from direct or indirect use.[88] Even prior to those restrictions the risk of criminal prosecution had to be real and not remote[89] and the court would often grant the order subject to the applicant's undertaking that it would not use the information obtained in criminal proceedings. The example orders attached to the harmonised practice notes require the plaintiff to give an undertaking not to use seized evidence for any other proceedings. For example, Federal Court Practice Note CM11 provides the following example of one of the undertakings that the plaintiff is required to give the court:

> The applicant will not, without leave of the Court, use any information, document or thing obtained as a result of the execution of this order for the purpose of any civil or criminal proceeding, either within or outside Australia, other than this proceeding.[90]

Dissolution

10.18   A search order may be discharged or dissolved if the defendant shows that one of the elements was not satisfied; or if insufficient or inadmissible[91] evidence was relied upon to support the order; or if the plaintiff failed to give full and frank disclosure at the ex parte hearing; or if the plaintiff failed to comply with the terms of the order.

Failure to make full and frank disclosure is the most common ground for dissolution. In *Thomas A Edison Ltd v Bullock* a case that predates search orders

85.   *Rank Film Distributors Ltd v Video Corp Centre* [1982] AC 380 (HL); *BPA Industries Ltd v Black* (1987) 11 NSWLR 609; *Istel Ltd v Tully* [1992] 3 WLR 344 (HL).

86.   Section 63 Evidence Act 2006 (NZ).

87.   See s 72 of the Supreme Court Act 1981 (UK) and *Universal City Studios Inc v Hubbard* [1984] Ch 225; see also s 31(1) of the Theft Act 1968 (UK).

88.   Section 128A of the Evidence Act 1995 (Cth), Evidence Act 1995 (NSW) and the Evidence Act 2008 (Vic).

89.   *Authors' Workshop v Bileru Pty Ltd* (1989) 88 ALR 211 (FCA).

90.   *Warman International Ltd v Envirotech (Aust) Pty Ltd* (1986) 67 ALR 253 (FCA); *PMSI Group v Wilson* [2003] NSWSC 263 at [13] per Campbell J; *Pathways Employment Services v West* [2004] NSWSC 903.

91.   See *Singtel Optus Pty Ltd v Almad Pty Ltd* [2011] NSWSC 492.

but has been applied to them, Isaacs J explained the plaintiff's obligation in
an ex parte hearing 'to bring under the notice of the Court all facts material
to the determination of his right to that injunction'.[92] The plaintiff has 'a duty
to the court to make full and frank disclosure of all material facts' including
possible defences and an inability to meet the undertaking as to damages.[93]
But, as with Mareva orders, not all omissions lead to dissolution.[94] In *Dormeuil
Freres v Nicolian International (Textiles) Ltd* Browne-Wilkinson VC observed:

> It is a basic principle, applicable to all *ex parte* applications, that a plaintiff
> seeking *ex parte* relief must make full disclosure to the court of all facts which
> are material to the exercise of the court's discretion whether or not to grant the
> relief. If such disclosure is not made by the plaintiff, the court may discharge
> the *ex parte* injunction on that ground alone. But if, in the circumstances
> existing when the matter comes before the court *inter partes*, justice requires
> an order either continuing the *ex parte* injunction or the grant of a fresh
> injunction, such an order can be made notwithstanding the earlier failure of
> the plaintiff to make such disclosure. Moreover … there is no absolute right
> to have an *ex parte* order obtained without due disclosure set aside; there is a
> discretion in the court whether to do so or not.[95]

It is unlikely that the order will be dissolved if the non-disclosure was
innocent and immaterial, in the sense that the injunction would still have
been granted even if the disclosure had been made.[96] The 'real question' at
the inter partes hearing 'should not be what happened in the past but what
should happen in the future'.[97] In *Universal Music Australia Pty Ltd v Sharman
License Holdings Ltd*[98] the respondents submitted that the order should have
been dissolved because the applicants failed to disclose that in similar US
proceedings the respondents had not attempted to destroy the evidence.
Wilcox J regarded this as a matter that 'ought to have been mentioned by
counsel in seeking the Anton Piller orders',[99] but held:

> Although the detail of the US proceedings was not disclosed to me on [the ex
> parte application], I have reached the conclusion that the non-disclosure was
> not material. The non-disclosed material would not have affected my decision
> to make the *Anton Piller* orders. Accordingly, there is no occasion for me to set
> aside those orders.[100]

---

92. (1912) 15 CLR 679 at 681 which has been applied to Anton Piller orders; see, for example, *Universal Music Australia Pty Ltd v Sharman License Holdings Ltd* (2004) 59 IPR 299 at [53]–[54] per Wilcox J.
93. Federal Court Practice Note CM11 (1 August 2011).
94. *Bank Mellat v Nikpour* [1985] FSR 87 at 90 per Lord Denning MR (CA).
95. [1989] FSR 256 at 261 (Ch D).
96. *Lloyd's Bowmaker Ltd v Brittania Arrow Holdings plc* [1988] 1 WLR 1337 at 1343–4 per Glidewell LJ; see also *Jabuna Pty Ltd v Hartley* (FCA, Beazley J, 18 April 1994, unreported); compare *Singtel Optus Pty Ltd v Almad Pty Ltd* [2011] NSWSC 492 at [67]–[68] per Bergin CJ in Equity.
97. *Dormeuil Freres v Nicolian International (Textiles) Ltd* [1989] FSR 256 at 261 per Browne-Wilkinson VC (Ch D); see also *Swedac Ltd v Magnet & Southerns plc* [1989] FSR 243 (Ch D).
98. (2004) 59 IPR 299.
99. (2004) 59 IPR 299 at [66].
100. (2004) 59 IPR 299 at [80]; and see *Bandaid Tyres Australia Pty Ltd v Williams* [2002] WASC 306 at [7]–[8] per Heenan J; *Liberty Financial Pty Ltd v Scott* [2002] FCA 345.

10.19   If the order is dissolved then, in accordance with the undertaking as to damages, the plaintiff will ordinarily have to pay compensation to the defendant and third parties who have suffered loss due to the order. In some cases the defendant may claim damages for trespass.[101] In *Foga Systems International AB v Shop & Display Equipment Pty Ltd*,[102] Hayne J awarded $230,000 in damages. The loss claimed, however, must be foreseeable, so his Honour refused to make an allowance for the emotional consequences and effects suffered by the defendant on the basis that such loss was not foreseeable. Hayne J did accept in *Foga*, citing *Columbia Picture Industries Ltd v Robinson*[103] in support, that exemplary damages may be available where the order was executed 'oppressively or in excess of the power granted by it'.

In Canada full indemnity costs were awarded against a plaintiff company which applied for a rolling or John Doe search order based on 'insufficient, careless and misleading' evidence.[104]

---

101. *Chappell v United Kingdom* [1989] FSR 617 at 625.

102. (SC(Vic), Hayne J, 14 April 1992, unreported); see also *Flocast Australia Pty Ltd v Purcell (No 2)* [1999] FCA 309 at [14] per Heerey J.

103. [1987] Ch 38.

104. *Vinod Chopra Films Private Limited v John Doe* [2010] FC 387 per Hughes J, Fed C of Canada.

CHAPTER

Equitable Compensation and Damages

INTRODUCTION

11.1 Arising from the historical division of jurisdiction between the Court of Chancery and the courts of common law before the Judicature Act 1873[1], damages developed primarily as a remedy of the common law. Damages at common law are awarded in respect of common law wrongs, including torts

---

1.   Supreme Court of Judicature Act 1873, 36 & 37 Vict c 66.

and breaches of contract. To discuss monetary compensation in equity, it is necessary to distinguish between the exclusive jurisdiction of equity in respect of purely equitable wrongs, and the auxiliary jurisdiction of equity in respect of common law and other wrongs.

EXCLUSIVE JURISDICTION

11.2   In respect of purely equitable wrongs, including breaches of trust and other fiduciary duties, equity has long exercised an inherent jurisdiction to award monetary compensation for loss.[2] To avoid confusion with the common law remedy of damages, monetary compensation awarded in the exclusive jurisdiction of equity is called 'equitable compensation'. In a passage that has been adopted by the High Court, the distinct nature of equitable compensation was explained by McLachlin J in *Canson Enterprises Ltd v Boughton & Co*:

> The basis of the fiduciary obligation and the rationale for equitable compensation are distinct from the tort of negligence and contract. In negligence and contract the parties are taken to be independent and equal actors, concerned primarily with their own self-interest. Consequently the law seeks a balance between enforcing obligations by awarding compensation and preserving optimum freedom for those involved in the relationship in question, communal or otherwise. The essence of a fiduciary relationship, by contrast, is that one party pledges itself to act in the best interest of the other. The fiduciary relationship has trust, not self-interest, at its core, and when breach occurs, the balance favours the person wronged.[3]

Irrespective of these differences, it has been said by the House of Lords that equitable compensation and damages in tort share the same fundamental purpose of compensation.[4] In both remedies, the plaintiff is to be put 'in the same position as he would have been in if he had not sustained the wrong for which he is now getting his compensation or reparation'.[5] Although there have been cases of equitable compensation where the plaintiff's loss was measured by the defendant's gain,[6] the appropriate restitutionary remedy in such cases of wrongful gains is an account of profits in the exclusive jurisdiction of equity: see Chapter 6. The plaintiff must elect between equitable compensation and an account of profits because they are alternative and inconsistent remedies.[7] Unlike damages in tort, exemplary damages cannot be awarded in the exclusive

2.   See I E Davidson, 'The Equitable Remedy of Compensation' (1982) 13 *MULR* 349.

3.   [1991] 3 SCR 534 at 543, quoted in *Youyang Pty Ltd v Minter Ellison Morris Fletcher* (2003) 212 CLR 484 at 501 per Gleeson CJ, McHugh, Gummow, Kirby and Hayne JJ.

4.   *Target Holdings Ltd v Redferns* [1996] 1 AC 421 at 432 per Lord Browne-Wilkinson. On the compensation principle in tort, see 2.1.

5.   *Livingstone v Rawyards Coal Co* (1880) 5 App Cas 25 at 39 per Lord Blackburn; quoted in *Target Holdings Ltd v Redferns* [1996] 1 AC 421 at 432 per Lord Browne-Wilkinson.

6.   *McKenzie v McDonald* [1927] VLR 134 at 146 per Dixon A-J; *Dempster v Mallina Holdings Ltd* (1994) 13 WAR 124 at 172 per Rowland J (Pidgeon and Seaman JJ agreeing).

7.   *Warman International Ltd v Dwyer* (1995) 182 CLR 544 at 559 per Mason CJ, Brennan, Deane, Dawson and Gaudron JJ; *Tang Man Sit v Capacious Investments Ltd* [1996] 1 AC 514 (PC).

jurisdiction of equity because equity 'abhors' penalties.[8] However, because aggravated damages are compensatory in nature,[9] these can be awarded in the exclusive jurisdiction.[10] Like all equitable remedies, equitable compensation is discretionary and can be awarded on terms.

In equity, as at common law, there must be a causal connection between the defendant's wrongdoing and the plaintiff's damage.[11] Beyond this, it is said that:

> Causation in equity is not … susceptible to the formulation of a single test. It is necessary to identify the purpose of the particular rule to determine the appropriate approach to issues of causation.[12]

The principles governing the award of equitable compensation in the exclusive jurisdiction of equity will be considered in three groups of cases: misapplication of trust assets, undisclosed conflicts of duty and interest, and breaches of equitable duties of care and skill. Many of the leading cases arise from the fiduciary relationship between solicitors and their clients.

Misapplication of trust assets

11.3 The principles governing the award of equitable compensation for misapplication of trust assets were restated by the House of Lords in *Target Holdings Ltd v Redferns*:

> [T]he basic rule is that a trustee in breach of trust must restore or pay to the trust estate either the assets which have been lost to the estate by reason of the breach or compensation for such loss. Courts of Equity did not award damages but, acting *in personam*, ordered the defaulting trustee to restore the trust estate: see *Nocton v Lord Ashburton*.[13] If specific restitution of the trust property is not possible, then the liability of the trustee is to pay sufficient compensation to the trust estate to put it back to what it would have been had the breach not been committed: *Caffrey v Darby*;[14] *Clough v Bond*.[15] Even if the immediate cause of the loss is the dishonesty or failure of a third party, the trustee is liable to make good that loss to the trust estate if, but for the breach, such loss would not have occurred: see … *Re Dawson (dec'd)*;[16] *Bartlett v Barclays Bank Trust Co Ltd (Nos 1 and 2)*.[17] Thus the common law rules of remoteness of damage and causation do not apply. However there does have to be some causal connection between the breach of trust and the loss to the trust estate

---

8.   *Harris v Digital Pulse Pty Ltd* (2003) 56 NSWLR 298. Contrast *Aquaculture Corp v New Zealand Green Mussel Co Ltd* [1990] 3 NZLR 299. On exemplary damages in tort, see **2.88**.

9.   *Uren v John Fairfax & Sons Ltd* (1966) 117 CLR 118 at 149 per Windeyer J.

10. *Giller v Procopets* (2008) 24 VR 1 at 34 per Ashley JA, at 105–6 per Neave JA.

11. On causation at common law, see **2.8–2.41, 3.6–3.13**.

12. *O'Halloran v R T Thomas and Family Pty Ltd* (1998) 45 NSWLR 262 at 274 per Spigelman CJ.

13. [1914] AC 932 at 952, 958 per Viscount Haldane LC.

14. (1801) 6 Ves 488; 31 ER 1159.

15. (1838) 3 My & Cr 490; 40 ER 1016.

16. [1966] 2 NSWLR 211.

17. [1980] Ch 515.

for which compensation is recoverable, *viz*, the fact that the loss would not have occurred but for the breach.[18]

In *Target Holdings Ltd v Redferns*, the plaintiff finance company had instructed the defendant firm of solicitors to act for it in the provision of a loan, to be secured by a charge over certain property. Target transferred the loan funds of £1,525,000 to Redferns, to be held on trust and released once the property was purchased and charged to Target. In breach of trust, Redferns prematurely released funds of £1,490,000 before the property was purchased and the charge was executed. However, the transaction was completed and the charge was executed and delivered within weeks. When, at a later time, the mortgagor defaulted, Target exercised its chargee's power of sale over the property, but the proceeds of sale were only £500,000. It was then revealed that Target had been defrauded by others about the true value of the property. To recover the loss, Target claimed equitable compensation from Redferns for breach of trust. Target argued successfully in the English Court of Appeal that Redferns were under an immediate duty as trustee to restore the trust funds upon breach, and that subsequent events which diminished the loss in fact suffered were irrelevant, allowing only for Target's proceeds of sale.[19] However, the House of Lords reversed the Court of Appeal's decision, holding unanimously that Target had 'suffered no compensatable loss'.[20] Lord Browne-Wilkinson said:

> A trustee who wrongly pays away trust money, like a trustee who makes an unauthorized investment, commits a breach of trust and comes under an immediate duty to remedy such breach. If immediate proceedings are brought, the court will make an immediate order requiring restoration to the trust fund of the assets wrongly distributed or, in the case of an unauthorized investment, will order the sale of the unauthorized investment and the payment of compensation for any loss suffered. But the fact that there is an accrued cause of action as soon as the breach is committed does not in my judgment mean that the quantum of the compensation payable is ultimately fixed as at the date when the breach occurred. The quantum is fixed at the date of judgment at which date, according to the circumstances then pertaining, the compensation is assessed at the figure then necessary to put the trust estate or the beneficiary back into the position it would have been in had there been no breach.[21]

In this case, 'Target obtained exactly what it would have obtained had no breach occurred, ie a valid security for the sum advanced'.[22] The insufficiency of the security was not to the point.

18.   [1996] 1 AC 421 at 434 per Lord Browne-Wilkinson.
19.   [1994] 2 All ER 337 at 351–3 per Peter Gibson LJ (Hirst LJ agreeing).
20.   [1996] 1 AC 421 at 440 per Lord Browne-Wilkinson (Lords Keith, Ackner, Jauncey and Lloyd agreeing).
21.   [1996] 1 AC 421 at 437.
22.   [1996] 1 AC 421 at 440 per Lord Browne-Wilkinson.

11.4 *Target Holdings Ltd v Redferns* was distinguished by the High Court in *Youyang Pty Ltd v Minter Ellison Morris Fletcher*.[23] In this case, the defendant firm of solicitors held $500,000 on trust for Youyang, for the purpose of subscribing for shares in a new investment company. In breach of trust, Minters released the funds in two instalments without obtaining the security of a negotiable bearer deposit certificate that was required under the terms of the trust. When the investment company later collapsed, Youyang lost the whole of its unsecured investment. In awarding equitable compensation for the whole amount, the High Court held that Youyang's loss would not have occurred but for Minters' breach of trust by releasing the funds. The High Court distinguished *Target Holdings Ltd v Redferns* on the facts.[24] Unlike the security that was provided to Target, albeit belatedly in breach of trust, Youyang was never provided with any security at all. The High Court rejected Minters' argument that supervening events after the share subscription were the true cause of Youyang's loss:

> It is not to the point that, in addition to the breaches of trust by Minters, there may also have been dishonest and discreditable subsequent acts by third parties which led to the loss of funds.[25]

As the High Court said in *Maguire v Makaronis*, 'there is no translation into this field of discourse of the doctrine of *novus actus interveniens*'.[26]

Undisclosed conflict of duty and interest

11.5 Compensation may be awarded in the exclusive jurisdiction of equity where a fiduciary has an undisclosed conflict of fiduciary duty and personal interest that is material to the beneficiary's loss. The leading authority is the judgment of the House of Lords in *Nocton v Lord Ashburton*.[27] In that case, the solicitor Nocton advised his client Lord Ashburton to partially release a first mortgage that Ashburton held over certain land. By acting on the advice, Ashburton unknowingly gave an advantage to Nocton by advancing Nocton's second-ranking security over the same land. When the mortgagor subsequently defaulted, Ashburton's diminished security was insufficient to secure the debt owed to Ashburton by the mortgagor. The House of Lords held that Nocton had breached his fiduciary duty as a solicitor by failing to disclose his personal interest in the transaction and by advancing his own interest at the expense of his client. Viscount Haldane LC confirmed the exclusive jurisdiction of equity to make monetary awards for breach of fiduciary duty 'to compensate the plaintiff

---

23.   (2003) 212 CLR 484.

24.   (2003) 212 CLR 484 at 503 per Gleeson CJ, McHugh, Gummow, Kirby and Hayne JJ. See also *Jessup v Lawyers Private Mortgages Ltd* [2006] QCA 432 at [59]–[63] per Keane JA.

25.   (2003) 212 CLR 484 at 507 per Gleeson CJ, McHugh, Gummow, Kirby and Hayne JJ.

26.   (1997) 188 CLR 449 at 469–70 per Brennan CJ, Gaudron, McHugh and Gummow JJ. On the doctrine of *novus actus interveniens* at common law, see **2.14, 3.11–3.13**.

27.   [1914] AC 932.

by putting him in as good a position pecuniarily as that in which he was before the injury'.[28]

11.6   The question of causation in cases of conflict between duty and interest was the subject of *obiter dicta* by the Privy Council (on appeal from the Supreme Court of Canada) in *Brickenden v London Loan and Savings Co.*[29] The case involved a loan made by the respondent lender that was to be secured by a mortgage over certain property. The appellant solicitor, who acted for both the lender and the borrower in the transaction, had an undisclosed personal interest in a prior mortgage over the property. The solicitor's failure to disclose this interest to the lender was a breach of fiduciary duty. As a result, the lender received a 'worthless security' for the loan, and subsequently suffered a loss. Although it was unnecessary for the disposition of the case, Lord Thankerton said:

> When a party, holding a fiduciary relationship, commits a breach of his duty by non-disclosure of material facts, which his constituent is entitled to know in connection with the transaction, he cannot be heard to maintain that disclosure would not have altered the decision to proceed with the transaction, because the constituent's action would be solely determined by some other factor, such as the valuation by another party of the property proposed to be mortgaged. Once the Court has determined that the non-disclosed facts were material, speculation as to what course the constituent, on disclosure, would have taken is not relevant.[30]

Writing extra-judicially, Justice Heydon has commented that the *Brickenden* principle operates 'without reference to issues of causation'.[31] However, as Kirby J explained later in *Maguire v Makaronis*,[32] the element of causation in the *Brickenden* principle resides in the 'materiality' of the undisclosed facts. The stringency of the principle is justified by 'the prophylactic consequence of discouraging fiduciary default. Such default is inherent in the temptations to which people in the position of fiduciaries are commonly exposed'.[33] The authority of *Brickenden* in Australia was left open by the majority of the High Court in *Maguire v Makaronis*[34] and *Youyang Pty Ltd v Minter Ellison Morris Fletcher*,[35] where it was unnecessary in either case to decide the point. However, *Brickenden* has otherwise been accepted as good authority in Australia.[36]

---

28. [1914] AC 932 at 952.

29. [1934] 3 DLR 465.

30. [1934] 3 DLR 465 at 469.

31. J D Heydon, 'Causal Relationships between a Fiduciary's Default and the Principal's Loss' (1994) 110 *LQR* 328 at 331.

32. (1997) 188 CLR 449 at 494. See also *Beach Petroleum NL v Kennedy* (1999) 48 NSWLR 1 at 92 per Spigelman CJ, Sheller and Stein JJA.

33. (1997) 188 CLR 449 at 492 per Kirby J.

34. (1997) 188 CLR 449 at 470–4 per Brennan CJ, Gaudron, McHugh and Gummow JJ.

35. (2003) 212 CLR 484 at 501 per Gleeson CJ, McHugh, Gummow, Kirby and Hayne JJ.

36. *Hill v Rose* [1990] VR 129 at 142 per Tadgell J; *Commonwealth Bank of Australia v Smith* (1991) 102 ALR 453 at 478–9 per Davies, Sheppard and Gummow JJ; *Wan v McDonald* (1992) 105 ALR 473 at 501–2 per Burchett J; *Gemstone Corporation of Australia Ltd v Grasso* (1994) 62 SASR 239 at 243 per Matheson J

11.7 The *Brickenden* principle stands in contrast with the judgment of the New Zealand Court of Appeal in *Day v Mead*.[37] In this case, the plaintiff client had acted upon the advice of the defendant solicitor to make an initial investment of $20,000, and later, a further investment of $80,000 to purchase shares in a company. The solicitor was a director and shareholder of the company. Although the client was aware of the solicitor's personal interest as a shareholder, the solicitor had failed to make 'explicit disclosure of the risks known to the defendant and the nature and extent of the possibly conflicting interests of other clients'.[38] When the company later went into liquidation, the client lost both investments. The Court of Appeal held that the solicitor was in breach of his fiduciary duty on both occasions by failing to disclose all the material facts to the client, and by failing to recommend independent advice. In respect of the client's initial investment of $20,000, the court awarded equitable compensation for the whole loss. However, in respect of the further investment of $80,000, the Court of Appeal held that the client was half responsible for his own loss, because he had acquired some knowledge of the company's affairs by then. The Court of Appeal took the unprecedented step of applying, by analogy, the apportionment legislation governing contributory negligence in tort to reduce by half the award of equitable compensation: see **2.16–2.19**. Cooke P said 'there appears to be no solid reason for denying jurisdiction to follow that obviously just course, especially now that law and equity have mingled or are interacting'.[39] Casey J explained the result in terms of equitable discretionary factors:

> … the basic ideal of controlling unconscionable conduct underlying the jurisdiction of equity justifies an approach aimed at awarding a party no more than the loss fairly attributable to the defendant.[40]

11.8 In Australia, however, the High Court in *Pilmer v Duke Group Ltd (in liq)*[41] has warned of 'the severe conceptual difficulties in the path of acceptance of notions of contributory negligence as applicable to diminish awards of equitable compensation for breach of fiduciary duty'. In particular, the court pointed out that 'contributory negligence focuses on the conduct of the plaintiff, fiduciary law upon the obligation by the defendant to act in the interests of the plaintiff'.

---

and at 252 per Olsson J; *Permanent Building Society (in liq) v Wheeler* (1994) 11 WAR 187 at 245–6 per Ipp J; *O'Halloran v R T Thomas & Family Pty Ltd* (1998) 45 NSWLR 262 at 276 per Spigelman CJ, at 280 per Priestley JA; *Beach Petroleum NL v Kennedy* (1999) 48 NSWLR 1 at 91–4 per Spigelman CJ, Sheller and Stein JJA; *Tenji v Henneberry & Associates Pty Ltd* (2000) 172 ALR 679 at 688 per French J; *Fexuto Pty Ltd v Bosnjak Holdings Pty Ltd* (2001) 37 ACSR 672 at 694 per Spigelman CJ; *Cassis v Kalfus (No 2)* [2004] NSWCA 315 at [42] per Hodgson JA, *Rigg v Sheridan* [2008] NSWCA 79 at [27] per Handley AJA, *Simpson v Donnybrook Properties Pty Ltd* [2010] NSWCA 229 at [100] per Young JA; *Watson v Ebsworth & Ebsworth* [2010] VSCA 335.

37. [1987] 2 NZLR 443.
38. [1987] 2 NZLR 443 at 448 per Cooke P.
39. [1987] 2 NZLR 443 at 451.
40. [1987] 2 NZLR 443 at 468.
41. (2001) 207 CLR 165 at 201 per McHugh, Gummow, Hayne and Callinan JJ.

Breach of equitable duty of care and skill

11.9   The same tensions between the equitable and common law principles of compensation have arisen in cases of breach of equitable duties of care and skill. In *Permanent Building Society (in liq) v Wheeler*, where a company liquidator claimed equitable compensation for breach of the defendant company director's equitable duty of care and skill, Ipp J said:

> It is essential to bear in mind that the existence of a fiduciary relationship does not mean that every duty owed by a fiduciary to the beneficiary is a fiduciary duty. In particular, a trustee's duty to exercise reasonable care, though equitable, is not specifically a fiduciary duty.[42]

This passage was quoted with approval by the English Court of Appeal in *Bristol and West Building Society v Mothew*.[43] In this case, the defendant solicitor had breached his equitable duty of care and skill, as well as his common law duties of care in tort and contract, by inadvertently providing incorrect information to his plaintiff client, in response to a telephone query. By a chain of subsequent events, the plaintiff argued that the solicitor was responsible for the loss of the plaintiff's loan funds in the transaction. In dispute before the Court of Appeal was the correct legal test of causation and remoteness of damage to apply to the plaintiff's claim. While the plaintiff's concurrent actions at common law for negligence and breach of the solicitor's retainer agreement were clearly subject to the common law rules on causation and remoteness of damage (see **2.8–2.52, 3.6–3.24**), the plaintiff argued unsuccessfully that the solicitor's equitable duty of care and skill was a fiduciary duty, hence the common law restrictions did not apply. The Court of Appeal held that the solicitor was not in breach of a fiduciary duty. Millett LJ (as he then was) said:

> It is inappropriate … to apply the expression ["fiduciary duty"] to the obligation of a trustee or other fiduciary to use proper skill and care in the discharge of his duties. If it is confined to cases where the fiduciary nature of the duty has special legal consequences, then the fact that the source of the duty is to be found in equity rather than the common law does not make it a fiduciary duty. The common law and equity each developed the duty of care, but they did so independently of each other and the standard of care required is not always the same. But they influenced each other, and today the substance of the resulting obligations is more significant than their particular historic origin … Although the remedy which equity makes available for breach of the equitable duty of skill and care is equitable compensation rather than damages, this is merely the product of history and in this context is in my opinion a distinction without a difference. Equitable compensation for breach of the duty of skill and care resembles common law damages in that it is awarded by way of compensation to the plaintiff for his loss. There is no reason in principle why the common law rules of causation, remoteness of

---

42.   (1994) 11 WAR 187 at 237 (Malcolm CJ and Seaman J agreeing). See also *Henderson v Merrett Syndicates Ltd* [1995] 2 AC 145 at 205 per Lord Browne-Wilkinson; *Breen v Williams* (1996) 186 CLR 71 at 82 per Brennan CJ. See: W M Heath, "The director's 'fiduciary' duty of care and skill: A misnomer" (2007) 25 *Company and Securities Law Journal* 370.

43.   [1998] Ch 1.

damage and measure of damage should not be applied by analogy in such a case.[44]

In Australia, however, the persuasive authority of *Mothew* must be doubted since the *obiter dicta* of the High Court in *Youyang Pty Ltd v Minter Ellison Morris Fletcher*. After quoting from the above passage, the High Court said:

> … there must be a real question whether the unique foundation and goals of equity, which has the institution of the trust at its heart, warrant any assimilation even in this limited way with the measure of compensatory damages in tort and contract. It may be thought strange to decide that trustees are to be kept by courts of equity up to their duty has an application limited to the observance by trustees of some only of their duties to beneficiaries in dealing with trust funds.[45]

AUXILIARY JURISDICTION

11.10   The modern jurisdiction of equity to award 'damages' in respect of common law and other wrongs is based largely upon statutory provisions that follow the drafting of s 2 of the Chancery Amendment Act 1858, known as 'Lord Cairns' Act'.[46] The Act, which preceded the Judicature system, supplemented the inherent jurisdiction of the Court of Chancery. In New South Wales, the modern equivalent is s 68 of the Supreme Court Act 1970:[47]

> Where the Court has power:
>
> (a) to grant an injunction against the breach of any covenant, contract or agreement, or against the commission or continuance of any wrongful act; or
>
> (b) to order the specific performance of any covenant, contract or agreement,
>
> the Court may award damages to the party injured either in addition to or in substitution for the injunction or specific performance.

It is apparent from the drafting of the Act that the court must have 'power' either to grant an injunction or to order specific performance before equitable damages can be awarded. In this chapter, the term 'specific relief' will be used to refer to both injunctions (see Chapters 8–10) and specific performance: see Chapter 7. Some authorities have interpreted equivalent statutory provisions to mean that damages are only available if all the conditions for the grant of specific relief are satisfied, including discretionary considerations.[48] However, the better view is that damages are available if the court has *jurisdiction* to grant specific relief, but declines to do so because

---

44.   [1998] Ch 1 at 16–17.

45.   (2003) 212 CLR 484 at 500 per Gleeson CJ, McHugh, Gummow, Kirby and Hayne JJ.

46.   21 & 22 Vict c 27. See, generally, P M McDermott, *Equitable Damages*, Butterworths, Sydney, 1994.

47.   The equivalent provisions in other jurisdictions are: Supreme Court Act 1933 (ACT) s 20; Supreme Court Act 1979 (NT) s 14(1)(b); Supreme Court Act 1995 (Qld) s 244; Supreme Court Act 1935 (SA) s 30; Supreme Court Civil Procedure Act 1932 (Tas) s 11(13); Supreme Court Act 1986 (Vic) s 38; Supreme Court Act 1935 (WA) s 25(10). See also: Corporations Act 2001 (Cth) Pt 9.5.

48.   *King v Poggioli* (1923) 32 CLR 222 at 247 per Starke J; *J C Williamson Ltd v Lukey and Mulholland* (1931) 45 CLR 282 at 295 per Dixon J.

of discretionary considerations.[49] As Millett LJ (as he then was) said in *Jaggard v Sawyer*, 'the question is whether, at the date of the writ, the court *could* have granted an injunction, not whether it *would* have done'.[50]

Jurisdiction to award damages

11.11   The better interpretation of s 68 of the Supreme Court Act 1970 (NSW), just discussed, and its statutory equivalents requires a distinction to be drawn between matters of jurisdiction and matters of discretion in granting specific relief.[51] Unfortunately, there is no obvious or logical distinction between matters of jurisdiction and matters of discretion: see also **7.34**. The tendency of modern authorities has been to treat everything as a matter of discretion, hence increasing the scope to award equitable damages. In *Wentworth v Woollahra Municipal Council*,[52] the High Court identified laches, acquiescence and hardship as matters of discretion. Absence of mutuality in specific performance is a matter of discretion.[53] Likewise, where mistake is a discretionary defence to specific performance, equitable damages may still be awarded.[54]

11.12   Impossibility of granting specific relief has been treated as a matter of jurisdiction. If a grant of specific relief was impossible when proceedings seeking relief were commenced, and remained so, there is no jurisdiction to award equitable damages. In *McMahon v Ambrose*,[55] specific performance was sought of a contract to assign a lease. Because the lease had expired before the commencement of proceedings, there was no jurisdiction to award specific performance or equitable damages. However, if a contract was capable of specific performance when proceedings seeking relief were commenced, the court does not lose its jurisdiction to award damages in substitution for specific performance if performance of the contract becomes impossible during the pendency of the litigation. That was so in *Johnson v Agnew*,[56] where specific performance of a contract for the sale of land became impossible because the vendors' mortgagees exercised their power to sell the property to another purchaser. The same principle applies in cases of prohibitory injunctions where, as in *Fritz v Hobson*,[57] the nuisance to be enjoined had

---

49.   *Goldsbrough Mort & Co Ltd v Quinn* (1910) 10 CLR 674 at 701 per Isaacs J; *Wentworth v Woollahra Municipal Council* (1982) 149 CLR 672 at 678–9 per Gibbs CJ, Mason, Murphy and Brennan JJ.

50.   [1995] 2 All ER 189 at 205. See also *Mills v Ruthol Pty Ltd* [2004] NSWSC 547 at [61]; (2004) 61 NSWLR 1 at 13 per Palmer J.

51.   I.C.F Spry, *The Principles of Equitable Remedies: Specific Performance, Injunctions, Rectification and Equitable Damages*, 8th ed, Law Book Co, Australia, 2010, p 627.

52.   (1982) 149 CLR 672 at 679 per Gibbs CJ, Mason, Murphy and Brennan JJ.

53.   *Price v Strange* [1978] Ch 337. Mutuality in relation to specific performance is discussed at **7.37–7.38**.

54.   *Goldsbrough Mort & Co Ltd v Quinn* (1910) 10 CLR 674 at 701 per Isaacs J.

55.   [1987] VR 817. See also *Jaggard v Sawyer* [1995] 2 All ER 189 at 205 per Millett LJ.

56.   [1980] AC 367. See also **7.14**.

57.   (1880) 14 Ch D 542.

abated after proceedings were commenced. Equitable damages in substitution for an injunction were awarded.

Discretion to award damages

11.13 An award of equitable damages under Lord Cairns' Act and its equivalents is discretionary in nature. Unlike damages at common law, equitable damages are not awarded as a matter of right. It follows that equitable damages may be reduced or denied because of equitable discretionary considerations, such as 'unclean hands', laches, or hardship to the defendant, that are irrelevant at common law. Under s 68 of the Supreme Court Act 1970 (NSW) and its statutory equivalents one of three outcomes is possible.

11.14 First, neither damages nor specific relief may be awarded. An equitable defence, such as acquiescence, may preclude both the grant of specific relief and an award of damages. That was the result in *Sayers v Collyer*,[58] where the plaintiff sought to enforce a restrictive covenant over land to restrain the defendant from using his premises as a beer shop. The defendant had been conducting his business there for three years without objection by the plaintiff, and the plaintiff himself had purchased beer from the defendant's shop. The English Court of Appeal held that the plaintiff's acquiescence disentitled him to an injunction or equitable damages.

11.15 Second, damages may be awarded *in addition to* specific relief. In these cases, the governing principle is to avoid duplication of relief. An illustration of damages being awarded in addition to specific performance is *Grant v Dawkins*,[59] where a purchaser contracted to buy a parcel of land free of encumbrances. The vendor failed to complete the contract because two mortgages remained outstanding over the land. The purchaser sought specific performance of the contract on the basis that he would discharge the mortgages himself. Goff J awarded equitable damages in addition to specific performance to compensate the purchaser for the mortgage liabilities.

11.16 The third possible outcome under s 68 of the Supreme Court Act 1970 (NSW) is that damages may be awarded *in substitution for* specific relief. As in *Johnson v Agnew*,[60] such damages may be awarded when specific relief has become impossible during the pendency of the litigation. However, damages in substitution for specific relief may still be awarded even when specific relief remains possible. In *Shelfer v City of London Electric Lighting Co*, AL Smith LJ proposed a 'good working rule' that:

(1) If the injury to the plaintiff's legal rights is small,

(2) And is one which is capable of being estimated in money,

(3) And is one which can be adequately compensated by a small money payment,

58.   (1884) 28 Ch D 103.
59.   [1973] 3 All ER 897.
60.   [1980] AC 367.

(4) And the case is one in which it would be oppressive to the defendant to grant an injunction; then

damages in substitution for an injunction may be given.[61]

In *Shelfer's* case, the plaintiff was the lessee under a 21-year lease of a house that became subject to continuing noise and vibration created by the defendant's works. While the plaintiff was successful in establishing a case of continuing nuisance, Kekewich J at first instance refused to grant the injunction which the plaintiff had sought, and awarded equitable damages instead. The English Court of Appeal reversed that judgment and granted an injunction, primarily because 'the injury to the plaintiff is certainly not small'.[62] As *Shelfer's* case shows, the courts have always been mindful of the criticism that Lord Cairns' Act conferred the 'power to legalize the commission of torts by any defendant who was able and willing to pay damages'.[63]

Shelfer's case was considered by the Victorian Court of Appeal in *Break Fast Investments Pty Ltd v PCH Melbourne Pty Ltd*.[64] In this case, the defendant had refurbished the exterior of its 12 storey office building in central Melbourne by attaching metal cladding to one of the walls. Inadvertently, the cladding encroached into the plaintiff's adjacent airspace by approximately 3–6 centimetres. The judge at first instance granted a mandatory injunction to remove the cladding because the trespassing encroachment was not 'trifling' or *de minimis* and it would permanently prevent the plaintiff from building up to the boundary in its proposed re-development of its site. On appeal, the defendant argued unsuccessfully that equitable damages should have been awarded instead of a mandatory injunction, relying upon *Shelfer's* case.

The Court of Appeal emphasised the exceptional nature of such awards, and reiterated the common misgiving of the courts in these cases that 'an award of damages in lieu would amount to a court-approved acquisition of property, against the consent and interests of the registered proprietor.'[65] In terms of the 'good working rule' in *Shelfer's* case, the Court of Appeal held that the defendant had failed to satisfy the last principle that 'the case is one in which it would be oppressive to the defendant to grant an injunction'.[66] On the meaning of oppression, the Court of Appeal said:

> Oppression in that context imports consideration of, inter alia, specific detriment, including disproportionate harm to the defendant relative to injury to the plaintiff, the deliberate or unintended quality of the trespass and all other relevant considerations.[67]

---

61. [1895] 1 Ch 287 at 322.
62. [1895] 1 Ch 287 at 323.
63. *Leeds Industrial Co-operative Society Ltd v Slack* [1924] AC 851 at 860 per Viscount Finlay; *Attorney-General v Blake* [2001] 1 AC 268 at 281 per Lord Nicholls.
64. (2007) 20 VR 311; [2007] VSCA 311.
65. (2007) 20 VR 311 at 319; [2007] VSCA 311, at [35] per Dodds-Streeton JA (Ashley and Cavanough JJA agreeing).
66. [1895] 1 Ch 287 at 322.
67. (2007) 20 VR 311 at 336; [2007] VSCA 311 at [135],.

The Court of Appeal made the crucial point, however, that oppression to the defendant requires more than the balance of convenience being in the defendant's favour.[68] In the particular circumstances of this case, the Court of Appeal held that the cost of approximately $300,000 to remove the cladding, and the 'loss of improved appearance', was not oppressive to this defendant.

Meaning of 'wrongful act'

11.17   Based upon the drafting used in Lord Cairns' Act, s 68(a) of the Supreme Court Act 1970 (NSW) provides that one of the occasions for awarding equitable damages is 'where the Court has power … to grant an injunction … against the commission or continuance of any wrongful act'. Clearly, wrongful acts include torts. The course of authority has identified other wrongful acts that may also give rise to an award of equitable damages.

Breaches of statutory prohibitions

11.18   The jurisdiction to award equitable damages for breaches of statutory prohibitions was considered by the High Court in *Wentworth v Woollahra Municipal Council*.[69] In that case, the plaintiff sought a mandatory injunction to demolish a neighbouring house which had been erected in breach of a local planning ordinance. It was conceded for the purposes of the appeal that the plaintiff had *locus standi* to seek an injunction. The plaintiff's standing was based upon special damage that consisted of having the views from her house obscured by the offending structure. Because the New South Wales Court of Appeal declined to grant the injunction on discretionary grounds, the plaintiff claimed equitable damages and argued that the breach of the statutory prohibition was a 'wrongful act' within the meaning of s 68(a) of the Supreme Court Act. In refusing the claim for damages, the High Court held that s 68 is 'exclusively preoccupied with private rights' and that the section 'was not intended to authorise the award of damages for breach of a statutory prohibition which manifests no intention to create a private cause of action for damages'.[70]

In *Matthews v ACP Publishing Pty Ltd*,[71] the prohibition was in s 35(5) of the Copyright Act 1968 (Cth). The section, as then enacted, effectively provided that where a photograph was commissioned for a particular purpose, 'the author is entitled to restrain the doing, otherwise than for that purpose, of any act comprised in the copyright in the work'. In this case, the plaintiff photographer had been commissioned by the defendant publisher to photograph a celebrity for the single purpose of publication on the cover of *Cleo* magazine. Without the consent of the plaintiff or any additional payment, the defendant then licensed the photograph to another company for publication on the cover

68.   (2007) 20 VR 311 at 326; [2007] VSCA 311 at [81]; *Jaggard v Sawyer* [1995] 2 All ER 189 at 203 per Sir Thomas Bingham MR (CA).

69.   (1982) 149 CLR 672.

70.   (1982) 149 CLR 672 at 683 per Gibbs CJ, Mason, Murphy and Brennan JJ.

71.   (1998) 157 ALR 564.

of another magazine. The plaintiff sought an injunction to restrain further publication of the photograph and equitable damages. Although s 35(5) of the Copyright Act contained no express provision for damages, Beaumont J held that the section 'manifests an intention to create a private cause of action in damages in lieu of or in addition to the grant of an injunction where the award of compensation is appropriate'. His Honour distinguished *Wentworth v Woollahra Municipal Council* for the reason that 'section 35(5) is not concerned with public rights'.[72] Accordingly, Beaumont J awarded equitable damages to the plaintiff, in addition to an injunction.

Equitable wrongs

11.19   There has been a question whether the phrase 'commission or continuance of any wrongful act', as used in Lord Cairns' Act and its modern equivalents, encompasses purely equitable wrongs. Meagher, Heydon and Leeming make a persuasive historical argument that Lord Cairns' Act 1858, which preceded the Judicature Act 1873, was intended to supplement the auxiliary jurisdiction of equity in aid of common law rights, and that 'wrongful acts' in this context meant torts.[73] Equitable wrongs were always matters for the exclusive jurisdiction, which did not require any supplementation by statute. The course of authority, however, has overtaken that view. The point is still significant because the common law principles of assessment are generally applied to the assessment of equitable damages under Lord Cairns' Act, including the common law standards of causation and remoteness of damage: see **11.22**.

In Australia, the inclusion of equitable wrongs has arguably been settled by *dicta* in *Wentworth v Woollahra Municipal Council*,[74] where the High Court observed that 'An incidental object of the Act was to enable the court to award damages in lieu of an injunction or specific performance, even in the case of a purely equitable claim'. Meagher, Heydon and Leeming reject the assumption that equity had lacked the inherent jurisdiction to do so.[75] However, it is consistent with the view expressed by the High Court that the authorities have recognised a jurisdiction to award equitable damages in substitution for an injunction in breach of confidence cases, where the obligation of confidence was purely equitable in nature. In *Attorney-General v Guardian Newspapers Ltd (No 2)*, the defendant newspaper proprietor had published extracts from the book *Spycatcher* in breach of an equitable duty of confidence owed to the Crown. Lord Goff referred to:

---

72.   (1998) 157 ALR 564 at 573.

73.   R P Meagher, J D Heydon and M J Leeming, *Meagher, Gummow and Lehane's Equity: Doctrines and Remedies*, 4th ed, LexisNexis Butterworths, Sydney, 2002, [23-105].

74.   (1982) 149 CLR 672 at 676 per Gibbs CJ, Mason, Murphy and Brennan JJ.

75.   R P Meagher, J D Heydon and M J Leeming, *Meagher, Gummow and Lehane's Equity: Doctrines and Remedies*, 4th ed, LexisNexis Butterworths, Sydney, 2002, [23-105]. See also P M McDermott, *Equitable Damages*, Butterworths, Sydney, 1994, pp 24–25.

… the remedy of damages, which in cases of breach of confidence is now available, despite the equitable nature of the wrong, through a beneficent interpretation of the Chancery Amendment Act 1858 (Lord Cairns' Act).[76]

These comments were *obiter* because the plaintiff elected for an account of profits: see **6.4**. Lord Goff's comments are best understood as a reference to equitable damages awarded in substitution for an injunction. In the *Spycatcher* case, the House of Lords refused to grant an injunction to restrain further publication because the information was already in the public domain.

11.20 In *Talbot v General Television Corp Pty Ltd*, the Victorian Supreme Court had earlier taken a similar view of the jurisdiction to award an injunction and equitable damages for breach of confidence. In that case, the defendant broadcaster had made an unauthorised use of a new program concept that the plaintiff producer had submitted to the defendant in confidence, for the purpose of evaluation only. The obligation of confidence was purely equitable because there was no contract between the parties. The plaintiff was awarded an injunction and an inquiry as to damages. In a judgment that was affirmed by the Full Court, Harris J said:

> The only question is whether there is jurisdiction to award damages as well as an injunction. As the action relies upon the equitable jurisdiction of the court, the most obvious source, and perhaps the only source, of power to award such damages is s 62(3) of the Supreme Court Act 1958.[77] The power there is given to award damages either in addition to or in substitution for an injunction …[78]

11.21 In the United Kingdom and in Victoria, but not in the other Australian jurisdictions, the modern equivalents of Lord Cairns' Act no longer refer to 'the commission or continuance of any wrongful act'. Section 38 of the Supreme Court Act 1986 (Vic), which is drafted in the same terms as s 50 of the Supreme Court Act 1981 (UK), provides:

> If the Court has jurisdiction to entertain an application for an injunction or specific performance, it may award damages in addition to, or in substitution for, an injunction or specific performance.

This drafting removes any residual doubt about the inclusion of equitable wrongs. In *Giller v Procopets*,[79] a case that was decided under this Act, the Victorian Court of Appeal upheld a claim for equitable damages in substitution for an injunction, arising from the breach of a purely equitable obligation of confidence. This case was, in part, about the defendant's distribution of an explicit videotape among the plaintiff's family and friends which showed various sexual encounters between the plaintiff and the defendant. In circumstances such as these, the action for breach of confidence has restrained the dissemination

76. [1990] 1 AC 109 at 286.
77. Repealed by the Supreme Court Act 1986 (Vic).
78. [1980] VR 224 at 241.
79. (2008) 24 VR 1; [2008] VSCA 236.

of personal and private images since the earliest cases.[80] The Court of Appeal accepted that the plaintiff would have been entitled to a restraining injunction, if copies of the tape had not already been distributed. Although the resulting harm to the plaintiff fell short of a recognized 'psychiatric injury' for the purposes of the law of torts,[81] the Court of Appeal awarded compensation of $40,000 for the plaintiff's 'mental distress'. This was recognized as a head of damage for breach of confidence by the House of Lords in *Campbell v MGN Ltd*.[82] Neave JA held that the award could be characterized either as equitable damages under Lord Cairns' Act or equitable compensation in the exclusive jurisdiction of equity.[83] Ashley JA concurred in awarding equitable damages in substitution for an injunction for the plaintiff's 'distress'.[84] Because the defendant's conduct was intended to harm the plaintiff in this way, and did so, Neave JA[85] and Ashley JA[86] each included a component for aggravation in the award of compensation, by analogy with the law of torts. However, the Court of Appeal refused to recognize a tort of 'invasion of privacy' in Australian law.

Assessment of damages

11.22 Applying the maxim *aequitas sequitur legem* (meaning 'equity follows the law'), the rule governing assessment of equitable damages in the auxiliary jurisdiction is that equity follows the common law principles of assessment. In *Johnson v Agnew*, Lord Wilberforce said that 'I find in the Act no warrant for the court awarding damages differently from common law damages'.[87] Two corollaries flow from that rule. First, the common law standards of causation and remoteness of damage are applied in the auxiliary jurisdiction of equity.[88] Second, and despite prior authority to the contrary,[89] there is no necessary difference between the common law and equity as to the date for assessment of damages, because both remedies are governed by the compensation principle.[90] However, it is the general practice to assess common

---

80. *Prince Albert v Strange* (1849) 2 De Gex & Sim 652, 41 ER 1171; *Pollard v Photographic Co* (1889) 40 Ch D 345.

81. See **2.46**.

82. [2004] UKHL 22, [2004] 2 AC 457. See also *Douglas v Hello! Ltd (No 2)* [2005] EWCA Civ 595, [2006] QB 125.

83. (2008) 24 VR 1 at 102; [2008] VSCA 236 at [431].

84. (2008) 24 VR 1 at 34; [2008] VSCA 236 at [159], Maxwell P (at 5) awarded damages for a new tort of 'intentional infliction of emotional distress'.

85. (2008) 24 VR 1 at 105; [2008] VSCA 236 at [442].

86. (2008) 24 VR 1 at 34; [2008] VSCA 236 at [158] per Ashley JA.

87. [1980] AC 367 at 400. See also *Attorney-General v Blake* [2001] 1 AC 268 at 281 per Lord Nicholls. The common law principles of assessment are discussed at **2.57–2.87** and **3.36–3.52**.

88. *Dillon v Nash* [1950] VLR 293 at 301 per Sholl J. The common law principles of remoteness are discussed at **2.37–2.52** and **3.14–3.24**.

89. *Wroth v Tyler* [1974] Ch 30 at 60 per Megarry J.

90. *Johnson v Agnew* [1980] AC 367 at 400–1 per Lord Wilberforce, cited with approval in *Johnson v Perez* (1988) 166 CLR 351 at 356 per Mason J. See also *Vieira v O'Shea* [2012] NSWCA 21 at [44] per Basten and Meagher JJA. The common law principles governing the date of assessment are discussed at **2.58** and **3.36–3.39**.

law damages by reference to the date on which the cause of action accrued, and to assess equitable damages as at the date of judgment, in order to be a true substitute for specific relief.[91]

11.23 The main qualification to the general rule that equitable damages follow the common law principles of assessment is that damages may be awarded under Lord Cairns' Act and its equivalents where no damages can be awarded at common law. Hence, the common law provides no direct analogue. This will be the case where purely equitable obligations have been breached, such as a breach of confidence, or an action to enforce an equitable easement.[92]

11.24 The assessment of equitable damages is most difficult in cases of threatened or apprehended injuries to legal rights where a *quia timet* injunction would lie, but the common law offers no remedy. In *Leeds Industrial Co-operative Society Ltd v Slack*,[93] the appellant was constructing buildings which, if completed according to plan, would have caused an actionable obstruction of the respondent's common law right to light. However, no such obstruction had actually occurred when the respondent commenced proceedings to seek a *quia timet* injunction to restrain the threatened injury: see **8.13**. When the injunction was refused on discretionary grounds, the question arose of whether equitable damages in substitution for an injunction could be awarded where the respondent had suffered no actual injury. Viscount Finlay stated what remains the position at common law:

> Such [common law] damages were given only in respect of a cause of action which had accrued at the date of commencement of the action. No damages could be recovered for injury that was merely threatened, but, of course, the damages might include compensation for consequences of the injury already completed which it was proved would occur in the future.[94]

A majority of the House of Lords held that Lord Cairns' Act enabled an award of equitable damages in substitution for an injunction, even where no injury had actually occurred.[95] As Viscount Finlay explained:

> ... if damages are given in substitution for an injunction they must necessarily cover not only injury already sustained but also injury that would be inflicted in the future by the commission of the act threatened. If no injury has yet been sustained the damages will be solely in respect of the damage to be sustained in the future by injuries which the injunction, if granted, would have prevented.[96]

---

91. *Madden v Kevereski* [1983] 1 NSWLR 305; *Mills v Ruthol Pty Ltd* (2004) 61 NSWLR 1 at 14; and *ASA Constructions Pty Ltd v Iwanov* [1975] 1 NSWLR 512 at 518.

92. *Gas & Fuel Corporation of Victoria v Barba* [1976] VR 755 at 766 per Crockett HJ.

93. [1924] AC 851. Approved in *Jamena Gas Networks (NSW) Ltd v Mine Subsidence Board* [2011] HCA 19 at [33].

94. [1924] AC 851 at 856. The 'once and for all' rule in awarding tort damages is discussed at **2.59–2.60**.

95. The position is different in Tasmania. Under the Supreme Court Civil Procedure Act 1932 (Tas) s 11(13)(b), there is no jurisdiction to award damages in substitution for specific relief where 'no breach of covenant, contract, or agreement, or no wrongful act ... *has been committed*'.

96. [1924] AC 851 at 857; cited with approval by the High Court in *Bankstown City Council v Alamdo Holdings Pty Ltd* (2005) 223 CLR 660 at 664 per Gleeson CJ, McHugh, Gummow, Hayne and Callinan JJ.

In *Attorney-General v Blake*, Lord Nicholls identified this capacity of equitable damages to compensate for both present and future injury as a key difference and advantage over common law damages. [97]

11.25   In conclusion, there is much force in Professor Burrows' criticism that:

> ... all these technical distinctions between common law damages, equitable compensation and equitable damages bring no credit to the legal system. They are the irrational historical residue of an unfused system ...'[98]

---

97.   [2001] 1 AC 268 at 281. See also *Barbagallo v J & F Catelan Pty Ltd* [1986] 1 Qd R 245 at 262–3 per Thomas J.

98.   A Burrows, *Remedies for Torts and Breach of Contract*, 3rd ed, Oxford University Press, Oxford, 2004, p 606.

CHAPTER 12

Rectification

NATURE OF THE REMEDY

12.1 At common law a written contract is effective according to its terms, the assumption being that it reflects the true intention or agreement of the parties. But what if the written terms fail to reflect the agreement that was actually reached by the parties? The equitable remedy of rectification is designed to provide relief in such cases. An example is found in *Bosaid v Andry*.[1] At the time of signing a contract for the sale of land, both parties intended that a property known as 'No 75' Alma Road, St Kilda be sold, but the written document said 'No 15'. The court rectified the document. So, rectification is available where

---

1.   [1963] VR 465.

both parties are agreed at the time of execution, but the written document recording the agreement fails to reflect this. The court strikes out the mistake and replaces it with the words that reflect the true agreement between the parties. As explained by Mason J in *Maralinga Pty Ltd v Major Enterprises Pty Ltd*:

> … the purpose of the remedy is to make the instrument conform to the true agreement of the parties where the writing by common mistake fails to express that agreement accurately. And there has been a firm insistence on the requirement that the mistake as to the writing must be common to the parties and not merely unilateral, except in cases of a special class to which I shall later refer.[2]

When this statement was made, nearly four decades ago, it was certainly true that rectification was primarily aimed at correcting common mistakes, that is, where both parties shared the same mistake about the contents of the written contract. As Mason J said in *Maralinga*, only in 'special' cases would the court rectify a unilateral mistake, that is, where just one of the contracting parties was mistaken. However, as discussed at **12.7**, this is no longer true. The courts now grant rectification for unilateral mistake where the enforcing party has unconscientiously taken advantage of the other party's mistake.

It is consistent with the reasoning in *Maralinga* that unconscientious conduct by the enforcing party has also been recognised as the rationale for granting rectification of contracts for common mistake. Most recently, in *Franklins Pty Ltd v Metcash Trading Ltd*, the New South Wales Court of Appeal held:

> In considering whether to grant rectification of a written contract… equity focuses on what it is unconscientious for a party to assert about the contract. The rationale is that it is unconscientious for a party to a contract to seek to apply the contract inconsistently with what he or she knows to be the common intention of the parties at the time that the written contract was entered. In other words, when a plaintiff succeeds in a claim for rectification, the plaintiff is found to have been justified in effect saying to the defendant "you and I both knew, when we entered this contract, what our intention was concerning it, and you cannot in conscience now try to enforce the contract in accordance with its terms in a way that is inconsistent with our common intention".[3]

Rectification proceedings in equity are generally commenced when one of the parties seeks to enforce the agreement according to its written terms. That party benefits from the strong presumption of fact and law that the written agreement is the true agreement between the parties. In order to rebut that presumption, the party seeking rectification must show that the written instrument was intended to record the true agreement of the parties but, due to a mistake, it failed to do so.[4]

---

2.   (1973) 128 CLR 336 at 350.

3.   (2009) 76 NSWLR 603 at 710; [2009] NSWCA 407at [444] (Allsop P and Giles JA concurring).

4.   *Maralinga Pty Ltd v Major Enterprises Pty Ltd* (1973) 128 CLR 336 at 351 per Mason J.

ELEMENTS

12.2   For the court to grant rectification in cases of common mistake, the plaintiff must 'clearly and convincingly' prove that:

a)   there is a *written instrument*;

b)   there was a *mistake* by the parties as to its contents or its effect;

c)   the parties' *intention* as to what the instrument should have contained was common or *concurrent* at the time of execution; and

d)   the *court's discretion* should be exercised in favour of granting relief.

A *unilateral* mistake will be sufficient where the defendant unconscientiously takes advantage of the mistake *and* there was a consensus as to what the document should have contained prior to the mistake.[5]

WRITTEN INSTRUMENT

12.3   The main area where the equitable remedy of rectification applies is contracts in writing, but it applies to most documents, except for the constitutions of companies,[6] and wills.[7] It includes, for example, deeds,[8] conveyances, leases,[9] options to purchase,[10] life insurance policies,[11] bonds, trusts[12] and documents conveying gifts.[13] Meagher, Heydon and Leeming state that a registered trade mark may be rectified in equity, but the authority they cite does not support that proposition.[14] Errors or defects in a trade mark's entry on the public register may be corrected by the court or registrar in statutory rectification proceedings.[15]

---

5.   *Leibler v Air New Zealand Ltd (No 2)* [1999] 1 VR 1 at 27 per Kenny JA.

6.   *Scott v Frank F Scott (London) Ltd* [1940] Ch 794 at 801; *National Roads and Motorists' Association Ltd v Parkin* [2004] NSWCA 153 at [85] per Ipp JA. These matters are governed by the Corporations Act 2001 (Cth).

7.   *Harter v Harter* (1873) LR 3 P&D 11; *Osborne v Smith* (1960) 105 CLR 153 at 162 per Kitto J. There is now a statutory power to rectify wills in most jurisdictions: Succession Act, 2006 (NSW) s 27; Wills Act 1968 (ACT) Pt 4; Wills Act (NT) s 27; Succession Act 1981 (Qld) s 31; Wills Act 1936 (SA) s 25AA; Wills Act 1992 (Tas) s 47; Wills Act 1997 (Vic) s 31.

8.   *Eroc Pty Ltd v Amalg Resources NL* [2003] QSC 74; *Pourzand v Home Building Society Ltd* [2004] WASC 127.

9.   *Stormriders Pty Ltd v Copperart Pty Ltd* [2004] NSWSC 809; *Aspro's Pty Ltd v Robert Frederick Hayter* [2005] NSWSC 512; compare *The Stuart Park (D580060) Reserve Trust v Esmibarb Pty Ltd* [2006] NSWSC 603.

10.   *Stewart Investments v Legge Building* [2003] NSWSC 193.

11.   *Metlife Insurance Ltd v Visy Board Pty Ltd* [2007] NSWSC 1481; compare *Permanent Trustee Australia Ltd v EAI General Insurance Co Ltd* (1998) 153 ALR 529 at 568–9.

12.   *Commissioner of Stamp Duties (NSW) v Carlenka Pty Ltd* (1995) 41 NSWLR 329; *Furey v Mackne* [1999] NSWSC 1298.

13.   *Re Butlin's Settlement Trusts* [1976] Ch 251.

14.   R P Meagher, J D Heydon and M J Leeming, *Meagher, Gummow & Lehane's Equity: Doctrines & Remedies*, 4th ed, LexisNexis Butterworths, Sydney, 2002, at [26 005], citing *Higgins Holdings Pty Ltd v Registrar of Trade Marks* (1995) 131 ALR 554.

15.   See Pt 8 (Amendment and cancellation of registration) and Pt 10 (Assignment and transmission of trade marks) Trade Marks Act 1995 (Cth).

Where, as a matter of formality, two written counterpart contracts are exchanged, but one of the contracts contains a mistake, rectification is generally available. However, it will be refused if the parties' intention is to be bound only by an exchange of identical contracts.[16]

MISTAKE

Construction and rectification

12.4 Not all mistakes require rectification. Difficulties and ambiguities on the face of the document, such as obvious typographical errors, spelling mistakes, deletions and insertions, can often be corrected simply as a matter of interpretation or construction. In *Fitzgerald v Masters*, the High Court said that 'words may generally supplied, omitted or corrected, in an instrument, where it is clearly necessary in order to avoid absurdity or inconsistency.'[17] Rectification and interpretation are not mutually exclusive remedies, and the plaintiff may plead both in the one claim.[18] However, they are distinguished by purpose. As Sheller JA explained in *National Australia Bank Ltd v Budget Stationary Supplies*:

> Whereas interpretation is concerned with the meaning of the language on the face of the contract and its ambiguities, rectification may be ordered when the meaning of the document is clear, but it fails to express the real intention of the parties.[19]

12.5 Where both construction and rectification are claimed, Atkinson J noted in *Décor Blinds Gold Coast Pty Ltd v Décor Blinds Australia Pty Ltd*:

> The question of rectification can safely be left until after the determination of the true meaning of the contract. The resolution of ambiguity may mean that it becomes unnecessary to consider rectification of the contract.[20]

Common mistake

12.6 Early last century, in *Bacchus Marsh Concentrated Milk Co Ltd v Joseph*,[21] Higgins J said equity would only grant rectification in exceptional cases, such as incorrect omission or inclusion of a word or words.[22] Both parties had to be mistaken about the content or form of the document. A mistake about its *effect* was insufficient. An example of the traditional view can be found in

---

16.   *Sindel v Georgiou* (1984) 154 CLR 661 at 666–7; see also *Hayward v Planet Projects Pty Ltd* [2000] NSWSC 1105; *Eid v Wollondilly Retirement Village Pty Ltd* [2003] NSWCA 109.

17.   (1956) 95 CLR 420 at 426-7 per Dixon CJ and Fullagar J.

18.   *Standard Portland Cement Pty Ltd v Good* [1982] 2 NSWLR 668; 47 ALR 151 (PC); *Metlife Insurance Ltd v Visy Board Pty Ltd* [2007] NSWSC 1481 at [22].

19.   (1997) 217 ALR 365 at 381, Mason P and Handley JA concurring.

20.   [2004] QSC 55 at [23].

21.   (1919) 26 CLR 410.

22.   (1919) 26 CLR 410 at 452.

Maralinga Pty Ltd v Major Enterprises Pty Ltd.[23] At an auction for the sale of land at Vaucluse Heights, Sydney, the auctioneer said that the vendor was offering finance requiring a cash payment of $75,000 and a three-year mortgage for the balance of the purchase price. The property was sold to the appellant, Maralinga, for $155,000. However, the draft contract did not refer to the finance offer and instead required the balance of the purchase price to be paid in cash upon completion. Maralinga, through its agent, Mr Mutton, was aware of that term and eventually signed the contract in that form. Later Maralinga sought to have the document rectified so as to include, inter alia, the mortgage, but the High Court refused to rectify the document. Mason J held:

> In these circumstances the statement that the written instrument was signed merely to record the terms of the oral bargain is, in my view, neither sufficient nor accurate. Both parties knew that the written instrument contained a provision for payment of cash on completion and that it differed from the terms of the antecedent bargain; yet they signed it. So in this respect the written instrument was not executed as the result of a mistaken belief as to what it contained. Mr Mutton was mistaken as to its effect but not as to its contents.[24]

Equity will now correct many mistakes beyond those envisaged by Higgins J in *Bacchus Marsh* and Mason J in *Maralinga*, including common mistakes about the *effect* of the document. In *Re Butlin's Settlement Trusts*[25] Brightman J held that rectification was available:

> ... not only in a case where particular words have been added, omitted or wrongly written as the result of careless copying or the like. It is also available where the words of the document were purposely used but it was mistakenly considered that they bore a different meaning from their correct meaning as a matter of true construction. In such a case, which is the present case, the Court will rectify the wording of the document so it expresses the true intention ...[26]

This reasoning was applied by the New South Wales Court of Appeal in *Commissioner of Stamp Duties (NSW) v Carlenka Pty Ltd.*[27] The parties in this case sought to amend a trust deed so that a company could become an income beneficiary of the trust. A solicitor was instructed to put that intention into effect, but due to inadvertence by the solicitor, the resulting amendment had the unintended effect of making the company a capital beneficiary as well, which attracted *ad valorem* stamp duty. The Court of Appeal ordered rectification because there was a 'disconformity between the form or effect of the document executed and the intention of the parties or party who executed it'.[28] Although the form of relief was not an issue in *Carlenka*, for a court to

23. (1973) 128 CLR 336.
24. (1973) 128 CLR 336 at 349.
25. [1976] Ch 251.
26. [1976] Ch 251 at 260.
27. (1995) 41 NSWLR 329.
28. (1995) 41 NSWLR 329 at 336 per Sheller JA; compare *Club Cape Schanck Resort Co Ltd v Cape Country Club Pty Ltd* (2001) 3 VR 526 (CA); *Permanent Trustee Australia Ltd v FAI General Insurance Co Ltd* (1998)

rectify a mistake about the effect of the document it must be able to determine clearly 'both the substance and the detail of the precise variation which needs to be made to the wording of the instrument'.[29]

In *Club Cape Schanck Resort Co Ltd v Cape Country Club Pty Ltd*,[30] the Victorian Court of Appeal distinguished *Carlenka*. This case was about a clause in a settlement agreement between two litigating parties which referred further disputes to a statutory tribunal. Unfortunately, as the parties later found out, the tribunal lacked the necessary jurisdiction. The plaintiff sought rectification of the clause to replace the tribunal with a named arbitrator, but the Court of Appeal refused. Tadgell JA said:

> It is true enough that the clause failed to achieve the parties' expectation, but that was not by reason of words that were used or omitted: there were, indeed, no words that could have been used to achieve the expectation, for the tribunal could not have jurisdiction conferred upon it by agreement …
>
> It cannot be right to say that, in those circumstances, the doctrine of rectification will provide, by way of insertion of some words, for the achievement of what the court, or one of the parties, considers to be the next best thing. So much I take to be axiomatic: it has never been the office of a decree of rectification to offer, as a kind of simulacrum, the nearest alternative to the thing to which the parties actually agreed.[31]

In *Carlenka*, by contrast, the parties' common intention was achievable by adding certain words and omitting others from the trust deed.

Unilateral mistake

12.7   Traditionally, rectification did not correct mistakes or defects in the transaction, only mistakes in how the transaction was recorded. As Sir William James VC said in *Mackenzie v Coulson*:

> Courts of Equity do not rectify contracts; they may and do rectify instruments purporting to have been made in pursuance of the terms of contracts.[32]

One of the effects of this general principle has been that courts have traditionally refused to grant rectification in cases of unilateral mistake.[33] However, the authorities came to recognise a 'special class' of rectification where one party is guilty of equitable fraud or unconscientiously taking advantage of a mistake in the written agreement.[34] As Mason J observed in *Maralinga*:

---

44 NSWLR 186 at 231 per Hodgson CJ (in Eq); *Oates Properties Pty Ltd v Commissioner of State Revenue* [2003] NSWSC 596.

29.   *Bush v National Australia Bank Ltd* (1992) 35 NSWLR 390 at 407; *Franklins Pty Ltd v Metcash Trading Ltd* [2009] NSWCA 407 at [446]; (2009) 76 NSWLR 603 at 711 per Campbell JA.

30.   (2001) 3 VR 526.

31.   (2001) 3 VR 526 at 531; and see *Baird v BCE Holdings Pty Ltd* (1996) 40 NSWLR 377.

32.   (1869) LR 8 Eq 368 at 375.

33.   *Slee v Warke* (1949) 86 CLR 271.

34.   *Stormriders Pty Ltd v Copperart Pty Ltd* [2004] NSWSC 809 at [61] per White J.

… if one party to a transaction knows that the instrument contains a mistake in his favour but does nothing to correct it, he will be precluded from asserting that the mistake is unilateral and not common …[35]

In these circumstances, the court may rectify the written agreement to relieve the plaintiff of the unilateral mistake.[36] Two qualifications, however, ensured that this branch of the law was rarely used. The first was that the defendant must have *actual* rather than constructive knowledge of the plaintiff's mistake. Certainly, it appears that Mason J in *Maralinga* is referring to actual knowledge of a mistake in one party's favour. In *Leibler v Air New Zealand Ltd* Kenny JA accepted that something less than actual knowledge may suffice, but her Honour declined to finally decide the issue.[37] Kenny JA stated the principles governing rectification of contracts for unilateral mistake in the following terms:

If (1) one party, A, makes an agreement under a misapprehension that the agreement contains a particular provision which the agreement does not in fact contain; and (2) the other party, B, knows of the omission and that it is due to a mistake on A's part; and (3) lets A remain under the misapprehension and concludes the agreement on the mistaken basis in circumstances where equity would require B to take some step or steps, depending on those circumstances, to bring the mistake to A's attention; then (4) B will be precluded from relying upon A's execution of the agreement to resist A's claim for rectification to give effect to A's intention …[38]

In *International Advisor Systems Pty Ltd v XYYX Pty Ltd,* Brereton J said:

An actual knowledge of the mistake is not required; it is sufficient that the other party "must have known" or "strongly suspect" that the first party is making a mistake.[39]

The second qualification restricting rectification in cases of unilateral mistake was described by McLelland J in *Tenceiro v First Mitmac Pty Ltd* as follows:

… unconscionable conduct sufficient to found a remedy of rescission is not necessarily sufficient to found a remedy by way of rectification. Furthermore, the elements of unconscionable conduct which would justify rectification for unilateral mistake must be proved to the same clear and convincing standard as the elements which would justify rectification for common mistake …[40]

However, it has now been accepted that unconscionable conduct sufficient to found a remedy of rescission (see 5.29) is also sufficient for rectification.

---

35. (1973) 128 CLR 336 at 351.

36. See D McLauchlan, 'The "Drastic" Remedy of Rectification for Unilateral Mistake' (2008) 124 *LQR* 608.

37. [1999] 1 VR 1 at 24 (CA); see also *P Ward Civil Engineering Pty Ltd v Lend Lease Property Services Pty Ltd* [1999] NSWSC 727; *Fox Entertainment Precinct Pty Ltd v Centennial Park and Moore Park Trust* [2004] NSWSC 214 at [24] per Barrett J; *Eroc Pty Ltd v Amalg Resources NL* [2003] QSC 74.

38. *Leibler v Air New Zealand Ltd (No 2)* [1999] 1 VR 1 at 14; and see *Agip Sp A v Navigazione Alta Italia Sp A* [1984] 1 Lloyd's Rep 353.

39. [2008] NSWSC 2 at [23].

40. (1997) 8 BPR 15,733; and see Chapter 5 for a discussion of rescission.

The New South Wales Court of Appeal in both *Tutt v Doyle*[41] and *Medsara Pty Ltd v Sande*[42] accepted that rectification of a unilateral mistake is based upon the doctrine in *Taylor v Johnson*,[43] the leading High Court authority on rescission for unilateral mistake. The 'real question' in both rescission and rectification for unilateral mistake is whether it is 'unconscionable for one party knowingly to take advantage of another party's mistake'.[44]

INTENTION

Continuing concurrent intention

12.8   In cases of common mistake it must be shown that the written instrument does not reflect the true and concurrent intention of both parties at the time of execution of the document or at the time the document came into force.[45] A concurrent intention at an earlier stage, such as during the negotiations, is not sufficient. In *Slee v Warke*[46] the owner of the Victoria Hotel, Benalla agreed that Warke could lease the hotel and that she was entitled to an option, exercisable *within* the first year of the lease, to purchase the hotel, provided that the purchase was not completed within that first year of the lease. The owner arranged for his solicitor to prepare a draft lease and for it to be sent to Warke. The draft did not include the option as agreed, but rather referred to an option to purchase being exercisable at any time *after* the expiry of the first year of the lease. Warke noticed the change but thought that the owner of the hotel had changed his intention. A formal lease agreement was drawn, including the error, and was executed on 12 March 1946. The hotel owner was not aware of the change. Warke exercised the option in accordance with the written agreement, after one year. The hotel owner refused to convey the hotel. Warke obtained a declaration that she was entitled to require the owner to sell the hotel in accordance with the written agreement. The owner of the hotel appealed to the High Court on the ground that the written agreement should be rectified. In refusing the appeal, Rich, Dixon and Williams JJ observed:

> We can find no concurrent intention of the parties existing at the date of the contract of 12 March 1946 that the option was to be an option exercisable at any time during the first year of the lease but only to be completed at the end of that year. At the date of the contract that intention was at most only the intention

---

41. (1997) 42 NSWLR 10.

42. [2005] NSWCA 40; see also *Fox Entertainment Precinct Pty Ltd v Centennial Park and Moore Park Trust* [2004] NSWSC 214 at [24]–[27] per Barrett J.

43. (1983) 151 CLR 422 at 432–3 and see **5.28–5.29**.

44. *Tutt v Doyle* (1997) 42 NSWLR 10 at 12–13 per Meagher JA.

45. *Slee v Warke* (1949) 86 CLR 271; *Maralinga Pty Ltd v Major Enterprises Pty Ltd* (1973) 128 CLR 336 at 349 per Mason J; *Pukallus v Cameron* (1982) 180 CLR 447 at 457 per Brennan J; *Ryledar Pty Ltd v Euphoric Pty Ltd* [2007] NSWCA 65 at [258]–[272], (2007) 69 NSWLR 603 at 655–658, per Campbell JA; *Franklins Pty Ltd v Metcash Trading Ltd* [2009] NSWCA 407 at [511]; (2009) 76 NSWLR 603 at 724 per Campbell JA.

46. (1949) 86 CLR 271.

of the appellants. The respondent never had such an intention. She had at most an intention at an early stage of the negotiations that the option should be an option to be exercised during the first year and immediately completed upon its exercise. But even that intention was not her intention at the date of the contract. Her intention then was in accordance with the contract.[47]

The mistake in *Slee v Warke* was a unilateral mistake that was not contributed to by the other party, so rectification was refused. The position is different in cases of equitable fraud, where one party has taken an unconscientious advantage of the other's mistake, and has, in that sense, contributed to the other party's mistake. However, even in these cases of rectification for unilateral mistake, the element of concurrent intention cannot be entirely absent. In *Leibler v Air New Zealand Ltd (No 2)* Kenny JA held:

> If ... a plaintiff establishes, by convincing proof, that the executed document does not conform with the intention shared by the parties prior to the mistake coming to the attention of the non-mistaken party and that intention is sufficiently precise and specific to be the subject of an order for rectification, then, rectification may, in appropriate circumstances, be granted.[48]

Antecedent contract unnecessary

12.9 Formerly, a party seeking rectification of a written contract needed to prove that there had been an effective antecedent contract between the parties. The antecedent contract was often oral in nature. The effect of the Statute of Frauds 1677 and its modern equivalents upon oral contracts may be noted here. Where the statute required the contract to be in writing in order to be enforceable, but the written contract embodied a mistake, there was no effective antecedent contract to enforce by rectification. Under the modern law of rectification, however, an effective antecedent contract is no longer required. In New South Wales the authority is *Montgomery v Beeby*,[49] and in Victoria see *Bosaid v Andry*.[50] The more liberal approach also found favour with the High Court in *Slee v Warke*,[51] *Maralinga Pty Ltd v Major Enterprises Pty Ltd*[52] and *Pukallus v Cameron*.[53]

12.10 In the United Kingdom, the liberal approach was approved by the English Court of Appeal in *Crane v Hegeman-Harris Co Inc*[54] and *Joscelyne v Nissen*.[55] In the latter case, Mr and Mrs Joscelyne were tenants in a house known as Martindale, from which Mr Joscelyne operated a car-hire business. When they received a notice to quit Martindale, their daughter decided to help

47.   (1949) 86 CLR 271 at 281.
48.   [1999] 1 VR 1 at 27 per Kenny JA.
49.   (1930) 30 SR (NSW) 394.
50.   [1963] VR 465.
51.   (1949) 86 CLR 271 at 280 per Rich, Dixon and Williams JJ.
52.   (1973) 128 CLR 336 at 350 per Mason J.
53.   (1982) 180 CLR 447.
54.   [1939] 4 All ER 68.
55.   [1970] 2 QB 86.

them by purchasing the house. The daughter and her husband moved into the upstairs of Martindale while the parents occupied the downstairs. Three years later in 1963, the mother fell ill and the father had to devote much of his time to caring for her, to the detriment of the car-hire business. Because of this, the father and daughter discussed a scheme which culminated in a written agreement being entered into on 18 June 1964, whereby the daughter took over the car-hire business on certain conditions, one of them being that the father could reside for the rest of his life in Martindale 'free of all rent and outgoings of every kind in any event'. For a time, the daughter paid the electricity, gas and coal bills. However, when trouble arose between the daughter and her parents, the daughter received professional advice that she was not obliged to pay these bills, as a matter of the true construction of the written agreement. So, she stopped doing so. In response, the father commenced proceedings seeking rectification of the written agreement to make clear the obligation to pay. The opposing legal arguments are encapsulated in a passage from the judgment of the Court of Appeal:

> For the daughter it is argued that the law says that the father cannot get rectification of the written instrument save to accord with a complete antecedent concluded oral contract with the daughter, and, as was found by the judge, there was none such here. For the father it is argued that if in the course of negotiation a firm accord has been expressly reached on a particular term of the proposed contract, and both parties continue minded that the contract should contain appropriate language to embrace that term, it matters not that the accord was not part of a complete antecedent oral contract.[56]

The Court of Appeal upheld the father's case for rectification. In a joint judgment, Russell, Sachs and Phillimore LJJ quoted with approval from the decision of Simonds J in *Crane v Hegeman-Harris Co Inc*:

> … in order that this court may exercise its jurisdiction to rectify a written instrument, it is not necessary to find a concluded and binding contract between the parties antecedent to the agreement which it is sought to rectify … it is sufficient to find a common continuing intention in regard to a particular provision or aspect of the agreement.[57]

However, the Court of Appeal in *Joscelyne v Nissen* added the qualification that there must be 'some outward expression of accord'.[58] The need for this objective test has been criticised[59] and was doubted in *Pukallus v Cameron*[60] by Wilson J who said, with Gibbs CJ and Murphy J concurring:

---

56. [1970] 2 QB 86 at 90.

57. [1939] 1 All ER 662 at 664; affirmed [1939] 4 All ER 68 at 72 per Sir Wilfred Greene, MR. (CA); *Chartbrook Ltd v Persimmon Homes Ltd* [2009] UKHL 38 at [59] per Lord Hoffmann.

58. [1970] 2 QB 86 at 98.

59. L J Bromley, 'Rectification in Equity' (1971) 87 *LQR* 532; compare M Smith, 'Rectification of Contracts for Common Mistake, *Joscelyne v Nissen*, and Subjective States of Mind' (2007) 23 *LQR* 116.

60. (1982) 180 CLR 447 at 452.

So long as there is a continuing common intention of the parties, it may not be necessary to show the accord found outward expression, notwithstanding views expressed to the contrary in *Joscelyne*,[61] and *Maralinga*.[62]

The New South Wales Court of Appeal rejected the need to prove an 'outward expression of accord' in *Ryledar Pty Ltd v Euphoric Pty Ltd*.[63] Tobias JA, with whom Mason P and Campbell JA concurred, held that evidence of 'intention may be ascertained not only from the external or outward expressions of the parties manifested by their objective words or conduct but also from evidence of their subjective states of mind'.[64]

By contrast with the Australian cases, in *Chartbrook Ltd v Persimmon Homes Ltd*, the House of Lords has recently upheld the objective approach taken in *Joscelyne v Nissen* to determine the common intention of the parties:

> In accordance with the general approach of English law, the terms of the prior consensus were what a reasonable observer would have understood them to be and not what one or even both of the parties believed them to be.[65]

This does not state the position under Australian law, where evidence of the parties' subjective states of mind is relevant and admissible.

Rectification and implied terms

12.11   Rectification seeks to give effect to the parties' actual intention, and not the parties' presumed intention. This had led to some confusion between the doctrine of rectification and that of implied terms. The difference between the two was explained by Mason J in *Codelfa Construction Pty Ltd v State Rail Authority of NSW*:

> The implication of a term is to be compared, and at the same time contrasted, with the rectification of a contract. In each case the problem is caused by a deficiency in the expression of the consensual agreement. A term which should have been included has been omitted. The difference is that with rectification the term which has been omitted and should have been included was actually agreed upon; with implication the term is one which it is presumed that the parties would have agreed upon had they turned their minds to it — it is not a term they have actually agreed upon. Thus, in the case of the implied term the deficiency in the expression of the consensual agreement is caused by the failure of the parties to direct their minds to a particular eventuality and to make explicit provision for it. Rectification ensures that the contract gives effect to the parties' actual intention; the implication of a term is designed to give effect to the parties' presumed intention.[66]

61.   [1970] 2 QB 86 at 98.

62.   (1973) 128 CLR 336 at 350; compare *Pourzand v Home Building Society Ltd* [2004] WASC 127 at [61] per Pullin J; *Stormriders Pty Ltd v Copperart Pty Ltd* [2004] NSWSC 809 at [46] per White J.

63.   [2007] NSWCA 65.

64.   [2007] NSWCA 65 at [182]. See also *NSW Medical Defence Union Ltd v Transport Industries Insurance Co Ltd* (1986) 6 NSWLR 740 at 752-3 per Clarke J.

65.   [2009] UKHL 38 at [57] per Lord Hoffmann. See R Buxton, 'Construction and Rectification After *Chartbrook*' [2010] CLJ 253.

66.   (1982) 149 CLR 337 at 346.

Evidence

12.12   The plaintiff must 'displace the hypothesis arising from execution of the written instrument, namely, that it is the true agreement of the parties'.[67] Accordingly, there must be 'convincing proof' that the written document fails to give effect to the parties' intention.[68] As noted by White J in *Stormriders Pty Ltd v Copperart Pty Ltd*:

> Although the standard of proof of such common intention remains the civil standard to the balance of probabilities, the authorities are replete with references to the need for a convincing proof, or clear and satisfactory proof, of that intent ... Such evidence may include direct evidence that the parties' intention was not reflected in the written agreement, and it may also consist of facts occurring both before and after the contract was made from which inferences can be drawn as to the particular intention of the parties at the time the contract was entered into.[69]

This standard applies both to rectification of common mistakes and rectification of unilateral mistakes.[70] The rationale for the standard was explained by Barrett J in *Fox Entertainment Precinct Pty Ltd v Centennial Park and Moore Park Trust* as follows:

> The insistence upon a high degree of proof in this area is a recognition of two realities: first, that persons who take the trouble to record their agreement in writing (particularly when they are, as here, assisted by lawyers) must generally be presumed to intend their written bargain to prevail over what they have not written; and, second, that it is easy for one such party, upon becoming dissatisfied after the event with some element of the written compact, to seek to brand it as inaccurate.[71]

Because the purpose of rectification is to reform the written agreement to conform with the parties' true intention, extrinsic evidence of the parties' subjective states of mind is admissible as an exception to the parol evidence rule.[72] The subjective intention of a corporation is shown 'by proving the intention of the person or persons who were relevantly its directing mind and will in the transaction'.[73]

---

67. *Maralinga Pty Ltd v Major Enterprises Pty Ltd* (1973) 128 CLR 336 at 351 per Mason J.

68. *Bacchus Marsh Concentrated Milk Co Ltd v Joseph* (1919) 26 CLR 410 at 433 per Isaacs J; *Joscelyne v Nissen* [1970] 2 QB 86 at 98 (CA); *Pukallus v Cameron* (1982) 180 CLR 447; *Australian Performing Right Association Ltd v Austarama Television Pty Ltd* (1972) 2 NSWLR 467 at 475 per Street J; *Franklins Pty Ltd v Metcash Trading Ltd* [2009] NSWCA 407 at [451]-[461], (2009) 76 NSWLR 603 at 712–714 per Campbell JA.

69. [2004] NSWSC 809 at [47].

70. *Terceiro v First Mitmac Pty Ltd* (1997) 8 BPR 15,733 (SC(NSW)); *Fox Entertainment Precinct Pty Ltd v Centennial Park and Moore Park Trust* [2004] NSWSC 214 at [28] per Barrett J.

71. [2004] NSWSC 214 at [30].

72. *Hoyt's Pty Ltd v Spencer* (1919) 27 CLR 133 at 139; *Bacchus Marsh Concentrated Milk Co Ltd v Joseph* (1919) 26 CLR 410 at 451–2 per Higgins J; *Codelfa Construction Pty Ltd v State Rail Authority of New South Wales* (1982) 149 CLR 337 at 402; *Whittet v State Bank of New South Wales* (1991) 24 NSWLR 146 at 151; *Equuscorp Pty Ltd v Glengallen Investments Pty Ltd* [2004] HCA 55 at [33].

73. *Pourzand v Home Building Society Ltd* [2004] WASC 127 at [61] per Pullin J; appeal dismissed in *Home Building Society Ltd v Pourzand* [2005] WASCA 242.

COURT'S DISCRETION AND DEFENCES

12.13   Rectification may be refused in the court's discretion, but only in 'exceptional cases', as observed by Crispin J in *Misner v Australian Capital Territory*:

> It is true that rectification is an equitable remedy subject to the discretion of the court which must, of course, be exercised according to general equitable principles … However, the discretion must commonly be exercised in a somewhat different context from those that attend other equitable remedies such as specific performance because damages or other forms of alternative relief are not normally available if rectification is refused. As a result an unsuccessful plaintiff may suffer significant hardship. Accordingly, it has been said that when the basis of a right to rectification has been established, relief will be refused on discretionary grounds only in exceptional cases.[74]

In such cases relief may be refused if there has been acquiescence, delay amounting to laches,[75] unclean hands or estoppel.[76] It will also be refused if, after execution of the document, third parties have for value and without notice obtained legal or equitable rights in property passed under the contract.[77] If the contract has been fully performed[78] or if it is incapable of performance, rectification is not possible.[79] If the parties' intention is illegal, rectification will be refused. For illegal contracts, there is the separate equitable remedy of delivery up and cancellation of the document, in order to prevent it 'continuing in existence as a source of confusion and possible fraud.'[80] If the plaintiff also has a right to rescission and prefers rescission, the court will follow the plaintiff's election.[81]

EFFECT OF RECTIFIED DOCUMENT

12.14   Once the court orders rectification it 'relates back so that the rights of the parties are treated as having always been in accordance with the contract as so rectified'.[82] Accordingly, a rectified contract will support an action for

74.   (2000) 146 ACTR 1 at [20].

75.   *Beale v Kyte* [1907] 1 Ch 564; *Segal v Fleming* [2002] NSWCA 262. For a discussion on the distinction between laches and acquiescence, see *Orr v Ford* (1989) 167 CLR 316 at 337–9 per Deane J.

76.   *Fredensen v Rothschild* [1941] 1 All ER 430; *Standard Portland Cement Pty Ltd v Good* [1982] 2 NSWLR 668; 47 ALR 151 (PC); compare *Market Terminal Pty Ltd v Dominion Insurance Co of Australia* [1982] 1 NSWLR 105 (plaintiff's suit on unrectified insurance contract did not amount to estoppel).

77.   *Garrard v Frankel* (1862) 30 Beav 445; 54 ER 961; *Smith v Jones* [1954] 1 WLR 1089; *Thames Guaranty Ltd v Campbell* [1985] QB 210; *Lyme Valley Squash Club Ltd v Newcastle-under-Lyme Borough Council* [1985] 2 All ER 405; *Westminster Bank Ltd v Lee* [1956] Ch 7; *National Provincial Bank Ltd v Ainsworth* [1965] AC 1175; *Latec Investments Ltd v Hotel Terrigal Pty Ltd* (1965) 113 CLR 265.

78.   *Caird v Moss* (1886) 33 Ch D 22.

79.   *Borrowman v Rossel* (1864) 16 CB (NS) 58; compare *Club Cape Schanck Resort Co Ltd v Cape Country Club Pty Ltd* (2001) 3 VR 526.

80.   *Money v Money (No 2)* [1966] 1 NSWR 348 at 351, per Jacobs J. See **Chapter 14**.

81.   *Taylor v Johnson* (1983) 151 CLR 422.

82.   *Re Jay O Bees; Rosseau v Jay O Bees* (2004) 50 ACSR 565; [2004] NSWSC 818 at [93] per Campbell J.

damages[83] or equitable compensation.[84] Subject to the principles governing specific performance (see **Chapter 7**), a rectified contract may be specifically enforced and both remedies may be obtained in the one action.[85] For example, in *Coset No 15 Pty Ltd v Blagojevic*,[86] Gzell J ordered the rectification of a contract for the sale of an apartment to exclude a car-parking space, and then ordered specific performance of the rectified contract.

---

83. *Bosaid v Andry* [1963] VR 465 at 468; *Spathis v Hanave Investment Co Pty Ltd* [2002] NSWSC 304 at [108]–[111] per Campbell J.
84. *Medsara Pty Ltd v Sande* [2005] NSWCA 40.
85. *United States of America v Motor Trucks Ltd* [1924] AC 196; *Medsara Pty Ltd v Sande* [2005] NSWCA 40.
86. [2003] NSWSC 418; (2003) 11 BPR 20,883.

CHAPTER 13

Declarations

NATURE OF THE REMEDY

13.1 A declaration of right is an order of the court that declares the respective rights and obligations of the parties in a dispute before the court. Historically, declarations were an equitable remedy granted in conjunction with specific relief in equity, such as an injunction or an order for specific performance. There was no inherent jurisdiction to grant so-called 'naked' declarations, meaning declarations that were not ancillary to a grant of specific relief. By a long process of statutory reform that began in the United Kingdom with the Chancery Act 1850,[1] all the historical limitations on the remedy have been removed. In New South Wales law, the modern jurisdiction to grant declarations is based upon s 75 of the Supreme Court Act 1970 (NSW), which provides:

> No proceedings shall be open to objection on the ground that a merely declaratory judgment or order is sought thereby and the Court may make

---

1. 13 & 14 Vict c 35. See P W Young, *Declaratory Orders*, 2nd ed, Butterworths, Sydney, 1984, Ch 3.

binding declarations of right whether any consequential relief is or could be claimed or not.[2]

ELEMENTS OF THE REMEDY

13.2 Declaratory relief may be ordered if the plaintiff satisfies three elements:

1. that the court has jurisdiction to grant the declaration;
2. that the plaintiff has *locus standi* to seek the declaration; and
3. there is no discretionary ground for refusing the declaration.

Jurisdictional limitations

13.3 Declarations may be made in respect of equitable, common law and statutory rights and obligations. Declarations may also be granted either with or without other forms of equitable, common law or statutory relief. Traditionally, the only true jurisdictional limitation upon the remedy is exclusion by statute. As Gibbs J stated in *Forster v Jododex Australia Pty Ltd*:

> The jurisdiction to make a declaration is a very wide one … However, the jurisdiction may be ousted by statute, although the right of a subject to apply to the court for a determination of his rights will not be held to be excluded except by clear words.[3]

In *Forster v Jododex*, Forster had applied for authority under the Mining Act 1906 (NSW) to enter certain land for the purpose of mineral exploration. To forestall Forster's application, Jododex obtained a declaration from the Supreme Court of New South Wales that Jododex was the holder of a prior valid exploration licence over the same land. That being so, the authority sought by Forster could not be granted. At the time when Jododex made its application to the Supreme Court for declaratory relief, proceedings were already on foot before the mining warden. According to the provisions of the Mining Act, the warden was under a duty to determine the issues in dispute. However, the authority of the warden under the statute was not expressed to be exclusive. In these circumstances, the High Court upheld the declaration granted at first instance. On the question of jurisdiction, each of the judges concurred with Gibbs J that the creation of a special tribunal under the Mining Act did not exclude by necessary implication the jurisdiction of the Supreme Court to make a declaration in respect of matters in dispute before the special tribunal.[4] Nevertheless, the existence of a specialised alternative

---

2.   Equivalent provisions are: Federal Court of Australia Act 1976 (Cth) s 21; Supreme Court Rules 1937 (ACT) O 29 r 5; Supreme Court Act 1979 (NT) s 18; Supreme Court Act 1995 (Qld) s 128; Supreme Court Act 1935 (SA) s 31; Supreme Court Rules 2000 (Tas) r 103; Supreme Court Act 1986 (Vic) s 36; Supreme Court Act 1935 (WA) s 25(6).

3.   (1972) 127 CLR 421 at 435–6 (McTiernan, Stephen and Mason JJ agreeing).

4.   (1972) 127 CLR 421 at 436.

tribunal was acknowledged as a matter of discretion that might influence the court to decline relief.[5]

Locus standi

13.4 Before the court may determine a claim for declaratory relief, the plaintiff must establish a sufficient interest in the subject matter of the dispute. This is known as the requirement of *locus standi*, which literally means 'place of standing'. For the purposes of *locus standi*, a distinction has been made between the determination of private rights and public rights.[6] A rare illustration of *locus standi* being denied in the case of private rights is the judgment of the English Court of Appeal in *Meadows Indemnity Co Ltd v Insurance Corp of Ireland plc*.[7] In that case, Meadows was denied standing to claim a declaration as to the validity of an insurance contract to which it was not a party.

13.5 Questions of *locus standi* have been most controversial in the area of public rights. The principles of *locus standi* are the same for both declarations and injunctions in relation to public rights.[8] The Attorney-General, as the principal law enforcement officer of the Crown, has been regarded as the proper plaintiff to enforce public rights. The Attorney-General may act in his or her own right, or at the relation of a third party.[9] Subject to statutory and common law exceptions,[10] the two circumstances in which a private plaintiff may act to enforce public rights without joining the Attorney-General were identified by Buckley J in *Boyce v Paddington Borough Council*:

> A plaintiff can sue without joining the Attorney-General in two cases: first, where the interference with the public right is such that some private right of his is at the same time interfered with ... and, secondly, where no private right is interfered with, but the plaintiff, in respect of his public right, suffers special damage peculiar to himself from the interference with the public right.[11]

13.6 The requirement of 'special damage' in the so-called second limb of the rule in *Boyce's* case has been considered by the High Court in a series of cases. In *Australian Conservation Foundation Inc v Commonwealth*[12] the High Court

---

5. (1972) 127 CLR 421 at 427 per Walsh J and 438 per Gibbs J. See also *Oil Basins Ltd v Commonwealth* (1993) 178 CLR 643; *Telstra Corp Ltd v Australian Telecommunications Authority* (1995) 133 ALR 417 at 426–7 per Lockhart J; *Philips Electronics NV v Remington Products Australia Pty Ltd* (1997) 150 ALR 355.

6. *Boyce v Paddington Borough Council* [1903] 1 Ch 109.

7. [1989] 2 Lloyd's Rep 298; followed in *CE Heath Casualty & General Insurance Ltd v Pyramid Building Society (in liq)* [1997] 2 VR 256 at 288 per Phillips JA.

8. *Australian Conservation Foundation Inc v Commonwealth* (1980) 146 CLR 493 at 526 per Gibbs J.

9. *Gouriet v Union of Post Office Workers* [1978] AC 435 at 477 per Lord Wilberforce, at 494 per Viscount Dilhorne, and at 502 per Lord Diplock. Compare *Bateman's Bay Local Aboriginal Land Council v Aboriginal Community Benefit Fund Pty Ltd* (1998) 194 CLR 247 at 257–64 per Gaudron, Gummow and Kirby JJ.

10. See *Truth About Motorways Pty Ltd v Macquarie Infrastructure Investment Management Ltd* (2000) 200 CLR 591 at 609 per Gaudron J, at 625–9 per Gummow J, at 651–3 per Kirby J, and at 665–6 per Callinan J.

11. [1903] 1 Ch 109 at 114.

12. (1980) 146 CLR 493.

refused the appellant standing to enforce the Environmental Protection (Impact of Proposals) Act 1974 (Cth) against the Commonwealth.

The appellant was an organisation formed to promote conservation of the environment. Gibbs J, with whom Stephen and Mason JJ gave concurring judgments, interpreted the requirement of special damage in *Boyce's* case as being equivalent to 'having a special interest in the subject matter of the action'.[13] Gibbs J explained the meaning of a special interest as follows:

> ... an interest, for present purposes, does not mean a mere intellectual or emotional concern. A person is not interested within the meaning of the rule, unless he is likely to gain some advantage, other than the satisfaction of righting a wrong, upholding a principle or winning a contest, if his action succeeds or to suffer some disadvantage, other than a sense of grievance or a debt for costs, if his action fails. A belief, however strongly felt, that the law generally, or a particular law, should be observed, or that conduct of a particular kind should be prevented, does not suffice to give its possessor *locus standi*. If that were not so, the rule requiring special interest would be meaningless.[14]

13.7   The High Court applied the same reasoning to reach the opposite result in *Onus v Alcoa of Australia Ltd*.[15] The appellants in that case were members of the local indigenous community where the respondent proposed to build an aluminium smelter. The appellants were granted standing to enforce the Archaeological and Aboriginal Relics Preservation Act 1972 (Vic) against the respondent. Gibbs CJ formulated the general principle as follows:

> A plaintiff has no standing to bring an action to prevent the violation of a public right if he has no interest in the subject matter beyond that of any other member of the public; if no private right of his is interfered with he has standing to sue only if he has a special interest in the subject matter of the action.[16]

13.8   The High Court has since affirmed the need for 'a special interest in the subject matter of the action'. In *Shop Distributive and Allied Employees Association v Minister for Industrial Affairs (SA)* the Full Court said that 'the rule is flexible and the nature and subject matter of the litigation will dictate what amounts to a special interest'.[17] In *Bateman's Bay Local Aboriginal Land Council v Aboriginal Community Benefit Fund Pty Ltd*, Gaudron, Gummow and Kirby JJ said that the criterion of a special interest 'is to be construed as an enabling, not a restrictive, procedural stipulation'.[18]

13.9   As well as a proper plaintiff with a special interest in the subject matter of the action, there must also be a proper defendant. As Lord Dunedin said

---

13. (1980) 146 CLR 493 at 527.

14. (1980) 146 CLR 493 at 530–1.

15. (1981) 149 CLR 27.

16. (1981) 149 CLR 27 at 35–6 (Mason J agreeing).

17. (1995) 183 CLR 552 at 558 per Brennan, Dawson, Toohey, Gaudron and McHugh JJ.

18. (1998) 194 CLR 247 at 267.

in *Russian Commercial & Industrial Bank v British Bank for Foreign Trade*, 'he [the plaintiff] must be able to secure a proper contradictor, that is to say, someone presently existing who has a true interest to oppose the declaration sought'.[19] Similarly, the courts are reluctant to grant declarations by consent of the parties. In *Wallersteiner v Moir*, Buckley LJ said that 'a declaration by the court [is] a judicial act, and ought not to be made on admissions of the parties or on consent, but only if the court was satisfied by evidence'.[20]

Discretionary considerations

13.10   Declarations are a discretionary remedy. However, in reviewing the decided cases, factors can be identified which influence courts in exercising that discretion. Traditionally, the courts have warned against treating discretionary factors that have resulted in a refusal to grant the remedy as being jurisdictional limitations. Typical of this approach is the view expressed by Gibbs J in *Forster v Jododex*, that:

> It is neither possible nor desirable to fetter the broad discretion ... by laying down rules as to the manner of its exercise.[21]

The matter was put more strongly by Street CJ of the New South Wales Court of Appeal in *Johnco Nominees Pty Ltd v Albury-Wodonga (NSW) Corp*:

> Factors and considerations leading to a discretionary refusal are an unsafe guide to marking out a jurisdictional boundary line. Cases in which it is said that one or another element will result in a situation in which the jurisdiction *should*, or *should not*, be exercised are not to be treated as establishing that such an element will result in a situation in which the jurisdiction *can*, or *cannot*, be exercised.[22]

13.11   However, in *Ainsworth v Criminal Justice Commission*,[23] the High Court seemed to qualify that view. In *Ainsworth* the appellants were granted a declaration that the Queensland Criminal Justice Commission had failed to observe procedural fairness in reporting adversely on the business activities of the appellants. After quoting with approval the above-mentioned passage from *Forster v Jododex*,[24] Mason CJ, Dawson, Toohey and Gaudron JJ, in a joint judgment, qualified that passage by adding that the discretionary power 'is confined by the considerations which mark out the boundaries of judicial power'.[25] If the High Court can be taken as saying that the recognised discretionary grounds for refusing declaratory relief have hardened into

19. [1921] 2 AC 438 at 448, quoted with approval in *Forster v Jododex Australia Pty Ltd* (1972) 127 CLR 421 at 437 per Gibbs J.
20. [1974] 1 WLR 991 at 1029, quoted with approval in *Australian Competition and Consumer Commission v Dataline.Net.Au Pty Ltd* [2006] FCA 1427 at [54]; (2006) 236 ALR 665 at 680 per Kiefel J; *Ajkay v Hickey & Co Pty Ltd* [2011] NSWSC 822.
21. (1972) 127 CLR 421 at 437.
22. [1977] 1 NSWLR 43 at 50-1.
23. (1992) 175 CLR 564.
24. (1972) 127 CLR 421 at 437.
25. (1992) 175 CLR 564 at 582.

jurisdictional limitations, that view marks a departure from previous authorities. In *Ainsworth*, the major discretionary considerations were stated in the following passage from the joint judgment of Mason CJ, Dawson, Toohey and Gaudron JJ:

> ... declaratory relief must be directed to the determination of legal controversies and not to answering abstract or hypothetical questions. The person seeking relief must have "a real interest" and relief will not be granted if the question "is purely hypothetical", if relief is "claimed in relation to circumstances that [have] not occurred and might never happen" or if "the Court's declaration will produce no foreseeable consequences for the parties".[26]

Apart from the requirement of *locus standi* considered at 13.4, the discretionary considerations identified by the High Court in *Ainsworth* will be considered in two broad categories that are likely to result in a refusal of declaratory relief. These are: hypothetical or non-justiciable issues, and lack of utility. These grounds are not, however, exhaustive.

Hypothetical questions

13.12   The general refusal by the courts to determine hypothetical questions manifests itself in at least three circumstances. *First*, there must be a dispute in existence. For example, in *Re Clay; Clay v Booth*[27] the English Court of Appeal refused to make a declaration that the petitioners were not liable to the defendant under a deed of indemnity. Swinfen Eady MR (with whom Duke LJ and Eve J agreed) held that the case was not a proper one for the making of a declaration because the defendant had made no claim under the deed against the petitioners. *Re Clay* has been approved by the High Court in *Hume v Munro (No 2)*[28] and *Toowoomba Foundry Pty Ltd v Commonwealth*.[29]

Second, as the High Court held in *University of New South Wales v Moorhouse*, declaratory relief will be refused where it is 'claimed in relation to circumstances that had not occurred and might never happen'.[30] However, a dispute is not hypothetical simply because it involves future rights and obligations. In *Commonwealth v Sterling Nicholas Duty Free Pty Ltd*[31] the respondent claimed a

---

26.   (1992) 175 CLR 564 at 582 (citations omitted).

27.   [1919] 1 Ch 66.

28.   (1943) 67 CLR 461 at 478 per Starke J.

29.   (1945) 71 CLR 545 at 572 per Latham CJ. See also *Re McKenzie* [1974] Qd R 171; *Renard Partners Pty Ltd v Quinn Villages Pty Ltd* [2001] QCA 538; *Madera v Commissioner of Taxation* (2004) 214 ALR 327; *Commonwealth of Australia v BIS Cleanaway Ltd* [2007] NSWSC 1075; *Weimann v Allphones Retail Pty Ltd* [2009] FCA 673 at [102] per Barker J. Contrast *Messier-Dowty Ltd v Sabena SA (No 2)* [2000] EWCA 25, [2001] 1 All ER 275.

30.   (1975) 133 CLR 1 at 10 per Gibbs J, quoted in *Ainsworth v Criminal Justice Commission* (1992) 175 CLR 564 at 582. See also *Aussie Airlines Pty Ltd v Australian Airlines Ltd* (1996) 68 FCR 406 at 414 per Lockhart J; *Mentha v GE Capital Ltd* (1997) 154 ALR 565 at 574–5 per Finkelstein J; *Lend Lease Insurances Ltd v Glenmont Investments Pty Ltd* (1999) 74 SASR 152 at 162 per Debelle J; *Hamersley Iron Pty Ltd v National Competition Council* (1999) 164 ALR 203 at 223–7 per Kenny J; *Copyright Agency Ltd v Charles Sturt University (No 2)* (2001) 53 IPR 383 at 396–8 per Lindgren J; *Rich v Lennox Palms Estate Pty Ltd* [2010] NSWCA 242.

31.   (1972) 126 CLR 297.

declaration that it was not prohibited by the Airports (Business Concessions) Act 1959 (Cth) from delivering goods to departing passengers at Sydney Airport. While the High Court was divided on the operation of the statute, the majority held that it was a case in which declaratory relief could be granted in the discretion of the court.[32] Barwick CJ said:

> The respondent undoubtedly desired and intended to do as he asked the court to declare he lawfully could do. The matter, in my opinion, was in no sense hypothetical, but in any case not hypothetical in a sense relevant to the exercise of this jurisdiction. Of its nature, the jurisdiction includes the power to declare that conduct which has not yet taken place will not be in breach of a contract or a law.[33]

In *Oil Basins Ltd v Commonwealth*,[34] Dawson J refused to dismiss the plaintiff's claim for a declaration that it was not liable for petroleum resource rent tax, even though the Commissioner of Taxation had not issued any notice of assessment against the plaintiff. Dawson J held that the 'question raised by the plaintiff is neither abstract nor hypothetical and the answer to that question will clearly produce consequences for the parties'.[35]

13.13 *Third*, the dispute must not be 'divorced from the facts'. For example, in *Australian Boot Trade Employees' Federation v Commonwealth*[36] the plaintiff claimed a declaration that certain amendments to the Conciliation and Arbitration Act 1904 (Cth) were beyond the powers of the Commonwealth Parliament. Although the amendments created a new offence, no prosecutions were pending or threatened. A majority of the High Court refused relief because the dispute was hypothetical. Similarly, the High Court affirmed in *Bass v Permanent Trustee Co Ltd* that 'where the dispute is divorced from the facts, it is considered hypothetical and not suitable for judicial resolution by way of declaration or otherwise'.[37]

By contrast, in *Croome v Tasmania*[38] the High Court refused to strike out the appellants' claim for a declaration that the criminalisation of homosexual acts under the Criminal Code (Tas) was inconsistent with the Human Rights (Sexual Conduct) Act 1994 (Cth), and therefore invalid under s 109 of the Constitution. Although the appellants had admitted to such acts, and had stated their intention of continuing to do such acts, none of the appellants had been prosecuted under the Code. In the absence of any pending or

---

32.   (1972) 126 CLR 297 at 305 per Barwick CJ, 315 per Windeyer J, and 311 per Menzies J. See also *Trustees of Church Property of the Diocese of Newcastle v Ebbeck* (1960) 104 CLR 394 at 400–1 per Dixon CJ.

33.   (1972) 126 CLR 297 at 305. See also *Bass v Permanent Trustee Co Ltd* (1999) 198 CLR 334 at 356 per Gleeson CJ, Gaudron, McHugh, Gummow, Hayne and Callinan JJ.

34.   (1993) 178 CLR 643.

35.   (1993) 178 CLR 643 at 649.

36.   (1954) 90 CLR 24.

37.   (1999) 198 CLR 334 at 356 per Gleeson CJ, Gaudron, McHugh, Gummow, Hayne and Callinan JJ.

38.   (1997) 191 CLR 119.

threatened prosecution, the respondent argued that the issue was hypothetical. In rejecting that argument, the High Court said:

> The State, by the Director of Public Prosecutions, has not prosecuted but, even if it were open for it to do so, it has not disabled itself from prosecuting hereafter. The DPP does not take the position that no offences have been committed nor that the offences do not continue.[39]

Non-justiciable issues

13.14   The issues in dispute must be 'justiciable', meaning that the dispute must be about legal rights and liabilities. This was not the case in *Johnco Nominees Pty Ltd v Albury- Wodonga (NSW) Corp*,[40] where the plaintiff sought a declaration that its land was affected by a policy statement issued jointly by three government departments. Although the New South Wales Court of Appeal held that it had the necessary jurisdiction to make the declaration sought, the Court refused to grant relief to the appellant because 'the declaration it seeks declares no legal right of the appellant, and can have no legal consequence to any right or disability of the appellant in respect of the land which it owns.'[41] As the High Court affirmed in *Egan v Willis*, 'declaratory relief should be directed to the determination of legal controversies concerning rights, liabilities and interests of a kind which are protected or enforced in the courts'.[42]

Lack of utility

13.15   A declaration will be refused where 'the Court's declaration will produce no foreseeable consequences for the parties'.[43] *A priori*, there can be no utility where the dispute is hypothetical or non-justiciable. Inutility is further illustrated by the judgment of the High Court in *Church of Scientology Inc v Woodward*,[44] where Mason J said:

> It is inconceivable that the Court would exercise its discretion so as to grant declaratory relief in respect of past acts long since completed under a statute which has since been repealed. The manifest inutility of making such a declaration makes the claim for relief academic.[45]

13.16   A less obvious instance of inutility is where the declaration will not conclude the dispute between the parties. This was so in *Neeta (Epping) Pty Ltd v Phillips*,[46] where the appellant claimed a declaration that the respondent had

---

39.   (1997) 191 CLR 119 at 138–9 per Gaudron, McHugh and Gummow JJ.

40.   [1977] 1 NSWLR 43.

41.   [1977] 1 NSWLR 43 at 59 per Street CJ.

42.   (1998) 195 CLR 424 at 439 per Gaudron, Gummow and Hayne JJ. See also *Thorpe v Commonwealth of Australia (No 3)* (1997) 144 ALR 677; *Direct Factory Outlets Pty Ltd v Westfield Management Ltd* (2003) 132 FCR 428.

43.   *Ainsworth v Criminal Justice Commission* (1992) 175 CLR 564 at 582 per Mason CJ, Dawson, Toohey and Gaudron JJ, quoting from *Gardner v Dairy Industry Authority (NSW)* (1977) 52 ALJR 180 at 188 per Mason J.

44.   (1982) 154 CLR 25.

45.   (1982) 154 CLR 25 at 62.

46.   (1974) 131 CLR 286.

not validly rescinded a contract for the sale of land between them. No further relief was claimed, except an order for costs. The High Court refused to make a declaration because:

> Unless the parties are agreed on the consequences which flow from a declaration that such a contract has or has not been validly rescinded it is generally undesirable that a court should so declare without any orders for consequential relief.[47]

Barwick CJ and Jacobs J based their reasoning partly upon their view that the power created by s 75 of the Supreme Court Act 1970 (NSW) to grant declarations must be exercised in conjunction with the duty imposed by s 63 of that Act to avoid a multiplicity of proceedings.[48]

Equitable defences

13.17 Because declarations were historically an equitable remedy, there has been a question whether equitable defences, especially unclean hands and refusal to do equity, have any relevance to the modern statutory jurisdiction. The question was considered by the High Court in *Mayfair Trading Co Pty Ltd v Dreyer*.[49] The appellant claimed, along with other relief, a declaration that certain loan contracts and promissory notes were unenforceable under the Money Lenders Act 1912 (WA). The appellant was the borrower and the respondent was the lender. One of the issues on appeal was whether, as a condition of granting declaratory relief, the borrower should be required to 'do equity' by repaying the outstanding balance of the loan. Dixon CJ (with whom McTiernan J agreed) distinguished declaratory relief from 'true equitable relief ', and held that the borrower was entitled to the declaration without being required to repay the loan.[50]

This distinction between declaratory relief and 'true equitable relief' was considered more recently by the Full Court of the Supreme Court of South Australia in *H Stanke and Sons Pty Ltd v O'Meara*.[51] The plaintiffs in this case sought declarations of certain equitable interests in land held by the defendants. One of the issues before the Full Court was to determine if the plaintiffs' unclean hands could be pleaded by the defendants as a defence to 'the whole of the plaintiffs' claim'. It seems that the defendants' case drew no distinction between the declarations and the equitable subject matter of the declarations. The plaintiffs argued that the defence should be struck-out because equitable relief was not being claimed, only declaratory relief under s 31 of the Supreme Court Act 1935 (SA). The Full Court allowed the pleading to stand:

---

47.   (1974) 131 CLR 286 at 307 per Barwick CJ and Jacobs J. See also *Sanderson Computers Pty Ltd v Urica Library Systems BV* (1998) 44 NSWLR 73.

48.   (1974) 131 CLR 286 at 296 and 307.

49.   (1958) 101 CLR 428. Compare *Maguire v Makaronis* (1997) 188 CLR 449 at 474–5 per Brennan CJ, Gaudron, McHugh and Gummow JJ.

50.   (1958) 101 CLR 428 at 454. See also *Chapman v Michaelson* [1909] 1 Ch 238.

51.   [2007] SASC 246; (2007) 98 SASR 450.

While it may be accepted that applications for mere declaratory relief cannot be regarded as seeking equitable relief, it is necessary to examine the pleadings in each case in order to determine the true nature of the relief sought. ... In these circumstances, the declaratory orders sought by the plaintiffs would simply express the result of the application of the relevant equitable principles. Whether or not this results in the declarations themselves being properly regarded as equitable, there is little doubt that the plaintiffs are seeking the aid of equity. Accordingly, there is no reason to exclude from the court's consideration other equitable principles such as the requirement as to clean hands.[52]

Declarations in criminal law

13.18 Courts exercising civil jurisdiction (as distinct from criminal jurisdiction) have traditionally been reluctant to make declarations concerning matters of criminal law, especially once criminal proceedings have commenced. There are a number of policy reasons why this is so. First, civil courts apply a lesser standard of proof than criminal courts in determining questions of fact. Second, the civil court may be usurping the functions of the criminal jury. Third, the making of a declaration may prejudice the result of the criminal trial; and fourth, the procedure of seeking a declaration is open to abuse as a tactic for delaying the conclusion of the criminal trial.[53]

13.19 However, in *Sankey v Whitlam*,[54] the High Court confirmed that the statutory jurisdiction to make declarations under s 75 of the Supreme Court Act 1970 (NSW) and equivalent provisions 'is not excluded because the matter as to which a declaration is sought may fall for decision in criminal proceedings'.[55] As a matter of discretion, however, the jurisdiction should be exercised sparingly. In the words of Gibbs ACJ:

> Once criminal proceedings have begun they should be allowed to follow their ordinary course unless it appears that for some special reason it is necessary in the interests of justice to make a declaratory order.[56]

Similarly, in *Gedeon v Commissioner of the New South Wales Crime Commission*, the High Court emphasised that 'the fragmentation of the criminal process is to be actively discouraged.'[57]

An exceptional example of a declaration as to the criminality of future conduct was granted by the House of Lords' in *Airedale NHS Trust v Bland*.[58] In *Airedale*, the plaintiff health authority was proposing to withdraw life-sustaining treatment from a patient in a persistent vegetative state. While

---

52.   [2007] SASC 246 at [39]–[41]; (2007) 98 SASR 450 at 459 per Duggan and White JJ (Kelly J agreeing).

53.   This paragraph, as it appeared in the fourth edition of this book, was cited with approval in *Cousins v Merringtons Pty Ltd* [2007] VSC 542 at [31] per Hansen J.

54.   (1978) 142 CLR 1.

55.   (1978) 142 CLR 1 at 20 per Gibbs ACJ.

56.   (1978) 142 CLR 1 at 26. See also *Crane v Gething* (2000) 169 ALR 727 at 737 per French J.

57.   [2008] HCA 43 at [23] per Gummow, Kirby, Hayne, Crennan and Kiefel JJ.

58.   [1993] AC 789.

Lord Browne-Wilkinson observed that 'in general the court sets its face against making declarations as to the criminality of proposed future actions', the particular facts of the case made it 'absolutely necessary' to do so.[59]

Airedale was cited by the Western Australia Supreme Court in *Brightwater Care Group (Inc) v Rossiter*,[60] which involved similar issues about the criminality of future conduct by a professional health care provider. In this case, a mentally competent quadriplegic patient had given a direction to withhold further nutrition and hydration. This would cause the patient's death by starvation, as he intended. In granting a declaration about the legal effect of the patient's direction, Martin CJ referred to:

> ... a vital distinction between making a declaration with respect to the lawfulness of conduct which is proposed but has not occurred, and making a declaration as to whether or not conduct which has occurred constitutes a criminal offence. Declarations in respect of proposed future conduct add to the practical utility of this jurisdiction, but a declaration in respect of conduct that has occurred has little practical utility and would usurp the jurisdiction and role of the criminal courts, and for those reasons, will not be made.[61]

---

59.   [1993] AC 789 at 880. See also *Re F (mental patient: sterilization)* [1990] 2 AC 1.

60.   [2009] WASC 229.

61.   [2009] WASC 229 at [19]. See also *H Ltd v J* [2010] SASC 176.

CHAPTER

Delivery Up

NATURE OF THE REMEDY

14.1   Delivery up is a remedy by which documents or other goods are delivered up to the custody of the court under oath for the purpose of cancellation or supervised destruction. Delivery up is an equitable remedy that is administered according to equitable principles. The remedy has two main areas of practical application. First, in relation to ineffective legal documents; and second, in relation to goods that infringe, or may be used to infringe, intellectual property rights.

INEFFECTIVE DOCUMENTS

14.2   The remedy of delivery up and cancellation may be ordered where a document that appears to be effective on its face is proven to be void or voidable,[1] or unenforceable[2] at common law or in equity. Forged documents

---

1.   *Bromley v Holland* (1802) 7 Ves Jun 3; 32 ER 2; *Duncan v Worrall* (1822) 10 Price 31; 147 ER 232; *Brooking v Maudslay Son & Field* (1888) 38 Ch D 636.
2.   *Mayfair Trading Co Pty Ltd v Dreyer* (1958) 101 CLR 428.

are one such case.[3] The remedy is not confined to contracts, but extends to other legal documents such as bonds, deeds and negotiable instruments.[4]

The rationale for the remedy was explained by Rich and Dixon JJ in *Langman v Handover*:

> The jurisdiction of Courts of equity to direct delivery up and cancellation of instruments which, although good on their face, are, in fact, void, is thoroughly established by decisions. "And these decisions are founded on the true principles of equity jurisprudence, which is not merely remedial, but is also preventive of injustice. If an instrument ought not to be used or enforced, it is against conscience for the party holding it to retain it; since he can only retain it for some sinister purpose".[5]

Discretionary grounds for refusal

14.3   As with all equitable remedies, delivery up may either be refused or ordered on terms, in the discretion of the court. There are at least four cases where delivery up will generally be refused. First, where the ineffective nature of the document is apparent on its face. This was so in *Gray v Mathias*,[6] which concerned a bond that was void at common law because it stated an immoral consideration. The Court of Exchequer Chamber held that delivery up was unnecessary for such an obviously ineffective document, and that such cases were 'not to be encouraged'.[7] Second, where the document is neither void nor voidable, the availability of a common law defence to an action based upon the document is insufficient to warrant delivery up in equity.[8] Third, delivery up will generally be refused where the document is only partially void. This was so in *Ideal Bedding Co Ltd v Holland*,[9] where the insolvent defendant had executed a settlement of property that was void only against the defendant's creditors. Fourth, in cases where the plaintiff would otherwise be entitled to delivery up, the remedy may be refused because of a general equitable defence, such as laches and acquiescence by the plaintiff. It is settled, however, that the presence of 'unclean hands' on the part of the plaintiff will not necessarily preclude an order for delivery up. The reason behind that proposition, which runs contrary to the normal rule, was stated by Lord Eldon LC in *Vauxhall Bridge Co v Earl of Spencer*:

> In the view I take of the case, it will not be an obstacle to the plaintiffs that they do not come with clean hands, for it is settled, that if a transaction be objectionable on grounds of public policy, the parties to it may be relieved; the relief not being given for their sake, but for the sake of the public.[10]

---

3.   *Peake v Highfield* (1826) 1 Russ 559; 38 ER 216.
4.   *Money v Money (No 2)* [1966] 1 NSWR 348 at 351 per Jacobs J.
5.   (1929) 43 CLR 334 at 352, quoting from Story's *Equity Jurisprudence*.
6.   (1800) 5 Ves Jun 286; 31 ER 591.
7.   (1800) 5 Ves Jun 286 at 294; 31 ER 591 at 595 per Macdonald CB.
8.   *Brooking v Maudslay Son & Field* (1888) 38 Ch D 636. Compare *Cooper v Joel* (1869) 27 Beav 313; 54 ER 122.
9.   [1907] 2 Ch 157 at 172-4 per Kekewich J.
10.   (1821) Jac 64 at 67; 37 ER 774 at 775.

14.4   The question of unclean hands has arisen most often in the case of illegal contracts where both parties have participated in the illegal enterprise. In *Money v Money (No 2)*[11] the plaintiff husband executed and delivered to the defendant wife a memorandum of transfer relating to Torrens title land in performance of an illegal and void contract between them. However, before the transfer was registered, the husband sought to escape the transaction. The husband claimed, along with other relief, delivery up and cancellation of the transfer. Having found that the illegal consideration for the transfer was not apparent on the face of the document, Jacobs J cited with approval the judgment of Lord Eldon LC in *Vauxhall Bridge Co v Earl of Spencer* and granted relief 'to prevent the memorandum of transfer continuing in existence as a source of confusion and possible fraud'.[12]

14.5   A related issue is whether a plaintiff seeking delivery up will always be required to 'do equity' as a condition of relief. The question has arisen in the context of illegal or unenforceable money-lending contracts. In *Lodge v National Union Investment Co Ltd*[13] the plaintiff borrower sought delivery up and cancellation of securities that he had given to the defendant lender in performance of a contract that was 'void for illegality' under the Money Lenders Act 1902 (UK). Parker J granted relief, but accepted the defendant's argument that 'this being an appeal to the equitable jurisdiction of the Court, the plaintiff can be put upon terms and not allowed to assert any equity unless he himself is prepared to do equity by repaying' the outstanding balance of the loan.[14] *Lodge v National Union Investment Co Ltd* was approved and applied to equivalent legislation by the High Court in *Langman v Handover*.[15]

In *Kasumu v Baba-Egbe*,[16] which involved delivery up of securities under an 'unenforceable' money-lending contract, the Privy Council distinguished *Lodge v National Union Investment Co Ltd* on the basis of different legislation that manifested a different legislative policy. The Nigerian legislation in *Kasumu v Baba-Egbe* provided that the defendant money lender 'shall not be entitled to enforce any claim in respect of any transaction in relation to which the default shall have been made'. In these circumstances, the Privy Council ordered delivery up without conditions because:

> … to impose terms of repayment as a condition of making any order for relief it would be expressing a policy of its own in regard to such transactions which is in direct conflict with the policy of the Acts themselves.[17]

In other words, the principle of 'doing equity' as a condition of equitable relief had been displaced by the legislation. Similarly, in *Mayfair Trading Co Pty*

11.   [1966] 1 NSWR 348.
12.   [1966] 1 NSWR at 351. See also *Nelson v Nelson* (1995) 184 CLR 538 at 563 per Deane and Gummow JJ.
13.   [1907] 1 Ch 300.
14.   [1907] 1 Ch 300 at 306.
15.   (1929) 43 CLR 334.
16.   [1956] AC 539.
17.   [1956] AC 539 at 552 per Lord Radcliffe.

Ltd v Dreyer,[18] the High Court concluded that the Money Lenders Act 1912 (WA) required the court to follow the reasoning in *Kasumu v Baba-Egbe*, and to distinguish its own reasoning in *Langman v Handover*. Accordingly, delivery up was ordered without conditions.[19]

INFRINGING GOODS

14.6 Delivery up and destruction of goods may be ordered where the manufacture or exploitation of the goods constitutes an infringement of a patent,[20] a registered design,[21] a registered trade mark[22] or a copyright.[23] The remedy is also available for breach of confidence[24] and passing off.[25]

Delivery up is usually ordered to perfect an injunction restraining infringement.[26] In every case, delivery up may be ordered, not only of the infringing goods, but also of the moulds, dies and plates used to manufacture the infringing goods,[27] as well as advertising and promotional materials.[28] With the possible exception of copyright infringement, the jurisdiction to order delivery up in such cases arises from the inherent equitable jurisdiction of the court. The general operation of the remedy, in the context of patent infringement, was explained by Cotton LJ in *Vavasseur v Krupp*:

> The property in articles which are made in violation of a patent is, notwithstanding the privilege of the patentee, in the infringer if he would otherwise have the property in them. The Court in a suit to restrain the infringement of a patent does not proceed on the footing that the Defendant proved to have infringed has no property in the articles; but, assuming the property to be in him, it prevents the use of those articles, either by removing that which constitutes the infringement, or by ordering, if necessary, a destruction of the articles so as to prevent them from being used in derogation of the Plaintiff's rights, and does this as the most effectual mode of protecting

---

18.   (1958) 101 CLR 428.

19.   See also *Barclay v Prospect Mortgages Ltd* [1974] 2 All ER 672; *Farrow Mortgage Services Pty Ltd (in liq) v Edgar* (1993) 114 ALR 1 at 12–13 and 18–19 per Lockhart, Gummow and Lee JJ; *Nelson v Nelson* (1995) 184 CLR 538 at 563–4 per Deane and Gummow JJ; *Fitzgerald v FJ Leonhardt Pty Ltd* (1997) 189 CLR 215 at 230–1 per McHugh and Gummow JJ.

20.   *Vavasseur v Krupp* (1878) 9 Ch D 351 at 360 per Cotton LJ.

21.   *Geodesic Constructions Pty Ltd v Gaston* (1976) 16 SASR 453 at 471 per Mitchell J.

22.   *Slazenger & Sons v Feltham & Co (No 2)* (1889) 6 RPC 531 at 538 per Lindley and Cotton LJJ.

23.   *Hole v Bradbury* (1879) 12 Ch D 886 at 903 per Fry J.

24.   *Industrial Furnaces Ltd v Reaves* [1970] RPC 605 at 627 per Graham J; *Ansell Rubber Co Pty Ltd v Allied Rubber Industries Pty Ltd* [1967] VR 37 at 52 per Gowans J.

25.   *Warwick Tyre Co Ltd v New Motor and General Rubber Co Ltd* (1910) 27 RPC 161 at 171 per Neville J.

26.   *Auguste Marechal and Ferdinand Ruchon v Neil M'Colgan* (1901) 18 RPC 262; *Warwick Tyre Co Ltd v New Motor and General Rubber Co Ltd* (1910) 27 RPC 161; *Peter Pan Manufacturing Corp v Corsets Silhouette Ltd* [1963] RPC 45.

27.   *Auguste Marechal and Ferdinand Ruchon v Neil M'Colgan* (1901) 18 RPC 262 at 264 per Chatterton VC; *Geodesic Constructions Pty Ltd v Gaston* (1976) 16 SASR 453 at 471 per Mitchell J.

28.   *Solarhart Industries Pty Ltd v Solar Shop Pty Ltd (No 2)* (2011) 282 ALR 43; [2011] FCA 780.

the Plaintiff's rights — not on the footing that there is no property in the Defendant.[29]

It follows from the judgment of Cotton LJ that, where the infringing part of the goods can be removed or obliterated (for example, by erasing a trade mark applied to the goods), that course of action will be preferred to an order for delivery up and complete destruction of the goods.[30]

14.7 For infringements of copyright, there are two alternative bases upon which an infringer may be deprived of property in infringing copies and devices. First, delivery up and destruction may be ordered in the inherent equitable jurisdiction of the court according to the principles outlined above.[31] Second, the copyright owner may bring a common law action in detinue for possession of the infringing copies and devices, based upon s 116(1)–(1A) of the Copyright Act 1968 (Cth). These subsections provide:

> (1) The owner of the copyright in a work or other subject-matter may bring an action for conversion or detention in relation to:
>
> (a) an infringing copy; or
>
> (b) a device (including a circumvention device) used or intended to be used for making infringing copies.
>
> (1A) In an action for conversion or detention, a court may grant to the owner of the copyright all or any of the remedies that are available in such an action as if:
>
> (a) the owner of the copyright had been the owner of the infringing copy since the time the copy was made; or
>
> (b) the owner of the copyright had been the owner of the device since the time when it was used or intended to be used for making infringing copies.

14.8 From the plaintiff's viewpoint, the distinction between an order for delivery up and an order for possession in detinue is that the former remedy 'is limited to delivery up for destruction, whereas an order in detinue gives possession of the copies to the copyright owner in virtue of his statutory property in them'[32]. It follows that where a copyright owner seeks possession of the infringing copies and devices under s 116(1), that remedy will be an alternative and inconsistent remedy to an order for delivery up.

---

29. (1878) 9 Ch D 351 at 360.

30. *Slazenger & Sons v Feltham & Co (No 2)* (1889) 6 RPC 531 at 538 per Lindley and Cotton LJJ; *Mergenthaler Linotype Co v Intertype Ltd* (1926) 43 RPC 381; *Roussel Uclaf v Pan Laboratories Pty Ltd* (1994) 29 IPR 556 at 559–60 per Einfeld J; *Milpurrurru v Indofurn Pty Ltd* (1994) 130 ALR 659 at 689–90 per von Doussa J; *Polygram Pty Ltd v Golden Editions Pty Ltd* (1997) 148 ALR 4 at 10–11 per Lockhart J.

31. *Hole v Bradbury* (1879) 12 Ch D 886 at 903 per Fry J.

32. *Sutherland Publishing Co Ltd v Caxton Publishing Co Ltd* [1936] 1 Ch 323 at 338 per Lord Wright MR.

Part 5

STATUTE

CHAPTER

Remedies under the Contracts Review Act

LEGISLATIVE PURPOSE

15.1   Neither the common law nor equity has developed a general doctrine of unjust contracts. The existing case law relating to unjust contracts is subject to two main limitations. First, plaintiffs seeking relief must bring themselves within one of the recognised common law or equitable doctrines of misrepresentation (see 5.5–5.17), mistake (see 5.19–5.29), duress (see 5.30–5.39), undue influence (see 5.40–5.50) or unconscionable dealing: see 5.51–5.56. Second, the primary form of relief in such cases is rescission. The remedy of rescission is, in itself, limited to cases where the parties can substantially be restored to their respective precontractual positions: see 5.59–5.61. Rescission also extinguishes any accrued right to contractual damages or specific performance of the contract: see 5.58. To address these perceived limitations in the common law and equity, the Contracts Review Act 1980 (NSW) was enacted. The Act is described in the preamble as:

> An Act with respect to the judicial review of certain contracts and the grant of relief in respect of harsh, oppressive, unconscionable or unjust contracts.

UNJUST CONTRACTS

15.2   The operation of the Act is triggered by a finding under s 7(1) that 'a contract or a provision of a contract'[1] was 'unjust in the circumstances relating to the contract at the time it was made'. 'Unjust' is defined in s 4(1) to include 'unconscionable, harsh or oppressive'. In making a finding of injustice under s 7(1), the court must take into consideration a list of factors, which are stated in s 9 as follows:

> (1) In determining whether a contract or a provision of a contract is unjust in the circumstances relating to the contract at the time it was made, the Court shall have regard to the public interest and to all the circumstances of the case, including such consequences or results as those arising in the event of:
>
> > (a) compliance with any or all of the provisions of the contract, or
> >
> > (b) non-compliance with, or contravention of, any or all of the provisions of the contract.
>
> (2) Without in any way affecting the generality of subsection (1), the matters to which the Court shall have regard shall, to the extent that they are relevant to the circumstances, include the following:
>
> > (a) whether or not there was any material inequality in bargaining power between the parties to the contract,
> >
> > (b) whether or not prior to or at the time the contract was made its provisions were the subject of negotiation,
> >
> > (c) whether or not it was reasonably practicable for the party seeking relief under this Act to negotiate for the alteration of or to reject any of the provisions of the contract,
> >
> > (d) whether or not any provisions of the contract impose conditions which are unreasonably difficult to comply with or not reasonably necessary for the protection of the legitimate interests of any party to the contract,
> >
> > (e) whether or not:
> >
> > > (i) any party to the contract (other than a corporation) was not reasonably able to protect his or her interests, or
> > >
> > > (ii) any person who represented any of the parties to the contract was not reasonably able to protect the interests of any party whom he or she represented,
> >
> > because of his or her age or the state of his or her physical or mental capacity,
> >
> > (f) the relative economic circumstances, educational background and literacy of:
> >
> > > (i) the parties to the contract (other than a corporation), and
> > >
> > > (ii) any person who represented any of the parties to the contract,

---

1.   There is no jurisdiction under the Act where there is no contract formed in law: *Ford v Perpetual Trustees Victoria Ltd* (2009) 75 NSWLR 42 at 68; [2009] NSWCA 186 at [91] per Allsop P and Young JA.

(g)   where the contract is wholly or partly in writing, the physical form of the contract, and the intelligibility of the language in which it is expressed,

(h)   whether or not and when independent legal or other expert advice was obtained by the party seeking relief under this Act,

(i)   the extent (if any) to which the provisions of the contract and their legal and practical effect were accurately explained by any person to the party seeking relief under this Act, and whether or not that party understood the provisions and their effect,

(j)   whether any undue influence, unfair pressure or unfair tactics were exerted on or used against the party seeking relief under this Act:

   (i)   by any other party to the contract,

   (ii)   by any person acting or appearing or purporting to act for or on behalf of any other party to the contract, or

   (iii)   by any person to the knowledge (at the time the contract was made) of any other party to the contract or of any person acting or appearing or purporting to act for or on behalf of any other party to the contract,

(k)   the conduct of the parties to the proceedings in relation to similar contracts or courses of dealing to which any of them has been a party, and

(l)   the commercial or other setting, purpose and effect of the contract.

15.3   In the judgment of the New South Wales Court of Appeal in *Perpetual Trustee Co Ltd v Khoshaba,*[2] Basten JA (with whom Handley JA agreed) formulated a three-stage approach to claims under the Act:

In considering an application for relief under s 7 of the Contracts Review Act 1980 (NSW) the Court must undertake a three stage process although, of course, the steps need not be taken in a particular order or necessarily identified as separate steps. The first step is to make findings of primary fact as to the circumstances revealed in the evidence …

The second step in the process is a finding that a contract or a provision of a contract is "unjust". This … is variously described in s 7(1) as a finding and in s 9(1) and (4) as a determination. On either description, the Court is not exercising a discretionary power, but making an evaluative judgment as to whether the facts as found satisfy a statutory description which in turn engages a discretionary power …

The third step involves the exercise of the power to grant relief which may, but need not, follow from the conclusion that a contract or a provision thereof is unjust. That is truly a discretionary power to be exercised if the Court "considers it just to do so, and for the purpose of avoiding as far as practicable an unjust consequence or result": s 7(1).[3]

---

2.   [2006] NSWCA 41.

3.   [2006] NSWCA 41 at [106]–[109], at [34]–[40] per Spigelman CJ. See also: *Kowalczuk v Accom Finance* (2008) 77 NSWLR 205 at 225; [2008] NSWCA 343 at [87] per Campbell JA (Hodgson and McColl JJA agreeing); *Brighton v Australia and New Zealand Banking Group Ltd* [2011] NSWCA 152 at [164] per Campbell JA (Giles and Hodgson JJA agreeing).

15.4   The leading authority on 'unjustness' under the Act is the judgment of the New South Wales Court of Appeal in *West v AGC (Advances) Ltd.*[4] In that case, West had borrowed $68,000 from AGC on ordinary commercial terms, secured by a mortgage over her home. To the knowledge of AGC, West loaned $38,000 of that amount to her husband's employer (Quiche) for the purposes of expanding its business. The loan from West to Quiche was interest-free, in consideration of Quiche paying the instalments owed by West to AGC. West was not otherwise in a financial position to pay these instalments herself. When Quiche's business failed, and West defaulted on her loan, AGC sought to enforce its security. West sought relief under the Act, which the Court of Appeal refused.

The judgment of the Court of Appeal in *West's* case is authority for a number of propositions about the concept of unjustness under the Act. First, 'the Contracts Review Act 1980 is beneficial legislation. It must be interpreted liberally'.[5] Second, the definition of 'unjust' in s 4(1) and the matters listed in s 9(2) are not exhaustive. As McHugh JA said:

> It is in my opinion a mistake to think that a contract or one of its terms is only unjust when it is unconscionable, harsh or oppressive. Contracts which fall within any of those categories will be "unjust". But the latter expression is not limited to the so-called "tautological trinity" … Moreover, the provisions of s 9(2) do not exhaustively indicate the criteria as to what can be taken into account in determining whether a contract or any of its provisions is unjust.[6]

Third, while s 9(2) codifies many of the case law principles relating to duress, undue influence and unconscionable dealing, the statutory concept of unjustness is not confined by analogous common law and equitable doctrines. This is fundamental. In *Elders Rural Finance Ltd v Smith,*[7] Mahoney P held that the loan contract in question 'was not, under the general law, "unconscionable, harsh or oppressive" '. However, that was no barrier to relief, because 'the Act was intended to set a standard less onerous than that required by the general law'.[8] Fourth, the Act addresses matters of both procedural and substantive injustice. As McHugh JA said in *West's* case:

> … a contract may be unjust under the Act because its terms, consequences or effects are unjust. This is substantive injustice. Or a contract may be unjust because of the unfairness of the methods used to make it. This is procedural injustice. Most unjust contracts will be the product of both procedural and substantive injustice.[9]

---

4.   (1986) 5 NSWLR 610.

5.   (1986) 5 NSWLR 610 at 631 per McHugh JA and 611 per Kirby P. See also *Beneficial Finance Corp Ltd v Karavas* (1991) 23 NSWLR 256 at 267 per Kirby P and 277 per Meagher JA.

6.   (1986) 5 NSWLR 610 at 620–1. See also *Antonovic v Volker* (1986) 7 NSWLR 151 at 168 per Mahoney JA.

7.   (1996) 41 NSWLR 296.

8.   (1996) 41 NSWLR 296 at 302. See also *Toscano v Holland Securities Pty Ltd* (1985) 1 NSWLR 145 at 151 per McLelland J; *S H Lock (Australia) Ltd v Kennedy* (1988) 12 NSWLR 482 at 494–5 per Priestley JA.

9.   (1986) 5 NSWLR 610 at 620. See also *Nguyen v Taylor* (1992) 27 NSWLR 48 at 69 per Sheller JA.

Although the transaction in *West's* case proved to be improvident for the claimant, in the absence of any substantive or procedural injustice 'relating to the contract at the time it was made',[10] the Court of Appeal held that the contract was not unjust within the meaning of the Act. In reaching that conclusion, McHugh JA made the point, which has been affirmed repeatedly in the later authorities, that 'the Contracts Review Act regulates contracts not investments'.[11] His Honour explained:

> If a defendant has not been engaged in conduct depriving the claimant of a real or informed choice to enter into a contract and the terms of the contract are reasonable between the parties, I do not see how that contract can be considered unjust simply because it was not in the interest of the claimant to make the contract or because she had no independent advice.[12]

15.5　The judgment of the New South Wales Court of Appeal in *Nguyen v Taylor*[13] is authority that a contract can be unjust within the meaning of the Act, even where the party seeking to enforce the contract is entirely innocent of that unjustness. In *Nguyen*, the respondent vendor sought to avoid an option contract for the sale of his home because the contract had been induced by misrepresentation. The vendor's *own* real estate agent had misrepresented to him that he 'could get out of the agreement within 30 days' if he changed his mind. The vendor changed his mind, but found that the contract was binding. Although the appellant purchasers were neither parties to the misrepresentation nor did they have any knowledge of it, the option contract was held by Kirby P, Sheller JA and, *semble*, by Meagher JA to be unjust in the circumstances.[14] There was no suggestion of unjustness in the terms of the contract. Kirby P affirmed his own observations in *Baltic Shipping Co v Dillon*[15] that:

> A contract may be "unjust" because of peculiarities inherent in the circumstances of one of the parties of which the other party was quite ignorant. It may be 'unjust' although the other party has acted quite honourably and lawfully.[16]

Notwithstanding the finding of unjustness in *Nguyen v Taylor*, the Court of Appeal unanimously denied relief to the vendor as a matter of discretion. Each of the judges emphasised, first, that the purchasers were entirely innocent of the unjustness; and second, that alternative remedies were likely to be available to the vendor against his real estate agent, who was not a

---

10.　Contracts Review Act 1980 (NSW) s 9(1).

11.　(1986) 5 NSWLR 610 at 621. See also *Beneficial Finance Corp Ltd v Karavas* (1991) 23 NSWLR 256 at 277 per Meagher JA; *Citicorp Australia Ltd v O'Brien* (1996) 40 NSWLR 398 at 419 per Sheller JA; *Elders Rural Finance Ltd v Smith* (1996) 41 NSWLR 296 at 298 per Mahoney P and at 304 per Meagher JA; *Esanda Finance Corp Ltd v Tong* (1997) 41 NSWLR 482 at 491 per Handley JA.

12.　(1986) 5 NSWLR 610 at 621. See also *PC Developments Pty Ltd v Revell* (1991) 22 NSWLR 615 at 638 per Mahoney JA; *Citicorp Australia Ltd v O'Brien* (1996) 40 NSWLR 398 at 420 per Sheller JA.

13.　(1992) 27 NSWLR 48.

14.　(1992) 27 NSWLR 48 at 55 per Kirby P, at 1 per Sheller JA, and at 61 per Meagher JA.

15.　(1991) 22 NSWLR 1 at 20.

16.　(1992) 27 NSWLR 48 at 54.

party to the proceedings. Sheller JA[17] cited with approval an observation by Meagher JA in *Beneficial Finance Corp Ltd v Karavas* that:

> There is jurisdiction under the Act to make orders in favour of a party to a contract who proves that … he suffers from a relevant disability even though the other party to the contract is unaware of that disability, although in general it would be unsound to exercise the jurisdiction in those circumstances.[18]

15.6 In *Elkofairi v Permanent Trustee Co Ltd*,[19] Beazley JA summed up the effect of the earlier authorities, as follows:

> It would appear that the trend of authority since *West* is that the Contracts Review Act permits a court not only to look at the terms of the contract per se, to see its terms are unjust, but to look at the circumstances in which the contract was made and its effect, having regard to those circumstances. It is not sufficient, however, for a claimant for relief under the Act merely to point to a loss or inopportune transaction. This approach, in my view, is not inconsistent with that of McHugh JA in *West*.[20]

In *Elkofairi*, the appellant borrower and her husband had entered into a loan and mortgage contract on ordinary commercial terms with the respondent lender to borrow the amount of $750,000. The loan was secured by a mortgage over the borrower's home that she owned jointly with her husband. The borrower had benefited from the loan because part of it was used to discharge an existing mortgage over the home. The balance was used by her husband for his own business purposes. The distinctive feature of the transaction was that the lender knew at the time that neither the borrower nor her husband had any income to repay the loan. The lender readily acknowledged that it had made the loan on the value of the asset only, and considered itself entitled to do so. This lending practice has become known as 'asset lending', typically where the borrower's only asset is their home.[21] When the lender later acted to enforce the transaction, the borrower sought relief under the Act.

Beazley JA (with whom Santow JA and Campbell AJA agreed) held that the contract was unjust in the circumstances in which it was made, primarily for two reasons. First, because the borrower was subject to the special disadvantages of being uneducated, illiterate in English, and oppressed by her husband, although the lender was unaware of these matters. She had also waived any independent legal advice. Second, because the lender was 'content to lend on the value of the security only', knowing that the borrower had no income or assets other than her home to repay the loan and interest.[22] For the same reasons, her Honour further held that the lender had acted 'unconscientiously'

---

17. (1992) 27 NSWLR 48 at 71.
18. (1991) 23 NSWLR 256 at 277.
19. [2002] NSWCA 413; (2003) 11 BPR 20,841.
20. [2002] NSWCA 413 at [78]; (2003) 11 BPR 20,841 at 20,855 (Santow JA and Campbell AJA agreeing).
21. See J M Paterson, 'Knowledge and Neglect in Asset-based Lending: When is it Unconscionable or Unjust to Lend to a Borrower Who Cannot Repay?' (2009) 20 *Journal of Banking and Finance Law and Practice*, 18.
22. [2002] NSWCA 413 at [79]; (2003) 11 BPR 20,841 at 20,855.

in making the loan. Her Honour exercised the court's discretion under s 7 of the Act to set aside the loan and mortgage, but (in agreement with Santow JA) required the borrower to repay the 'unwarranted benefit' retained by her at the lender's expense, being her half share of the amount used to discharge the earlier mortgage.

15.7   The reasoning in *Elkofairi* was applied to similar facts by the Court of Appeal in *Perpetual Trustee Co Ltd v Khoshaba*.[23] The respondent borrowers in this case were an elderly pair of migrants, for whom English was their second language. Neither of the borrowers had any business or investment experience. They entered into an agreement on ordinary commercial terms with the appellant lender to borrow the amount of $120,000. The loan was secured by a mortgage over their only asset, their home.

In granting the loan, the lender had failed to follow its internal lending guidelines in at least two respects. First, the lender had failed to verify the borrowers' employment and income. These had been fraudulently misrepresented in the loan application form that had been prepared and submitted on the borrowers' behalf by a third-party mortgage broker. In truth, the borrowers were retired pensioners with no other income. Moreover, the signature of one borrower had been forged on the application form. Second, the lender had failed to establish the purpose of the loan. The relevant section of the loan application form had been left blank, and the lender had failed to follow up the omission. The borrowers had, in fact, borrowed the money to invest the amount of $100,000 through their daughter in a pyramid investment scheme that was being promoted amongst the local Assyrian community. In ignorance of the borrowers' purpose, the lender had failed to recommend independent advice. A failure by the lender to observe its internal lending guidelines is a recurring feature of these cases.[24] When the investment scheme later collapsed, and the borrowers defaulted on the loan, the lender sought to enforce its security. The borrowers sought relief under the Contracts Review Act.

As in *Elkofairi*, the Court of Appeal approached the question of unjustness by considering 'the commercial or other setting, purpose and effect of the contract' as required by s 9(2)(l) of the Act. The distinctive feature of this judgment is that the Court of Appeal attached particular relevance to establishing the purpose of the loan. Of the lender's failures to observe its lending guidelines, Spigelman CJ said:

> ... the most significant, in my opinion, is the fact that the section of the standard form application about the purpose of the loan was left blank. This indicates that, as in *Elkofairi*, the Appellant "was content to lend on the

23.   [2006] NSWCA 41.

24.   *Spina v Permanent Custodians Ltd* [2009] NSWCA 206; *Permanent Trustee Co Ltd v O'Donnell* [2009] NSWSC 902; *Tonto Home Loans Australia Pty Ltd v Tavares* [2011] NSWCA 389.

value of the security".[25] In my opinion, that approach is entitled to significant weight in the determination of unjustness.[26]

Basten JA similarly condemned the lender's conduct:

> To engage in pure asset lending, namely to lend money without regard to the ability of the borrower to repay by instalments under the contract, in the knowledge that adequate security is available in the event of default, is to engage in a potentially fruitless enterprise, simply because there is no risk of loss. At least where the security is the sole residence of the borrower, there is a public interest in treating such contracts as unjust, at least in circumstances where the borrowers can be said to have demonstrated an inability reasonably to protect their own interests, for the purposes of, for example s 9(2)(e) or (f). That does not mean that the Act will permit intervention merely where the borrower has been foolish, gullible or greedy.[27]

As a result, the Court of Appeal held that the loan and mortgage contract was unjust in the circumstances in which it was made. The court exercised its discretion in this case to grant relief to the borrowers. Of the principal loan amount of $120,000, the borrowers owed the amount of $87,572 in principal and accrued interest at the time of the trial. Through a series of calculations based upon the notional 'total benefit' of the loan to the borrowers, and the amount outstanding, the court reduced the indebtedness to the amount of $29,803.

Since *Elkofairi* and *Khoshaba*, a number of decisions have considered the practice of asset lending, where it has been treated as relevant to the substantive unjustness of the contract under s 9 of the Act.[28] However, the practice is neither illegal nor 'presumptively unjust'.[29] It is only one factor to be considered in all of the relevant circumstances of the case.

EXCLUSIONS

15.8   Certain categories of plaintiffs and certain categories of contracts are excluded from the operation of the Act. In relation to plaintiffs, s 6(1) provides that:

> The Crown, a public or local authority or a corporation may not be granted relief under this Act.

This subsection does not preclude a claim for relief under the Act being made *against* the Crown, a public or local authority, or a corporation.

---

25.   [2002] NSWCA 413 at [79]; (2003) 11 BPR 20,841 at 20,855 per Beazley JA.

26.   [2006] NSWCA 41 at [82].

27.   [2006] NSWCA 41 at [128]. See also *Teachers Health Investments Pty Ltd v Wynne* (1996) NSW ConvR 55-785 at 56,033 per Beazley JA.

28.   *Kowalczuk v Accom Finance Pty Ltd* (2008) 77 NSWLR 205, [2008] NSWCA 343; *Permanent Trustee Co Ltd v O'Donnell* [2009] NSWSC 902; *Fast Fix Loans Pty Ltd v Samardzic* [2011] NSWCA 260. Contrast *Perpetual Trustees Victoria Ltd v Kirkbride* [2009] NSWSC 377.

29.   *Ford v Perpetual Trustees Victoria Ltd* (2009) 75 NSWLR 42 at 68, [2009] NSWCA 186 at [111] per Allsop P and Young JA.

15.9   In relation to categories of contracts, the most important exclusion is the so-called 'commercial contracts' exclusion in s 6(2) of the Act:

> A person may not be granted relief under this Act in relation to a contract so far as the contract was entered into in the course of or for the purpose of a trade, business or profession carried on by the person or proposed to be carried on by the person, other than a farming undertaking (including, but not limited to, an agricultural, pastoral, horticultural, orcharding or viticultural undertaking) carried on by the person or proposed to be carried on by the person wholly or principally in New South Wales.

The commercial contracts exclusion has been interpreted narrowly, hence extending the scope of the Act. In particular, contracts entered into for the purpose of a trade, business or profession carried on by a person *other* than the person seeking relief under the Act are not excluded from the operation of the Act. The most striking illustration of this proposition is the judgment of McLelland J in *Toscano v Holland Securities Pty Ltd*.[30] In *Toscano* a business formerly carried on in partnership by the two personal plaintiffs was subsequently transferred to a company in which the two plaintiffs were the sole shareholders. In these circumstances, contracts made personally by the plaintiffs after transfer of their business to the company, and which related to the company's business, were not treated as contracts 'entered into in the course of or for the purpose of a trade, business or profession carried on by' the plaintiffs. Instead, the contracts were entered into for the purpose of a business carried on by another person, being the company. Accordingly, the contracts were not excluded by the Act. Likewise, in *Australian Bank Ltd v Stokes*,[31] a contract of guarantee made by the defendants in relation to the liabilities of a trading company controlled by them was held to be within the operation of the Act. As Rogers J said: 'the defendants were not carrying on any relevant trade, business or profession; they were utilising the form of enterprise known as the limited company for the purpose of engaging in a business activity'.[32]

Conversely, the inclusion within the Act of contracts 'entered into in the course of or for the purpose of … a farming undertaking (including, but not limited to an agricultural, pastoral, horticultural, orcharding or viticultural undertaking)' has been interpreted broadly. In *Ellison v Vukicevic* Young J said that 'the words of the section make it quite clear that farming is to be used in a greatly extended sense'.[33] Accordingly, his Honour held that quarrying works on the plaintiff's land were a 'farming undertaking' within the meaning of the Act.

---

30.   (1985) 1 NSWLR 145.
31.   (1985) 3 NSWLR 174.
32.   (1985) 3 NSWLR 174 at 176.
33.   (1986) 7 NSWLR 104 at 111.

15.10   The second category of contracts excluded from the operation of the Act is contracts of service to the extent that they include provisions that conform to an applicable industrial award.[34]

15.11   Finally, it is not possible to 'exclude, restrict or modify' the operation of the Act by contract.[35] Moreover, to include a provision in a contract that 'purports to exclude, restrict or modify' the operation of the Act is an offence under s 18(1).

RELIEF

15.12   The grant of relief under the Act is discretionary. Once the court has made a finding of injustice in relation to a contract, s 7(1) provides, in part, that:

> ... the Court may, if it considers it just to do so, and for the purpose of avoiding as far as practicable an unjust consequence or result, do any one or more of the following:
>
> (a) it may decide to refuse to enforce any or all of the provisions of the contract,
>
> (b) it may make an order declaring the contract void, in whole or in part,
>
> (c) it may make an order varying, in whole or in part, any provision of the contract ...

The proper interpretation of s 7(1) was explained by Handley JA in *Esanda Finance Corporation Ltd v Tong*:

> Section 7 gives the Court powers to grant civil remedies to remove injustice. These powers are neither penal nor disciplinary, and should not be exercised for such purposes. Once injustice to the weaker party has been remedied, the Court should not further interfere with the rights of the parties. Interference beyond that point will cause injustice to the other party, and is not authorised by the section.[36]

In addition to orders for principal relief under s 7(1), s 8 of the Act provides for the grant of ancillary relief. Schedule 1 sets out a range of ancillary orders that may be granted under s 8, including orders for the making of any disposition of property, the payment of money (whether or not by way of compensation) to a party to the contract, the compensation of a person who is not a party to the contract and whose interest might otherwise be prejudiced by a decision or order under the Act, the supply or repair of goods, the supply of services, the sale or other realisation of property, the disposal of the proceeds of sale or other realisation of property, the creation of a charge on property in favour of any person, the enforcement of a charge so created, and

---

34.   Contracts Review Act 1980 (NSW) s 21(1).
35.   Contracts Review Act 1980 (NSW) s 17(1).
36.   (1997) 41 NSWLR 482 at 489. See also *S H Lock (Australia) Ltd v Kennedy* (1988) 12 NSWLR 482 at 492 per Priestley JA.

the appointment of a receiver of property. However, the forms of ancillary relief set out in Sch 1 are not exhaustive, and the court may make 'such orders in connection with the proceedings as may be just in the circumstances'.

CHAPTER

16

Remedies under the Competition and Consumer Act

INTRODUCTION

16.1 A significant change to Australian competition and consumer law occurred in January 2011 when the Trade Practices Act 1974 (Cth) (the TPA) was replaced by the Competition and Consumer Act 2010 (Cth) (the CCA). While the new Act retained many TPA provisions, it also improved and extended the TPA. Perhaps the most dramatic change was the replacement of the consumer protection provisions with a uniform national regime known as the Australian Consumer Law (the 'ACL'). The ACL is promulgated as a schedule to the CCA. While it thus operates as a law of the Commonwealth,[1] the words of the schedule are also adopted by legislation in each of the States and Territories.[2] The ACL thus functions both as a law of the Commonwealth and an 'applied law' of the States and Territories. While there were transitional arrangements, for the most part the CCA applies to transactions occurring on or after 1 January 2011. For transactions before this date, the previous national, State and Territory provisions continue to apply.[3]

The new regime replaces previously inconsistent provisions in the various State and Territory Fair Trading Acts. It also adopts approaches that had been taken under some State and Territory Acts, notably the approaches to unfair contract terms and unsolicited consumer contracts. Administration is shared by the Australian Competition and Consumer Commission (ACCC) and the consumer law agencies in each of the States and Territories—referred to generically as 'regulators'. All Australian courts and tribunals, including State and Territory courts, have jurisdiction. Since most of the provisions in the

---

1. See CCA Pt XI ss 131–131G. A reference to the CCA will thus include the ACL unless the context indicates otherwise.
2. CCA ss 140–140K; and see Fair Trading (Australian Consumer Law) Act 1992 (ACT) ss 6–7; Fair Trading Act 1987 (NSW) ss 27–28; Consumer Affairs and Fair Trading Act (NT) ss 26–27; Fair Trading Act 1989 (Qld) ss 15–16; Fair Trading Act 1987 (SA) ss 13–14; Australian Consumer Law (Tasmania) Act 2010 ss 5–6; Fair Trading Act 1989 (Vic) ss 8–9; Fair Trading Act 2010 (WA) ss 18–19.
3. The Trade Practices Amendment (Australian Consumer Law) Act (No 1) 2010 introduced the ACCC's increased powers as from March 2010 and the unfair contracts regime from July 2010. The Trade Practices Amendment (Australian Consumer Law) Act (No 2) 2010 replaced and renamed the TPA and set the ACL commencement date from January 2011. Schedule 7 of the Trade Practices Amendment (Australian Consumer Law) Act (No 2) 2010 contains many specific transitional arrangements dealing, for example, with what is to happen to investigations started or orders made under the old provisions.

CCA have come from similarly worded provisions in the TPA, past decisions interpreting the TPA will, to a large extent, continue to be relevant.

16.2 Since the ACL is shared across all the States and Territories, it undoubtedly simplifies what was an extraordinarily complex mix of Commonwealth, State and Territory law. However, it has complexities of its own. Not all the TPA provisions were repealed. Some, such as those in Part IVB relating to industry codes, have remained under the ACCC's exclusive regulation and thus appear in the body of the CCA rather than in the shared ACL. The States and Territories may also 'facilitate the application of the ACL'[4] by supplementary or additional provisions contained in their own legislation. While most of these additional provisions deal with administrative arrangements relevant only in that particular jurisdiction, such as the creation of a regulator and the appointment and powers of inspectors, some supplementary substantive or remedial provisions may subsist. This means one still needs to consider both the ACL and the relevant enabling statute in each jurisdiction to know the applicable consumer law. Due to limitations of space, this chapter will not consider the State and Territory Acts. It will focus on the civil remedies available under the ACL as a law of the Commonwealth; and the more important remedial provisions in the CCA that carry over from the TPA or refer to and supplement the ACL.

16.3 The ACL draws a clear distinction between criminal proceedings brought under Ch 4 and contraventions of the consumer protection provisions in Chs 2 and 3.[5] However, from the remedies perspective, there is increased overlap between private enforcement and the remedies available under the enforcement powers of investigative bodies. The new regime gives the ACCC increased powers to investigate and address infringements by issuing infringement notices, seeking civil pecuniary penalties and issuing substantiation notices. Civil pecuniary penalties in particular allow regulators to seek penalties and redress for consumers in the same proceedings. When it comes to private enforcement, however, the remedies that previously applied under the TPA continue to exist, although many of them have been rephrased in an attempt at simplification. Thus the power to issue injunctions, previously in TPA s 80, is now in ACL s 232; the power to award damages, previously in TPA s 82, is now in ACL s 236; and the remedial orders previously in TPA s 87 are now in ACL ss 237–239 (as read with s 243). These provisions are the primary focus of this chapter.

16.4 While Ch 5 of the ACL (like Part VI of the TPA before) is headed 'Enforcement and Remedies', it does not provide a complete code on the available remedies for the various causes of action. Initially, when interpreting the TPA, this led to many general law remedial principles being imported, usually by way of analogy. But this approach drew criticism. In *Akron Securities*

---

4.   Explanatory Memorandum, Trade Practices Amendment (Australian Consumer Law) Act (No 2) 2010 (Cth) at [18.1].

5.   ACL s 217.

v Iliffe Mason P said that the courts should not fear 'to move far from the familiar coastline of traditional common law and equitable approaches'.[6] After approving this dictum in *Marks v GIO Australia Holdings Ltd*, Gummow J concluded that '[a]nalogy, like the rules of procedure, is a servant not a master'.[7]

Even though many remedies under the CCA do have counterparts in general law such as injunctions under ACL s 232, damages under ACL ss 236, 237 and 238, rescission, restitution, rectification and specific performance under ACL ss 237, 238 and 239 and declarations under CCA s 163A, there are also many remedies that have no such equivalent. Indeed, in *Akron*, referring to the previous TPA s 87, the President said that courts are faced with a 'remedial smorgasbord'.[8] He pointed out that the section supported, for example, 'remedies dismantling a series of interlocking contractual arrangements' and such orders 'may be made not only against parties to the contract but also against third parties'.[9] It also permitted a damages award to be 'married' with an order varying a contract.[10] The same comments apply to the powers given to courts by the replacement sections in the ACL.

One can only speculate where this voyage 'from the familiar coastline' will take the courts. Hopefully far from the semantic sea, to adapt the words of Lord Denning.[11] But what is sure is that the various remedies under the CCA will continue their 'rise and rise'.[12] Still, one general law remedy that does not appear to be available under the CCA is an account of profits.[13]

DAMAGES

Introduction

16.5 The ACL gives a claimant a right of action to recover loss or damage suffered because of contraventions of its provisions. Section 236(1) provides:

> If:
>
> (a) a person (the claimant) suffers loss or damage because of the conduct of another person; and
>
> (b) the conduct contravened a provision of Chapter 2 or 3;

---

6.   (1997) 41 NSWLR 353 at 364 (CA).

7.   (1998) 196 CLR 494 at [103] per Gummow J; approved in *Henville v Walker* (2001) 206 CLR 459; [2001] HCA 52 at [130] per McHugh J.

8.   (1997) 41 NSWLR 353 at 364.

9.   (1997) 41 NSWLR 353 at 366.

10.   *Akron Securities v Iliffe* (1997) 41 NSWLR 353 at 365 per Mason P; *I & L Securities Pty Ltd v HTW Valuers (Brisbane) Pty Ltd* (2002) 210 CLR 109; [2002] HCA 41 at [108] per McHugh J.

11.   *H Parsons (Livestock) Ltd v Uttley Ingham & Co* [1978] QB 791 at 802.

12.   See Diane Skapinker, 'Other Remedies Under the Trade Practices Act—The Rise and Rise of Section 87' (1995) *21 Mon L Rev* 188; cited by Mason P in *Akron Securities v Iliffe* (1997) 41 NSWLR 353 at 364.

13.   *C Shirt Pty Ltd v Barnett Marketing and Management Pty Ltd* [1996] FCA 1079; *Multigroup Distribution Services Pty Ltd v TNT Australia Pty Ltd* [2001] FCA 226 at [35]–[42] per Gyles J.

the claimant may recover the amount of the loss or damage by action against that other person, or against any person involved in the contravention.

Section 236(1) is almost identical to TPA s 82(1) and the 'existing jurisprudence should continue to apply'.[14] The phrase 'to recover loss or damage' indicates that the aim of the section is compensatory. It is not, however, the only section that allows a court to make compensatory orders.

Sections 237 and 238 give the courts wide powers to make a range of remedial orders,[15] one of the purposes of which may be compensation. Remedial orders under both sections may also be made for the purpose of preventing or reducing loss or damage.[16] To the extent that the aim of a remedial order is compensation (a 'compensation order'), there is obvious overlap with s 236. For this reason, it is convenient to discuss the principles applicable to both types of compensatory claims in this section on damages: see **16.5–16.29**. Other possible remedial orders will be described separately after dealing with damages: see **16.30–16.34**.

16.6　When interpreting TPA s 82(1), courts applied the fundamental principle in common law damages;[17] that is, the plaintiff should be placed, so far as money can, in the position that would have been occupied had the wrong not been committed.[18] This fundamental principle does not necessarily apply to the 'compensation order' provisions because, while s 236(1) (like its predecessor) provides 'a right to complete recovery of loss or damage',[19] ss 237 and 238 allow compensation to be awarded either in 'whole or *in part* for the loss or damage'[20] suffered. This and other significant differences between ACL ss 236, 237 and 238 are examined in more detail at **16.10**.

'Loss or damage' is not confined to economic loss. Interpreting the previous TPA provisions, the High Court held in *Murphy v Overton Investments Pty Ltd* that:

> The Act's references to "loss or damage" can be given no narrow meaning. Section 4K of the Act provides that loss or damage includes a reference

---

14.　Explanatory Memorandum, Trade Practices Amendment (Australian Consumer Law) Act (No 2) 2010 (Cth) at [15.14]. See also the corresponding provisions now replaced: Fair Trading Act 1992 (ACT) s 46; Fair Trading Act 1987 (NSW) s 68(1); Consumer Affairs and Fair Trading Act (NT) s 91; Fair Trading Act 1989 (Qld) s 99; Fair Trading Act 1987 (SA) s 84; Fair Trading Act 1990 (Tas) s 37; Fair Trading Act 1999 (Vic) s 159; Fair Trading Act 1987 (WA) s 79.

15.　As read with s 243. These sections replace TPA s 87. Note ACL s 259(4) (dealing with remedies for consumer guarantees) also allows damages to be recovered: see **16.58**.

16.　ACL ss 237(2) and 238(2). The equivalent purpose of s 239 is to 'redress' the loss or damage, rather than compensate. See **16.31**.

17.　See **Chapters 2** and **3**.

18.　See *Brown v Jam Factory Pty Ltd* (1981) 53 FLR 340 at 351 per Fox J (FCA); *Gates v City Mutual Life Assurance Society Ltd* (1986) 160 CLR 1 at 13 per Mason, Wilson and Dawson JJ; *Wardley Australia Ltd v State of Western Australia* (1992) 175 CLR 514 at 526 per Mason CJ, Dawson, Gaudron and McHugh JJ; compare *Elna Australia Pty Ltd v International Computers (Australia) Pty Ltd (No 2)* (1987) 16 FCR 410 at 420–1 per Gummow J (FCA).

19.　*Mayne Nickless Ltd v Multigroup Distribution Services Pty Ltd* (2001) 114 FCR 108 at [58] per Wilcox, French and Drummond JJ interpreting TPA s 82.

20.　Italics added.

to injury. It follows that the loss or damage spoken of in ss 82 and 87 is not confined to economic loss. What kinds of detriment constitute loss or damage, when a detriment is to be identified as occurring or likely to occur, and what remedies are to be awarded, may all raise further difficult questions. Especially is that so when it is recalled that remedies may be awarded to compensate, prevent or reduce loss or damage that has been or is likely to be suffered by conduct in contravention of the Act.[21]

The CCA continues to make it clear that 'loss or damage' includes an injury.[22] However, shortly after the civil liability statutes imposed limits on personal injury claims,[23] similar limits were introduced into the TPA.[24] These provisions endure as a law of the Commonwealth in the CCA.[25] They apply to contraventions of ACL Pt 2-2 (unconscionable conduct), 3-3 (safety of consumer goods and product related services), 3-4 (information standards), 3-5 (liability of manufacturers for goods with safety defects), and Div 2 of Pt 5-4 (actions for damages against manufacturers of goods). And, like the civil liability statutes, they include such things as changing the limitation periods for certain claims; imposing caps on non-economic loss and loss of earnings; and introducing thresholds for gratuitous care. The definition of 'personal injury' includes 'pre-natal injury', 'impairment of a person's physical or mental condition' provided it is a 'recognised psychiatric illness' and 'disease'.[26]

To succeed in a compensation claim, the plaintiff must generally show that he or she is in fact 'worse off' as a result of the contravention, something that could not be shown in *Marks v GIO Australia Holdings Pty Ltd*.[27] The appellants entered into loan agreements with the GIO, which represented that it would charge interest at a base rate plus a fixed margin of 1.25 per cent. But the loan contracts allowed for a variable margin, and the GIO exercised that variation by increasing the margin to 2.25 per cent. Despite the GIO conceding a breach of s 52, it won. Even with the increase, the GIO loan was the best available. The appellants could not prove that they were 'worse off' as a result of the contravention.[28]

16.7   While accepting the general common law aim of compensation, when interpreting TPA s 82 courts have been careful to avoid applying the common law principles *mutatis mutandis*. For example, Gummow J in *Elna Australia Pty Ltd v International Computers (Aust) Pty Ltd (No 2)*, said tort and contract

---

21.   *Murphy v Overton Investments Pty Ltd* (2004) 216 CLR 388; [2004] HCA 3 at [45].

22.   CCA s 4K; ACL s 13.

23.   See Civil Law (Wrongs) Act 2002 (ACT); Personal Injuries (Liabilities and Damages) Act 2003 (NT); Civil Liability Act 2002 (NSW); Civil Liability Act 2003 (Qld); Civil Liability Act 1936 (SA); Civil Liability Act 2002 (Tas); Wrongs Act 1958 (Vic); Civil Liability Act 2002 (WA); and the discussion of the effect of these statutes in Chapter 2.

24.   See Pt VIB inserted by the Trade Practices Amendment (Personal Injuries and Death) Act (No 2) 2004.

25.   See CCA Pt VIB.

26.   CCA s 4.

27.   (1998) 196 CLR 494.

28.   *Marks v GIO Australia Holdings Ltd* (1998) 196 CLR 494 at [52] per McHugh, Callinan and Hayne JJ.

damages do not comprise 'the universe of analogues offered by the general law', and that equitable principles may also be relevant to claims under TPA ss 52 and 82.[29]

Courts have also been careful to avoid drawing an analogy with a particular tort; and then applying it inflexibly to all cases. In a joint judgment in *Wardley Australia Ltd v Western Australia*, Mason CJ, Dawson, Gaudron and McHugh JJ held:

> … it would not be right to conclude that the measure of damages recoverable under [s 82(1)] necessarily coincides with the measure of damages applicable in an action for deceit or in an action for negligent misrepresentation. The measure of damages recoverable under s 82(1) can only be fully ascertained after a thorough analysis of those provisions in Pts IV and V of the Act for contravention of which the statutory cause of action may be maintained. But the common law measure of damages will in many cases be an appropriate guide, though it will always be necessary to look to the provisions of the Act with a view to ascertaining the existence of any relevant legislative intention.[30]

In *Murphy v Overton Investments Pty Ltd* the High Court again cautioned against being guided too closely by analogies with a particular common law claim:

> This court has now said more than once that it is wrong to approach the operation of those provisions of Pt VI of the Act which deal with remedies for contravention of the Act by beginning the inquiry with an attempt to draw some analogy with any particular form of claim under the general law. No doubt analogies may be helpful, but it would be wrong to argue from the content of the general law that has developed in connection, for example, with the tort of deceit, to a conclusion about the construction or application of provisions of Pt VI of the Act. To do so distracts attention from the primary task of construing the relevant provisions of the Act.[31]

Elements

16.8 While courts have not been prepared to draw inflexible analogies with particular torts, they have found the familiar common law elements for damages claims to be helpful.[32] It will be recalled that the common law elements are:

a) a cause of action;

b) causation;

c) the damage must not be too remote; and

d) the plaintiff should take reasonable steps to mitigate the damage.

---

29. (1987) 16 FCR 410 (FCA) at 420–1.

30. (1992) 175 CLR 514 at 526; compare *Henville v Walker* (2001) 206 CLR 459; [2001] HCA 52 at [130] per McHugh J.

31. (2004) 216 CLR 388; [2004] HCA 3 at [44].

32. See *Munchies Management Pty Ltd v Belperio* (1988) 84 ALR 700 at 712–13 (Full FC); *Paper Products Pty Ltd v Tomlinsons (Rochdale) Ltd* (FCA, French J, 24 January 1994, unreported).

At common law, the onus of proving the first three elements rests on the plaintiff. The same is true under the Act. As Gaudron J observed in *Marks v GIO Australia Holdings Pty Ltd*:

> There being nothing in the Act to suggest otherwise, it is for an applicant for relief under s 82 or s 87 to establish what he or she has lost or, in the case of s 87, what he or she is likely to lose …[33]

Each element is discussed in turn below, followed by an examination of assessment issues.

Cause of action

16.9   Chapters 2 and 3 of the ACL cover a wide variety of causes of action supporting claims for damages. Most of the consumer protection provisions formerly in the TPA are in these chapters. Chapter 2 is titled 'General protections' and deals with misleading and deceptive conduct, unconscionable conduct and unfair contract terms. Chapter 3 is titled 'Specific protections' and covers such things as bait advertising, unsolicited supplies, pyramid schemes and product safety. Chapter 3 also includes the guarantees (previously known as warranties) in respect of consumer goods and services.

There are also some causes of action that have remained under the sole supervision of the ACCC (the Commonwealth regulator) and thus appear in the CCA instead of the ACL's national scheme. They cover contraventions of CCA Pt IV (restrictive trade practices) and Div 2 of Pt IVB (contraventions of industry codes). The sections enabling compensatory awards in these cases still bear the same section numbers and use the same words as the old TPA provisions, ss 82 and 87.

16.10   One of the difficult issues under the TPA was the apparent overlap between the damages provision (s 82) and the compensation order provision (s 87). The ACL sections have been split up and reworded in simpler language. As a result, the procedural form required under each section is now clearer. Section 236 gives a 'claimant' a right of action, that is, a right to originate litigation by making a claim. Section 237 contemplates an application — as opposed to a claim — being made by an 'injured person' or by a regulator on his or her behalf. The application may be made 'by way of motion'[34] during enforcement proceedings; or as a separate originating application, whether as a result of a finding in an enforcement proceeding, or 'even if an enforcement proceeding … has not been instituted'.[35] Section 238 makes no mention of a claim or application — it merely enables a court to make a compensatory (or other remedial) order where appropriate as a result of a finding during criminal or other enforcement proceedings. Sections 237 and

---

33.   (1998) 196 CLR 494 at [19].

34.   Explanatory Memorandum, Trade Practices Amendment (Australian Consumer Law) Act (No 2) 2010 (Cth) at [15.77].

35.   ACL s 242(1); and see the Explanatory Memorandum, Trade Practices Amendment (Australian Consumer Law) Act (No 2) 2010 (Cth) at [15.77].

238 also contemplate orders being made as a result of contraventions of the criminal offence provisions in Chapter 4, whereas the damages section (s 236) does not.

In addition to these procedural differences, there remain a number of other important differences between the sections. First, as noted by the Full Federal Court in *Western Australia v Wardley Australia Ltd*, s 82 created both 'a right and a remedy'.[36] But, '[u]nlike s 82, which provides a right of action, the remedies under s 87 [now ss 237 and 238] are discretionary'.[37] This discretion is 'very wide' because it 'enables orders to be made that could not be made at common law or in equity'.[38] Second, as discussed below, damage is the gist of the action under s 236, whereas under ss 237 and 238 the court is empowered to make an order not only for loss suffered, but also loss 'likely to be suffered': see **16.29**. Third, s 236 'provides a right to complete recovery of loss or damage' whereas 'the relief that may be awarded under s 87(1) [now ss 237 and 238] includes relief which compensates only in part for loss or damage suffered'.[39] Fourth, ss 237 and 238 allow for orders which reduce or prevent likely loss or damage and this 'remedy' is not available under s 236.[40] Given these differences, the compensatory order provisions (ss 237 and 238) will continue to be seen as independent of the damages provision (s 236); that is, each will not be read as restricting the other.[41]

16.11   The approach under all three provisions is first to determine whether the defendant's conduct is in contravention of the relevant provision of the Act. The defendant may be any person involved in the contravention.[42] But, for the purpose of s 236, a contravention of a relevant provision by the defendant clearly does not constitute or complete the cause of action. The plaintiff has to have suffered damage.[43] In this respect, s 236, unlike ss 237 and 238 (which do not require proof of actual loss),[44] resembles the

---

36. (1991) 30 FCR 245 at 257; and see *I & L Securities Pty Ltd v HTW Valuers (Brisbane) Pty Ltd* (2002) 210 CLR 109; [2002] HCA 41 at [50] per Gaudron, Gummow and Hayne JJ; *Arnotts Ltd v Trade Practices Commission (No 1)* (1989) 21 FCR 297 at 303–4.

37. *I & L Securities Pty Ltd v HTW Valuers (Brisbane) Pty Ltd* (2002) 210 CLR 109; [2002] HCA 41 at [106] per McHugh J; see also *Marks v GIO Australia Holdings Pty Ltd* (1998) 196 CLR 494 at [109] per Gummow J.

38. *I & L Securities Pty Ltd v HTW Valuers (Brisbane) Pty Ltd* (2002) 210 CLR 109; [2002] HCA 41 at [106] per McHugh J; and see **16.33**.

39. *Mayne Nickless Ltd v Multigroup Distribution Services Pty Ltd* (2001) 114 FCR 108 at [58] per Wilcox, French and Drummond JJ.

40. (2001) 114 FCR 108 at [58] per Wilcox, French and Drummond JJ.

41. *I & L Securities Pty Ltd v HTW Valuers (Brisbane) Pty Ltd* (2002) 210 CLR 109; [2002] HCA 41.

42. ACL ss 236(1), 237(1) and 238(1) and see *Western Australia v Wardley Australia Ltd* (1991) 30 FCR 245 at 257 (Full FC).

43. *Wardley Australia Ltd v Western Australia* (1992) 175 CLR 514 at 551 per Toohey J interpreting TPA s 82.

44. *Marks v GIO Holdings Pty Ltd* (1998) 196 CLR 494 at [22] per Gaudron J, at [45] per McHugh, Hayne and Callinan JJ interpreting the equivalent TPA provisions.

tort of negligence because 'loss or damage' is the 'gist of the action'.[45] As with negligence, in order for this 'loss or damage' to be proved the plaintiff must show that it has in fact been caused by the defendant's contravention and that it is not too remote; and if the plaintiff has failed to mitigate loss then the quantum may be reduced. These principles are discussed below.

Causation

16.12   The courts consistently held that the use of the phrase 'suffers loss or damage by conduct of another person' in TPA s 82(1) meant that there must be a causal connection between the breach and the loss or damage for which the plaintiff sought compensation.[46] In *Wardley Australia Ltd v Western Australia*,[47] Mason CJ, Dawson, Gaudron and McHugh JJ were of the view that 'by' was a 'curious word to use' in s 82(1) because:

> One might have expected "by means of", "by reason of", "in consequence of" or "as a result of".[48]

Notwithstanding this, their Honours concluded that the word 'by':

> ... clearly expresses the notion of causation without defining or elucidating it. In this situation, s 82(1) should be understood as taking up the common law practical or common-sense concept of causation recently discussed by this court in *March v E & M H Stramare Pty Ltd*,[49] except in so far as that concept is modified or supplemented expressly or impliedly by the provisions of the Act. Had parliament intended to say something else, it would have been natural and easy to have said so.[50]

The wording in ACL s 236 has changed to 'suffers loss or damage because of the conduct of another person'. This change merely emphasises the need for a causal connection.

Again, caution ought to be exercised when considering the extent to which common law approaches to causation are relevant. In *Elna Australia Pty Ltd v International Computers (Aust) Pty Ltd (No 2)*, Gummow J pointed out that, in relation to:

> ... statutory rights and obligations it would be an error to translate automatically to the particular statute what appeared the closest analogue from the common law 'rules' as to causation. It is rather a question of statutory construction ... That process of statutory construction calls for an examination of the terms of

---

45.   *Elna Australia Pty Ltd v International Computers (Australia) Pty Ltd (No 2)* (1987) 16 FCR 410 at 18 per Gummow J (FCA); cited with approval in *Wardley Australia Ltd v Western Australia* (1992) 175 CLR 514 at 525 per Mason CJ, Dawson, Gaudron and McHugh JJ; *Sellars v Adelaide Petroleum NL* (1994) 120 ALR 16 at 24 and 27 per Mason CJ, Dawson, Toohey and Gaudron JJ.

46.   *I & L Securities Pty Ltd v HTW Valuers (Brisbane) Pty Ltd* (2002) 210 CLR 109; [2002] HCA 41; *Henville v Walker* (2001) 206 CLR 459; [2001] HCA 52; *Brown v The Jam Factory Pty Ltd* (1981) 53 FLR 340 at 350–1 (FCA); *Elna Australia Pty Ltd v International Computers (Australia) Pty Ltd (No 2)* (1987) 16 FCR 410 at 418 per Gummow J (FCA).

47.   (1992) 175 CLR 514.

48.   (1992) 175 CLR 514 at 525.

49.   (1991) 171 CLR 506.

50.   (1992) 175 CLR 514 at 525.

the statute in their context, using "context" to embrace the other provisions of the statute, the pre-existing state of the law, other statutes in pari materia, and the mischief the court can discern as that the statute was intended to remedy.[51]

16.13   To what extent will a defendant's liability for a contravention of the ACL be reduced by the plaintiff's contributory negligence, a *nova causa interveniens*, or vicissitudes or contingencies of life? In its original form, s 82 did not contain a 'direct provision to apportion responsibility for loss or damage between [the] applicant and respondent or third parties'.[52] Notwithstanding this, prior to *Henville v Walker*[53] and *I & L Securities Pty Ltd v HTW Valuers (Brisbane) Pty Ltd*[54] there was a view that, if the defendant's contravention played only a minor part in the loss caused, the court had a discretion under either s 82 or s 87 to reduce the quantum.[55] In *S & U Constructions Pty Ltd v Westworld Property Holdings Pty Ltd*[56] Pincus J held that damages under s 87 could be apportioned because, unlike s 82, the court has the express power to award compensation 'in part for the loss or damage'.[57] This line of authority was rejected by the High Court in *Henville* and *I & L Securities*.

However, the TPA was subsequently amended to allow for apportionment as a result of contributory negligence in certain circumstances.[58] These amendments endure in the CCA and are discussed below: see **16.15–16.16**. Further, in *Murphy v Overton Investments Pty Ltd*[59] the High Court in considering how damages are to be measured found that it was relevant to consider the impact of the vicissitudes of life.[60]

Intervening causes

16.14   In cases concerning the entry into a contract following a misrepresentation that breaches the misleading and deceptive conduct provision (now ACL s 18), the plaintiff has to show reliance on the misrepresentation in order to recover damages.[61] If other reasons or causes contributed to the plaintiff's loss this may not be fatal, because the defendant's

51. (1987) 16 FCR 410 at 418. See also *Henville v Walker* [2001] HCA 52 at [18], [96] and [164]–[165]; *I & L Securities Pty Ltd v HTW Valuers (Brisbane) Pty Ltd* [2002] HCA 41 at [26], [50] and [84]; *Travel Compensation Fund v Robert Tambree t/as R Tambree and Associates* [2005] HCA 69 at [29]–[30].

52. *Elna Australia Pty Ltd v International Computers (Aust) Pty Ltd (No 2)* (1987) 16 FCR 410 at 419 per Gummow J.

53. (2001) 206 CLR 459; [2001] HCA 52.

54. (2002) 210 CLR 109; [2002] HCA 41.

55. See, for example, *Brown v The Jam Factory Pty Ltd* (1981) 53 FLR 340, where Fox J discounted the plaintiff's damages by 20 per cent.

56. (1988) ATPR 40–854.

57. However, *S & U Constructions Pty Ltd v Westworld Property Holdings Pty Ltd* (1988) ATPR 40–854 was questioned in *Tefbao Pty Ltd v Stannic Securities Pty Ltd* (1993) ALR 565.

58. Corporate Law Economic Reform Program (Audit Reform and Corporate Disclosure) Act 2004 (Cth).

59. (2004) 216 CLR 388; [2004] HCA 3.

60. (2004) 216 CLR 388; [2004] HCA 3 at [66]–[71].

61. *Gould v Vaggelas* (1985) 157 CLR 215 at 236 per Wilson J; *Henjo Investments Pty Ltd v Collins Marrickville Pty Ltd* (1988) 79 ALR 83 at 95–6 per Lockhart J (Full FC); *Argy v Blunts and Lane Cove Real Estate* (1990) 26 FCR 112; *Futuretronics International Pty Ltd v Gadzhis* [1992] VR 209 at 242 per Ormiston J.

contravention need not be the *sole* cause of the plaintiff's loss.[62] Indeed, to 'search for the single cause of an event is … to pursue an illusion'.[63] It is sufficient if the contravention was *a* cause[64] or if it played 'some part even if only a minor part in contributing to the formation of the contract'.[65] Obviously, if the plaintiff did not in any way rely on the defendant's breach this will be a complete bar to damages.[66]

Contributory negligence

16.15   At common law, and under ACL s 236(1), if the plaintiff fails to 'take reasonable care' of his or her 'own interests' this may break the chain of causation and bar relief.[67] Merely failing to check the accuracy of the defendant's representation is not sufficient;[68] 'grossly unreasonable conduct',[69] 'gross negligence' or 'extraordinary stupidity' is necessary before the chain of causation can be broken.[70] In *Argy v Blunts and Lane Cove Real Estate* Hill J observed:

> … an applicant may be so negligent in protecting his own interests that there will be a finding of fact that the representation complained of was not in the circumstances a real inducement to his entering into a contract. In such a case the element of causation between the misrepresentation and damage will have been severed by the intervention of the negligence of the applicant.[71]

Conduct short of gross negligence, namely contributory negligence, may in some cases lead to an apportionment of damages. TPA s 82(1B), introduced in 2004 after *Henville v Walker*[72] and *I & L Securities Pty Ltd v HTW Valuers (Brisbane) Pty Ltd*,[73] endures in the CCA. It provides:

---

62.   *Gould v Vaggelas* (1985) 157 CLR 215 at 236; *Brown v Southport Motors Pty Ltd* (1982) 1 TPR 441; *I & L Securities Pty Ltd v HTW Valuers (Brisbane) Pty Ltd* (2002) 210 CLR 109, [2002] HCA 41 at [25] and [33] per Gleeson CJ.

63.   *I & L Securities Pty Ltd v HTW Valuers (Brisbane) Pty Ltd* (2002) 210 CLR 109; [2002] HCA 41 at [56] per Gaudron, Gummow and Hayne JJ.

64.   *Marks v GIO Australia Holdings Pty Ltd* (1998) 196 CLR 494; *Henville v Walker* (2001) 206 CLR 459; [2001] HCA 52; *I & L Securities Pty Ltd v HTW Valuers (Brisbane) Pty Ltd* (2002) 210 CLR 109; [2002] HCA 41 at [57] per Gaudron, Gummow and Hayne JJ.

65.   *Gould v Vaggelas* (1985) 157 CLR 215 at 236; *Henjo Investments Pty Ltd v Collins Marrickville Pty Ltd* (1988) 79 ALR 83 at 96 per Lockhart J (Full FC).

66.   *Mister Figgins Pty Ltd v Centrepoint Freeholds Pty Ltd* (1981) 36 ALR 23 at 48 per Northrop J (FCA); *Henville v Walker* (2001) 206 CLR 459; [2001] HCA 52 at [17]; *I & L Securities Pty Ltd v HTW Valuers (Brisbane) Pty Ltd* (2002) 210 CLR 109; [2002] HCA 41 at [27]–[28] per Gleeson CJ.

67.   *Parkdale Custom Built Furniture Pty Ltd v Puxu Pty Ltd* (1982) 149 CLR 191 at 198–9 per Gibbs CJ; *Elders Trustee & Executor Co Ltd v EG Reeves Pty Ltd* (1987) 78 ALR 193 at 241 per Gummow J (FCA).

68.   *Henville v Walker* (2001) 206 CLR 459; [2001] HCA 52 at [128] per McHugh J; *Sutton v AJ Thompson Pty Ltd* (1987) 73 ALR 233; *Nielsen v Hempston Holdings Pty Ltd* (1986) 65 ALR 302; *Henjo Investments Pty Ltd v Collins Marrickville Pty Ltd* (1988) 79 ALR 83.

69.   *I & L Securities Pty Ltd v HTW Valuers (Brisbane) Pty Ltd* (2002) 210 CLR 109; [2002] HCA 41 at [27] per Gleeson CJ.

70.   See, for example, *Taco Co of Australia Inc v Taco Bell Pty Ltd* (1982) 42 ALR 177 at 181 per Franki J (FCA).

71.   (1990) 26 FCR 112 at 138; 94 ALR 719 at 144 (FCA).

72.   (2001) 206 CLR 459; [2001] HCA 52.

73.   (2002) 210 CLR 109; [2002] HCA 41.

137B Reduction of the amount of loss or damage if the claimant fails to take reasonable care

If:

(a) a person (the claimant) makes a claim under subsection 236(1) of the Australian Consumer Law in relation to economic loss, or damage to property, suffered by the claimant because of the conduct of another person; and

(b) the conduct contravened section 18 of the Australian Consumer Law; and

(c) the claimant suffered the loss or damage as result:

(i) partly of the claimant's failure to take reasonable care; and

(ii) partly of the conduct of the other person; and

(d) the other person did not intend to cause the loss or damage and did not fraudulently cause the loss or damage;

the amount of the loss or damage that the claimant may recover under subsection 236(1) of the Australian Consumer Law is to be reduced to the extent to which a court thinks just and equitable having regard to the claimant's share in the responsibility for the loss or damage.

Thus, in misleading and deceptive conduct claims, the plaintiff's failure to take reasonable care may lead to a reduction in damages 'to the extent that the court thinks just and equitable' having regard to the plaintiff's share in the responsibility for the loss or damage. This is the same apportionment test that applies in tort (see **2.15–2.20**) and some contract cases see **3.9–3.10**. There will, however, be no apportionment if the defendant intentionally or fraudulently caused the loss or damage. Nor will damages be apportioned in those rare cases where the plaintiff has suffered a personal injury due to a breach of ACL s 18 because CCA s 137B is confined to 'economic loss' and 'damage to property'.

Contribution and proportionate liability

16.16 Prior to the reforms in 2004 there was no provision which allowed liability or damages to be apportioned between multiple defendants who had jointly or concurrently engaged in misleading and deceptive conduct. Nor did the Act allow a court to limit the defendant's liability to its contribution to the loss.[74] The harsh result was that a claimant could recover the total loss from any defendant, and that defendant would then have to seek contribution from the other defendants.

Proportionate liability reforms were enacted for damages in tort (see **2.22**) and these have been repeated for concurrent wrongdoers breaching the misleading and deceptive conduct provision.[75] Section 87CD(1) in Pt VIA in the CCA provides:

---

74. *Burke v LFOT* (2002) 209 CLR 282; [2002] HCA 17.

75. Corporate Law Economic Reform Program (Audit Reform and Corporate Disclosure) Act 2004 (Cth) inserted a new Pt VIA into the Trade Practices Act.

87CD Proportionate liability for apportionable claims

(1) In any proceedings involving an apportionable claim:

(a) the liability of a defendant who is a concurrent wrongdoer in relation to that claim is limited to an amount reflecting that proportion of the damage or loss claimed that the court considers just having regard to the extent of the defendant's responsibility for the damage or loss; and

(b) the court may give judgment against the defendant for not more than that amount.

A 'concurrent wrongdoer' is defined in s 87CB(3) as:

… a person who is one of 2 or more persons whose acts or omissions (or act or omission) caused, independently of each other or jointly, the damage or loss that is the subject of the claim.

There are several restrictions on the breadth of proportionate liability under the CCA. First, under s 87CB(1) it applies only to claims for damages under s 236 of the ACL 'caused by conduct that was done in a contravention of section 18'.[76] Second, Pt VIA allows for apportionment only where the claim is for either 'economic loss' or 'damage to property'.[77] Third, there is no apportionment if the concurrent wrongdoer intentionally or fraudulently caused the loss or damage.[78]

Remoteness

16.17   In cases of breach of TPA Pt V, especially in misleading and deceptive conduct cases, the High Court said that the appropriate measure of damages will usually, but not necessarily, be the same as those in the tort of deceit.[79] So, in *Wardley Australia Ltd v Western Australia*,[80] Mason CJ, Dawson, Gaudron and McHugh JJ adopted the direct causation test as it applies in deceit; that is, the plaintiff is entitled to recover all loss directly flowing from the contravention of the Act.[81] However, the court left open the question of whether the reasonable foreseeability test of remoteness (see **2.37–2.40**) is applicable in a claim for consequential losses under TPA s 82(1) where there is a negligent misrepresentation inducing the purchase of property.[82] But in *Henville v Walker* McHugh J held:

Given the long history of the common law's recognition of the concept of remoteness in assessing damages in contract and tort and its relationship with the issue of causation, it seems proper to read the term 'by' in s 82 as including

---

76.   Section 87CB(1).

77.   Section 87CB(1)(a) and (b).

78.   Section 87CC.

79.   *Gates v City Mutual Assurance Society Ltd* (1986) 160 CLR 1; *Henville v Walker* (2001) 206 CLR 459; [2001] HCA 52.

80.   (1992) 175 CLR 514.

81.   (1992) 175 CLR 514 at 526.

82.   (1992) 175 CLR 514 at 526.

the concept of remoteness. By remoteness, I mean that the loss or damage was not reasonably foreseeable even in a general way by the contravenor.[83]

Whether there is any difference between the 'foreseeability' test of remoteness and the direct causation test is a moot point (see **2.37–2.40**). But of course no definitive choice needs to be made under the CCA because these general law analogies are merely servants, not masters.[84] In *HTW Valuers (Central Qld) Pty Ltd v Astonland Pty Ltd* the High Court noted that '[a]nalysis of the test for remoteness of damage in contract, in tort and under s 82 may make a difference on the particular facts of some cases',[85] but the court did not elaborate on this difference or the appropriate test under the Act.

16.18   In Chapter 2 there was a discussion of the rule restricting the recovery of 'pure' economic loss in some torts: see **2.49–2.52**. There is no such rule under s 236(1). Economic loss is clearly recoverable,[86] irrespective of the issue of damage to the plaintiff's property or person.[87] CCA ss 87CB(1) and 137B(1), which deal with contributory negligence and proportionate liability, also envisage pure economic loss claims.

Mitigation

16.19   As in tort and contract, there is a duty on the plaintiff to take reasonable steps to mitigate loss flowing from the contravention of the Act.[88] In *Murphy v Overton Investments Pty Ltd*[89] the High Court did not need to resolve an issue relating to mitigation of damages in a claim under TPA ss 52 and 82. Nonetheless, it accepted, first, that this was a relevant consideration in assessing damages and, second, that the onus of proof rests on the defendant to show that the plaintiff has failed to discharge this duty.[90] If there has been a reasonable attempt to mitigate loss and the plaintiff actually makes the loss worse, this extra loss is recoverable.[91] In cases analogous to breach of contract, there may in fact be a duty to take reasonable steps in mitigation, even where the plaintiff affirms the contract.[92] In *Crystal Auburn Pty Ltd v I L Wollermann Pty Ltd* Crystal Auburn on 19 December 1997 paid $550,000 for a theme park

---

83. (2001) 206 CLR 459; [2001] HCA 52 at [136]; compare Gleeson CJ at [21]–[35] and Gaudron J at [66].

84. To adapt the words of Gummow J in *Marks v GIO Australia Holdings* (1998) 196 CLR 494 at [103].

85. [2004] HCA 54 at [14] per Gleeson CJ, McHugh, Gummow, Kirby and Heydon JJ.

86. *Murphy v Overton Investments Pty Ltd* (2004) 216 CLR 388; [2004] HCA 3 at [45].

87. *Wardley Australia Ltd v Western Australia* (1992) 175 CLR 514 at 525–6 per Mason CJ, Dawson, Gaudron and McHugh JJ.

88. *Murphy v Overton Investments Pty Ltd* (2004) 216 CLR 388; [2004] HCA 3 at [70]; *Crystal Auburn Pty Ltd v I L Wollermann Pty Ltd* [2004] FCA 821; *Finucane v New South Wales Egg Corp* (1988) 80 ALR 486; *Munchies Management Pty Ltd v Belperio* (1988) 84 ALR 700 (Full FC); *Futuretronics International Pty Ltd v Gadzhis* [1992] VR 209 at 245 per Ormiston J; *Corbidge v Bakery Fun Shop Pty Ltd* (1984) ATPR 40–493 per Beaumont J; compare *I & L Securities Pty Ltd v HTW Valuers (Brisbane) Pty Ltd* (2002) 210 CLR 109; [2002] HCA 41 at [29] per Gleeson CJ and [88] per McHugh J.

89. (2004) 216 CLR 388; [2004] HCA 3.

90. *Murphy v Overton Investments Pty Ltd* (2004) 216 CLR 388; [2004] HCA 3 at [70]; see also *Hubbards Pty Ltd v Simpson Ltd* (1982) 41 ALR 509.

91. *Hellyer Drilling Co v MacDonald Hamilton & Co Pty Ltd* (1983) 51 ALR 177.

92. *Tiplady v Gold Coast Carlton Pty Ltd* (1984) ATPR 40–472; compare **3.31–3.35**.

known as Wobbies World. It was on seven acres of land in Springvale Road, Nunawading and featured a monorail, miniature trams and fire trucks on rails, minigolf and trampolines. Before the sale the respondents misleadingly inflated the park's attendance figures. Despite Crystal Auburn receiving legal advice in April 1998 that it could rescind the contract, it affirmed the contract by putting the park on the market and treating the contract as if it remained on foot. Such conduct 'was a declaration of ownership of the business and a desire to pass that ownership to a buyer'.[93] Crystal Auburn vacated the park in August 1998. The respondents were found to be in contravention of the Act, but they submitted at the trial that once Crystal Auburn had 'affirmed the contract they were obliged to take reasonable steps to mitigate their loss and that their conduct was so unreasonable as [to] break the chain of causation'.[94] They raised several matters in support of this argument, including a failure to sell the park, plant and equipment, and allowing it to deteriorate after vacating. They relied on the following observation by Lee J in *Henjo Investments Pty Ltd v Collins Marrickville Pty Ltd (No 2)*:

> Under the general law, a person who affirmed the contract induced by deceit would lose the right to rescind but not the right to recover damages for the tort of deceit. The act of affirming the contract would make no difference in itself to the right to recover damages for the misrepresentation inducing the contract.[95] There would, however, be an obligation upon the party affirming the contract to take reasonable steps to mitigate the loss resulting from the deceit. The actual or imputed affirmation may be treated as the point at which it becomes unreasonable for consequential damages to continue to accrue if no steps to mitigate the loss are taken thereafter or if affirmation of the contract was not the reasonable course to have followed.[96]

Goldberg J held that even though the contract to purchase the park had been affirmed, Crystal Auburn was still under a duty to mitigate its loss. But it had not breached this duty because it had acted reasonably in its efforts to sell the park and the equipment. Thus, it was 'entitled to recover the difference between the amount paid for the business and its true value at the purchase date'.[97]

Assessment of damages

16.20 The general principle to be applied in assessing quantum is that of compensation; that is, to put the plaintiff in the same position, so far as money can, that would have been occupied had the breach of the Act not occurred.[98]

---

93.   [2004] FCA 821 at [16].

94.   [2004] FCA 821 at [27].

95.   Citing *S Gormley & Co Pty Ltd v Cubit* [1964] NSWR 557.

96.   (1989) 40 FCR 76 at 90–1 citing *Mister Figgins Pty Ltd v Centrepoint Freeholds Pty Ltd* (1981) 36 ALR 23 at 60; *TN Lucas Pty Ltd v Centrepoint Freeholds Pty Ltd* (1984) 1 FCR 110 at 118.

97.   [2004] FCA 821 at [27] and [69].

98.   See **16.6** and *Mayne Nickless Ltd v Multigroup Distribution Services Pty Ltd* (2001) 114 FCR 108; *Multigroup Distribution Services Pty Ltd v TNT Australia Pty Ltd* (2001) 109 FCR 528 at [35]–[42] per Gyles J; *Snyman v Cooper* (1989) 16 IPR 585 at 610 per von Doussa J (FCA); compare *Munchies Management Pty*

The common law rule against double recovery is also applicable to claims under the Act.[99] However, the rule that damages are awarded 'once-and-for-all' in a lump sum (see **2.59–2.60** and **3.40**), does not necessarily apply. Dealing with contraventions of TPA Pt V in *Murphy v Overton Investments Pty Ltd* the High Court held:

> It would be wrong … to assume that, where a person is induced by misleading or deceptive conduct to undertake a continuing future obligation, the remedy to be awarded for a contravention of Pt V of the Act must be, or even ordinarily will be, a lump sum award of damages. There will be cases in which that will be the appropriate remedy. But that is a conclusion to be reached only after identifying the loss or damage which has been or will likely be suffered. That loss or damage may take several forms. It may be incurred at different times. Whether damages are to be awarded in compensation may depend upon what other forms of relief are to be awarded. In particular it will be much affected by what orders to prevent or reduce the loss or damage are made under s 87.[100]

The CCA continues to allow for structured settlements (as opposed to lump sum awards) for certain death and personal injury claims. These are available where the claim arises as a result of contraventions of ACL Pt 2-2 (unconscionable conduct), 3-3 (safety of consumer goods and product related services), 3-4 (information standards), 3-5 (liability of manufacturers for goods with safety defects), or Div 2 of Pt 5-4 (actions for damages against manufacturers of goods).[101]

Date of assessment

16.21   In tort (see **2.58**) and contract (see **3.36**), damages are ordinarily assessed at the date of breach, except where that defeats the compensation principle. No date is expressed in the Act as to when damages are to be assessed but, like the common law, whatever date is selected it should not defeat the 'overriding compensatory rule'.[102]

So far as ACL s 236(1) is concerned, damages will usually not be assessed at the date of breach because, like negligence, the cause of action does not accrue until actual loss or damage is suffered.[103] Prior to that happening, the loss is merely contingent: see **16.28**. In *HTW Valuers (Central Qld) Pty Ltd v Astonland Pty Ltd*[104] the High Court held that under TPA s 82 damages for a misleading statement are to be assessed at the date some loss or damage has been suffered, but as with 'many fields of law' the court may take into

Ltd v Belperio (1988) 84 ALR 700, where the Full Federal Court left open the question of whether restitutionary damages are available under ss 82 and 87.

99.   *Murphy v Overton Investments Pty Ltd* (2004) 216 CLR 388; [2004] HCA 3 at [50].

100. (2004) 216 CLR 388; [2004] HCA 3 at [52].

101. CCA s 87ZC arw s 87E.

102. *HTW Valuers (Central Qld) Pty Ltd v Astonland Pty Ltd* [2004] HCA 54 at [63]–[64].

103. *Wardley Australia Ltd v Western Australia* (1992) 175 CLR 514 at 525 per Mason CJ, Dawson, Gaudron and McHugh JJ.

104. [2004] HCA 54.

account 'all matters known by the later date when the court's assessment is being carried out'.[105] In support it cited its earlier decision in *Kizbeau Pty Ltd v WG & B Pty Ltd* where it was held:

> In an action for damages for deceit for inducing a person to enter a contract of purchase, which is an action that is closely analogous to an action for damages for breach of s 52, the courts have consistently held that the proper measure of damages is the difference between the real value of the thing acquired as at the date of acquisition and the price paid for it. Nevertheless, although the value is assessed as at the date of the acquisition, subsequent events may be looked at in so far as they illuminate the value of the thing as at that date. A distinction is drawn, however, between subsequent events that arise from the nature or use of the thing itself and subsequent events that affect the value of the thing but arise from sources supervening upon or extraneous to the fraudulent inducement. Events falling into the former category are admissible to prove the value of the thing, those falling into the latter category are inadmissible for that purpose. Thus, the takings of a business subsequent to purchase are generally admissible, not only to prove that a representation concerning the takings was false but also to prove the true value of the business as at the date of purchase. Even when some difference exists between the conditions under which the business was conducted before and after purchase, evidence of subsequent takings may be admissible, "subject to due allowance being made for any differences in relevant conditions". But if it is established that the decline in takings has been caused by business ineptitude or unexpected competition, evidence of subsequent takings is not admissible to prove the value of the business as at that date, events such as ineptitude and unexpected competition being regarded as supervening events. In some cases of deceit, it may also be proper to compensate the defrauded party not only for the difference between the value of the thing acquired and the price paid for it but also for losses induced by the fraud and directly incurred in conducting the business. All of these principles are appropriate to the assessment of damages under s 82 where a breach of s 52 of the Act has induced a person to purchase a business.[106]

While this approach was approved in *Astonland*, the High Court did indicate that the 'width of s 82' permits damages to be assessed 'at the time of the trial' provided it worked 'no injustice'.[107] In that case Astonland Pty Ltd bought a small shopping arcade of eight shops known as the Plaza for $485,000 on 28 April 1997 after obtaining advice about the demand for retail tenancies from HTW Valuers. The advice was that current rental levels were maintainable despite a shopping centre being built nearby. When the shopping centre opened in mid-1998, the Plaza's gross rentals 'held up reasonably well to about March 1999 and then collapsed'.[108] Astonland tried to sell the Plaza without success and by March 2000 several shops were vacant. Astonland sued HTW in the Queensland Supreme Court for negligent advice, breach of contract and misleading conduct under s 52 of the Act.

---

105. [2004] HCA 54 at [39].
106. (1995) 184 CLR 281 at 291.
107. [2004] HCA 54 at [64]–[65] per Gleeson CJ, McHugh, Gummow, Kirby and Heydon JJ.
108. [2004] HCA 54 at [8] citing Dutney J.

Dutney J found that the collapse in rentals was mainly due to the opening of the nearby shopping centre; and that HTW was negligent in failing to qualify its opinion by cautioning that the effect of the new shopping centre was uncertain. The evidence showed that the arcade was worth $400,000 at the date of the purchase in April 1997; $375,000 when the purchase was completed in July 1997; and $130,000 by 1999. HTW argued that its damages should only be $85,000, based on the difference between the purchase price and the April 1997 valuation; or $110,000 based on the July 1997 valuation. Dutney J, however, awarded Astonland $355,000 in damages representing the difference between the price paid for the Plaza and its realistic value in early 1999. HTW's appeals to the Full Court and the High Court against the award of $355,000 were dismissed. The High Court considered that the plaintiff had suffered a loss from the moment it bought the arcade in April 1997 because it paid $485,000 and its value was at best $400,000. But, 'with the benefit of hindsight operating from the time of the trial in 2001, it can be seen that that loss was much greater'.[109] In a unanimous judgment the court held:

> Thus, in assessing damages in this case, the court is not limited to the assessment of risk as at 28 April 1997, but is entitled to take account of how those risks had evolved into certainties at dates after the date on which the comparison of price and true value was being made.[110]

While that reasoning was sufficient to dismiss the appeal in *Astonland*, the High Court indicated that the plaintiff's alternative approach of assessing damages by recovering the purchase price of $485,000 less whatever was 'left in its hands' did not 'lack merit'. The qualification, stemming from the House of Lords majority speech in *Smith New Court Securities Ltd v Scrimgeour Vickers (Asset Management) Ltd*,[111] was that the plaintiff must have acted reasonably in retaining the asset. The High Court then explained:

> *Advantages of the approach.* While here the plaintiff cannot bring into account the actual proceeds of sale of the Plaza, because, despite its best efforts, it has not succeeded in effecting a sale, the principle would permit the value of the Plaza at the time of the trial to be the relevant figure.
>
> There is certainly no reason why an approach of that kind is not open under s 82 of the Act. The deduction of true value at the acquisition date from the price paid is no more than a guide to the assessment of damages under s 82. Section 82 does not in terms refer to that method, and the width of s 82 permits other approaches to the assessment of damages so long as they work no injustice. The alternative approach advocated by the plaintiff has particular appropriateness in the present circumstances. That is because a primary reason for the common adoption, in assessing damages in deceit, of the test of comparing the price paid for an asset with its true value when acquired is the desirability of separating out losses resulting from extraneous factors in the later history of the asset. Here, the trial judge found that the decline in value of the Plaza had no cause other than the completion of the

---

109. [2004] HCA 54 at [44].
110. [2004] HCA 54 at [45].
111. [1997] AC 254 at 265.

Beach Rd Shopping Centre. The present case is from that point of view an unusually pure one. Since there are no losses resulting from extraneous factors to separate out, there is correspondingly less need to look to a comparison of purchase price and real value on acquisition as the appropriate approach.[112]

Expectation loss

16.22   While refusing to be constrained by analogy with a particular tort, in misleading and deceptive conduct cases the courts have often found it appropriate to apply the principles of damages as they apply in tort,[113] particularly deceit.[114] Therefore, damages for expectation loss, a measure of damages in contract for the loss of a bargain, are not available.[115] Nonetheless, damages may be available for the loss of an opportunity, as discussed below.

Loss of opportunity

16.23   Lost opportunity or lost chance damages are clearly recoverable under both s 236 and the 'compensation order' provisions (ss 237 and 238). In *Gates v City Mutual Assurance Society Ltd*,[116] Mason, Wilson and Dawson JJ held that if the reliance on the statutory contravention has deprived the plaintiff of 'a different contract' where a profit would have been made, then that lost profit or benefit is recoverable.[117] The onus is on the plaintiff to prove such a loss.[118] In *Sellars v Adelaide Petroleum NL*, the majority in the High Court confirmed that loss of chance damages are available where a contravention of the TPA deprived the plaintiff of an alternative commercial opportunity.[119] This is so even if the alternative opportunity only had a 40 per cent chance of being realised.[120]

Mental stress

16.24   The court awarded damages for mental stress and emotional suffering in *Steiner v Magic Carpet Tours Pty Ltd*[121] and *Zoneff v Elcom Credit Union Ltd*[122]

---

112.   [2004] HCA 54 at [64]–[65].

113.   *Henville v Walker* (2001) 206 CLR 459; [2001] HCA 52 at [130] per McHugh J.

114.   *Marks v GIO Australia Holdings Pty Ltd* (1998) 196 CLR 494 at [41] per McHugh, Hayne and Callinan JJ.

115.   *Gates v City Mutual Assurance Society Ltd* (1986) 160 CLR 1; *Henville v Walker* (2001) 206 CLR 459; [2001] HCA 52 at [132] per McHugh J; *Futuretronics International Pty Ltd v Gadzhis* [1992] VR 209 at 244 per Ormiston J; *Marks v GIO Australia Holdings Pty Ltd* (1998) 196 CLR 494; *Gough & Gilmour Holdings Pty Ltd (No 2) v Peter Campbell Earthmoving Pty Ltd* [2007] NSWSC 172; *Haryn Pty Ltd v Webster* [2005] NSWCA 182.

116.   (1986) 160 CLR 1.

117.   (1986) 160 CLR 1 at 13; *Marks v GIO Australia Holdings Pty Ltd* (1998) 196 CLR 494; *Warnock v ANZ* (1989) ATPR 40-928.

118.   (1986) 160 CLR 1 at 13 and 15.

119.   (1994) 179 CLR 332 per Mason CJ, Dawson, Toohey and Gaudron JJ.

120.   (1994) 179 CLR 332 at 349 and 355–6 per Mason CJ, Dawson, Toohey and Gaudron JJ. See also the discussion at 2.28–2.30 and 3.46.

121.   (1984) ATPR 40-490.

122.   (1990) 94 ALR 445; see also *Nixon v Slater & Gordon* (2000) 175 ALR 15 (Fed C of A), where Merkel J awarded damages to two surgeons for, inter alia, the 'hurt' caused by a defamatory and misleading medical malpractice brochure.

---

but they were refused in *Argy v Blunts and Lane Cove Real Estate*.[123] In order to claim such a loss, the plaintiff must be a natural person.[124] Personal injury claims can also be made for a recognised psychiatric illness or disease.[125]

Reputation

16.25   The court has awarded damages for injury to reputation in actions resembling defamation[126] and passing off.[127] So far as passing off is concerned, Beaumont J in *Prince Manufacturing Inc v ABAC Corp Australia Pty Ltd*[128] observed that:

> ... where the conduct which constitutes a contravention of s 52 also constitutes the tort of passing off and a claim is made under s 82 for damages, it is appropriate to apply a measure of damages similar to that applied under the general law of passing off ... In particular, in my view, general damages for loss of business profits may, in a proper case, be recovered under s 82. By general damages is meant damages which are not capable of precise proof and calculation but which could be expected to result in the normal course of things from a particular type of conduct. Damages of this kind may be awarded even though a claimant does not produce evidence of particular losses from particular transactions.[129]

Interest

16.26   Subject to any prohibition in the Act, an award for interest can be made under the various statutes regulating the courts that can hear and determine actions under the Act.[130] CCA s 87ZA prohibits the awarding of interest on various heads of damage for personal injury claims including non-economic loss (pain and suffering, loss of amenities of life, loss of expectation of life and disfigurement) and gratuitous attendant care services.

Exemplary and aggravated damages

16.27   Prior to 2004, it was clear that an exemplary or punitive damages award could neither be made under s 82 nor under s 87, because the aim under those sections was to compensate the plaintiff rather than penalise the defendant.[131] By the same reasoning, aggravated damages were available because their

---

123. (1990) 26 FCR 112; 94 ALR 719.
124. *T N Lucas Pty Ltd v Centrepoint Freeholds Pty Ltd* (1984) 1 FCR 110.
125. See CCA s 4 definition of personal injury and **16.6**.
126. *Nixon v Slater & Gordon* (2000) 175 ALR 15 at 33 per Merkel J (FCA); *Brabazon v Western Mail Ltd* (1985) 58 ALR 712.
127. *Flamingo Park Pty Ltd v Dolly Dolly Creations Pty Ltd* (1986) 6 IPR 431.
128. (1984) 4 FCR 288; 4 IPR 104.
129. (1984) 4 FCR 288 at 294; 4 IPR 104 at 111.
130. See, for example, s 51A of the Federal Court of Australia Act 1976 (Cth); *Smallacombe v Lockyer Investment Co Pty Ltd* (1993) 114 ALR 568. See also **2.82**.
131. *Musca v Astle Corp Pty Ltd* (1988) 80 ALR 251 at 262 (FCA); applied in *Snyman v Cooper* (1989) 16 IPR 585 at 610 per von Doussa J (FCA); see also *Marks v GIO Australia Holdings Pty Ltd* (1998) 196 CLR 494 at [9] per Gaudron J; *Munchies Management Pty Ltd v Belperio* (1988) 84 ALR 700 (Full FC).

purpose was to compensate the plaintiff.[132] The TPA was changed in 2004; and this change is carried over in CCA s 87ZB which provides:

87ZB Exemplary and aggravated damages

(1) A court must not, in a proceeding to which this Part applies, award exemplary damages or aggravated damages in respect of death or personal injury.

(2) This section does not affect whether a court has power to award exemplary damages or aggravated damages:

    (a) otherwise than in respect of death or personal injury; or

    (b) in a proceeding other than a proceeding to which this Part applies.

While CCA s 87ZB(1) prohibits exemplary and aggravated damages for death and personal injury claims, s 87ZB(2)(a) contemplates that the court has power to award such damages 'otherwise than in respect of death or personal injury'. Section 87ZB(2)(b) also provides that exemplary and aggravated damages may be available 'in a proceeding other than a proceeding to which this Part applies'. In this regard, s 87E(1) provides:

(1) This Part applies to proceedings taken under the Australian Consumer Law:

    (a) that relate to Part 2-2, 3-3, 3-4 or 3-5, or Division 2 of Part 5-4, of the Australian Consumer Law; and

    (b) in which the plaintiff is seeking an award of personal injury damages; and

    (c) that are not proceedings in respect of the death of or personal injury to a person resulting from smoking or other use of tobacco products.

Presumably the reference in s 87ZB to the court's 'power to award exemplary damages' is a reference to the general law as there is no express provision in the Act allowing exemplary damages to be awarded. The relevant parts of the ACL deal with unconscionable conduct (Pt 2-2), safety of consumer goods and product related services (Pt 3-3), information standards (Pt 3-4), liability of manufacturers for goods with safety defects (Pt 3-5) and actions for damages against manufacturers of goods (Div 2 of Pt 5-4).

Limitation period

16.28 ACL s 236(2) provides:

An action under subsection (1) may be commenced at any time within 6 years after the day on which the cause of action that relates to the conduct accrued.

Since loss or damage is the 'gist of the action' under s 236(1), the cause of action does not accrue until the applicant actually suffers loss or damage.[133] The mere fact that the defendant's contravention has induced the plaintiff to enter

---

132. *Collings Construction Co Pty Ltd v Australian Competition and Consumer Commission* (1998) 43 NSWLR 131 (CA); *Philip Morris (Aust) Pty Ltd v Nixon* (2000) 170 ALR 487; and see **2.84–2.87**.

133. *Wardley Australia Ltd v Western Australia* (1992) 175 CLR 514 at 525 per Mason CJ, Dawson, Gaudron and McHugh JJ.

into a contract does not mean that the plaintiff has suffered damage at that date.[134] After discussing the various authorities, Mason CJ, Dawson, Gaudron and McHugh JJ in *Wardley Australia Ltd v Western Australia*[135] concluded:

> If … the English decisions properly understood support the proposition that where, as a result of the defendant's negligent misrepresentation, the plaintiff enters into a contract which exposes him or her to a contingent loss or liability, the plaintiff first suffers loss or damage on entry into the contract, we do not agree with them. In our opinion in such a case, the plaintiff sustains no actual damage until the contingency is fulfilled and the loss becomes actual; until that happens the loss is prospective and may never be incurred.[136]

The High Court reconsidered the issue in *Murphy v Overton Investments Pty Ltd*.[137] In 1992 the appellants, Mr and Mrs Murphy, were induced to enter into a retirement village lease and obliged to pay a levy for outgoings including rates, insurance premiums, maintenance and operating costs. The initial estimate of outgoings was $55.71 per week. While the lease made it plain that this was only an estimate, it was calculated without regard to all expenditure actually being incurred in the operation of the village. In July 1994 the levy was increased by more than 18 per cent and in November 1996 the respondents told the tenants that it would thereafter charge all operational costs. On appeal, the respondents accepted the finding of misleading and deceptive conduct in relation to the additional charges. While there was no evidence that the appellants had paid an excessive amount for their leasehold interest in 1992 they had, nonetheless, suffered a contingent loss. As later explained by the High Court when considering *Murphy* in *HTW Valuers (Central Qld) Pty Ltd v Astonland Pty Ltd*:

> Whether the charges would rise above the level stated before the applicants entered the lease was contingent in the sense that it was not inevitable: the contingency could never eventuate unless the respondent exercised its discretion to increase the charges. There was thus a contingency hidden by the respondent's conduct which might or might not come to pass.[138]

Following *Wardley*, the court concluded in *Murphy* that the cause of action did not accrue until actual damage had been suffered. That was not on the date of entry into the lease but, rather, when the respondents departed from their 1992 representation and charged for all outgoings.[139]

---

134. *Murphy v Overton Investments Pty Ltd* (2004) 216 CLR 388; [2004] HCA 3 at [54]–[56].

135. (1992) 175 CLR 514.

136. (1992) 175 CLR 514 at 532; applied in *Murphy v Overton Investments Pty Ltd* (2004) 216 CLR 388; [2004] HCA 3 at [46] and [55] per Gleeson CJ, McHugh, Gummow, Kirby, Hayne, Callinan and Heydon JJ.

137. (2004) 216 CLR 388; [2004] HCA 3.

138. [2004] HCA 54 at [30].

139. [2004] HCA 54 at [55].

Generally, the onus will fall on the defendant to plead and prove the expiration of the limitation period in s 236(2).[140] The defendant may be deemed to have waived the point if it is not pleaded.[141]

16.29   Like s 236(2), the limitation period under s 237(3) is also six years.[142] But the Full Federal Court in *Western Australia v Wardley Australia Ltd* has noted that 'the action … may accrue as soon as loss or damage is likely to be suffered', meaning that the time bar has a 'different operation' to that in s 236.[143] The court found it unnecessary 'to determine precisely what is meant … by the expression "likely to be suffered"' but nonetheless indicated that it meant 'a real chance or possibility'.[144] The onus is on the defendant to prove that the plaintiff's claim is statute-barred under s 237.[145]

REMEDIAL ORDERS

16.30   As pointed out at 16.5, ss 237 and 238 not only permit compensation orders, but also a range of other remedial orders. The causes of action that enliven remedial orders differ slightly from s 236. They are not restricted to contraventions of the provisions in Chs 2 and 3, but include contraventions of Ch 4 (the criminal offences). They also include conduct that 'constitutes applying or relying on, or purporting to apply or rely on, a term of a consumer contract that has been declared under section 250 to be an unfair term'.[146]

16.31   In addition to ss 237 and 238, one other section enables remedial orders. ACL s 239 gives the court power to make orders on the application of the regulator in favour of a class of consumers who are not party to the proceedings. Subsections (1) to (3) provide:

(1) If:

　(a) a person:

　　(i)   engaged in conduct (the *contravening conduct*) in contravention of a provision of Chapter 2, Part 3-1, Division 2, 3 or 4 of Part 3-2 or Chapter 4; or

　　(ii) is a party to a consumer contract who is advantaged by a term (the *declared term*) of the contract in relation to which a court has made a declaration under section 250; and

　(b) the contravening conduct or declared term caused, or is likely to cause, a class of persons to suffer loss or damage; and

---

140. *Murphy v Overton Investments Pty Ltd* (2004) 216 CLR 388; [2004] HCA 3 at [56].

141. *Western Australia v Wardley Australia Ltd* (1991) 30 FCR 245 (Full FC).

142. ACL s 237(3).

143. *Western Australia v Wardley Australia Ltd* (1991) 30 FCR 245 (Full FC); compare *Magman International Pty Ltd v Westpac Banking Corp* (1991) 32 FCR 1 (Full FC).

144. (1991) 30 FCR 245 at 261 (Full FC); *Marks v GIO Australia Holdings Pty Ltd* (1998) 196 CLR 494 at [22] per Gaudron J.

145. *Murphy v Overton Investments Pty Ltd* (2004) 216 CLR 388; [2004] HCA 3 at [56].

146. ACL ss 237(1) and 238(1); and see ACL ss 23–28 relating to unfair contract terms.

(c) the class includes persons who are non-party consumers in relation to the contravening conduct or declared term;

a court may, on the application of the regulator, make such order or orders (other than an award of damages) as the court thinks appropriate against a person referred to in subsection (2) of this section.

(2) An order under subsection (1) may be made against:

(a) if subsection (1)(a)(i) applies — the person who engaged in the contravening conduct, or a person involved in that conduct; or

(b) if subsection (1)(a)(ii) applies — a party to the contract who is advantaged by the declared term.

(3) The order must be an order that the court considers will:

(a) redress, in whole or in part, the loss or damage suffered by the non-party consumers in relation to the contravening conduct or declared term; or

(b) prevent or reduce the loss or damage suffered, or likely to be suffered, by the non-party consumers in relation to the contravening conduct or declared term.

This section does not permit compensation orders — it allows orders 'other than damages', provided the aim is to redress, prevent or reduce loss or damage. Non-party consumers are bound by the order once they accept the redress, prevention or reduction; and then do not have an independent claim against the person contravening the relevant provisions.[147]

16.32 As mentioned earlier, the range of orders available under s 87 of the TPA were described by Mason P as a 'remedial smorgasbord'.[148] The same is equally true of the remedial orders available under the ACL. Section 243 lists some of the orders a court may make:

Without limiting section 237(1), 238(1) or 239(1), the orders that a court may make under any of those sections against a person (the respondent) include all or any of the following:

(a) an order declaring the whole or any part of a contract made between the respondent and a person (the injured person) who suffered, or is likely to suffer, the loss or damage referred to in that section, or of a collateral arrangement relating to such a contract:

(i) to be void; and

(ii) if the court thinks fit — to have been void ab initio or void at all times on and after such date as is specified in the order (which may be a date that is before the date on which the order is made);

(b) an order:

(i) varying such a contract or arrangement in such manner as is specified in the order; and

(ii) if the court thinks fit — declaring the contract or arrangement to have had effect as so varied on and after such date as is specified in

---

147. ACL s 241.
148. *Akron Securities v Iliffe* [1997] NSWSC 106; (1997) 41 NSWLR at 364 (CA).

the order (which may be a date that is before the date on which the order is made);

(c) an order refusing to enforce any or all of the provisions of such a contract or arrangement;

(d) an order directing the respondent to refund money or return property to the injured person;

(e) except if the order is to be made under section 239(1) — an order directing the respondent to pay the injured person the amount of the loss or damage;

(f) an order directing the respondent, at his or her own expense, to repair, or provide parts for, goods that had been supplied by the respondent to the injured person;

(g) an order directing the respondent, at his or her own expense, to supply specified services to the injured person;

(h) an order, in relation to an instrument creating or transferring an interest in land, directing the respondent to execute an instrument that:

    (i) varies, or has the effect of varying, the first mentioned instrument; or

    (ii) terminates or otherwise affects, or has the effect of terminating or otherwise affecting, the operation or effect of the first mentioned instrument.

16.33 Not only can the court make 'any or all' of the orders listed in this section, but it can also make orders in combination with injunctions, damages awards and certain more specific orders.[149] More specific orders are provided for in ss 246–248. They include 'non-punitive' orders to perform a service for the benefit of the community; to establish compliance, education or training programs for employees; to revise the internal operations of a business; to disclose information to specified persons; and to publish an advertisement. There are also powers to make adverse publicity orders and to disqualify a person from managing a corporation. The court is able to choose from this 'remedial smorgasbord' and, for example, marry a damages award with an order rewriting or rescinding the contract;[150] dismantle a series of interlocking contractual arrangements;[151] vary parts of the contract; order the refund of money, the return of property, the repair of goods or the supply of services; and even make orders against third parties.[152]

16.34 While orders under these sections can achieve results that would be impossible under common law, it is still useful to consider the extent to which

---

149. ACL s 244.

150. *Kizbeau Pty Ltd v W G & B Pty Ltd* (1995) 184 CLR 281 at 299; *I & L Securities Pty Ltd v HTW Valuers (Brisbane) Pty Ltd* (2002) 210 CLR 109; [2002] HCA 41 at [108] per McHugh J.

151. *Akron Securities v Iliffe* (1997) 41 NSWLR 353 at 366 per Mason P (CA).

152. *Demagogue Pty Ltd v Ramensky* (1992) 110 ALR 608 (FCA); *Akron Securities v Iliffe* (1997) 41 NSWLR at 366 per Mason P; *I & L Securities Pty Ltd v HTW Valuers (Brisbane) Pty Ltd* (2002) 210 CLR 109; [2002] HCA 41 at [107] per McHugh J.

the court can achieve some of the familiar remedies discussed in the previous chapters of this book.

RESCISSION

16.35 The term 'rescission'[153] is no longer used in the CCA. The confusing reference to 'rescission' in s 75A of the TPA (when the remedy described there was more accurately a 'termination') has been removed. However, the remedial order provisions are wide enough to allow a court to effect a rescission. Under s 243(c) the court may refuse to enforce a contract or any of its provisions. Obviously, if a court refuses to enforce the whole contract this is akin to rescission. A necessary corollary to this is the refund of money or return of the property which is allowed under s 243(d).

In *Munchies Management Pty Ltd v Belperio*[154] the Full Federal Court (Fisher, Gummow and Lee JJ) accepted that the equitable principles governing rescission (see **Chapter 5**) 'give safe, if not necessarily exclusive, guidance' under TPA s 87; and in *Henjo Investments Pty Ltd v Collins Marrickville Pty Ltd*,[155] an order for rescission was refused following the equitable principle that *restitutio in integrum*[156] was no longer possible.[157] Still, in *Akron Securities v Iliffe*, Mason P held:

> In granting a remedy under s 87, the Court is not restricted by the limitations under the general law upon a party's right to rescind for misrepresentation ... Nor is the court restricted in granting a remedy under s 87 by the general law's limitations upon a party's right to rescind for breach of contract ... These include the limitations deriving from the much criticised decision in *Seddon v North Eastern Salt Co Ltd* ...[158]

SPECIFIC PERFORMANCE

16.36 Specific performance is not mentioned in the Act. Nonetheless, a mandatory injunction may be granted under s 232 (see **16.41**). In addition, ss 237–239 provide that, where a person 'has suffered or is likely to suffer, loss or damage', the remedial orders a court may make include an order that a person repair, or supply parts for, supplied goods (s 243(f)) or supply specified services (s 243(g)).

But, unlike the equitable remedy of specific performance, orders under these sections will be limited to the purposes described in whichever section

---

153. See the discussion of rescission and the discretionary remedy of *restitutio in integrum* in **Chapter 5**.
154. (1988) 84 ALR 700 at 714; see also *Akron Securities v Iliffe* (1997) 41 NSWLR 353 at 367 per Mason P.
155. (1988) 79 ALR 83 (Full FC).
156. This principle is discussed at **5.59–5.61**.
157. (1988) 79 ALR 83 at 102 per Lockhart J.
158. *Akron Securities v Iliffe* (1997) 41 NSWLR 353 at 366 per Mason P (CA). The rule in *Seddon's* case is discussed at **5.16**.

enlivens the court's discretion—that is compensating, redressing, preventing or reducing the loss or damage.[159] So, in *Futuretronics International Pty Ltd v Gadzhis*,[160] Ormiston J refused to order specific performance under the corresponding Victorian section[161] because such an order was not, in the circumstances of the case, a substitute for compensation.[162]

The ordinary rule that specific performance will not be granted when the contract is to lend money does not apply to remedial orders, but the court may take into account the principles behind the rule.[163]

INJUNCTIONS

Introduction

16.37 The power to grant an injunction comes primarily from ACL s 232. The relevant subsections provide:

(1) A court may grant an injunction, in such terms as the court considers appropriate, if the court is satisfied that a person has engaged, or is proposing to engage, in conduct that constitutes or would constitute:

(a) a contravention of a provision of Chapter 2, 3 or 4; or

(b) attempting to contravene such a provision; or

(c) aiding, abetting, counselling or procuring a person to contravene such a provision; or

(d) inducing, or attempting to induce, whether by threats, promises or otherwise, a person to contravene such a provision; or

(e) being in any way, directly or indirectly, knowingly concerned in, or party to, the contravention by a person of such a provision; or

(f) conspiring with others to contravene such a provision.

(2) The court may grant the injunction on application by the regulator or any other person.

Section 232 does not fully replace the previous injunctive power in TPA s 80. Some residual powers remain in the Commonwealth Act — see CCA s 80. They relate to restrictive trade practices and contraventions of industry codes of practice. The associated investigative and enforcement powers are still with the ACCC rather than a generic 'regulator' — hence there was no need for these to be included in the national ACL regime. While CCA s 80 also allows 'any other person' to seek an injunction, the discussion that follows will focus on the ACL as the more common source of injunctive

---

159. Sections 237(2), 238(2) and 239(3); *Finucane v New South Wales Egg Corp* (1988) 80 ALR 486 at 519; *Frith v Gold Coast Mineral Springs Pty Ltd* (1983) 47 ALR 547.

160. [1992] VR 209.

161. Fair Trading Act 1985 (Vic) s 41 (now repealed): see Fair Trading Act 1999 (Vic) s 158.

162. [1992] VR 209 at 244–5; see also *Mikhas Investments Pty Ltd v Larkin* (1989) ATPR 40956 cited by his Honour in support.

163. *Angelatos v National Australia Bank* (1994) 51 FCR 574.

relief. However, the principles discussed will also be equally relevant to CCA s 80.

A number of preliminary points might be made. First, the wording of ACL s 232 is almost identical to the previous TPA s 80, so the body of case law interpreting TPA s 80 is likely to be equally relevant. Second, standing to apply for an injunction is given to the regulator and 'any other person'. This results in a 'significant broadening of locus standi'[164] compared with equitable injunctions: see **16.38**. Third, there is a wide range of injunctions available: see the discussion at **16.40–16.49**. Fourth, the injunctive power is enlivened where a person engages in conduct or proposes to engage in conduct that contravenes a provision of Chs 2, 3 or 4. As discussed at **16.9**, contraventions of Chs 2 and 3 also enliven an action for damages. These provisions cover 'General protections', such as misleading or deceptive conduct, unconscionable conduct and unfair contract terms; and 'Specific protections' such as bait advertising, unsolicited supplies, pyramid schemes, product safety and the guarantees (previously known as warranties) in respect of consumer goods and services. The inclusion here of Ch 4 in the list of enlivening events means that injunctions can also be obtained where the conduct or proposed conduct amounts to a criminal offence under the Act. Injunctions are also available where someone is applying or relying on — or proposing to apply or rely on — a term in a standard form consumer contract declared to be unfair.[165]

Injunctions granted under the ACL are capable of having an extra-territorial effect. In a domain name case concerning the Sydney Opera House Trust, *Australian Competition and Consumer Commission v Chen*, Sackville J held:

> There is nothing in this language that imposes an implied territorial limitation on the power of the court. On the contrary, not only is the language of s 80(1) broad enough to permit the court to prohibit or mandate acts abroad … there is good reason to interpret it in this way.

> Section 6(2) of the TP Act extends the application of Pt V (and other provisions) to conduct in trade or commerce between Australia and places outside Australia. In enacting this provision, parliament has relied on the trade and commerce power conferred by s 51(i) of the Constitution. The extended application of the TP Act has the effect that a person outside Australia (but subject to the jurisdiction of the court under provisions such as FCR O 8 r 2) might well contravene provisions of the Act and thereby enliven the power conferred on the court by s 80(1). In these circumstances, in my opinion, s 80 should be read as contemplating that an injunction may be granted prohibiting or requiring the performance of acts outside Australia. I should add that the

---

164. *ICI Ltd v Trade Practices Commission* (1992) 38 FCR 248 at 266 per Gummow J (Full FC).

165. ACL s 232(3). This event does not enliven an action for damages, although it may give rise to an application for a compensation or other remedial order: see **16.54** and compare ACL s 236 with ss 237(1)(a)(ii), 238(1)(a)(ii) and 239(1)(a)(ii).

court may have a similar power pursuant to s 23 of the Federal Court of Australia Act 1976 (Cth) ...[166]

Standing

16.38 An injunction may be sought under ACL s 232(2) by the 'regulator or any other person'.[167] The equivalent phrase in the TPA was interpreted broadly.[168] It extends the range of people entitled to apply beyond the scope of equitable injunctions. In *Phelps v Western Mining Corporation*[169] Bowen CJ was of the view that there was 'no room for implying any qualification' on the words 'any other person'.[170] In the same case, Deane J agreed with Bowen CJ, and observed:

> As a matter of ordinary language, the phrase "any other person" connotes any other person whatsoever.[171]

This reasoning was upheld by the High Court in *Truth About Motorways Pty Ltd v Macquarie Infrastructure Investment Management Ltd*. The Court confirmed that even a person who had no special interest in a matter could seek an injunction.[172]

General requirements

16.39 The requirements for the various types of injunction generally available were discussed in **Chapter 8**. To summarise those principles, an injunction is a discretionary equitable remedy and, at least when a court is exercising auxiliary jurisdiction, will not be granted where damages would be adequate. In considering whether to exercise its discretion, a court will take account of the equitable maxims, such as whether there has been undue delay (laches) and whether the applicant has 'clean hands'.

To what extent are these equitable principles applicable when the power to grant injunctions is given by statute? The High Court considered this broad question in *Cardile v LED Builders Pty Ltd* and came to the conclusion that:

> The term "injunction" is used in numerous statutes to identify a particular species of order, the making of which the law in question provides as part of a new regulatory or other regime, which may be supported by penal provisions.

---

166. (2003) 132 FCR 309 at [41]–[42]. The facts are considered at **16.56**. See also *ACCC v Sensaslim Australia Pty Ltd (in liq) (No 1)* [2011] FCA 1012.

167. Compare CCA s 80(1A) and (1AAA) which contain limited exceptions where no one other than the Commissioner or Minister may apply.

168. See *Truth About Motorways Pty Ltd v Macquarie Infrastructure Investment Management Ltd* (2000) 200 CLR 591; *Phelps v Western Mining Corp* (1978) 33 FLR 327; 20 ALR 183 (Full FC); *R v Federal Court of Australia; Ex parte Pilkington ACI (Operations) Pty Ltd* (1978) 142 CLR 113 at 128 per Mason J; *Trade Practices Commission v Mobil Oil Australia Ltd* (1984) 4 FCR 296 at 300 per Toohey J (FCA); *Tobacco Institute of Australia Ltd v Australian Federation of Consumer Organisations Inc* (1988) 19 FCR 469.

169. (1978) 33 FLR 327; 20 ALR 183 (Full FC).

170. (1978) 33 FLR 327 at 332.

171. (1978) 33 FLR 327 at 333.

172. (2000) 200 CLR 591 at [13]–[15] per Gleeson CJ and McHugh J, and [120] per Gummow J.

Notable examples in statutes presently in force nationally are found in s 80 of the Trade Practices Act (Cth) ("the Trade Practices Act"), s 114 of the Family Law Act 1975 (Cth), s 1324 of the Corporations Law (Cth) and s 170NG of the Workplace Relations Act 1996 (Cth). These provisions empower courts to give a remedy in many cases where none would have been available in a court of equity in the exercise of its jurisdiction, whether to protect the legal (including statutory) or equitable rights of the plaintiff, the administration of a trust for charitable purposes, or the observance of public law at the suit of the Attorney-General, with or without a relator, or at the suit of a person with a sufficient interest.

In these situations, the term "injunction" takes its content from the provisions of the particular statute in question. In other laws, for example Div 2 (ss 43–65) of Pt III of the Proceeds of Crime Act 1987 (Cth), where the term "restraining order" is used, remedies having some characteristics of injunctions as understood in courts of equity are given their own particular statutory designation. [Footnotes omitted][173]

This does not mean that the equitable principles are irrelevant.[174] Firstly, the equitable principles are not static. As observed by Gleeson CJ, Gaudron and Gummow JJ in *ACCC v Edensor Nominees Pty Ltd*, 'the injunctive remedy is still the subject of development in courts of equity, particularly in public law'. And secondly, as their Honours went on to point out, the 'remedies created by legislation … are not fundamentally distinct from the equitable remedy'.[175]

The main difference between equitable injunctions and those under the ACL is that equity is said to act *in personam*; that is, it is concerned predominantly with the interests of the parties before the court. The ACL, on the other hand, is more concerned with protection of the public[176] — particularly when an application is brought by the regulator. Consequently, injunctions have been granted even where the plaintiff will not suffer damage,[177] the relevant damage to be considered being 'possible damage to consumers'[178] or the 'public interest'.[179] Injunctions are also possible whether or not damages would be an adequate remedy;[180] and whether or not there is evidence that further contraventions are contemplated or likely.[181] Another contrast can be found

---

173. [1999] HCA 18; 162 ALR 294 at [27]–[28].

174. *ICI Australia v Trade Practices Commission* [1992] FCA 474; *ACCC v Wilson Parking 1992 Pty Ltd* [2009] FCA 1580 at [41].

175. [2001] HCA 1; 75 ALJR 363 at [45].

176. *Truth About Motorways Pty Ltd v Macquarie Infrastructure Investment Management Ltd* (2000) 200 CLR 591 at [121] per Gummow J.

177. See *World Series Cricket Pty Ltd v Parish* (1977) 16 ALR 181 at 186 per Bowen CJ (Full FC); *Tobacco Institute of Australia Ltd v Australian Federation of Consumer Organisations Inc* (1993) ATPR 41–222 per Sheppard J (Full FC).

178. *World Series Cricket Pty Ltd v Parish* (1977) 16 ALR 181 at 191 per Bowen CJ.

179. *Truth About Motorways Pty Ltd v Macquarie Infrastructure Investment Management Ltd* (2000) 200 CLR 591 at [121] per Gummow J.

180. *World Series Cricket Pty Ltd v Parish* (1977) 16 ALR 181.

181. *ACCC v Vassallo* [2009] FCA 954; *Procter and Gamble Australia Pty Ltd v Energizer Pty Ltd (No 2)* [2011] FCA 1446.

in the fact that delay matters less under the Act than it does in equity, because of the importance of the public interest.[182]

There must obviously be a connection between the contravention and the injunction sought. As observed by Vickery J in *Blackman v Gant*:

> There is, however, a limit on the power to grant injunctions pursuant to s 80 which is considered by the case law to impose a requirement beyond the initial threshold of an alleged or actual contravention of the Act — there must be a sufficient nexus between the alleged or actual contravention relied upon and the injunction granted.[183]

Types of injunction

The ACL gives a court broad power to grant an injunction 'in such terms as the court considers appropriate'. What types of injunction are possible?

Prohibitory injunctions

16.40   The broad power to grant an injunction clearly enables prohibitory injunctions. Subsection (4) also makes it clear that the power to grant prohibitory injunctions is not limited to situations where the contravening conduct has occurred in the past or is likely to continue. It provides:

> The power of the court to grant an injunction under subsection (1) restraining a person from engaging in conduct may be exercised:
>
> (a) whether or not it appears to the court that the person intends to engage again, or to continue to engage, in conduct of a kind referred to in that subsection; and
>
> (b) whether or not the person has previously engaged in conduct of that kind; and
>
> (c) whether or not there is an imminent danger of substantial damage to any other person if the person engages in conduct of that kind.

In *Trade Practices Commission v Mobil Oil Australia Ltd*,[184] Toohey J held:

> It is clear therefore that in determining whether to grant an injunction the court is not restricted because the factors mentioned in subs (4) are absent. The question must still be asked — where those factors are absent, what purpose is the injunction intended to serve?[185]

So, despite these provisions, if there is no public interest being served and no deterrent effect of the injunction, courts are still inclined to take into account the likelihood that the conduct will be repeated in assessing the purpose of, or the need to grant, the injunction.[186]

---

182. See *World Series Cricket Pty Ltd v Parish* (1977) 16 ALR 181 at 190 per Bowen CJ (Full FC); *ICI Ltd v Trade Practices Commission* (1992) 38 FCR 248 (Full FC).

183. [2010] VSC 229 at [165]. See also *ACCC v Z-Tek Computer Pty Ltd* [1997] FCA 871 and *ACCC v Real Estate Institute of WA Inc* [1999] FCA 18.

184. (1984) 4 FCR 296.

185. (1984) 4 FCR 296 at 300.

186. See *Australian Competition & Consumer Commission v Universal Music Australia Pty Ltd (No 2)* [2002] FCA 192 at [46]–[50] per Hill J; *Dickson v Gallagher* (1985) ATPR 40550; *Gull Petroleum*

Mandatory injunctions

16.41 The broad power to grant injunctions 'in such terms as the court considers appropriate' would be sufficient for the grant of a mandatory injunction.[187] Two subsections also specifically countenance mandatory injunctions. They provide:

> (6) Without limiting subsection (1), the court may grant an injunction under that subsection requiring a person to do any of the following:
>
>   (a) refund money;
>   (b) transfer property;
>   (c) honour a promise;
>   (d) destroy or dispose of goods.
>
> (7) The power of the court to grant an injunction under subsection (1) requiring a person to do an act or thing may be exercised:
>
>   (a) whether or not it appears to the court that the person intends to refuse or fail again, or to continue to refuse or fail, to do that act or thing; and
>   (b) whether or not the person has previously refused or failed to do that act or thing; and
>   (c) whether or not there is an imminent danger of substantial damage to any other person if the person refuses or fails to do that act or thing.

Courts have awarded mandatory injunctions, for example, directing the defendant to publish corrective advertisements.[188] Many of the injunctions granted by courts are interlocutory: see **16.43**. There is also some overlap with the non-punitive and adverse publicity orders that may be applied for by the regulator under ss 246 and 247, which are akin to mandatory injunctions. For example, the court can order a person to establish a compliance program or an education and training program for employees; or to disclose or publish information.

16.42 Under ACL s 243(g), the court has a discretion to make orders compelling the defendant to provide services. Such an order will in some cases be akin to a mandatory injunction compelling the specific performance of a contract: see **8.66**. The purpose of the order, however, will be limited by the purpose described in whichever section (237, 238 or 239) enlivens the court's discretion to make the order — that is compensation, redress, or the reduction or prevention of loss or damage: see **16.36**.

(WA) Pty Ltd v Povey Corp Pty Ltd (1988) ATPR 40–842; compare *Australian Competition and Consumer Commission v Lux Pty Ltd* [2004] FCA 926 at [138].

187. See *Orison Pty Ltd v Strategic Minerals Corp NL* (1987) 77 ALR 141 (FCA); compare *Truth About Motorways Pty Ltd v Macquarie Infrastructure Investment Management Ltd* (2000) 200 CLR 591 at [80] per Gummow J; *Health Insurance Commission v Hospitals' Contribution Fund of Australia* (1981) 36 ALR 204 (FCA).

188. *Janssen Pharmaceutical Pty Ltd v Pfizer Pty Ltd* (1986) ATPR 40–654; *Hospitals Contribution Fund (Aust) Ltd v Switzerland Australia Health Fund Pty Ltd* (1987) 78 ALR 483; (1988) ATPR 40–834; *Trotman Australia Pty Ltd v Hobsons Press (Australia) Pty Ltd* (1991) 22 IPR 397; compare *Q Promotions Pty Ltd v Queensland Bloodstock Breeders and Sales Pty Ltd* (FCA, Drummond J, 16 July 1993, unreported).

Interlocutory and interim injunctions

16.43   While the ACL does not use the term 'interlocutory injunction', the court is given express power under s 234(1) to grant an interim injunction 'pending the determination of the application'.

The orthodox approach in equity in deciding whether to grant such injunctions is to ask, first, whether there is a prima facie case or a serious question to be tried; and second, whether the balance of convenience favours the grant. This approach has been adopted under TPA s 80(2)[189] but, as mentioned earlier, there is no need to show that damages will be an inadequate remedy. While this issue is often of prime importance to the balance of convenience in equity (see **8.57**) the focus here is rather on the public interest.[190]

16.44   Courts have also been prepared to grant mandatory interlocutory injunctions where appropriate. In *Aerospatiale Societe Nationale Industrielle v Aerospatiale Helicopters Pty Ltd*[191] Wilcox J granted a mandatory interlocutory injunction directing the defendant to change its name where the use of that name would have amounted to passing off and a contravention of the prohibition against misleading or deceptive conduct (TPA s 52). By contrast, in *Q Promotions Pty Ltd v Queensland Bloodstock Breeders and Sales Pty Ltd*,[192] a mandatory interlocutory injunction compelling corrective advertising was refused in a case analogous to passing off. The main damage caused by the offending conduct would have been to reputation, and this was described by Drummond J as being 'irrelevant' to s 52; thus, there was not a 'serious issue to be tried'.

16.45   As with injunctions in equity, the remedy under s 80(2) is clearly discretionary. In *World Series Cricket Pty Ltd v Parish*,[193] Bowen CJ noted that:

> The court is given jurisdiction to grant an interim injunction under s 80(2) where, in its opinion, "it is desirable to do so". These words confer a judicial discretion of the widest kind upon the court. It is not an arbitrary discretion but one to be exercised judicially in accordance with principle. The principles concerning the grant of interlocutory injunctions were developed in the Court of Chancery, but have been moulded to what is appropriate for different jurisdictions in which interlocutory relief may be obtained.[194]

16.46   As discussed in Chapter 8, a prerequisite for the grant of an interlocutory injunction in equity is that the plaintiff must give an 'undertaking as to damages': see **8.60–8.62**. For the most part, this is also true of injunctions under the s 232. In some cases, however, the Minister may give an undertaking

---

189.   See, for example, *Ricegrowers' Co-operative Mills Ltd v Howling Success Australia Pty Ltd* (1987) ATPR 40-778 per Gummow J.

190.   *CBA v Insurance Brokers' Association* (1977) 16 ALR 161 at 168 (Full FC); *Truth About Motorways Pty Ltd v Macquarie Infrastructure Investment Management Ltd* (2000) 200 CLR 591 at [121] per Gummow J.

191.   (1986) 11 FCR 37; 6 IPR 219.

192.   (FCA, Drummond J, 16 July 1993, unreported).

193.   (1977) 16 ALR 181.

194.   (1977) 16 ALR 181 at 185.

as to damages for a suit brought by another person; but if the application is made by the Minister or the ACCC no undertaking is required.[195]

16.47 As an alternative to the grant of the interlocutory injunction, the court may accept an undertaking from the defendant not to engage in certain conduct. In *Thomson Australian Holdings Pty Ltd v Trade Practices Commission*[196] the High Court observed that the Federal Court has power to accept such an undertaking in interlocutory proceedings, 'even though it is not in a form which falls within s 80', so long as it reasonably relates 'to the orderly procedure of the court or the subject matter of the litigation'.[197] Such an undertaking is enforceable in the same way as an injunction.[198]

Injunctions by consent

16.48 Where an application is made for an injunction, the court may grant an injunction with the consent of all the parties, whether or not it is satisfied that the conduct that would normally enliven the injunctive power under s 232(1) has taken place.[199] The court still needs to be satisfied that the admitted facts 'disclose a sufficient nexus between the conduct alleged and the orders sought' and that 'the proposed injunction is sufficiently clearly and precisely stated to be capable of being complied with and would not require Court supervision'.[200]

Mareva orders

16.49 The Minister and the ACCC are given the express power to apply for a Mareva-type order in s 137F of the CCA.[201] A private litigant may also obtain a Mareva order, but here the power to make the order is not found in the Act, but in the statutory or inherent power of the court.[202]

Varying or discharging injunctions

16.50 The power to vary or discharge an injunction is also specifically granted. ACL s 235 provides:

> The Court may vary or discharge an injunction (including an interim injunction) granted under this Division.

---

195. ACL s 243(2) and (3).

196. (1981) 148 CLR 150.

197. (1981) 148 CLR 150 at 165.

198. (1981) 148 CLR 150 at 165.

199. ACL s 233.

200. *ACCC v Wilson Parking 1992 Pty Ltd* [2009] FCA 1580 at [44]–[45]. See also *ACCC v Z-Tek Computer Pty Ltd* [1997] FCA 871; *ACCC v Real Estate Institute of Western Australia Inc* [1999] FCA 18; (1999) 161 ALR 79 at [26].

201. See, for example, *Australian Competition & Consumer Commission v Giraffe World Australia Pty Ltd (in liq)* [1999] FCA 1476.

202. See *Jackson v Sterling Industries Ltd* (1987) 162 CLR 612; *Australian Competition and Consumer Commission v Giraffe World Australia Pty Ltd* (1998) 156 ALR 273; and see **Chapter 9**.

The operation of the similarly-worded provision in the TPA was considered by Gummow J in the Full Court of the Federal Court in *ICI Ltd v Trade Practices Commission* where his Honour observed:

> ... s 80(3) authorises the court to rescind or vary not only an interim injunction but a final injunction. ... [I]t remains a question under the general law as to when a final injunction may be discharged otherwise than by consent. However, the generality of the circumstances in which an injunction may be granted under s 80 made it highly expedient for the Parliament to place beyond doubt the power of the court to rescind or vary both interim and final injunctions.[203]

Either the plaintiff or the defendant may apply to have the injunction set aside. In *Caltex Petroleum Pty Ltd v Australian Competition and Consumer Commission*[204] the court allowed the defendant's application to set aside an injunction that was granted 27 years earlier.

RECTIFICATION

16.51   The 'remedial smorgasbord'[205] provided by ss 237–239 (as read with s 243) include orders akin to the equitable remedy of rectification[206] discussed in Chapter 12. For example, s 243(b), (c) and (h) allow courts to rectify or vary contracts, arrangements and instruments transferring land. The relevant parts of s 243 provide that a court can make:

(b) an order:

    (i)   varying such a contract or arrangement in such manner as is specified in the order; and

    (ii) if the court thinks fit — declaring the contract or arrangement to have had effect as so varied on and after such date as is specified in the order (which may be a date that is before the date on which the order is made);

(c) an order refusing to enforce any or all of the provisions of such a contract or arrangement;

...

(h) an order, in relation to an instrument creating or transferring an interest in land, directing the respondent to execute an instrument that:

    (i)   varies, or has the effect of varying, the first mentioned instrument; or

    (ii) terminates or otherwise affects, or has the effect of terminating or otherwise affecting, the operation or effect of the first mentioned instrument.

Like the equitable remedy, an order under these provisions is discretionary; but, as noted by Gummow J in *Marks v GIO Holdings Pty Ltd*:

---

203. *ICI Ltd v Trade Practices Commission* (1992) 38 FCR 248 at 266.

204. [2001] FCA 1503.

205. *Akron Securities v Iliffe* [1997] NSWSC 106; (1997) 41 NSWLR at 364 per Mason P (CA).

206. See *Marks v GIO Holdings Pty Ltd* (1998) 196 CLR 494 at [116] per Gummow J.

[The] paragraphs of s 87(2) … create new remedies which have an affinity to the equitable remedies of rescission and rectification … The principles regulating the administration of equitable remedies afford guidance for, but do not dictate, the exercise of the statutory discretion conferred by s 87.[207]

An important difference is that, unlike equitable rectification, an order varying a contract can only be made if the court considers that it will achieve the objects of ss 237–239, namely to compensate, prevent, reduce or redress the loss or damage.[208]

DECLARATIONS

16.52   There are a number of provisions that enable a court to issue declarations. A 'person', meaning *any* person,[209] can seek declaratory relief under s 163A of the CCA.[210] Section 163A provides:

163A Declarations and orders

(1) Subject to this section, a person may, in relation to a matter arising under this Act, institute a proceeding in a court having jurisdiction to hear and determine proceedings under this section seeking the making of:

  (a) a declaration in relation to the operation or effect of any provision of this Act other than the following provisions:

   (ii) Part XIB;

   (iii) Part XIC; or

  (aaa) a declaration in relation to the operation or effect of any provision of the Australian Consumer law other than Division 1 of Part 3-2 or Part 5-4; or

  (aa) a declaration in relation to the validity of any act or thing done, proposed to be done or purporting to have been done under this Act; or

  (b) an order by way of, or in the nature of, prohibition, certiorari or mandamus;

  or both such a declaration and such an order.

(1A) Subsection (1) does not apply in relation to a matter arising under Part IIIAA.

Later subsections make it clear that the ACCC and the Minister also have standing to apply for declarations in certain circumstances; and they clarify jurisdictional issues between Federal, State and Territory courts.[211]

---

207. (1998) 196 CLR 494 at [116].

208. See *Marks v GIO Holdings Pty Ltd* (1998) 196 CLR 494 at [43] per McHugh, Hayne and Callinan JJ.

209. *Truth About Motorways Pty Ltd v Macquarie Infrastructure Investment Management Ltd* (2000) 200 CLR 591 at [74] and [120] per Gummow J.

210. See also *Polgardy v AGC Ltd* (1981) 52 FLR 240; *Tobacco Institute of Australia Ltd v Australian Federation of Consumer Organisations Inc* (1993) ATPR 41–222 (Full FC); *Bray v F Hoffman-La Roche Ltd* (2003) 200 ALR 607.

211. CCA s 163A(2)–163A(4E).

16.53   The list of remedial orders in ACL s 243 includes a declaratory power. Section 243(a) provides that the court can make declarations that the whole or any part of a contract or a collateral arrangement is void, void ab initio or void on and after a certain date. The declaration will have to satisfy the objectives in ss 237–239, that is, the order must either compensate, prevent, reduce or, in the case of s 239, redress the loss or damage.

16.54   The court has power to make declarations in respect of the new provisions relating to unfair terms in standard form consumer contracts (ACL ss 23–28). Section 250 provides:

250 Declarations relating to consumer contracts

(1)   A court may, on the application of a party to a consumer contract or on the application of the regulator, declare that a term of such a contract is an unfair term.

(2)   Subsection (1) does not apply unless the consumer contract is a standard form contract.

(3)   Subsection (1) does not limit any other power of the court to make declarations.

A declaration under this section may enliven an application for a compensation or other remedial order,[212] or for an injunction,[213] but not an action for damages under s 236.

16.55   These specific provisions do not, however, form a complete code on the availability of declarations under the Act[214] and do 'not … provide a charter for the granting of declarations in the same way as s 80 does for the granting of injunctions'.[215] As a matter of practice, for example, the courts often declare whether conduct is in breach of the misleading and deceptive conduct provision before determining whether a remedy is available.[216] Such declarations 'which simply reflect findings of contravention are not always warranted, but … they may be useful in public interest litigation where they serve to vindicate legislation aimed at the protection of consumers'.[217] In *Tobacco Institute of Australia Ltd v Australian Federation of Consumer Organisations Inc*,[218] the Full Court relied on s 21 of the Federal Court of Australia Act 1976 (Cth) in deciding that a declaration could be made in respect of conduct in contravention of s 52 of the TPA irrespective of injunctive relief being

---

212.   ACL ss 237(1)(a)(ii), 238(1)(a)(ii) and 239(1)(a)(ii).

213.   ACL s 232(3).

214.   *FAI General Insurance Co Ltd v RAIA Insurance Brokers Ltd* (1992) 108 ALR 479 at 507–8 per Foster J; *Tobacco Institute of Australia Ltd v Australian Federation of Consumer Organisations Inc (No 2)* (1993) 41 FCR 89; 113 ALR 257.

215.   *FAI General Insurance Co Ltd v RAIA Insurance Brokers Ltd* (1992) 108 ALR 479 at 507 per Foster J.

216.   See *RAIA Insurance Brokers Ltd v FAI General Insurance Co Ltd* (1993) 112 ALR 511; compare *Australian Competition & Consumer Commission v Francis* [2004] FCA 487.

217.   *Australian Competition and Consumer Commission v Oceana Commercial Pty Ltd* [2003] FCA 1516 at [343] per Kiefel J.

218.   (1993) ATPR 41-222.

granted under s 80.[219] Section 21 of the Federal Court of Australia Act provides:

Declarations of right

21 (1) The Court may, in relation to a matter in which it has original jurisdiction, make binding declarations of right, whether or not any consequential relief is or could be claimed.

(2) A suit is not open to objection on the ground that a declaratory order only is sought.[220]

16.56   In *Australian Competition and Consumer Commission v Chen*[221] the respondent, a United States resident, registered and operated three domain names and websites including <www.sydneyopera.org>. The applicant alleged Chen had in breach of Pt V falsely represented that the sites were affiliated with the Sydney Opera House Trust and that the sale of tickets to events at the Opera House through the sites was approved or permitted by the trust. Despite extensive investigations the applicant failed to ascertain Chen's whereabouts and serve him with any documents. The applicant sought a declaration that Chen had contravened ss 52, 53 and 55 of the Trade Practices Act. It also sought various mandatory and negative injunctions under s 80. Sackville J granted the declaration in respect of ss 52 and 55 of the Act and held:

> Section 21(1) of the Federal Court of Australia Act 1976 (Cth) (the Federal Court Act) confers power on the court in any matter in which it has original jurisdiction to make binding declarations of right, whether or not consequential relief is claimed. In *Tobacco Institute of Australia Ltd v Australian Federation of Consumer Organisations Inc (No 2)* …, the Full Court held that the court has power under s 21 of the Federal Court Act to make a declaration of right in proceedings for injunctive relief [brought] under s 80 of the TP Act, regardless of whether injunctive relief is granted. The declaration, if made, is a declaration of right because the right declared is a public right, namely the right of the public not to be misled or deceived by misrepresentations[222] … Sheppard J specifically recognised[223] … that the policy of the TP Act, concerned as it is with the public interest, warrants the court, in an appropriate case, exercising its power to grant declaratory relief to mark its disapproval of particular conduct contravening the TP Act.
>
> Hill J in the same case rejected an argument that a declaration should not be made to the effect that the publication of an advertisement relating to passive smoking contravened s 52 of the TP Act because to do so would be futile. His Honour considered[224] that it was in the public interest that the court indicate

---

219. See also *Australian Competition and Consumer Commission v Chen* (2003) 132 FCR 309 at [35]–[36] per Sackville J.
220. Equivalent provisions are considered in **Chapter 13**.
221. (2003) 132 FCR 309.
222. (1993) 41 FCR 89 at 98; 113 ALR 257 at 266 per Sheppard J; at FCR 110; ALR 278 per Hill J.
223. (1993) 41 FCR 89 at 100; 113 ALR 257 at 268.
224. (1993) 41 FCR 89 at 107; 113 ALR 257 at 276.

the result of the case by making an order binding on the parties …[225] On this reasoning, it is open in the present case to grant an appropriately framed declaration to mark disapproval of the respondent's conduct whether or not injunctive relief is granted to restrain repetition of that conduct …

A declaration also marks the court's disapproval of the respondent's conduct and, if appropriate, can be used to inform consumers of the dangers posed by the respondent's operation of the sites. I think that these considerations justify making a declaration in the present case …[226]

REMEDIES RELATING TO CONSUMER GUARANTEES

16.57   The ACL replaces the TPA's 'implied terms' with 'consumer guarantees'.[227] Under the 'implied terms' approach, aggrieved consumers did not have access to the TPA's remedies because breach of an implied term was not seen as a contravention of the Act. The consumer had to institute proceedings for breach of contract. Under the new regime, there are a variety of remedies available to a consumer against suppliers of goods and services and manufacturers.[228] The following paragraphs provide a brief description.

16.58   The crucial provision dealing with suppliers of goods is s 259. It provides:

> **259 Action against suppliers of goods**
>
> (1)   A consumer may take action under this section if:
>
>   (a)   a person (the *supplier*) supplies, in trade or commerce, goods to the consumer; and
>
>   (b)   a guarantee that applies to the supply under Subdivision A of Division 1 of Part 3-2 (other than sections 58 and 59(1)) is not complied with.
>
> (2)   If the failure to comply with the guarantee can be remedied and is not a major failure:
>
>   (a)   the consumer may require the supplier to remedy the failure within a reasonable time; or
>
>   (b)   if such a requirement is made of the supplier but the supplier refuses or fails to comply with the requirement, or fails to comply with the requirement within a reasonable time — the consumer may:
>
>   (i)   otherwise have the failure remedied and, by action against the supplier, recover all reasonable costs incurred by the consumer in having the failure so remedied; or
>
>   (ii)   subject to section 262, notify the supplier that the consumer rejects the goods and of the ground or grounds for the rejection.

---

225.   Citing (1993) 41 FCR 89 at 106; 113 ALR 257 at 274 per Foster J; *Australian Competition and Consumer Commission v IMB Group Pty Ltd (in liq)* (1999) ATPR 41-688 at 42,803-4 per Drummond J.

226.   (2003) 132 FCR 309 at [35]-[36] and [48].

227.   ACL Chapter 3, ss 51 to 68.

228.   ACL Chapter 5, ss 259-277.

(3) If the failure to comply with the guarantee cannot be remedied or is a major failure, the consumer may:

    (a) subject to section 262, notify the supplier that the consumer rejects the goods and of the ground or grounds for the rejection; or

    (b) by action against the supplier, recover compensation for any reduction in the value of the goods below the price paid or payable by the consumer for the goods.

(4) The consumer may, by action against the supplier, recover damages for any loss or damage suffered by the consumer because of the failure to comply with the guarantee if it was reasonably foreseeable that the consumer would suffer such loss or damage as a result of such a failure.

(5) Subsection (4) does not apply if the failure to comply with the guarantee occurred only because of a cause independent of human control that occurred after the goods left the control of the supplier.

(6) To avoid doubt, subsection (4) applies in addition to subsections (2) and (3).

(7) The consumer may take action under this section whether or not the goods are in their original packaging.

The consumer guarantees to which the section applies are in ACL ss 51–57. They include guarantees as to title, undisturbed possession, undisclosed securities, acceptable quality, fitness for any disclosed purpose, supply of goods by description or sample and demonstration models.

Section 259 differentiates between minor and major failures to comply with these consumer guarantees. Section 260 explains what is meant by a major failure and, by implication, anything that does not amount to a major failure is a minor failure. Major failures include situations where goods would not have been acquired by a reasonable consumer who knew of the failure; where goods depart in a 'significant respect' from their description or sample; where goods are 'substantially unfit' for their common purpose and cannot be remedied easily and within a reasonable time; and where goods are unsafe. It is noteworthy that, in cases of major failure or unremedied minor failure, there is a right similar to rescission to reject the goods; and for major failure, where the goods are retained, an action to recover compensation for any reduced value. Whether the failure was minor or major, there is also an action to recover damages under s 259(4) if the (presumably consequential) loss or damage was reasonably foreseeable.

A supplier can remedy a failure to comply with a guarantee by curing a defect in title (where the failure relates to title), repairing or replacing the goods, or providing a refund.[229] While s 259(2) and (3) give a consumer a right to reject goods, this right may be lost where a reasonable time within which the failure should have become apparent has lapsed; or the goods have been lost, destroyed, disposed of or damaged after delivery; or the goods have been attached to other property and cannot be detached without damaging them.[230]

---

229. ACL s 261.
230. ACL s 262.

These provisions are reminiscent of the equitable bars to rescission discussed at 5.59–5.61.

16.59 The approach is similar in the case of suppliers of services. The relevant consumer guarantees are in ACL ss 60–63. They include guarantees that the services will be provided with due care and skill, fit for their particular purpose and supplied within a reasonable time. The remedies also depend on whether the failure to comply with the guarantees is minor or major. Section 267(2) provides:

> (2) If the failure to comply with the guarantee can be remedied and is not a major failure:
>
> (a) the consumer may require the supplier to remedy the failure within a reasonable time; or
>
> (b) if such a requirement is made of the supplier but the supplier refuses or fails to comply with the requirement, or fails to comply with the requirement within a reasonable time — the consumer may:
>
> > (i)   otherwise have the failure remedied and, by action against the supplier, recover all reasonable costs incurred by the consumer in having the failure so remedied; or
> >
> > (ii) terminate the contract for the supply of the services.
>
> (3) If the failure to comply with the guarantee cannot be remedied or is a major failure, the consumer may:
>
> (a) terminate the contract for the supply of the services; or
>
> (b) by action against the supplier, recover compensation for any reduction in the value of the services below the price paid or payable by the consumer for the services.
>
> (4) The consumer may, by action against the supplier, recover damages for any loss or damage suffered by the consumer because of the failure to comply with the guarantee if it was reasonably foreseeable that the consumer would suffer such loss or damage as a result of such a failure.
>
> (5) To avoid doubt, subsection (4) applies in addition to subsections (2) and (3).

The major failures are described in similar terms to those that apply to the supply of goods.[231]

16.60 Consumers will normally proceed against suppliers for defective goods or goods that do not match their description. The ACL gives such a supplier some indemnification as against the manufacturer of the goods.[232] To cover situations where a successful action against a supplier is unlikely, such as where the supplier is insolvent or out of business, the ACL also gives the consumer a right to recover damages directly from the manufacturer.[233] The action can include recovery of the price paid for the goods and any loss

---

231. ACL s 268.

232. ACL s 274.

233. ACL s 271(1).

reasonably foreseeable as a result of the failure.[234] There is also a right to seek damages where a manufacturer fails to make spare parts and repairs reasonably available.[235]

PUBLIC ENFORCEMENT OF CIVIL REMEDIES

16.61   While the focus of this chapter has been on private enforcement of civil remedies, it was noted at the outset that the distinction between private and public enforcement has become increasingly blurred. While the offences described in Chapter 4 of the ACL require proof beyond reasonable doubt, regulators can seek civil pecuniary penalties for non-criminal breaches that only require proof on a balance of probabilities. As a final comment, then, it is worth emphasising that civil remedies might arise from public enforcement proceedings. Regulators can in certain circumstances apply for civil remedies on behalf of private individuals; and, during proceedings involving criminal offences or pecuniary penalties, the court may make orders that directly benefit a party to the proceedings, or even a class of non-party consumers.[236]

---

234. ACL s 272(1).
235. ACL s 271(5).
236. ACL ss 238 and 239.

Index

References are to paragraphs

Aggravated damages – *cont'd*
overview 2.84
trespass to land 2.84

Anticipatory breach
damages 3.5, 3.32
date of assessment 3.39
mitigation 3.31–3.34, 3.39
overview 3.31
right to affirm or repudiate 3.31, 3.32, 3.35, 3.39
specific performance 3.35, 7.12

Anton Piller orders
acquiescence 10.15
availability 10.5
contempt 10.7, 10.16
courts' discretion 10.15
dissolution 10.18
effect of dissolution 10.19
elements 10.9
ex parte orders 8.46
exemplary damages, and 10.19
failure to comply 10.16
form or order 10.14
historical background 10.4, 10.5
jurisdiction 10.7
likely destruction of evidence 10.12
nature of remedy 8.1, 10.1–10.3
patents 10.10
prima facie case 8.51, 10.10
principles 8.2
privilege against self-incrimination 10.15, 10.17
recent developments 10.6
representative orders 10.6
safeguards 10.8
serious damage 10.11
statutory power 10.7
supervising solicitor 10.13
trade marks 10.10
unclean hands 10.15
undertakings 10.13

Assault
aggravated damages 2.84
exemplary damages 2.89
injunctions 8.24

Australian Consumer Law *see* **Competition and Consumer Act**

Battery
exemplary damages 2.89

Breach of confidence
accounts of profits 6.4, 6.6
innocent breach 6.10
damages in equity 11.19, 11.20

Breach of contract *see* **Damages in contract; Rescission; Specific performance**

Breach of fiduciary duty *see* **Fiduciary duty**

Breach of trust *see* **Trust**

Building contracts
exemplary damages 3.54
restitution 4.44, 4.51, 4.52

Burden of proof *see* **Onus of proof**

Causation
'but for' test 2.8–2.11, 2.32, 2.34
application in contract 3.7
Competition and Consumer Act 16.12
contributory negligence 16.13, 16.15
intervening causes 16.13, 16.14
role of policy 16.12
concurrent tortfeasors 2.21
proportionate liability 2.24
right of contribution 2.21
settlement with one tortfeasor 2.23
solidary liability 2.21
statutory reforms 2.21, 2.22, 2.24
subsequent actions 2.22
contributory negligence 2.15
apportionment provisions 2.15–2.17, 2.20
Competition and Consumer Act 16.13, 16.15
contract, and 3.6, 3.9, 3.10
degree of culpability 2.18, 2.19
successive tortfeasors 2.27

consideration, total failure
.... 4.19–4.31, 4.88
specific performance *see* **Specific performance**
Contracts Review Act
approach to claims 15.3
excluded contracts 15.8
commercial contracts 15.9
service contracts 15.10
excluded plaintiffs 15.8
exclusion clauses 15.11
grant of relief 15.12
legislative purpose 15.1
unjust contracts 15.2
circumstances of contract 15.6, 15.7
considerations 15.2
definition 15.2
innocence of unjustness 15.5
unjustness, concept 15.4
Contribution, right of
apportionment of damages 2.57
Competition and Consumer Act
.... 16.16
concurrent tortfeasors 2.21
Contributory negligence
apportionment provisions 2.15
application of provisions 2.16, 2.17
defeat of claims 2.20
New South Wales 2.16
assessment of damages 2.57
causation 2.15
apportionment provisions
.... 2.15–2.17, 2.20
Competition and Consumer Act
.... 16.13, 16.15
contract 3.6, 3.9, 3.10
degree of culpability 2.18, 2.19
successive tortfeasors 2.21
Competition and Consumer Act
.... 16.13, 16.15
damages in contract 3.6, 3.9
chain of causation 3.10
equitable compensation 11.8
conflict of interests, and 11.7, 11.8

onus of proof 2.6
successive tortfeasors 2.27
Conversion *see also* **Trespass to goods**
cause of action 2.7
exemplary damages 2.89
injunctions 8.23, 8.31
reasonable foreseeability 2.43
restitution 4.35
Copyright
account of profits 6.6, 6.7
innocent infringement 6.14
Anton Piller orders 10.4, 10.10
delivery up 14.6
alternative bases 14.7, 14.8
detinue 14.7, 14.8
exemplary damages 2.92
injunctions 8.29
specific performance 7.28
unnecessary or oppressive terms
.... 7.29
Damages
anticipatory breach 3.5, 3.32
date of assessment 3.39
mitigation 3.31–3.34, 3.39
Competition and Consumer Act
.... 16.46
assessment of damages 3.46, 16.20–16.27
causation 16.12–16.16
cause of action 16.9–16.11
consumer guarantees, remedies
relation to 16.60
contributory negligence 16.13, 16.15
economic loss 16.18
elements 16.8
intervening causes 16.13, 16.14
limitation period 16.28, 16.29
mitigation of damage 16.19
mutatis mutandis 16.7
overview 16.5–16.7
personal injuries 16.6
proportionate liability 16.16
remedial orders, and 16.10, 16.33
remoteness of damage 16.17